Lecture Notes in Computer Science   11577

Commenced Publication in 1973
Founding and Former Series Editors:
Gerhard Goos, Juris Hartmanis, and Jan van Leeuwen

Editorial Board Members

Pei-Luen Patrick Rau (Ed.)

Cross-Cultural Design

Culture and Society

11th International Conference, CCD 2019
Held as Part of the 21st HCI International Conference, HCII 2019
Orlando, FL, USA, July 26–31, 2019
Proceedings, Part II

 Springer

Editor
Pei-Luen Patrick Rau
Tsinghua University
Beijing, China

ISSN 0302-9743 ISSN 1611-3349 (electronic)
Lecture Notes in Computer Science
ISBN 978-3-030-22579-7 ISBN 978-3-030-22580-3 (eBook)
https://doi.org/10.1007/978-3-030-22580-3

LNCS Sublibrary: SL3 – Information Systems and Applications, incl. Internet/Web, and HCI

This Springer imprint is published by the registered company Springer Nature Switzerland AG
The registered company address is: Gewerbestrasse 11, 6330 Cham, Switzerland

Foreword

The 21st International Conference on Human-Computer Interaction, HCI International 2019, was held in Orlando, FL, USA, during July 26–31, 2019. The event incorporated the 18 thematic areas and affiliated conferences listed on the following page.

A total of 5,029 individuals from academia, research institutes, industry, and governmental agencies from 73 countries submitted contributions, and 1,274 papers and 209 posters were included in the pre-conference proceedings. These contributions address the latest research and development efforts and highlight the human aspects of design and use of computing systems. The contributions thoroughly cover the entire field of human-computer interaction, addressing major advances in knowledge and effective use of computers in a variety of application areas. The volumes constituting the full set of the pre-conference proceedings are listed in the following pages.

This year the HCI International (HCII) conference introduced the new option of "late-breaking work." This applies both for papers and posters and the corresponding volume(s) of the proceedings will be published just after the conference. Full papers will be included in the *HCII 2019 Late-Breaking Work Papers Proceedings* volume of the proceedings to be published in the Springer LNCS series, while poster extended abstracts will be included as short papers in the HCII 2019 *Late-Breaking Work Poster Extended Abstracts* volume to be published in the Springer CCIS series.

I would like to thank the program board chairs and the members of the program boards of all thematic areas and affiliated conferences for their contribution to the highest scientific quality and the overall success of the HCI International 2019 conference.

This conference would not have been possible without the continuous and unwavering support and advice of the founder, Conference General Chair Emeritus and Conference Scientific Advisor Prof. Gavriel Salvendy. For his outstanding efforts, I would like to express my appreciation to the communications chair and editor of *HCI International News*, Dr. Abbas Moallem.

July 2019   Constantine Stephanidis

HCI International 2019 Thematic Areas and Affiliated Conferences

Thematic areas:

- HCI 2019: Human-Computer Interaction
- HIMI 2019: Human Interface and the Management of Information

Affiliated conferences:

- EPCE 2019: 16th International Conference on Engineering Psychology and Cognitive Ergonomics
- UAHCI 2019: 13th International Conference on Universal Access in Human-Computer Interaction
- VAMR 2019: 11th International Conference on Virtual, Augmented and Mixed Reality
- CCD 2019: 11th International Conference on Cross-Cultural Design
- SCSM 2019: 11th International Conference on Social Computing and Social Media
- AC 2019: 13th International Conference on Augmented Cognition
- DHM 2019: 10th International Conference on Digital Human Modeling and Applications in Health, Safety, Ergonomics and Risk Management
- DUXU 2019: 8th International Conference on Design, User Experience, and Usability
- DAPI 2019: 7th International Conference on Distributed, Ambient and Pervasive Interactions
- HCIBGO 2019: 6th International Conference on HCI in Business, Government and Organizations
- LCT 2019: 6th International Conference on Learning and Collaboration Technologies
- ITAP 2019: 5th International Conference on Human Aspects of IT for the Aged Population
- HCI-CPT 2019: First International Conference on HCI for Cybersecurity, Privacy and Trust
- HCI-Games 2019: First International Conference on HCI in Games
- MobiTAS 2019: First International Conference on HCI in Mobility, Transport, and Automotive Systems
- AIS 2019: First International Conference on Adaptive Instructional Systems

Pre-conference Proceedings Volumes Full List

1. LNCS 11566, Human-Computer Interaction: Perspectives on Design (Part I), edited by Masaaki Kurosu
2. LNCS 11567, Human-Computer Interaction: Recognition and Interaction Technologies (Part II), edited by Masaaki Kurosu
3. LNCS 11568, Human-Computer Interaction: Design Practice in Contemporary Societies (Part III), edited by Masaaki Kurosu
4. LNCS 11569, Human Interface and the Management of Information: Visual Information and Knowledge Management (Part I), edited by Sakae Yamamoto and Hirohiko Mori
5. LNCS 11570, Human Interface and the Management of Information: Information in Intelligent Systems (Part II), edited by Sakae Yamamoto and Hirohiko Mori
6. LNAI 11571, Engineering Psychology and Cognitive Ergonomics, edited by Don Harris
7. LNCS 11572, Universal Access in Human-Computer Interaction: Theory, Methods and Tools (Part I), edited by Margherita Antona and Constantine Stephanidis
8. LNCS 11573, Universal Access in Human-Computer Interaction: Multimodality and Assistive Environments (Part II), edited by Margherita Antona and Constantine Stephanidis
9. LNCS 11574, Virtual, Augmented and Mixed Reality: Multimodal Interaction (Part I), edited by Jessie Y. C. Chen and Gino Fragomeni
10. LNCS 11575, Virtual, Augmented and Mixed Reality: Applications and Case Studies (Part II), edited by Jessie Y. C. Chen and Gino Fragomeni
11. LNCS 11576, Cross-Cultural Design: Methods, Tools and User Experience (Part I), edited by P. L. Patrick Rau
12. LNCS 11577, Cross-Cultural Design: Culture and Society (Part II), edited by P. L. Patrick Rau
13. LNCS 11578, Social Computing and Social Media: Design, Human Behavior and Analytics (Part I), edited by Gabriele Meiselwitz
14. LNCS 11579, Social Computing and Social Media: Communication and Social Communities (Part II), edited by Gabriele Meiselwitz
15. LNAI 11580, Augmented Cognition, edited by Dylan D. Schmorrow and Cali M. Fidopiastis
16. LNCS 11581, Digital Human Modeling and Applications in Health, Safety, Ergonomics and Risk Management: Human Body and Motion (Part I), edited by Vincent G. Duffy

http://2019.hci.international/proceedings

11th International Conference on Cross-Cultural Design (CCD 2019)

Program Board Chair(s): **Pei-Luen Patrick Rau,** *P.R. China*

- Sangwoo Bahn, South Korea
- Chien-Chi Chang, Taiwan
- Na Chen, P.R. China
- Zhe Chen, P.R. China
- Zhiyong Fu, P.R. China
- Paul Fu, USA
- Toshikazu Kato, Japan
- Rungtai Lin, Taiwan
- Dyi-Yih Michael Lin, Taiwan
- Na Liu, P.R. China
- Cheng-Hung Lo, P.R. China
- Yongqi Lou, P.R. China
- Liang Ma, P.R. China
- Alexander Mädche, Germany
- Katsuhiko Ogawa, Japan
- Taezoon Park, South Korea
- Chunyi Shen, Taiwan
- Huatong Sun, USA
- Hao Tan, P.R. China
- Pei-Lee Teh, Malaysia
- Lin Wang, South Korea
- Hsiu-Ping Yueh, Taiwan

The full list with the Program Board Chairs and the members of the Program Boards of all thematic areas and affiliated conferences is available online at:

http://www.hci.international/board-members-2019.php

HCI International 2020

The 22nd International Conference on Human-Computer Interaction, HCI International 2020, will be held jointly with the affiliated conferences in Copenhagen, Denmark, at the Bella Center Copenhagen, July 19–24, 2020. It will cover a broad spectrum of themes related to HCI, including theoretical issues, methods, tools, processes, and case studies in HCI design, as well as novel interaction techniques, interfaces, and applications. The proceedings will be published by Springer. More information will be available on the conference website: http://2020.hci.international/.

General Chair
Prof. Constantine Stephanidis
University of Crete and ICS-FORTH
Heraklion, Crete, Greece
E-mail: general_chair@hcii2020.org

http://2020.hci.international/

Contents – Part II

Cross-Cultural Product and Service Design

Intercultural Learning

Contents – Part I

Cross-Cultural User Experience

Cultural Differences, Usability and Design

Cultural Products, Experiences and Creativity

A Framework of Experiential Service Design in Creative Tourism

Shu-Hua Chang[1(✉)] and Rungtai Lin[2(✉)]

[1] Department of Arts and Creative Industries,
National Dong Hwa University, Hualien, Taiwan
iamcsh0222@gms.ndhu.edu.tw
[2] Graduate School of Creative Industry Design, College of Design,
National Taiwan University of Arts, New Taipei City, Taiwan
rtlin@mail.ntua.edu.tw

Abstract. This study explored experiential service design in creative tourism from the perspective of tourists. Service design methods, collated observations, and a questionnaire were employed to form multiple case studies regarding three sites of creative tourism destinations in Taiwan. The findings are as follows: (1) tourists learn not only through participating in activities but also through related creative people, stylish works/featured products, and aesthetic atmosphere; (2) service facilities, such as descriptions of exhibits, and displays equipment, are important peripheral experiences that may affect tourists' learning in the core experience; (3) the storytelling experiences include not only the norms, shared values, etc., but also the activation of local culture and contributions to local development are demonstrated as important elements; and (4) the study combines gain/pain points of empathy mapping and customer journey mapping with creative tourism experiences that provides in-depth insights into the tourists' experiences. Therefore, regarding the service design principles, the pain and gain points can be transformed into key elements of the tourism experiences through an experiential service design for creative tourism.

Keywords: Experience economy · Creative tourism · Experiential service design · Service design

1   Introduction

The term "creative tourism" refers to a new generation of tourism [1] and has been posed as an extension of "cultural tourism" [2, 3]. UNESCO [1] advocated that creative tourism should be linked to the living culture of a location and aim to drive local enterprises that offer cultural experiences. Smith [4] argued that development of the creative industries and accompanying experiential forms of tourism can lead to exciting new products.

Several studies have examined the value of creative tourism in promoting local skills, expertise, and traditional culture [3, 5]. Active tourists are especially important for successful creative tourism because they must participate in cultural activities such as painting, photography, crafts, dancing, and cookery [4]. To meet the ever-changing

© Springer Nature Switzerland AG 2019
P.-L. P. Rau (Ed.): HCII 2019, LNCS 11577, pp. 3–16, 2019.
https://doi.org/10.1007/978-3-030-22580-3_1

interests of tourists, tourism-related enterprises must be aware and proud of their strengths, and they should be willing to share experiences through creative products and services. Therefore, it is essential to understand how creative experiences for creative tourism are formed.

The concept of an experience economy is as an emerging paradigm encompassing a variety of industries, including the tourism and hospitality sectors [6, 7]. The experience economy has been increasingly applied as a framework for the arts, culture, and creative industries, including music, performing arts, and cultural festivals [8]. Tourism is seen as the biggest producer of experiences [9], wherein values can be created through various elements within tourism related services and products [10]. Pine II and Gilmore [11] proposed that experience industries use services as a stage and products as props to spur individual consumers' participation. Experience designers provide not only products or services but also experiences and memories elicited by the product or service.

In the tourism literature, tourist experience has been emphasized as an essential creator of competition in the tourism industry [12–15]. Several studies have explored and evaluated tourism experiences by using service design approaches and tools [14–18]. For example, Tussyadiah [14] developed a theoretical foundation for experience design in tourism and proposed a human-oriented, iterative designing process for producing a holistic experience concept. The concept of creativity in creative tourism has been discussed, and the factors resulting in creative experiences have been developed [19, 20]. However, few studies have examined the creative experience of designing experiential products or services in creative tourism. On the basis of the aforementioned studies, tool for designing tourist experiences and methods emerging from different disciplines should be integrated to provide a framework for experiential service design in creative tourism.

The following section provides a brief review of the literature on creative tourism, service design, and tourism experience. In the next section, a theoretical model is proposed through multiple case studies of creative tourism in Taiwan. Last, the theoretical findings and limitations of the study and future directions for research are discussed. This study is important for both theory and practice. The purpose of this paper is to capture the elements affecting the tourists' experiences in creative tourism. Regarding tourists' views, these factors are analyzed and discussed in order to establish a framework for designing experiential products and services in creative tourism.

2 Theoretical Background

2.1 Creative Tourism

Creative tourism is an extension of cultural tourism that reflects a changing demand in tourism style [2, 3]. Creative tourism has been defined by UNESCO [1] as "travel directed toward an engaged and authentic experience, with participative learning in the arts, heritage, or special character of a place, and it provides a connection with those who reside in this place and create this living culture". People are increasingly interested in cultural activities (e.g. painting, photography, crafts, dancing, cookery, pottery, and music), and they hope to develop their creative potential through creative tourism [4, 21].

Recent studies have explored the essence of creative experiences in creative tourism from the perspective of tourists. Tan et al. [20] proposed that outer interactions and inner reflections are the key factors for modeling tourists' creative experiences. Entrepreneurs should understand the key factors to tourists' experiences in creative tourism and devise appropriate design methods to facilitate a unique tourism experience. An empirical study by Ali, Ryu, and Hussain [22] examined the effect of creative tourists' experiences on their memories, satisfaction, and behavioral intentions. The results demonstrated the importance of overall experience in forming creative tourists' memories, satisfaction, and behavioral intentions. Therefore, creative tourism enterprises must offer tourists opportunities to develop their creativity through active participation in various activities.

2.2 Tourism Experience

In the design of experiences, Pine II and Gilmore [11] proposed that encompassing more realms of the experience economy increases the likelihood of producing an experience "sweet spot," with the likelihood highest if an experience incorporates all four realms. They proposed five steps to experience design: (1) defining the theme, (2) blending the experience with positive cues, (3) eliminating negative cues, (4) associating with memorability, and (5) integrating sensory stimulation. These steps indicate that even after determining the realm of an experience, experiential cues and sensory stimulation must be employed to enhance customer experience.

Recent research on tourism has examined creating and managing tourism experiences through design research or methods [14–18]. Stickdorn and Frischhut [16] proposed that tourism experiences can be facilitated through peak tourism experiences, supporting consumer experiences, and daily routine experiences. Supporting experiences include activities such as eating and sleeping; if failure points occur with the supporting experiences, then the total customer experiences can be damaged irrespective of the strength of the peak experience [16]. The study performed by Lee, Tussyadiah, and Zach [23] explored tourist experiences through user diaries. Trischler and Zehrer [18] applied personas and service scenarios to develop tourism experiences at theme parks.

Tussyadiah [14] proposed that design tools such as touchpoints and customer journeys as stand-alone items are too simplistic for application in tourism. Hence, tourism experience design (TED) research was conducted. The theoretical framework of TED includes two steps: a meta-concept and an operational concept of tourism experience. The meta-concept of tourism experience emphasizes positioning strategy, meaning that propositions transform into the core and peripheral experiences, supported by the storytelling of these experiences at the society level (i.e., interpretation of experiences that is guided by norms, shared values, etc.). The operational concept of tourism experience focuses on integrating design elements such as touchpoints and functional and emotional clues to generate more favorable tourism experiences [14].

From the aforementioned studies on tourism design, creative tourism experiences should be well developed and enable tourists to reach a "sweet spot" [11] or "peak experience" [16].

2.3 Service Design

Service design is a multidisciplinary field that incorporates knowledge from the management, marketing, design, and research fields. The goal of service design is to provide users with holistic services by integrating various design techniques, management styles, and engineering processes. Service design must be performed from a consumer perspective to ensure that a service interface features differentiating characteristics that are feasible, useful, effective, and conform to customer expectations [24]. Service design emphasizes user-centered, co-creative, sequencing, evidencing, and holistic principles [25].

Overall, service design is the planning and designing of systems and processes through an integration of tangible and intangible media to provide customers with comprehensive and meticulous service experiences [25]. Service design can be viewed as a way to design experiences that allow customers to perceive the value of the overall process through various touchpoints [26]. Related studies have discussed how to construct the customer service journey, such as through moment mapping [27]. Service design methods and tools have been proposed by various monographs, such as stakeholder mapping, customer journey mapping, cultural probing, empathy mapping, and service blueprints. These methods and tools are applied to different aspects with different objectives. In the service process, each touchpoint that represents customer contact can be viewed as a stage of the customer experience journey. The empathy map tool helps to build up a broader understanding of what a person thinks, feels, sees, hears and does as well as his/her pain and gain points [28].

Cook et al. [29] asserted that to establish a competitive edge, service providers should emphasize interactive experiences at service touchpoints and customer emotions, behaviors, and expectations through design and management. Visualization tools can transform ideas and concepts into visible dimensions that may create greater clarity about the service design process [24]. This study also uses customer journey mapping for illustrating findings.

3 Methodology

This study applied the service design methods and tools of observation, questionnaire survey, pain and gain points of empathy mapping, and customer journey mapping at Jioufen Gallery, Ceramic Art Workshop, and Artist Teahouse in Taiwan as multiple case studies. Valuable insights from multiple target case studies are more suitable for descriptive analyses or theory construction [30]. Based on previous studies, a research framework combining service design methods and TED model [14] is put forth to explore the elements of experiential service design in creative tourism, as shown in Fig. 1.

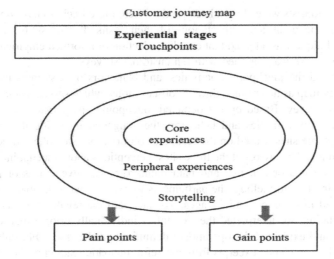

Fig. 1. Research framework

Data were collected from different creative tourism contexts: painting, pottery, and tea culture. The Jioufen Gallery displays works by local artists and serves as a platform for artists. Ceramic Art Workshop is the first of its kind in Jiufen and produces ceramics themed on the old mining atmosphere. The Artist Teahouse is located near the most beautiful seascape in Jiufen and serves as a platform for interactions between artists and collectors. In Jiufen, the Artist Teahouse is known to be very unique with red brick and selected by the New Taipei City Government as the "model building." The various tea programs and ceramic works present the passion of the founder toward tea culture. The three cases represent local art, craft, and traditional tea culture and offer specific cultural experiences that can be categorized as creative tourism. This study is therefore suitable for exploring the elements of experiential service design for creative tourism with multiple themes.

First, the founder of the target of case studies was interviewed and documentary analysis was employed to determine the core, peripheral, and storytelling aspects of the experiences offered by the Jioufen Gallery, Ceramic Art Workshop, and Artist Teahouse. The documents used in the study included news reports, books interviews, and formal reports. These can be regarded as "mute evidence" and can provide useful information for the case studies by covering event details [31]. Subsequently, observations and questionnaires were conducted at the three sites. By using observation, the observer may have a clear picture of the customer journey in mind when following the tourist through the service experience [17] and the tourists' experiences were directly examined. This study also employed nonparticipant observations to avoid influencing the respondents and creating bias. This data triangulation strengthens findings and increases internal validity and reliability [32]. The open-ended questionnaire avoided interference with the respondents and enabled them to express their internal thoughts and opinions freely. When necessary, interviews were conducted by the author to clarify any questions and respond to feedback.

Purposive tourists were chosen because they were more likely to have opinions and beliefs about the goals and expectations of their visits. In this study, a purposive sampling technique was adopted that enabled selection of informed empirical materials [32], and each case was supplied with ten customer surveys.

We depicted the touchpoints, activities, and behaviors of customers using a customer journey map as determined through observations, which served as the basis for a questionnaire survey. Based on the depicted touchpoints, participants were asked to describe what key activities and behaviors they engaged in during the experiential stages at the three sites. Based on the results of observation, we collected descriptions of the respondents' behaviors at the three sites; perceptions about touchpoints with gain points (i.e., rewards or benefits) and pain points (i.e., inconveniences or problems). Next, regarding the storytelling, the participants were asked what the main experiences they perceived in the experiential stages. To safeguard the reliability of data analysis and interpretation, we interpreted the exemplars individually prior to participating in the research and explained the operational definitions of the study. For data analysis, we identified respondents' excerpts from a careful, thematic reading of their transcripts to reflect the respondents' perceptions and opinions relevant to the study.

4 Results

In the experiential stages, we identified the behaviors, activities, and touchpoints of the respondents as they experienced their destinations visit. For ease of interpretation, the results from the aforementioned research questions are summarized in Figs. 2, 3, and 4. The three journeys incorporate tourism experience and gain/pain points into all touchpoints the visitor had during the Jioufen Gallery, Ceramic Art Workshop, and Artist Teahouse. The sections counted '+N' in the customer journey represent frequencies of gain points with good experiences, '−N' represent frequencies of negative experiences, resulting in dissatisfaction and negative reactions. The gain/pain points line indicate how satisfied/dissatisfied the visitors were at certain stages of the tourism experiences.

4.1 The Jioufen Gallery

The core experiences provided at the Jioufen Gallery included tea sets, pottery works, and oil paintings of Taiwan's local artists. As shown in Fig. 2, among the respondents, most frequently mentioned aesthetic pleasure, story of collection, and guide as their gain points within the core experiences, indicating that they perceived aesthetics, professional guide, narratives of exhibits as important elements to strengthen their core experiences. It was found that most respondents had a great experience while the professional guide to introduce the stories behind the exhibits. A respondent stated that "the tour guides provided professional and clear explanations that enhanced understanding of the connection between the exhibits and the display space as well as the backgrounds, stories, and values of the works."

Some respondents mentioned signage, indistinctive characteristics of the gallery, circulation, artwork descriptions, and light effect as the pain points within the

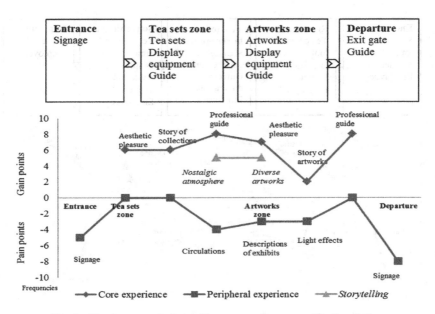

Fig. 2. Tourism experiences with customer journey at Jioufen Gallery

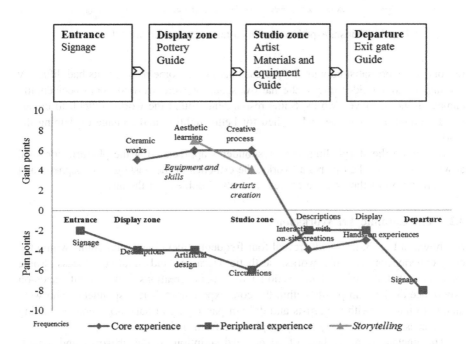

Fig. 3. Tourism experiences with customer journey at Ceramic Art Workshop

peripheral experiences, indicating that respondents were dissatisfied with the facilities, infrastructure, etc., to support the achievement of the core experiences. Although most

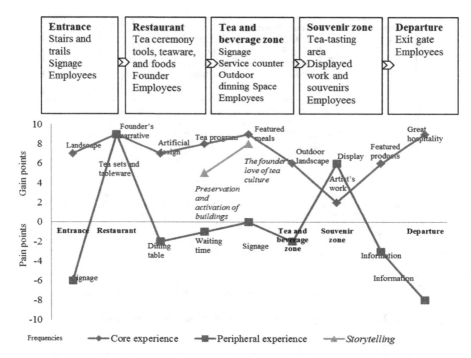

Fig. 4. Tourism experiences with customer journey at Artist Teahouse

respondents were satisfied with the professional guide, some respondents had difficulty hearing the tour guides due to the narrow space or were worried about accidentally damaging the displayed works. Some respondents found the works difficult to understand without a tour guide and wished for better lighting and signage explaining the works.

Regarding the storytelling, most respondents appreciated at the platform for local artworks—such as the diverse artworks, the esthetics of the nostalgic atmosphere, and an appreciation of the creative process and philosophies—at the site.

4.2   The Ceramic Art Workshop

As shown in Fig. 3, the results reveal four frequently mentioned gain points within the core experiences: ceramic works, aesthetic learning, and creative process. Some mentioned that the lack of interaction with on-site creations and without hands-on experience as the pain points within the core experiences. The respondents who were unable to interact with the artists and did not participate in hands-on ceramic making experiences were less likely to report pleasure from their visits.

The unclear signage, lack of adequate description of the artworks and award-winning pieces, artificial design, and display were the pain points within the peripheral experiences. Because passageways in the workshop are narrow, some respondents felt the workshop was not a place to linger for fear of accidentally damaging the ceramics. Some respondents also felt that the workshop displayed too many items, and the placement of items on shelves lacked design, indicating that the artificial design, facilities, and infrastructure affected the core experiences.

Regarding the storytelling, Ceramic Art Workshop is the first studio of pottery works in Jiufen and the one only where makes and sells its own products. Some respondents felt that the artist's creations, equipment and skills displayed in the ceramic making process at the workshop constituted the value of local art life.

4.3 The Artist Teahouse

Among the three cases, the respondents described the greatest variety of gain points and the most memorable impressions at the Artist Teahouse as shown in Fig. 4. Most respondents perceived landscape, the founder's narratives, beautifully furnished space, tea and food tasting, artist works, featured products, and great hospitality as their gain points within the core experiences. A respondent stated that "through skillful planning and design of the topography, the beauty of the natural scenery was blended with the beauty of the artistic creations." Most respondents had pleasant dining experiences and could sense the care that went into each step of the service design. A respondent stated that "the communal tea bowl was a unique ritual from among all of our tea-drinking experiences, and the teapot shaped like Keelung Mountain was one of the founder's original creations." Some of the products were derivative products created by the business founder that demonstrated his lifestyle. A respondent stated that "viewing these items was like viewing artistic works. The majority of the practical items on display demonstrated aesthetic appeal."

The pain points included unclear service signage, information and a need for improvement in the comfort level of the meal service. Some respondents felt that the signage for the teahouse was also difficult to see when they approached the Artist House. In the dining and tea ceremony area, a respondent discovered that it was inconvenient to serve tea because the tables were too long. Moreover, one respondent felt that the waiting time for food was too long. After completing their visit, some respondents discovered that the exit was relatively far away from the entrance and were therefore confused about how to leave the building.

Most respondents appreciated the founder's love of tea and tea culture, as well as the beauty of his efforts to preserve and activate the historical building that contributed the storytelling of these experiences.

5 Discussion

This study explored the essence of experiential service design in creative tourism from perspective of tourists. Through cross-analyses of the pain and gain points of customer journeys, we proposed the important elements of the core experiences, peripheral experiences, and storytelling of these experiences as shown in Fig. 5. Regarding the experiential stages, the findings show that creative people, thematic activities, aesthetic atmosphere, and stylish works/featured products together construct the dimensions of core experiences in creative tourism. Service and exhibition facilities are identified in this work as important dimensions of peripheral experiences. Preservation and activation of traditional building, contribution to local development, and activation of local culture are demonstrated as important dimensions of storytelling of these experiences to support the achievement of the core and peripheral experiences.

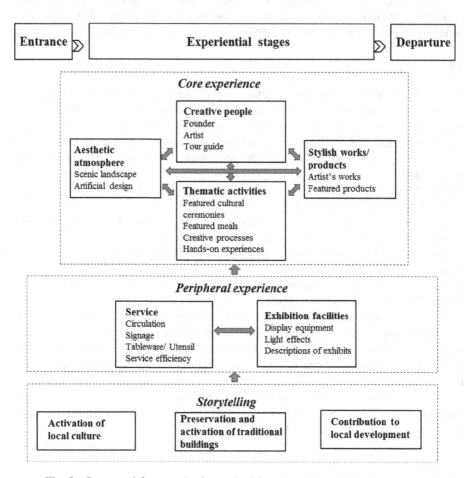

Fig. 5. Conceptual framework of experiential service design in creative tourism

First, the current findings indicate that tourists learn not only through participating in activities [4, 21] but also through related creative people, stylish works/featured products, and aesthetic atmosphere which contribute the core experiences at creative tourism destinations. This study extends the literature on the related activities enable tourists to learn about the local skills, expertise, traditions, and unique qualities of a location for the purposes of creative tourism [3].

The findings show that interaction with creative people (i.e., the founders, artists, guides) of the destinations plays a very important role in creative tourism experiences. This study also extends the literature on interaction between tourists and the physical elements of the destinations, interactions with the social elements of the destinations (i.e., interactions with other tourists, locals, tourism employees, and other social networks associated with the destinations) [14]. However, distinct from other studies, this study finds that stylish works/featured products play an important role in differentiating from other tourism experiences. For example, respondents appreciated at the Ceramic Art Workshop produces ceramics themed on the old mining atmosphere of Jiufen and products such as tea sets. In this study, tourists are now searching for aesthetic and authentic experiences through the use of products at creative tourism destinations. The story, aesthetic design, award-winning objects, and stylish dimensions of products should be essential design elements of creative tourism that cause active participation by tourists.

The result with regard to learning activities demonstrated that in addition to the interactive elements consistent with Tussyadiah [14], participating in daily life activities is crucial for tourists wishing to experience a local living environment. Regarding local daily life, the study identified special cultural ceremonies (i.e., tea culture experiences), featured meals, and hands-on experiences as important elements of 'thematic activities' which enhance tourists' active participation. Favorable tourism experiences can be facilitated by identifying peak tourism experiences and supporting consumer experiences and daily routine experiences, as proposed by Stickdorn and Frischhut [16]. Supporting experiences are eating and sleeping. This study differs from earlier work because the findings reveal that eating can be considered peak experiences. For example, respondents perceived peak or "sweet spot" experiences when using utensils and tableware associated with tasting and dining to gain more experience regarding tea and food culture. This finding indicates the importance of designing authentic engagement with local daily life in creative tourism.

Second, the respondents' pain points mostly reflected peripheral experiences; some tourists could not hear the tour guides' presentations, which might have influenced achievement of the core experiences [14]. For example, most respondents perceived esthetics within the core experiences at the three sites, but peripheral experiences were insufficient or there was a lack of explanation regarding exhibitions and inconvenient tea experience might that created pain points for some tourists. This finding is consistent with the literature, with a previous study noting that if failure points occur with the supporting experiences, the experience value could be jeopardized regardless of the strength of the peak experience [16]. Therefore, creative tourism enterprises should focus on integrating various design elements with the peripheral experiences to allow for valuable tourism experiences. Therefore, practitioners who wish to enhance tourists' total experiences should pay more attention to these elements. Exhibition facilities, such as descriptions of exhibits, light effects, and display equipment, are important peripheral experiences that may affect tourists' learning in the core experience.

Third, the findings show that the preservation and activation of traditional buildings is consistent with Tussyadiah [14], which proposed that storytelling experiences at the society level were guided by norms, shared values, etc. This study extends the literature on storytelling experiences at the society level by identified the norms, shared values, etc., in the meta-concept of tourism experiences by Tussyadiah [14].

Our results also imply that the storytelling experiences include not only the norms, shared values, etc., but also the activation of local culture and contributions to local development are demonstrated as important elements. For example, while tourists listen to the story of the Artist Teahouse, the featured products, such as the Keelung Mountain teapot or the communal tea bowl, can be provided to the tourists for brewing tea themselves.

Finally, the use of pain and gain points within a customer journey as a visualization tool made the results interpretable. The study combines gain/pain points of empathy maps [28] and customer journey maps [25] with creative tourism experiences that provides in-depth insights into the tourists' experiences, implies that the proposed method recognizes reality as it is and applies service design tools to analyze and visualize tourist experiences [24]. The findings imply that pain and gain points encountered by the tourists at the touchpoints were mostly equivalent to the core and peripheral experiences. The results demonstrated that the core experiences largely reflected the reported gain points in behavior or activities in the process of interacting with the touchpoints. Respondents' pain points mostly reflected unfulfilled expectations regarding the core and peripheral experiences with the touchpoints. The pain and gain points can be transformed into key elements of the tourism experiences through an experiential service design for creative tourism.

6 Conclusion and Implications

From an academic perspective, the findings of this study contribute to the literature on tourism experience in the creative tourism field, and within it developed a framework of experiential service design from the tourists' perspective. This study has both theoretical and managerial implications.

First, creative tourists prefer active involvement, and they not only actively gain knowledge to develop their own skills [3] but also endeavor to enrich their minds and life experiences. Regarding the key elements of creative experience, outer interactions refer to tourists' interactions with the environment, people, and products/services/experiences [20]. In designing touchpoints, creative tourism enterprises should focus on providing useful facilities and devices for tourists' experiences because peripheral experiences support the achievement of core experiences.

Second, tourists gradually incline toward cultural activities [4, 21] with participative learning in the arts, heritage, or special characteristics of a place, and this provides an opportunity to create the living culture [1]. Regarding the service design principles of user-centrism, co-creation, sequencing, evidencing, and holism [25], in addition to emphasizing thematic learning activities, the importance of local daily life experiences, such as food culture and featured culture ceremonies, should be designed as core experiences in creative tourism.

The study was concentrated on the one small county of Taiwan. Thus, it has limitations. The study used qualitative research methods in the specific creative tourism contexts and collected empirical data. Hence, conclusions that are generally applicable to creative tourism in other countries cannot be easily drawn. Creative tourism has a wide range of connotations. We recommend that the framework developed in this study be applied to other creative tourism contexts, including travel experiences of museums, cultural assets, etc. The value of applying this research model in other relevant fields should be discussed.

References

1. UNESDCO homepage. http://unesdoc.unesco.org/images/0015/001598/159811E.pdf. Accessed 25 Oct 2018
2. Richards, G.: Creativity: a new strategic resource for tourism. In: Swarbrooke, J., Smith, M., Onderwater, L. (eds.) Tourism, Creativity and Development: ATLAS Reflections 2005, pp. 11–22. Association for Tourism and Leisure Education, Arnhem (2005)
3. Richards, G., Wilson, J.: Developing creativity in tourist experiences: a solution to the serial reproduction of culture? Tour. Manag. **27**, 1408–1413 (2006)
4. Smith, M.K.: Issues in Cultural Tourism Studies, 2nd edn. Routledge, New York (2009)
5. Binkhorst, E.: The experience economy and creativity, towards the co-creation tourism experience? In: The ATLAS Annual Conference 2005: Tourism Creativity and Development, Barcelona (2005)
6. Gilmore, H.J., Pine II, B.J.: The experience is the marketing. Brown Herron Publishing (2002). Amazon.com, eDoc
7. Gilmore, H.J., Pine II, B.J.: Differentiating hospitality operations via experiences: why selling services is not enough. Cornell Hotel Restaur. Adm. Q. **43**(3), 87–96 (2002)
8. United Nations homepage. https://unctad.org/en/pages/publicationarchive.aspx?publicationid=946. Accessed 20 Dec 2018
9. Binkhorst, E., den Dekker, T.: Towards the co-creation tourism experience. J. Hosp. Mark. Manag. **18**(2–3), 311–327 (2009)
10. Diller, S., Shedroff, N., Rhea, D.: Making Meaning: How Successful Businesses Deliver Meaningful Customer Experiences. New Riders, Berkeley (2008)
11. Pine II, B.J., Gilmore, J.H.: The Experience Economy: Work Is Theatre & Every Business a Stage. Harvard Business School Press, Boston (1999)
12. Ellis, G.D., Rossman, J.R.: Creating value for participants through experience staging: parks, recreation, and tourism in the experience industry. J. Park Recreat. Adm. **26**(4), 1–20 (2008)
13. Stamboulis, Y., Skayannis, P.: Innovation strategies and technology for experienced based tourism. Tour. Manag. **24**, 35–43 (2003)
14. Tussyadiah, I.P.: Toward a theoretical foundation for experience design in tourism. J. Travel Res. **53**(5), 543–564 (2014)
15. Zehrer, A.: Service experience and service design: concepts and application in tourism SMEs'. Manag. Serv. Qual. **19**(3), 332–349 (2009)
16. Stickdorn, M., Frischhut, B.: Service Design and Tourism: Case Studies of Applied Research Projects on Mobile Ethnography for Tourism Destinations. Books on Demand GmbH, Norderstedt (2012)
17. Stickdorn, M., Zehrer, A.: Service design in tourism: customer experience driven destination management. In: The First Nordic Conference on Service Design and Service Innovation, Oslo, Norway (2009)
18. Trischler, J., Zehrer, A.: Service design: suggesting a qualitative multi-step approach for analyzing and examining theme park experiences. J. Vacat. Mark. **18**(1), 57–71 (2012)
19. Richards, G.: Creativity and tourism: the state of the art. Ann. Tour. Res. **38**(4), 1225–1253 (2011)
20. Tan, S.-K., Kung, S.-F., Luh, D.-B.: A model of "creative experience" in creative tourism. Ann. Tour. Res. **41**, 153–174 (2013)
21. Richards, G., Raymond, C.: Creative tourism. ATLAS News **23**, 16–20 (2000)
22. Ali, F., Ryu, K., Hussain, K.: Influence of experiences on memories, satisfaction and behavioral intentions: a study of creative tourism. J. Travel Tour. Mark. **33**(1), 85–100 (2016)

23. Lee, G., Tussyadiah, I.P., Zach, F.: A visitor-focused assessment of new product launch: the case of Quilt Gardens Tour^{SM} in Northern Indiana's Amish Country. J. Travel Tour. Mark. **27**(7), 723–735 (2010)
24. Mager, B.: Service design as an emerging field. In: Miettinen, S., Koivisto, M. (eds.) Designing Services with Innovative Methods, pp. 28–42. Taik Publications, Helsinki (2009)
25. Stickdorn, M., Schneider, J.: This Is Service Design Thinking: Basics, Tools, Cases. Wiley, New York (2012)
26. Ho, S.-S., Sung, T.-J.: The development of academic research in service design: a meta-analysis. J. Des. **19**(2), 45–66 (2014)
27. Shaw, C., Ivens, J.: Building Great Customer Experiences. Palgrave Macmillan, Basingstoke (2002)
28. Osterwalder, A., Pigneur, Y., Bernarda, G., Smith, A., Papadakos, T.: Value Proposition Design: How to Create Products and Services Customers Want. Wiley, Hoboken (2014)
29. Cook, L.S., Bowen, D.E., Chase, R.B., Dasu, S., Stewart, D.M., Tansik, D.A.: Human issues in service design. J. Oper. Manag. **20**(2), 159–174 (2002)
30. Benbasat, I., Goldstein, D., Mead, M.: The case research strategies in studies of information system. MIS Q. **11**(3), 369–374 (1987)
31. Yin, R.K.: Case Study Research: Design and Methods, 3rd edn. Sage, London (2003)
32. Patton, M.Q.: Qualitative Research and Evaluation Methods, 3rd edn. Sage, London (2002)

Museum and Cultural Products Co-creation Brand Value

Taking the Innovative Cultural Products of Ningbo Port Museum as an Example

Ching-Wen Chang[(⊠)]

Graduate Institute of Creative Industries, Shih Chien University, Taipei, Taiwan
lizchang@cycu.org.tw

Abstract. In the 21st century, the emotional era is coming; the new art exhibition trend will be accompanied by the viewer/consumer experience, and the viewer/consumer's expectation for the future, compatible with the three connotations of culture, design and marketing. Cultural products that conform to the brand image of the museum can make the public more willing to return and pay attention to the pulse of the museum. Under the function of the education, research, performance and entertainment of traditional museums, is the museum brand image limited to the collection of museums? With the advent of the digital era, is there any opportunity or aspect for the extension of brand imagery? Brand value can be given to the museum with more attractive brand charm under the sharing and creation of museums and their derivative cultural products. In addition, museums with a lot of space for growth in the creative industry, could be create more industries or service niches through the enhancement of brand value.

This study starts from interdisciplinary co-creation cases between Taiwan and China students. By participating in, observing and analyzing cases with Interpretive case study [17], interpretation of Commercial Design of CYCU and Industrial Design of NIT design teams, through the cooperation with the Ningbo Port Museum and the introduction of the design thinking workshop, how to interpret the product connotation from different levels, to re-recognize the brand value, sort out the consensus of the cognitive level, and derive the insight of the new product.

Keywords: Museum brand · Cultural products design EDCBA · Co-creation value

1 Introduction

Under the function of the education, research, performance and entertainment of traditional museums, is the museum brand image limited to the collection of museums? With the advent of the digital era, is there any opportunity for the extension of brand image to be more possibilities? Brand value, under the sharing and creation of museums and their derivative cultural products, can the museum be given more

© Springer Nature Switzerland AG 2019
P.-L. P. Rau (Ed.): HCII 2019, LNCS 11577, pp. 17–32, 2019.
https://doi.org/10.1007/978-3-030-22580-3_2

attractive brand charm? In addition, museums with a lot of growing space in the creative industry, such as create more industries or service niches through the enhancement of brand value.

Over time, the function and design philosophy of the museum has also changed. The traditional concept of museum has evolved into the concept of community development of the ecological museum, and the spirit of design has also changed from the finished art to the creative communication mode with independent thinking. The systematic evolution of museum and design has contributed to the development of cultural products with brand spirit, and at the same time has become the core connotation of the creative industry's primary concern.

1.1   Eco Museum

In the 1970s, the student movement in France mainly reflected the anti-state machine of French intellectuals and the anti-centralization of a claim. Under the influence of this trend, two French museum scientists: Georges Henri Rivière and Hugiles de Varine have proposed the concept of "decentralization of museums", arguing that museums should go to the people, not the products of centralization. According to Georges Henri Rivière: "Eco museums are tools that are cultivated, shaped and operated by the public sector (local government) and local residents. Local museums provide librarians, equipment and resources, and local people show their ambitions, knowledge and personal strength, so the Eco-Museum is a mirror for local people to take care of themselves, to find the image of self, to seek an explanation of the life of the ancestors living in this field, regardless of the natural or human heritage. At the same time, it is also a mirror that allows visitors to take a deeper understanding of local industries, customs and characteristics." [1].

The museum's operational base is not limited to museum collections, displays, or educational activities. In fact, the natural and human assets of the entire region within the reach of museum organization are covered. The definition of museum audiences has also expanded, with the exception of visitors to the museum, including visitors to the museum, community people and future generations. In the organization of museums, museum professionals are no longer the only core of power, the community representatives, volunteers, museum friends, etc., will form a partnership relationship with professionals. In summary, we can extract the following five concepts from the development of the Eco-Museum: (1) It has changed from a "top-down" of central authority to a localization of "bottom-up." (2) From the traditional "from the inside out" to the "outside-in" business approach. (3) Abandoning grand theory or grand discourse. (4) The operating base of the museum has changed from "object-oriented" to "person-oriented". (5) From past-oriented to present or future-oriented. The museum is no longer a nostalgic institution, it should participate in social changes as a catalyst for social change. In other words, the development strategy of the Eco-Museum is not about what happened in the past, but about changing the present and even creating a new future [2].

1.2   Museum Culture Product

The cultural store is usually the "last exhibition hall" of the museum. It was raised in the European and American museums in the 1950s, and it was brought late in China and Taiwan [3]. The souvenirs in the store carry the culture and philosophy of the museum, and because of its popular, practical and fluent nature, it brings a sense of consumer satisfaction to visitors, inspiring visitors' interest and enthusiasm [4]; at the same time, it also increases visitors. Touching the closeness of the museum culture and further expanding the educational function of the museum. In addition, by creating business income, the museum can also achieve a virtuous circle of self and ensure the sustainability of the museum [5].

Derivatives are commemorative products derived from the cultural resources of the museum itself, combined with creative design, aesthetics of life and popular elements [3]. It is usually a product that maintains the original shape, but is made of different materials and specifications. Or, it is the performance characteristic of the original, combined with other functional products to form a new cultural and creative products, such as: bookmarks, U disk, fan, cup, stationery, umbrella, clothing, etc. In general, artifacts and works of art are far away for the public. The former is limited by ownership, and the latter is expensive because of the fact that the public can only stay at the distance of appreciation. Derivative products allow cultural relics and artworks to enter the daily life of the public, and also realize the process of creative design transformation and sales, explore the potential value of cultural relics and artworks, promote the educational functions of the museum, and enhance the brand influence of the museum [5].

1.3   Museum Brand

Brand is an important asset of the industry. In addition to good quality and convenient access, excellent brand image enables enterprises to quickly obtain excellent profits and achieve growth goals. The Aaker Model five-star conceptual model created by American organization theory expert David Aaker regards brand equity as a combination of brand awareness, brand recognition, brand loyalty, brand association and other brand-specific assets, from products, organizations, people and the symbol is four perspectives to interpret the brand. Aaker thinks: "The brand is the main source of competitive advantage and valuable strategic wealth." [6].

The connotation of the brand includes the association of the organization; the place of production, the image of the user, the value of emotional attachment, the value of self-expression, brand characteristics, symbols (logo), the brand and customer relationship, the product (including scope, attributes, quality, and function), that is, the brand contains the product. It may be abstract, a feeling, a trust, a service or a general experience, and its foundation is derived from the product itself. "You will not be satisfied with having the best brand; you want the only brand", "the brand that grasps the market demand, people will want to buy; seize the brand of the customer's heart, they will be loyal", Do not Let your brand become an enemy and obstacle for the organization to move forward [7].

Therefore, in the era of multi-information marketing, brand management as an asset management method will help the product to break away from the best method of price war. "Marketing" is the most important function of the company; "Brand" is the core of marketing. Therefore, erecting unique brand characteristics, focusing on brand positioning and spirit, and defining a unified visual language are important foundations for construction [8]. In addition, from the input to the output process, all processes of research analysis, transformation, and integration must be carefully handled in order to establish a system that conforms to the spirit of the brand under the cultural language of the museum. At the same time, from the strategy, planning, design, execution, to the business stage, we must also rely on the same system to create memories and maximize the brand's charm (see Fig. 1).

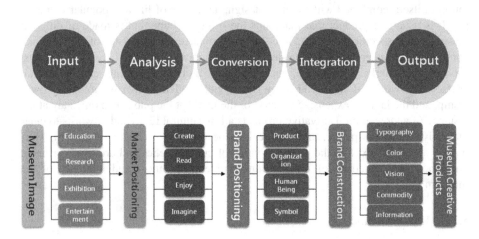

Fig. 1. Museum cultural products brand derivative system

The museum is regarded as a brand. All the collections are the core values of the brand, and the goods can be regarded as vehicles. Through the innovative creation mode, the cultural codes and core values can be fully conveyed, that is, culture goods. With the docking between the two, the successful establishment of the museum image can also lead to the valuable museum culture creative brand.

Museums of a New Century (CMNC, 1984), a famous collection of American museums, reminds everyone of the importance of museum education: "If the collection is the heart of the museum, education is the soul of the museum" [9]. Art can exist for all, resonate with community life, and awaken human collective historical memory. Cultural creative products that conform to the brand image of the museum use aesthetic education to match the visual art design and museum functions of the creative industry, to enhance the public get closer, reversal, and always pay attention to the museum, thus creating more museum business opportunities and laying the museum brand image with "Uniquely". This is also the creators of contemporary art-related fields who are eager to carry out brand marketing, glamour communication and effective implementation in response to changes in the times.

2 Literature Review

The era of change, the design concept that changes with the social form, has a new challenge and framework for the evolution of design thinking and the concept of traditional museum fields. The biggest change in the design environment is the need to integrate the connotation of culture and emphasize the feasibility of sustainable development; the discussion of design thinking must be based on the culture of the era, interpret the diversity of design and diversity of interdisciplinary scales, and focus on the nature of design image, the meaning of design completion, the diversified environment, the experience value of reflecting history, and the culture of geographical design; as for the place, the ecological museum that emphasizes the development of the community becomes a new manifestation; and the economic view of the museum industry which is the pre-foundation of cultural heritage, field and marketing model as industrialization.

2.1 Cultural Product Innovation Design

From the perspective of the evolution of creative life industry and design, the evolution of industrial value proposed by scholar Lin Rung-Tai divides this evolution into a cultural economy based on manufacturing economy, service economy, experience economy and even cultural goods. It can be found that product design has a certain correspondence with consumer demand, from a manufacturing economy that emphasizes product function prices to a service economy that emphasizes consumer demand and a unique customization, and then emphasizes user experience (UX), user interface (UI) or the experience economy of life style mode develops into today's cultural economy. Product design emphasizes culture, consumer demand pursues aesthetic experience. In the traditional product development process, there is obviously no introduction and design of this cultural concept. There is no need for other innovative processes to assist [10].

Professor Lin Rung-Tai believes that "culture" is a life style, "design" is a taste of life, "creative" is a kind of touched identity, and "industry" is a medium, means or method for realizing cultural creativity. On the cultural level, it is the design that through the cultural creativity, through the industry to achieve a design taste, to form a life style. If the 21st century is based on "humanity", the design of "culture" is even more important. How to convert "culture" into "creative" and value-added products "design", that is, how to "culture creativity" Value design is the main topic of cultural innovation design [11].

2.2 Design Thinking

With the design thinking training of Hasso Plattner Institute of Design at Stanford University (D-School), put forward the spirit that should be possessed in design thinking; 1. People-oriented: the starting point of human design, experience from the user's point of view, to treat him the feeling is to achieve the design that is closest to the user. 2. Early failure: It is better to invest in a relatively small amount of early cost and time, know the failure early, and make corresponding corrections. 3. Cross-domain teamwork: Members of different backgrounds have different expertise and different perspectives on things. Therefore, a cross-domain innovation team is not only able to achieve cross-domain integration results, but also more possibility in inspire innovation. 4. Learning from the process: hands-on learning, and to make prototypes, regardless of success or failure, we can learn more from the process of implementation. 5. Empathy: Look at the world from the same angle as the user, to feel the same experience. 6. Rapid Prototyping: Prototype production begins with a rough and simple model, completed quickly for quick and repeated corrections [12].

2.3 Co-creation Value

From the concept of "product value" first proposed by Sobel Rothenberg's Creative Value, 1980, the value of the product is based on emphasis on originality, value, and integrity [13]. Michael Porter then put forward the concept of "value chain" in 1985, arguing that products can give more industrial profits because of the linkage of value chains. By identifying the various activities in the process from feed, manufacturing to service, we identify the main and value-added activities of the company's value creation to match the company's resources to develop competitive advantage [14]. In 2004, Prahalad and Ramaswamy put forward the idea of "value creation", thinking that value is not only defined by the product side, but contains existing consumers, potential markets, online emerging markets, and has the opportunity to become co-creation. It is mainly divided into two categories of value creation (production, service) and consumption (consumer alone, consumer interaction with enterprise, consumer interaction with consumer) [15].

In view of the literature discussion of value, this research will further supplement the research gap, which means that while discussing the value of products, we should inject a more layered cultural analysis to explore the life propositions and overalls released by the niche consumer groups, and the lifestyle tastes guided by the product form, also even extend the life style traits implied by large-scale cultural rituals. This is the reference the chairman of the former Taiwan Creative Design Center, Professor Lin Rung-Tai proposed in 2011: the creative design of the creative industry, which "begins with culture, is shaped by products, used for life, and becomes a brand" [16]. Rethinking the definition of value, advancing with the times and creating (string) a model must rely on the addition and subtraction of the experience combing comb, as for the theoretical gap, it is corrected by a more detailed layer-by-layer completeness. This is also the value and significance of this research.

Looking at the above, regardless of the ecological museum or design thinking, the essence is based on "people". It is necessary to give a layered cultural connotation, deepen the prototype of brand memory, and the brand value created by museums and cultural goods can be specific. The practical operation of this case study in this research is based on the concept of cross-domain cooperation in design thinking, stimulating more innovation and thinking on the museum cultural goods, through the repeated test and correction of the run-in, this study finally derives the cultural products design principles EDCBA which model can help museums, cultural products development, consumers, innovation or experience the unique brand image and value of the museum.

3 Research Methods

3.1 Interpretive Case Study

This study begins with the Interpretive case study [17], emphasizing that the number of cases is fine, its focus on re-recognizing the problem, the angle determines the resolution, the reasoning must be integrated into the dialectic, and saw that didn't see it before [17]. The case object is for the Ningbo Port Museum of China. Students from both sides of Taiwan and China will create a unique cultural and creative product that meets the image of the museum. Through the participation of the group, in-depth observation and analysis of the case, interpretation of CYCD and NITID design teams, how to interpret product connotations from different cultural levels under the introduction of Port museum professional guides and design thinking workshops, so as to re-recognize the value of the brand, sort out the meaning of the cognitive level, and derive the insight into the design of the new product.

Then, discuss with the museum staff and workshop training instructors, in addition to layering the comments, while studying the cognitive attributes, emotional depth and design value of various new works in the hearts of consumers, designers and enterprises, with cultural level (physical/tangible material, social/interpersonal behavior, spiritual/inner feeling), cultural meaning (external/intuitive, intermediate/behavior, internal/emotional), design attributes (external/intuitive, function/behavior, feelings/humanity), summarizing product positioning levels and new attributes.

3.2 Case Object: Port Museum and Cross-School Student Team

The Port Museum is located Chunxiao Town, Beilun District, Ningbo, Zhejiang Province. The Museum was founded in October 2014, it has a total land area of 51,966 m^2, and a total construction area of 40,987 m^2. With port culture as its theme, the China Port Museum integrates exhibition, education, collection, research, tourism, international exchanges as well as other functions. Embodying internationalism, professionalism and interactivity, the largest and uppermost port theme museum in China has become a cultural base to inherit port history & culture and spread ocean civilization and a cultural fulcrum of the Maritime Silk Road in the new century.

The port museum carries the cultural connotation of "Ports Leading to the world". The whole hall is divided into seven exhibition halls. It is different from the traditional museum model with the collection of "historical artifacts" and focuses on creating a new and more youthful "modern museum". Its provide an academic exchange platform for scholars who study the history of China's ports and explore the future of the port at home and abroad; provide an in-depth learning environment for visitors to understand the development process of China's ports and master port knowledge; provide a deep understanding of the port's development and foster interest in the port for the majority of young people; provide a comprehensive display and in-depth research space for the dissemination and promotion of marine civilization and port culture.

College of Commercial Design, Chung Yuan Christian University (Taiwan), CYCD is based on humanity and digital technology courses, working with design and marketing courses to develop students' critical thinking skills to have a successful career in marketing and visual communication design.

College of Industrial Design, Ninbo Institute of Technology, Zhejiang University (China), NITID is recognized as one of the Key Majors in the city of Ningbo. The mission is to be a cradle of creativity for talented students of journalism, advertising, design, film, and animation. The vision can be summarized as emphasizing creativity in media and design to create a more vital society, instill positive values, and to express the aesthetics and soul of our nation.

3.3 Design Thinking Workshop

This study starts from the cross-domain creation of students from both sides of Taiwan and China. Through the in-depth tour of the museum, the students can understand the history of the museum, the story behind each cultural relic, the curatorial spirit and the concept of cultural goods management. According to this hierarchical concept, the museum image is recognized, the product orientation is drawn up, and in the workshop implementation, the two backgrounds of commercial design and industrial design are combined across the domain to create a prototype of nine new cultural products. Cross-domain collaboration of new products has three processing stages: First, based on five steps of design thinking process: Empathize, Define, Ideate, Prototype, Test. We encourage young designers across the different background to brainstorming stimulates more possibilities creativity. Second, citing Professor Lin Rung-Tai's creative connotation essence ABCDE to the industry profit model ABCDE structure [18], in the way of storytelling, find the design attributes that can best highlight the museum image. Third, in the process of translating design into knowledge, we quote the term "sense, start from knowledge" of Designer Mizuno [19], define the shape of the product, adopt the common rules of common points, and establish the level of behavior, it is necessary to conduct research and fully understand the current and popularity trend, and before creating products rich in inner spiritual level, you must rely on the classics. The design concept and results are as follows Table 1.

Table 1. Ningbo Port Museum innovation cultural products with design thinking, create by CYCD (Taiwan) and NITID (China) students.

Design Thinking Stage
Empathize→Define→Ideate→Prototype→Test
Case object / Workshop Team

Ningbo Port Museum, China.

CYCD: College of Commercial Design, Chung Yuan Christian University (Taiwan).
NITID: College of Industrial Design, Ninbo Institute of Technoloty, Zhejiang Universty (China).

NO.	Product Name	3D Model Diagram	Design Concept
P1	Fishing chopsticks cage combination		Each set of chopsticks has a pattern derived from the port fish coin. The upper ceramic part is composed of three layers of 12 ceramic chopstick holders, which can be removed separately or connected by magnets.
P2	Coloring Book: The museum is wonderful		Simplify the story of the museum into an ink coloring book, and let the children easily interpret the story of Mazu(one of the most popular goddess in China) while painting and reading the story.
P3	Silver bottled water		Inspired by the silver cocktail bottle of the Port Museum, the classic bottle is transformed into a modern mineral water bottle.
P4	Through-ear bottle style Tableware		It is converted into a combination of wine glasses and bowls, which can be freely disassembled and superposed, using the shape and meaning of the Yuan Dynasty(A.D.1217) Shou-Shan Fu-Hai pattern ear bottle.

(*Continued*)

Table 1. (*Continued*)

P5	Chime key case		The Western Zhou Dynasty's(B.C.1122) chime is transformed into a key bag that can be carried daily, and the keys collide with each other, and the jingle is like a musical piece of the millennium. The packaging and collection museum red, black and gold are the main colors.
P6	Helm		In the Song Dynasty(A.D. 960), the rudder of the hull was controlled, and a series of drinking tools were produced: a stir bar, a wine spoon, and a tea maker. When the product is placed in a cup, the beverage cup is like the same boat, and the drinker is like the captain controlling the ship.
P7	Temperature mug		With the deep sea archaeological diver costume as a creative idea, the cartoon version of the Q version is designed to pour hot water into the cup. The temperature mug will turn dark, like the image of a diver diving into the sea.
P8	Child mirror		Taking children as the main target group, and taking the flower and bird bronze mirror as the imagination, the ancient bronze mirror can also become an interesting deformation mirror.
P9	Treasure cup		Inspired by the copper bird pot, the bottom of the cup is placed in the treasure of the port museum town hall: "Heyi-Ru" wreck. The drinker blows the straw and gets bubbles, just like the diver enters the underwater for archaeology and exploration.

4 Results and Discussion

4.1 Cultural Innovation Value-Added Design Model

From the design results of the cross-domain workshop, this study continues to extend the application of the three-level analytical culture design module proposed by Professor Lin, [20] combined with the core spirit of the eco-museum: (1) From user's view, the museum is a tool for the government to communicate with the public. (2) Challenge the concept of relics preservation institutions serving a small number of

Table 2. Cultural level, cultural meaning, design attributes and product preference survey of cross-domain innovation products (n = 125)

Factor	NO.								
	P1	P2	P3	P4	P5	P6	P7	P8	P9
Physical/ (understand) tangible substance	3.63	4.33	4.08	3.68	**4.20**	3.82	4.17	3.99	3.82
External/ (sincere) intuitive meaning	3.87	3.84	3.84	3.70	3.63	3.87	**3.92**	3.57	3.92
External/ (function) intuitive design	3.84	3.73	**4.20**	3.55	3.60	3.45	3.92	3.64	3.35
Sociality/ (durable) people behavior	3.84	3.05	3.46	3.64	3.63	3.90	4.03	**3.85**	3.55
Intermediate/ (environment) behavioral meaning	3.87	**3.65**	3.15	3.42	3.39	3.67	3.74	3.28	3.65
Function/ (innovative) behavioral pattern	3.88	3.05	3.96	**3.85**	3.50	3.99	3.20	3.46	4.16
Spirituality/ (aesthetic) inner feeling	4.14	3.96	4.35	3.95	3.68	**4.35**	3.33	3.58	4.20
Inner/ (introverted) emotional meaning	3.74	3.46	3.51	3.68	3.41	3.59	3.35	3.35	**4.02**
Feeling/ (thoughtful) human nature	**4.10**	3.40	3.42	3.60	3.36	3.46	3.48	3.40	3.59
Degree of preference	19%	4%	16%	6%	2%	12%	2%	3%	**31%**

social elites. (3) The museum should based on humanity, serve the people, serve now, and divided into three stages according to the formation process of life style, users (life proposition) Form (product, lifestyle taste), ceremony (culture, lifestyle), and then corresponding to the three levels of cultural level, cultural meaning, and design attributes, nine sets of design patterns with different emotional levels are formed. Through

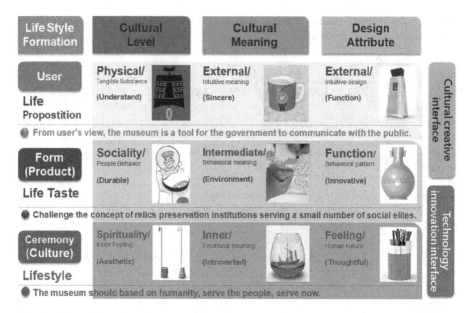

Fig. 2. Cultural innovation value-added design model from cultural level to design attribute.

the questionnaire survey (see Table 2), the nine sets of new achievements of the workshop will be placed in the grids. The closer the products are to the upper level, the more emphasis will be placed on the external visual and cultural creative interface. The lower level will pay more attention to the inner spirit and technological innovation interface. The survey also found that viewers' preference for new products is more or less close to the emotional level, or closer to the story of the museum, worthy of attention. The results form a cultural innovation value-added design pattern from cultural level to design attributes. (see Fig. 2)

4.2   Cultural Products Design Principles EDCBA Model

Combining the essence of three major external frameworks: creative connotation ABCDE (Attractiveness, Beauty, Creativity, Delicacy, and Engineering perception), and profit model ABCDE (Art aesthetics, cultural Business, Creative first, precise Design, and E-commerce) [18] and design Knowledge [19], this study finally derived the "cultural product design EDCBA principles" model to verify whether new products are eligible for niche Evaluation? Can you increase the fun of interaction through Dynamic aesthetics? Is there a concept of sustainable management that considers Cycling design? Eventually, the product has the Brand's memory and thus the Achievement prototype.

The cultural product design EDCBA is the experience of this cross-domain cooperation experiment and research. At the beginning of design thinking, it should be based on the creative connotation and profit model, and the process of translating in the middle layer, applying more complete design and The reinforcement of knowledge

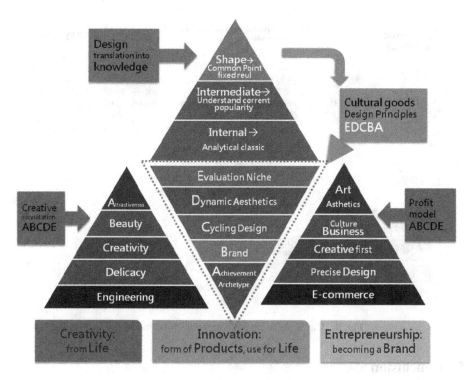

Fig. 3. From the creative ABCDE to the industrial ABCDE translation of the cultural products design principles EDCBA

theory can better conform to the process of cultural product design, and will also help to coordinate with museum managers to create a deep memory and value of the museum brand (see Fig. 3).

4.3 Circular Economy Co-creation Value Model

Cultural and creative products do not simply apply cultural totems directly to commodities, but ignore the culture and cultural heritage, which is rich in cultural human factors engineering, a life style, and the basis for analytical cultural identification. In the process of transforming the museum into design information and design elements, it is necessary to accurately explain the subjective creative performance and external and objective innovations in order to become a design module that can be used repeatedly. More importantly, in order to achieve the ultimate mission of sustainable development, a complete cultural and creative product should be prudently used with limited resources and maximize its added value in order to be regarded as a creative economy that respects the environment and ecology. The full-mode cycle accumulation, correction, and multiplication are the most difficult survival issues in the first century. They are also designed through circulation to achieve an important manifestation of the Circular economy (see Fig. 4).

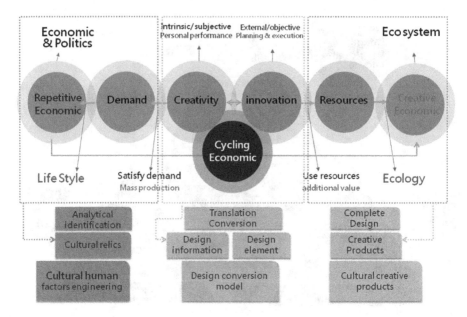

Fig. 4. Circular economy co-creation value model.

5   Conclusion

Through the verification of cross-domain cooperation of innovative products, this study summarizes the museum's functions, performance forms and brand image, the new creation principle of media and cultural products design, the profit model of creative industry, and the creation of the brand value of museums and cultural products model. Look forward to a brand convergence culture, a culture-based industry, and an industry-added economy. Through the process from cultural creativity to design innovation, we have achieved the brand entrepreneurship process and practiced the beliefs of "beginning with culture, shaping products, using for life, and becoming a brand" [21, 22].

Also, fully constructing: First, The cultural value-added with "Transforming" from the museum to culture; Second, The innovation value-added with "Change" from cultural records to the brand; Third, The economic value-added with "Conversion" from branding to the cyclical model of cultural creative products. Provided to cultural product creators or museum managers, in the future management of art and design, carefully consider the need for a sense of common sense, beauty, and invitation, while at the same time working to extend the benefits of the exhibition in the surrounding cultural goods derived from it, let museum brand no longer stays in the past one-way rigid output, but can have more value to create.

With the advent of the digital era, the extension of brand image is bound to be presented in multiple dimensions. The brand value, under the sharing and creation of the museum and its derivative cultural products, can certainly be deeply rooted in the form of both rationality and sensibility. When designers have a deeper understanding of the museum's cultural narrative system, it will inevitably lead to culture in the field of creative industries, constitute the most beautiful social design services and commercial niches. When the museum not only ends with the display function, but the goods are no longer just the superficial work of the art, and as the foundation of sustainable development, the brand value can be Co-created.

References

1. Rivière, G.H.: The ecomuseum: an evolutive definition. Mus. Int. **37**(4), 182 (1985)
2. Chang, Y.-T.: The planning concept and case analysis of the Eco-Museum. Mus. Q. **10**(1), 9–10 (1996)
3. Li, J.-C., Ho, M.-C.: Rethinking about the cultural products of a museum: perspectives across disciplines. J. Des. **14**(4), 69–84 (2009)
4. Cheng, X.-F.: Museum culture creative: from "acting cute" to "the last exhibition hall". Artron Art Network (Reprinted by Phoenix Culture), 21 May 2016
5. Han, B.-D.: Can the museum be creative? National Policy Research Foundation, 24 February 2014
6. Aaker, D.A.: Building Strong Brands, p. 7. The Free Press, New York (1996)
7. Aaker, D.A., Keller, K.L.: Consumer evaluations of brand extension. J. Mark. **54**(11), 27–41 (1990)
8. Editor-in-Chief of the Museum of the Republic of China. Museum Branding. CAM, Taipei (2016)
9. Wan-Chen, L.: Between virtuality and reality: the opportunity of museum education reform. Mus. Q. **18**(1), 20–27 (2004)
10. Yang, J.-H.: Wenchuang products open innovation model classification, service innovation e-newsletter Innoservice Homepage, 16 September 2014. https://innoservice.org/3993/
11. Lin, R.-T.: Cultural and creative product design: from the perspective of emotional technology, human design and cultural creativity. Humanit. Soc. Sci. Newsl. Q. **11**(1), 32–42 (2005)
12. Brown, T.: Design Thinking. Harvard Business Review, Brighton (2008)
13. Sobel, R.S., Rothenberg, A.: Artistic creation as stimulated by superimposed versus separated visual images. J. Pers. Soc. Psychol. **39**(5), 953–961 (1980)
14. Porter, M.: Competitive Advantage: Creating and Sustaining Superior Performance. Free Press, New York (1985)
15. Prahalad, C.K., Ramaswamy, V.: Co-creation experiences: the next practice in value creation. J. Interact. Mark. **18**(3), 5–14 (2004)
16. Lin, R.-T.: The essence and research of cultural and creative industries. Des. J. **16**(4), 1–18 (2011)
17. Dyer, W.G., Wilkins, A.L.: Better stories, not better constructs, to generate better theory: a rejoinder to Eisenhardt. Acad. Manag. Rev. **16**(3), 613–619 (1991)
18. Lin, R.T.: Transforming Taiwan aboriginal cultural features into modern product design: a case study of a cross-cultural product design model. Int. J. Des. **1**(2), 45–53 (2007)
19. Mizuno, M.: Sense Starts from Knowledge. Asahi Shimbun Publishing, Tokyo (2014)
20. Lin, R.T.: Cultural and creative product design: talking about emotional technology, human design and cultural creativity. Humanit. Soc. Sci. Newsl. Q. **11**(1), 32–42 (2009)

21. Hsu, C.-H., Lin, C.-L., Lin, R.: A study of framework and process development for cultural product design. In: Rau, P.L.P. (ed.) IDGD 2011. LNCS, vol. 6775, pp. 55–64. Springer, Heidelberg (2011). https://doi.org/10.1007/978-3-642-21660-2_7
22. Lin, R., Sun, M.-X., Chang, Y.-P., Chan, Y.-C., Hsieh, Y.-C., Huang, Y.-C.: Designing "culture" into modern product: a case study of cultural product design. In: Aykin, N. (ed.) UI-HCII 2007. LNCS, vol. 4559, pp. 146–153. Springer, Heidelberg (2007). https://doi.org/10.1007/978-3-540-73287-7_19

Communication Between Artist and Audience: A Case Study of Creation Journey

Yajuan Gao[1(✉)], Jiede Wu[2(✉)], Sandy Lee[3(✉)], and Rungtai Lin[2(✉)]

[1] School of Fine Arts and Design, Guangzhou University,
Guangzhou, People's Republic of China
78343821@qq.com
[2] Graduate School of Creative Industry Design,
National Taiwan University of Arts, New Taipei City, Taiwan
125082357@qq.com, rtlin@mail.ntua.edu.tw
[3] Sandy Art Studio, New Taipei City, Taiwan
slee195600@gmail.com

Abstract. This study is intended to propose a framework focusing on how the conception of the artist affects the creation process and how the creation process is understood by the audience. The artist's creation activities were analyzed through the framework of four steps using case study intended to turn "the feeling of home" to "the visual form of paintings." The results showed that the approach can be applied to understanding paintings and provides artists with an idea how to concentrate their efforts at the creation stage, the easier to communicate with their audience. In addition, the research framework seems to provide a better way to explore the understanding of how verbal meaning transforms into non-verbal forms, which is clearly worthy of further study.

Keywords: Communication · Cognitive human factors · Poetry · Painting

1 Introduction

Recently, there are many studies exploring the meaning of home within various disciplines such as sociology, anthropology, psychology, architecture and philosophy etc. [6, 13]. Many studies identified home as a multidimensional concept requiring interdisciplinary research [29, 30]. There has been little research on performance arts and the concept of "home" research. For example, how the function of "house" in verbal expression transfers to the "feeling of home" in visual artwork [6, 7]. This paper focuses on exploring the relationships between verbal expression (e.g. poetry, prose) and nonverbal expression (e.g. painting, music) by focusing on Dewey's model of "art as experience" and Collingwood's model of "art as language" [7, 8, 16, 36].

For verbal expression, the question used was, "What's the difference between a house and a home [12]?" It is easy to communicate the question with the audience using verbal expression to convey semantic meaning. The main difference between home and house is that house is tangible. House refers to a building in which someone lives. In contrast, a home can refer either to a building or to any location that a person thinks of as the place where she (he) lives and that belongs to her (him). A home can

© Springer Nature Switzerland AG 2019
P.-L. P. Rau (Ed.): HCII 2019, LNCS 11577, pp. 33–44, 2019.
https://doi.org/10.1007/978-3-030-22580-3_3

even be something abstract, a place in your mind. When you say, "Let's go home," you are probably not talking simply about going to the physical structure where you live. You are talking about being in the special place where you feel most comfortable and that belongs to you [6, 12, 29, 30].

In the early 20th century, artists began to experiment with nonrepresentational art, in which formal qualities such as line, color, and form were explored rather than subject contents. Today, painting vacillates between representational and nonrepresentational forms [1, 2, 27]. Thus, the artists expected to transfer the concept of "the feeling of home" by doing and acting together, whereas the audience had a more traditional view of the "the function of house", seeing it as the transfer of semantic information. The difference highlights the need for the artists to reflect on the nature of "home" based on the various ways in which one learns; the key is to create a verbal learning context and to nurture rather than manage artwork creation [7, 8, 29, 30].

For non-verbal expression, artists apply these to a variety of artistic media, symbols, and metaphors in order to independently create and perform expressions of their own ideas and to communicate their life experience. Hence, the arts are the media which provide powerful and essential means of social communication [15]. On the other hand, painting is a form of visual art, which is a mode of creative expression consisting of representational, imaginative, or abstract designs produced by the application of color to two-dimensional artworks [7, 8, 16]. For example, a poem creates visual images in the reader's mind, just as a painting creates images in the viewer's eyes. While a great painting has much more below the surface than the first impression, a poem is a painting made with words. In the analysis of poems and paintings, it is important to consider whether or not the texts are situated in the poems in a way that is analogous to the illustrations of the paintings [9, 11, 20].

Lin et al. [25] argued that the idea of turning poetry into painting should be interdisciplinary, as well as mentally challenging and creative [28]. When a viewer is faced with a painting, the audience is presumably required to interpret the elements provided by decoding and then constructing meaning by encoding [10]. The audience has to discover or construct a meaning and then attribute that meaning to what is in the painting [3, 20]. Mare [26] explored whether or not visual images and works of art can be "read," and raised important questions as to whether the description and interpretation of a work of visual art can be referred to as the "reading" of that work.

The use of information technology in multimedia is becoming common and accessible to users. The arts are the media which provide powerful and essential means of communication [26]. So, this paper is intended to bring together and examine the artist creation and recurring ideas about "the feeling of home" represented in the creative process [6–8, 12]. It raises the question whether or not home is the feeling and/or a verbal function of being in the communication between artist and audience? Many authors consider notions of creating or making artworks as an unknown "black box". In an effort to facilitate interdisciplinary communication about the meaning and experience of artwork creation each of these processes are briefly considered in this paper [29].

Thinking about art as a process of social interaction, how the artist's performances are conceived, developed, delivered and received, and how the viewer is attracted to, accurately, and are affected by the artwork need to be studied [15]. Therefore, the purpose of this study is to proposal a framework that affect artwork creation, and to propose a framework for communicating between artist and audience [26].

2 Framework for Communication Research

Lin et al. [25] explored a better understanding of artist-audience communication not just in the social context, but also for developing the interactive experience between artist and audience [14, 38]. Lin et al. [21, 22] proposed a framework with three levels of problems as identified in the study of communication: technical, semantic, and effectiveness. In addition, six constitutive factors were proposed with six functions in a Jakobson's [18] communication model. The six constitutive factors are as follows: addresser, addressee, context, message, contact, and code. Each of these factors determines a different function in each act of communication: emotive, conative, referential, poetic, phatic, and metalingual [17–19]. The framework also uses Norman's [31] conceptual model that includes three parts: design model, user's model, and system image. Furthermore, Norman's [31] emotional design was adopted with three levels of design processing—visceral, behavioral, and reflective design that represents three kinds of user's experience that is aesthetic, meaningful, and emotional experience. Based on previous studies [23–25], a research framework combining communication theory with communication and mental models was proposed to explore the communication matrix as shown in Fig. 1 [15].

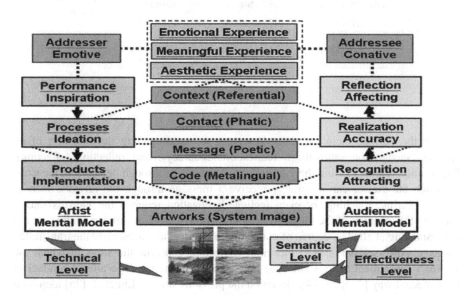

Fig. 1. A framework for communication research

For communication research between artist and audience, there are three key stages involved in the artist expressing significance through his or her artworks: performance (inspiration), process (ideation), and product (implementation). Performance is the inspiration to produce a kind of significance that the artist's intentions can be expressed through the artwork. Process represents the artist's ideation that through the artwork and the artist's imagination, thoughts, and feelings can be reproduced. Product is the implementation of signification and expression which can be transmitted to the viewer when the artist's and the viewer's thoughts are identical [22–24].

Table 1. The communication matrix for communicate between artist and audience

	ARTIST (CODING)			
	Performance Inspiration	Processes Ideation	Products Implementation	
Level C	C7-1: Topic and Acknowledgement C7-2: Going beyond Reality C7-3: Affluence in Life	C8-1: Thought Provoking C8-2: Deep Planting C8-3: Immersion	C9-1: Emotional Resonance C9-2: Authentic Experience C9-3: Mental Simpatico	Reflection Affecting
Level B	B4-1: Curiosity Raising B4-2: Desire Exploring B4-3: Emotion Stirring	B5-1: Moving Stories B5-2: Mood Changing B5-3: Atmosphere Bulging	B6-1: Richly Culturally-Loaded B6-2: Realistic Characteristics B6-3: Role Identity	Realization Accuracy
Level A	A1-1: Appropriately Captured A1-2: Creative and Clever A1-3: Video Effects	A2-1: Well-Paced A2-2: Touching Plot A2-3: Sensitive Settings	A3-1: Well Defined Personalities A3-2: Skillful and Appealing A3-3: Warm Touching	Recognition Attraction
	Aesthetic Experience	Meaningful Experience	Emotional Experience	
	AUDIENCE (DECODING)			

For the viewer, there are three key steps to understanding the meaning of an artwork: recognition (attracting), realization (accuracy), and reflection (affecting). Recognition requires letting the viewer receive a message through perception, the ways in which the viewer can accurately receive a message through the artwork such as seeing, hearing, touching, or even feeling. Realization requires the viewers understanding the meaning of the message without misinterpreting, misunderstanding, or not understanding at all. The degree of realization measures how accurately the transmitted message expresses the desired meaning. Reflection concerns the ways in which the viewer's subsequent actions showing how effectively the message affects conduct in the expected way [4, 5, 23, 24]. Based on the previous studies, Lin et al. [25] identified the factors that affect the communication between artist and audience as shown in Table 1 and Fig. 2. This study was designed to take into account the changing nature of social communication issues, resistance to artworks creation of the artist and the context for appreciation and evaluation of audience.

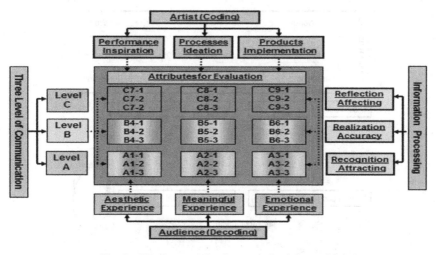

Fig. 2. The framework of communication matrix

3   Methodology

Recently, connections between artist and audience have become increasingly close. For the artworks to be understood in communication, they need to be meaningful, understandable, memorable, etc. [34]. Gao et al. [15] used poetry as an example of how to transfer poetry to a painting, in a form of verbal art that uses the aesthetic qualities of language. Poetry has been more generally regarded as a fundamentally creative act employing language. Poetry uses forms and conventions to suggest different interpretations of words or to evoke emotive responses [23]. Turning poetry into painting deals with complex objects which are interdisciplinary in their nature. This nature appears to be suitable for an opening to "read" in different ways and multiple perspectives are available to analyze them [11, 22, 23].

Based on Lin's studies [21], Gao et al. [15] proposed a framework for turning poetry into painting which consists of three main parts: poetic works, creation model and artworks. The creation model focuses on how to extract the semantic features from poetic works and then transfer these features into the painting. The creation model consists of three steps; identification, translation and implementation to finally create a painting. The creation model is described as follows: Identification, Translation and Implementation phases as shown in Fig. 3 [15].

The amateur painter Ms. Lee [15] experimented with turning poetry into painting. She developed the poetic titles based on the framework shown in Fig. 3 and expressed her own feelings about the painting and focused on whether the poetic title expressed the mood of the painting. The abstract paintings were painted according to the selected poetry following the four steps for turning poetry into paintings of illustration, interpretation, reaction and reflection. Figure 4 [15] showed the process of turning a poem entitled – I set out with a farewell to Bai-Di Town glittered with morning clouds, to a painting [4, 5, 23].

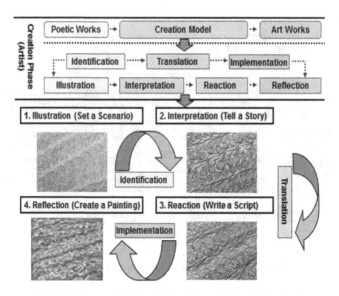

Fig. 3. Framework for turning "poetry" into "painting"

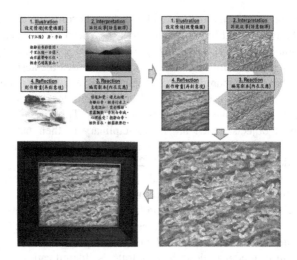

Fig. 4. The process of turning poetry into painting

The importance of communication studies is shown in several studies on evaluating artworks. However, despite the recognized importance of social interaction between artist and audience, they lack a systematic approach to explore this [33, 35, 37]. Therefore, the purpose of this paper is to study factors affecting the appreciation of artworks. Then, these factors are analyzed and discussed in order to establish a communication matrix to understand the perceptions of artist and audience. By combining

Figs. 1, 2 and 3, a research method combining the previous studies was proposed to explore the issue of turning poetry into painting as shown in Fig. 5 [15].

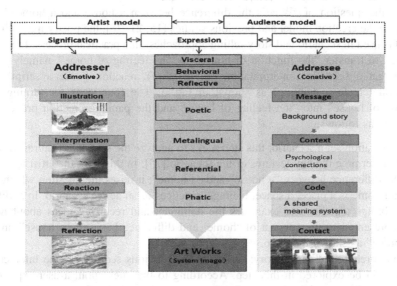

Fig. 5. Research framework for study turning poetry into painting

4   Case Study: What's the Difference Between a House and a Home?

An artwork must fulfill three functions in order to express its significance through the symbol system: signification, expression and communication. Thus, the idiom of "home sweet home", which is suggestive of verbal and non-verbal qualities, is used as the criteria to evaluate a visual painting [39]. A verbal artwork (e.g. poetry) creates visual images in the reader's mind, just as a painting creates images in the viewer's eyes [7, 8]. A great painting has much more below the surface than the first impression [9]. When a viewer is faced with a painting, they are required to interpret the elements provided by decoding meaning and then construct meaning by encoding it [19]. Thus, the audience has to discover or construct a meaning and then attribute that meaning to what is in the painting [3, 20]. A poem is a painting made with words. In the analysis of poems and paintings, it is important to consider whether or not the texts are situated in the poems in a way that is analogous to the illustrations of the paintings [20].

It has been argued that the idea of turning poetry into painting should be inter-disciplinary, as well as mentally challenging and creative [28]. Mare [26] explored whether or not visual images and works of art can be "read," and raised important questions as to whether the description and interpretation of a work of visual art can be referred to as the "reading" of that work. Turning poetry into painting involves com-plex issues that are interdisciplinary in nature. This nature appears to be suitable for "reading" in different ways, and multiple perspectives are available through which to analyze them. Based on the above discussions, the research framework can be used in a continuous search for a deeper understanding of the nature of turning poetry into painting, in which some conjectures can be tested.

For the question of "What's the difference between a house and a home?" [12] Based on the creation model and previous studies [15, 21, 28], the poetry into painting model is used in scenario and story-telling approaches. In a practical process, four steps are used to transfer "the function of house" to "the feeling of home", namely; illustration (set a scenario), interpretation (tell a story), reaction (write a script), and reflection (create a painting) as shown in Fig. 3. The four steps for turning "the function of house" into "the feeling of home" and the painting creation process are described as follows:

(1) Illustration/set a scenario: this step seeks to analyze the semantic features in order to determine the key features of the scenario [15]. In this step, the artist identifies the difference between "a house" and "a home"; it raises the question whether or not home is a place, a space, feelings, practices or an active scenario. In addition, it brings together and examines the dominant and recurring ideas about home represented in the concept of 'home' and difference between "a house" and "a home" as shown in Fig. 6.

(2) Interpretation/telling a story: based on the previous scenario, some interactions should be explored in this step. According to the interaction, a user-experience approach is used to describe the features of the painting by story-telling [15]. Home is variously described in the literature as conflated with or related to house, family, joy and journeying. The artist also considers notions of being-at-home, creating or making a home and the ideal home. Figure 7 showed the artist trying to tell a story about "home" for a family.

Fig. 6. Creation process of illustration   **Fig. 7.** Creation process of interpretation

(3) Reaction/write a script: this step is to develop an idea sketch in text or pictograph form based on the developed scenario and story. During this step, the scenario and story might require modification in order to transform the semantic meaning into a painting [15]. The artist is trying to facilitate "the house" and convey the meaning

and experience of home, and each of these themes is briefly addressed in the script. So, the key issue is how to combine "the function of house" and "the feeling of home" as shown in Fig. 8.

(4) Reflection/creating a painting: this step deals with previously identified semantic features and the context of the painting. At this point, all semantic features should be listed in a matrix table which will help the artist check the cultural features of the creation process [15]. Many researchers understand home as a multidimensional concept and acknowledge the presence of and need for multidisciplinary research in the field. There has been little sustained reflection and critique of the multidisciplinary field of home research, as in the artworks shown in Fig. 9.

Fig. 8. Creation process of reaction   **Fig. 9.** Creation process of reflection

5 Conclusions and Suggestions

In order to evaluate artworks, it is necessary to identify the cognitive factors affecting them. These factors can then be used by the artist as the basis for evaluating their artworks during the creation stage. Most of the studies are focused on evaluation after the artworks is completed and very few have ever mentioned the approaches of artworks evaluation at the creation stage to assess artworks for communication [38]. The importance of communication studies is shown repeatedly in several studies of evaluating artworks. Despite the recognized importance of social interaction between artist and audience, they lack a systematic approach to explore it [33, 35, 37, 38]. Hence, the purpose of this paper is to propose a framework that can help the artist evaluating their artworks which was then analyzed and practiced in order to establish a communication matrix to understand the perceptions of artist and audience for communication.

Taking artwork as a media of social communication, this study aims to understand how the relationship between the artist and the audience is potentially altered by social communication. Three levels are identified in the study of communication between artist and audience, namely technical, semantic and effectiveness levels [10, 21]. For turning "the function of a house" into "the feeling of a home", the artist (addresser) wanted to successfully communicate with the audience (addressee), and the functions of communication were studied to understand the conceptual difference between artist and audience. The communication approach appears to have an advantage over the subjective interpretation of artworks. For combined Figs. 2 and 3, a research framework for exploring the creation process of turning "verbal form" into "nonverbal artwork" was proposed as shown in Fig. 10.

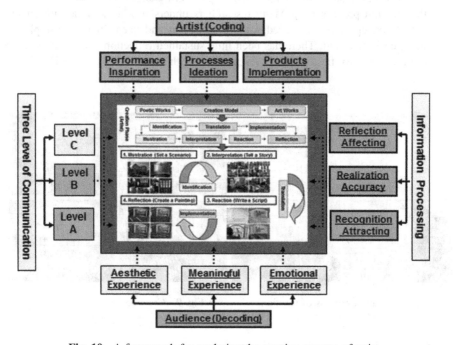

Fig. 10. A framework for exploring the creation process of artist

This study proposed a research framework which could be used for a deeper understanding of the nature of communication between artist and audience. Although the idea of using a communication approach to explore the evaluation of artworks both for the artist and audience is quite simple, this study is only the first step in testing the utility of communication between artist and audience as an approach for understanding the creation and recognition of turning "semantics" into "artworks" and is clearly worthy of more in-depth study. Furthermore, the results suggested that the approach will be validated in more testing and evaluating of artworks communication between artist and audience in further study.

Acknowledgments. This study was rewritten based on the previous research [15, 26]. The authors would like to thank those who make this research possible. Special thanks to Sandy Lee of Sandy Art Studio for authorizing the use of her paintings in this study.

References

1. Beatty, E.L.: The intersection of poetry and design. In: 8th ACM Conference on Creativity and Cognition, C&C 2011, pp. 449–450. ACM, New York (2011)
2. Beatty, E.L., Ball, L.J.: Poetic design: an exploration of the parallels between expert poetry composition and Innovation design practices. In: 1st DESIRE Network Conference on Creativity and Innovation in Design, pp. 62–71. Desire Network, Lancaster (2010)
3. Cantoia, M., Antonietti, A.: To see a painting versus to walk in a painting: an experiment on sense-making through virtual reality. Comput. Educ. **34**(3), 213–223 (2000)
4. Chen, S.J., Lin, C.L., Lin, R.: The study of match degree evaluation between poetry and paint. In: 5th Asian Conference on the Arts and Humanities (ACAH 2014), Osaka, Japan (2014)
5. Chen, S.J., Lin, C.L., Lin, R.: A cognition study of turning poetry into abstract painting. In: The Fifth Asian Conference on Cultural Studies (ACCS 2015), Kobe, Japan (2015)
6. Collins, C.: Home sweet home. In: NYU WPL, vol. 1, pp. 1–34 (2007)
7. Dewey, J.: Art as Experience. Penguin, London (2005)
8. Dorn, C.M.: Mind in Art: Cognitive Foundations in Art Education. Routledge, London (1999)
9. Emerson, R.W.: Poetry and imagination. Lett. Soc. Aims **8**, 3–4 (1883)
10. Fiske, J.: Introduction to Communication Studies. Routledge, London (2010)
11. Frankel, H.H.: Poetry and paintings: Chinese and western views of their convertibility. Comp. Lit. **9**(4), 289–307 (1957)
12. Hamza, P.: What's the difference between a house and a home. http://www.learnersdictionary.com/qa/what-s-the-difference-between-a-house-and-a-home. Accessed 21 July 2018
13. Hecht, A.: Home sweet home: tangible memories of an uprooted childhood. In: Home Possessions, pp. 123–148 (2001)
14. Goldman, A.: Evaluating art. In: The Blackwell Guide to Aesthetics, pp. 93–108 (2004)
15. Gao, Y.-J., Chen, L.-Y., Lee, S., Lin, R., Jin, Y.: A study of communication in turning "poetry" into "painting". In: Rau, P.-L.P. (ed.) CCD 2017. LNCS, vol. 10281, pp. 37–48. Springer, Cham (2017). https://doi.org/10.1007/978-3-319-57931-3_4
16. Hagberg, G.L.: Art as Language: Wittgenstein, Meaning, and Aesthetic Theory. Cornell University Press, Ithaca (1998)
17. Hsu, C.-H., Lin, C.-L., Lin, R.: A study of framework and process development for cultural product design. In: Rau, P.L.P. (ed.) IDGD 2011. LNCS, vol. 6775, pp. 55–64. Springer, Heidelberg (2011). https://doi.org/10.1007/978-3-642-21660-2_7
18. Jakobson, R.: Language in Literature. The Belknap Press of Harvard University Press, Cambridge (1987)
19. Fiske, J.: Introduction to Communication Studies. Routledge, London (1990)
20. Laude, J., Denomme, R.: On the analysis of poems and paintings. New Lit. Hist. **3**(3), 471–486 (1972)
21. Lin, R.: Transforming Taiwan aboriginal cultural features into modern product design: a case study of a cross-cultural product design model. Int. J. Des. **1**(2), 45–53 (2007)
22. Lin, R., Lin, P.-H., Shiao, W.-S., Lin, S.-H.: Cultural aspect of interaction design beyond human-computer interaction. In: Aykin, N. (ed.) IDGD 2009. LNCS, vol. 5623, pp. 49–58. Springer, Heidelberg (2009). https://doi.org/10.1007/978-3-642-02767-3_6
23. Lin, C.L., Chen, J.L., Chen, S.J., Lin, R.: The cognition of turning poetry into painting. J. US-China Educ. Rev. B **5**(8), 471–487 (2015)

24. Lin, R., Hsieh, H.-Y., Sun, M.-X., Gao, Y.-J.: From ideality to reality-a case study of mondrian style. In: Rau, P.-L.P. (ed.) CCD 2016. LNCS, vol. 9741, pp. 365–376. Springer, Cham (2016). https://doi.org/10.1007/978-3-319-40093-8_37

25. Lin, R., Qian, F., Wu, J., Fang, W.-T., Jin, Y.: A pilot study of communication matrix for evaluating artworks. In: Rau, P.-L.P. (ed.) CCD 2017. LNCS, vol. 10281, pp. 356–368. Springer, Cham (2017). https://doi.org/10.1007/978-3-319-57931-3_29

26. Mare, E.A.: Can one "read" a visual work of art? S. Afr. J. Art Hist. 25(2), 58–68 (2010)

27. Michel, K.F.: Turning poetry into paintings: an experiment in visualization. Art Educ. Pract. Art Educ. 52(3), 6–12 (1999)

28. Mallett, S.: Understanding home: a critical review of the literature. Sociol. Rev. 52(1), 62–89 (2004)

29. Modesti, S.: Home sweet home: tattoo parlors as postmodern spaces of agency. West. J. Commun. 72(3), 197–212 (2008)

30. Norman, D.A.: Emotional Design: Why We Love or Hate Everyday Things. Basic Books, New York (2005)

31. Norman, D.A.: The Design of Everyday Things: Revised and Expanded. Basic Books, New York (2013)

32. Peterson, R.A.: Sociology of the arts exploring fine and popular forms. Contemp. Sociol. J. Rev. 33(4), 454–455 (2004)

33. Porter, A., McMaken, J., Hwang, J., Yang, R.: Common core standards the new US intended curriculum. Educ. Res. 40(3), 103–116 (2011)

34. Pratt, H.J.: Categories and comparisons of artworks. Br. J. Aesthet. 52(1), 45–59 (2012)

35. Sawyer, R.K.: Improvisation and the creative process: dewey, collingwood, and the aesthetics of spontaneity. J. Aesthet. Art Crit. 58(2), 149–161 (2000)

36. Shelley, J.: The character and role of principles in the evaluation of art. Br. J. Aesthet. 42(1), 37–51 (2002)

37. Trivedi, S.: Artist-audience communication: tolstoy reclaimed. J. Aesthet. Educ. 38(2), 38–52 (2004)

38. Yeh, M.L., Lin, P.H.: Beyond claims of truth. J. Arts Humanit. 3(1), 98–109 (2014)

39. Yeh, M.L., Lin, R., Wang, M.S., Lin, P.H.: Transforming the hair color design industry by using paintings: from art to e-business. Int. J. E-Bus. Dev. 4(1), 12–20 (2014)

Analysis of Cover Design Styles of Magazines

Taking *THE SHORT STORY MAGAZINE* (1910–1932) as an Example

Jianping Huang[1(✉)], Si Chen[2(✉)], Jiede Wu[1,3(✉)],
and Rungtai Lin[1(✉)]

[1] Graduate School of Creative Industry Design,
National Taiwan University of Arts, New Taipei City, Taiwan
50516059@qq.com, rtlin@mail.ntua.edu.tw
[2] Fuzhou University of International Studies and Trade, Fuzhou 350202, China
731553247@qq.com
[3] Department of Animation, School of Journalism and Communication,
Anhui Normal University, Wuhu 241002, China
125082357@qq.com

Abstract. Magazine cover design is usually an epitome of such factors as historical background, politics and economy, social aesthetics and crowd psychology. The culture showed a landscape of diversity in the turbulent and complex times in the earlier period of the Republic of China. This research takes the cover design of the magazine *THE SHORT STORY MAGAZINE* (1910–1932) as an Example and adopting a quantitative empirical research method, the paper studies the cognitive pattern of the contemporary readers towards the magazine cover design style in the context of past times. Design style shows the characteristics of "periodic circle development". Therefore, the research is of great significance to the formation of design styles at present and in the future. The results of the research reveal: 1. The cover design of magazines in the Chinese mainland in the early 20th century displayed six styles. 2. Among the cover designs of magazines in history, the contemporary audience prefer the design styles with distinctive characteristics. 3. Among the style attributes, the harmonious, regular and elegant design styles are most popular among the contemporary audience. Hopefully the results of the research will provide references for the field of design at present and in the future.

Keywords: Historical context · Cover design · Magazine cover · Design style · Cognition of style

1 Introduction

It is widely believed that the mainstream modern design history started at the turn of the 19th and 20th century. In this period, the world was turbulent and restless politically and economically and the trend of culture and ideology was surging. It was the most impacting era in the humankind's history when two World Wars happened, the population declined abruptly, economic crisis and unemployment were serious. In this

© Springer Nature Switzerland AG 2019
P.-L. P. Rau (Ed.): HCII 2019, LNCS 11577, pp. 45–59, 2019.
https://doi.org/10.1007/978-3-030-22580-3_4

special era, the design trend of "Modernism" developed rapidly. Starting from the mid-19th century, the trend of complicated decoration style was prevailing, represented by fine arts and new artistic design, behind which was the fact that the European powers plundered wealth from the colonies and concentrated the wealth in the European continent and made their own politics, economy and culture reach a summit. By the early 20th century, the world's economic crisis broke out in 1907, the World War I broke out in 1914, a second global economic crisis happened in 1929 and the World War II took place in 1939. The economic depression forced the design style to shift to simple and practical styles. Under such a context, design styles of modernism such as Bauhaus that stressed "ornament is a crime" came into being. However, the US and France, two beneficiary countries in the World War I, refused concise forms as their politics and economy were flourishing. As a result, complicated decorative artistic design continued to develop. The World War II was over in 1945, the Korean War broke out in 1950 and the African-American Civil Rights Movement was launched in 1955. In the turbulence of the times and political situation, the concise and simple abstractionist design developed and its influence swept the whole world. After 1980, as science and technology, civilization and economy were growing rapidly, the abstractionism was replaced by the complicated post-modernism design style which became the mainstream design style in this period. The aforesaid indicates that the development of design styles is closely related with the historical background of the society.

The historical background not only covers political and economic aspects, but also covers the crowd psychology, which is also an important factor. Design is a link in our social activities. Kawazoe Noboru, a Japanese scholar, proposed a "Kawazoe Noboru" program in the book What is Design, taking "human, nature and society" as three constituents of the world and pointing out that the three fields are linked up by design [16]. A fourth turning was ushered in by the traditional design style history studies in the early 20th century, which shifted from the research of external forms to the research of internal ceremony, from narrative research to analytical research, and from the research of individual psychology to crowd psychology of the society. Historians no longer viewed psychology as a consistent, constant, permanent and fixed foundation for interpreting the behaviors of the humankind, but as an aspect of the social environment, which must be interpreted with all other aspects under the historical background [22]. Therefore, the research at the level of crowd psychology of the society is also an important aspect in the exploration of the factors of design styles.

The magazine covers in the early 20th century are selected by the research for the exploration of the cognitive pattern of design styles for three reasons. First, under the historical background of the early 20th century, the turbulent and complex political and economic situations brought rich and diversified cultural thoughts. Second, design thoughts were surging at the turning of 19th and 20th centuries when different design styles developed along a spiral in the alternation of complex and simple. Third, in the period when science and technology were still undeveloped, the magazines and periodicals were the most effective media for the communication between the authors and the readers. The magazine THE SHORT STORY MAGAZINE was initiated in 1910 and ceased publication in 1932, which had gone through the two decades when the Chinese mainland was war-ridden and cultural thoughts were surging. Among the magazines and periodicals published in this period, it boasted the biggest number of issues, the largest amount of distribution and the longest operation history. The five editors-in-chief in its history were either traditional writers or reformative scholars. In the face of the impact from the Western thoughts of modern design, they not only maintained the traditional aesthetic orientation and values of China, but also showed the eagerness to reform and innovate [12]. Therefore, the cover design styles of *THE SHORT STORY MAGAZINE* showed inclusiveness and diversity blending the Eastern and Western characteristics. Yang called it the "No. 1 magazine of novels in the 1920s" [20]. Taking *THE SHORT STORY MAGAZINE*, a literary magazine of Chinese mainland in the early 20th century, as the subject of research and adopting the methods of historical interpretation and contents analysis, the research conducts a qualitative analysis on the correlation between historical background and design styles in the specific period. By applying the quantitative empirical research method, the research conducts a questionnaire survey in two stages among experts in a semi-open manner and the public to understand the cognitive pattern of the contemporary readers with the cover design styles in the historical context.

We can seek wisdom from the ancients and realize our shortcomings from the comments of others. Since design style develops with the times, which becomes complex in a wealthy era and simple in a poor era. It shows a periodic spiral development pattern [22]. Previous design styles may overlay with the current ones, or re-emerge at some point in the future. Therefore, it is of important significance for the construction of design styles at present and in the future to study the cognitive pattern of contemporary audience with the magazine design styles in a historical context. We will understand the evolution course of design style history by analyzing the correlation between historical context and design styles. We will understand the crowd psychology of the contemporary society and perceive the trend of design by studying the cognitive pattern of the contemporary audience with cover design styles of magazines in the history. Hopefully this research will be helpful to the development of an evolution history of design styles, explore the cognitive psychology of the contemporary audience with design styles and provide references for the field of design.

The paper aims to explore the following two aspects.

1. The correlation of politics and economy, crowd psychology and design styles under a specific historical context.
2. The contemporary audience's evaluation of the cover design styles of magazines under a specific historical context and the correlation between the evaluation results and their preferences.

2 Literature Review

2.1 Design Style

As a French motto goes, "Style is the writer", it indicates the importance of style in some certain fields. The term style originates from Latin word Stilus, which originally meant a writing tool of the ancient Rome and later extended to refer to handwriting, literary form and style of writing and was used in mixture with "Pattern" and

"Maniera" (the individual style of an artist). After the Renaissance in the 16th century, people began to uphold artistic style and pursue the liberation of individuality. The term "Applied Arts" emerged in the 17th century. By the 18th century, style was defined as "some constant pattern of arts". By the mid-19th century, style, as a research methodology, had become a core concept in the foundation of art history studies. By the 20th century, scholars in the field of arts had developed a clearer picture of style. Kenwa Tamu, a Japanese scholar, argued that style is a unique form of expression of elements following different constituent grammars and a manifestation mode with characteristics of the times or a region [18]. By the 21st century, scholars have come up with new definitions of style. Chen Junzhi argued that in terms of artistic creation, different intentions of the authors will create different characteristics. Such kind of difference is classified as some feature or image based on its characteristics, which is also known as "style" [3]. Arts are a manifestation of culture, while style is the most distinctive characteristic of the culture [2]. Cultural meanings are expressed by applying cultural symbols [13]. Lin [9] pointed out that only works with distinctive styles can be competitive in the market. Nowadays the demands of customers in products have shifted from attention to pragmatic functions and appearances to a pursuit of the meanings and recognition behind the products, or the ideas and concepts, lifestyle or spiritual resonance conveyed by the works [19]. Therefore, the research of styles is an exploration of the similarity and difference of works [15].

Viewed from the vein of historical development, there is not a clear boundary between the fields of arts and design. The development trend of design history can also be perceived in the changes of artistic styles. Saguchi, a Japanese scholar (1990), stated on the close relationship between arts and design in this way, "Arts influence design, while design is an extension of arts." John A. Walker, a design historian of the UK, also argued in The History of Design, "The history of design derives from the history of arts." Many historians of Europe and America nod at such views. Arts usually take the lead in the era subject to no constraint of conditions in reality and also directly leads the development of design. This has been proven by the influence of Cubism on modern design and the influence of Pop arts on post-Modernist design [22]. Therefore, in exploring the design styles of a specific historical period, it is inevitable for us to analyze the artistic styles of the periods before and after the specific period. This is a basic principle for the discourse of the research.

2.2   Correlation Between Historical Background and Design Style

The formation of design styles, in the description of design history studies for a long period in the past, was mainly attributed to the achievements of some design team or some designer, while the impact of the historical background of the society had been neglected. W. Pevsner who was honored as "Father of Design History" argued that "Modernism" is an ideal ultimate perfect form in the book Pioneers of Modern Design: From William Morris to Walter Gropius. He praised the pioneers that met the standard of high morality, but hated other non-Modern pioneers [14]. Such discourses that neglect social background, and confine the subject of design to Modernist morality limit the scope of design styles and the research of design history.

As the environment and soil, the historical background provides design styles in the history with topics and patterns. Edward said, the contemporary design is closely related with the life of the public [11]. The historical background usually covers the crowd psychology, politics and economy of the specific era. The formation of design styles is closely related with the development of the society and times. C. K. Simonton searched for the "social variables" that influenced creativity in an 8-year research "Correlation between Creativity of Famous People and Social Factors" and verified the correlation and causal model between creativity and historical background of the society [1]. Through a systematic research of social psychology, the research proves that the historical background of the society is the initial driving force and ultimate destination for the formation of design styles. Feng Yonghua and Yang Yufu have ever sorted out a correlation chart between the initiating country of a design style and the political and economic strength of the country (see Table 1).

Table 1. Correlation chart between the initiating country of a design style and the historical background at that time.

Time	Initiating country (region)	Style	Political and economic strength
	Greece and Rome	Greek and Roman styles	Greece developed a mature classical style after winning the victory in the Persian wars. Rome was an empire spanning across three continents, Europe, Asia and Africa, with trade flourishing.
1495-1525	Italy	Renaissance style	Italy was an important hub of politics, religion and economy of Europe at that time.
1600-1750	France	Baroque style	Louis XIV dynasty of France was the most powerful country of Europe at that time
1715-1815	France	Rococo & Neo-classical styles	The politics and economy of France reached the global summit in the Napoleonic era
1820-1901	The UK	Victorian style	The UK developed rapidly and set the trend of the century after the Industrial Revolution
1859-1900	The UK	Art & Craft Movement	The UK continued to be honored as "the empire on which the sun never sets" in this period
1890-1910	European countries	Art Nouveau	By plundering wealth from colonies, the European powers became the strongest region in the world
1919-1933	Germany	Bauhaus (Modern style)	Prime Minister Bismarck who took office in 1895 adopted the policy of "Blood and Iron", and turned Prussia into a strong Reich of militarism.

(Source of data: Feng Yonghua, Yang Yufu (2006). Research on Factors for Formation of Design Styles. Journal of Design)

The data indicates that a strong culture of arts and design is usually initiated by a country or region with powerful politics and economy. Under the action of Butterfly Effect, it will affect and lead the global cultural trend. The formation of a design style cannot be achieved by one or two designers or design teams. The spirit of the times is transformed into a design style with distinctive characteristics of the times with the work of the designers. Therefore, in analyzing the design style of a specific period, it is inevitable for us to explore the historical background of the specific period, thereby exploring the fundamental cause of its formation.

G. Plekhanov, a Russian aesthetician, ever remarked on the relationship between design styles and social psychology, "The economic and political relations of the society play a decisive role in arts, while the latter reflects the former via the link of social psychology." "Without deeply studying and understanding social psychology, it is impossible to understand the literary thought history or art history of a country or interpret the historical materialism of its ideology system" [8]. The economic and political relations of the social influence the design styles via the medium of "social psychology". G. Barraclough, a British historian, argued that the focus of historical studies shifted from individual psychology to social psychology. Historians no longer viewed psychology as a consistent, constant, permanent and fixed foundation for interpreting the behaviors of the humankind, but as an aspect of the social environment, which must be interpreted with all other aspects under the historical background [17]. Funai Nobukatsu of Japan, reputed as a "God of Operation Guidance", explained the social effect aroused by crowd psychology like this. The information generated by a monkey is first passed to the entire team. When the number of recipients reaches a certain level, the information will be expanded and reach another team far away. Under an unconscious state, a crowd can be aroused a sympathy with a "specific magnetic field" [21]. At the end of 19th century, Gustave Le Bon, a social psychologist of France, described the psychology changes after a crowd effect was achieved by individual psychology, "Their feelings and thoughts are all steered to the same direction as their conscious individuality vanishes, forming a collective mentality. When the conscious personality vanishes and the unconscious personality becomes dominant, their feelings and thoughts will be steered to the same direction under the actions of hinting and mutual influence [6] ". Therefore, to explore the formation of design styles under a specific historical background, other than analyzing the political and economic relations of the society, we cannot neglect the analysis of crowd psychology of the society.

2.3   Communication Model of Design Styles

The aforesaid indicates that the formation of design styles cannot be separated from the political and economic conditions and crowd psychology of the whole society. However, the formation does not mean Communication, what is the path of communication? Under the specific historical background, what factors are required to achieve an effective communication? According to the school of process in the communication theory, now the factors for a successful communication are divided into three levels, which are technology level, semantic level and effect level [4, 5, 7]. The technology level means that the author achieves an external manifestation of the design works with the use of technology. The semantic level means that the author expresses the meanings of the works through the external level. The effect level means that the information of form and meaning is received by the readers and turned into their reflection, which effectively affects their anticipated behaviors. Scholars like Lin Rongtai has developed a new research framework by combining the theoretical frameworks of communication and semantic cognition of mental model, thereby exploring the related aspects of the communication of artistic styles [10] (See Fig. 1).

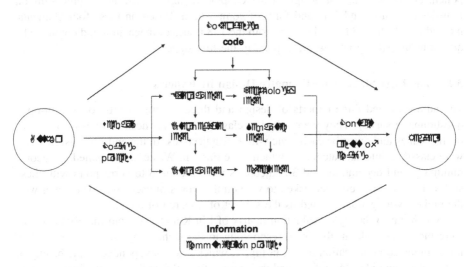

Fig. 1. Creation and communication model of design styles (source of data: Lin Rongtai, Lin Boxian, 2009)

Jakobson [7] has ever proposed six elements for communication model, which are the sender, the recipient, scenario, information, contact and code, which respectively correspond to different functions of communication. In the current research, the cover design styles of the magazine *THE SHORT STORY MAGAZINE* are taken as an example. The sender refers to the cover designer; the recipient refers to the target readers; the scenario refers to the turbulent political and economic environment of the Chinese mainland and the cultural background of surging thoughts in early 20th century; information refers to the information formed at technology and semantic levels; contact refers to the magazine *THE SHORT STORY MAGAZINE* itself; code refers to the sympathy code system formed from the understanding shared by the author and readers. In this way, effective communication and cognition are achieved. Therefore, the communication model of design styles provides corresponding theoretical foundations for the research.

3 Methodology

The research attempts to verify the research hypothesis by employing qualitative research methods of historical interpretation and contents analysis and quantitative empirical research methods in the form of a questionnaire survey. First of all, the research collected the covers of 178 issues of the magazine *THE SHORT STORY MAGAZINE* for around 20 years from 1910 to 1932. According to the 4 basic component elements of layout design in the Graphic Design, which are graphic symbol, font design, color rendering and form of composition. Based on these four elements, the author selected 33 typical covers from the 178 issues of magazines and conducted a questionnaire survey among the experts in the first stage.

3.1 The First Stage: Questionnaire Design by Experts

The author invited three experts of design and three experts of arts for a semi-open questionnaire survey. They were asked to classify the cover design styles of 33 issues of magazines and describe each style with five adjectives. In the end, the design styles were classified into six categories, which were Eastern, Western, diversified, gorgeous, minimalist and decorative, and 30 adjectives were proposed to correspond with these styles. The experts were then asked to vote on the works of each style. The cover with the highest voting was selected as the subject of research of a style.

According to the style evaluation matrix of Lin Rongtai, 9 from the 30 adjectives were picked as style attributes corresponding to the technology, semantic and effect levels in the communication model in Fig. 1, which also corresponded to the beauty of form, image and idea and interpreted the process from the coding in artistic creation to the decoding of the readers (see Table 2).

Table 2. Evaluation matrix of cover design styles

Artistic Creation				
Designer (Coding)				
	Designer	Design Process	Presentation of Implication	
Technology level	Elaborate (Eastern)	Clear and intelligible (concrete)	Decorative patterns (graphic)	Beauty of form
Semantic level	Strong contrast (conflict)	Traditional interpretation (conventional)	Reformative (modern)	Beauty of image
Effect level	Refined (elegant)	Conservative (regular)	Artistic values (thoughts)	Beauty of idea
	Aesthetic experience	Meaning experience	Emotional experience	
Readers (decoding)				
Style interpretation				

3.2   The Second Stage: Question Survey Among the Public

In the expert questionnaire survey in the first stage, the expert panel came up with six styles and nine adjectives from the evaluation matrix. In the second stage of the research, a questionnaire survey was conducted among the public. The nine adjectives and their antonyms were taken as 18 style attributes, which were Eastern vs Western, conventional vs avant-garde, elegant vs vulgar, conflicting vs harmonious, regular vs chaotic, graphic vs stereoscopic, concrete vs abstract, contemporary vs historical, artistic vs worldly. These style attributes were taken as evaluation criteria and labeled as f1 to f9. 108 respondents from different backgrounds were invited to score the works of the six styles based on the 18 style attributes adopting a five-point scale. Taking Eastern vs Western as an example, 1 point represents the strongest Eastern attribute, and 5 points represent the strongest Western attribute. Finally taking preference as the overall evaluation indicator, the respondents were asked to pick a favorite style from the six cover design styles.

The questionnaire was finished online by providing a QR code for the respondents to scan and answer. The website of the questionnaire is:

https://docs.google.com/forms/d/1JYe4IH-v-6xL3s3D15G4TTy7oECPPfMdq7jzersxN8E/edit?usp=forms_home&ths=true

3.3   Respondents

108 valid questionnaires were obtained, including 39 males (36.1%) and 69 females (63.9%). Their ages: 30 respondents ages below 19 (27.8%), 49 ages between 20 and 29 (45.4%), 7 ages between 30 and 39 (6.4%), 12 ages between 40 and 49 (11.1%), 10 ages above 50 (9.3%). Their professional backgrounds: 97 are related with arts or design (89.8%), 11 with other backgrounds (10.2%). Their education background: 81 bachelors (75%), 10 masters (9.3%) and 17 doctors (15.7%).

4   Results and Discussion

4.1   Reliability and Validity Analysis

The validity analysis reveals that the KMO coefficient is .691, with a certain value, Sig value is .000, a distinctive strength, the eigenvalue is 12.407, which can interpret 22.976% of the variances of default usage. The factor loading of each question ranges from .344 to .632 and the communality ranges from .119 to .396. The questionnaire presents a good construction validity. The reliability analysis of the questionnaire is made to evaluate the internal consistency of each perspective of the questionnaire and the reduction of Cronbachα coefficient in each dimension after a single question is deleted, which is used as a reference standard for the selection of questions and evaluating the reliability of the questionnaire. The analysis of the questionnaire reveals: the Cronbachα coefficient is .892. The total correlation between each perspective of styles and characteristics and the correction of a single question ranges from .173 to .977. The Cronbachα coefficient after the deletion of a single question ranges from .849

to .905. This indicates that some questions are problematic, but the majority of questions are highly consistent internally, so the setting of most questions is reasonable.

4.2 Analysis of Styles

A matrix was established with the original data. The mean score of the six cover designs in 18 attributes was worked out. Through MDS analysis, our purpose was to analyze their distribution by employing the perceptual map and study the cognitive space of six covers with different styles and 18 attributes. The results of MDS analysis reveal that the stress coefficient is .12259, which indicates that the stress coefficient and adaptability are good. The determination coefficient RSQ value is .95035, near 1.0. Therefore, in deploying the original attribute data, it shows a rather high conformity, indicating that two dimensions are suitable for depicting the spatial relation between the six works and 18 attributes.

The two-dimension spatial axial diagram of the six covers is shown as Fig. 2. The included angle of the axial diagram of each attribute was analyzed with multiple regression to obtain the cognitive spatial map of 18 attributes. It reveals: (1) P3, P4, and P6 rest on the third quadrant forming a cluster and showing similarity. (2) P1, P2 and P5 respectively rest on the first, second and fourth quadrant, whose style is distinctively different from that of other works. After drawing a spatial map of attributes, the degree of style attributes of each cover was further explored. The distance between the projection point from each cover to the attribute vector and the original point was worked out. The OD distance in the MSD map was the distance from the cover to the level of attributes. The formula for working out OD distance was shown in Fig. 3. The value of b2/b1 was the slope of the vector. The vector projection of D on the original point showed the strength of characteristic, with the vector contributing to the attributes of the works.

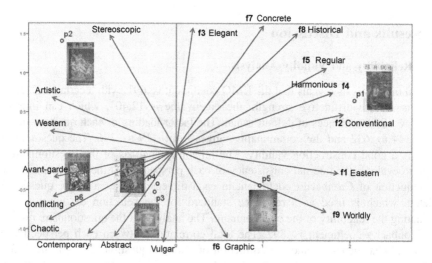

Fig. 2. MDS spatial distribution map of six cover designs and 18 style attributes

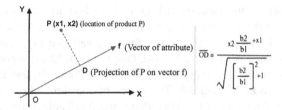

Fig. 3. Cognitive space distribution of the 9 dances and eight fundamental relations

Table 3 shows the OD distance values of six cover designs in the vectors of 18 attributes. Taking P1 as an example, its distance from Eastern and Western attributes (f1) is the largest, presenting a strong Eastern style, while the distance of P2 is the largest in the opposite direction in the same attributes, showing a strong Western style.

Table 3. Distance between projection point from five landscape paintings to style attribute vectors and the original point.

		P1 Chinese style	P2 Western style	P3 diversi-fied style	P4 gor-geous style	P5 mini-malist style	P6 decora-tive style
Eastern-Western	F1	1.96	-1.49	-0.19	-0.17	1.01	-1.12
Conventional-avant-garde	F2	2.14	-1.01	-0.36	-0.30	0.85	-1.32
Elegant-vulgar	F3	0.95	1.20	-0.55	-0.44	-0.29	-0.86
Conflicting-harmonious	F4	2.15	-0.76	-0.42	-0.35	0.75	-1.37
Regular-chaotic	F5	2.12	-0.53	-0.47	-0.39	0.65	-1.39
Graphic-stereoscopic	F6	0.48	-1.89	0.32	0.25	0.86	-0.02
Concrete-abstract	F7	1.73	0.37	-0.57	-0.47	0.21	-1.26
Contemporary-historical	F8	1.94	0.00	-0.54	-0.45	0.40	-1.35
Artistic-worldly	F9	1.65	-1.77	-0.03	-0.04	1.06	-0.86

The exploratory factor analysis (EFA) was applied to detect the relations of potential variables in the nine pairs of style attributes. The characteristic value extracted from three factors is bigger or equal to 1, the total variance explained is 57.83. As shown in Table 4, three clusters are formed. One is f7, f8, f2 corresponding to works P1 and P6; one is f6, f9, f1, corresponding to works P2 and P5; one is f4, f5 and f3, corresponding to works P3 and P4. The styles of the three clusters are internally correlated. Based on the scores of style attributes listed in Table 3, we can further learn about the specific style attribute of each cover (see Table 4).

Table 4. Factors analysis of 18 style attributes

Style Attributes		Factor Loading			Typical Works			
		Factor 1	Factor 2	Factor 3	Works 1		Works 2	
Concrete-Abstract	F7	.950	-.089	.297		Concrete		Abstract
Contemporary-Historical	F8	-.947	-.093	-.306		Historical		Contemporary
Conventional-Avant-garde	F2	.693	.549	.463		Conventional		Avant-garde
Graphic-Stereoscopic	F6	-.300	.932	.008		Graphic		Stereoscopic
Artistic-Worldly	F9	-.358	-.922	-.080		Worldly		Artistic
Eastern-Western	F1	.364	.745	.547		Eastern		Western
Conflicting-Harmonious	F4	-.209	-.155	-.965		Conflicting		Harmonious
Regular-Chaotic	F5	.383	.127	.914		Chaotic		Regular
Elegant-Vulgar	F3	.420	-.593	.668		Vulgar		Elegant
Characteristic Value		5.21	2.69	1.00				
Explained Variance %		57.83	29.87	11.15				
Cumulative Explained Variance %		57.83	87.71	98.85				

4.3   General Evaluation of the Works

The respondents were asked to select a favorite one from the six covers. The result is shown in Table 5, which indicates P4 > P1 > P2 > P6 > P5 > P3. Based on Table 4, it indicates that the audience favor harmonious, regular and elegant attributes, followed by the concrete, historical and conventional attributes and the stereoscopic, artistic and Western attributes ranked third. The abstract, contemporary and avant-garde attributes ranked fourth. The audience did not accept graphic, worldly and Eastern attributes quite well and disliked the conflicting, chaotic and vulgar attributes.

Table 5. Percentage ranking of favorite works

Rank	1	2	3	4	5	6
No	P4>	P1>	P2>	P6>	P5>	P3
Product						
Number of respond ents (%)	32 (29.6%)	21 (19.4%)	20 (18.5%)	14 (13%)	12 (11.1%)	9 (8.4%)

5   Conclusions and Suggestions

Taking the cover designs of the magazine *THE SHORT STORY MAGAZINE* in the Chinese mainland in the early 20th century from 1910 to 1932 as the subject of research, the research explores the cognitive pattern of the contemporary audience with the cover design styles of magazines under a historical context. The author picked the covers of 33 issues from the covers of 178 issues published in 20 years based on four basic elements of graphic design. The styles were evaluated by experts. 108 respondents were invited to perceive and evaluate the 18 style attributes to explore the cover design styles of magazines under the context of a specific period and the correlation between the evaluation results and preferences. The results of the research are stated as follows.

a. The covers of 178 issues of the magazine *THE SHORT STORY MAGAZINE* from 1910 to 1932 show inclusive and diversified design styles, which not only include traditional themes of paintings by Chinese scholars and modern ornamentation of the West, but also include the thoughts of patriotism and Western Romanticism. Under the historical background, Chinese mainland received an impact from Western modern design trend. A unique design style was developed gradually in its social environment in the traditional aesthetic tendency of China and the wish to reform and innovate;

b. After a multiple regression analysis was made on the aforesaid pattern, it reveals that the 18 attributes corresponding to the six styles show certain clustering effect. The conventional, harmonious, regular, historical, concrete and elegant attributes are classified as one category; the stereoscopic, artistic and Western attributes are classified as one category; the avant-garde, conflicting, chaotic, contemporary, abstract and vulgar attributes are classified as one category; the Eastern, worldly and graphic attributes are classified as one category;

c. Through further evaluation with factors analysis, the 18 attributes can cover the six styles, which indicates that the 18 attributes are valid in the evaluation of the six cover design styles;

d. According to the favorite works selected by the audience, it reveals that the audience favor the harmonious, regular and elegant attributes best, followed by concrete, historical and conventional attributes. The stereoscopic, artistic, Western, abstract, contemporary and avant-garde attributes cannot arouse many cognitive emotions. And the audience dislike the graphic, worldly, Eastern, conflicting, chaotic and vulgar attributes;

e. The ranking of average score of preferences reveals that the contemporary audience favor the design works with distinctive characteristics of the times best.

Since design styles are "periodic" [22], they always develop with the society and times according to a certain law and show some relevant cyclic changes. Therefore, by studying the cognitive patterns of the contemporary audience with the cover design styles under the historical context, we can reflect on the design styles at present and infer the future design styles. It can help the establishment of an evolution history of cover design styles of magazines, and provide references for the field of design at present and in the future.

The research only conducts an exploratory research on the contemporary audience's cognition of the cover design styles of the magazine THE SHORT STORY MAGAZINE from 1910 to 1932. The differences of the audience's overall cognition with the six design styles and the reasons for the difference of cognition of respondents from different backgrounds with the cover design styles of the THE SHORT STORY MAGAZINE, etc. need to be further studied.

References

1. Amabile, T.M.: Creative Social Psychology. Shanghai Academy of Social Sciences Press, Shanghai (1987)
2. Chen, C.H., Cheng, Y.P.: A study on side and arm chairs of ming dynasty using the theory of style. J. Des. 10(4), 87–105 (2005)
3. Chen, C.C.: Exploring style cognition and identification of Chinese and western design-using chair designs as example. J. Des. 6(2), 79–99 (2001)
4. Craig, R.T.: Communication theory as a field. Commun. Theory 9(2), 119–161 (1999)
5. Fiske, J.: Introduction to Communication Studies. Routledge, London (2010)
6. Zhang, G.Z., Zhou, B.: Psychological History. Yang Chih Culture, Taipei (2001)
7. Jakobson, R.: Language in Literature. The Belknap Press of Harvard University Press, Cambridge (1987)

8. Zhang, L.G.: Modern Design Sociology, p. 85. Hunan Science and Technology Press, Changsha (2005)
9. Lin, R.T.: From service innovation to qualia product design. J. Des. Sci. **14**(S), 13–31 (2011)
10. Lin, R., Lin, P.-H., Shiao, W.-S., Lin, S.-H.: Cultural aspect of interaction design beyond human-computer interaction. In: Aykin, N. (ed.) IDGD 2009. LNCS, vol. 5623, pp. 49–58. Springer, Heidelberg (2009). https://doi.org/10.1007/978-3-642-02767-3_6
11. Edward, L.S.: A History of Industrial Design, p. 117. Phaidon Press Limited, Oxford (1983)
12. Peng, L.: A combination of Chinese and western style: binding and design of "fiction monthly" in 1910–1920. Art Obs. (08), 101–107 (2009)
13. Hung, P.H., Lin, P.H.: The style of Taiwan cultural and creative products. J. Arts (101), 79–105 (2017)
14. Nikolaus, P.: Pioneers of Modern Design, p. 84. Museum of Modern Art, New York (1949)
15. Ross, S.D.: A Theory of Art, pp. 41–45. State University of New York, New York (1982)
16. Nanaro, S.: Introduction to Design, p. 36. Yifengtang Publisher, Taipei (1990)
17. Sparke, P.: An Introduction to Design & Culture in the 20th Century, p. 74. Unwin Hyman Ltd., London (1986)
18. Kagiwata, W.C.: Edited and translated by Editorial Department: Design History. Yi feng tang Publisher, Taipei (1991)
19. Yen, H.Y., Lin, P.S., Lin, R.T.: Qualia characteristics of cultural and creative products. J. Kansei **2**(1), 34–61 (2014)
20. Yang, Y.: A Illustrated Book of Chinese New Literature (I), p. 140. People's Publishing House (1998)
21. Funai, Y.K.: The Hundredth Monkey, pp. 94–95. Taipei, Hong's Foundation (1997)
22. Feng, Y.H., Yang, Y.F.: The research of forming factors of the design styles. J. Des. **11**(3), 99–115 (2006)

Contrast Research on Cognitive Differences Between Design End and Consumption End in Cultural Products

Bo Li, Chao Ma, Xingyi Zhong, and Ting Han[✉]

School of Design, Shanghai Jiao Tong University, Shanghai, China
hanting@sjtu.edu.cn

Abstract. Cultural products of today have become an important embodiment of people's spiritual life, and serve as a medium between designers and consumers. Due to the differences between designers and consumers in terms of age, education and cultural backgrounds, however, the cultural connotations the designers give to cultural products may fail to be well communicated to consumers and do not always match the needs of particular consumers. This paper explored possible methods of improving communication between the design end and the consumption end in China by studying and comparing the overall perception of cultural products at the two ends based on in-depth interviews, focus group interviews, and online questionnaires. Differences between the design end and the consumption end in the definition, value, marketing strategies, and purchasing strategies of cultural products, as well as the changes in the lifestyle of contemporary Chinese people were analyzed in this paper.

Keywords: Cultural product · Design end · Consumption end · Lifestyle

1 Introduction

Developing the cultural and creative industries has become an important economic strategy, which could not only help promote local and regional economic development, but also raise the quality of people's cultural life [1]. Cultural uniqueness and innovation have become the core competencies of a country. Nowadays, with social and economic development, people's basic needs have been generally satisfied. The functionality gap between products has been narrowing, and thus the product competition in cultural connotation has become increasingly fierce. Cultural products have been exerting more and more impact on people's lives.

Many definitions have been given to the term cultural products. In a broad sense, all products produced by humans are cultural products, as they all have cultural connotations; in a narrow sense, products produced by humans should be divided into material products and cultural products, the latter of which refer to products that satisfy people's spiritual needs. This paper mainly studies cultural products in its narrow sense. According to UNESCO, cultural products generally refer to those consumer products for the transmission of thought, symbol and lifestyle.

P.-L. P. Rau (Ed.): HCII 2019, LNCS 11577, pp. 60–70, 2019.
https://doi.org/10.1007/978-3-030-22580-3_5

At present, related research on cultural products mainly focuses on the design end. Li et al. drew attention to design methods by introducing the design method and application of DNA in the design of cultural creative products through the example of traditional Chinese lion dance [2]. In the study by Chow et al., the design flow and design method based on literature survey, interviews, questionnaires, mind mapping, participatory design and value opportunity analysis were proposed [3]. In terms of design strategy, Chen et al. investigated how to maintain the balance between "commercialization" and "preservation of the spirit of cultural connotation" in the process of developing cultural and creative products [4]. In the study of Chen, the product life cycle model of cultural creative product industrialization was explored and established [5].

Cultural products need to communicate to consumers their cultural connotations, which are given by designers through various design methods and expression techniques. But consumption experience is "a primarily subjective state of consciousness with a variety of symbolic meanings, hedonic responses, and aesthetic criteria", and an objective evaluation of products is difficult to realize [6]. Therefore, designers should not only study how to bring cultural elements to cultural products, but also adapt to the market environment and consumers.

This research aims to improve the communication of perception, value and expectations of cultural products between the design end and the consumption end based on their perceptions of cultural products. This research mainly focuses on: (1) a contrast study on cultural product definition, characteristics and value of the design end and the consumption end; (2) design and marketing strategies of the design end; (3) motivation, purchasing stages and decision-making basis of cultural product consumers; (4) changes in the lifestyle of contemporary Chinese people.

2 Method

2.1 Research Methods

This research used in-depth interviews to explore individuals' perceptions of cultural products and marketing strategies of the design end, as these participants all have unique characteristics and a group interview is difficult to coordinate [7]. At the consumption end, this research adopted interview and questionnaire survey methods, as the large consumer group makes it easier to find participants and conduct group interviews. Group interaction of young consumers with unconventional thinking may spark new insights and perspectives to the research. Therefore, focus group methods were used in the consumer interviews [8]. Quantitative analysis of the qualitative answers obtained from focus group interviews was conducted through the online questionnaire survey methods. The research methods and sampling methods are shown in Fig. 1.

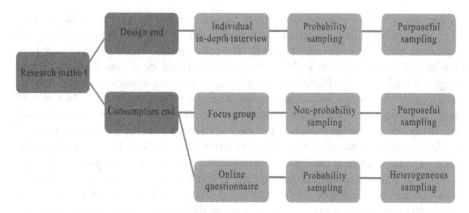

Fig. 1. Research methods and sampling methods

2.2 Design End Research

Based on the purposeful sampling method, specific sampling conditions of the participants are determined as follows:

1. At the design end to produce or study related contents of cultural products.
2. Representativeness: produce products or study topics that are designed for young consumers and have successful cases (see Table 1).

Table 1. Information of participants from the design end

Number	Occupation	Related working experience	Interview time (minutes)
1	Teacher at School of Design, SJTU (Shanghai Jiao Tong University)	Related studies on creative industry and its competitiveness	61
2	Teacher at School of Design, SJTU	Vehicle interaction and navigation systems	36
3	Teacher at School of Media and Communication, SJTU	Studies on cultural and creative products	55
4	Manager of Wanwu SJTU	Shop management and operation	40

2.3 Consumption End Research

Highly-educated groups with sophisticated aesthetic tastes and more money to spend enjoy the greatest potential in the consumption of cultural products. Hence, young consumers with higher education levels were selected as participants from the consumer side.

Based on the methods of purposeful sampling and heterogeneous sampling adopted in the focus group interviews, specific sampling conditions of the participants are set as follows:

1. Consumers of cultural products;
2. Have different professional backgrounds and are currently at different stages of life (students, workers, entrepreneurs, etc.) to ensure that the composition of the research participants is not too limited;

Tables 2 and 3 list the participants of two focus groups:

Table 2. Participant information of focus group one

Number	Occupation	Related work	Years of working
1	Civil servant	Marketing	0.5
2	Programmer	Electronic information	0.5
3	Financial worker	Audit	1
4	Startup company founder	Computing	2

Table 3. Participant information of focus group two

Number	Occupation	School	Grade
1	Student	School of Electronic Information and Electrical Engineering, SJTU	First-year graduate student
2	Student	School of Foreign Languages, SJTU	First-year graduate student
3	Student	School of Electronic Information and Electrical Engineering, SJTU	Third-year doctoral student
4	Student	School of Design, SJTU	First-year graduate student
5	Student	School of Design, SJTU	First-year graduate student

2.4   Interview Outline and Questionnaire Design

Question design should be consistent with the possibility of participants' answers, as questions over or below participants' actual capability will fail to reflect the actual conditions [10]. Based on this principle, question options were designed using some of the options mentioned by participants in focus group interviews. The consumption-end questionnaire is listed in Table 4.

Table 4. Consumption-end research questionnaire

Number	Question	Question type
1	Gender	Multiple choice
2	Age	Multiple choice
3	Education	Multiple choice
4	What do you think is a cultural product?	Multiple choice (more than one possible answers)
5	Your purchase frequency of cultural products	Multiple choice
6	What do you think is the greatest value of cultural products?	Multiple choice
7	What characteristics do you think an ideal cultural product should have?	Multiple choice (more than one possible answers)
8	Select the top three channels you use to access information of cultural products?	Multiple choice (more than one possible answers)
9	Select your top three motivations for purchasing cultural products	Multiple choice (more than one possible answers)
10	Factors affecting your choice of cultural products	Multiple choice

Interview outline of the research was prepared based on the semi-structured interview method. During the interview, the interviewer asked questions and topics in different ways for different participants based on the interview context and participants' answers [9]. The interview process was recorded with participants' permission, which lasted for about an hour. The interview outline for the design end and the consumption end is listed in Table 5.

Table 5. Interview outline for the design end and the consumption end

Item	Design end	Consumption end
Basic information of participants	Company profile, project experience, etc.	Professions, hobbies, etc.
Definitions, characteristics, and value of cultural products	1. What characteristics do you think cultural products should have? 2. What aspects do you pay most attention to when designing cultural products? 3. What value do you think cultural products have for consumers?	1. Please talk about your understanding of cultural products 2. Have you ever purchased cultural products before? If any, what did you purchase? What do you think could also be classified as cultural products?
Design-end marketing strategy—consumption-end purchasing process	1. What do you think is the most distinguishing feature of your company's products/research projects? 2. What are the target groups of your products/projects?	**Core discussion:** Please share your own purchasing experience of cultural products. **Related questions:** 1. What motivates you to buy cultural products?

(*continued*)

Table 5. (*continued*)

Item	Design end	Consumption end
	3. How did you establish contacts with the target groups when designing the products? 4. What are the main marketing plans and strategies of the design end? 5. What are the main marketing channels of your company? 6. According to your observation, what are consumers' key considerations when purchasing cultural products?	2. What provides you access to information of cultural product? 3. What are the most popular channels to purchase cultural products? 4. What affects your choice of cultural products? 5. What's your user experience of the cultural products you have purchased?
Changes in lifestyle	What are the significant differences between young people and the previous generation in terms of lifestyle and consumption habits?	

3   Result and Discussion

Data of the research were collected and analyzed using the content analysis method in three processes: (1) data restoration: transcribe the recording into text and compress the data through coding, summarization and classification; (2) data display: based on quantitative principles of the content analysis and questionnaire results, the frequency and intensity of the analytical units were measured, and the compressed data were recombined using statistical methods; (3) results obtainment: analyze and interpret the results [11]. The final results are shown in Tables 6 and 7.

Table 6. Research results of the design end

Subject	Description	
Perception of cultural products	Definition	• Products with cultural contents • Products for cultural guidance • Products that meet both material and spiritual needs
	Characteristics	• Culture as the primary element of products • Lead the thoughts of people • Meet people's lifestyle today

(*continued*)

Table 6. (*continued*)

Subject	Description	
		• Culturally recognizable (regional) • Give people a sense of belonging • Give people spiritual satisfaction
Design end's view of cultural products' value for consumers		• Sense of identity • Sense of belonging • Functional value • Collection value • Spiritual value
Design end's view of factors affecting consumers' purchase of cultural products		• Practicality • Quality • Aesthetic value • Creativity • Technical added value • Cultural added value
Marketing strategies of the design end	Establishing relationships with target groups	• Explore cultural connotations in the new era • Explore cultural identity of target users • Consider use context
	Marketing	• Impress consumers with stories • Experiential consumption

Table 7. Research results of the design end

Subject	Description	
Perception of cultural products	Definition	• Cultural symbols and traditional culture • Books and newspapers • Derivative products • Contents and stories
	Characteristics	• Give certain cultural identity • Enhance consumers' understanding of a culture through purchase • Spiritual comfort • Aesthetic value • Collection value

(*continued*)

Table 7. (*continued*)

Subject	Description			
				• Demonstrate personal taste and help build personal image • Social function: convey emotions
Factors affecting consumers' choice of cultural products				• Aesthetic value • Function • Price • Humor • Emotion
Purchase Stages Of cultural products	Before purchase	Ways to obtain information		• Recommendation of friends and relatives • Information delivered on the internet • Shopping • Tourist attractions • Variety shows
		Motivation	Sudden	• Attracted by appearance • Attracted by the stories • As a gift
			Non-sudden	• Like the product itself • Interested in the cultural connotation of the product • To demonstrate personal taste
	During purchase	Decision making		• Appearance • Interest • Influence of the media • Memorial meaning • Influence of friends and relatives
		Purchase method		• Online shopping • Offline shopping
	After purchase	Good experience		• Quality guaranteed • Emotional factors
		Bad experience		• Poor quality • Become idle items that no longer be needed
Changes of contemporary people's lifestyle and their influence on cultural products	Change			• Advanced concepts • Focus not only on functions • Stronger urge to buy • Increased money cost and reduced time cost
	Influence			• Products should satisfy more than functional demands • Impulse purchases increase

In terms of the definition and characteristics of cultural products, the biggest difference between the design end and the consumption end is that the design end believes what cultural products carry in essence is modern culture or modernized traditional culture, but the consumption end always unconsciously adds a traditional culture label to the cultural products, as products on which traditional culture is forced still reach much more consumers under the influence of surrounding environments.

In terms of consumers' perception of the value of cultural products, the design end believes that consumers could demonstrate their aesthetic taste, economic power, and social status through the purchase of cultural products, that is, consumers strengthen the personal image they want to build through cultural products. This agrees with consumers' need for the social functions of cultural products. However, the attention designers of today pay to the educational value of cultural products is far from enough. Consumers may be motivated to buy certain cultural products because the cultural connotation carried by such cultural products is relatively unfamiliar but intriguing. As for the marketing strategies of the design end, the narrative method can create immersive experiences for consumers to promote sales and increase the added value of the products. This also confirms the fact that nowadays people's requirements for products have shifted from physical attributes to cultural attributes. At the same time, as disposable costs increase, purchases of cultural products at the consumption end are mainly impulse purchases, for which cultural atmosphere created by the experiential marketing of the design end is precisely the best catalyst (see Table 8).

Table 8. Comparison of the perception of cultural products between the design end and the consumption end

Subject	Design end	Consumption end
Definitions and characteristics of cultural products	Carry tangible or intangible culture	Carry traditional culture (mostly tangible)
		Various manifestation
	Satisfy spiritual need	Humanistic edification
Value of cultural products	Gain social respect: higher-level need Build personal image	Demonstrate personality: social function
		Gain knowledge of a certain culture: educational function
Design-end marketing strategy—consumption-end purchasing process	Communicate in a highly accessible way: story telling	Love the stories behind products
	Weak correlation marketing: experiential marketing	Impulse purchases
	Multi-channel	Keep up with hot topics

4   Redesign

The Shanghai Hero Pen, known for its Hero fountain pens, is a time-honored brand founded in 1931. Since 1958, the Hero Pen has formed its unique "heroic spirit", the core value of which is "striving to surpass", and its brand slogan is "the pen of success". The Hero Pen has been used several times as the national gifts and signature pens of the Party and the state leaders. In the 1980s and 1990s, Hero Pen enjoyed a market share of about 70%, and reached buyers overseas. But today, its market share reaches a miserably low record of 5%. Hero Pen now suffers from years of heavy loss and grim operation.

Based on the investigation of Hero Pen and the results of this research, it is found that both the brand image and the actual products of Hero Pen have become disjointed with the young consumers. The advertising of "the pen of success" no longer matches young people's communication style and demands. And Hero Pen's product appearance has long been criticized by consumers for its cheap and mature looking.

Therefore, in the redesign of Hero Pen, students aged 15 to 25 were selected as target consumers, and product design was positioned as modern, vibrant and personalized. Figure 2 gives the final redesign plan of Hero Pen.

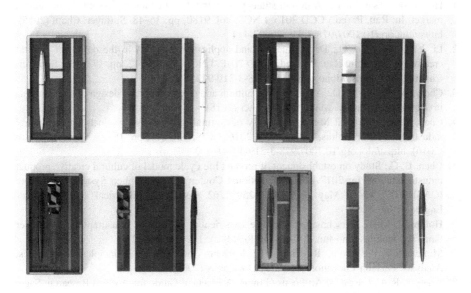

Fig. 2. Redesign of Hero Pen

5   Conclusion and Future Work

This research mainly found that: (1) the appearance, function, price, and cultural spiritual value of cultural products are the common concerns of consumers and designers; (2) young consumers today value the social and educational function of cultural products, and cultural products with humorous contents are more popular with the public. Designers, however, tend to ignore the educational value of cultural products; (3) young people tend to be impulse spenders, and storytelling and experiential marketing can attract consumers quickly. Findings of this research could, to some extent, enable the design end to better reach consumers in cultural product design and marketing.

Future studies could be conducted in the following directions: (1) segmentation research of the consumption end that focuses on small market segments, such as cross-regional cognitive research, cross-label-property research (ACGN, social media savvy), etc. (2) research on the social attributes of cultural products. The importance of the social attributes of cultural products is recognized by both the design end and the consumption end. Future research could investigate how social attributes are given to cultural products by designers, then communicated to consumers, and finally delivered to people in the social circle of the consumers, which in turn reflect consumers' personal image.

References

1. Hsu, C.-H., Tsai, W.-C.: A design strategy of cultural and creative products on the global market. In: Rau, P. (ed.) CCD 2015. LNCS, vol. 9180, pp. 36–48. Springer, Cham (2015). https://doi.org/10.1007/978-3-319-20907-4_4
2. Li, Y., Li, J., Yan, Q.: Design method and application of DNA in the design of cultural creative products. In: Rau, P.L. (ed.) CCD 2018. LNCS, vol. 10912, pp. 172–185. Springer, Cham (2018). https://doi.org/10.1007/978-3-319-92252-2_13
3. Chow, W., Shieh, M.-D.: A study of the cultural and creative product design of phalaenopsis in Taiwan. J. Interdisc. Math. **21**, 389–395 (2018)
4. Chen, C.H., Lin, S.C.: Message delivery of cultural and creative products under cultural industries. In: Stephanidis, C. (ed.) HCI 2016. CCIS, vol. 617, pp. 15–23. Springer, Cham (2016). https://doi.org/10.1007/978-3-319-40548-3_3
5. Chen, B.-C.: Study on establishment of product life cycle model of cultural creative product industrialization. In: 2017 IEEE International Conference on Applied System Innovation, ICASI 2017, 13–17 May 2017, pp. 1259–1262. Institute of Electrical and Electronics Engineers Inc. (2017)
6. Holbrook, M.B., Hirschman, E.C.: The experiential aspects of consumption: consumer fantasies, feelings, and fun. J. Consum. Res. **9**(2), 132–140 (1982)
7. Minichiello, V., Aroni, R., Hays, T.: In-Depth Interviewing: Principles, Techniques. Analysis. Pearson Education Australia, Docklands (2008)
8. Krueger, R.A., Casey, M.A.: Focus Groups: A Practical Guide for Applied Research. Sage, Thousand Oaks (2014)
9. Ayres, L.: Semi-structured interview. In: The SAGE Encyclopedia of Qualitative Research Methods, pp. 811–813 (2008)
10. Suskie, L.A.: Questionnaire Survey Research: What Works. Resources for Institutional Research, Number Six (1992)
11. Neuendorf, K.A.: The Content Analysis Guidebook. Sage, Thousand Oaks (2016)

The Display of Intangible Cultural Landscape Based on the Concept of Eco-Museum

Jiayi Liu[1(✉)] and Ruiguang Tan[2]

[1] Donghua University, Shanghai, China
elynliu@foxmail.com
[2] East China University of Science and Technology, Shanghai, China
artrayt@qq.com

Abstract. The rapid development of industrialization and urbanization brought about changes in the economic structure, forms of production and lifestyle, resulting in deterioration of the natural and human environment, as well as many intangible cultural landscape degradation. To display intangible cultural heritage landscape in the form of eco-museum aims to achieve harmony between man and nature and human environment. Eco-museum with community residents' participation in live state display is the way to retain the cultural heritage, is a means of protecting intangible cultural heritage and tradition.

In this paper, based on the concept of ecological museum theory and practice, the author makes an overview of the history of establishment of eco-museums in accordance with our national conditions, to avoid the homogenization of intangible cultural heritage display modes, and to improve the cultural landscape heterogeneity and retain historical memory of diverse cultures, to protect natural and cultural environment of the country.

Keywords: Environment · Eco-museum · Intangible · Landscape · Display

1 Introduction

With the rapid industrialization and urbanization process in China, as some local governments place too much emphasis on GDP or short-term economic benefits, a growing number of historical and cultural heritages are disappearing in the process. These heritages, due to social economic transformation, the new social consumption patterns and tourism commercial involvement, are losing survival foundation and destroying ecological nature, which has brought about irreversible changes.

Intangible cultural heritage is the result of development and accumulation of human civilization activities. The level of protection, scope, quality and social benefits generated, reflect the level of civilization and culture of a country as a whole. Also it is the only way to carry down human civilization and cultural heritage. So how to combine the local natural and cultural environment, authenticity, a panoramic view of the various intangible cultural landscape displays, is the purpose to protect and pass on the heritage which should not be ignored, and need an urgent study.

Traditional museums which display intangible cultural heritage landscape have played an important role, but as they are enclosed in particular buildings (such as a

© Springer Nature Switzerland AG 2019
P.-L. P. Rau (Ed.): HCII 2019, LNCS 11577, pp. 71–79, 2019.
https://doi.org/10.1007/978-3-030-22580-3_6

museum hall), with little or no participation of indigenous people, they can not demonstrate intangible, non-form aspects, therefore they can not completely show really intangible cultural heritage landscape, and the aim of this landscape display is precisely to better protect these heritages.

Given the limitations of the traditional museum display of intangible cultural heritage landscape, governments in many countries and in many parts of our country have conducted a lot of theoretical study and practical experiments, such as the proposal of eco-museum concept and its practice, with a connotation of ecological community museums and specialized ecological museums, etc., to solve this problem provides a useful theoretical basis and practical experience, but also for our country to develop a useful idea for the display of intangible cultural heritage landscape, and conservation of intangible cultural heritage.

2   Characteristics of Intangible Cultural Heritage and Its Landscape Display

Intangible cultural heritage refers to a variety of cultural expressions and cultural spaces to be inherited for generations, and closely related to people's life [1]. It refers to, regarded by communities, groups, and sometimes persons, the social practice as parts of their cultural heritage representations, expressions, knowledge, skills, and associated instruments, objects, art work and cultural places [2]. The intangible cultural heritage is an intangible, local and a living culture.

This kind of culture and heritage, only through the involvement of people or groups in human behavior and mental activities, expressed in dynamic behavior or the way of information transfer, can only be expressed with visual and non-visual, tangible and intangible, while it can be felt, in a living state and with dynamic characteristics.

In summary, the landscape display of intangible cultural heritage, must have the following factors: the unique quality of the natural landscape, authenticity of its rendering process, integrity, continuity of cultural heritage, and people's participation.

Thus people are exploring new forms of panoramic display of intangible cultural heritage landscape. Looking at the history and social development process, intangible cultural heritage is always inherited in change and development. Many of the "original" heritages that people now protect are not entirely the originally ecological state in their own sense, but the "originally ecological state" identified in today's historical section. In the process of inheritance, people make adaptive adjustments, improvements and innovations according to changes in social productivity. Therefore, it is necessary to protect the living environment according to changes in the social and cultural environment.

3   Theory and Practice of Intangible Cultural Heritage Display

Eco-Museum Proposals and Its Connotation. A series of theoretical exploration and operation practices have been carried out, and achieved gratifying results at abroad, in order to better display, conserve, make research on inheriting intangible cultural heritage.

In 1950, Albert Parr the American Museum of Natural History curator, first put forward the concept of the museum to be repositioned, adapt to changes in the environment, and adapt to social development. In the 20 years that followed, scholars have come to realize that museums must be adapt to social development, outgrow the traditional model, and proposed the concept that museums should show more things outside their architecture and the surrounding environment concerning such intangible factors as political, cultural, economic, social or folk, humane and natural environment.

From the seventies and eighties of the last century, George Henry Riviera proposed and gradually improved the definition of eco-museum, which is the famous "Riviera definition", pointing out that eco-museum does not specifically refer to the natural ecological related museums, its focus is on community and its residents. Hugo de Kovalam, founder of eco-museum theory, further explained it as follows: "Eco" in Ecological Museum (eco-museum) does not refer to ecology itself, but the social environment equalization system.

International Museum of Natural History Committee recommended the definition of eco-museum as follows: Eco-museum through scientific, educational, or generally cultural means of management, makes research and development of a particular community, including the whole tradition of its natural and cultural environment [3].

The French government enacted an clearer definition in 1981, that in a permanent way, on a particular land, along with people's participation, to ensure its research, conservation and display functions, emphasizing the natural and cultural heritage as a whole, in order to show the inherited lifestyle in a representative field.

The interpretation of these definitions and connotations emphasizes the protection of intangible cultural heritage in the original place instead of removing to museums. These theories point out to us a way of displaying the intangible cultural heritage, which should not be displayed in the traditional museum, because once intangible heritage disappears in a place, it will fade in the history. People of next generations can not actually feel their existence, thus destroys the original, local, natural or human environment.

Display of Intangible Cultural Heritage Landscape and Practice of Eco-Museums. France is the first eco-museum practice site.

In 1967, France established a "local natural park in France," which reserves intangible cultural heritage or restores to its original state, focusing on a comprehensive education to people the relationship between people and environment, preserving the memory of tradition in the region. Participation of community residents makes the protection of intangible cultural heritage remain in the local natural and humane environment.

The opening of "Ke Laisuo Montessori Eco-museum", retains the folk religion and industrial buildings passing down from the 18th century, showing the original historical characteristics of lifestyle and cultural environment of the region and so on. Community participation plays an important role in its authenticity and sustainable development.

Built in 1986, France's "Bo Laisai Eco-museum" is a representative case of the French eco-museums in the nineties of the last century. It perfects the concept of eco-museum, cares to preserve local ecological environment; carries out preservation, protection and comprehensive study on intangible cultural heritage. Community residents participate in and guide visitors to arouse their interest in cultural and natural heritage and so on. Through these means, the cultural heritage can be displayed, studied and inherited in its genuine, originally ecological environment.

Since the eighties of the last century in some regions of Norway, Sweden, Britain and other countries, more ecological museums have also been established to reserve original humane and natural ecological environment, providing a local recognition platform for intangible cultural heritage, a display of the entire process, a conservation and inheritance measure. With these eco-museum exhibitions, they train people and motivate their interest in the natural environment and historical heritage, and responsibility to protect local natural and cultural environment, and people's lives reach the harmony between people's lifestyle and production mode.

Since 1980, the eco-museum concept has been accepted by many countries in the French, Spanish, Portuguese, Italian and Latin America, and its ideas have gained popularity in Europe, North America, South America, Africa, Oceania and Asia. There has been a rapid development. By the 1990s, the number of ecological museums in the world had reached more than 300.

4 Domestic Intangible Cultural Heritage Landscape Display Mode

In 2003, UNESCO adopted the "International Convention on the Protection of Intangible Cultural Heritage," In 2004 China formally joined the international conventions, and in 2005 the first national intangible cultural heritage list recommendation project started, paying increasingly attention to the intangible cultural heritage display and protection. Ways and means to its landscape display have been improved steadily along with the development of science and technology [4].

Intangible cultural heritage landscape display experienced from the scratch, from the local regions to the whole country, from the plane mode to the three-dimensional process. The display has also experienced a single "picture + word" to "audio + video" up to the "three-dimensional images + multimedia stereo" and other technological means of sound, light, images.

However, these landscape display format, mostly confined to the museum halls in the traditional sense, while the enclosed display in the form of a traditional museum has been unable to fully accomplish the tasks of panoramic display, audience participation, and protection of tradition, especially the unique customs, popular in certain settlements, and traditional oral culture, production techniques and processes. With the progress of urbanization, as well as impacts of local over-exploitation from an economic perspective, over- development of ancient towns has resulted in a lack of historical and cultural memory and cultural convergence.

Successful practice of titled eco-museums or specialized museums without the title of eco-museum but have a content of eco-museum, and community museums provide us with an example of the display of intangible cultural heritage landscape, e.g. Bo Laisai ecological museum in France, and Figure Raton Museum of Norway, Borg Sagan ecological museum in Sweden. Specialized museums with eco-museum concept and community museums, even ancient towns and villages, provide a comprehensive display of traditional handicraft production process, such as the show of traditional glass-making process in Otaru, Hokkaido, Japan, shown in an European style street, are excellent examples.

5 Principles for Designing Landscape Display of Intangible Cultural Heritage

Regional Nature of Natural Landscape. No culture can exist in real life from the environment on which it depends. The living culture is nurtured in the local social, natural and cultural environment. To preserve it, it must be coordinated with the sociocultural ecology in which it is located.

The Authenticity and Integrity of the Restoration Process. Intangible cultural heritage is a unique cultural landscape that reflects production, lifestyle and activities in a specific region or in a specific environment. The original display of intangible cultural heritage is a different way from the "solid" and "static" protection and display of traditional museums. It is more "live" and "dynamic" as a way of display, in order to fully and truly demonstrate its complete process.

Inheritance of Cultural Heritage. The main carrier of intangible cultural heritage is people. It is the community residents, artisans and artists who engage in this cultural activity. They are people-oriented, and they are passed on from generation to generation, from masters to apprentices, and from the inheritance of human beings. The natural cultural heritage will naturally die out without people's participation.

People's Participation. Intangible cultural heritage is created and passed down by people in local social production activities. The participation of community residents and active people is very important. Through self-management, direct or indirect economic benefits, the participation enthusiasm is continuously improved. It plays a key role in display and protection.

6 Design Method of Intangible Cultural Heritage Landscape Display

The design of intangible cultural heritage landscape display has the following methods: live display, scene reproduction, and interactive inheritance.

Living Display. The live demonstration of intangible cultural heritage is actually a way of designing its existence and activities in the original ecological environment. The most fundamental difference between it and the traditional, solid-state display type is that it is not a static display of objects on the materialized level of a historical geographical node, but an intangible cultural dynamic display of the non-materialized level of society in the development process. By establishing an ecological museum display in traditional villages, it is possible to better protect some natural villages in relatively remote and sheltered areas. In the restoration, protection and development of ancient villages, ancient towns and ancient streets, the local cultural landscape is organically displayed. This local, original and original lively display of the local cultural landscape has played a very important role.

Scene Reproduction, or Context Restoration. The particularity of the display of intangible cultural heritage is that it realizes the reappearance of the scene through the organization of the space environment and the human environment. Through the scene, the audience creates a space environment and a human environment that can truly explain the exhibits of intangible cultural heritage.In the professional museum, the panoramic reproduction shows the unique cultural landscape of the area. Using some of the factory's early production equipment and process flow, the audience will get an overall, original impression. For example, the ancient canal block in Wuxi City, Jiangsu Province, uses the original silk factory, the professional museum built in the ancient kiln group of Ming and Qing Dynasties, and the community museum established by the residents of the Xianyudun community in Wuxi, and also vividly displayed the local silk and brick production lines. Cultural process and cultural environment can thus be restored production lines such as production process and folk activities in the area of southern Yangtze River Delta.

Interactive Inheritance. The display of intangible cultural heritage is not a one-way transmission of material heritage, but through the activities of individuals or groups of people, to participate, express and experience in person, in the process of achieving the smooth communication of intangible cultural information, to achieve the purpose of inheritance. It is embodied in the use of ancient villages, ancient towns, ancient streets to repair, protect and develop cultural landscapes. The local combination of ecological construction, excavation of cultural diversity, and promotion and development of local tourism development, through the display of various technological techniques, such as the blue print fabric production process of Wuzhen, Zhejiang, the clay figurine production of Huishan Ancient Town, Wuxi, Jiangsu, the batik of Dali, Yunnan, Suzhou's Su embroidery in the ancient towns, etc., to promote people's personal participation, thereby increasing people's interest in these skills, and finally achieve the effect of inheritance.

7   Demonstration of Intangible Cultural Heritage Landscape Display

Establish Eco-Museum for Display. Eco-museum practice in China started in the mid-1990s. Local governments made exploration to protect the traditional settlements in this period, such as Tunxi Ancient Street in Anhui, Xu Village in Shexian, Xiuning in Anhui and other ancient towns were listed in the provincial areas of historical and cultural protection. Guizhou Province launched the "Ethnic Cultural Villages" experimental protection program, and Zhouzhuang, Tongli, Jiangsu, Wuzhen, in Zhejiang and ancient towns in other provinces were listed in the ancient town protection projects. In the southwestern regions of Guizhou and Guangxi, under the influence of international "eco-museum" reputation effects, the display and protection have been strengthened, becoming major provinces to implement eco-museum projects, e.g., Suxia Miao eco-museum, the town of Buyi ecological museum in Zhenshan. This natural village eco-museums are commonly seen in relatively remote and transportation backward Western regions.

Display Specialized Museum and Community Museum. There are many places, taking advantage of a variety of specialized museums, panoramically display unique local cultural landscape, such as Qingdao Beer Museum, making use of the workflow and equipment of the former Tsingtao Brewery, a beer manufacturer of Germany in China, allowing viewers to get a whole, living impression of its workflow.

Wuxi's Ancient Canal blocks turned the original silk reeling mills and the site of ancient kilns built in the Ming and Qing Dynasties into specialized museums and community museums. The community of Xian Li Tun, Wuxi built a community museum, vividly demonstrating the local reeling, brick making and other folk cultural landscape and human environment in the Southern Yangtze River Delta.

Display Cultural Landscape along with the Renovation, Protection and Development of Ancient Towns, Villages and Street Blocks. In recent years, in accordance with ecological construction, restoration, protection and development of ancient local villages, ancient towns, ancient streets, people excavate cultural diversity in them, organically show the local cultural landscape, which in the local community, the approach of native, original, and living display of local cultural landscape has played a good role, such as the blue print cloth production process in Wuzhen in Zhejiang, clay figurines making procedure in Huishan, Wuxi, Jiangsu, wax-dying technique in Dali, Yunnan, embroidery of Mudu town, Suzhou, etc. These kinds of display have better preserved local cultural environment.

8   Thoughts on the Intangible Cultural Landscape Display

Display of intangible cultural landscape is a matter of museology, landscape designing, architecture, environment sciences, ecology and other interdisciplinary topics, which are involved in many government departments concerned, the current economic development and cultural landscape display and protection of environment. There is often a conflict between the current economic development and the protection of the local natural environment, which needs to be considered in a long-term, scientific way.

Local governments with sufficient conditions can formulate projects and programs to build ecological museums, such as eco-museum project in the southwestern region. Also the economic entities such as tourism development companies, by means of exploitation and development of ancient streets and towns, can donate or fund to establish specialized museums. And also, a number of industrial and mining enterprises and farms with profound historical and cultural heritage, can protect, study the unique production techniques, production processes, through current production flows in some factories, workshops, cultural landscape is showing to tourists, where workers are still making products, and the audience can witness, experience, and some can even participate personally. Such as ancient salt and sugar making wine brewing process, and other places where the production process is shown and the effective protection of the original ecological environment can be obtained.

At present, considering from eco-museum concept, there is much improvement in displaying cultural landscape.

Natural environment has been constructively damaged in some places. In the cultural landscape of environmental restoration, too much attention has been paid to appealing aesthetic factors and the attraction of tourists. The natural environment and cultural landscape have been made excessive use, the use of modern technology and materials in repairing, such as cement repaired facades, aluminum alloy windowsills, air-conditioning machines fixed on the walls, all of which destroyed the authenticity of landscape. The same kind of exterior repair and decoration destroyed the heterogeneity of the local natural and cultural environment.

Low degree of participation of community residents occur in some places, all the original residents moved to other places and the excessive commercial exploitation and the introduction of too many commercial projects, cause residents participation reduce or even no participation, people come and go in the daytime and the block becomes empty shell town at night. These have destroyed the historical memory of the original human environment. Ecological theory tells us that people need not only economic development, improved material life, but also need to meet the needs of the natural environment. Modern ecology science, environmental science take shape and develop leading people to establish a more equilibrium and harmony between man and nature, urban development and ecological environment [5].

Living display of intangible cultural landscape is not given proper consideration. When they display cultural landscape in the museums in some places, the authorities still maintain the traditional thinking, focusing on static display in a still state, but not showing the whole process of the cultural heritage as a whole. As a result, the living display of human environment has been turned into a static exhibition.

Therefore, in the design of the exhibition of intangible cultural landscape, we take care of avoiding the above deficiencies. Take the Huishan Ancient Town Project, which is currently being repaired and listed in the "Application for World Heritage" in Wuxi, Jiangsu Province as an example. Let us discuss the following aspects:

Excavate a main line and an auxiliary line to display the local historical and cultural landscape in all directions. Taking the ancestral culture as the main line, it shows the connotation of the local filial piety culture and the farming culture that has been passed down for thousands of years. With Huishan clay figurine, Huiquan yellow wine, Huishan oil crisp cakes and Wuxi Opera, and "small heat" comic dialogue as two auxiliary lines, together with the display of the food and developed by the public activities such as the ancestral temple worship and the Huishan temple fair. Cultural achievements such as performing arts and exhibitions showcase the unique culture, characteristic handicrafts and special diets of Wuxi Huishan through the front sales space and back workshops, family production, and the participation of the masses.

Use policy tilt or economic leverage to attract aboriginal and non-genetic people and families to move back, form a non-legacy cultural display block, and have non-genetic inheritors such as the original residents and Huishan clay figurines, Huishan oil cake production, etc. The active participation of community residents or craftsmen can reflect the display of the eco-museum.

Using civil society to carry out research on intangible culture, Wuxi Huishan ancestral Culture Research Association has played such a role, and in the future it will attract more academic groups to participate in various research, such as genealogical research, production technology research and so on.

Avoid excessive commercial development and homogenization. The display of intangible cultural landscape should avoid the influence of excessive commercial development and its destruction into a one-person, one-size-fits-all antique street. The development such as Mudu and Luxiang Ancient Village, in Suzhou should be the road to sustainable development.

9 Conclusions

Researches and practices in cultural landscapes display of the intangible cultural heritage have been carried on at home and abroad for many years. From the view point of the theory and concept of ecological museum, this paper proposes cultural landscape ecologic display based on the concept of eco-museum, to the protection of historical and cultural environment, and promote harmony between man and natural human environment, and various forms of inheritance of intangible cultural heritage and its development can be guaranteed.

References

1. Xu, Z.: Intangible Cultural Heritage is an Important Resource and the Way to the Features and Formation of Grassroots Museums, p. 154. Regional Specialized and Small Museums, Heritage Press (2011)
2. Yang, X., Gan, Y.: On the Intangible Cultural Heritage and Dynamic Cultural Heritage a Research on Cultural Heritage Protection from the Outlook of Scientific Development, p. 205. Regional Specialized and Small Museums, Heritage Press (2011)
3. Yu, Y.: Protection of Traditional Settlements in the Southwest Regions from the Field of Landscape View. Tongji University Press (2012)
4. Zhou, L.: Active Protection on Historical and Cultural Cities and their Whole Creation. Science Press (2009)
5. Li, Z.: Urban Construction, Garden landscape and Environment. China Building Industry Press (2010)

What Makes for Successful Game Storytelling in Different Countries? A Comparison Between Japan, Korea and China

Bingcheng Wang, Yun Gong, and Pei-Luen Patrick Rau$^{(\boxtimes)}$

Tsinghua University, Beijing, China
rpl@tsinghua.edu.cn

Abstract. This paper aims to explore the factors that influence the attitude of players from different countries towards video games. Three steps were taken in this study: (1) Survey construction and distribution to collect players' ratings of the importance of each variable to a game story, and (2) exploratory factor analysis to extract a concise model from the variables. (3) compare the result of three different countries: Japan, Korea and China. One hundred ninety-two data were collected from Korea, and 393 were from Japan. Factor analysis indicates that players from different countries have different factors to consider when judging the story of a game. Chinese players tend to judge a game story from many aspects, such as engagement, scriptwriting, distance from reality, autonomy, values, empathy, competition, multi-challenge, power, physical attractiveness and familiarity. Korea players have fewer factors to considerate. Seven factors have been found through factor analysis: engagement, familiarity, competition, power, empathy, scriptwriting and physical attractiveness. Japan has the least factors in three countries. Only four factors were found in the games: world settings, familiarity, competition and autonomy. The potential implementation of the study is to guide game story writing, selection and adaption.

Keywords: Game story-telling · Culture difference · Exploratory factor analysis

1 Introduction

The video game industry has been proved to be a vast and promising industry with more than 100 billion dollars in revenue each year. According to gamesindustry.biz [1], global games market value rose to 134.9 billion dollars in 2018. More and more game developers focus their attention on the narrative of the story instead of the gameplay, for example, Telltale Games and Quantio Dream are companies known for their storytelling video games. There are mainly three reasons for the emergence of storytelling video games. First, the story is a fundamental part of the video game, and many games are built around a story to communicate emotion, convey values and enhance immersion. Even for online games that do not pay much attention to stories, such as League of Legends, the game also has backgrounds and stories related to each hero. Second, the rise of the live streaming platform has enabled more and more players to

© Springer Nature Switzerland AG 2019
P.-L. P. Rau (Ed.): HCII 2019, LNCS 11577, pp. 80–90, 2019.
https://doi.org/10.1007/978-3-030-22580-3_7

experience the game by watching other people's play. In this way, the game story has become an important factor affecting the viewer's watching experience. Third, with the increasing awareness of intellectual property, a good story can promote the development and sales of peripheral game products.

Modern evaluation model of a game story lies in three aspects: scriptwriting in the traditional movie industry [2], game immersion and playability [3–7], and game motivation studies [8, 9]. However, these models do not involve the creation, selection and adaption of game stories. Unlike the script of the movie, the script of the game is relatively open and free [10], and the plot of the game needs to be modified according to the task design and game design. Especially in the now favourite open world games, the non-linear plot design is also one of the unique charms of the game. So how to design or adapt a good game story is a very worthwhile topic.

Gong et al. [11] proposed a model of eleven dimensions to describe the game-adaptability of stories: engage and explore, script writing, distance from reality, autonomy, values, empathy, competition, multi-challenge, power, physical attractiveness, familiarity. However, because the data was collects only from China, the results of the research may be affected by cultural differences. Besides, previous research on the narrative of the game story is not sufficient, especially the discussion of the game in East Asia is very few. We want to look into this subject and compare the differences between China, Japan and Korea.

This paper aims to compare the factors of the stories that influence game adaptability between China, Japan and Korea. Four steps were taken in this study: (1) Determine variables based on literature and empirical studies, including content analysis and interviews; (2) Survey construction and distribution to collect players' ratings of the importance of each variable to game playability; and (3) exploratory factor analysis to extract a concise model from the variables. (4) Compare the result of three different countries: Japan, Korea and China. The potential implementation of the study is to guide game story writing, selection and adaption, not only for game designers but also for the leads of gamification projects on a broader domain.

2 Related Works

2.1 Game Design Evaluation

Previous research proposed several video game design and evaluation heuristics for enhancing the immersion, playability, enjoyment of gameplay [3–7]. Malone [3] first introduced a heuristics model for video games including three features: challenge, fantasy and curiosity. Clanton [4] suggested a series of usability guideline for video games from three aspects: game interface, game mechanics and gameplay. Federoff [7] then enriched the list of guidelines based on a case study of a game design team. In his research, Federoff recommended a user-centred approach to game design, which includes prototyping, postmortems, expert evaluations, and resources to implement usability. In Heuristic Evaluation for Playability model [5], game story was included as one of the evaluation categories. Game flow was first introduced by Sweetser and Wyeth [6], which focus on player enjoyment in games rather than usability. Eight elements were included in the model: Concentration, challenge, skills, control, clear goals, feedback, immersion, and social interaction. Gong et al. [11] conducted an exploratory factor analysis (EFA) and proposed a model of eleven dimensions to describe the game-adaptability of stories: engage and explore, script writing, distance from reality, autonomy, values, empathy, competition, multi-challenge, power, physical attractiveness, familiarity. In this model, engage and explore are the most significant factors.

2.2 Game Motivation

Both empirical literature [9, 12] and theoretical research [13] found that games can offer experiences that fulfil people needs. Bartle [12] first proposed a player type model and the players were categorised into four types: explorers, achievers, killers and socialisers. Explorers' motivation is the curiosity for knowledge of the internal contents and machinations of the game. Achievers tend to accomplish game-related goals, advance to higher levels and gather treasures and points. Killers are fulfilled when they cause massive distress to other players. Socialisers are more willing to maintain inter-player relationships. Based on the player type model, Yee [9] conducted a factor analysis study on the motivation for gameplay. A principal component analysis revealed ten factors, which fit into three categories: Achievement, Social and Immersion. Achievement players seek advancement, and they want to learn mechanics and enjoy competition. Social players prefer in-game relationships and teamwork. Immersion players enjoy the experience in exploring the virtual world, customising their characters and escaping from the real world. Theoretical works [13] on the motivations for game playing are mainly rooted in self-determination theory. According to self-determination theory, both intrinsic motivation and extrinsic motivation are important for understanding what people want out of a game. Intrinsic motivation refers to the fundamental needs of human beings such as competence, autonomy and relatedness whereas extrinsic motivation comes from external sources such as reward, punishment or self-esteem pressure. In Ryan and Deci's work [8], they proposed three aspects of intrinsic motivation: competence, autonomy and relatedness. Competence needs refer to the necessity of challenge and feelings of capability. Autonomy needs refer to feel that decision making will impact results. Relatedness needs refer to the needs for social interaction.

2.3 Culture Difference

One of the most famous culture difference models is Hofstede's cultural dimensions theory [14]. In this theory, Hofstede proposed six dimensions to describe culture difference: power distance, individualism/collectivism, uncertainty avoidance, masculinity/femininity, long/short-term orientation, indulgence/restraint. Many researchers [15–17] have found that gender plays a vital role in video games, which are related to masculinity/femininity in Hofstede's model. Some other researchers [18] also found that individualism/collectivism also contribute to the culture difference in the games. Many eastern players in games are more collectivism whereas western players prefer to act alone. Although some works have been done in the field, further culture difference in video games storytelling still needs investigation.

3 Methodology

In this study, we collected data through survey and expounded the results by exploratory factor analysis. The purpose of exploratory factor analysis is to reduce the dimensionality of the data so that we can more accurately find the difference in the attitude of players in different countries to the game story.

The questionnaire used in the experiment was from Gong's et al. [11] research. In this study, the researchers obtained 45 factors related to the narrative of the game story through literature research, expert interviews, and content analysis. The 45 factors are shown in Table 1. The questionnaire also includes demographic information, game preference, maximum game-playing frequency, current game-playing frequency, subjective ratings on expertise, overall rating on the importance of storytelling in gameplay, and ratings on the importance of each variable with a statement. A 7-point Likert scale was adopted for each question requiring a rating of attitude. One represented strongly disagree, and seven represented strongly agree.

Table 1. Items in the questionnaires

Storytelling	Game design	Game motivation	Others
Main plot	Comprehension	Advancement	Power
Subplot	Challenge & skills	Competition	Heroism
Character	Curiosity	Discover	Rival camp
personality	Concentration	Role-play	Counter strike
Character	Control	Socialising	Strategy
preference	Empathy	Teamwork	Romance
Structure	Empathy 2	Customisation	Attractive female
Logic	Familiar events	Escape	character
Ending	Familiar conception of world	Autonomy	Attractive male
World	Familiar character	Relatedness	character
conception	Adapt from famous history	Relatedness 2	
Goal	Adapt from famous literature,	Competency	
Profound insight	films, TV	Violence	
Values	Adapted into films, literature, films, TV		

In our survey, experienced game players were targeted as participants. To filter inexperienced game players, the following pre-screening requirement was added: love video games; spend much time on video games; have played video games with stories. Those who failed to meet the requirements were filtered out. The questionnaire was introduced as an "investigation of game preferences in Japan/Korea", without informing participants of the actual purpose of the study.

4 Result and Analysis

4.1 Japan

The results of the Japanese data were commissioned by a questionnaire company. A total of 393 valid data were collected. Exploratory factor analysis was conducted to find the structural characteristics of the questionnaire. We used Kaiser Test (KMO = 0.97) to reveal the significant correlation between items, which means that the items have enough common information. The EFA enabled the reduction of the items into factors that are comparatively less correlated. The procedure of EFA is as follows. First, factors with an eigenvalue larger than 1 were extracted. A component matrix was calculated and rotated relative to orthogonal rotation for further interpretation. Quartimax rotation was adopted in this study to get factors with lower correlation. After the calculation, the following conditions were imposed: (1) the communality should be larger than 1 for most variables; (2) the total variance should be larger than 0.5; (3) The factor loading of each item should be larger than 0.45, and (4) there should be no items with two factor loadings larger than 0.45. If these conditions were not satisfied, the items violating the conditions were deleted one by one until all of the conditions were met. As a result, four factors were extracted. The results of EFA were shown in Table 2.

Table 2. Rotation matrix of Japanese data

Items	Components			
	1	2	3	4
World conception	0.87			
Structure	0.84			
Character preference	0.82			
Main plot	0.82			
Logic	0.81			
Goal	0.81			
Values	0.78			
Subplot	0.77			
Character personality	0.74			
Curiosity	0.72			
Profound insight	0.72			
Comprehension	0.69			
Empathy	0.66			
Empathy 2	0.6			
Challenge & skills	0.58			
Advancement	0.57			
Concentration	0.56			
Ending	0.53			

(*continued*)

Table 2. (*continued*)

Items	Components			
	1	2	3	4
Escape	0.52			
Adapt from famous history		0.87		
Adapted into films, literature, films, TV		0.86		
Adapt from famous literature, films, TV		0.85		
Familiar character		0.81		
Familiar conception of world		0.8		
Familiar events		0.68		
Teamwork		0.65		
Control		0.54		
Socialising		0.49		
Attractive female character			0.76	
Counter strike			0.73	
Rival camp			0.69	
Heroism			0.68	
Attractive male character			0.66	
Violence			0.64	
Power			0.6	
Strategy			0.58	
Romance			0.58	
Competency			0.57	
Competition			0.56	
Relatedness				0.64
Relatedness 2				0.55
Discover				0.53
Role-play				0.52
Customisation				0.52
Autonomy				0.49

4.2 South Korea

The results of the Japanese data were collected at a university in South Korea. A total of 192 valid data were collected. Exploratory factor analysis was conducted to find the structural characteristics of the questionnaire. We used Kaiser Test (KMO = 0.93) to reveal the significant correlation between items, which means that the items have enough common information. The EFA enabled the reduction of the items into factors that are comparatively less correlated. The procedure of EFA is as follows. First, factors with an eigenvalue larger than 1 were extracted. A component matrix was calculated and rotated relative to orthogonal rotation for further interpretation. Quartimax rotation was adopted in this study to get factors with lower correlation. After the calculation, the following conditions were imposed: (1) the communality should be larger than 1 for most variables; (2) the total variance should be larger than 0.5; (3) The factor loading of each item should be larger than 0.45; (4) there should be no items with two factor loadings larger than 0.45. If these conditions were not satisfied, the items violating the conditions were deleted one by one until all of the conditions were met. Following the procedure, power, relatedness, concentration was eliminated. As a result, seven factors were extracted. The results of EFA were shown in Table 3.

Table 3. The results of EFA

Items	Components						
	1	2	3	4	5	6	7
Structure	0.85						
Logic	0.84						
Main plot	0.84						
Character personality	0.81						
Subplot	0.8						
World conception	0.79						
Profound insight	0.62						
Ending	0.62						
Challenge & skills	0.61						
Curiosity	0.58						
Goal	0.58						
Character preference	0.57						
Values	0.55						
Customisation	0.52						
Empathy	0.52						
Discover	0.46						
Adapted into films, literature, films, TV		0.84					
Adapt from famous literature, films, TV		0.83					
Familiar character		0.83					
Adapt from famous history		0.81					
Familiar conception of world		0.81					
Familiar events		0.78					
Competency			0.76				
Violence			0.7				
Relatedness 2			0.65				
Empathy 2			0.58				
Advancement			0.45				
Heroism				0.84			
Counter strike				0.68			
Competition				0.63			
Rival camp				0.58			

(*continued*)

Table 3. (*continued*)

Items	Components						
	1	2	3	4	5	6	7
Teamwork				0.51			
Escape					0.58		
Socialising					0.54		
Autonomy					0.54		
Role-play					0.53		
Control						0.71	
Comprehension						0.55	
Strategy						0.51	
Romance						0.67	
Attractive male character							0.78
Attractive female character							0.56

5 Discussion

5.1 Evaluating the Game-Adaptability of Stories in Japan

The result proposes an evaluation model with four factors based on players' ratings to measure the game-adaptability of stories in Japan. The first factor is mainly about scriptwriting, which includes many items like world conception, structure, character preference, main plot, logic, goal, values, subplot, character personality, curiosity, profound insight, comprehension, empathy, challenge & skills, advancement, concentration, ending, escape. The second important factor from the perspective of the Japanese player is familiarity. Japanese players are more willing to play the games adapted from famous history, literature, films and TVs. Familiar character, event and world conception also contribute to the popularity of games in Japan. Social items like teamwork, socialising is also categorised into this factor mainly because player think that a game from a familiar story may help them find a common topic. The third important factor from the perspective of Japan is character and power. Japanese players are attracted by the charm of the characters in games, especially female characters. The character power also attracts them in games such as counter strike, rival camp, heroism, violence, power, strategy, romance, competency and competition. Autonomy is the last factors taken into account why Japanese players choose a video game. This factor includes relatedness, discover, role-play, customisation and autonomy.

5.2 Evaluating the Game-Adaptability of Stories in Korea

The result of EFA indicates that the evaluation model for game-adaptability in Korea consists of seven factors: scriptwriting, familiarity, empathy, competition, autonomy, comprehension and physical attractiveness. Scriptwriting includes structure, logic, main plot, character personality, subplot, world conception, profound insight, ending challenge & skills, curiosity, goal, character preference, values, customisation, empathy, discover. Korean players are also willing to play the games adapted from famous history, literature, films and TVs. Korean players think that empathy is an essential factor when they play video games, and they are more likely to be influenced by emotion in games. Korean player also like competition which includes heroism, counter strike, competition, rival camp and teamwork. Factor autonomy consists of escape, socialising, autonomy and role-play. Factor comprehension includes control, comprehension, strategy and romance. The last factor is physical attractiveness which includes attractive male characters and attractive female characters.

5.3   Comparison Between Japan, South Korea and China

In previous research, Gong et al. [11] proposed an evaluation model of 11 factors for Chinese players: engage and explore, script writing, distance from reality, autonomy, values, empathy, competition, multi-challenge, power, physical attractiveness, familiarity. Because the study shared the same questionnaires and methods used in our research, the results are comparable to some degree. Thus, we compared the differences in preferences between China, Japan and Korea in game story-telling.

A comprehensive comparison of the factor analysis results of the three countries of China, Japan and Korea shows that the number of factors in the three countries is different. There are up to 11 factors in China. The number of factors in Japan is the least, only four. The number of factors reflects the variety of evaluation criteria for a game story. A large number of factors indicates that the player will think more from a perspective when he or she evaluates a story into a game, and the small number of factors means that the player the taste of the game story is more consistent. The difference between China, Japan and South Korea may be due to the different degrees of development of the game industry in the three countries. Japan started too early in the game field and produced many excellent games. Therefore, Japanese players have more experience in evaluating the quality of a game story, and they are more likely to reach a consensus. For players in China and South Korea, the history of the game industry is not as long as that of Japan, so there will be less experience in this area. Besides, with the development of mobile technology, more and more emerging players are starting to play games on mobile phones, and there are many differences between mobile games and traditional stand-alone games. These various reasons have caused differences between the three countries.

6   Conclusion

This paper aims to explore the factors that influence the attitude of players from different countries towards video games. Factor analysis indicates that players from different countries have different factors to consider when judging a story of a game. Chinese players tend to judge a game story from many aspects, such as engagement, scriptwriting, distance from reality, autonomy, values, empathy, competition, multi-challenge, power, physical attractiveness and familiarity. Korea players have fewer factors to considerate. Seven factors have been found through factor analysis: engagement, familiarity, competition, power, empathy, scriptwriting and physical attractiveness. Japan has the least factors in three countries. Only four factors were found in the games: world settings, familiarity, competition and autonomy. The difference between the three countries is related to the culture difference and their experience in game story-telling. There are some limitations to this research. First, we only compare the differences between China, Japan and South Korea. There are many similarities between the three countries. The differences between the East and West for game stories have not been studied. We believe that comparing the differences between the East and the West in game story-telling will give us more insights. Second, we study their preference for storytelling from the perspective of the player, and game developers and game companies might hold a different idea toward a game story. Therefore, considering this issue from their perspective should also be one of the research directions.

References

1. James, B.: Global games market value rising to $134.9bn in 2018. https://www.gamesindustry.biz/articles/2018-12-18-global-games-market-value-rose-to-usd134-9bn-in-2018
2. Glassner, A.: Interactive storytelling: people, stories, and games. In: Balet, O., Subsol, G., Torguet, P. (eds.) ICVS 2001. LNCS, vol. 2197, pp. 51–60. Springer, Heidelberg (2001). https://doi.org/10.1007/3-540-45420-9_7
3. Malone, T.W.: Heuristics for designing enjoyable user interfaces: lessons from computer games. In: Proceedings of the 1982 Conference on Human Factors in Computing Systems, pp. 63–68. ACM, New York (1982)
4. Clanton, C.: An interpreted demonstration of computer game design. In: CHI 1998 Conference Summary on Human Factors in Computing Systems, pp. 1–2. ACM, New York (1998)
5. Desurvire, H., Caplan, M., Toth, J.A.: Using heuristics to evaluate the playability of games. In: CHI 2004 Extended Abstracts on Human Factors in Computing Systems, pp. 1509–1512. ACM, New York (2004)
6. Sweetser, P., Wyeth, P.: GameFlow: a model for evaluating player enjoyment in games. Comput. Entertain. **3**, 3 (2005)
7. Federoff, M.A., Federoff, M.A.: Heuristics and usability guidelines for the creation and evaluation of fun in video games. Indiana University, Bloomington (2002)
8. Deci, E.L., Ryan, R.M.: The "What" and "Why" of goal pursuits: human needs and the self-determination of behavior. Psychol. Inq. **11**, 227–268 (2000)
9. Yee, N.: Motivations for play in online games. CyberPsychol. Behav. **9**, 772–775 (2006)
10. Qin, H., Rau, P.-L.P., Salvendy, G.: Measuring player immersion in the computer game narrative. Int. J. Hum.-Comput. Interact. **25**, 107–133 (2009)
11. Gong, Y., Wang, B., Rau, P.-L.P., Huang, D.: What makes for successful game storytelling? A model for evaluating game-adaptability of stories in China. In: Rau, P.-L.P. (ed.) CCD 2018. LNCS, vol. 10912, pp. 30–45. Springer, Cham (2018). https://doi.org/10.1007/978-3-319-92252-2_3
12. Bartle, R.: Hearts, clubs, diamonds, spades: players who suit MUDs. J. MUD Res. **1**, 19 (1996)
13. Ryan, R.M., Rigby, C.S., Przybylski, A.: The motivational pull of video games: a self-determination theory approach. Motiv Emot. **30**, 344–360 (2006)

Research on Creation Architecture of Opera Cartoons

Jiede Wu[1,2(✉)], Jianping Huang[1,2(✉)], and Rungtai Lin[2(✉)]

[1] Department of Animation, School of Journalism and Communication, Anhui Normal University, Wuhu 22058, People's Republic of China
125082357@qq.com, 50516059@qq.com
[2] Graduate School of Creative Industry Design, National Taiwan University of Arts, Xinpei 22058, Taiwan
rtlin@mail.ntua.edu.tw

Abstract. As the traditional culture is declining gradually nowadays, it is an issue that needs to be addressed urgently to preserve its inherent essence and transform its external forms to be better adapted to the demands under the context of times. Cartoons are a form of creation popular among the youth of today and are in an ascendant in the digital era. How can we transform the forms of traditional culture with the aid of development and advantages of cartoons to spread the traditional culture in the forms that are better adapted to the times? Taking Chinese traditional operas as an example, the research attempts to blend opera elements into the creation of cartoons and mine the culture and aesthetics of Chinese traditional operas by analyzing and extracting opera elements. Opera cartoons are created by applying the expressive forms of cartoons such as modeling, lines and colors and the concepts of Eastern painting such as form, spirit and freehand to analyze and explore the creation concepts, techniques of expressions and creation methods of opera cartoons. Taking cognitive pattern as its theoretical foundation, this paper attempts to explore the coding process of the creation methods of opera cartoons through rational cognition and perceptual aesthetic experience and study how the decoding process of the audience to see how they interpret the thoughts of the author and understand the essence of creation. The main purpose of this paper is to establish a model for the creation and evaluation of cartoons based on the ideas "reflecting form with form", "reflecting spirit with form", "reflecting the conception with spirit" and "expressing conception and neglecting form". Hopefully this research is referential to the innovation of the ways to spread traditional culture and provides references to the field of cartoon creation.

Keywords: Opera cartoons · Form · Spirit and conception · Aesthetic experience · Cognitive factors

1 Introduction

Chinese opera culture boasts a long history and rich essences as an important component of Chinese culture. However, since it does not make progress and is divorced from today's aesthetic demands, it is gradually faded into oblivion. The governments

© Springer Nature Switzerland AG 2019
P.-L. P. Rau (Ed.): HCII 2019, LNCS 11577, pp. 91–106, 2019.
https://doi.org/10.1007/978-3-030-22580-3_8

have tried to rescue Chinese opera culture, but no big success has been made. With unique elements of exaggeration, abstraction and fun, cartoons are popular among the youth, whose derivative applications also echo with artistic creation or design creativity [1]. However, while cartoons develop rapidly, they are faced with increasingly serious problems such as homogeneity of contents and visual styles and low ages of the audience. It has become hot topics discussed by the society today how to revitalize the opera arts through new paths and how to extend and innovate cartoon arts in terms of themes and contents. This is not only necessary for the inheritance of opera culture, but also necessary for the diffusion and development of cartoon arts today [2].

Cartoon is a form of arts and an important way to express emotions. It is an interesting, complex and dialectical topic worth exploring how the authors of cartoons express their creation concepts with external forms, guide the audience to understand the works and realize communication between the authors and audience [3–5]. For a long time, the communication model for artistic works is mainly explored and interpreted from the perspective of abstract aesthetic feelings. Most Western philosophers of past times opposed to conducting a rational research on the issue from the perspective of cognitive pattern. However, Efland believed that without the use of cognition theory, it is impossible to study the communication model [6]. Therefore, based on the cognition theory, this research attempts to achieve a marriage between operas and cartoons, blend the elements of Chinese operas into the creation of cartoons, apply the principles and categories of Chinese classical aesthetics such as form, spirit and freehand to mine the rational principles behind the perceptual forms of traditional operas. Starting from the external characteristics of roles in operas, the research attempts to analyze the semantic directionality of dressing-up and actions of characters in the operas, create opera cartoons following the principles of Chinese aesthetics and aesthetic paradigms of traditional opera culture. From the perspective of cognition and communication theory, the research explores the factors that influence the aesthetic experience, preference and cognition of the audience and explores the perceptual aesthetic experience through rational cognition, so as to make up the gap of exchange between the authors and the audience [7]. It is also an important aspect explored by the research how the authors of cartoons express the context and conception of creation and how the audience perceive and understand the creativity of the authors. The essence of creation is the core thinking in the creativity of the authors. Cognition is a process for the audience to understand and feel the works. Cartoon works set up a bridge between the authors and the audience.

Nowadays digitization has brought numerous forms of arts to enrich our audio-visual life. Our aesthetic mindset is also changing quietly. The cultural forms inherited from Chinese civilization over thousands of years are now subject to an unprecedented impact from such forms of arts ranging from deep and immersive experiences to fast food style stimulus and enjoyment. It has become a mission and responsibility of every Chinese to carry forward the traditional culture and revitalize Chinese culture in the new era. This research attempts to apply the traditional esthetic philosophy of China in the expression methods and spiritual content of cartoon creation and innovate the creativeness of opera cartoons to enhance the methods, strategy and artistic state of opera cartoon creation, with an expectation to provide helpful experience for the diffusion and development of cartoon creation and operas.

The two major purposes of the research are: (1) Exploring how to transform the thoughts and principles of Chinese classical aesthetics into specific creation architecture; (2) Understanding the sympathy of the audience in the "flexible adaption" and providing references to the authors of opera cartoons.

2   Literature Review

Opera arts blend literature, dancing, music and opera, while cartoon arts integrate story, exaggeration, comedy and imagery. The former reveals details in movement, while the latter manifests feelings in stillness, each carrying its own fun. The two forms of art evolve with the passage of time and can spread and manifest the cultural spirit and aesthetic styles of Chinese people, both of which are related and connected with the core spirit of Chinese aesthetics. Therefore, by referring to Chinese classical aesthetics and the categories of aesthetics such as form, spirit and conception, the research will analyze and develop the creative concepts of opera cartoons.

"Form" represents the body of a person, the material body of a life and the physical features of a character. "Spirit" represents the mind of a person, which is the commander of life and the inherent spirit of a character [8]. "Conception" is a topic with a long history in Chinese traditional aesthetics, which conveys the unique principles of Chinese traditional aesthetics and its aesthetic charm valuing the artistic conception from the perspectives of its functionality and the aesthetic flavors of the authors. In the process of creation, the authors of Chinese paintings focus on expressing their subjective feelings in the objective world. They do not pursue "formal" accuracy, but pay much more attention to the expression of "conception". However, the authors of cartoon works pay more attention to the presentation of skills and techniques but neglect the substance of creativity in the process of creation [9]. The communication model between authors and the audience is exploring the "substance of creativity" from the coding of creative conception to decoding of cognition and feelings. The authors present their "creativity" from a concept, while the audience interact with the works and develop semantic cognition in the works based on their own cultural background and experience. This is a complex cognition process [10].

The roles of operas have undergone an evolution of different stages in history. At present, most operas feature four basic roles, which are male roles, female roles, painted roles and clown roles, of which female roles display distinctive characteristics, which are generally played by young females. Such type of roles usually features a smart and charming figure. In the process of performing, they can reflect the softness, lightness and flexibility of the roles, which are very suitable for cartoons. The image of female roles is summarized by Bai Yunsheng, an opera master, as "tender", "lively" and "genuine". For this reason, the research selects the female roles in operas as the main object of research to create cartoons, which makes the cartoon works closer to life and humanity [11]. Following the three levels of the "essence" of artistic works, namely, the technology level of appearance and perception, the semantic level of cognition of the meaning, and the effect level of inner feelings [12, 13], the research starts from the image building of operas and apply the techniques of cartoons to manifest the form and spirit of opera characters. How to realize form and spirit can be analyzed from the practice of cartoon creation. Following the four steps of creation proposed by Lin, namely, setting the scenario, telling the story, writing the play and cartoon creation [14], the research creates cartoons containing opera elements by reflecting form with form, reflecting spirit with form, expressing conception with spirit [15], extended to a creation model of reflecting the conception and neglecting the form.

2.1   Reflecting Form with Form

Shi Zhang of Qing Dynasty proposed in Painting Theory, "For a beginner of imitating, it's forbidden to separate from the antiquity, otherwise form will be lost." By observing and imitating the features and posture of the characters, the authors of cartoons try their best to approach the dynamic posture of the characters with their skillful painting techniques and observation and mastery of the images of operas. By observing the characters, the authors turn their features into the attributes of the cartoon. Their core thinking is objective depiction and direct expression, emphasizing the basis of form and respecting the form of the object. Such a way of manifestation aims to achieve a vivid resemblance with the "form" of the characters, also known as "reflecting form with form" (Fig. 1).

Fig. 1. Creation concept of reflecting form with form

2.2   Reflecting Spirit with Form

It is recorded in the article *Craftsmanship* in the book *A New Account of the Tales of the World*, "When Gu Changkang was creating figure paintings, he did not paint the eyes for some figures over the years. When asked why, Gu answered, 'The beauty or ugliness of the body is originally unrelated with the eyes. To make the figure lifelike, the key lies in the eyes" [16]. Generally speaking, form is the carrier of spirit. Without the form, spirit will not be conveyed at all. Form and spirit are in a precedence and subordination relationship. Kaizhi Gu, a painter of Eastern Jin Dynasty, pointed out that the core of figure paintings lies in conveying the spirit of the figure, or "vivid portrayal". He stressed that a painter must respect the object on the basis of form and continue to refine and recreate to convey the spirit while achieving an aesthetic effect in the form. The painters should manifest the inherent essence of a figure and pursue the spirit through the form of painting. The portrayal of "form" surrounds and serves the center of "spirit", whose substance is emphasizing likeness in spirit. Its value lies in highlighting the spirit of the figure rather than simply be overcritical with the resemblance in appearance, which is also known as reflecting spirit with form (Fig. 2).

Fig. 2. Creative concept of reflecting spirit with form

2.3 Reflecting Conception with Spirit

As the top of "six techniques" proposed by He Xie, "lively spirit and charm" is the first aesthetic principle for the evaluation of paintings. "Spirit and charm" refers to the inherent spirit of the paintings. The expression of artistic conception emphasizes the exhibition of spiritual temperament, which focuses on the liveliness and vividness of the figures painted. Traditional Chinese paintings reveal that due to the subjectivity of "freehand", different painters have different understanding and cognition in "conception". The artistic realm originates from imagination and goes beyond the image. Therefore, painting should value the artistic state rather than resemblance of appearance [5]. Freehand is one of the important techniques of Chinese painting. A freehand painting does not pursue vividness of details, but manifests the fun of the object and interest of the painters with simple and vigorous painting techniques [17]. Conception is a topic with a long history in the Chinese traditional aesthetics, which conveys the unique principles of Chinese traditional aesthetics and its aesthetic charm valuing the artistic conception from the perspectives of its functionality and the aesthetic flavors of the authors. When cartoon creation encounters implied opera elements, naturally it will add some semantic effects. The form and spirit of operas will form some symbolic visual images and highlight the implied characteristics of opera culture, which is also known as reflecting conception with spirit (Fig. 3).

Fig. 3. Creative concept of reflecting conception with spirit

2.4   Expressing Conception and Neglecting Form

Chinese traditional philosophy is a poetic philosophy and artistic philosophy, pursuing "implication beyond the lines", "image beyond the images" and "purport beyond the tastes". The ideas of Confucianism like "comparison to virtues" and "expression of aspiration", the ideas of Taoism like "Tao models itself after the nature" and "great resemblance is formless", and the pursuit of "realm" by the Chan sect of Buddhism, and the like, are all an interpretation of the Chinese aesthetic philosophy that values conception but neglects form. Ouyang Xiu, a poet of Song Dynasty, also took the spiritual substance as the fundamental, but paid little attention to resemblance of appearance, claiming, "The ancient paintings pursue conception and neglect form". Kaizhi Gu, a painter of Eastern Jin Dynasty, proposed "imagination" in the Comments on Painting. He argued that painting required a process of "imagination" and blended the subjective and objective world on the basis of grasping the appearance features and spiritual essence of the object to create a wonderful artistic image. How to convey the rich essence of operas to the audience without any loss by simply drawing the lines of the figures? By reshaping the figures in reality and simplifying the object with an attitude of aesthetic feelings, the cartoon creation restores the full picture of the spirit of operas. Reflecting the conception and neglecting the form, the cartoon becomes a recreation of the objects and a symbolic image (Fig. 4).

Fig. 4. Creative concept of reflecting conception and neglecting form

3 Methodology

3.1 Creation and Analysis Model for Cartoons

The creation of opera cartoons also has to follow certain methods and procedures. It builds its own languages from the aesthetic principles unique to arts such as harmony, symmetry, balance, comparison, changes, mildness, spirit and charm and artistic rules such as circular and curve, movement and stillness, fullness and emptiness, high and low. Conscious transformation is performed on the basis of observing. The final cartoon effect is created. The specific method and process as follows. The process can be roughly divided into two stages, i.e., operating interface and process analysis. The author searches for the elements that can best reflect the characteristics and traits of the object such as identity and manner, costume and head-wear, movement, facial expressions and charm by observing the visual feelings, inner feelings, actions and facial expressions and personality of the object and figure, and create the cartoons by means of observing and imagination, construction of scenario, reflecting the spirit with form, making choice and refinement, so as to realize the effects of harmony and symmetry, balance and changes, emotional appeal and cultural implications. Now the creation and analysis model for opera cartoons is briefly introduced as follows (Fig. 5).

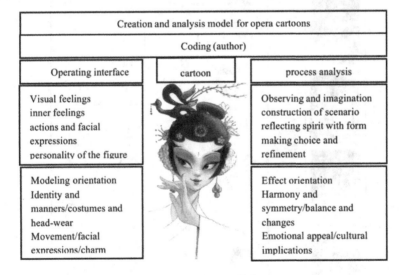

Fig. 5. Creation and analysis model for opera cartoons

After evolving for hundreds of years, the actions and body languages of roles in operas imply a high refinement of beauty. The cartoon creation not only should create vivid and lively figures, but also should be particular in the aesthetic effect of painting. The audience should be able to perceive the external images of opera cartoons and taste the aesthetic effect of the modelling of cartoons. The cartoons should manifest the elements of operas with a form suitable for the contemporary context by combining the creation thoughts and essence, so as to enable the audience to understand, recognize, accept and widely apply the works [18].

3.2   Object of Research

Starting from the perspective of aesthetics theory and based on the analysis model for cartoon creation, the author sorts their relations into creative models, "reflecting form with form", "reflecting spirit with form", "reflecting conception with spirit" and "reflecting conception and neglecting form" and creates cartoons by referring to the pictures of opera figures. Four cartoon works are created for each picture, which cover the four said processes. So 16 works are created in four groups, which are respectively labeled from 1 to 16, shown below.

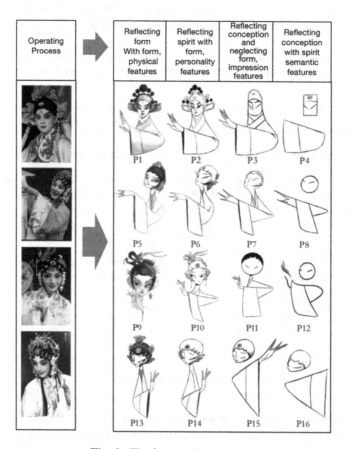

Fig. 6.   The four creative concepts

3.3   Questionnaire Design

Taking the creative models in Fig. 6 as an architecture, the research studies how general audience understand and perceive the creative concepts of artists and the essence of creative models [14]. The stimulus samples are the 16 works listed in Fig. 6. The evaluation methods for two stages are proposed. In the first stage the creative attributes of cartoon works was explored and the appropriateness of transformation according to creative thinking was evaluated Table 1. The understanding and preferences of respondents in the opera cartoons were evaluated in Q1 to Q5. Four questions easy to be understood by the public were raised based on the creative thinking models from Q6 to Q9 to evaluate the creative thinking model of the cartoon author and the sympathy of the audience.

Table 1. Evaluation attributes of cartoon works

Cartoon Options	Questions	
	P1. Which cartoon is simplified to a most appropriate degree do you think?	P6. Which works do you think stresses the resemblance of "form" on the basis of form?
	P2. Which cartoon can best express the creativity?	P7. Which works convey the spirit with the use of skillful techniques and emotional experience?
	P3. Which works shows the richest elements of a cartoon?	P8. Which works highlight the cultural characteristics by forming visual images of symbols through form and spirit?
	P4. Which works has the best overall expression?	P9. Which works reflects the conception and neglects the form and becomes an objective symbolic image?
	P5. Which works you like best in terms of expression approach?	

Respondents were asked to score the 16 cartoon works in the second stage on a 5-point scale, 5 points given to the works that is most consistent with each evaluation factor and 1 point given to the works most inconsistent with evaluation factors. The evaluation factors include concise appearance (D1), mastery of facial expressions (D2), bold exaggeration (D3) and creativity (D4) (Table 2). The stimulus samples are the 16 cartoon works shown in Table 2.

Table 2. Questionnaire design for the evaluation of opera comics

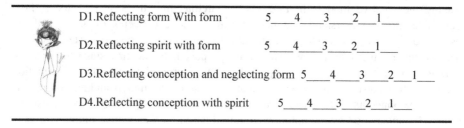

D1.Reflecting form With form	5___ 4___ 3___ 2___ 1___
D2.Reflecting spirit with form	5___ 4___ 3___ 2___ 1___
D3.Reflecting conception and neglecting form	5___ 4___ 3___ 2___ 1___
D4.Reflecting conception with spirit	5___ 4___ 3___ 2___ 1___

3.4   Respondents

With the aid of an online questionnaire survey, the research has collected a total of 176 questionnaires, of which 163 are valid. Among the respondents, 48 are males (29.5%) and 115 are females (70.6%). In terms of ages, 35 respondents age below 20 (21.7%), 104 age between 21 and 40 (63.8%), 19 age between 41 and 60 (11.7%), 5 age older than 61 (3.1%). In terms of education background, 28 respondents are postgraduates (17.2%), 91 are undergraduates (55.8%) and 44 are from other education backgrounds (27.0%). As to professional backgrounds, 69 respondents are related with the field of arts (42.3%), 64 are from the field of design (39.3%), and 30 from other fields (18.4%).

4   Research Results and Discussion

4.1   Evaluation in First Stage

In the first stage, frequency was adopted to evaluate the selection of evaluation attributes of cartoon works Q1 to Q9 by the respondents.

Table 3. The selection frequency and percentage of evaluation attribute questions

Q1	P10 > P3 > P13 > P15 > P12 > P9 > P6 > P2 > P7 > P4 > P1 > P16 > P14 > P11 > P5 > P8
%	18.2 > 10.4 > 7.8 > 6.5 > 6.5 > 6.5 > 6.5 > 6.5 > 5.2 > 5.2 > 5.2 > 3.9 > 3.9 > 2.6 > 2.6 > 1.3 > 1.3
Q2	P6 > P12 > P4 > P15 > P10 > P9 > P7 > P14 > P13 > P11 > P2 > P1 > P5 > P3 > P16 > P8
%	16.9 > 15.6 > 11.7 > 10.4 > 6.5 > 6.5 > 6.5 > 3.9 > 3.9 > 3.9 > 3.9 > 3.9 > 2.6 > 2.6 > 1.3 > 0
Q3	P14 > P10 > P11 > P3 > P6 > P9 > P1 > P5 > P15 > P4 > P12 > P11 > P2 > P16 > P7 > P8
%	15.6 > 14.3 > 11.7 > 9.1 > 9.1 > 7.8 > 7.8 > 6.5 > 3.9 > 3.9 > 2.6 > 2.6 > 2.6 > 1.3 > 1.3 > 0
Q4	P9 > P10 > P1 > P2 > P6 > P14 > P5 > P15 > P13 > P12 > P11 > P3 > P16 > P7 > P4 > P8
%	29.9 > 15.6 > 11.7 > 7.8 > 6.5 > 5.2 > 5.2 > 3.9 > 2.6 > 2.6 > 2.6 > 2.6 > 1.3 > 1.3 > 1.3 > 0

(*continued*)

Table 3. *(continued)*

Q5	P9 > P10 > P14 > P6 > P5 > P15 > P13 > P2 > P12 > P4 > P3 > P5 > P1 > P7 > P8 > P11
%	22.1 > 18.2 > 10.4 > 7.8 > 7.8 > 6.5 > 6.5 > 6.5 > 5.2 > 3.9 > 2.6 > 1.3 > 1.3 > 0>0 > 0
Q6	P9 > P12 > P3 > P15 > P10 > P5 > P1 > P4 > P14 > P2 > P16 > P13 > P11 > P8 > P7 > P6
%	22.1 > 10.4 > 10.4 > 7.8 > 6.5 > 6.5 > 6.5 > 5.2 > 3.9 > 3.9 > 2.6 > 2.6 > 2.6 > 2.6 > 2.6 > 2.6
Q7	P9 > P10 > P15 > P5 > P6 > P2 > P14 > P7 > P3 > P13 > P1 > P16 > P12 > P8 > P4 > P11
%	29.9 > 11.7 > 10.4 > 7.8 > 6.5 > 6.5 > 5.2 > 5.2 > 5.2 > 3.9 > 2.6 > 1.3 > 1.3 > 1.3 > 1.3 > 0
Q8	P1 > P9 > P5 > P15 > P14 > P3 > P10 > P6 > P2 > P16 > P13 > P12 > P11 > P8 > P4 > P7
%	15.6 > 14.3 > 14.3 > 10.4 > 7.8 > 7.8 > 6.5 > 5.2 > 5.2 > 3.9 > 3.9 > 2.6 > 1.3 > 1.3 > 0>0
Q9	P16 > P4 > P12 > P15 > P11 > P1 > P6 > P3 > P13 > P7 > P8 > P14 > P10 > P9 > P2 > P5
%	18.2 > 16.9 > 13 > 9.1 > 7.8 > 7.8 > 6.5 > 5.2 > 3.9 > 3.9 > 2.6 > 1.3 > 1.3 > 1.3 > 1.3 > 0

The above table indicates that among the samples of attribute Q1, 18.2% selected "P10". Among the samples of attribute Q2, 16.9% selected "P6", among the samples of attribute Q3, 15.6% selected P14, and among the samples of attribute Q4, 29.9% selected P9. Among samples of attribute Q5, 22.1% selected P9 (Fig. 7).

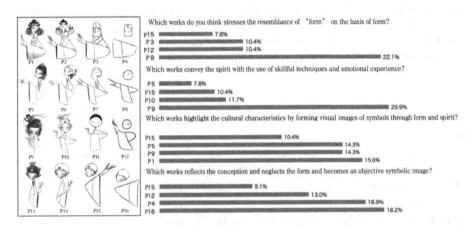

Fig. 7. Top four of the 16 samples in terms of preference

Among samples of attribute Q6, more than 20% selected P9. Among samples of attribute Q7, 29.9% selected P9. Among samples of attribute Q8, more than 10% selected P1. For Q9, the proportion of P16 was as high as 18.2%. In Table 3, the evaluation of Q6 to Q9 matched the opera cartoons with creative thinking models. Since the respondents were highly uncertain, or had different understanding of creative thinking model of the cartoon authors, significant inconsistency was observed between the matrix formed from the data of reference evaluation and the evaluation results of respondents. That is to say, significant difference was observed between the creative thinking models to be expressed by the author and the cognition of respondents. It is worth further exploration how to explore the factors for such difference according to these objective evaluation data.

4.2   Evaluation in Second Stage

In the second stage, the scoring of 16 cartoon works by the respondents was evaluated with the "t appraisal" and "ANOVA" according to the evaluation model. Table 4 shows the mean value and standard deviation of all respondents for 16 works in terms of 4 evaluation attributes. For example, the mean value of appropriateness D1 of works 1 by all respondents (concise appearance) was 3.23, with a standard deviation of 1.16; the mean value of appropriateness D2 (mastery of facial expression) of works 2 was 3.29, with a standard deviation of 0.87.

Table 4. Mean value and standard deviation of 16 works in 4 factors

	P1	P2	P3	P4	P5	P6	P7	P8	P9	P10	P11	P12	P13	P14	P15	P16
D1	3.23	3.79	4.38	4.49	3.36	3.91	4.27	4.47	3.16	3.84	4.12	4.33	3.13	3.94	4.40	4.58
	1.16	0.92	0.92	1.03	0.97	0.81	0.82	0.94	1.18	0.83	0.87	1.14	1.28	0.86	0.83	0.84
D2	3.95	3.29	2.70	2.33	4.17	3.74	3.44	2.51	4.08	3.71	2.94	2.26	4.44	4.20	2.79	2.55
	0.93	0.87	1.17	1.16	0.85	1.06	0.98	1.11	0.90	0.93	1.09	1.12	0.72	0.81	1.08	1.30
D3	3.01	3.35	3.31	3.44	3.79	3.58	3.56	3.30	3.33	3.64	3.31	3.17	3.27	3.58	3.43	3.39
	0.91	0.92	1.23	1.34	0.95	0.89	0.97	1.33	0.85	0.93	1.10	1.36	1.06	0.89	1.16	1.34
D4	3.29	3.38	3.27	3.18	3.82	3.82	3.56	3.08	3.48	3.64	3.31	2.94	3.68	3.78	3.14	3.36
	1.09	0.89	1.17	1.32	0.90	0.85	1.06	1.23	1.00	0.87	1.06	1.37	1.01	0.88	1.14	1.34

Table 5. Analysis of the difference of evaluation attributes of opera cartoons by different genders

Works	Factor	Gender	Number of respondents	Mean value	Standard deviation	t	Contrast
P12	D2(mastery of facial expression)	Male	26	2.65	1.09	2.27*	Male > female
		Feale	51	2.06	1.08		

*$p < .05$. **$p < .01$. ***$p < .001$. (Gender: (1) male; (2) female)

Table 5 indicates: t was used to study the difference of evaluation attribute D2 by different genders for works P12, which showed distinctive difference in one factor only. The mean value of males was 2.65, which was higher than the mean value of female (2.06).

Table 6. Analysis of evaluation attributes of opera cartoons by different genders (ANOVA)

Works	Factor	Variation	SS	Df	MS	F	Contrast
P1	D1(concise appearance)	Between groups	17.50	3	5.83	5.05**	2 > 1
		Within groups	84.29	73	1.15		
		Total	101.79	76			
P9	D2(mastery of facial expression)	Between groups	6.68	3	2.23	2.96*	3 > 4 > 1 > 2
		Within groups	54.85	73	.75		
		Total	61.53	76			
P9	D4(creativity)	Between groups	7.79	3	2.60	2.81*	4 > 3 > 1 > 2
		Within groups	67.43	73	.92		
		Total	75.22	76			

$*p < .05.$ $**p < .01.$ $***p < .001.$ (ages: (1) below 20; (2) between 21 and 40; (3) between 41 and 60; (4) above 61)

Table 6 indicates that according to an analysis of the evaluation difference of opera cartoons by different ages (ANOVA), a distinctive difference was observed in three factors, namely, D1 concise appearance in works P1, D2 mastery of facial expression in P9, and D4 creativity in P9. P1 (D1): (2) 21–40 > (1) below 20; P9 (D2): (3) 41–60 > (4) above 61 > (1) below 20 years > 21–40; P9 (D4): P9 (D4): (4) above 61 > (3) 41–60 > (1) below 20 > (2) 21–40.

Table 7. Analysis of difference of evaluation attributes by different education backgrounds (ANOVA)

Works	Factor	Variation	SS	Df	MS	F	Contrast
P6	D2(mastery of facial expression)	Between groups	9.14	2	4.57	4.47*	3 > 2
		Within groups	75.67	74	1.02		
		Total	84.81	76			
P6	D3(bold exaggeration)	Between groups	5.99	2	2.99	4.05*	3 > 2
		Within groups	54.72	74	.74		
		Total	60.70	76			
P9	D2(mastery of facial expression)	Between groups	6.83	2	3.42	4.62*	3 > 1
		Within groups	54.70	74	.74		
		Total	61.53	76			

$*p < .05.$ $**p < .01.$ $***p < .001.$ (education background: (1) others; (2) junior college; (3) graduate school).

Table 7 indicates that distinctive different is observed in three factors, namely, P6 (D2) mastery of facial expressions, P6 (D3) bold exaggeration and P9 (D2) mastery of facial expression. P6 (D2): (3) Graduates > (2) junior college; P6 (D3): (3) graduates > (2) junior college; P9 (D2): (3) Graduates > (1) junior college and below.

Table 8. Analysis of difference of evaluation attributes by different backgrounds (ANOVA)

Works	Factor	Variation	SS	Df	MS	F	Contrast
P12	D2(mastery of facial expression)	Between Groups	7.38	2	3.69	3.12*	1 > 2
		Within Groups	87.41	74	1.18		
		Total	94.81	76			
P16	D4(creativity)	Between Groups	12.66	2	6.33	3.80*	1 > 2
		Within Groups	123.16	74	1.66		
		Total	135.82	76			

*$p < .05$. **$p < .01$. ***$p < .001$. Professional backgrounds: (1) Related with design: (2) Related with arts; (3) Other professions

Table 8 indicates that distinctive difference is observed in two factors, namely, P12 (D2) mastery of facial expression and P16 (D4) creativity. P12 (D2): (1) Related with design > (2) Related with arts; P16 (D4): (1) Related with design > (2) Related with arts.

5   Conclusion and Suggestions

Following the creative thoughts and principles of Chinese traditional aesthetics, the research creates opera cartoons, establishes four creative thinking models. Using a quantitative research method of subjective cognition, the research proposes an operable evaluation model and makes an attempt to set up a bridge of communication between the author of cartoons and the audience based on the cognitive difference of preference evaluation. The main purpose of the research is to explore how to transform the principles and thoughts of Chinese classical aesthetics into specific creation architectures and understand whether the audience can reach sympathy with the creative thinking models for creation architectures. Though it is not so detailed, preliminary research findings will be provided as reference to the authors and audience of cartoons. The evaluation results of 16 opera cartoon works by 77 respondents indicate that:

1. Related data indicates that the consistency gap between creative attributes and preference evaluation is distinctive, which may be because the authors of cartoons do not thoroughly understand the creation principles of Chinese aesthetics, the creative thinking model is not so consistent with the forms of cartoons, the skills

and experience of the authors are not rich enough. Too much stress is put on the concrete external forms. The essence of thinking model is not expressed in depth. The cognition is simpler than the understanding of intrinsic meaning.

2. The understanding of the audience in thinking model is different from that of the author. It is worth further exploration how the author can evaluate the external forms of opera cartoons with the intrinsic meaning of creative thinking model, how to explore the factors for the difference based on these objective evaluation data.

3. The mean score given by males to D2 facial expression of works P12 is higher than that of females. And no distinctive difference is observed between males and females for other works and questions.

4. The data indicates that the score given by older respondents is obviously higher than that given by younger respondents for works P1 and P9 in different evaluation attributes. And no distinctive difference is observed in other works and questions.

5. In terms of education background, the data reveals that distinctive difference is observed in different questions between works P6 and P9, which indicates that the mean value of graduates is significantly higher than that of other education backgrounds. No distinctive difference is observed among different education backgrounds for other works and questions.

6. The data indicates that the highest score of four questions: Q4. Which works has the best overall expression? Q5. Which works you like best in terms of expression approach? Q6. Which works do you think stresses the resemblance of "form" on the basis of form? Q7. Which works conveys the spirit with the use of skillful techniques and emotional experience? It also indicates that the favorite works and expression method of the audience is also the most vivid and lifelike works. The reason is worth further exploration.

References

1. Gavil, A.I.: Moving Beyond Caricature and Characterization: The Modern Rule of Reason in Practice (2012)
2. Wu, J.D.: Integration and innovation—"Manga cartoonization" drama character creation exploration. Painting and calligraphy world (2018)
3. Ayu, P.: Designing caricature in teaching writing for EFL learners. Res. Engl. Educ. J. 1(1), 1–9 (2016)
4. Flyvbjerg, B.: Five misunderstandings about case-study research. Qual. Inq. 12(2), 219–245 (2006)
5. Chen, X.M.: On the principle of "Flexibility" in the system of literary criteria. Relig. Philos. 65–66 (2013)
6. Efland, A. Imagination in cognition: the purpose of the arts. The Ohio State University, Ohio (2003). Acesso em, 25
7. Lin, R.T., Li, X.M.: Poetic and Picturesque–Sharing of Working Experience of Beauty of Xianyun. National Taiwan University of Arts, New Taipei City (2015)
8. Chen, W.H.: History of Chinese Classical Aesthetics (Upper Volume), p. 340. Wuhan University Press, Hubei (2007)

9. Cohn, N.: Un-defining "Comics": separating the cultural from the structural in 'Comics'. Int. J. Comic Art **7**(2), 236–248 (2005)
10. Montola, M.: The invisible rules of role-playing: the social framework of role-playing process. Int. J. Role-Play. **1**(1), 22–36 (2009)
11. Kreifeldt, J., Lin, R., Chuang, M.C.: The importance of "Feel" in product design feel, the neglected aesthetic "DO NOT TOUCH". In: Rau, P.L.P. (ed.) Internationalization, Design and Global Development, IDGD 2011. Lecture Notes in Computer Science, vol. 6775, pp. 312–321. Springer, Heidelberg (2011). https://doi.org/10.1007/978-3-642-21660-2_35
12. Fiske, J.: Introduction to Communication Studies. Routledge, London (1990)
13. Jakobson, R.: Language in Literature. The Belknap Press of Harvard University Press, Cambridge (1987)
14. Lin, R.T.: Transforming Taiwan aboriginal cultural features into modern product design: a case study of a cross - cultural product design model. Int. J. Des. **1**(2), 45–53 (2007)
15. Ye, M.L.: Creative design application of poetry culture. An Unpublished Doctoral Dissertation. Creative Industry Design Research Institute of National Taiwan University of Arts, Taipei (2014)
16. Liu, Y.Q.: A New Account of the Tales of the World, vol. 195. Zhejiang Ancient Books Publishing House, Zhejiang (2011)
17. Zeng, F.R.: Artificial Creation Totally Natural–Aesthetic Concept of Landscape Garden and Its Contemporary Values, Literature and Art Studies, **7**, 107–116 (2018)
18. Lin, R.T.: Preface–essence and research of cultural creativity industry. J. Des. **16**(4), 1–4 (2011)

Design for Social Change and Development

Emo-View: Convey the Emotion of the Back-Seat Passenger with an Emoji in Rear-View Mirror to the Driver

Chiju Chao, Xue He, and Zhiyong Fu[✉]

Department of Information Art and Design, Tsinghua University,
Beijing 100084, China
478925410@qq.com, hexue1991@foxmail.com,
fuzhiyong@tsinghua.edu.cn

Abstract. With the development of the self-driving technology, more diverse in-car interaction design has become an essential tendency for the future. In order to enhance the interaction experience between driver and back-seat passenger, we propose the concept of "AEIC" (Augmented Emoji in Car). By modifying the existing in-car equipment with information augment, we can offer multi-modal ways of interaction inside the car for the driver and back-seat passenger, so that they can have a better mutual understanding of each other under the premise of safe drive regulations. By optimizing the current central rear-view mirror, the mood of back-seat passenger can be detected and judged by means of facial recognition. Though the sound, light and Emoji, the passenger's current emotional state will be fed back to the driver. In order to test the designed scheme, we constructed a vehicle driving simulator experimental platform with highly free scalability to obtain interactive data to conduct the user research. We invited 20 participants to participate in our prototype test, by observing them simulating the driving scenes we designed in the platform, their interactive feedback information can be precisely collected. Then we conducted depth interviews with the users about the earlier experience of interactions in the simulated scenario to obtain the reference information for further design iterations.

On the basis of these results we concluded that: a. With the conversion of light source color and the intervention of Emoji (symbolic expression), the driver can have a better understanding of the back-seat passenger's emotional state. b. The information interface, which is designed based on the attention span and short-term memory, can optimizing information output in the car without increasing the cognitive load. However, we found that there are significant differences in interactive feedbacks of different user combinations in scenario simulation. Accordingly, we should design according to different users. At the same time, we believe that the experiments based on the vehicle driving simulator platform is conducive to the preliminary basic research on in-car interaction. By amplifying interaction feedback in the driving scenes, the designers can identify the potential design needs more conveniently. Therefore, we will continue to use the platform to conduct the simulation experiments on the design prototype in the follow-up research to gradually address the gap in the interaction between the front-seat driver and back-seat passenger.

© Springer Nature Switzerland AG 2019
P.-L. P. Rau (Ed.): HCII 2019, LNCS 11577, pp. 109–121, 2019.
https://doi.org/10.1007/978-3-030-22580-3_9

Keywords: Interaction · Emoji · Emotion · Communication · Driver · Passenger · Attention

1 Introduction

1.1 In-car Interaction Change Caused by the Development of Self-driving Technology

With the popularization of L1 and L2 self-driving technology, the driving system are gradually taking on the driving tasks [18]. The relationship among drivers, passengers and system has been changed fundamentally [11]. Which means that the role of driving system for drivers will gradually change from a tool to the collaborative partner [7]. Predictably, with the reduction of driving tasks, there will be more communication between drivers and passengers in the car, therefore, the design for back-seat passengers need to be devoted to more attention on it.

However, to date the design for back-seat passengers are mainly based on players and game consoles. Compared with other aspects of the car, many auto manufacturing companies only offer limited possibilities of personalization and adaptability for the back seat [3], which is due to the current in-car interaction design, which is trying to avoid the interference from the back to the front. However, such an idea shall not apply to the future self-driving. We should work on eliminating the gap between the front-seat driver and the back-seat passenger, and offer more opportunities to the interaction between them.

1.2 In-car Interaction: Difficulties in Communication

Driving can be regarded as a social activity, since we do not drive the car alone in most cases, sometimes passengers may distract the driver's attention, or help the driver complete the task [3]. Sharing the same space by multiple people in a car can be considered as a kind of social activities. However, the space arrangement of the car weakens the observation between the people in it. For example, the design of seats makes people unable to see each other's face due to the visual barriers, which results the fragility and distrust of the in-car social communication. The interior space of a car can be divided into the following areas: driver, front seat passenger and rear seat. Because of the space barrier, it is generally agreed that there is little communication between the front-seat and the back-seat people [9]. Moreover, we also find that there is obvious difference between their conversation experience during driving: In fact, it's difficult for people in the car to truly understand what the other side said as a result of the driving noise, the acoustic characteristics of in-car space and the facial orientation of passengers [2].

1.3 Difficulties in Emotional Understanding of Language Dialogue

Human communication is naturally influenced by emotions [14]. Darwin believed that the face is the most important medium of emotional expression for human beings. Facial expressions can express all the predominant emotions, as well as every subtle change of them [16]. People are used to integrating facial and voice information to manage the emotional cognition, lacking either of them may lead to some misunderstandings [10]. However, the barrier between the front and back seats makes it impossible for people to judge others' emotions based on their faces, which is relatively easier to cause the in-car interaction develops to negative direction.

Accordingly, we put forward the concept of AEIC (Augmented Emoji in Car). By displaying simple symbols which represent the expressions of the back-seat passengers in the central rear-view mirror, we can enhance driver's comprehension of the emotions from the back-seat passengers without increasing the cognitive load. We expect to make up for the "neglected" back-seat scenarios in the current in-car interaction field to propose some valuable design directions and targets, as well as study their pain points by exploring the interactive scenes of the communication among people in a car. We made a prototype according to the design schemes and invite users to experiment with it, and draw conclusions through analyzing the data and interviews to support further design.

2 Related Work

In this section, we present an overview of related work on driver, front seat passenger and rear seat. These cases either introduce how to enhance the information exchange among people in a car or how to provide some activities for passengers to improve the riding experience:

nICE is an in-car game played by everyone in a car, including the driver, in accordance with their capabilities [17]. But it is mainly is designed to pass the long-distance travel time, rather than enhance the emotional communication.

HomeCar Organiser is a connected system that enables families to coordinate schedules, activities, and artifacts between the home and activities placed in the car [8]. However, it is mainly used for sharing information among families and eliminating the boundary between the home and family car to create a seamless experience rather than enhancing emotional connections.

RiddleRide investigated the activities and the technology usage in the rear seat as social and physical space by a cultural probing study [9], but the interaction between the rear seat and the driver has remained to be explored.

Backseat Games is an in-car augmented reality game [6]. It is designed to entertain children during long journeys. Unlike it mainly focus on the passengers' experience rather than the driver's participation, we extended our researches into the relationship between passengers and drivers.

Although these works are based on similar requirements with Emo-view, such as improving passengers' experience or facilitating communication among people in a car. But very few of these works have been resolved the problems of emotional communication during riding. So far, little attention has been devoted to study and test the emotional communication between front and rear seats and driving efficiency of drivers. We focus on the driver to test and compare the prototypes to explore how to enhance in-car emotional communication to achieve good emotional interaction and driving experience in the premise of reasonable driver's attention distribution.

3 Concept

Based on our design motivation and previous research, we believe that the interaction design for the car should be based on the following concepts:

1. Our design allows drivers to complete our experiments while doing the main task without completely changing their visual focus, so the prototype needs to be at a similar level to the driver's eyes. By locating the information in the driver's line of sight, we can minimize his/her scanning distance from the road to the mirror [4]. On the basis of this concept, we believe that we can modify the existing equipment, rather than adding new pieces of equipment and interactions to reduce the driver's visual burden.

2. We consider that taking simple Emoji, color and voice interaction as the main features is more suitable and reliable for the driving. Given that the way of in-car interaction must adapt to the automation era of high development, it is difficult for traditional user interfaces to produce a coherent user experience in this complex environment [12], so we should consider multi-modal ways of interaction as the main method. We should not simply add more information on the screen, but adopt a simpler as well as more effective way to enhance the information in the car.

3. Taking the safety into account, the key is to distribute the driver's attention which is ought to have for the driving task after following information display and interaction control [17]. Based on Wickens' research on multi-resource load theory [22], and the fixed capacity hypothesis [24], it can be concluded that it is more likely to lead to the shortage of cognitive resources in a mobile environment [5]. Therefore, the design should offer the least information that requires drivers to pay attention to [15]. We suggest that by limiting the number of the focus points, the visual scanning time can be reduced to allow the driver focus on the main task (driving task) [21], so as to enhance the in-car information output without increasing the cognitive load.

4 Design

We consider that the key to in-car interactions is the ways of emotional communication and expression, since the improper understanding of emotions may lead to obstacles in language communication [19]. Using the Emoji, especially the positive one, properly is beneficial to the formation of interpersonal relationships and cognitive understanding. They not only help participants express emotions and manage relationships, but also serve as the words to help people understand information [20]. Based on the concept of AEIC, we modified the central rear-view mirror to make it as an output interface to enhance the Emoji information.

Our design is also called Emo-view, which can detect the emotional state of the back-seat passenger by facial recognition, and display the Emoji on the left side of central rear-view mirror to show the emotions of them. Emo-view means the combination of Emoji and the view of the driver, as well as the concept of AEIC to allow drivers look in their rear-view mirror along with the information enhancement, rather than increasement during usual driving.

5 Prototype and Test

5.1 Introduction of Prototype

This prototype is assembled by Microduino's mCookie suite, and the display function of it is realized by LED Strip and Dot Matrix-Color (see Fig. 1).

The LED Strip is attached on the bottom left side of the rear-view mirror, close to the driver. If the back-seat passenger is in the positive mood, it will turn green, or yellow if he/she is in the neutral mood, and red represents the negative mood.

The Dot Matrix-Color is installed on the left side of the rear-view mirror, which can display 6 emotions: calm, happy, exciting, bored, lost and angry.

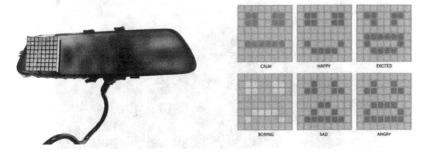

Fig. 1. Prototype of Emo-view and 6 emotions. (Color figure online)

5.2 The Experimental Platform

For evaluation of interaction design and user experience (UX), using laboratory equipment to capture and record the subjective performance of real users dynamically is particularly important and effective, which is also the advantage of field and laboratory experiments [23]. However, it's unrealistic for the early prototype to have the early field test, due to the high cost and low efficiency, lack of conditional control, the difficulties in making prototypes, high-risk to participants and so on. Especially in the experiment of automobile interaction technology, security issues of participants will be extraordinarily magnified. Therefore, these studies mainly rely on laboratory experiments [1].

We hence determine to build a driving simulator platform for product tests and user experience experiments in the laboratory (see Fig. 2). The driving platform is equipped with large screens and speakers to simulate different scenarios, and placeholders of steering wheel, touchable screen and rear-view mirror to ensure multiple diversified tests.

In order to simulate the main task of driving, it is also necessary to record the accuracy and response time of the users' driving tasks. The platform contains a unique driving task simulation system to finish the main task of driving simulation through a pedal and animations on the screen. If a red light (or any custom event) appears in these animations, the driver needs to step on the pedal, and the system will record the reaction time of it. The red light shows up randomly in this experiment, and the driver need to step on the pedal within 3 s after it appears.

Fig. 2. Driving simulator platform (Color figure online)

5.3   Introduction of Experiments

Research Through Design. User-centered design is aimed to develop products that meet users' needs, the point is identifying and providing solutions to meet users' needs. We adopt the concept of research through design to explore users' needs, and take our design as the experimental subject to explore them through experiments.

Our experiment was conducted in Haidian District, Beijing, China. 8 groups of experiments had been done, each of them consists 1 driver and 1 back-seat passenger, with a total of 16 people, whose age ranged from 19 to 30, including 10 females and 6 males.

Wizard of Oz (WoZ) is a technique for prototyping and experimenting dynamically with a system's performance that uses a human in the design loop. It was originally developed by HCI researchers in the area of speech and natural language interfaces as a means to understand how to design systems before the underlying speech recognition or response generation systems were mature [13].

We use Wizard of OZ to understand the real-time characteristics of our design for in-car interaction so that we can get the response during driving simulation. We arrange human "wizard" to play the driving environment and sound, the back-seat passenger to simulate his/her emotions with sound, and the driver to participate in natural language dialogue for observation.

Each group of users has 2 free conversations, each for 5 min in the test. The back-seat passenger needs to deduce 3 kinds of emotions according to the prompt in every conversation, and every time the driver should take the simulated driving as the main task while communicating with the back-seat passenger. The difference between 2 tests is that for the first time, there is no Emo-view, and for the second time, Emo-view was added.

6 Analysis

After the experiments, we analyze the results by data analysis and video analysis and conducted unstructured interviews with each group of subjects.

1. First of all, we analyzed the overall response time of the main task with or without Emo-view. On the basis of single factor analysis of variance we concluded that the response time of main task with Emo-view (M = 180.89, SD = 55.51) was significantly shorter than that without Emo-view (M = 211.26, SD + 96.45), $F(1,297) = 46.327$, $P < 0.001$). Soon afterward, by observing the distribution of reaction time, we found that in most cases, the reaction time of the main task is more stable in the early stage, and fluctuates greatly in the later stage. Therefore, we compared the response time of the first 1/3 and the last 1/3 of the experiments, it can be concluded that when there was no Emo-view, the response time of main task in early stage (M = 182.47, SD = +58.52) was significantly shorter than that in later stage (M = 245.83, SD = +120.64), $F(1,98) = 40.375$, $P < 0.001$; and when there was Emo-view, the response time of main task in early stage (M = 184.36, SD = +52.13) had no significant difference ($F(1,98) = 0.073$, $p = 0.787$) with that in later stage (M = 183.12, SD = +6. 1.12). From the results we have obtained, one can conclude that his/her fatigue effect will show up as the experiment is carried out, which can lead to a longer reaction time without Emo-view, in contrast, with the help of Emo-view, the driver's cognitive processing of the back-seat passenger's emotion can be easier, which can be helpful to relieve his/her fatigue effect.

2. We take the driver as the main object of observation and record the performance of each group on the timeline, which includes the change of the back-seat passenger's emotion, speaking, the point-in-time when the driver looks at Emo-view, and the reaction time he/she used to complete the main task. Here are 3 typical timelines (Fig. 3).

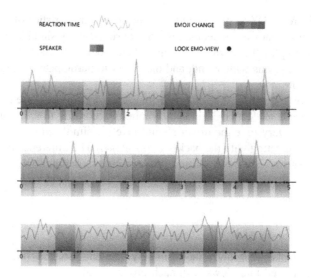

Fig. 3. Timeline of the experimental process

We analyzed the timelines of each group, mainly the situation of drivers watching Emo-view:

a. Drivers' reaction time of driving task has no obvious relationship with mood change, with or without Emo-view and dialogue.

b. When drivers look at Emo-view, 67.5% of these actions occur when they speak and 27.3% when they listen. It can be concluded that drivers need to pay more attention to the emotion of the back-seat passenger when expressing their views.

c. 78.8% of the cases in which drivers look at Emo-view while whey talk occurred at the beginning (32.7%) and the end (46.1%). We conclude that drivers need to confirm the effect of their conversation by observing the passenger's emotion when they start and end a topic.

d. 61.9% of the cases in which drivers look at Emo-view while they listening occurred in the middle period. It can be assumed that in most cases, the driver feel they need to rely on Emo-view to judge the emotion of the back-seat passenger during the listening.

e. When drivers look at Emo-view, only 36.3% of the cases occur when Emo-view is switching emotion, which leads us to conclude that Emo-view doesn't cause the drivers do not often notice switching, so it can be inferred that Emo-view does not cause the excessive cognitive load.

3. The content of our interviews is aimed at the cognitive difference between drivers and back-seat passengers about the dialogic emotion and the driver's actual user experience. Each group was interviewed for about 3–5 min after the experiment. The results can be summarized as follows:

a. With the help of Emo-view, the driver's perception of the back-seat passenger's emotion can be more accurate and reliable. The emotional cognition of both sides become more consistent.

b. Drivers think that with the help of Emo-view, they can change the topic according to the emotional state of the back-seat passenger, so as to lead the topic to a more positive one.

c. Emo-view can help drivers understand the back-seat passenger more easily and reduce the distraction cost of drivers. Some drivers said that without Emo-view it would affect their driving task when considering the emotion of the back-seat passenger.

d. Drivers generally believe that Emo-view will not cause too much psychological burden. They only need to look at it when necessary and ignore it in normal times.

The analysis showed that Emo-view did not occupy the driver's attention resource allocation, nor did it cause the driver's cognitive load. And users generally believe that Emo-view is helpful for in-car communication, and the driver is more dependent on Emo-view when expressing.

7 Discussion and Future Work

According to the test of real users, without changing the space arrangement of the car, that is, the driver can not face the back-seat passenger directly, Emo-view can still be positive and effective. We have considered comprehensively whether it can assist the front and back seats to understand each other better, in which cases it is more needed by the driver, and whether it will affect the safety of driving.

First of all, the data makes us conclude that Emo-view won't occupy the driver's attention allocation, nor does it cause his/her cognition load. Since the interaction design of cars has always been accompanied with the severe safety problems, we concentrate the driver's perception of emotional understanding into a simple Emoji based on the attention span theory and let the interaction happens in the driver's most comfortable parallel line of sight, that is, the central rear-view mirror. So the driver does not need to do the additional interactive operation when looking at Emo-view, he/she can complete the action of viewing it and understand the emotions it expressed instantaneously at the same time in normal driving situations.

Secondly, on the basis of video analysis and interviews, we concluded that drivers need Emo-view. They generally believe that with the help of Emo-view, they can communicate better with the back-seat passenger and managed to bring the conversation to positive topics. However, without Emo-view, some drivers may ignore the driving task because of the deep thinking. And we find that Emo-view can be a reference for drivers' in-car conversation. They will subconsciously look at Emo-view to confirm whether they have "wrong-talking" when they want to start or end a conversation.

However, Emo-view doesn't take into account the relationship within the dialogue. We think that there should be different responses when they are parents, friends, couples, and strangers, since not everyone wants the driver to observe their emotions, and some people prefer to show positive emotions. Therefore, the future work will focus on the following aspects to make some breakthroughs:

a. In order to make Emo-view applicable for people with different relationships, we set up several Emo-view modes, and invite participants with different relationships to take experiments to estimate the referentiality of interpersonal relationships to Emo-view modes' settings.
b. Considering that the back-seat passengers can debug Emo-view themselves during the experiment, such as avoid displaying emotions on certain topics. Emo-view can gradually learn the expression habits of back-seat passengers after several operations. Emo-view can be customized to adapt to any back-seat user.
c. Particular emphasis should be placed on parent-child users. The car is the most frequent way for children to travel, and when the front and back seats are in a parent-child relationship, the driver will pay much more attention to the back-seat passenger than an ordinary one. Thus, we believe that parent-child users need Emo-view more than ordinary ones.

In view of the encouraging results of experiments in laboratory environment presented by now, we will continue to test in a higher fidelity environment in the future, as well as in a car for real world testing. Although laboratory testing has many advantages and is safer, we believe that the real driving environment can help us to reveal new discoveries about the application effect of Emo-view.

8   Implications for In-car Interaction

Our research inspired and expanded the possibility of the interaction between the front and back seats. We believe that the primary issue of in-car interaction is "how to make the communication between front and back seats more smoothly". To improve the situation, we conducted a survey, and locate the main problem at the emotional understanding of the passengers in the car. The experiments demonstrate that Emo-view is effective and needed, and it won't distract but optimize the driver's concentration on driving tasks. We believe that our main design findings are as follows:

First, the output of emotional expression from the back-seat passenger based on the concept of AEIC can indeed lead the communication between the front and the back seats to a positive state. Drivers can be well accustomed to using Emo-view as a reference for conversation when expressing their views.

Second, minimizing the realizing focal points and the amount of information based on the attention span theory can almost eliminate the driver's extra cognitive allocation beyond driving tasks. And the data shows that drivers' observation of Emo-view can actually lighten their cognitive burden of back-seat emotions.

Third, modifying existing equipment to display information in it can minimize the driver's scanning distance, so as to reduce the difficulties in operation and visual burden of the driver.

Last, for in-car interaction experiments, laboratory testing would be a better choice. Indoor driving simulator platform cannot only guarantee participants'safety, but also allow researchers to customize many scenarios and variable conditions, and observe more detailed interactive data of subjects.

9 Conclusion

In order to adapt to the development of self-driving, we consider that as a social space, the in-car interaction will face notable variations. So we designed Emo-view to assist the communication between the front and back seats. With the help of Emo-view, the driver can easily observe the emotional state of the back-seat passenger in the rear-view mirror to have a more active dialogue with he/she. In this paper, we use Arduino to build a simple prototype, set up 6 emotional characteristics, and build a driving simulator platform to do some test by means of Wizards of OZ.

The good results of Emo-view make us confident about the concept of AEIC. From the results of indoor driving simulator platform we have obtained, it can be concluded that if we pay attention to both cognitive load theory and human-machine interaction design theory, we can enhance the in-car information output to drivers without increasing the cognitive load to ensure safe driving, as well as improve the dialogue experience between the front and back seats.

Future work will focus on the comprehension of emotions and interaction among the front and back seats. Not only study the applicability of Emo-view in various other situations, but also explore a range of possibilities of more different ways of interaction to gradually fill the gap in the in-car interaction design for the front and back seats.

Acknowledgments. This research is a phased achievement of "Smart R&D Design System for Professional Technology" project and supported by the Special Project of National Key R&D Program——"Research and Application Demonstration of Full Chain Collaborative Innovation Incubation Service Platform Based on Internet+" (Question ID: 2017YFB1402000), "Study on the Construction of Incubation Service Platforms for Professional Technology Fields" sub-project (Subject No. 2017YFB1402004).

References

1. Soro, A., Rakotonirainy, A., Schroeter, R., Wollstädter, S.: Using augmented video to test in-car user experiences of context analog HUDs. In: Adjunct Proceedings of the 6th International Conference on Automotive User Interfaces and Interactive Vehicular Applications, pp. 1–6. ACM, New York (2014). https://doi.org/10.1145/2667239.2667302
2. Mahr, A., Pentcheva, M., Müller, C.: Towards system-mediated car passenger communication. In: Proceedings of the 1st International Conference on Automotive User Interfaces and Interactive Vehicular Applications, pp. 79–80. ACM, New York (2009). https://doi.org/10.1145/1620509.1620525
3. Meschtscherjakov, A., et al.: Active corners: collaborative in-car interaction design. In: Proceedings of the 2016 ACM Conference on Designing Interactive Systems, pp. 1136–1147. ACM, New York (2016). https://doi.org/10.1145/2901790.2901872
4. Meschtscherjakov, A., Wilfinger, D., Gridling, N., Neureiter, K., Tscheligi, M.: Capture the car!: qualitative in-situ methods to grasp the automotive context. In: Proceedings of the 3rd International Conference on Automotive User Interfaces and Interactive Vehicular Applications, pp. 105–112. ACM, New York (2011). https://doi.org/10.1145/2381416.2381434

5. Oulasvirta, A., Tamminen, S., Roto, V., Kuorelahti, J.: Interaction in 4-second bursts: the fragmented nature of attentional resources in mobile HCI. In: Proceedings of the SIGCHI Conference on Human Factors in Computing Systems, pp. 919–928. ACM, New York (2005). https://doi.org/10.1145/1054972.1055101
6. Brown, B., Laurier, E.: The trouble with autopilots: assisted and autonomous driving on the social road. In: Proceedings of the 2017 CHI Conference on Human Factors in Computing Systems, pp. 416–429. ACM, New York (2017). https://doi.org/10.1145/3025453.3025462
7. Brunnberg, L., Hulterström, K.: Designing for physical interaction and contingent encounters in a mobile gaming situation (2003)
8. Cycil, C., Eardley, R., Perry, M.: The HomeCar organiser: designing for blurring home-car boundaries. In: Proceedings of the 2014 ACM International Joint Conference on Pervasive and Ubiquitous Computing: Adjunct Publication, pp. 955–962. ACM Press, New York (2014). https://doi.org/10.1145/2638728.2641556
9. Wilfinger, D., Meschtscherjakov, A., Murer, M., Osswald, S., Tscheligi, M.: Are we there yet? A probing study to inform design for the rear seat of family cars. In: Campos, P., Graham, N., Jorge, J., Nunes, N., Palanque, P., Winckler, M. (eds.) INTERACT 2011. LNCS, vol. 6947, pp. 657–674. Springer, Heidelberg (2011). https://doi.org/10.1007/978-3-642-23771-3_48
10. De Gelder, G.B., Böcker, K.B., Tuomainen, J., Hensen, M., Vroomen, J.: The combined perception of emotion from voice and face: early interaction revealed by human electric brain responses. Neurosci. Lett. **260**(2), 133–136 (1999). https://doi.org/10.1016/S0304-3940(98)00963-X
11. Flemisch, F., Heesen, M., Hesse, T., Kelsch, J., Schieben, A., Beller, J.: Towards a dynamic balance between humans and automation: authority, ability, responsibility and control in shared and cooperative control situations. Cogn. Technol. Work **14**(1), 3–18 (2012). https://doi.org/10.1007/s10111-011-0191-6
12. Pettersson, I., Ju, W.: Design techniques for exploring automotive interaction in the drive towards automation. In: Proceedings of the 2017 Conference on Designing Interactive Systems, pp. 147–160. ACM, New York (2017). https://doi.org/10.1145/3064663.3064666
13. Kelley, J.F.: An empirical methodology for writing user-friendly natural language computer applications. In: Proceedings of the SIGCHI Conference on Human Factors in Computing Systems, pp. 193–196. ACM, New York (1983). https://doi.org/10.1145/800045.801609
14. Lubis, N., Sakti, S., Neubig, G., Toda, T., Purwarianti, A., Nakamura, S.: Emotion and its triggers in human spoken dialogue: recognition and analysis. In: Rudnicky, A., Raux, A., Lane, I., Misu, T. (eds.) Situated Dialog in Speech-Based Human-Computer Interaction. SCT, pp. 103–110. Springer, Cham (2016). https://doi.org/10.1007/978-3-319-21834-2_10
15. Sodhi, M., Reimer, B., Cohen, J.L., Vastenburg, E., Kaars, R., Kirschenbaum, S.: On-road driver eye movement tracking using head-mounted devices. In: Proceedings of the 2002 Symposium on Eye Tracking Research & Applications, pp. 61–68. ACM, New York (2002). https://doi.org/10.1145/507072.507086
16. Newmark, C.: Charles Darwin: the expression of the emotions in man and animals. In: Senge, K., Schützeichel, R. (eds.) Hauptwerke der Emotionssoziologie, pp. 85–88. Springer, Wiesbaden (2013). https://doi.org/10.1007/978-3-531-93439-6_11
17. Broy, N., et al.: A cooperative in-car game for heterogeneous players. In: Proceedings of the 3rd International Conference on Automotive User Interfaces and Interactive Vehicular Applications, pp. 167–176. ACM Press, New York (2011). https://doi.org/10.1145/2381416.2381443

18. van der Heiden, R.M.A., Iqbal, S.T., Janssen, C.P.: Priming drivers before handover in semi-autonomous cars. In: Proceedings of the 2017 CHI Conference on Human Factors in Computing Systems, pp. 392–404. ACM, New York (2017). https://doi.org/10.1145/3025453.3025507

19. Saarni, C., Buckley, M.: Children's understanding of emotion communication in families. Marriage Fam. Rev. **34**(3–4), 213–242 (2002). https://doi.org/10.1300/J002v34n03_02

20. Tang, Y., Hew, K.F.: Emoticon, emoji, and sticker use in computer-mediated communications: understanding its communicative function, impact, user behavior, and motive. In: Deng, L., Ma, W.W.K., Fong, C.W.R. (eds.) New Media for Educational Change. ECTY, pp. 191–201. Springer, Singapore (2018). https://doi.org/10.1007/978-981-10-8896-4_16

21. Mancuso, V.: Take me home: designing safer in-vehicle navigation devices. In: Extended Abstracts on Human Factors in Computing Systems, CHI 2009, pp. 4591–4596. ACM, New York (2009). https://doi.org/10.1145/1520340.1520705

22. Wickens, C.D.: Processing resources in attention. In: Parasuraman, R., Davies, R. (eds.) Varieties of Attention. Academic Press, New York (1984)

23. Sun, X., May, A.: A comparison of field-based and lab-based experiments to evaluate user experience of personalised mobile devices. Adv. Hum.-Comput. Int. **2013**, 1, Article no. 2 (2013). https://doi.org/10.1155/2013/619767

24. Young, M.S., Stanton, N.A.: Malleable attentional resources theory: a new explanation for the effects of mental underload on performance. Hum. Factors: J. Hum. Factors Ergon. Soc. **44**(3), 365–375 (2002). https://doi.org/10.1518/0018720024497709

New Impression of Beijing Hutongs: A Microscale Urban Emotion Measurement Method

Zhiyong Fu[⊠] and LingChyi Chan

Department of Information Art and Design, Tsinghua University,
Beijing 100084, People's Republic of China
fuzhiyong@tsinghua.edu.cn,
chenlql8@mails.tsinghua.edu.cn

Abstract. Urban emotion is a critical aspect for the human-centered city in the Smart City context. As a general approach of public emotion, measuring happiness has is an active focus with great marketing potential since actually, it concerned prominently by the government in recent years. Different authors have measured urban emotion in a variety of ways. Prior spatial-oriented urban emotion measurement tools practice on the macroscale level for the nation and mesoscale level for community result in a lack of microscale level for the street. This paper presents a spatial-oriented microscale measurement approach of urban emotion based on the Artificial Intelligence (AI) technology, which enables a data collection and visualization from human emotion recognition and object recognition technology. By comparing the data visualization maps, the gradual improvement of urban facilities is one of the manifestations elements of urban development, but emotion of citizens is mostly neutral. These results attempt to reveal the structure and interpret a particular connection between urban emotions and facilities. In the sensor-rich future cities, various data can be accumulated from the recognized data proposals and then transferred to contribute in a reference or feedback for the process of urban planning.

Keywords: Smart city · Urban emotion · Microscale · Spatial-oriented · AI

1 Introduction

The development of human-centered smart cities provides a new opportunity for the acquisition of real-time spatial data and a new attention to human emotions. Urban emotion, not only the important aspects of smart city, but also a human-centered approach, was emerging rapidly in the recent years. It integrates various disciplines such as spatial planning, geographic information system, computational linguistics, sensor technology methods, and real-world data [1, 2]. It aims to understand how people's feelings get affected by urban or geographical factors [2], and it has many functions, for instance, as decision support or evaluation criteria in the ongoing urban planning process, more reliable results can be obtained than the existing urban analysis approaches [3], and the perception of citizens can be managed, and so on.

P.-L. P. Rau (Ed.): HCII 2019, LNCS 11577, pp. 122–134, 2019.
https://doi.org/10.1007/978-3-030-22580-3_10

In the current era of rapid development, big data is no longer a strange word, sensor devices are becoming smaller, cheaper and more powerful. Ubiquitous sensors make humans machine-readable [4]. Human activity, appearance and emotional states will be recognized, recorded and processed [3]. This vast amount of human data has to be used. In this paper, a microscale urban emotion measurement method is proposed. This method recognizes a large number of photos which collected by external sensors through artificial intelligence identification technology, and the identified data can be used for visualization. Although the type of emotional data in this method is fixed and immutable, it can be applied different spatial scales projects according to practical and actual needs. In the future, real-time data visualization can be realized in combination with big data.

2 Related Work

There are two types of urban emotion research projects: user-oriented and spatial-oriented. The user-oriented projects target users, on the other hand, spatial-oriented projects target geographical space. Each of these projects contains two types of data: spatial data and emotional data.

Spatial data mostly refers to geographic location data which detects by sensors. These data are usually measured and recorded for visualization and mapping. Emotional data mostly refers to basic human emotions, happiness [5, 7], anxiety [8], perceptions [10, 11], stress [16], etc. These data are either detected by sensor or judged by user, and there are several measurement modes: tagging based on GPS, extracting from social media, ground-truthing, psychophysiological monitoring [12, 13], questionnaires, etc. Each emotional data will match with geographical location data.

Besides, the emotional data can be classified or derived from different criteria before calculation. For instance, the emotional data in Choudhury's Majitar project [1] are divided into six parts according to facilities, including educational, entertainment, health, industrialization, shopping mart, transportation. World Happiness Report [5] used the Gallup World Poll questionnaire, which covering 14 fields, such as economic, education, government, safety, health, work, etc.

2.1 Spatial-Oriented

According the difference size of the location, spatial-oriented projects can be divided into macroscale, mesoscale and microscale. Macroscale spatial-oriented projects refer to projects at the global or national levels, such as World Happiness Report [5, 6] and Personal Wellbeing Three Year Dataset Maps [8] which recorded the emotional data based on United Kingdom. Mesoscale spatial-oriented projects refer to projects at the city or community levels, such as Christian Nold's Emotion Map [9] and Choudhury's Majitar project [1]. Microscale spatial-oriented projects refer to projects at the street levels.

Macroscale. This type of project refers to the study of emotional data in a large scale urban space, such as at the global and national levels.

World Happiness Reports [5]. A landmark global happiness survey, has quantified and ranked the subjective senses of happiness and well-being in more than 150 countries. The data used for the country rankings came from the Gallup World Poll questionnaire, and there have six variables, included GDP per capita, social support, healthy life expectancy, freedom to make life choices, generosity, and perceptions of corruption. These six key variables were used to explain the variation of happiness across countries. They revealed a populated-weighted average score called the happiness score, which was tracked over time and compared with other countries. All these data are mapped and visualized [6].

Personal Well-Being Interactive Maps [8]. This is a study by Office for National Statistics (ONS) on local happiness and the geographies of subjective well-being in United Kingdom from 2012 to 2016. The data on life satisfaction, happiness, worthwhile and anxiety were collected using the Annual Population Survey (APS) and weighted average. The interactive maps were mapped and visualized from the weighted average data across the United Kingdom [17].

Mesoscale. This type of project refers to the study of emotional data in a medium scale urban space, such as at the city and community levels.

Christian Nold's Emotion Map [9]. The maps are the outcomes of the series of 'Bio Mapping' project, which has involved thousands of participants in over 16 different countries to explore the political, social and cultural implications of visualizing biometric data and emotions since 2004. A simple biometric sensor measuring Galvanic Skin Response and a GPS device was used to build the Bio Mapping device, which is portable and wearable tool. The bio-sensor, which based on a lie-detector, measures the sweat changes levels and assuming those changes are an indicator of emotional intensity. GPS part record the geographical location. The data were visualized and mapped by geographical mapping software at a city level, such as Stockport Emotion Map, East Paris Emotion Map, San Francisco Emotion Map, Greenwich Emotion Map, etc. [9].

K-Means Algorithm [1] and K-Nearest Algorithm [15]. The emotional data of Majitar, a small village in East Sikkim in the Indian state of Sikkim, were measured and determined in two separate projects. K-means is used in the unsupervised learning method project and k-nearest is used in the supervised learning method project. The emotional data are collected through questionnaire and can be divided into six facilities: education, entertainment, health, industrialization, shopping mart and transportation. The calculation results were drawn in six ANOVA tables according to six different facilities.

Microscale. This type of project refers to the study of emotional data in a small scale urban space, such as at the street levels.

Human Sensory Assessment Methods [10]. Eastern Harbor Promenade, main promenade of Alexandria, is an average of a 4.0 km stretch along the water front. It can be divided to inner side and outer side of the path. The surrounding impacts that influence peoples' perceptions can be identified using the data obtained by measuring stress reaction of local participants and foreigner participants when they are walking through the two pathways. The GPS tracker automatically synchronizes the geo-data when the stress reaction is identified. The identified stress points are stored as geological data and visualized in the stress hotspot heat map. This study not only proposed that different cultural backgrounds might affect the perception of the participants in different urban spaces, but also presented a method to investigate the relationship of stress emotion and environment.

2.2 User-Oriented

There are many user-oriented projects, which mainly study the emotions generated by users in different urban spaces, especially public spaces. This type of project focuses on the user emotion and perception rather than urban space. For instance, EmoCycling project [16] focuses on traffic safety and detects the subjective safety by measures the negative arousals of a cyclist riding a bike in the city. RADAR SENSING app [14] adopts the tagging [12] method, and People as sensors app [3] using the ground-truthing method [12] to measure and record the human basic emotions in the urban context and these emotional data is mapped. Walking & talking method [18] probed the relationship between people and places through walking interviews, and conducted in-situ emotions identification through the Plutchik Emotion Wheel.

All the above cases focus on individual's subjective emotion and perception to the urban space. Most of the emotional data here refer to basic human emotions, like relax, happy, sad, angry, stress, etc. These projects are generally small in scale and directly focus on the emotions of users, whether they are subjective experience and provided by users or detected by external sensors. Subsequently, the emotional and geographic data were recorded and visualized for analysis.

3 Microscale Measurement Method

The user-oriented project is a study of the users' emotions on a given topic. The macroscale and mesoscale spatial-oriented projects do not directly concern the personal emotions of users or citizens. Microscale projects which need to study the street, due to the its small scale, a large number of streets need to be collected and studied to form effective data for comparison. Therefore, this paper provides a method for microscale spatial-oriented project to collect and study a large quantities emotional data of different streets. The 'micro' of this microscale spatial-oriented method not only represents the small space as street, but also represents that the emotional aspect of this method will directly focus on the personal emotions of citizens. This method introduces a way that can collect a large amount of emotional data in a street and use the data for visualization. After collecting a large number of streets through the ubiquitous sensors in the future, mesoscale or macroscale projects can be gradually formed according street number.

3.1 Preparation

This paper proposes a micro scale spatial-oriented measurement method of urban emotion based on artificial intelligence technology, namely emotion recognition and object recognition. There are five streets in this project is selected from Beijing hutongs. In terms of emotion, seven emotions commonly used in current emotion recognition technologies are selected. These emotional data will be compared with the element data which come from the object recognition in the hutongs.

Hutong Selection. Hutongs from the Mongolian word "gudum", narrow street which recorded the history of Beijing, well regarded for the local customs, practices and numerous cultural attractions. The Old Beijing was divided into four walls, namely the outer city, the inner city, the imperial city and the Forbidden City. There are many famous hutong areas in inner city and outer city. The famous hutong areas in inner city included Beiluo area, Nanluo area, Shichahai area, etc. The famous hutong areas in outer city included Dashilan area, South hall, Temple of Heaven, etc.

The Shichahai hutong area and Dashilan hutong area was chosen from the inner city and the outer city respectively. From Shichahai hutong area, the Yangmeizhu Xiejie as long as 496 m, the Yingtao Xiejieas long as 579.4 m and the Tieshu Xiejieas long as 551 m were selected. From Dashilan hutong area, the Yangfang Hutong as long as 470 m and the Luoer Hutong as long as 285 m were selected.

The Hutong selected by this project has not been fully developed or completely abandoned. These hutongs not only have new and old residential houses, new and old stores but also include the style and appearances of the hutongs before and after the Beijing Hutong Renovation Project. In addition, the length of hutongs will affect the number of photos, so it is better to have similar length.

Emotion Group and Element Group. The project began by taking a large number of photos and identifying two groups of data: the emotion group and the element group. The emotional group obtains emotional data by recognizing people's expressions in the photos; the element group identifies the hutong elements in the photograph through object recognition technology based on Beijing Hutong ontology (see Fig. 1).

Emotion Group. The emotional data were drawn from seven emotions commonly used in current emotion recognition technologies: happiness, sadness, anger, neutral, fear, surprise and disgust. Besides, age and gender can also be identified. Each photo identifies only one person.

Element Group. As shown in Fig. 1, the elements in Beijing Hutong photos are classified in detail according to dynamic and constant characteristics. The constant categories include five subcategories: sky, green (plant), building, facility, and road. The dynamic categories include two subcategories: people and vehicle. Each of subcategories contains many elements. Several elements are selected as key objects for object recognition. One of key elements is tuktuk (see Fig. 2), a tricycle, which is a common means of transportation in Beijing Hutong.

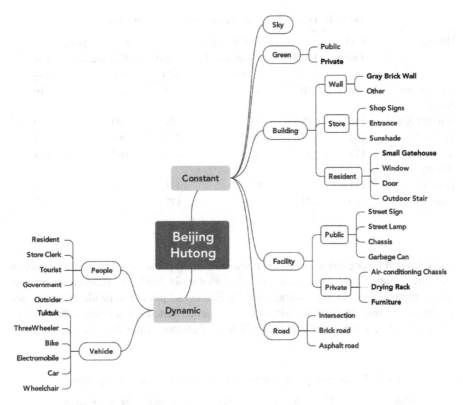

Fig. 1. Hutong Beijing ontology

3.2 Proposed Approach

This approach is divided into three steps: photo collection, AI recognition, and data visualization. The collected photos will identify two groups of data, emotion and element, and finally visualize the data.

Step 1: Data Collection. In this phase, GoPro was used to collect hutong images. The GoPro was set to shoot every five seconds and was attached to a bracket. Holding the GoPro bracket and walking slowly back and forth in a hutong. After walking slowly back and forth through those five selected hutongs, a total of 750 photos were taken. After deleting the overexposed and unoccupied photos, a total of 503 valid photos were obtained.

The 503 photos identified two sets of data using two recognition techniques. Each photo can recognize a set of emotional data and a set of element data. The unrecognizable photos and valid data sets are deleted. The photos and valid data of each hutong are summarized as shown in the following Table 1.

Table 1. Data collection and the number of valid data.

Hutong	Photo		Emotion group		Element group	
	Taken	Valid photo	Recognized photo	Valid data	Recognized photo	Valid data
Yangmeizhu Xiejie	112	70	45	315	36	16
Yingtao Xiejie	168	75	41	287	60	36
Tieshu Xiejie	162	127	39	273	89	44
Yangfang Hutong	177	133	65	455	162	158
LuoErHutong	131	98	63	441	125	123
Total	750	**503**	-	**1771**	-	**377**

Step 2: Data Recognition. After the photo collection phase, two kinds of recognition (see Figs. 2 and 3) are carried out, and the data are obtained. The recognition process is accomplished by calling commercial API. Each valid photo can be identified one set of data (see Table 2). Next, the identified data can be sorted into a table, with a total of 1771 sets of emotion valid data and 377 sets of element valid data (see Table 1).

Table 2. An example of one valid data set from emotion recognition.

Photo	Emotion	e_value	Sex	Age	a_range	Smile	s_range
LuoErHuTong1	Sadness	2.599	Male	77	71–80	0.174	0–10
LuoErHuTong1	Neutral	75.747	Male	77	71–80	0.174	0–10
LuoErHuTong1	Disgust	0.183	Male	77	71–80	0.174	0–10
LuoErHuTong1	Anger	0.183	Male	77	71–80	0.174	0–10
LuoErHuTong1	Surprise	6.337	Male	77	71–80	0.174	0–10
LuoErHuTong1	Fear	14.766	Male	77	71–80	0.174	0–10
LuoErHuTong1	Happiness	0.183	Male	77	71–80	0.174	0–10

Step 3: Data Visualization. The 1771 sets of emotion valid data and 377 sets of element valid data are drawn into four visualization maps by visualization tools, such as RAW Graphs. The visualized maps are not map-based because there is a small geographic information gap between each street's data.

Fig. 2. Object recognition of photo 'Yangmeizhu Xiejie 17'

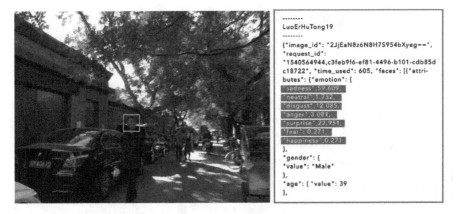

Fig. 3. Emotion recognition of photo 'LuoErHuTong 19'

4   The Visualization Maps

The data visualization maps included Classification of the Elements in Hutongs (Fig. 4), Gender-based Emotional Information of Hutong Residents (Fig. 5), The Key Elements in Hutongs (Fig. 6), and Emotional Information of Hutong Residents (Fig. 7).

The Classification of the Elements in Hutongs (Fig. 4) categorizes the data of element groups according to hutong, subcategories of hutong ontology, and time. Yangfang hutong has the most effective data. Basically, each hutong contains the same proportion of subcategories, with the largest proportion of transportation (vehicles), followed by people, then architecture, greening and equipment.

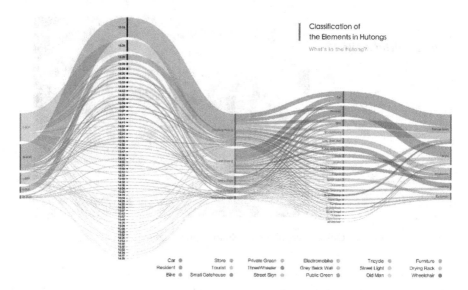

Fig. 4. Classification of the elements in Hutongs

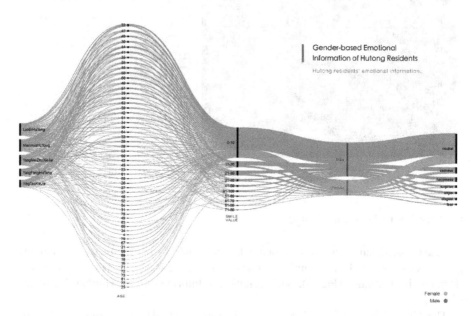

Fig. 5. Gender-based emotional information of Hutong residents

Fig. 6. The key elements in Hutongs (Color figure online)

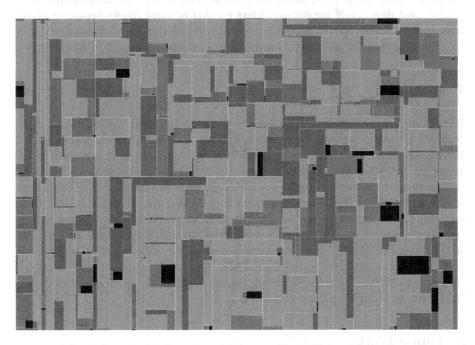

Fig. 7. Emotional information of Hutong residents (Color figure online)

The Gender-based Emotional Information of Hutong Residents (Fig. 5) show the basic emotion, age and gender information of citizen in different hutong. This visualized map shows two important messages. First, the ratio of male to female is approximately 7:3, there are more boys than girls. Secondly, the most common of the seven emotions of citizen was neutral, followed by sadness and happiness.

The Key Elements in Hutongs (Fig. 6) show the key element, such as tuktuk (blue color), private green (green color), small gatehouse (purple color), and drying rack (orange color). Tuktuk was chosen because it is the main means of transportation in the hutongs. The small gatehouse is a symbol of ancient Chinese architecture. The choice of drying rack, or we called clothes hangers, can only be placed on the roof, outside the door, and other public space because of the lack of space in the hutongs. Private greening in narrow space hutong is represent a phenomenon that old men how to spend their time and pursue green life in hutong. The colors represent the objects identified, while the number of blocks represents the number of objects identified. The blocks are hierarchical. First, divide the artboard into 5 large blocks according to 5 hutongs, and then divide the corresponding number of middle blocks according to the number of valid photos of each hutong. Finally, according to number of objects identified in the photo, the middle blocks is divided into small blocks and filled with color.

The Emotional Information of Hutong Residents (Fig. 7) show the sadness (blue color), neutral (gray color), disgust (violet color), anger (red color), surprise (orange color), fear (black color), and happiness (green color) of citizen in five hutong. The blocks are hierarchical. First, divide the artboard into 5 large blocks according to 5 hutongs, and then divide the corresponding number of small blocks according to the value of emotional data of each photo and filled with color. In this visualized map, it is not difficult to find out that the gray neutral is the majority, followed by blue sadness.

5 Discussion

These comparison between the visualized map explore the relationship between urban emotions and urban facilities. For instance, The Key Elements in Hutongs (Fig. 6) and The Emotional Information of Hutong Residents (Fig. 7) can be used to analysis at the same time. In the Key Elements in Hutongs (Fig. 6), the numerous blocks shown in this picture means the numerous objects was identified, while in The Emotional Information of Hutong Residents (Fig. 7), the gray neutral is the majority. Both result came from the same set of photos. In the half-developed hutongs, there are numerous hutong elements, which represent the current perfection of hutongs' facilities, equipment, tools and environment. Although these things are not necessarily excellent and advanced, but certainly to meet the basic needs of residents. Even so, hutong residents are mostly neutral and sadness. The most interesting finding was that the development of city or hutong has failed to bring happiness to citizen.

6 Future Work

As a spatial-oriented project, these data results are from half-developed hutongs. Several years later, when the hutong reconstruction project was completed, the residents' emotional information was collected again for comparison with the data this time, so that feedback from the citizen could be obtained. In the long term, the results are used in decision support in urban planning and the evaluation system in the ongoing processes. In the sensor-rich future cities, a large amount of data can be formed by accumulating the recognized data. These data can be used as a reference, feedback or evaluation criteria in the urban planning, such as street reconstruction, policy implementation and so on.

Acknowledgement. This work was supported by Tsinghua University Institute of Service Design. Sincerely thanks to Ms. He Xue for her visualization work. Finally, sincere appreciation also goes to the teachers and students from B466 Academy of Arts & Design of Tsinghua University, who participated this study with great cooperation.

References

1. Choudhury, S., Pradhan, M.P., Sharma, P., Kar, S.K.: Determining urban emotion using an unsupervised learning approach: a case study around Majitar, East District, Sikkim. In: 2016 International Conference on Energy Efficient Technologies for Sustainability (ICEETS), pp. 134–141. IEEE, Nagercoil (2016)
2. Choudhury, S., Pradhan, M.P., Kar, S.K.: A survey on determining urban emotions using geo-data classification: a case study around Majitar, East District, Sikkim. Int. J. Comput. Appl. **135**(2), 26–29 (2016)
3. Resch, B., Summa, A., Sagl, G., Zeile, P., Exner, J.-P.: Urban emotions—geo-semantic emotion extraction from technical sensors, human sensors and crowdsourced data. In: Gartner, G., Huang, H. (eds.) Progress in Location-Based Services 2014. LNGC, pp. 199–212. Springer, Cham (2015). https://doi.org/10.1007/978-3-319-11879-6_14
4. Smyth, M., Helgason, I.: Tangible possibilities—envisioning interactions in public space. Digit. Creat. **24**(1), 75–87 (2013)
5. World Happiness Report. http://worldhappiness.report/. Accessed 16 Jan 2019
6. StatPlanet. https://cloud.statsilk.com/statsilk/statworld/happiness.html. Accessed 23 Jan 2019
7. Pykett, J., Cromby, J.: Mapping happiness, managing urban emotions. In: Higgins, V., Larner, W. (eds.) Assembling Neoliberalism, pp. 195–216. Palgrave Macmillan, New York (2017)
8. Office for National Statistics (ONS) Personal Wellbeing Three Year Dataset Maps. http://webarchive.nationalarchives.gov.uk/20160105160709/, http://www.ons.gov.uk/ons/rel/wellbeing/measuring-national-well-being/personal-well-being-in-the-uk–three-year-data-2011-2014/rpt-personal-well-being2.html. Accessed 16 Jan 2019
9. Bio Mapping/Emotion Mapping by Christian Nold, BioMapping.net. Accessed 22 Jan 2019
10. Bergner, B.S., et al.: Human sensory assessment methods in urban planning – a case study in Alexandria. In: Schrenk, M., Popovich, V.V., Zeile, P., Elisei, P. (eds.) REAL CORP 2013, pp. 407–417 (2013)
11. Okulicz-kozaryn, A.: City life: rankings (livability) versus perceptions (satisfaction). Soc. Indic. Res. **110**(2), 433–451 (2013)
12. Zeile, P., et al.: Urban emotions – tools of integrating people's perception into urban planning. In: Schrenk, M., Popovich, V.V., Zeile, P., Elisei, P. (eds.) REAL CORP 2015, pp. 905–912 (2015)

13. Zeile, P., Resch, B., Exner, J.-P., Sagl, G.: Urban emotions: benefits and risks in using human sensory assessment for the extraction of contextual emotion information in urban planning. In: Geertman, S., Ferreira, J., Goodspeed, R., Stillwell, J. (eds.) Planning Support Systems and Smart Cities. LNGC, pp. 209–225. Springer, Cham (2015). https://doi.org/10.1007/978-3-319-18368-8_11

14. Zeile, P., Memmel, M., Exner, J.P.: A new urban sensing and monitoring approach: tagging the city with the RADAR SENSING app. In: Schrenk, M., Popovich, V.V., Zeile, P., Elisei, P. (eds.) REAL CORP 2012, pp. 17–25 (2012)

15. Choudhury, S., Pradhan, M.P., Sharma, P., Kar, S.K.: Determining urban emotion using a supervised learning approach: a case study around Majitar, East. Int. J. Comput. Appl. **144** (5), 37–44 (2016)

16. Höffken, S., Wilhelm, J., Groß, D., Bergner, B.S., Zeile, P.: EmoCycling—Analysen von Radwegen mittels Humansensorik und wearable computing. In: Schrenk, M., Popovich, V. V., Zeile, P., Elisei, P. (eds.) REAL CORP 2014, pp. 851–860 (2014)

17. Personal well-being in the UK: local authority update, 2015 to 2016. https://www.ons.gov.uk/peoplepopulationandcommunity/wellbeing/bulletins/measuringnationalwellbeing/localauthorityupdate2015to2016#how-do-people-rate-their-personal-well-being-in-your-area . Accessed 23 Jan 2019

18. Stals, S., Smyth, M., Ijsselsteijn, W.: Walking & talking: probing the urban lived experience mobile. In: Proceedings of the Nordi CHI 2014: The 8th Nordic Conference on Human-Computer Interaction: Fun, Fast, Foundational, pp. 737–746 (2014)

User Experience in Older Adults Using Tablets for Neuropsicological Tests in Mexico City

Erika Hernández-Rubio[1]([⊠]), Amilcar Meneses-Viveros[2],
and Laura Muñoz Salazar[1]

[1] Instituto Politécnico Nacional, SEPI-ESCOM, Mexico City, Mexico
{ehernandezru,lmunozs}@ipn.mx
[2] Departamento de Computación, CINVESTAV-IPN, Mexico City, Mexico
ameneses@cs.cinvestav.mx

Abstract. In Mexico, the health gap has increased, so that the population with health problems exceeds the capacity of the available medical specialists. The population sector of the elderly has difficulty moving to medical care sites to undergo treatments. The use of eHealthy tools can help reduce the problem of the health gap by expanding the coverage of medical care to sectors of the population that have difficulties accessing health services. Neuropsychological tests can be digitized on mobile devices and help in the area of neuropsychology. It has been detected that tablets are an ideal mobile device for older adults due to the size of their screen and the different types of interaction they offer. Several neuropsychological tests have been developed: 10-word learning, Poppelreuter and Raven, among others, in tablets. In this paper we present the results of user experiences when testing these applications in seniors in various centers for older adults in Mexico City.

Keywords: eHealth · Mobile devices · Neuropsicological tests · Older adults · User experience

1 Introduction

Mexico has become an urban country. The concentration of elderly population in urban areas of Mexico has increased [16,19]. Currently, the municipal authorities are those that attend the programs of the third age. The increase in demographic aging is due to three main factors: the fall of the fertility rate, decrease in mortality and migratory phenomena [4,23]. The developing countries have greater growth in their population of older adults [11].

The authors thank financial support given by National Polytechnic Institute through SIP project 20181095, for encouragement and facilities provided to accomplish this publication.

P.-L. P. Rau (Ed.): HCII 2019, LNCS 11577, pp. 135–149, 2019.
https://doi.org/10.1007/978-3-030-22580-3_11

Many government policies on old age assistance provide for older adults with disabilities to remain at home as much as possible. This allows problems of exclusion by keeping them in their current environment. Therefore, a home care network is proposed. In the United Kingdom, this solution has proven to be the most economical for the care of the elderly [24].

In Mexico, some programs aimed at providing care to the elderly through the community have been developed, such as the cases of the "Comparte" program (which arises as a result of the 1985 earthquakes) implemented in the Tepito area in Mexico City, in this program only the female gender will be used to care for the elderly [7]. Another approach are the "clubs of the third age" under the direction of the Municipal System for the Integral Development of the Family (DIF) and National Institute of Senescence INAMAP. In the meetings of these clubs, the elderly practice dancing, they are given talks of self-esteem, health and hygiene, legal advice, among others activities [7,8].

In Mexico, the family continues to be the main institution responsible for the care of the elderly. However, social changes (such as the increase of women in working life) increase the number of older adults who do not have any type of company, loneliness affects 9.8% of older adults [23].

In Mexico in 2005 the 7.1% of the population are older adults. The 27% of the elderly (2.2 million people) are older than 75 years old and present more risks of dependency. According to the National Institute of Statistics and Geography (INEGI) of Mexico, 30% of older adults can not read and write, and the 70% of this group are women.

Projections for Mexico indicate that by 2030 the proportion of people over 60 years old will be 18% and in 2050 the proportion will be 28%. 73% of the concentration of older adults live in cities that have more than half a million inhabitants, 23% live in rural populations and 4% live in cities with less than 500 thousand population. The cities with more than 500 thousand population (Mexico City, Puebla, Monterrey, and Guadalajara to mention a few) concentrate hospitals and specialty clinics for the elderly. The states with the highest increase in older adults are: Chiapas, Veracruz, Oaxaca, Mexico City and Sinaloa [23]. The states with the largest concentration of older adults are the State of Mexico, Veracruz, Mexico City and Jalisco [23].

Although in the cities in Mexico where there is more concentration of older adults are those who have more medical services for this group of people, coverage is not enough to provide care to everyone. 44% of the population is not guaranteed access to medical services. This situation increases in rural communities and in small cities.

One option is to develop e-health tools to increase health coverage for older adults in Mexico. In particular, the area of neuropsychology can benefit from the use of e-Health. Neuropsychology, studies the relationship between the mental and behavioral processes of the brain [5]. Many older adults may have neuropsychological problems, due to cognitive impairments that occur with age. Neuropsychological tests that are used in older adults can be implemented in tablet-type mobile devices. Thus, specialists can attend to more patients in person or remotely, follow up on the system's reports. Mobile applications of neuropsychological tests have been created, such as the word-learning test, Poppelreuters, Raven, and Yerkes, and Luria's test for memory [3,9,10,15].

To prove that it is feasible to use Luria's tests as eHealthy technologies in older adults, it is necessary to know what is the acceptance and the user experience that this group have with the neuropsychological tests that have been implemented as applications for tablets. In this paper we present the results of usability and user experience (UX) evaluations of applications in tablets of some neuropsychological tests of Luria in older adults in Mexico City. These tests have been designed by an interdisciplinary group of professionals from IPN, Cinvestav and UNAM in Mexico. Our experiments allow us to see that there is no resistance to the use of eHealth technologies.

2   Healthy Gap Problem in Mexico

The resources allocated for health services in Mexico are not enough to cover the demand. For example, the Mexican Social Security Institute (IMSS) in 2017 provided medical care for more than 53% of the Mexican population. Only 18.3% of the medical staff is specialized to treat chronic generative diseases. The IMSS has foreseen that the population of beneficiaries will continue to increase, so measures must be taken to provide medical attention to all those who require it [2].

Although there are social security institutions in Mexico such as IMSS or ISSSTE, which provide medical care to a high percentage of the population in Mexico and government programs have been announced to expand coverage, 44% of the total of older adults is not guaranteed access to health services. In urban areas the lack of protection for older adults is 30.4%, and in metropolitan areas it is 30%. Also, 28.4% of older adults are illiterate and 63% are functionally illiterate (without completed studies) [23]. Of the illiterate group, 65% are women. There is a 69% correlation between illiterate people and people who do not have medical coverage in metropolitan areas [23].

Older adults are a sector of the population that is affected by the problem of health gap. Elderly people represent 21.5% of the population of the Mexican Republic [2] and due to their advanced age, they may suffer from physical and mental health problems [18].

The State is committed to providing health services, in order to help improve their quality of life [1]. The IMSS offers services to the elderly, in fact, in the year 2017 the population was 12.5% of the total of beneficiaries. The IMSS made a report in which it shows that the growth rate of the elderly was 45.9% in a span of 8 years, so that the demand for services by people older than 65 years old increased, but the service provided by the institute, has not increased its infrastructure and human resources proportional [2].

3 Neuropsicological Test App for Older Adults

The Soviet neurologist Alexander Romanovich Luria (1902–1977), studied the higher cortical functions in man and his relationship with the cerebral mechanisms. Functions such as perception, memorization, language, thinking, writing, reading and arithmetic can not be considered as isolated or indivisible faculties, since they are usually the result of interaction between different areas of the brain. The main purpose of these tests is to analyze and to understand the structure of psychic phenomena. This analysis helps to diagnose abnormalities of the central nervous system, and to rehabilitate superior cortical functions [6]. Luria visual perception tests are used in the diagnosis of different affections or diseases, for example visual agnosia, which is the inability to recognize objects with the naked eye, but once the patient takes them and manipulates them, recognizes them. This visual condition is due to a dysfunction between the brain and the vision that makes everything around the individual continually new. For example, if a tennis racket is shown to a patient with visual agnosia, he will not know what that object is or what it is used for. Only when using it, the patient will know that it is a racket and that serves to hit a ball. This visual disability is associated with a brain injury caused by traumatic brain injury or stroke and even meningitis.

The application of these tests is carried out by mental health specialists and are usually applied with the help of printed images, audio tracks, interviews, text analysis and even body movements.

In this paper we describe six Luria tests: Poppelreuter 1, Poppelreuter 2, Raven, Words learning, Visual afterimages and Mediate memory. The images used for their description come from the book by Luria [14] and Raven's progressive matrix manual [20].

Poppelreuter Test 1. This test begins by showing the patient the image of the outline of an object, later it will be shown more images containing the original object, but now the outline is mixed with strokes or lines that can confuse the patient. The specialist will request that the outline of the original object be marked, ignoring the additional lines, which are classified as visual noise. The test consists of displaying different images, with different objects and different types of visual noise. Figure 1 shows an example of test images where the original object is a bottle and next to it we see two images with visual noise, the extra strokes can be straight lines or curves.

Poppelreuter Test 2. This test consists of displaying images that contain the outline of different objects. Unlike Poppelreuter 1, this test uses visual noise, but it does overlap the contour of different objects. In this test, there are various objects, all the strokes displayed belong to a general drawing and all objects must be identified. The specialist will ask the patient to distinguish objects. In case the patient shows problems to list them he can use his finger and try to point them out. Figure 2 shows four examples with objects that are easily identified.

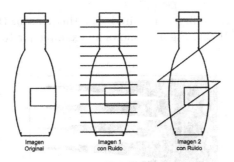

Fig. 1. Example of the Poppelreuter 1 test.

This is important because if uncommon objects are included, the patient will have trouble naming objects and the cause is not a visual disability [17].

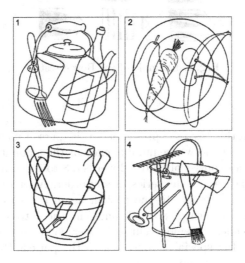

Fig. 2. Example of the Poppelreuter 2 test.

Raven Test. The Raven test is used to evaluate visual abilities and cognitive abilities. It consists of the patient observing a certain visual structure, which is incomplete. The patient can choose between six or eight possible options, but only one is correct. In some cases, the specialist will ask the patient to differentiate the answers from the others. To do this, the patient must identify the pattern of each option.

The complete Raven test consists of three series, each with twelve different test matrices whose difficulty progressively progresses. The advantage of employing Raven to evaluate cognitive abilities is that no grammatical knowledge or complex mathematical ability is required. For this reason, this test is used in children and adults [21, 22]. Figure 3 shows an example for Raven test matrix.

Fig. 3. Example of the Reven test.

Words Learning. In this test, are presented to the person many words or numbers, not linked to each and whose number exceeds the amount that can remember. Usually the series consist of 10 to 12 words o 8 to 10 numbers. The patient is asked to recall and repeat the series in any order. After recording the number of items retained, presents to the patient again the series and record the results. This process is repeated 8 to 10 times and the data obtained are shown in graphical form called "memory curve". After complete all repetitions and spent 50 to 60 min, the specialist must ask to the patient the series of words without mentioning it to the patient again.

Mediate Memory. It is proposed the subject to remember a series composed of 12 to 15 words, using appropriate images that will serve as support for memorization. The images doesn't must directly represent the meaning of the words, the patient selects the images by setting a certain relationship between the meaning of the word and image. The number of images must be of 15 to 20. Once the patient has chosen an image to associate with a word, specialist must ask the patient why chose that image, this relationship should be considered and the patient must remember this association. After 40 min, the specialist should show to the patient the selected pictures and asked to mention the word that associate with that image.

Visual Afterimages Test. Consists in presenting the patient with 3 or 4 bright red geometric figures over a heterogeneous background (white or gray) for 15 or 20 s each one. After this, the patient must be draw the figures that can remember.

For testing visual footprints, it is possible to present 3 or 4 random geometric figures (square, circle, pentagon, etc.) bright red on the mobile device display, indicating that remain for 15 to 20 s and must be indicated in the instructions that the patient should remain viewing this pictures during this time. The application solicit to the patient to draw the figures that was showed before.

3.1   Older Adults Computer Interaction

GUI Design for Older Adults. Interface design for seniors considered possible natural damage they may have. These impairments are visual, auditory, movement and cognitive.

Vision. Physiological changes to the eye related to aging result in less light reaching the retina, yellowing of the lens (making blue a difficult to discern color), and even the beginning stages of cataracts result in blurriness. The eye muscles are also affected; it can be more difficult for older adults to quickly change focus or get used to fast-changing brightness. Some solutions for design include: conspicuity can be enhanced by enhanced contrast and taking advantage of preattentive processes, and effortful visual search can be lessened through application of Gestalt laws.

Effect of vision. How the visual aspects of the web can interact with aging to produce difficulties.

Background images should be used sparingly if at all because they create visual clutter in displays. High contrast should be maintained between important text or controls and the background. Older users vary greatly in their perceptual capabilities; thus interfaces should convey information through multiple modalities (vision, hearing, touch) and even within modalities (color, organization, size, volume, texture). Within a website, consistency should be the highest priority in terms of button appearance and positioning, spatial layout, and interaction behavior. Older users are likely to have a reduced tolerance for discovery and quit instead of hunting.

Information should be presented in small, screen-sized chunks so that the page does not require extensive scrolling. If this cannot be helped, alternative ways of navigating (such as table of contents) or persistent navigation that follows the user as they scroll be provided.

Hearing. A wide variety of changes can occur to hearing. A good auditory design considers both the physical changes in sound perception and the cognitive changes in the comprehension that comes from initial perception. Keeping informational sounds above background noise requires a study of the display environments. The loudness of a sound is truly individual, but can be approximated through the sound pressure levels (dB) and frequencies typically maintained in the aging ear. When hearing loss is severe enough that users wear an aid, consider how those aids interact with the interface.

List of general design guidelines that can be used to improve the design of auditory menus. Calculate loudness levels. Consider potential background noise For tones, use low-tom-mid-range frequencies When designing a display device, consider physical proximity ti the ear and interactions with hearing aids. Avoid computer-generated voices Use prosody Provide succinct prompts Provide context.

Cognition. The main objective in the design of displays is that they are easy to understand. It is intended that the interface is effective, that is, to help users to complete tasks with less confusion and less possible error. To achieve this, we consider some user skills such as: working memory, spatial skills and perceptual speed. Working memory allows the user to recall situations or things in a short period of time. Spatial ability refers to the user to have a location-based representation of the environment where it interacts, in our case, the state of the application. The perceptual speed indicates the rate at which it perceives and processes information. It is known that these skills decline with age, so the design should not be confused with the instructions or the information presented.

For this reason they have only information related to the test. It ensures that each task selection, display, are associated with their own display. Generating an intuitive workflow. In each display the action to take as a central element occurs, this allows the user to hold the attention.

Movement. The movement is an essential part of many means of interaction, because a series movements, perform an action to complete a task. Motion control refers to the accuracy and response time of a movement of a human. The accuracy and response time decay with age, for various reasons, mainly due to illness, such as Parkinson or arthritis. From [18], it is suggested that there is sufficient time for inputs, have feedback by other means (auditory, visual, haptic). Simplifying the number of target elements with which the user must interact. And use words instead of images.

3.2   Design Considerations for Tablets of Neuropsychological Tests

Following the ideas of design for older adults, the designs of the tests were made with a linear navigation, example of this is the Mockup of the application of the Word Learning test that is shown in the Fig. 4.

Applications development considers orientation in landscape and portrait. However, once the test is initialized in an orientation it can not be changed until the test is completed. Luria's memory test applications have two o more combinations of interaction modalities.

Vision-Haptic. In this combination of modalities, the application presents the series on the touch screen and after the presentation, the user must type the words or figure using the virtual touch keyboard.

Vision-Voice. In this case, the application displays the words or the test format on the touch screen and the user indicates the words by voice.

Audition-Haptic. In this combination, the applications says the series and the user must type the series using the virtual touch keyboard.

Audition-Voice. In this case, the applications says the words and the user indicates the words by voice.

Vision-Touch. In this combination of modalities, application shows the format and the users use the finger to draw an image on the touch screen.

Vision-Stylus. In this combination of modalities, application shows the format and the users use the stylus to draw an image on the touch screen.

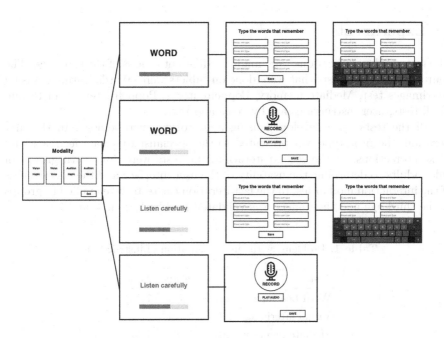

Fig. 4. Mockups for Word Learning tests with interaction modalities.

4   UX Evaluation

According to [25] the relationship between user experience and usability is very close. Usability is more objective because it evaluates the execution of tasks by the user in an interface. UX is more subjective and try to study the experiences lived. From this point of view we can see that the usability evaluation methods help to obtain credentials and understand the UX for a specific problem.

Although it has been about usability and UX, usability and UX are closely linked to the evolution of software, from the point of view of prototypes. The types of dynamic GUIs that appear on devices such as tablets make textual descriptions and diagrams insufficient for a properly designed GUI. Rapid prototyping with user participation is appropriate for the development of these applications. The end user evaluates the prototype using usability questionnaires based on the Likert scale [13] and semantic differential [12]. In this way, we obtain quantitative data for usability and UX in the development of prototypes. The development by prototypes would basically have two or three iterations before an evaluation of UX.

Afterwards, the tests are carried out with the groups of end users. The objectives of the tests are explained to them, a demonstration of the application is made and each user is asked to perform different tasks. In the end, they are given a questionnaire with questions with Likert and semantic differential scales.

5   Experiments

The tests of the applications were made by different groups of the third age. The neuropsychological tests that were done on tablets were: Words learning, Visual afterimages test, Mediate memory, Poppelreuter 1, Poppelreuter 2 and Raven. In all tests, user instructions are by voice and text.

All the tests were developed using a prototype methodology. In the first iteration, the prototype was presented to the specialist to obtain feedback and make corrections. In the second iteration, the tests were done with groups of older adults to determine the usability of the user interface and the effectiveness of the interaction modalities. In the last iteration the tests were applied to groups of the third age and their effect was validated (Tables 1, 2, 3, 4, and 5).

Table 1. Problems with the presentation of instructions.

Test	Text	Audio	None
Word Learning	20.5%	2.5%	77%
Visual afterimage	20.5%	2.5%	77%
Mediate memory	20.5%	2.5%	77%
Poppelreuter 1	12%	4%	84%
Poppelreuter 2	12%	4%	84%
Raven	12%	4%	84%

The memory tests applications for learning words, visual afterimages and mediate memory were applied to 39 seniors with an average age of 70 years old. The 90% is female and 10% is male. In this group, 12% have a some vision problem, 2.5% have a audio problem, 7.6% have arthritis, 2.6% have Alzheimer y and 12% are illiterate. Raven, Poppelreuter 1 and 2 were applied to 25 seniors with an average of 74 years old. In this group, 22 people are female and 3 are male. Three member of this group have a vision problem (12%) and 1 senior have a audio problem (4%).

Table 2. Preferences in the orientation Tablet.

Test	Landscape	Portrait	Both
Word Learning	100%	0%	0%
Visual afterimage	100%	0%	0%
Mediate memory	100%	0%	0%
Poppelreuter 1	64%	28%	8%
Poppelreuter 2	68%	28%	4%
Raven	88%	8%	4%

In all tests, user instructions are by voice and text. As show in Table 2 the groups present a similar behavior in the different tests. The reader can see that the users who performed the Word Learning, Visual Afterimage and Mediate Memory tests have greater difficulty when presenting the instructions by text. The correlation of people who presented this difficulty and who have problems with vision or who can not read and write is 98%. The correlation of users who perform Poppelreuter 1, Poppelreuter 2 and Raven tests with difficulty with text instructions and users with vision problems is 100%. In all test, the users with problems with Audio modality. The correlation, in all the tests, of the users with problems with the modality of interaction of audio and hearing problems is 100%.

Table 2 shows the preference in the orientation (portrait or landscape), of the Tablet to make the tests. Clearly it is appreciated that Landscape orientation was the best acceptance among users.

To evaluate the usability, measurements were obtained through questionnaire qualification using Likert scales and semantic differential scale. Both scales allow us get an evaluation about UX. The questionnaire assesses the understanding of the instructions, the interaction and response of the application. For the questionnaires of all the tests, we asked about the size of the images, buttons, the easy identification of them, preference for interaction modalities and preferences in the use of the application. The possible results are in the range of 4 to 18, and 11 is de medium value. This medium value (11) allows us to divide the results into two sectors, on the left values that indicate less usability and on the right those that reflect good usability levels. In Table 3 we notice that Median and Average are far to the medium value and we can conclude that applications have a good usability for older adults.

For the analysis of time, we only consider the Poppelreuter tests, since they involve a drawing action. From Table 4, we can notice that when the interaction

Table 3. Values of usability.

Test	Minimum	First quartile	Median	Average	Third quartile	Maximum
Word Learning	12	13	16	16.1	18	18
Visual afterimage	12	14	16	15.8	17	18
Mediate memory	11	13	16	15.7	17	18
Poppelreuter 1	11	13	16	15.4	18	18
Poppelreuter 2	12	14	16	15.8	18	18
Raven	12	13	16	15.8	18	18

mode is by voice, the time is very short compared to the modalities of touch
and stylus. This behavior is due to the fact that in the touch and stylus modes
the user must identify and highlight the figure through a drawing. This makes
the user consume more time. Also its possible see that the use of stylus consume
more time for older adults because they can have a better definition and try to
do it in more detail.

Table 4. Performance for Poppelreuter 1 and 2.

Test	Minimun	First quartile	Median	Third quartile	Maximum
Poppelreuter 1	16.7	26.6	43.2	54.5	145.7
Poppelreuter 2 with voice	9	10	12	15	19
Poppelreuter 2 with touch	69.3	107.7	108.2	145.2	148.7
Poppelreuter 2 with stylus	108.7	143	166.9	192.7	250.1

Table 5 shows the preference interaction modalities. With the exception of
the Raven test, the other tests have two or more modes of interaction. The combination of interaction modalities easier to implement is that of Vision-Haptic,
however for Word Learning, Visual Afterimage and Mediate Memory tests, it
was not the preferred combination of modalities. It is observed that there is a
strong preference for the combinations Vision-Voice and Audition-Voice, that
is, the interaction between the participant and the tablet through the voice is
the most preferred. The interaction through Stylus in the Poppelreuter 1 test
has greater acceptance, mainly because this modality allows having a greater
definition in the identification of the objects that are presented to the user. The
relationship between participants who did not like any modalities of interaction
with illiteracy is 40% and with people with vision or hearing problems is 86%.
Interestingly, people with arthritis did not think negatively about modalities,
they prefer hearing and voice and voice vision. In the Poppelreuter 1 and 2 and
Raven tests, people with visual or hearing impairment did not have problems

with the interaction modalities. There were participants who could not finish some tests of Word Learning, Visual afterimage and Mediate Memory. These people have Alzheimer or have two problems in vision, hearing, illiteracy or arthritis.

Table 5. Preferences in the orientation of Tablet.

Test	Vision haptic	Vision voice	Audition haptic	Audition voice	Vision touch	Vision stylus	None
Word Learning	0%	38.4%	12.8%	38.4%	—	—	10.25%
Visual afterimage	0%	38.4%	15.38%	38.4%	—	—	12.8%
Mediate memory	0%	38.4%	12.8%	38.4%	—	—	10.25%
Poppelreuter 1	—	—	—	—	20%	80%	0%
Poppelreuter 2	—	80%	—	—	4%	16%	0%
Raven	100%	—	—	—	—	—	0%

6   Conclusions

There is a problem of health gap in Mexico. Older adults are a vulnerable sector of the population and a high percentage of this group does not have access to health services, although they live in urban areas. The increase of health services in Mexico is not proportional to the growth of the population that requires its services. IT services, through e-Health can help increase health coverage in older adults for certain conditions.

In the clubs of the third age of the DIF and INAPAM there is more participation of women of the third age than of men. And a 10% of illiterate people was detected.

Older adults have presented a favorable acceptance to the use of neuropsychological test applications in tablets. Not all users who used the test applications had previous experience with the use of mobile devices. The use of these applications was an incentive to use mobile devices.

Application developers should be careful with the graphic user interface designs for these tests, since the natural deteriorations of older adults should be considered. In addition to the design considerations that exist in the literature, with our exercises we could verify that older adults prefer voice and audio as interactions modalities.

There were participants who could not finish some tests. These people have Alzheimer or have two problems in vision, hearing, illiteracy or arthritis. It was proven that the tablet applications of the Poppelreuters and Raven tests are as effective as if they were done in the traditional way. Older adults take longer to perform some tests when they are digitized, mainly because they are focused on doing things well, rather than finishing them in short times.

References

1. Estadísticas a propósito del día internacional de las personas de la tercera edad (1 de octubre). Technical report, Instituto Nacional de Estadística y Geografía, Aguascalientes, Aguascalientes, September 2014
2. Informe al ejecutivo federal y al congreso de la unión sobre la situación financiera y los riesgos del instituto mexicano del seguro social 2017–2018. Technical report, Instituto Mexicano del Seguro Social, Instituto Mexicano del Seguro Social Reforma No. 476, Colonia Juárez 06600, Ciudad de México (2018)
3. Cruz Caballero, P., Meneses-Viveros, A., Hernández-Rubio, E., Zamora Arévalo, O.: Distributed user interfaces for Poppelreuters and Raven visual tests. In: Zhou, J., Salvendy, G. (eds.) ITAP 2017. LNCS, vol. 10298, pp. 325–338. Springer, Cham (2017). https://doi.org/10.1007/978-3-319-58536-9_26
4. Castillo Fernández, D., Vela Peón, F.: Envejecimiento demográfico en México: evaluación de los datos censales por edad y sexo, 1970–2000. Papeles de población **11**(45), 107–141 (2005)
5. Gathercole, S.E.: Neuropsychology and working memory: a review. Neuropsychology **8**(4), 494 (1994)
6. Glozman, J.: La valoración cuantitativa de los datos de la evaluación neuropsicológica de Luria. Revista española de neuropsicología **4**(2), 179–196 (2002)
7. Goicoechea, J.: Adultos mayores en México. Iztapalapa, Revista de Ciencias Sociales y Humanidades, no. 71 (2011)
8. González Llamas, J.C.: Evaluación de las acciones del INAPAM; avances y retos. Salud Pública de México **49**, 349–352 (2007)
9. Hernández-Rubio, E., Meneses-Viveros, A., Mancera-Serralde, E., Flores-Ortiz, J.: Combinations of modalities for the words learning memory test implemented on tablets for seniors. In: Zhou, J., Salvendy, G. (eds.) ITAP 2016. LNCS, vol. 9754, pp. 309–319. Springer, Cham (2016). https://doi.org/10.1007/978-3-319-39943-0_30
10. Guerrero Huerta, A.G., Hernández Rubio, E., Meneses Viveros, A.: Augmented reality in tablets for the Yerkes test for older adults. In: Zhou, J., Salvendy, G. (eds.) ITAP 2018. LNCS, vol. 10927, pp. 36–48. Springer, Cham (2018). https://doi.org/10.1007/978-3-319-92037-5_4
11. Kinsella, K., Velkoff, V.A.: US census Bureau, series P95/01-1, an aging world: 2001 (2001)
12. Lim, Y., et al.: Emotional experience and interaction design. In: Peter, C., Beale, R. (eds.) Affect and Emotion in Human-Computer Interaction. LNCS, vol. 4868, pp. 116–129. Springer, Heidelberg (2008). https://doi.org/10.1007/978-3-540-85099-1_10
13. Love, S.: Understanding Mobile Human-Computer Interaction. Elsevier, Amsterdam (2005)
14. Luria, A.: Las funciones corticales superiores del hombre: (y sus alteraciones por lesiones locales del cerebro). (Breviarios de conducta humana. Psicología, Psiquiatría y salud). Martínez Roca (1983)
15. Miranda, J.A.H., Hernàndez Rubio, E., Meneses Viveros, A.: Analysis of Luria memory tests for development on mobile devices. In: Duffy, V.G. (ed.) DHM 2014. LNCS, vol. 8529, pp. 546–557. Springer, Cham (2014). https://doi.org/10.1007/978-3-319-07725-3_54
16. Montes de Oca, V.: El envejecimiento en el debate mundial: reflexión académica y política. Papeles de población **9**(35), 77–100 (2003)

17. Muñoz, M.I.T.: Evaluación neuropsicológica y plan de tratamiento de un caso de demencia tipo Alzheimer. Revista de Discapacidad, Clínica y Neurociencias: (RDCN) 1(1), 1–16 (2014)
18. Pak, R., McLaughlin, A.: Designing Displays for Older Adults. CRC Press, Boca Raton (2010)
19. Partida Bush, V.: La transición demográfica y el proceso de envejecimiento en México. Papeles de población 11(45), 9–27 (2005)
20. Raven, J., et al.: Test de matrices progresivas: manual/Manual for Raven's progressive matrices and vocabulary scalesTest de matrices progresivas. Number 159.9. 072. e-libro, Corp. (1993)
21. Raven, J.C., Raven, J.: Test de matrices progresivas: escala coloreada/Cuaderno de matrices. Number 159.9. 072. Paidós (2009)
22. Rojas, L.Q., Lázaro, E., Solovieva, Y.: Evaluación neurospicológica de escolares rurales y urbanos desde la aproximación a Luria. Revista española de neuropsicología 4(2), 217–235 (2002)
23. Sánchez, D.: Envejecimiento demográfico urbano y sus repercusiones socioespaciales en méxico: Retos de la planeación gerontológica. Revista de Geografía Norte Grande 38, 45–61 (2007)
24. Thane, P.: Memorandum submitted to the house of commons' health committee inquiry: social care October 2009. Pat (2009)
25. Vermeeren, A.P., Law, E.L.-C., Roto, V., Obrist, M., Hoonhout, J., Väänänen-Vainio-Mattila, K.: User experience evaluation methods: current state and development needs. In: Proceedings of the 6th Nordic Conference on Human-Computer Interaction: Extending Boundaries, pp. 521–530. ACM (2010)

Parallel Orientation Assistant, a Vehicle System Based on Voice Interaction and Multi-screen Interaction

Nan Jiang and Zhiyong Fu[✉]

Department of Information Art and Design,
Tsinghua University, Beijing 100084, China
jiangn17@mails.tsinghua.edu.cn,
fuzhiyong@tsinghua.edu.cn

Abstract. With the development of smart transportation, more and more private cars become the carrier of People's Daily travel. While the information interaction technology advances, automobile driving is also more and more multi-screen oriented, while the study of the interaction pattern between the driver and the co-pilot in the car is often ignored. Under the people-oriented and interactive design concept, a multi-screen interactive vehicle interaction model based on vehicle center, mobile phone, and in-car head-up display navigation is designed. In order to verify the design, the prototype test was carried out in the simulated city self-driving tour. Under the driver's simulated driving task, the two subjects communicated with each other on the topic we designed before. The interactive feedback information of the subjects was collected simultaneously through qualitative and quantitative (reaction delay experimental data of the main driving task). Starting from the user experience aspect, this paper discusses whether the information interface based on multi-screen interaction and voice interaction can enhance the information output of the car without increasing the cognitive load of the driver. Through two kinds of mode user feedback different characteristics for tasks, trying to construct a more natural way to strengthen the pilot and the co-pilot interaction, improve the efficiency of driving, building multi-driving tasks switching model. Finally, based on the above information, the design iterative references of future vehicle assistant in artificial intelligence (AI), natural language understanding (NLU) and human-machine interaction interface (HMI) are summarized, so as to better experience for users.

Keywords: Vehicle system · Co-decision · Multi-screen interactive mode · HCI

1 Introduction

Multi-screen vehicle system is the development trend of automatic driving and semi-automatic driving. With the popularization of L1 and L2 autonomous driving technologies, the driving system gradually assumes the driver's driving tasks [1]. At the same time, the vehicle central system is no longer isolated in the form of the central

© Springer Nature Switzerland AG 2019
P.-L. P. Rau (Ed.): HCII 2019, LNCS 11577, pp. 150–158, 2019.
https://doi.org/10.1007/978-3-030-22580-3_12

control screen, but gradually transformed into multiple screens to assist driving tasks. For example, jaguar's new XFL, audi's new Q7 and other models all have four screens, including the central control screen, the dashboard display screen and two screens in the rear seat area. These four screens are not divided, but a whole that can display information together. The new seven is also based on four screens, adding a screen at the rear center armrest that can interact with the center panel [2].

Driving task should not only be undertaken by the driver alone, there is an objective need for social interaction in the car [3]. Contemporary car design must not only focus on technology supporting the driver and the driving task: it needs to create positive experiences for drivers and passengers alike [4]. Today a huge number of different driving assistance and navigation systems are available on the market. Often these systems fail to take into account the social nature and collaborative mechanism of driving [5]. Informing the development of future automotive user interface designs we need to develop a deeper understanding of collaboration in general. In addition, we need to develop an understanding of how, and in what way, other platforms (e.g., the mobile phones) are and will be used in combination with these systems while driving [6].

2 Related Work

The existing design and research mainly focus on the information exchange between cars and cars, or between drivers and cars, but often ignore the information exchange between drivers and passengers, the main driving pressure is still on the driver.

Case1: Information Interaction Between Drivers and Drivers
Due to an increasing level of automation whilst driving, users will gain additional spare time while travelling in the future. This allows passengers to indulge in non-driving activities, e.g. staying socially connected with their friends or entertaining themselves via mobile devices [7]. With everywhere available connectivity and the broad penetration of social network services, the relationship between drivers on the road may gain more transparency, enabling social information to pass through the steel shell of the cars and giving opportunities to reduce anonymity and strengthen empathy. The author utilized the "Four Side" communication model to describe different dimensions of information exchanging between drivers, which would be enhanced by the latest Vehicle to Vehicle communication technology [8]. Through this model, the driver can share music through adjacent vehicles. When the vehicle behind him needs to overtake due to an emergency (catching a plane), the driver can know the reason for speeding through the system, thus increasing the empathy between different drivers on the road.

Case2: Information Interaction Between Drivers and Pedestrians
One of the major challenges that autonomous cars are facing today is driving in urban environments. To make it a reality, autonomous vehicles require the ability to communicate with other road users and understand their intentions. Such interactions are essential between the vehicles and pedestrians as the most vulnerable road users [9].

In this case, the author designed a novel interface called "eyes on a car" to establish eye contact between self-driving cars and pedestrians. The concept behind the "look at the car" interface is to convey the intention of the car to pedestrians as they prepare to cross the road. The results show that pedestrians can make the right decision to cross the road "faster" and feel "safer" if the approaching vehicle has eyes and is watching them. This study details a potential and reasonable way of communication between cars and pedestrians. It provides a new perspective for vehicle and pedestrian communication [10].

3   Concept

Based on our design motivation and previous research, we believe that the interaction design between drivers and passengers for the car should be based on the following concepts:

With the appearance of apple CarPlay, Android Auto, Mirrorlink, etc., the driver's cellular phone and the on-board interconnect have become big trend [11]. Our design hopes to transform the existing equipment on the basis of not increasing the co-pilot learning cost, strengthen the co-pilot and driver communication, and connect the co-pilot mobile terminal platform with the vehicle center to participate in the driving information decision-making. Based on this concept, we believe that it is necessary to improve the existing vehicle-mounted systems and portable devices, rather than add new devices and interactions to increase the learning and visual pressure of drivers.

The interactive mode must adapt to the future development direction of L3, L4 autonomous driving, it is difficult for the traditional user interface to generate good user experience in this complex environment. Therefore, we should take the multi-mode interactive mode as the main design direction. This design assists the voice-based interface and visual feedback on the vehicle center [12]. The display should have the minimum amount of information for users to pay attention to [13]. It's a natural way of interacting with a multi-screen interactive system to enhance the interaction between drivers and copilot, and the decision-making skills of passengers and drivers.

To sum up, this design needs to ensure that the driver's main task is not disturbed, follow the logic of information display and interactive control, and meet the communication decision-making and social needs between the driver and the passengers in the car.

4   Prototype and Test

4.1   Experimental Environment

In order to simulate the main driving task, the user's accuracy and response time to the driving task should also be recorded. On the established vehicle-mounted platform, we play traffic lights animations and other customized events on the screen to give the driver a sense of tension to simulate the real driving situation. When a red light (or any custom event) appears in the road animation on the screen, the driver needs to step on the pedal, and the system will record the response of the driver when he steps on the pedal. In this experiment, the occurrence of red light is random, and it is set that it must be stepped down within 3 s after the occurrence (Fig. 1).

Fig. 1. The experimental environment (Color figure online)

4.2   Experimental Process

Venue: A205 zhizao avenue
Number of persons: 2 (one acts as the driver and one acts as the co-pilot) * 10 pairs,
a total of 20 persons
Test duration: 5 * 2 min for discussion in driving task, and 5 min for user interview
after completion.

The wizard of oz approach is an effective way to examine the user's interaction
with the computer and facilitate rapid iterative development of dialogue phrasing and
logic [14]. The phrase, the wizard of oz, has entered common usage in the field of
experimental psychology in laboratory Settings, simulating the behavior of theoretical
intelligent computer applications [15].

This experiment using The Wizard of Oz method, two subjects are played by a
driver, one vice driving, background for making a scene in city design experiment,
discussion topic for the pilot and the co-pilot common decision to select the destination
nearby restaurants and dishes, and two tasks were five 5 min (respectively, two different interactive mode based on The same task), after The experiment, interview
subjects for 5 min.

In the first task scenario, only voice interaction is adopted, and the co-pilot and the
driver interact with each other by voice to select the dish result. In the second task

scenario, a multi-mode interactive environment with multi-screen interaction and voice interaction is added. The co-pilot's mobile phone is connected to the vehicle center. When the co-pilot queries the information, the information will be displayed synchronously on the vehicle center, and the driver will complete the task under the voice and image information.

5 Analysis

5.1 Data Analysis

We selected three sets of data of typical users' simulated driving and drew them into line graphs. According to the data graph, in the 5 min driving experiment, user I encountered a red light [or any custom event] 99 times. The driving delay in the single interactive mode was 149.08 ms and 162.75 ms in the multi-mode interactive mode. User 2: there were 87 times of red light [or any custom event], and the average driving delay was 695.59 ms and 714.65 ms, respectively. User 3: a total of 90 times of red light [or any custom event] was encountered, and the average driving delay was 165.75 ms and 169.63 ms respectively.

By data we can see that different users of driving a delayed reaction rate is different, there are even bigger differences, but based on the same user interactive mode of different driving trend is the same, delayed reaction rate in multimodal interactive mode and the single interactive mode (voice interaction only) the reaction time of the mean difference of 37.15 ms, which can be concluded that compared the multimodal interaction mode for the user driving behavior will slow response speed, but the impact is very small, the amplitude. It will not interfere with the fluency of the driver's main driving task and thus cause driving burden (Fig. 2).

Through video analysis: orange-red is the time period for drivers to see the multiscreen interactive information. From the time dimension, we can see that in the multimode interactive mode, the viewing of the multi-screen interactive information by users is basically positively correlated with the driving delay.

Through 10 sets of experimental data, it can be found that when the driver and copilot enter the topic, at the beginning of the conversation, the driver will not pay special attention to visual interaction information, and the driver and co-pilot mainly focus on voice interaction. However, starting from the latter part of the test time, when the median total time length of the total experimental data is 37.4%, the visual interaction information of the vehicle center will become the main influence in the driving process, and arouse the interest of the driver and co-driver to participate in the decision-making together (starting from 37.4% of the total test time, the single time and total frequency of drivers staring at the screen are increasing). Then, when the decision is about to be made, at the end of the experiment (starts from 86.2%), the driver will change the driver's attention from the multi-screen interactive information to the co-driver's voice interaction.

At the same time, it can be concluded from the ten experimental videos that the frequency of using multi-mode interaction is very high. In task two, drivers spend more

■ Red is the line chart of user simulated driving response delay in the mode of voice interaction and multi–screen interaction

■ Blue is the line chart of user simulated driving response delay in voice interaction mode only

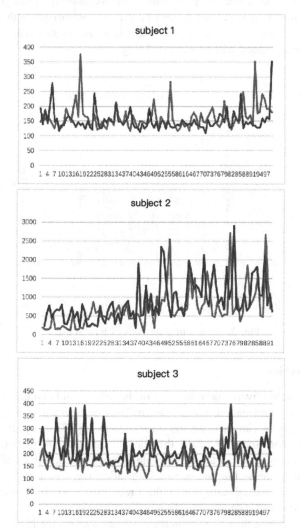

Fig. 2. Typical data for three users in two different modes of interaction (Color figure online)

than two-thirds of their time watching interactive information on multiple screens to participate in decision-making.

By video analysis we can conclude that in the process of driving, the driver is tend to seek help from a co-pilot to common decision, in the whole topic discussion, the driver's preferences trends are starting tendency voice interaction, and tendency of voice and the interaction of multiple screen information multimodal interaction, finally returned to voice interaction of volatility process.

Through the analysis, it is found that the multi-screen interactive information will have a major impact when the decision-making output is near, and the length and frequency of the driver's staring at the screen will increase. Interestingly, when multimodal interaction is an important factor (the driver is immersed in the screen information), the voice communication between the driver and co-pilot will be reduced, but the decision-making speed will be increased (Fig. 3).

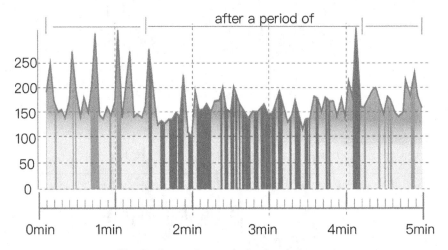

Fig. 3. Screen time analysis of typical users

5.2   User Interview

In the interview with drivers, more than 2/3 of the drivers said that the information can be more intuitively understood through the multi-mode interaction, and the co-pilot's auxiliary participation can increase the decision-making efficiency. In the interview with the driver, more than 2/3 of the drivers said that the information can be more intuitively understood through the multi-mode interaction, and the co-pilot's auxiliary participation can increase the decision-making efficiency. Compared with the single voice mode, the biggest advantage of multi-screen interaction for drivers is that they can let the co-pilot make decisions with more confidence.

When they feel that they need to make affirmation or choice in the task, they can more quickly participate in the task through the visual information in front of the screen to understand the progress. From this dimension, although the delay rate of driving will slightly increase, the overall driving efficiency will increase.

Compared with the co-pilot holding the mobile phone to search for information by himself, in the multi-screen interactive mode, the interaction between the driver and the co-driver will increase due to the information sharing. The main driver and co-driver can be more involved in the communication, increasing the sociality in the car and the information flow.

6 Conclusion

Based on the development of intelligent transportation, the design of vehicle-mounted system tends to be multi-screen, and the mode of information interaction tends to be multi-mode. From the perspective of user experience, this paper designs a task switching model of multi-driving task interaction to improve driving efficiency in multi-screen interaction and voice interaction mode. This system aims to strengthen the task flow between drivers and passengers, so that both drivers and passengers in the car can be more involved in the communication, increasing the social degree in the car, the information flow, and the efficiency of decision-making in the car. Although it has been verified by experiments that the response of driving tasks will be slightly delayed through multi-mode interaction, with the development of automatic driving, the response delay of driving tasks in the future can be ignored in the design.

Acknowledgments. This research is a phased achievement of "Smart R&D Design System for Professional Technology" project and supported by the Special Project of National Key R&D Program——"Research and Application Demonstration of Full Chain Collaborative Innovation Incubation Service Platform Based on Internet+" (Question ID: 2017YFB1402000), "Study on the Construction of Incubation Service Platforms for Professional Technology Fields" sub-project (Subject No. 2017YFB1402004).

References

1. van der Heiden, R.M.A., Iqbal, S., Janssen, C.P.: Priming drivers before handover in semi-autonomous cars. In: CHI Conference on Human Factors in Computing Systems. ACM (2017)
2. Car Home. https://chejiahao.autohome.com.cn/info/1580542
3. Rakotonirainy, A., Schroeter, R., Soro, A.: Three social car visions to improve driver behaviour. Pervasive Mob. Comput. **14**, 147–160 (2014)
4. Knobel, M., Hassenzahl, M., Lamara, M., et al.: Clique trip: feeling related in different cars. In: Designing Interactive Systems Conference. ACM (2012)
5. Gridling, N., Meschtscherjakov, A., Tscheligi, M.: I need help!: exploring collaboration in the car. In: ACM Conference on Computer Supported Cooperative Work Companion. ACM (2012)
6. Perterer, N., Sundström, P., Meschtscherjakov, A., et al.: Come drive with me: an ethnographic study of driver-passenger pairs to inform future in-car assistance. In: Conference on Computer Supported Cooperative Work (2013)
7. Winkler, A., Baumann, K., Huber, S., et al.: Evaluation of an application based on conceptual metaphors for social interaction between vehicles. In: Proceedings of the 2016 ACM Conference on Designing Interactive Systems, DIS 2016, Brisbane, QLD, Australia, 04–08 June 2016, pp. 1148–1159. ACM Press (2016)

8. Wang, C., Terken, J., Hu, J., et al.: Improving connectedness between drivers by digital augmentation. In: Adjunct International Conference on Automotive User Interfaces & Interactive Vehicular Applications. ACM (2016)
9. Rasouli, A., Tsotsos, J.K.: Autonomous vehicles that interact with pedestrians: a survey of theory and practice (2018)
10. Chang, C.M., Toda, K., Sakamoto, D., et al.: Eyes on a car: an interface design for communication between an autonomous car and a pedestrian. In: The 9th International Conference. ACM (2017)
11. Internet of vehicles/mobile Internet. https://baike.pcauto.com.cn/1920.html
12. Angelini, L., Carrino, F., Carrino, S., et al.: A comparison of three interaction modalities in the car: gestures, voice and touch. In: Actes De La 28ième Conférence Francophone Sur Linteraction Homme-machine. ACM (2016)
13. Sodhi, M., Reimer, B., Cohen, J.L., et al.: On-road driver eye movement tracking using head-mounted devices. In: Proceedings of the Symposium on Eye Tracking Research & Applications, ETRA 2002. Louisiana Eye Tracking Research & Applications Symposium, New Orleans, Louisiana, 25–27 March 2002, p. 61. ACM Press (2002)
14. Green, P., Wei-Haas, L.: The rapid development of user interfaces: experience with the Wizard of OZ method. In: Human Factors & Ergonomics Society Annual Meeting Proceedings, vol. 29, no. 5, pp. 470–474 (1985)
15. Wizard of Oz experiment. https://en.wikipedia.org/wiki/Wizard_of_Oz_experiment#Concept

Can Virtual Reality Satisfy Entertainment Needs of the Elderly? The Application of a VR Headset in Elderly Care

Xiaojun Lai[✉], Xin Lei[✉], Xuanwei Chen[✉],
and Pei-Luen Patrick Rau[✉]

Department of Industrial Engineering, Tsinghua University, Beijing, China
{laixjl5,lei-xl6,Chen-xwl8}@mails.tsinghua.edu.cn,
rpl@mail.tsinghua.edu.cn

Abstract. Aging has become one of the most significant population trends, and eldercare, particularly regarding emotional and entertainment needs, has become a challenge and an opportunity. Virtual reality (VR) can offer more direct and effective entertainment methods for the elderly. We interviewed ten elderly people in aging community to further know about their social cycles and entertainment activities and concluded their requirements. Then we conducted an experimental study where fourteen elderly people played three selected VR applications while their emotional state and attitude toward the applications were recorded. Results indicate that participants had more positive valence and higher arousal of emotion when they were playing the VR application, and applications related to tourism and easy-to-play games are favored by the elderly. Based on the insights from the user interviews and experimental study, we propose some guidelines of VR applications for the elderly. For example, the contents should be closer to actual life.

Keywords: Elderly entertainment · Virtual reality · Application design · Elderly care

1 Introduction

Ageing has been one of the most significant population trends in the 21st century owing to the decreased death and birth rates. Furthermore, this process is taking place in nearly every country in the world, particularly in developing nations, as continued pressure contributes to limiting fertility. Consequently, the number and proportion of older people in society is increasing, and eldercare is becoming both a new opportunity and a challenge. In addition to basic assistance with daily activities and health care, more attention must be paid to the emotional and entertainment needs of the elderly. However, a difficulty arises, one with two principal aspects. First, the physical and cognitive condition of the elderly makes it difficult for them to achieve their various wishes. Second, the economic situation limits the possibility of eldercare, especially services such as nursing homes to provide abundant activities for the elderly.

Virtual reality (VR) offers potential new possibilities for eldercare in entertainment. For example, the elderly can directly visit scenic sites in virtual reality and gain a

© Springer Nature Switzerland AG 2019
P.-L. P. Rau (Ed.): HCII 2019, LNCS 11577, pp. 159–172, 2019.
https://doi.org/10.1007/978-3-030-22580-3_13

feeling of actually being there without the complex and tiresome process of travelling. Besides, they can interact with different objects and change scenes freely. In addition to horizon-broadening experiences like tourism, VR also offers opportunities for gaining knowledge and doing physical exercise. The easy and fun games in VR can properly guide the elderly through exercises and provide them with a sense of achievement; while inexpensive educational applications can facilitate the learning process.

The present paper explores the application of VR for the elderly in the following conditions: to satisfy their entertainment needs, and to improve their emotional state. First, we researched on relevant literatures and interviewed some elderly people in order to define a set of typical requirements. Second, we evaluated and selected suitable applications. Third, we conducted an experimental study, where fourteen elderly were invited to play with the selected VR applications. The valence and arousal related to the emotions and attitudes of the participants before and during each application experience were measured. We discovered that different categories of applications led to different impacts; thus, guidelines for the design of VR applications for the elderly were proposed. The following sections describe the related research, user interviews, application selection, and experimental study.

2 Related Research

2.1 Characteristics of the Elderly

Previous studies indicate that the distinguishing characteristics of the elderly could be divided into three aspects.

First, for the physical dimension of aging, the structure and functions of each sensory system of people over 65 years old have undergone degenerative changes, mainly including the decline of visual acuity, hearing [1] and tactility, which affects the reception of information from the surrounding environment and leads to slow response [2]. In addition, double stance time increases with age, gait velocity (i.e. speed of walking) slows after 70 years old [3], and poor balance increases the frequency of falls, resulting in the elderly being unable to perform overabundant movements.

Second, aging of cognitive abilities generally includes changes in perception, memory, attention, and intelligence. Awareness is the first step in the process of human cognition, and the slowing down of perception is an important manifestation of aging [4]. In addition, working memory and spatial memory decline, and attention aging prevents the elderly from focusing on one task for a long time. Consequently, it takes longer time to perform familiar tasks and acquire new information [5], which leads to a decline in the learning ability of the elderly and a lack of confidence in using new technologies [1]. As a result, they need to seek for help and this dependence makes them feel incompetent and worthless [6].

Third, with respect to the social life, the death of a spouse, friends, and relatives, together with social disengagement after retirement can be considered as a loss of important relationships, which makes them feel neglected and lonely [7] and contributes to feelings of emptiness and depression [8, 9]. In addition, the prevalence of depressive disorders, which increases with age [10], may be associated with a reduction in cognitive functions [11].

2.2   The Role and Potential of VR in Elderly Care

Published research has shown that virtual reality is a potential technical application to help identify and rehabilitate cognitive disorders in the elderly, such as dementia [12], stroke risk [13], and Parkinson's disease [14], and memory decline [15]. Regarding the emotional care of the elderly, some institutions and individuals abroad have already conducted related research and exploration. For example, Kahana spent six months visiting community centers for field work and directed a series of films, BettVR With Age, to explore how VR can serve the elderly [16]. In addition, Maplewood Nursing Home utilized a VR system for the elderly, which not only improved memory and social skills, but also reduced their stress and anxiety, as well as strengthening their connection with the world [17]. VR-based scenarios can become more comprehensive, safer, and more functional; however, they can also be more expensive, more complex, and more difficult to be used by the elderly [18].

3   User Interview

3.1   Method

Ten elderly people from the Yijia aging community in Beijing Ganjiakou were invited for the interview. The sample included 9 females and one male, since few men participated in community activities. Participants aged from 64 to 80 years ($M = 71.5$, $SD = 5.44$). The majority of them ($N = 7$) had received a middle or high school education, while there were 2 subjects with university degrees, and 1 subject with elementary school education. They could live independently and most of them ($N = 7$) were living with their wives and children. Physical inconvenience was prevalent and some of them suffered from occupational diseases such as spine and lumbar aches.

Owing to the diverse nature of the interviewee backgrounds, their interviews were conducted in a semi-structured format. In the interviews, the elderly answered basic questions, including their educational background and physical conditions, and then introduced his or her current social cycles and entertainment activities. Ultimately, they shared their opinions after watching panoramic videos in VR and expressed their requirements.

3.2   Results

The results indicated that degenerative changes of sensory systems limit the daily activities of the elderly. According to the user interview, user requirements focused on connecting with their family or friends, experiencing and learning new things.

Limited Social Cycles. The social cycles of the elderly generally consist of three parts:

First, the most important relationship is their spouse and children (Fig. 1). The widowed elderly accounted for a large part among the interviewees; the rest were either mutually supported and understood, or generally in a harmonious relationship with some small friction. For those who lived with their children, they would help do housework and provide respect and understanding to reduce the pressure of their children, while in turn, their children would offer guidance to their parents, such as mobile app teaching. For those distanced from their children, the connection between them mainly relied on phone calls and WeChat, and their children would visit regularly on weekends or vacations.

Second, they would keep contact with old friends, classmates, or colleagues, and would get together during holidays. However, only few were close enough to share secrets such as family gossip.

Third, they were familiar with their neighbors and staff of the aging community through daily interactions, and the topics between them were mainly their physical condition and social events.

Furthermore, most of them were not willing to make more friends. *"One or two close friends are enough, and the more involved, the more energy they demand. It is very tiresome."* In addition, elderly people that lived alone had a stronger desire to pour out, *"I really need someone to talk to, and I hope you can come here more often."*

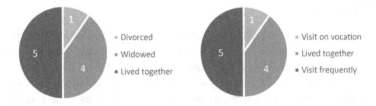

Fig. 1. Relationship with spouse (left) and children (right)

Relatively Monotonous Entertainment Activities. Activities organized by the community included health talks, physiotherapy, lessons of chorus, singing, dancing, calligraphy, and weaving. The population included a large proportion of female seniors. Generally, daily entertainment for the elderly was classified as follows:

Female (N = 9): in the morning, the female elders would take a walk in the nearby park, sing and dance. In the afternoon, they might listen to health lectures, do physical therapy, practice calligraphy, or learn to weave in the aging community. At night, they usually watched TV programs or soap operas at home.

Male (N = 3, two of the results are from the description of their wife): in the morning, the male elders would also exercise in the park, but they tended to go to some distant places such as Xiangshan. They would help do housework and watch the news more often.

Of course, on the basis of the activities above, the elderly would have their personal hobbies. For example, a calligraphy teacher often went to the exhibitions; the one fond of literature often listened to audiobooks at home; and one old lady played games on iPad in order to forget a widow's pain. Moreover, elderly people in a good financial situation and good physical condition would travel with their spouses or children in self-help tours or group tours; south or warm places near the sea were favored.

Unavoidable Entertainment Restrictions. The daily entertainment activities of the elderly are relatively simple, mainly for the following reasons:

Community Management Difficulties. At present, the aging communities were mostly non-government organizations. It was difficult to operate and had low profits. *"I think the activities are great, but they have to save for the aging community at first. The staff is very unstable because of the low pay; the space here is also limited."*

Family Factors or Limited Economic Conditions. Some elderly had to help babysit their grandchildren at home, do housework, take care of their parents, or were under economic pressure, so that no free time and money was available for entertainment.

Poor Physical Condition. Most elderly cannot walk for a long time because of physical inconvenience. One interviewee said, *"As far as my physical condition is concerned, I can't participate in many activities although I strongly desire to. And I have too many family affairs so that no more energy to spend on the activities. I am not young anymore."* The other interviewees originally planned to publish a book and run an exhibition, but his wife said, *"We have to go first, otherwise I can't travel any more as I get older and older."*

Different Learning Ability. In addition to TV, the other electronic product that the elderly were familiar with was the mobile phone. Most of them (n = 7) only used their phone to answer calls, send voice messages, and share their moments on WeChat, *"I just cannot remember any more operations no matter how many times my child tries teaching me"*. The minority with higher education had better learning ability and understood different kinds of software functions. For example, they downloaded audiobooks on the app and shared new technology information with friends.

Different VR Experience Feedback. After watching the panoramic videos of the starry sky and the sea in VR, their views were polarized:

More Negative. For those that had a higher level of education or richer life experiences, they were more hesitant when experiencing new technology equipment. Besides, some of them were sensitive to the HMDs with discomfort. *"Occasionally use might be fine, but it was more convenient and comfortable to watch TV, since it was inconsistent with the reality, and some people might not adapt to it. They would get nervous and anxious physically, and the HMDs was not that comfortable to wear."*

More Positive. For those with lower education, less familiarity with technology products, and more limited life experience, they were amazed at VR HMDs and had a passionate discussion with other elderly people after the experience. Besides, less discomfort occurred in this case. *"I think this scene is pretty good; you can watch it in bed at night. It's amazingly beautiful and has a strong three-dimensional effect."*

Diverse Requirements. When it comes to the expectations of the VR scene, the elderly put forward some ideas. *"There are so many things that you have never* *experienced, things that broad your mind, like natural scenery or animal worlds";* *"Scenes that are less about history or memory but funny."* Thus, a requirement list was defined based on the above results:

- Fit their physical and cognitive conditions;
- Connect with family and friends;
- Experience new or interesting things;
- Learn new things.

4   Application Research

4.1   Method

Applications available on VR stores, such as Viveport, and Steam, were played and evaluated according to the requirement list. Then, we defined the categories of the applications and selected three typical ones among them for further study.

4.2   Results

Categories of Available VR Applications. Based on the contents and forms, we divided the VR applications into three categories:

Games. They enhance the realistic effects of the game and further immerse players by three-dimensionalizing traditional games. The contents include sports, music, adventure, action, simulation, racing, strategy, and role play. Additionally, they support stand-alone or online multiplayer. Players perform tasks in the game to continuously improve their level, and meanwhile gain pleasure from the interaction and even acquire new knowledge.

Panoramic Videos. Panoramic videos are videos that record the live environment with professional VR photography equipment and then post-process it through a computer to realize a three-dimensional space display effect. Unlike the single viewing angle of traditional video, VR videos allow users to move around while watching the video, making the experience immersive. There are movies, dramas, documentaries, short films, and more. In addition to panoramic video, some video platforms have built private viewing rooms by combining 2D & 3D movies in the repository and virtual giant screen theaters.

Tools. Tool applications are mainly built for specific needs of all walks of life, including real estate, museums, education, family, shopping, simulation training, tourism exploration, conference rooms, etc. Users can experience and learn in the virtual reality environment, thus effectively reducing manpower and resource costs.

Applications Selected. We chose The Blu, Fruit Ninja, and Tilt Brush as the materials for the further experiment (Fig. 2).

The Blu. It brings users into the ocean with various habitats, which expanded their range of interests. Users are able to interact with the creatures through the handle, such as making the coral open and close, shrinking the jellyfish, etc. This agrees with the fact that the elderly enjoy travelling and think highly of the sea scene, according to the previous interview.

Fruit Ninja. It is an easy-to-play game where users can cut, throw, and string up fruits from any view. This allows users to easily achieve a sense of accomplishment. In addition, it is suitable for the elderly to exercise responsiveness and body coordination through moderate movements during the game.

Tilt Brush. It has a three-dimensional canvas for the elderly, which helps them learn to draw and develop their creativity. According to the interview results above, the elderly usually participated in calligraphy, dance, singing, weaving, and other cultural activities held by the aging community, and still retain the enthusiasm of learning in their daily life.

The Blu   Fruit Ninja   Tilt Brush

Fig. 2. The three VR applications selected for the elderly

5   Experimental Study

Based on the understanding of the characteristics and requirements of the elderly and the selection of suitable VR applications, we further conducted an experiential study to explore the application of virtual reality in meeting the entertainment needs of the elderly and improving their emotional state. The specific study questions were the following:

- What is the impact of playing VR applications or not?
- What is the impact of different categories of applications played?
- What is the impact of different education backgrounds on the feedback about the same applications?

5.1   Method

Participants. Fourteen elderly people from the Ganjiakou aging community in Beijing were invited, including 5 males and 9 females. Participants aged from 54 to 82 years ($M = 71$, SD = 8.13). The education background was divided into two categories: below high school education (N = 7) and high school education or above (N = 7).

Materials and Tasks. In this phase, participants firstly answered questions about their basic information such as educational background and daily emotional state. Then, they played one of the three different VR applications, i.e., The Blu, Fruit Ninja, and Tilt Brush, which appeared in a random order. The VR HMDs used were Vive Pro. Afterwards, they expressed their opinions about the applications and rested for 10 min before experiencing the next VR application. Empatica E4 was used for physiological measurements (Figs. 3 and 4).

Fig. 3. Task of experiential study

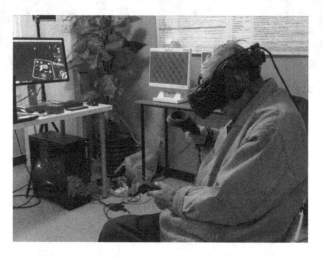

Fig. 4. An elderly person playing a VR application

Variables and Measurement Method. There were three independent variables in this study. The first one was whether to experience the virtual reality; the second one was the type of VR application, which contained 3 levels: The Blu, Fruit Ninja, and Tilt Brush; the last one was the education background of the users: below high school education and high school education or above. The dependent variables included emotions and attitudes, and the detailed dimension contained self-report and different indicators of physiological measurement. The evaluation methods for each dimension are listed below (Table 1).

Self-report. Questionnaires were used to measure the subjective feelings of the user. We gathered the information and basic situation of the users before the study. Then, after each VR application experience, the users were asked to fill in the questionnaire again to measure the impact of each application. Different questionnaires measured different aspects of the impact, including users' emotions and attitudes towards the applications and equipment.

Heartbeat Process. The heartbeat process recorded the rate at which the heart beat, usually using heart rate (HR) and heart rate variability (HRV) as measurements. The heartbeat process is controlled by the nervous system, which is related to the automatic response of humans to external stimuli and the state of calm and relaxation of the person. For example, the higher the heart rate, the higher the emotional arousal of the user.

Electrodermal Activity. The EDA measurement method is a method in which a pair of electrodes are placed on the surface of the skin and the minute currents passing through the surface are measured by a variety of electrical methods including skin potential, electrical resistance, conductance, admittance, and impedance. As a direct indicator of sympathetic nervous system function, EDA can indicate the brain arousal indirectly.

Table 1. Measurement method

Dimensions		Method	Description	Indicator
Emotion	Valence	HRV	Measures the specific change in time (in milliseconds) between consecutive beats of heart	The larger the HRV decrement, the more positive the valence of the emotion
		SAM scale	Scale for emotion assessment	The lower the score, the more positive the valence of the emotion
	Arousal	EDA	Measures the skin conductance level & reaction	The larger the EDA increment, the higher the arousal of the emotion
		HR	Number of heartbeats/min	The higher the HR, the higher the arousal of the emotion
		SAM scale	Scale for emotion assessment	The lower the score, the higher the arousal of the emotion
Attitude		Subjective scale	Scale for measuring the user attitudes	The higher the score, the greater the satisfaction of the application and the device

Statistics Method. A paired t-test was used to analyze the impact of playing VR applications or not and different educational backgrounds on the same applications. ANOVA was used to analyze the impact of different categories of VR applications.

5.2 Results

Playing VR Applications Increases Arousal Significantly. (Table 2).

Valence of Emotion. The pre-experiment scores of SAM scale were 1.71 in average, reflecting the participants were generally happy in their daily lives. The t-test results of the SAM scale indicated that users had insignificantly more positive valence of emotion when they experienced The Blu and Fruit Ninja. In addition, the results of HRV showed that users had significantly more positive valence in Fruit Ninja than pre-experience ($t_2 = 2.83$, $p_2 = 0.020$).

Arousal of Emotion. The pre-experiment scores of SAM scale were 3.86 in average, reflecting the participants were generally unaroused in their daily lives. The t-test results of the SAM scale indicated that users had significantly higher arousal of emotion after they experienced the VR application ($t_1 = -5.95$, $p_1 = 0.000$; $t_2 = -4.37$, $p_2 = 0.001$; $t_3 = -2.79$, $p_3 = 0.015$). In addition, the results of EDA ($t_2 = 2.67$, $p_2 = 0.019$) and HR ($t_2 = 5.25$, $p_2 = 0.001$) showed arousal was significantly higher in Fruit Ninja.

Table 2. Statistics results of paired t-test on emotion before and during the experiences

Emotion	Measurements	Application	M	SD	T	p-value
Valence	HRV	1 (The Blu)	0.010	0.047	0.68	0.515
		2 (Fruit Ninja)	-0.064	0.072	-2.83	0.020**
		3 (Tilt Brush)	-0.003	0.024	0.43	0.675
	SAM scale	1	-0.357	1.082	-1.24	0.239
		2	-0.357	1.008	-1.33	0.208
		3	0.357	0.929	1.44	0.174
Arousal	EDA	1	-0.110	0.303	-1.36	0.197
		2	0.457	0.638	2.67	0.019**
		3	0.461	1.654	1.04	0.316
	HR	1	-1.031	5.56	-0.59	0.572
		2	10.57	6.34	5.25	0.001**
		3	-0.432	4.32	-0.35	0.737
	SAM scale	1	-1.857	1.167	-5.95	0.000**
		2	-1.786	1.528	-4.37	0.001**
		3	-1.071	1.439	-2.79	0.015**

Applications of Tourism and Games Led to Better Emotional State and Satisfaction. (Table 3).

Valence of Emotion. The results of HRV indicated that the users had significantly more positive valence in Fruit Ninja than the other two applications ($F = 5.91$, $p = 0.007$), whereas the results of the SAM scale were insignificant.

Arousal of Emotion. The results of EDA ($F = 5.08$, $p = 0.011$) and HR ($F = 14.17$, $p = 0.000$) indicated that the users had significantly different arousal increments, and that the arousal of emotion was the highest while experiencing Fruit Ninja, followed by Tilt Brush, and lastly The Blu. The SAM scale results were not significantly different.

Satisfaction of Applications. The results of the five-point Likert scales showed that users had significantly higher content ($F = 8.94$, $p = 0.001$) and interaction ($F = 3.45$, $p = 0.042$) satisfaction of The Blu and Fruit Ninja, but not significantly stronger re-

Table 3. Statistics results of ANOVAs on feedback of different categories of applications

Emotion	Measurements	F	p-value
Valence	HRV	5.91	0.007**
	SAM scale	2.34	0.109
Arousal	EDA	5.08	0.011**
	HR	14.17	0.000**
	SAM scale	1.37	0.265
Satisfaction & Willingness	Content	8.94	0.001**
	Interaction	3.45	0.042**
	Re-experience	3.18	0.053
	Recommendation	1.75	0.187

experiencing and recommending willingness. Therefore, although The Blu and Fruit Ninja scored with higher satisfaction, users were still willing to re-experience and recommend Tilt Brush.

Higher Educational Background, Higher Preference of Educational Application
Different education background did not lead to significant difference in valence and arousal of emotion when playing the same VR applications. However, the interaction satisfaction of Tilt Brush for users without high-school levels of education was significantly lower than for the other two applications; whereas, this was not the case for users with high-school levels of education or above.

For the application preference, the elderly's favorite was The Blu, followed by Fruit Ninja, and lastly Tilt Brush. Particularly, users with high school education or above showed the same preference for Fruit Ninja and Tilt Brush (Fig. 5).

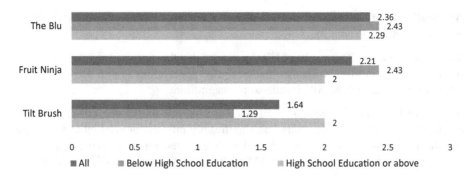

Fig. 5. Application preference

Application Feedback and Requirements

Overall, the elderly users hoped that the content was able to broaden their horizon, the operation would be simple and easy to learn, and the interaction had enough participation and feedback (Table 4).

Table 4. Application evaluation

Application	Evaluation	
	Positive	Negative
The Blu	The open sea world and the various creatures inside had wonderfully brought the immersion and further broadened their horizon and improved their mood	The biotypes and scene models were not abundant enough and the participation and exploration required further improvement *"The whales are too scary, and I will have a nightmare"* *"I want a sense of touch on the hand as feedback in interaction, like soft or hard"*
Fruit Ninja	It was relatively simple but interesting and exciting because the users had to concentrate and react quickly in the game. They got a sense of achievement and could exercise at the same time	*"Waving swords is too intense for me. Maybe something gentler, you know, like picking apples"*
Tilt Brush	The interaction was very fun and particularly free; for example, the color was beautiful and easy to adjust. The users practiced drawing inside, and they believed they could make it after trying for a few times *"I think painting is the best application among these and it is good for the elderly. They will progress little by little in learning painting and the interaction"*	They did not like painting and were not good at it either. Besides, it was too complicated to remember the operation. In addition, the space was too large, and the feeling and effect of three-dimensional painting were quite different from the traditional

First, the applications of tourism were the most demanding, and eleven participants mentioned that they hoped to see more scenes related to scenery and animals, such as the sea, grassland, forest, country, as a compensation for not being able to explore the vast world, or as a pre-study for field trips. Some users also proposed possible new improvements to the scenes. For example, a place is selected on the map to enter a specific spot, and then relevant travel routes are provided according to their demand, so that they could go walking and sightseeing.

Second, the content of educational applications should be closer to the actual lives of the elderly, such as calligraphy, musical instruments, singing, dancing, costume collocation, popular science information, the food characteristics of each place, or the common knowledge of physical health.

Third, the game applications should be edutainment in which the elderly could acquire interesting knowledge from recreation. There could be proper challenges and exercises, but not too much intensity. They could be practical experiences of real life, such as cooking, babysitting children, etc. The elderly should gain a sense of accomplishment in the games, and some guidance for the actual lives.

6   Conclusion and Discussion

The aging characteristics of the elderly consist of the physiological and the psychological aspects, which contributes to the feeling of uselessness and loneliness. The selected applications essentially took their physical condition into account and covered their entertainment needs. The experimental results indicated that the elderly had insignificantly more positive valence of emotion and significantly higher arousal of emotion during VR experience, especially in the game application Fruit Ninja. In addition, they were particularly satisfied with the tourism application The Blu, as well as the game application Fruit Ninja. However, the elderly encountered some frustration in the educational application Tilt Brush, particularly for those with lower education background and learning ability.

According to the above results, we propose some principles of VR application design for the elderly.

First, the contents should be closer to actual life. For example, they could improve and rehabilitate the physical function. Through the use of the brain and the movement of body parts, they could achieve physical fitness, and prevent or treat dementia or other related diseases while relaxing at the same time. In addition, by participating in a virtual world, they could broaden their horizons, such as unknown scenic spots, learn to sing, dance, cook, etc. Therefore, they could be able to further practice in actual lives to spend their twilight years more meaningfully.

Second, interaction should be more suitable and natural due to the physical and cognitive aging. For example, it is necessary to ensure that the scale of movements is small, and the scene should not be too intense so that the elderly can experience the applications from a sitting posture in most cases. In addition, the interaction with the scene should be simple and clear, and easy to remember, so that they can achieve a sense of accomplishment in the experience process rather than frustration. What is more, the feedback should be similar to the daily experience to eliminate the strangeness brought about by new technology. For example, more feedback should be available on the basis of enhancing the visual, auditory, and tactile experience.

References

1. Older Adults' Health and Age-Related Changes. https://www.apa.org/pi/aging/resources/guides/older.aspx. Accessed 30 Nov 2018
2. Spirduso, W.W., Francis, K.L., MacRae, P.G.: Physical Dimensions of Aging. Human Kinetics, Champaign (IL) (2005)
3. Gait Disorders in the Elderly. https://www.merckmanuals.com/professional/geriatrics/gait-disorders-in-the-elderly/gait-disorders-in-the-elderly. Accessed 30 Nov 2018
4. Christensen, H.: What cognitive changes can be expected with normal ageing? Aust. N. Z. J. Psychiatry **35**(6), 768–775 (2001)
5. Memory loss: When to seek help. https://www.mayoclinic.org/diseases-conditions/alzheimers-disease/in-depth/memory-loss/art-20046326. Accessed 30 Nov 2018
6. Berk, L.E.: Development Through the Lifespan, 2nd edn. Allyn and Bacon, Boston (2001)
7. Singh, A., Misra, N.: Loneliness, depression and sociability in old age. Ind. Psychiatry J. **18**(1), 51–55 (2009)
8. Hansson, R., Carpenter, B.: Relationships in Old Age: Coping with the Challenge of Transition. Guilford Press, New York (1994)
9. Green, B.H., et al.: Risk factors for depression in elderly people: a prospective study. Acta Psychiatrica Scandinavica **86**(3), 213–217 (1992)
10. Kennedy, G.J.: The epidemiology of late-life depression. In: Kennedy, G.J. (ed.) Suicide and Depression in Late Life: Critical Issues in Treatment, Research and Public Policy, pp. 23–37. Wiley, New York (1996)
11. Speck, C.E., Kukull, W.A., Brenner, D.E., et al.: History of depression as a risk factor for Alzheimer's disease. Epidemiology **6**, 366–369 (1995)
12. Mendez, M.F., Joshi, A., Jimenez, E.: Virtual reality for the assessment of frontotemporal dementia, a feasibility study. Disabil. Rehabil. Assist. Technol. **10**, 160–164 (2015)
13. Kang, Y.J.: Development and clinical trial of virtual reality-based cognitive assessment in people with stroke: preliminary study. CyberPsychol. Behav. **11**(3), 329–339 (2008)
14. Klinger, E., Chemin, I., Lebreton, S., Marié, R.-M.: Virtual action planning in Parkinson's disease: a control study. CyberPsychol. Behav. **9**(3), 342–347 (2006)
15. Optale, G., et al.: Controlling memory impairment in elderly adults using virtual reality memory training: a randomized controlled pilot study. Neurorehabil. Neural Repair **24**(4), 348–357 (2010)
16. For senior citizens, the future of VR lies in the past. https://www.wired.com/2017/04/vr-for-seniors/. Accessed 30 Nov 2018
17. Maplewood Using VR To Enhance Senior Living. https://www.vrfocus.com/2017/09/maplewood-using-vr-to-enhance-senior-living/. Accessed 30 Nov 2018
18. Cherniack, E.P.: Not just fun and games: applications of virtual reality in the identification and rehabilitation of cognitive disorders of the elderly. Disabil. Rehabil. Assist. Technol. **6**, 283–289 (2011)

Cross-Cultural Recycling and Design Methodology; to Prove the Effectiveness of the Three-Stage Design Method of Cross-Cultural Recycling "Why-What-How"

Dong Yeong Lee[✉] and Jee Yeon Ha

Hanyang University, Seoul, Republic of Korea
dannylee@hanyang.ac.kr

Abstract. From a traditional standpoint, recycling has commonly been summarized within the so-called 4Rs: Reduce, Reuse, Recycle and Refuse, however, today's multi-disciplinary and multi-cultural society encourage us to seek solutions beyond the traditional 4-Rs. This paper starts from the belief that recycling is cultural activity which can fuse various intangible - social, theoretical and cultural aspects of people's lives such as lifestyle, art, culture and ethics, a condition which we refer to as "Cross-Cultural Recycling". Therefore, this paper aims; (1) to academically prove that recycling is a cultural activity, (2) to determine whether the consideration of cultural dimensions in the design process of recycling results in more contextualised design, and finally, (3) to establish how to define the design factors related to Cross-Cultural Recycling, which we call "Cross-Cultural Recycling Design methodology" through practical design projects from 4 recycling design workshops between 2017 and 2018 at the Hanyang University Interior Design graduate course where we applied Cross-Cultural Design Methodology in accordance with the context of recycling design. As a result of the theoretical investigation and findings from 4 design workshops, this paper proposes a three-stage Cross-Cultural Recycling Design Method; Why-What-How. The first stage, "why" deals with the three main factors considered with regards to the motivation for recycling, the environmental, economic and cultural considerations and implications. The second stage, "what" is about to define "waste" to be recycled and offers 4 key concepts; forgotten, wasted, abandoned and misplaced. The third stage, "how" provides 6 keywords, and their concepts, which are pivotal in the future direction of this design approach; use, craft, technological, design, art and culture.

Keywords: Recycling · Cross-culture · Design education · Design methodology

1 Introduction

The matter of environmental degradation is undoubtedly one of the most critical global problems in the 21st century with "recycling" being one of the key issues that has been constantly discussed in line with this issue. As such, nowadays there is vast array of

© Springer Nature Switzerland AG 2019
P.-L. P. Rau (Ed.): HCII 2019, LNCS 11577, pp. 173–185, 2019.
https://doi.org/10.1007/978-3-030-22580-3_14

waste management and recycling techniques available in the market. From a traditional standpoint, recycling has commonly been summarized within the so-called 4Rs: Reduce, Reuse, Recycle and Refuse. The first 3 Rs are definite factors, and the last R – Refuse varies depending on the focusing values, for example, some say recovery, depending on the context. Recently, at the Grand Master Class 2019, one of the biggest annual forums in Korea which was held in Seoul from the 26th to the 27th of January under the title "Future for us", Prof. Jae Chun, Choe, who is currently the professor at the Faculty of Biological Science, Ewha Womans University, Korea[1] made a speech on the first day about how we should approach environmental issues in order to secure a "future for us". In the speech, Prof. Choe proposed a new paradigm for recycling as an improvement to the traditional 4-R concept of recycling (Reduce, Reuse, Recycle, Refuse). Here, he suggested 2 new keywords – Reflect and Restore, which he noted emphasised the importance of people's attitude and participation (Fig. 1).

Fig. 1. Prof. Jae Chun Choe at the Forum <Grand Master Class 2019 "Future for us">

Environmental problems are global issues which are not impossible to solve if governments take a very definite stance and implement measures to deal with them. For example, the Chinese government banned the presence of factories within the metropolitan region of Beijing as well as strictly limiting the numbers of cars found in Beijing city centre for a few months before the Beijing Olympics in order to improve the air quality during the Olympic period. However, not a lot of governments are able to take such a drastic and decisive measure because of the different complexities of each country's economic, social and cultural factors. As such, heavy governmental intervention and control within this field is not the best solution. Therefore, many scholars and activists including Prof. Choe repeatedly emphasise the need for awareness about the seriousness of the environmental problems. Here, a pro-attitude, active and constant participation at the individual level becomes critical. Prof. Choe made it clear that "there is a certain limit to what the government alone can solve when it comes to tackling the environmental problems. Thus, each one of us should change" (NEWS

---

[1] Prof. Choe is also the President of the Ecological Society of Korea, Alternate President of Convention on Biological Diversity (CBD), and the Founding Director of National Institute of Ecology.

2018). Whilst most of the responsibility of waste is born to consumers and society (Jones 2010), comprehensive solutions won't be found unless each one of us, who are actually stakeholders of all activities happening in our society, change. The technological development and design, and commercialising of those requires finance and time, and its application is still limited, but changing people's awareness and attitude, which continues to an increased people's action can have better – more effective impact. According to Gay Hawkins, recycling possesses emotional value; he argues that people at its simplest level, recycling can make them feel "good" which he calls as "ethical self-improvement" (Hawkins 2006). In the similar note, Kendall and Koster also argues that people "launder our collective consciousness" when we recycle bottles and paper etc. (Kendall and Koster 2007).

Therefore, it is critical to understand not only environmental issues but also recycling activity from a social and cultural perspective. In this standpoint, the role of design and designers becomes crucial. If viewed from a socio-cultural perspective, where environmental and recycling problems result from a lack of "consciousness" and positive "attitude" to solving the issue, design is not a technical factor for actual production; rather, it can play a more valuable role in improving people's awareness and encouraging people's motivation. Design is not only a problem-solving process, but also an expression of intention.

This paper starts from the belief that recycling is cultural activity which can fuse various intangible - social, theoretical and cultural aspects of people's lives such as lifestyle, art, culture and ethics, a condition which we refer to as "Cross-Cultural Recycling."

This paper aims; (1) to academically prove that recycling is a cultural activity, (2) to determine whether the consideration of cultural dimensions in the design process of recycling results in more contextualised design, and finally, (3) to establish how to define the design factors related to Cross-Cultural Recycling, which we call "Cross-Cultural Recycling Design methodology" through practical design projects.

2 Recycling as a Cultural Activity

For the past few decades, the word "recycling" has been mainly associated with recycling our waste, excess and re-usuable goods mainly for environmental reasons. (Kendall and Koster 2007) A lot of dictionary definitions of the word "recycling" associate it with "recycling waste"; for example, the Cambridge Dictionary defines "recycling" as [the process of collecting and changing old paper, glass, plastic, etc. so that it can be used again]. Similarly, the Oxford Dictionary defines it as [The action or process of converting waste into reusable material]. However, recycling as a pure activity should not be necessarily associated with only waste; recycling as an activity has been practiced throughout human history for economic, artistic and technological reasons, not only for saving environment.

In the art realm, many artists and craftsmen also often use existing objects, which are not necessarily waste and are commonly referred to as 'found-objects' or 'ready-made' (terms used in the contemporary pop art), as their material for their art works. Responding to the demands of today, especially considering an action's impact on the environmental crisis we are currently facing, the concept of "recycling" has somewhat evolved into a "green" movement, but the essence of "recycling" as an activity is rather on the action itself of "changing" or "converting", which requires a more contextualised understanding of surroundings.

Although there are not many who gives an insight into the word "recycling" from a non-environmental dimension, particularly when it comes its relationship with cultural boundaries. Tina S. Kendall and Kristin Koster from the University of California are one of the very few who tackle this topic. Kendall and Koster launched a journal called "Cultural Recycling" on their e-journal "Other Voices" back in 2007. In their discussion into the issue of "Cultural Recycling", Kendall and Koster give an apt and probably the only insight into the cultural dimensions of recycling. According to the duo, the term "recycling" has now made "a conspicuous appearance within academic discourse, emerging as a paradigm for understanding the way that artistic, literary, or cultural environments function" and "the rhetoric of recycling spills over into other levels of social discourse, from the aesthetic and historical to the legal and technological." (Kendall and Koster 2007). Kendall and Koster advance the concept of recycling into areas of social and cultural reproduction, where recycling becomes more ideological with "conflicting values of continuity and change". In this conceptual understanding of "recycling", defining recycling will always be complicated and the definition may need changing; as such it is crucial to place emphasises on the importance of understanding "recycling" contextually. The contextual understanding of recycling might seem difficult however it is simply about relating oneself to the socio-cultural surroundings of his/her location to the recycling activity, which means that every recycling case should be built on its own context. In the same vein, Jacques Derrida has noted that a "deconstructive understanding of history can be achieved through the critic's efforts of going back to the expelled, rejected and repressed elements of historical memory and recycling these histories, genres and voices" (Kendall and Koster 2007). Recycling in its very essence involves some type of conversion or fusion, which creates new value out of different objects; recycling in the traditional understanding is more about hardware improvement, but today, recycling refers to a more software approach, in other term, it denotes cultural dimensions which can fuse different parts from various objects, which is where we derived the term "Cross-Cultural Recycling". Overall, it is true that recycling is both a cultural and creative activity, and thus an interdisciplinary approach towards recycling is required and becomes urgent.

As we now realize that recycling is not just about dealing with abandoned waste, it becomes crucial to come up with guidelines on how to "recycle" culturally, and this is where the role of "design" plays a pivotal part. William McDonough and Michael Braungart's latest book <Upcycling> is noteworthy in discussing the matter of design within the context of recycling. Through this book, McDonough and Braungart encourage us to seek solutions beyond the traditional 4-Rs (Reduce, Reuse, Recycle, Refuse), since they view them as limiting creativity. William McDonough and Michael Braungart propose "an ideal scenario in the quest to solve the ecological crisis we are currently facing" by asserting that "resource scarcity and sustainability is a matter that has more to do with design." As McDonough and Braungart argued, today's environmental problems can be solved via design improvement and so a more careful approach to design details is critical; however, it is not easy to change all products and more ultimately human activity into a form that is optimised for recycling. (McDonough and Braungart 2013) Therefore, the role of design is to broaden the approach to recycling by understanding people and their different contexts when it comes to environmental issues; the meaning of waste can vary from person to person and from region to region. In this sense, we tried to establish a Pro-attitude by attaching the Cross- concept to existing Cultural Recycling. To us, Cross- is an intention and an active attitude.

Since the concept of "Cross-Cultural Recycling" is newly defined by us, definition is as follows;

1. Recycling is an "awareness of the problems" associated with our socio-cultural background and taking necessary step to improve consciousness of different local contexts when dealing with waste.

>> Why

2. Recycling is a complex process and its definition is constantly changing, so it is necessary to actively understand this problem according to the circumstances of each individual. Therefore, defining recycling will always be complicated and the definition may need changing.

>> What

3. Recycling has many complex facets so it is vital that, when addressing the issue, people focus on both the cultural and artistic aspects of our lifestyles in order to develop aesthetic ideas and artistic approaches.

>> How

This is our definition of the term "Cross-Cultural Recycling Design" as well as the explanation of our 3 step "Cross-Cultural Recycling Design method"; Why-What-How.

3 Methodology

Since last 2010, we have been conducting actual design workshop at Goldsmiths University in the UK where we focused on examining Cross-Cultural Design processes and Practical Methodologies. Cross-Cultural Design is a methodology that understands the socio-cultural context in the design process and concentrates on the process of why, what and how to design it. Our methodology is based on Dong Young Lee's Cross-Cultural Design Methodology (Lee 2016). We tried to finance this cross-cultural design methodology by introducing it for the purposes of understanding the cultural dimension of recycling design.

Following the theoretical introduction of the subject, in order to establish the practicality of the Cross-Cultural Recycling Design Methodology, we conducted 4 recycling design workshops between 2017 and 2018 during the graduate design course of the Hanyang University Interior Design course. We constructed the Cross-Cultural Design Methodology in accordance with the context of recycling design (Table 1).

In this process, we set up a three-step design method called Why-What-How based on the concept of extensibility of recycling as a cultural entity discussed above in Sect. 2. During each term, we conducted design workshops with about 7–12 graduate design students to design 3 dimensional objects, which had both practical and artistic

Table 1. Summary of 4 recycling design workshops

Workshop 1	Workshop 2	Workshop 3	Workshop 4
Individual projects		Team projects	
1st Term, 2017	2nd Term, 2017	1st Term, 2018	2nd Term, 2018
8 students, 7 teams	6 students, 5 teams	6 students, 3 teams	6 students, 3 teams

qualities, within the recycling design boundary. The workshop intended to invite the participating students to adopt the 3 stage design process of "Why-What-How" when designing their own projects that involved coming with their own definition of what waste is. Each term lasted for 4 months and the weekly design workshop was for 4 h each time. Participating students worked individually for the Workshop 1 and 2 and then in groups of 2-3 for the Workshop 3 and 4 in order to improve the quality of design and production. Each term had 3 main sessions – 1, how to define waste and understand recycling. 2, practically selecting what to recycle. 3, the actual prototyping.

Through the actual design outcomes from the design workshops, the concrete language of Why-What- How was established as presented in the chapter of Findings.

4   Findings

From 4 Cross-Cultural Recycling Design Workshops, we produced 21 projects. Table 2 is a summary of the projects. Each project is explained with the following information; (1) Type of object, (2) Why: Motivation, (3) What 1: Chosen Material, (4) What 2: Definition of Waste and (5) How: Design Method.

One interesting finding is that working individually or in a team affected the motivation of the project. The projects from the workshop 1 and 2 where participating students worked individually showed more personalised choice of material to recycle, for example, old go board (Project 1-4), comic books (Project 1-2) or Xylophone (Project 1-7), and Old Duvet set (Project 2-2) which the students defined "wasted" as "forgotten". These old objects are not necessarily something they want to throw out, but rather keep and remember. Project 2-2 transforms old duvet set into a stool, interestingly trying to symbolically show the fusion of sitting culture of the East and standing culture of the West through this recycling design. Some international students tried to reflect their unique lifestyle of being abroad and living in a temporary accommodation, for example, Project 1-3 started from the scene the student often sees in her neighbourhood with many foreign residents using mattress only and dumping it out on the street when moving out. This student retranslated "waste" as "misplaced". On the contrary, the projects from the workshop 3 and 4 where the students work in a group showed more socially and culturally directed motivation, for example, Project 3-3 started the project from the increasing volume of paper waste with an in-depth study of the recent trend of being digital. This team also defined "waste" as "misplaced". Project 4-2 was specifically directed to how to technically and practically recycle a huge volume of daily plastic consumption from the university campus. The details of each project are documented in Table 2.

Table 2. Summary of projects from 4 Cross-Cultural Recycling Design Workshops

	Workshop 1	Workshop 2	Workshop 3	Workshop 4
Final design				
Project no.	Project 1-1	Project 2-1	Project 3-1	Project 4-1
Type of object Why:Motivation What 1:Material What 2:Definition How:Method	Lighting Reuse Wasted Shower Balls Wasted Hand craft	Vase Reuse, Show- case of New technology Abandoned PET bottles Abandoned, Wasted Laser Cutting	Partition Wall Reuse Abandoned plywood from construction site Abandoned Laser cutting	Vase Reuse/ Showcase of New technology Abandoned PET bottles Abandone/ Wast- ed 3D printing
Final design				
Project no.	Project 1-2	Project 2-2	Project 3-2	Project 4-2
Type of object Why:Motivation What 1:Material What 2:Definition How:Method	Lighting Remember/ Reuse Old comic books Forgotten Handcraft	Stool Remember/ Reuse Old duvet Forgotten Handcraft	Tea table Reuse/ technolog- ical intervention Wooden Plates Wasted 3D Printing	Wall tile units Reuse/Social Message PE,PET plastic caps Wasted/ Aban- doned Mechanical
Final design				
Project no.	Project 1-3	Project 2-3	Project 3-3	Project 4-3
Type of object Why:Motivation What 1:Material What 2:Definition How:Method	Storage Reuse Mattress Springs Wasted/ abandoned handcraft	Tea table Reuse Cloth Hanger Wasted Handcraft	Tea Table Reuse/ Social message Paper magazines, leaflets Wasted/ Aban- doned/ Misplaced Handcraft	Lighting Reuse/ Social Message PET bottles Wasted/ Abandoned Handcraft
Final design				
Project no.	Project 1-4	Project 2-4		
Type of object Why:Motivation	Small table Remember/ Reuse	Lighting Abandoned/		

What 1:Material What 2:Definition How:Method	Old go board Abandoned/ Forgotten Handcraft	Wasted Leftover acrylic pieces Wasted/ Abandoned Handcraft
Final design		
Project no.	Project 1-5	Project 2-5
Type of object Why:Motivation What 1:Material What 2:Definition How:Method	Stool units Reuse Drain pipes Abandoned Handcraft	Lighting Reuse Wooden Chop- sticks Wasted Handcraft
Final design		
Project no.	Project 1-6	
Type of object Why:Motivation What 1:Material What 2:Definition How:Method	Stool units Reuse Drain pipes Abandoned Handcraft	
Final design		
Project no.	Project 1-7	
Type of object Why:Motivation What 1:Material What 2:Definition How:Method	Wall decoration Remember/ Abandoned Xylophone Forgotten/ Mechnical, Hand- craft	

5   Discussion

To summarise, the Cross-Cultural recycling design tools <Why-What-How> are applied to our recycling design workshops in order to empirically test the role and the influence of cultural dimensions within the recycling design.

The fundamentals of the Why-What-How process are the basis of Lee (2016)'s cross-cultural design method mentioned above. The Motive and Action tools are the core pillars of the Cross-Cultural Design method which focuses on encouraging designers to figure out how develop their own design approach as well as identifying the reasons for it (Fig. 2).

Fig. 2. Cross-Cultural Design <Motive-Action> Tools, 2016 (Lee 2016)

We redefined Lee's Motive – Action tool of the Cross-cultural design process for recycling design as the why → what → how process. While in the previous Cross-cultural design method we provided designers with the "what" to design totally on their findings from the motive stage, the Cross-cultural recycling design method clearly incorporates the "what" stage in order to encourage designers to re-define their own definition of waste in reflection of the context of where they are located (Table 3).

Table 3. Comparison of Cross-Cultural design method & Cross-Cultural recycling design method

Cross-Cultural Design method	MOTIVE		→		ACTION
Cross-Cultural recycling design method	WHY	→	WHAT	→	HOW

(1) Why

Here, 'Why' is another term for Motive, which is what gives people a reason and rational to start a project. It is almost universally accepted that there is a positive correlation between motivation and learning, and design education is not an exception. Dewey (1966), an influential education reformer in the traditional education scene, stated that the most important attitude in education is to plant in students a desire to learn. The more motivated a person is about a given subject, the more likely it is that they will learn about it. Malone (1981) claims that intrinsically motivated students may spend more time and effort learning, feel better about that learning, and use that learning more in the future. The Why method has 2 levels; the first level involves setting an aim, which is the initial reason for recycling whilst considering – (1) environmental, (2) economic and (3) cultural implications. The second level is to identify an objective, it is more about identifying an actual goal to achieve and it has five factors - (1) Promote, (2) Share, (3) Adopt, (4) Protect and (5) Deny. The second level of Why is adopted the Motive too of Lee's Cross-cultural design method (Table 4).

Table 4. Keywords of MOTIVE of Cross-Cultural Recycling design method

Motive 1 AIM	Environmental		Economic		Cultural	
Motive 2 objective	Promote	Share	Adopt	Protect	Deny

(2) What

Traditionally, identifying what had to be recycled was a very straight forward process especially if we look at examples like disposable plastic cups, straws, used paper, broken furniture and various construction waste. Today, however, there is a wide array of garbage which requires different methods to recycle. As a result of the rapid change of socio-cultural backgrounds of our living environment, the traditional understanding of "waste" no longer works. Today, waste cannot be simply understood as "plastic cups in a rubbish bin". For example, there has been a lot of controversy about how to deal recently with "E-Waste" (electronic waste) which refers to discarded electrical or electronic devices. E-Waste has dire effects on the environment in many parts of the world and it is the result of rapid development of technology. Furthermore, because today's global society is frequently crossing geographical borders, there is an increase in the number of prefabricated packed furniture, which overall leads to the discarding of the packaging along with the used furniture as waste. Moreover, these migrations tend to increase the number of households in a invariably increasing the amount of garbage and here it is important to note that this new, increased waste is different from the usual one and so the understanding of its implications on the local contexts have not been established.

As such, the discarding of waste is a very cultural process and it is the basis of Cross-Cultural Recycling design which is a process of having a deeper understanding and insight on our society and lifestyles. In fact, the cultural aspect refers to the process of subjectively exploring, understanding and accepting the contexts of various societies, and this process is also a process of self-learning. Therefore, the idea of cultural recycling should not simply follow an aesthetical, technical or economical approach; it has to redefine garbage from a new perspective. The normal definition of recycling does not fully address the complexity of the problem since it does not really touch on the consumer's behaviours. The Cross-Cultural Recycling Design method defines 4 categories in the What section that tackle this issue; (1) forgotten, (2) wasted, (3) abandoned and (4) misplaced based on the findings from analysing the projects from design workshops.

(3) How

The term 'How' is also understood from a similar perspective. There are various ways to approach where recycling activity and techniques developed from and the reasons for it. (1) Creating a new use, (2) Creating a new look and purpose from a craft perspective, (3) Technological conversion, (4) Improving the quality of the design manner and (5) Artistic Re-invention. The initial stage of the recycling process has to do with the manner in which the waste is collected. The second stage is about how to reuse the waste which brings about the matter of design. As such, the first stage of recycling refers to the physical re-usage of the waste; giving a new purpose to waste which is recoverable and has no major damage by making the most of the morpho-logical and material characteristics of the existing product. Here, D.I.Y activities can be employed. Converting waste back into raw materials is also one of the most common methods of recycling; for example, collected waste paper and plastic bottles can be converted into raw materials like paper pulp and liquefied plastic respectively. As a result of the many recent technological developments in today's world, there are easier, more effective and specialised ways of recycling materials available in the market. A different aspect of recycling deals with more theoretical aspects of the waste which involves improving the look of the product by integrating concepts and artistic values, along with integrating social intentions. For example, Sonic Fabric designed by the sound and conceptual artist Alyce Santoro weaves cassette tape with polyester thread to create a textile that can play sounds from the tape. 'Sonic Fabric' perhaps is not viable for immediate use as a final product, however it shows the possible future direction of recycling, arouses people's interest in recycling and refreshes people's understanding of the products made from recycled materials. Of course, these methods have not developed chronologically, but the latest issue now is about how to (6) culturally recycle (Figs. 3, 4 and 5).

1) USE: giving a new use
2) CRAFT: giving a new look and purpose in a craft manner
3)TECHNOLOGICAL: technologically converting
4) DESIGN: improving the quality in a design manner
5) ART: artistically re-inventing
6) CULTURE: culturally recycle

Fig. 3. Words of HOW of Cross-Cultural Recycling Design Method

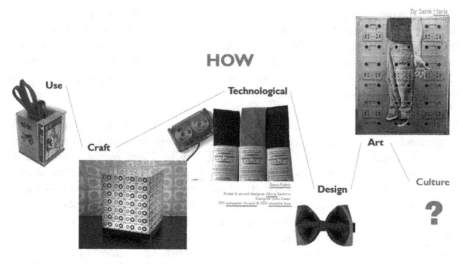

Fig. 4. A map for Cross-Cultural Recycling Design tool <How> – lecture materials

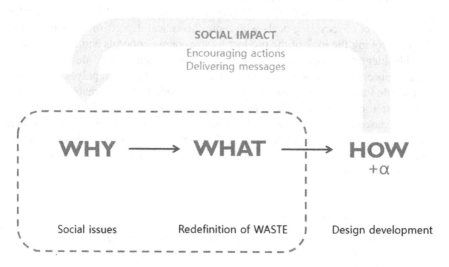

Fig. 5. Cross-Cultural Recycling Design Process

6   Conclusion

As a result of this theoretical investigation and projects from 4 design workshops, this paper proposes a design method which employs a three stage Cross-Cultural Recycling design process; Why-What-How. The first stage, "why," deals with the three main factors considered with regards to the motivation for recycling, the environmental, economic and cultural considerations and implications. The second stage "what" offers 4 key concepts; forgotten, wasted, abandoned and misplaced. This stage is all about how to define the "waste" to be recycled whilst paying attention to today's cultural and social contexts which have been largely influenced by age, industry, lifestyle change and frequent migration, which is one of the core elements of our "Cross-Cultural Recycling" design process. We believe that this stage will refresh people's understanding of waste and widen the boundary of recycling activity. The third stage, "how" provides 6 keywords, and their concepts, which are pivotal in the future direction of this design approach; use, craft, technological, design, art and culture.

As a result, this paper concluded on two main outcomes. From the feedback of the design projects from the workshops, using the "Cross-Cultural Recycling" design process of Why-What-How helps designers to design more contextualised and culturally viable design. It also helped them find a new way to understand and interpret different cultures and develop new design concepts and directions. The second core outcome is the effectiveness of the proposed cultural recycling design process; Why-What-How.

Acknowledgment. This public performance was supported by the research fund of Hanyang University (HY-2017).

References

Dewey, J.: Experience & Education. The Macmillan Company, New York (1966)

Hawkins, G.: The Ethics of Waste: How We Relate to Rubbish. Rowman & Litttlefield, Lanham (2006)

Jones, C.: The subject supposed to recycle. Philos. Today **54**, 30–39 (2010)

Kendall, T., Koster, K.: Critical approaches to cultural recycling. Other Voices **3**(1), 165 (2007)

Lee, D.Y.: Cross-Cultural Design (CCD) Learning Model: The development and implementation of CCD design education in South Korean higher education. University of London, Goldsmiths, Ph.D. dissertation (2016)

Malone, T.W.: Toward a theory of intrinsically motivating instruction. Cogn. Sci. **5**(4), 333–369 (1981)

McDonough, W., Braungart, M.: The Upcycle: Beyond Sustainability-Designing for Abundance. North Point Press, New York (2013)

MK News: [Q&A] Prof. Choi Jae-chun "Personal action is important in solving environmental problems" (2018). http://news.mk.co.kr/newsRead.php?year=2018&no=551813. Accessed 27 Jan 2019

Mobility-as-a-Service: A Critical Review and the Generalized Multi-modal Transport Experience

Yuanjun Li[✉], Andrew May, and Sharon Cook

Loughborough Design School, Leicestershire, UK
y.li5@lboro.ac.uk

Abstract. Considering MaaS still lacks a widely accepted definition, several pilots were launched without a solid reference, which has given rise to an unclear situation in market. This paper aims to help researchers and stakeholders to have an overall comprehension of MaaS and grasp a critical review on present concept by analysing the generalized multi-modal transport experience, service offerings of MaaS pilots and the knowledge raise by researchers and academic organizations, and then to summarize an generalized user experience map base on Multi-Level Service Design (MSD) model to narrow down the concept boundary and support further User-centred Design related researches.

Keywords: Mobility-as-a-Service · Urban transport · Service design

1 Introduction

In the result of customers' altering requirements, development of modern technologies and the transformation of industry, ITS (Intelligent Transport System) has contributed to a wider spectrum of possibility on urban transport and promoted the utilization of various resources from current market. In order to release the pressure brought by the issues such as transport congestion and management in urban cities, the policy makers were urged to come up with a holistic solution.

"Mobility-as-a-Service (MaaS)" is a new business model, which was proposed as "Using a digital interface to source and manage the provision of a transport service(s) which meets the requirements of customer (CATAPULT 2016)". This model aims to provide a more flexible, efficient and user-oriented mobility solution to customers by offering them the multi-modal transport experiences through a related one-stop services platform.

The concept of MaaS is discussed lively in most of European countries, but it is still on the initial phase of development, while the understanding is changing over time. Some organizations and newly-established firms have launched pilots to probe the possibilities of cooperation but are mainly taking service providers' value proposition at the centre. In previous studies, limited evidence has been collected about users' actual requirements in this service system. The reason might be, firstly, the stakeholders haven't attached importance to the gap between different propositions of service

P.-L. P. Rau (Ed.): HCII 2019, LNCS 11577, pp. 186–206, 2019.
https://doi.org/10.1007/978-3-030-22580-3_15

providers and end users. Secondly, it's still lacking a systematic and generalized tool to undertake the relevant researches.

In this paper, the understanding of MaaS service system have been updated slightly from previous studies', including the definition of Actors and Integration Approaches in service system. As a result of analysis, the transport service offerings established on Transport Integration were taken as the basis to develop the generalized multi-modal transport user experience map. By exploring the hidden idea of MaaS service design, 3 main Logic Lines are summarized to explain how the MaaS user experience is generated in current market.

By fitting the result into Multi-Level Service Design (MSD) model, the opportunities of service innovation can be observed on each level of MaaS service system. And meanwhile, any innovation on upper level may all effect users' actual experiences on the bottom. Therefore, future researches can be expected to be carried out on this basis with focus on end users' requirements and apply User-centred Design approach to probe the sustainable way for future service iteration.

2   Understanding MaaS

2.1   What Is MaaS?

Mobility-as-a-Service (MaaS) is a practical development of "collaborative transport", which stands for buying mobility services as a package based on customers' needs instead of buying the means of transport (Kamargianni et al. 2016). The idea behind MaaS is the integrated and seamless transport service (Hietanen 2014; Motta et al. 2013; Preston 2012; Schade et al. 2014) provided through an end-user digital interface (MaaSLab 2018), where different sectors in market are encouraged to co-operate and interconnected to work as an Eco-system (Hietanen 2014; CATAPULT 2015).

In the context of recent social generation, people who have similar experience and childhood that grow up in digital era have shown their increasing interests in multi-modal mobility (Heikkilä 2014) and reflects the change to a more light-asset lifestyle. With MaaS, customers don't need to have their own car but can get access to all travel modes, so that the fragments of customers' end-to-end journey can be covered.

In MaaS's early prospective (Fig. 1), its envisioned framework may contain both public and private sectors, including the operators under crowd-sourced logistics such as car-sharing and rental, transport fleet and infrastructure; trip planner, booking and payment; real-time traffic management and inter-connectivity information among service platform; as well as relevant value-added services. All the data from operators are integrated to background algorithm, so that the customer could receive the results of multi-modal routes and personalized information with real-time updates.

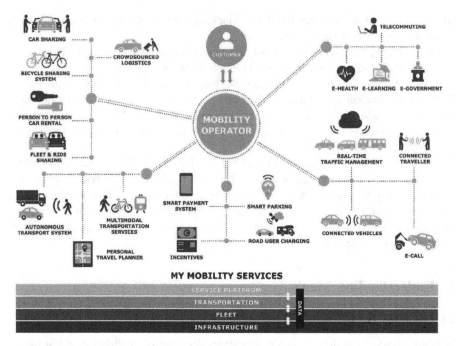

Fig. 1. MaaS autonomous vehicles-IoT (Source: Ecosystem report, synocus oy)

Referring to literature and report reading, the holistic thinking has overall high-lighted 2 features of MaaS, which are Transport Integration and Sharing Economy.

Transport Integration. The integration of MaaS can be distinguished into partial and advance level (Kamarginanni et al. 2016) and realized as physical, operating and managerial, which mainly states the integration in 3 fields: Transport Integration, Organizational-economic Integration and Tariff Integration (Poliaková 2013).

In partial level, integration refers to ICT, payment and the corresponding favour-able prices. It could be further extended to partial integration in ticketing, which means the user only need to purchase once with one ticket and lower price for one return tour or a trip with transfer. While the advance integration occurs systematically to the completed integration of ICT, institution and tailored mobility package on a higher level, where the establishment of the unified backstage platform and agreement among operators are the precondition. As the result, one could be released from concerning of specific routes or modes to simply expecting a seamless journey from A to B with enhanced options based on their own preference of time, cost and comfort demands (Kamarginaniet al. 2015; CATAPULT 2015). It provides an alter option for travellers who are confront with the transformation of transport modes to think about a collabo-rate solution (Sochor et al. 2015). Customers could pay for their total usage before ahead for a month or a season, which is not only more cost-effective (IET 2014), but could also leave flexibility for their temporary adjustment.

An example of current MaaS practice in Transport Integration is Whim, a mobile phone-based application released in Helsinki from 2016. This App helps customers to focus on travel essentials by offering integrated platform of planning, booking and payment for all modes of public and private transports, including train, taxi, bus, car-sharing, bike-sharing, and other city transport modes collaboratively operation from A to B.

By typing-in the destination, customer could get the information such as transport modes' availability, optimal routes and cost of time and money. And after departure, the enroute real-time information would deliver to them like the "live post". Whim has designed several service packages to cater different customers' needs, and all the operations could be completed as a one-stop process by one single App.

Sharing Economy. "Sharing economy" is usually being mentioned together with another concept - "collaborative consumption", which is defined as "those events in which one or more persons consume economic goods or services in the process of engaging in joint activities with one or more others (Felson and Speath 1978)". In information era, collaborative consumption is characterized by the backstage internet-mediated platform to support sharing behaviour as a new economic model and works by (1) trust between strangers; (2) power of idling capacity; (3) belief in the commons; and (4) critical mass (Botsman and Rogers 2011). It is assumed to open possibilities for new types of travel, reduce car ownership by making profit from "mobility services" (Karlsson et al. 2016; Sochor et al. 2014). It has also made little-used resources more productive, therefore, it can stimulate the opportunities to make private sectors joining urban transportation system.

An example is OfO Bicycle Sharing. Customers use mobile phone to unlock bicycle from anywhere around city through searching on OfO App. Service could be offered anytime throughout the day without restriction of fixed location of transport stop/station.

More examples like Uber and Lyft are both delivering on-demand transport service through a dedicated App. Users can choose to be service provider or receiver by accomplishing the registration and verification process online. In this case, the service platform is acting as a broker to guarantee and protect the interests for both parties.

MaaS takes in these companies accompanied with traditional transports as inter-mediary agent to link fragmented trips. However, many problems are raised along with its development. Firstly, high scrap rate of bicycles and the disordered situation of parking has been reported to bring about new issues to urban transport and environment. Secondly, the security issues of users and the coexistence problem among service providers have also brought challenge to urban transport management. All of these sort of problems also points out the important role of MaaS in urban transport management, but there were rare report and literature of previous studies has provided an systematic perspective to solve these issues.

2.2   MaaS Service System

Service Offerings. By exploring the developing trajectory of Intelligent Mobility, CATAPULT (2015) concluded Four Concurrent Transformational Theme through to 2030: Access, Demand and Supply, Integration and Automation (Fig. 2), and highlight the first consider question of MaaS is "Access".

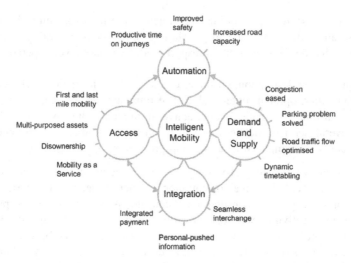

Fig. 2. Four themes of intelligent mobility (CATAPULT 2015) (Source: Expert panel workshop, expert interview, and CVA analysis)

"Access" refers to providing more possible channels and options for customers of their travel demands. As it relies much on existing devices, technologies and mobility asset, CATAPULT (2015) indicates the future majority developments in this theme would relate to business model innovations rather than technical innovations. Currently, the value delivery of MaaS is much depending on mobile phone-based App as the customer interface to realize most of the functions, because it can achieve "Access" of both physical and digital ways.

Several literatures have identified the key service offering of MaaS as: Easy Payment, Route Planning, Journey Booking & Reserving, Uniform Ticket, Easy Transfer & Last Mile Service, Service Package Subscription, Multi-modal Journey and Real-time Information & Navigation (CATAPULT 2015; Kamargianni et al. 2016; Jennia et al. 2018) (Fig. 3).

What makes the realization of those functions are the integration of different aspects resources: Ticket Integration, Payment Integration, Transport Integration and ICT Integration. The levels of integration could be regarded as the standard to value the service capability, which means the service offerings that contains more integration aspects refers to the higher level of capability to perform in customers' experience.

Territory of Actors. CATAPULT (2016) defined 4 key actors of MaaS Eco-system: MaaS Customer, MaaS Provider, Data Provider and Transport Operator. Similarly, Matyas and Kamargianni (2017) defined the actors as Political Actors, Mobility Service Providers (MSPs), MaaS Operator (MO) and End Users.

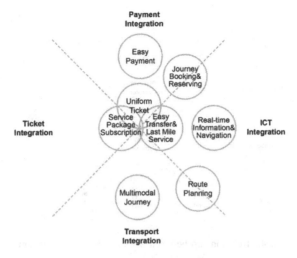

Fig. 3. Key service offerings of MaaS

Take Whim as an example, it doesn't provide service directly to customers, but set up an interface that enables communications between customers and suppliers. Referring to CATAPULT (2016)'s definition, Apps like Whim in current Eco-system are taking the role of MaaS Provider. Data Provider and Transport Operators are the fundamental actors in system. Data Provider undertakes the tasks of background algorithm on route planning, ticketing and payment. Transport Operator refers to the mobility operator who can provide access to mobility asset and actual physical services of both public and private sectors, covering traditional public transport, airlines, road and parking authorities, as well as private operators like individual citizens who register to share their own vehicles.

However, early launched pilots have proved that, an individual company may take multiple identities. For example, service providers like Uber can produce their own data (as Data Provider) while offering car-sharing services (as Transport Operator). Matyas and Kamargianni (2017) suggested a new identification of actor- MO, which shift the understanding slightly different (Smith et al. 2018). It further distinguishes the tasks of resource integrator and service operator in MaaS system. Integrator takes the role to match service resources, while the Operator comprise these services as a bundle of offering and deliver it to End Users.

In current market, the role of MO is basically implemented in the form of a unified platform. It is similar to mobile communication system where different mobile telecom carriers are allowed to sell their packages of calls and traffic data. The integrator of MaaS Eco-system variant according to local context. In consequence, different Integrators can be expected to coexist on the same platform to meet multiple market demands.

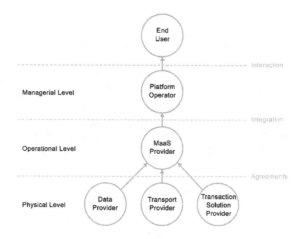

Fig. 4. Relationship between actors in MaaS eco-system

Established on previous studies, the key Actors in this paper are defined into 6 categories to clarify the responsibilities: End User, Platform Operator, MaaS Provider, Data Provider, Transport Provider and Transaction Solution Provider (Fig. 4), simultaneously matches the Integration in physical, operational and managerial layer (Poliaková 2013) (Similar figure can be found in Smith et al. 2018). Firstly, Transport, Data and Transaction Providers undertake and assist the physical services, which can be integrated by MaaS Provider or directly linked to the platform as an independent service resource. MaaS Provider above this works like a travel agent that designs theses integrated resources into offerings that meet travellers' requirements and promote the result to Platform Operator. The common practice of platform is using account/profile to do customer management that supports recording personal data and feedback to provide appropriate service. Any cooperation cross levels would need agreements to specify the boundary of share data and the division of functions.

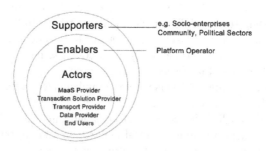

Fig. 5. Hierarchy of actors in wider MaaS environment

However, if put the model into a wider environment (Fig. 5), the other value-added service providers, as well as social communities, institutions and organization, such as political sector (Maytas and Kamargianni 2017) would also play an important part in MaaS Eco-system to extend service content, increase integration level and promote user experience.

3 Service Integration Approaches

Even though the concept of MaaS has been lively discussed, the actual user experience is still unclear because the market has not matured. In current development status, it's an urgent need of researchers to set up a generalized user experience framework to support further researches. The reasons are: (1) Current service system of MaaS is mainly guided by the value proposition of service providers, it might cause a discrepancy between service and the actual user requirements, but (2) MaaS should be customers' need based (Hietanen 2014). Taking the consideration of User-centred Design, a generalized user experience framework could provide a basic tool for further service innovation.

Given the diversity of current MaaS pilots, lacking the consensus among companies is the prior difficulty for generating the generalized framework of MaaS user experience is. To find this answer, this paper would step back to a wider concept and stand on the essential of MaaS - multi-modal transport experience - to clarify the boundary of current MaaS concept in market.

Reviewing on the methods used by Kamargianniet al. (2016), here analysed 15 integrated transport schemes by the integration types of Ticket Integration, Payment Integration, ICT Integration (Heikkilä 2014) (Table 1). Comparing with the original format, this table has decomposed "Ticket Integration" into "e-ticket" and "Smart Card"; "Payment Integration" into "Pay-as-you-go" and pay "Monthly"; "ICT Integration" into "Real-time Information" and "Planning and Booking Information"; as well as "Mobility Package Integration" and "Transport Integration", in order to add more details for analysing.

The horizontal header of Table 1 presents the categories of integration. 15 schemes can be divided three classes based on different integration approaches: Transport Integration (scheme No. 1–9), Transaction Integration (scheme No. 10–13), and Regional Integration (scheme No. 14 & 15).

As shown in Table 1, scheme No. 1–9 have the features of Transport Integration in common, are mostly newly established firms that integrate transport related services. Schemes No. 10–13 issue payment card or virtual card to integrate payment channels as a preliminary step, and then indirectly integrate transport services. Schemes No. 14 & 15 are regional transport services that have a long history of development, which has gradually grown up a locally adapted solution for citizens' needs.

Table 1. Summary of MaaS schemes' level of integration

No	Approaches for Integrated Transport Experience (Area)	Ticket Integration		Payment Integration		ICT Integration		Mobility Package Integration	Transport Integration	Accessible Modes					
		e-ticket	Smart card	Pay-as-you-go	monthly	Real-time info	Planning and booking info			1*	2*	3*	4*	5*	6*
1.	Qixxit app+web (Berlin, Germany)					x	x		x	x	x	x	x	x	+Plane; +Bike rental
2.	Metropia app +DUO Social Carpooling +MOOE (US)			x		x	x		x	x	x	x	x	x	+Parking
3.	Simobility JustGo app +CiCo +BiBo (Swiss Southeastern)	NA		x		x	x		x	x	x	x	x		
4.	Moovel app + Moovel transit + RideTap (Stuttgart/Berlin/Hamburg, Germany)	x		x		x	x		x	x	x	x	x	x	
5.	SMILE app (Vienna, Austria)	x		x	x	x		x	x	x	x	x	x	x	+Bike rental
6.	UbiGo (project) (Gothenburg, Sweden)	x		x		x		x	x	x	x		x		x
7.	Whim app (Helsinki, Finland; West midland, UK)	x		x	x	x	x	x	x	x	x		x		
8.	NaviGoGo project (Dundee/Fife, Scotland)	x		x	x	x	x	x	x	x	x		x		
9.	Switchh app+web +HVV (Hamburg, Germany)	x	x	x	x	x	x	x	x	x				x	+Parking
10.	Alipay app+web + (China)	x	x	x			x	NA		x	x	x	x	x	+Plane;
11.	Visa Global Transit Solution +TFL Network (London)		x	x				NA		x	x	x	x	x	Depends on TFL Network
12.	PayPal Access Card +TFL Network (London)		x	x				NA		x	x	x	x	x	Depends on TFL Network
13.	Mobility Mixx web +OV chip card (Netherlands)		x	x				x		x	x		x	x	+Parking
14.	STIB-MIVB app+web (Brussels, Belgium)	x	x	x	x	x	x	x	x	x	x	x	x		+Bike rental
15.	GVH (Hannover area,)					x		x	x	x	x	x	x	x	+ Parking

* Urban Public Transport (PT); 2* Taxi; 3* Rail; 4* Car Rental & Car Sharing; 5* Bike Sharing; 6* Others

3.1 Transport Integration (No. 1–9)

In terms of integration level, Transport Integration can be subdivided into Partial Integration, Advanced Integration and Advanced Integration with Mobility Packages (Kamargianni et al. 2016). Schemes under this category are mostly those identified as MaaS system in current market, but the result is slightly different from previous study because of some added details.

Partial Integration. On this level, service schemes partially possess Ticket Integration, Payment Integration and ICT Integration, which means travellers still can't fully join the fragments of journey on all aspects. The examples are: Qixxit (No. 1 in Table 1) has journey planning, booking and real-time information through its App, but customers are unable to grasp a through ticket to pay at once for a lump sum of fees; Metropia (No. 2 in Table 1) has Payment and ICT Integration, but the tickets are offered by Transport Providers separately.

Advanced Integration. Schemes of Advanced Integration should possess in full of Ticket, Payment and ICT Integration, the examples are SiMobility, Moovel and SMILE (No. 3–5 in Table 1).

Even though SiMobility doesn't has Ticket Integration, but a new technique was applied to fill the gap. As described in SiMobility JustGo project, the App installed in smart phone could detect Bluetooth transmitter in vehicle and sent the data to backend. Passengers would be charged automatically according to the trip made without the needs to buy tickets.

Kamargianni et al. (2016) has classified Moovel into the Partial Integration level as it doesn't support Ticket Integration among different transport modes. But considering it offers e-tickets- an QR code sent to smart-phone which replaced the separate ticket for each journey fragments do not actually make differences with customers' experience of through ticket, it can be regarded as having the equal function of advanced integration level.

Advanced Integration with Mobility Packages. Services in this level are: UbiGo, Whim, NaviGoGo and Switch (No. 6–9 in Table 1). These services have all designed packages for different traveller groups. On the basis of Advanced Integration, these schemes have further designed service packages for customer to choose from. Considering different travel purposes (e.g. commuting, leisure), each package contains different amount usage of travel by different transport modes to fit individual's habit and preferences. And the overall cost is lower than the original prices.

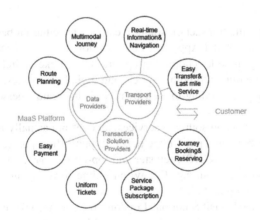

Fig. 6. Transport integration approach

As can be seen in Table 1, schemes No. 1–9 are all established on the base of transport integration to develop other features. Companies undertake the role of both MaaS Provider and Platform Operator. And Transaction Solutions, Data and Transport Providers are all integrated in this single platform (Fig. 6).

This platform possesses (or partially possess) the features of Easy Payment, Uniform ticket, Service Package, Journey Booking & Reserving, Easy Transfer & Last Mile service, Real-time Information & Navigation, Multi-modal Journey and Route Planning. The platform works as a central processor but also a 3rd party brokerage that exist individually, so that customers only need to interact with this single interface.

3.2   Transaction Solution Integration (No. 10–13)

Under this approach, one unique transaction solution plays as the common thread adopted by providers or platforms. Examples are Alipay, Visa Global Transit Solution, Paypal Access Card and Mobility Mixx (No. 10–13 in Table 1).

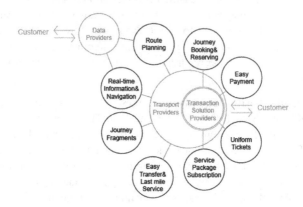

Fig. 7. Transaction integration approach

In Fig. 7, the specific transaction solution can be viewed as embedding in different service system. Alipay Wallet App serves the functions of bank account management, P2P transfer, prepay mobile phone top-up, transport ticket purchase, food order, insurance and the like linked to both physical and digital companies. It allows users to edit the service options according to their own needs to create a personalized one-stop shop interface.

Alipay Wallet recruits outsourcing services but does not actually integrate transport data. Customers can book and pay for the ticket for public transport (e.g. Air&Rail) and private transport (e.g. Uber&OfO), register and top-up bus pass, and search for travel recommendations and discount(e.g. Fliggy, an online travel agent). The QR code is generated within the App as tickets.

As for Visa Global Transit Solution (London), the core technique is the contactless payment, which aims to save time at fare gate and help customers to be unobstructed with different transport modes in urban city or around the world by taking the advantages of the widely used Visa Credit Card. Visa has created the MaaS Transit Transaction model, a back-office framework to manage contactless payment, which allows mass operators to offer flexible fares and also guarantees the features like fare cappping, concessions and delay refunds. Similarly, Paypal has extend its service to a physical card - Paypal Access Card. This card can be used on Tube, buses, tram, DLR, London Overground and the most National Rail in London.

Mobility Mixx, a subsidiary of Leaseplan Netherland, features in business trip including a wide range of mobility solutions covering mobility public transport, taxis, car rental, bike rental, parking and fuelling. This service aims at helping employers to control their employees' travel expenses by using a nationally effective Mobility Mixx business OV chip card that works as a budget. Employees are given a fixed annual allowance for all business travel to release the burden of management for employers. It doesn't integrate transports, but has all fees prepaid, so it has the same function of transaction integration.

Services above are deemed to take Transaction Integration as the precondition to realize multi-modal transport experience. In this case, Transaction Solution Providers operate the unified platform. For an individual transport provider (e.g. Uber), it can choose to link several Transaction Solution Providers to do payment if customer access through individual service's interface.

3.3   Regional Integration (No. 14 & 15)

Regional integration refers to the Transport Providers within a certain geographic area have agreements or hold shares of one common association in a strategic way. The association act as the Platform Operator and MaaS Provider to design transport services for local resident's needs (Fig. 8). Examples are Brussels Intercommunal Transport Company (STIB-MIVB) in Belgium, and "Großraum-Verkehr Hannover GmbH (GVH) in German Hannover area. (No. 14 & 15 in Table 1).

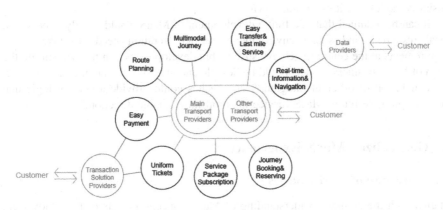

Fig. 8. Regional integration approach

STIB is the local public transport operator in Brussels covering service of metro, tram and bus. It serves offerings for multiple journeys and group journeys through an App and website where customers can choose the billing methods by various fare structures or load fares to smart card-MOBIB for each time payment.

Similarly, the main operators of GVH are Üstra (tram&bus), DB Regio (Commuter train) and RegioBus (bus). Other public Transport Providers, like Hannover Stadtbahn (light rail) and Hannover S-Bahn (Railway), are not belong to GVH association, but they issue and accept the tickets of GVH tariff. To private companies(e.g. car-sharing, taxi), platform allows the open access by providing quick links for customers to have an overall consideration of different travel modes.

Regional Integration is localized and non-copyable with high social approval degree among local citizens. As it's normally administrated by public sectors, the private transport service start-ups might need some efforts to fit-in the existing system. It reflects a prior concern of stakeholders about who should be responsible and how to supervise the system that can promote the development of urban transport system in a more sustainable and environmentally friendly way.

3.4 Summary

The above three integration approaches describe the ways that customers could have in current market to obtain the multi-modal transport experiences. Schemes No. 1–9 are specifically designed following the concept of MaaS which take transport integration as the basis, but it's just one of many approaches to achieve the desired goal.

Beside the approaches mentioned above, the multi-modal experience in future may also take "travel distance" as one criterion to consider the collaboration of transport modes. In America, Uber and Lyft (car sharing companies) has acquired Jump Bikes and Motivation (bike sharing companies) respectively to expand the service, since they found the market vacancy of the frequent use of bike and scooter for short-distance trips in urban centre. This might lead to an opportunity for a new form of MaaS business model, but it's still unknown.

It can be assumed that, the future development of MaaS would largely depends on local resources and social environment. Service iteration needs to take users' requirements at the centre to achieve sustainable developments. On this viewpoint, the form of MaaS business model should be flexible and alter by actual context. Therefore, the conclusion of different integration approaches could provide a general logic that helps to promote future MaaS service iteration into suitable direction.

4 Generalized MaaS Experience

4.1 Structure of Service Stages

Started with the common understanding of MaaS concept, objects of this study were narrowed down to scheme No. 1–9 to carry out the following content analysis. The reason is, the schemes divided into Transport Integration Approach have all take the responsibility of MaaS Operator and works as an independent platform to achieve overall planning. It matches the common understanding by most stakeholders and research institutions at present, so that it can be put forward to the practical analysis. In this process, a basic framework of MaaS user experience was initially summarized. Then a series of open-ended questions were raised according to this framework to interview the professionals from relevant schemes. These interviews aim to figure out the hidden idea of service design of MaaS in current market.

There are 2 important layers of customers' interaction with MaaS service system: (1) the interaction with service platform and (2) the interaction with multiple touch-points during journey.

Established on service experience cycle, which is composed of Pre-core service encounter period, Core service encounter period and Post-core encounter period (Voorhees et al. 2017), the user experience of MaaS could be refined as an embedded structure as shown in Fig. 9, the Core service encounter period also contains: Pre-journey, During journey and Post journey phases.

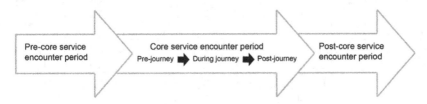

Fig. 9. Structure of service stages

Taking this structure as framework to raise questions of interviews, the data collected could have "time" as the main axle that make the analysis tractable.

4.2   Multi-level Service Model of MaaS

Customers today can create value by combining service offerings from different companies within complex service systems (Maglio et al. 2009). Multi-Level Service Design (MSD) Model is raised as an interdisciplinary method to probe the opportunities for service innovation in this context. It has divided service system into hierarchical levels: (1) Service Concept, (2) Service Structure and (3) Service Encounter (Patrício et al. 2011), and visualized the overall performance of service offering by linking the disconnected service fragments from multiple providers. Under the diagram of User-centred Design, service innovation could be clearly observed on every level that covers the system components and the network of relationships (Patrício et al. 2011). Then the co-operators can combine the result with the resources they possess to increase the feasibility of innovation proposals.

In this process, 5 professionals in related MaaS companies are interviewed with open-ended questions about the design idea of service concept and offerings, the details of cooperation networks and the tasks that users need to accomplish during journeys. The following entries (key words) were abstracted from the interviews, which are fitted into the 3 levels of MSD (Fig. 10).

On Concept and Touch-point Level, this process has obtained the similar result with previous literature that proved the key service offerings of MaaS and the smart phone's monopoly on touch-point interaction. While on Structure Level, 3 main logic lines are concluded:

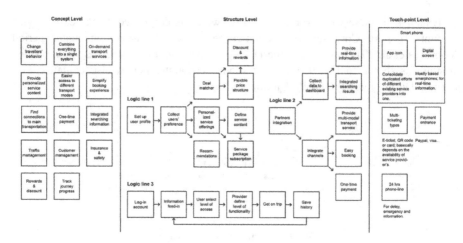

Fig. 10. Key elements and logics of MaaS MSD (Appendix 1)

Logic Line 1: Customer Profile and Function Layers. In most MaaS schemes, registering user account is regarded as a pre-requisite step to access service platform. Platform Operators use this data to filter the most appropriate service to individual customer, including travel recommendation, personalized service content and price discounts. For example, MaaS platform would record whether the customer has student card, senior card or disabled certification, then the search results and related offering would be modified to fit better with their needs.

Logic Line 2: Integration. This logic describes how the integrated resources from Data and Transport Providers are generated to service offerings. Multi-source data are integrated on the dashboard for different algorithm purposes. The output supports channel integration of transports or payment, so that the functions of multi-modal transport journey and one-stop service of booking and payment can be realized.

Logic Line 3: Overall Customer Management Loop. Corresponding to Logic Line 1, this line describes the overall management loop of MaaS service system. Normally, MaaS Operators would classify the offerings into different levels that matches the integrity of customers' data. It records the history of each trip, including the preference of transport modes and destinations, so that the user experience could be in a closed loop and every next trip would study from the previous ones to improve service performance.

Fit these elements above in with MSD model along with timeline, the following figure can be obtained.

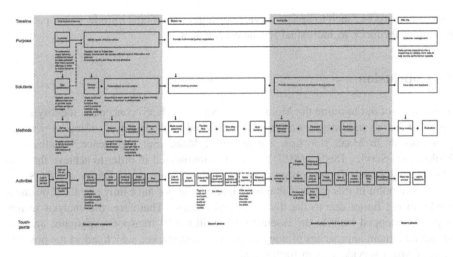

Fig. 11. Decomposition of customer activities for different levels of MaaS user experience (Appendix 2)

Comparing to the original format, this model has added Timeline and further divided Concept Level into: (1) Purpose, (2) Solutions and (3) Method to clarify some important details.

This is a top-down model. The common understanding of MaaS concept provides the general idea to relevant companies, while the logic of service system's establishment is largely depending on how they apply their resources to achieve the purposes. Then the solution and methods are the direct cause that effect customer activities and user experience.

Firstly, the ultimate purposes of MaaS concept are: the one-stop service and multi-modal transport experience. Firms need to collect individual user information to classify the layers of functions that matches the extent of customer involvement, where the greater involvement leads to the more personalized service content. To achieve the purpose, "unified platform" is raised as the solution to support customer management and provide the channel to deliver service content, for example, to simplify the booking process (e.g. Easy Payment, Uniform Ticket, Journey Booking & Reserving) and to provide necessary support during journey (e.g. Route Planning, Real-time Information & Navigation, Easy Transfer & Last Mile Service).

Since the service content is supplied by Data and Transport Providers, MaaS Provider and Platform Operator could not change the activity content or interaction modes of each touch-points, because these are lying on service context and the technical progress of terminal devices. Therefore, the granularity of service innovation may be utmostly focus on upgrading service concept, solutions and methods on upper levels.

Figure 11 can be used as a tool for user-centred research to figure out customers' requirements and the opportunities in each level to innovate service. Combined with existing resources, the framework of MaaS Eco-system can have alternative solutions fora same purpose, such to update service concept or solutions, introduce new partners, or deliver feedback to individual resource providers.

5 Conclusion

This paper set out to refine the Mobility-as-a-Service (MaaS) concept by identifying its involved Actors and Integration Approaches. Based on data analysis of interviews with professionals in MaaS start-ups, a generalized MaaS user experience visualized by Multi-Level Service Design (MSD) model is summarized in order to achieve the goal of obtaining a basic framework to carry out future User-centred Design of MaaS.

A core point in this paper is that the MaaS would not have only one fixed business model in the future due to the diverse social context. Therefore, the analysis in this paper has stepped back to the essentials of multi-modal transport experience and has identified 3 main approaches of integration in current market, which reflect the possible path of MaaS service system further innovation.

This study indicates that, the common understanding of MaaS in current market is inadequate, which is largely affected by the past experiences of similar complex service system. For this reason, early pilots are more likely to explore user requirements of the new service during the later iteration process rather than taking their proposition at the centre from the very beginning. It can be seen according to MSD is that the difference between two approaches would probably lead to the differences on the overall service system structure and end users' activity-based user experience. So, at the early stage of MaaS development, it's necessary to adopt a series of User-centred Design approach/tool that support service to find the most suitable iteration direction.

Currently, MaaS services in general sense are mainly delivered through account management, while the information transmitted through personal accounts is regarded as the basis that supports the whole service process. This method can make the service delivery become more effective, but on some other aspect, the information types could be transmitted through digital interface might be limited. And this could be a "ceiling" of MaaS to extend its service content in the future.

As can be seen from the MSD model, current service system is designed from the top (Concept Level) to the bottom (Touch-points Level), and the interactive mode is single. Take the older people as an example, they might be excluded from the service only because they have difficulties using smart phone. Considering this, this paper suggests exploring a more appropriate way to do service design by taking MSD model as the basis to solve the problems.

The last but not the least, there is no solid evidence has approved that, the emerging of MaaS has affected on customers' choices on travel planning, travel purpose or daily activities arrangement. This could be another direction for future research, because it can reveal the substantial impacts that MaaS brings to customers. In that condition, MaaS concept might need another innovation based on customers' updated value propositions.

Appendix 1. Key Elements and Logics of MaaS MSD

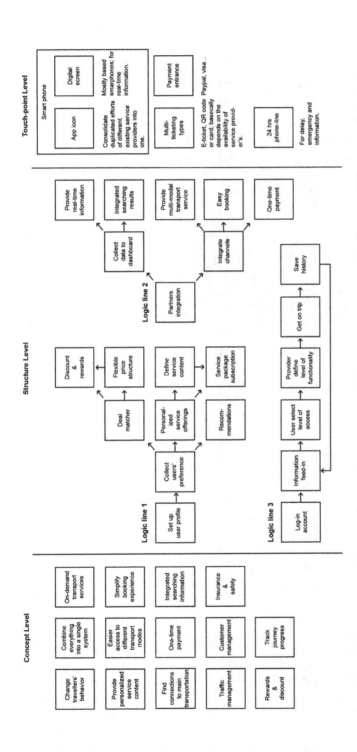

Appendix 2. Decomposition of Customer Activities for Different Levels of MaaS User Experience

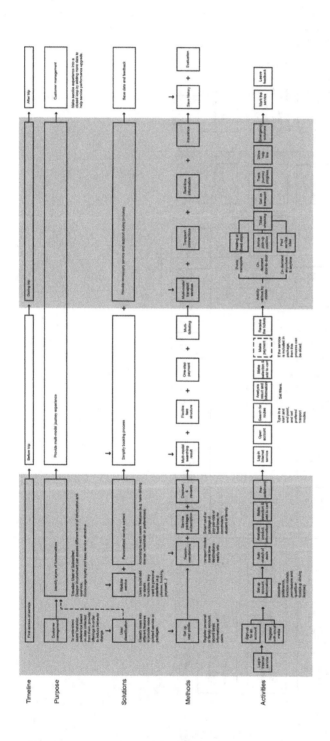

References

Botsman, R., Rogers, R.: What's Mine is Yours: How Collaborative Consumption is Changing the Way We Live, vol. 5. Collins, London (2011)

Felson, M., Spaeth, J.L.: Community structure and collaborative consumption: a routine activity approach. Am. Behav. Sci. **21**(4), 614–624 (1978)

Heikkilä, S.: Mobility as a Service-A proposal for action for the public administration. Case Helsinki (2014)

Hietanen, S.: Mobility as a service. New Transp. Model 2–4 (2014)

Jennia, E., Akia, A., Lassea, N., Janab, S., MariAnneb, K., Davidc, K.: The European roadmap 2025 for mobility as a service. In: Proceedings of 7th Transport Research Arena, TRA 2018 (2018)

Kamargianni, M., Li, W., Matyas, M., Schäfer, A.: A critical review of new mobility services for urban transport. Transp. Res. Procedia **14**, 3294–3303 (2016)

Kamargianni, M., Matyas, M., Li, W., Schäfer, A.: Feasibility Study for "Mobility as a Service" concept in London. UCL Energy Institute (2015)

Karlsson, I.M., Sochor, J., Strömberg, H.: Developing the 'Service' in mobility as a service: experiences from a field trial of an innovative travel brokerage. Transp. Res. Procedia **14**, 3265–3273 (2016)

MaaSLab: The MaaS Dictionary (2018). www.maaslab.org

Maglio, P.P., Vargo, S.L., Caswell, N., Spohrer, J.: The service system is the basic abstraction of service science. Inf. Syst. e-Bus. Manag. **7**(4), 395–406 (2009)

Matyas, M.B., Kamargianni, M.: A Holistic Overview of the Mobility-as-a-Service. Hungarian Transport Research Conference, March 2017

Motta, G., Ferrara, A., Sacco, D., You, L., Cugola, G.: Integrated mobility: a research in progress. J. Softw. Eng. Appl. **6**(03), 97 (2013)

Patrício, L., Fisk, R.P., Falcão e Cunha, J., Constantine, L.: Multilevel service design: from customer value constellation to service experience blueprinting. J. Serv. Res. **14**(2), 180–200 (2011)

Poliaková, B.: Key success factors of integrated transport systems. In: Proceedings of the 13th International Conference Reliability and Statistics in Transportation and Communication (RelStat 13), Riga, Latvia, pp. 83–90. Transport and Telecommunication Institute, Riga, October 2013

Schade, W., Krail, M., Kühn, A.: New mobility concepts: myth or emerging reality. In: Transport Research Arena-TRA 2014, 5th Conference-Transport Solutions: From Research to Deployment, April 2014

Smith, G., Sochor, J., Karlsson, I.M.: Mobility as a service: development scenarios and implications for public transport. Res. Transp. Econ. **69**, 592–599 (2018)

Sochor, J.L., Strömberg, H., Karlsson, M.: Travelers' motives for adopting a new, innovative travel service: insights from the UbiGo field operational test in Gothenburg, Sweden. In: 21st World Congress on Intelligent Transport Systems, Detroit, 7–11 September 2014 (2014)

Sochor, J.L., Strömberg, H., Karlsson, M.: An innovative mobility service to facilitate changes in travel behavior and mode choice. In: 22nd World Congress on Intelligent Transportation Systems, Bordeaux, 5–9 October 2015 (2015)

The Institution of Engineering and Technology (IET): Local Authority Guide to Emerging Transport Technology 2017–2018 (2014)

Transport System Catapult: Travellers Needs and UK Capability Study-Supporting the realization of Intelligent Mobility in the UK, October 2015.https://ts.catapult.org.uk/wp-content/uploads/2016/04/Traveller-Needs-Study.pdf

Transport System Catapult: Mobility as a Service- Exploring the Opportunity for Mobility as a Service in the UK, July 2016. https://ts.catapult.org.uk/wp-content/uploads/2016/07/Mobility-as-a-Service_Exploring-the-Opportunity-for-MaaS-in-the-UK-Web.pdf

Voorhees, C.M., et al.: Service encounters, experiences and the customer journey: defining the field and a call to expand our lens. J. Bus. Res. **79**, 269–280 (2017)

Design for Urban Resilience: A Case of Community-led Placemaking Approach in Shanghai China

Minqing Ni[(⊠)] and Tiziano Cattaneo

College of Design and Innovation, Tongji University, Shanghai, China
{niminqing, tiziano.cattaneo}@tongji.edu.cn

Abstract. This paper presents a recent design activism initiative named Open Your Space in Chinese urban context. The project aims to help the urban community acquire a better sense of sustainability, comfortability, and accessibility to public space, where citizens, place managers and local government could connect together through socially engaged and participatory process. The paper advocates the design initiative influence of public space in culture, social context and social system, analyses how to use public space design intervention strategies to modeling resilient community mechanism. By synthesizing ideas of resilience, the paper uses the community-led placemaking approach in order to create the third place and a new paradigm of spatial and social resilience.

Keywords: Urban resilience · Design activism ·
Community-led placemaking · Social resilience · Public space ·
Resilient community

1 Introduction

Shanghai is a city with speedy urban sprawl, rapid urbanization has greatly accelerated environmental and social development. The challenges follow up like the DesignX introduced that the complex sociotechnical systems such as healthcare, transportation, governmental policy, and environmental protection [1]. Urbanization in Shanghai has also created numerous problems ranging from the local to the global scale: migration, housing, urban pressures, social inequality, social disconnection etc.

Shanghai's population was 89.3% (20.6 million) urban and 10.7% (2.5 million) rural. More than 39% of Shanghai's residents are long-term migrants, a number that has tripled in ten years. Migrants from the rural areas of the country turned to Shanghai, giving the city the growth it was after [2]. The housing price of Shanghai have been rising precipitously for a decade, a standard apartment can cost multiple millions of yuan to purchase, and thousands of yuan to rent, making housing affordability the top concern of most low- and middle- income households. The house price-income ratio classifies much of China as "severely unaffordable" [3]. Those problems have been appeared and influenced in the everyday life, lack of social cohesion and low degree of social resilience is evident and damage the quality of living condition [4].

© Springer Nature Switzerland AG 2019
P.-L. P. Rau (Ed.): HCII 2019, LNCS 11577, pp. 207–222, 2019.
https://doi.org/10.1007/978-3-030-22580-3_16

How the designers attempted to combine their professional skills toward social change? How the design school becomes effective agents of change in the contexts where they are situated? Design activism is the one of them encompasses a wide range of socially and environmentally responsible actions in design. As Lou Yongqi argued that design requires a new, more proactive approach to economic and social change. Design must shift from passive to active [5].

In May 2015, a research and design initiative entitled "Open Your Space (OYS)" was launched under this background. The project aims to help the urban community acquire a better sense of sustainability, comfortability, and accessibility to public space. The goal is not to explore new undeveloped spaces, but to regenerate existing spaces and prioritizing design of the social functions of how to integrate space and demand, to study "people" in the community's living conditions and methods as the main core, in order to practice design-driven social innovation strategies for Chinese urban community-building and resilient transformation.

After experiencing a rapid urbanization process, Shanghai has been transformed from incremental to inventory development [6]. Activating neglected urban public space is the great opportunity for enhancing the quality of urban life, the project adopts to engage in social and political issues and develop solutions through small, incremental steps. The project carry out the research focuses on urban communities in a local context and aims to upgrade community cohesion through sustainable development on a more daily and microscopic perspective.

The project its significance includes the importance of people as both objective and subjective. The "object" emphasizes the living condition need to be renewal, and the "subject" emphasizes the initiative that the residents can play the big role in the community building process. The case not only roots on placemaking experiments, but also pays attention to the community-led empowerment, toward to a new paradigm of spatial and social resilience.

2   Urban Resilience Context

The concept of resilience originated in ecology, by the Canadian scholar Crawford Stanley Holling [7], and then began to intervene in different disciplines, now extended to the ecological, technical, social and economic four-dimensional perspective. The concept of resilient city was initially applied to disaster preparedness, especially the urban facilities to respond and recover from dangerous conditions. In recent years, this concept has been expanded, resilience is the capacity of a social-ecological system to absorb or withstand perturbations and other stressors such that the system remains within the same regime, essentially maintaining its structure and functions. It describes the degree to which the system is capable of self-organization, learning and adaptation [8]. Resilience and sustainable city as the development direction for the next 30 years, urban community is facing environmental, economic and social well-being and other adaptive problems, put forward to use of renovation, repair and other urban rehabilitation methods to make the community more healthy and more dynamic [9].

The 'resilience movement' has gained traction all over the world as organizations and governments attempt to address the widespread challenges of the 21st century that are becoming harder to ignore. The Paris Agreement, the 2030 Agenda for Sustainable Development, 100 Resilient Cities and the New Urban Agenda (adopted at Habitat III in 2016) all represent the desire and capacity of humanity to work together and plan ahead [10].

Urban resilience is a concept that recognises the capacity of humanity to adapt, grow and survive in the face of change and upheaval [10]. Social resilience was operationalized as social systems ability to maintain function while promoting social trust, reciprocity, collaboration, and character between networks of varying scales [11]. Keck and Sakdapolrak define social resilience across three main dimensions: coping capacities, adaptive capacities and transformative capacities [12]. Manzini considers that contemporary societies are fragile. This fragility has different causes, but a major factor is played by the lack of social cohesion within societies, or more precisely, by their low degree of social resilience [13].

How to use design intervention strategies to create resilient community toward spatial, system and social change? By synthesizing ideas of resilience, a design action has been taken and shifting the reaction to preparation, we believe design activism as a term to denote creative practices that invoke social and political issues, it shows more and more evidence that the initiative has been undertaken by design professionals who choose to pursue socially responsible practices. Open your space project is the case will be discussed by following, the project is created to explore the potential of placemaking approach for social resilience, connecting community in place, empowering the citizens through social engagement and participatory process.

3   A Design Activism Initiative Achieves Big Social Impact

The OYS project has been taken place at the community named Siping, locates in the midwest of Yangpu district of Shanghai, it is 2.75 km^2 in area and has a population of over a hundred thousand. Siping community includes one of Shanghai's first workers village called Anshan village. It was built in the 50's of last century and become one of the largest villages in Shanghai at that time. After continuous expansion, it now includes 8 villages (Fig. 1). In the community, two thirds of the buildings recognized as an old community due to housing condition, outdated infrastructure, and lacking of quality in public space, and the neighborhood looks less vital and strength. In the same time, there is lots of leftover space and hidden space has not been used very well.

What can design add and what can the designers contribute while enhancing problem-finding and observational skills? How design could address the complex issues in the built environment? After the observation and preliminary research, the team of OYS project proactively submitted a proposal to local government in 2015, which presents the studies of the residual public space and how to improve the public life of the Siping community, by involving the administrative office, local residents and students, designers and artists. Fortunately, the project gained full support from the government smoothly, the design intervention strategy starts to influence the version of top down strategy.

"Open Your Space: Design intervention in Siping community" as a pilot project has been launched in 2015, till now already 4 years. It becomes annual project contains

Fig. 1. Siping community includes one of Shanghai's first workers villages, which built in the 50's of last century.

physical spaces with social and cultural significance. The project strives to be a sociocultural framework that represents a special design attitude for collective space and public activities. "Open" as a keyword of the project due to its numerous meanings, such as: physical, cultural, emotional, inclusive, sustainable, connected, shared and interactive. The term "open", together with the term "space" involves co-creation, this is an emerging paradigm that advocates new procedures in imagining the public space. Like the Design Harvests project, OYS adapted the similar acupunctural design approach, a series of small but connected design intervention, to generate systemic changes [14].

The project was the collateral event of 2015 Bi-City Biennale of Urbanism \Architecture. This initiative brought along with a case exhibition, site-specific projects and micro design interventions as well as a community creative festival and several cultural activities. Fifteen site-specific projects and more than sixty micro design interventions have been spread across outdoor public space within the center of Siping community, by providing perspectives on how design activism and placemaking approach inspires people to create and improve their public places (Fig. 2). OYS project follows three main design strategies: empower multiple-stakeholders to drive local change, encourage creativity and new appropriation, and enhance the diversity of the community environment (Fig. 3).

OYS focuses on moving beyond design activism as a curiosity, to make a conscious effort to work toward a social and culture stance. The active intervention on public space is a part of social innovation strategy in Chinese context. Many community workshops together with local residents have been held, residents shared their concerns

Fig. 2. The sidewalk propaganda slogan wall has been replaced with the residents' portrait of Siping community in 2015.

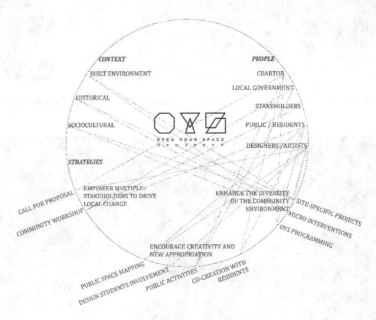

Fig. 3. Open Your Space concept map.

about public spaces were used in the community (Fig. 4). pointed out the positive and negative space and built ideal models of the public spaces they would like to see. The young generations also have been invited into the workshop, they were exciting about those activities and same time they contributed their imagination of the future public space in community (Fig. 5). Co-creation as a design tool to involves the residents fully in the process and helps boost the chances of engagement by pulling the residents further into the fold.

The team firmly believe that the success of public spaces can largely be attributed to the activities, events, recreational uses and social gatherings that take place there,

Fig. 4. Local residents shared their concerns about public spaces in the community.

Fig. 5. The young generations participated in the workshop express their wishes for the community public space.

whether planned or spontaneous, ongoing or temporary. Beside the design interventions, the OYS public program including exhibitions, forums, movie night and festival (Figs. 6 and 7).

Fig. 6. One of Open street festival booth that organized by the community school in 2017.

Fig. 7. The poster of Open your space 4th edition in 2018 with residents portraits.

The design workshops and programming were embracing the principles of activism. The evolvement of the design students was also a challenge to let them to rethink as the activist designers (Fig. 8). Design plays an active role to connect public sector and people in order to trigger more participation. Rooted in community-based participation, OYS explores the possibility of design thinking for innovative problem solving and generating new vision. Those actions totally change the image the community used to be, they meet together, listen and express for the same goal of community building, we believe this is the foundation of resilient community. Design activism principle help produce design interventions, events and services that are capable of generating meaningful encounters and resilience, sustainable ways of being and doing. Design has played a very important role during China's transition and "development" of opportunities. Design has shifted from the previously concerns about the material world to gradually expanding to non-material areas. The objects of design are also extended: from symbols to objects, to activities, to relationships, to services and processes, to systems, environments, and mechanisms. Real innovation is often learning by doing [15].

Fig. 8. Design intervention in residential common space co-design workshop with Design students and local residents.

4   Building the Resilient Community Through Community-led Placemaking Solution

Shanghai Playscape is a new public space, a micro-intervention and low cost project. It has been realized as part of the 4th edition of Open Your Space (OYS) in 2018. The project area is located at the core of Siping community which is essentially a residential area built in 60 s (Fig. 9). 80 m long, 3 m wide obsolete walking path in Fuxin Road, is turned into a stylish pocket park as well as the playground (Fig. 10). The project retains the original greenery layout, add the letters combines with initial name of College of Design and Innovation (D&I) and "四平 (siping)" in Chinese characters. The three dimensional letters represent the collaboration between the college and community, which are composed by logogram and has been merged along with a slide, swing, benches and photo shooting points (Fig. 11). The logogram becomes the new symbol of the pocket garden. Five letters with playful facilities, "D" with seating area, "&" with slide, "I" with swing, "四(si)" becomes a corridor with window, "平 (ping)" together with a seesaw, consistent with in Chinese means balance (Fig. 12). Identification and graphic treatments were designed to serve as placemaking features and enhanced the quality of residential public space.

Fig. 9. 80 m long, 3 m wide obsolete walking path in Fuxin Road, Shanghai, China.

The placemaking solution associating the letters with playful facilities, a bright, colorful pavement provides a new walking experience (Fig. 13). The solution creates an overlay of signage and interactive experience which offer the space a visual continuity while activate overall space. The remained 6 flowerbeds have been replaced with new flowers and self managed by the local residents, schools and enterprises. This action creates long-term community engagement for this place. The project has achieved a positive impact to the local community, co-creation as a design tool involves the residents fully in the process and helps boost the chances of engagement.

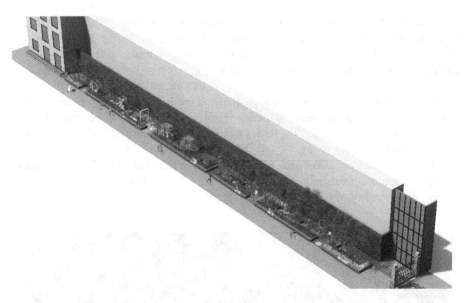

Fig. 10. The walking path is turned into a stylish pocket park as well as the playground, rendering bird view.

Fig. 11. Logogram has been merged along with a slide, swing, benches and photo shooting points.

It gives the identity to the community and contributes to activating the space beyond merely being a signage. The bottom up initiative pays particular attention to the physical, cultural, and social identities that define a place and support its ongoing progress.

Fig. 12. The logogram becomes the new symbol of the public space, "D" creates relax seating area.

Fig. 13. The placemaking solution associating the letters with playful facilities and a bright, colorful pavement, it turned to the pocket garden and playground.

Public spaces is for everyone's enjoyment, and if the possess a clear identity, should become "places". Building or rebuilding a place is important from various points of view, as Manzini states; recognizing the value of places goes hand in hand with the emergence of a new idea of well-being – a sustainable well-being. Questioning to what extent places contribute to quality of life could be a major driver of the placemaking dynamism [16]. Every public space should be designed with full consideration for diversity, and as the "third place" for bringing out features to maintain, enhance, and communicate [17]. Urban Intervention in public space has been associated with a changed understanding of the relationship between the social and the spatial [18].

We consider the Shanghai Playscape project as a collective project with well-organized participatory process. Three different participants have been involved in this project:

1. Siping sub-district office: as a representative from public sector, they play a significant role in financial and policy decision. Three departments from the office are involved: Department of Party and Government Affairs, Department of Culture, and Department of Administrative. They pays important role for negotiating with different public sectors. The idea to associate with local government's top down strategy could be get the process smooth.
2. Local residents in Siping community, the actual users of the public space. During the workshop, they were encouraged to express their memories, life stories and wishes related to local community (Fig. 14). For the long-term strategy for the place, the self-managed garden evolved different groups of the residents, transform the space to more creative and authentic places and build the social connection (Fig. 15).

Fig. 14. The father brings his daughter to participate the design workshop and sharing the story how the family activities around the community.

Fig. 15. The high school students were planting in one of the flowerbed managed by their school.

3. Professional designers, researchers, PhD students and students from Tongji University along with professional fabricators and construction companies. They created the great platform for the neighborhood, insured the quality of the place and more about inspiring them to do-it-themselves.

   In contrast to the state control of urban design and planning prevalent in China, this bottom-up action suggest an alternative mode of development that embodies the subjectivity and agency of urban dwellers. The place becomes the center of collective life, expressing a community's cultural diversity and a foundation of their identity, and it shows that key elements for individual and communal social well-being in the community. It is through the creation of these places the physical, social, environmental, connections, and economic health of urban communities can be nurtured [19].

5   Conclusion

The radical shifts are needed to allow any form of activism to evolve. Design as thought and action for solving problems and imagining new futures. OYS project start with problem finding by the designers and consistently works toward developing innovative solutions to benefit the community. During the entire process, the project team has gone through substantial negotiation with the local government that could be absorbed in the historical and cultural context of the community space. All the actions rather than give the form but more beneficial content for the community. It is a social constructive process of citizen engagement through design activism and community participation. The design interventions have helped engage local residents and other social assets in the process of local development, transformed the public spaces in Siping area into both fun and functional, an organic community with a good balance of old and new resources [20].

The negotiations, mediations, compromises, collaborations, and conflicts have left a meaningful footprint of the project. The major difficulties were in implementation with complex social issues. In OYS project, the team has to deal with government, designers and residents, the process involve complex human and social elements, especially in Chinese context. Each community has their own unique background and range of challenges. This is why we believe in that empowering multiple stakeholders for local level, community-led solutions. Placemaking, incorporates the role as agent contributing in an original way to social building of places. OYS dedicated to helping people create and sustain public spaces that build stronger communities and also try to help citizens transform their public spaces into vital places that highlight local assets, spur rejuvenation and serve common needs.

We believe that building the social equality, community connection and social cohesion are the foundation of urban resilience. Rooted in community-based participation, OYS explores the possibility of design thinking for innovative problem solving and generating new vision. Design activism principle help produce design interventions, events and services that are capable of generating meaningful encounters and resilience, sustainable ways of being and doing.

Through the OYS project, we've proved that giving people a shared goal and good place are a successful way of creating social cohesion. As described by Manzini, resilient systems are characterized by diversity, redundancy, feedback, and continuous experimentation in order to make the viability of the public space more visible and tangible [21]. The existence of a multiplicity and variety of places is a precondition of a more resilient natural, social, and productive system. The research and practices explore the potential of design intervention to reimagine, reinvigorate, and revitalize urban public space, although, design problems are "indeterminate" and "wicked" [22].

OYS project focused on clarifying and characterizing social resilience by creating good place and the community building process. The design solution requires collaboration and agreement of multiple social entities and political actors. These eventually constraints require compromises. But fortunately, the concept of "open" is embodied in the open motion and open the wide version of the local government by providing complete flexibility to the design team, also it is reflected in the highly open design process: multidimensional contribution and participation of students, designers, architects, artists, and local residents. The project collectively redefines ideas of public space and its multiple functions. It has convened scholars, artists, architects, and planners to engage contemporary critical discourses and practices on urban space. The practice investigated the definitions of public space across disciplines and the tools, tactics and consequences of reclaiming [13].

China's undergoing transition, the social, political, cultural, and economic relations are negotiated amidst rapidly changing urban space [23]. The composition of public space itself is a contested and contextualized category. Stimulated by the changing waves of urbanization, OYS project is working on a possible solution to ensure resilient community by promoting social resilience in a variety of urban systems and processes. The project also hope to contribute resilient community in Chinese context by facilitating the creation and activation of urban places that encourage people to participate in the design process and public awareness social understanding; Assembling citizens to lead community led placemaking; Creating an enabling environment to support local leaders and equipping communities with the tools and know-how to develop and maintain their own community projects. The changes can not happened in one day, follow the steps by years, we aim to encourage communities to support and connect each other in times of need and be prepared for whatever challenges the future may hold.

References

1. Norman, D.A., Stappers, P.J.: DesignX: complex sociotechnical systems. SheJi: J. Des. Econ. Innov. **1**(2), 83–106 (2015)
2. World Population Review Shanghai Population (2019). http://worldpopulationreview.com/world-cities/shanghai-population/. Accessed 10 Feb 2019
3. Lack of affordable housing threatens China's urban dream. https://www.chinadialogue.net/article/show/single/en/6365-Lack-of-affordable-housing-threatens-China-s-urban-dream. Accessed 10 Feb 2019
4. Manzini, E., Thorpe, A.: Weaving people and places: art and design for resilient communities. Sheji: J. Des. Econ. Innov. **4**(1), 1–9 (2018)
5. Lou, Y.: Enabling society: new design processes in China the case of chongming. J. Des. Strat. **4**(1), 22–28 (2010)
6. Shanghai master plan 2017–2035. Striving for the excellent global city. http://www.shanghai.gov.cn/newshanghai/xxgkfj/2035004.pdf. Accessed 10 Feb 2019
7. Holling, C.S.: Resilience and stability of ecological systems. Ann. Rev. Ecol. Syst. **4**, 1–23 (1973)
8. Gunderson, L.H., Holling, C.S. (eds.): Panarchy: Understanding Transformations in Systems of Humans and Nature. Island Press, Washington DC (2002)
9. Pearson, L., Newton, P., Roberts, P. (eds.): Resilient Sustainable Cities: A Future. Routledge, New York (2014)
10. Urban Resilience and the Importance of Community. https://codesignstudio.com.au/urban-resilience-and-the-importance-of-community/?lpw=2140. Accessed 11 Feb 2019
11. Putnam, R.D.: Bowling alone: America's declining social capital. J. Democr. **6**(1), 65–78 (1995)
12. Keck, M., Sakdapolrak, P.: What is Social Resilience? Lessons Learned and Ways Forward. Bd. 67, H. 1, pp. 5–19, Erdkunde, Bonn (2013)
13. Ni, M.: Introduction. In: Ni, M., Zhu, M. (eds.) Open Your Space: Design Intervention for Urban Resilience, pp. 23–31. Tongji University Press, Shanghai (2017)
14. Lou, Y., Valsecchi, F., Diaz, C.: Design Harvests: An Acupunctural Design Approach Towards Sustainability. Mistra Urban Futures, Gothenburg (2013)
15. Lou, Y.: Design activism in an era of transformation. Art Des. **7**, 17–19 (2015). (in Chinese)
16. Manzini, E.: Design, When Everybody Designs: An Introduction to Design for Social Innovation, p. 189. The MIT Press, Boston (2015)
17. Oldenburg, R.: The Great Good Place, p. 14. Da Capo Press, Boston (1999)

18. Charter of Public Space. http://www.biennalespaziopubblico.it/wp-content/uploads/2013/11/CHARTER-OF-PUBLIC-SPACE_June-2013_pdf-.pdf. Accessed 14 Feb 2019
19. Ni, M.: Open your space: a design-driven initiative in Chinese urban community. In: Ni, M., Zhu, M. (eds.) Open Your Space: Design Intervention for Urban Resilience, pp. 83–115. Tongji University Press, Shanghai (2017)
20. Ni, M.: Open your space: a design activism initiative in chinese urban community. In: Rau, P.-L.P. (ed.) CCD 2017. LNCS, vol. 10281, pp. 412–431. Springer, Cham (2017). https://doi.org/10.1007/978-3-319-57931-3_33
21. Manzini, E., Till, J. (eds.): Cultures of Resilience: Ideas, p. 9. Hato Press, London (2015)
22. Buchanan, R.: Wicked problems in design thinking. Des. Issues **8**(2), 5–21 (1992)
23. Cattaneo, T., Giorgi, E., Ni, M.: Landscape, architecture and environmental regeneration: a research by design approach for inclusive tourism in a rural village in China. Sustainability **11**(1), 128 (2018)

"We Are Actively Reaching Out to Different Organizations and Folks to Come in": Collective Design of the Vancouver Tool Library Project

Xiaolan Wang[1](✉) and Ron Wakkary[2](✉)

[1] Guangdong University of Technology, Guangzhou, Guangdong, China
wangxiaolan@gdut.edu.cn
[2] Simon Fraser University, Surrey, BC, Canada
rwakkary@sfu.ca

Abstract. This paper reports on a case study that describes the collective design process of the Vancouver Tool Library, a non-profit community service cooperative that provides tools to its members in the city of Vancouver. By using the theory of infrastructuring in relation to the theoretical framework publics (Le Dantec 2016), we describe the project through its confronted issues and the emerged work of infrastructuring in the project. We also reflect on the infrastructuring work and analyze the characteristics of the collective design in the Vancouver Tool Library project. On the one hand, this research highlights the aspects of the design process in which interaction designers can play a significant role and further support the collective design in a community-based project. On the other hand, applying the notion of infrastructuring to the collective design of community-based project provides an opportunity to extend the understanding of design toward a more dynamic and open-ended process where conflicts, standards, and adaptions are interwoven within an infrastructuring process.

Keywords: Infrastructuring · Collective design · Community-based project · Case study · Interaction design

1 Introduction

Today, an increasing number of people, from different cultures, are collectively designing their projects to create their own lifestyles based on their own ideas of well-being. These new ideas not only meet people's needs but also create new social relationships or collaborations [18]. However, very few researchers in interaction design have explored and investigated the underlying design processes of those projects, and fewer have reflected on how interaction design can support such processes.

In this work, we apply the theory of infrastructuring in relation to the theoretical framework publics [16] in understanding the collective design of a community-based project – Vancouver Tool Library. We draw on the framework proposed by Le Dantec because it provides a practical analytical tool that is an alternative to other related

© Springer Nature Switzerland AG 2019
P.-L. P. Rau (Ed.): HCII 2019, LNCS 11577, pp. 223–240, 2019.
https://doi.org/10.1007/978-3-030-22580-3_17

infrastructuring frameworks (e.g., technology driven infrastructuring). Le Dantec's framing can be easily situated in and developed further through interaction design research.

The question this study aims to address is: How does the theory of infrastructuring in relation to the theoretical framework of publics [16] effectively describe the collective design of community-based projects in an urban Canadian city? To answer this question, we apply qualitative case study as our research methodology. The case we selected is the Vancouver Tool Library project, which is a non-profit community service cooperative that provides tools to its members. The goal of the Vancouver Tool Library project is to contribute to a more sustainable life style and enable its community to access a rich collection of tools without having to buy or rent them.

The purpose of this study is to validate the effectiveness of the theory of infrastructuring in relation to the theoretical framework of publics [16] in describing the design process of the community-based project and to further uncover the characteristics of the design process that interaction designers can support. In what follows, we describe an overview of related work on infrastructuring theory. We then describe findings from our case study. We conclude with a discussion of the characteristics of the collective design of the project and opportunities for interaction design to support such community-rooted projects.

2   Research Background

2.1   The Concept of Infrastructuring

The term 'Infrastructuring', or 'artful infrastructuring', coined by Karasti and collaborators [12, 14], is an attempt to build a sensitive understanding of community participatory design. Karasti and Syrjänen characterized infrastructuring as a continuous process that is constantly becoming, and as the integration of new tools and technologies with existing people, materials and tools [14].

Infrastructuring draws on the notion of infrastructure [23, 24] and Suchman's notion of "artful integrations" [25:99]. By the notion of "artful integrations", Suchman highlights the significance of the integrations across artifacts and the integrations between devices and the settings of their use, rather than the discrete or decontextualized artifacts [25]. Through artful integrations, she argues, innovation and change is no longer merely brought about by professional designers but also could be made by everyday practitioners. Building on the above two notions, infrastructuring refers to a continuous process in which multiple relations are developing and socio-material assembly is constantly becoming.

More recently, researchers have worked at the intersections of infrastructuring, information and communications technology, and participatory design. For instance, to describe the dynamics in the infrastructuring process of cyberinfrastructure projects, Edwards et al. denoted three types dynamics - reverse salients, gateways, and path dependence [8]. The three dynamics have been embraced and developed by many researchers on information technology (e.g., [13, 26]). Also, focusing on infrastructuring in the field of information technology, in his book A Vast Machine, Edward proposed "infrastructural inversion", which emphasizes models and data of climate and the relationships between them [7]. In addition, the concept of infrastructuring has been applied by participatory design researchers in the workplace [21], in communities with open, and heterogeneous structures (e.g., [2, 3, 9]), and the context of jurisdictional identity schemes [4]. The works mentioned above show that the theory of infrastructuring is powerful. However, the majority of the studies confined themselves to technology design and the social aspects are overlooked. Furthermore, these examples limited the understandings of continuous infrastructure development to its longevity, but are short on articulation of the dynamics, changes and the evolutions that happened in it.

In our use of the term infrastructuring, we turn chiefly to Le Dantec, who investigated the application of infrastructuring in the formation of publics at particular groups [5]. We selected Le Dantec's framework over other related frameworks of infrastructuring because Le Dantec's framing can be more easily located within, operated, and developed further through interaction design research. It provides a practical lens for interpreting the dynamics in community-based projects and offers scaffolding that other related (and even design-oriented) frameworks of infrastructuring do not provide. In the section below, we will provide a brief overview of the framework of publics. Particularly, we will present how the infrastructuring is defined regards to publics.

2.2   Infrastructuring and Publics

Public, a conception from Dewey [6], is defined as a particular configuration of people bound by common cause in confronting a shared issue. They are not a priori social groups. A public "seeks to work constructively within the messy and contentious reality of discourse where all voices – from mainstream to marginal – jockey to participate and arrive at desired outcomes" [16:15]. The frame of publics thus provides an issue-oriented focus of relevance in community-based work. Furthermore, it provides "a pragmatic perspective and authority dynamics form complex and fluid social alignments" [5:246].

The frame of publics includes three elements – issues, attachments, and infrastructures. First, a basic element to form a public is issues. Issues determine the individuals who get involved, thus shaping the public. The evolution of issues drives the "dynamic and contingent nature of publics" [16:18]. Second, attachments are the "organizing force" that makes actors, institutions, and artifacts affected by an issue gather and take actions toward a common end. Attachments include multiple relations and motivations, central to which is the interplay between "dependency on" and "commitment to" [19]. Attachments are important because they build out the collective capacities to act on issues [16:63].

Based on the concepts of publics, issues, and attachments, in his book, Le Dantec articulated that the process that a public integrates social and technical resources to act towards issues is a process of infrastructuring:

As a public identifies and marshals the social and technical resources to contend with social issues, these resources become a form of infrastructure for the public: a durable and ready-to-hand support that enables constituents of a public to act. The work of creating it is a process described succinctly as infrastructuring, in which the infrastructure arises out of the relations and the resources entangled in the present issues and attachments [16:26].

According to Le Dantec, what infrastructuring does, is "move from a focus on creating a particular artifact (and the attendant fixity of context and artifact) to design as constituting a public in which issues and attachments are conjoined into sociotechnical networks for addressing present and future conditions" [16:28]. With respect to publics, Le Dantec sought to define infrastructuring as "the work of integrating sociotechnical resources – via existing and newly articulate attachments – that enable adoption and appropriation beyond the initial scope of the design space" [16:26].

This notion of infrastructuring provides us a perspective for understanding how individuals, artifacts, and institutions gather around a set of issues in community-based settings. It offers a vantage point to articulate and interpret the ongoing and dynamic process of the development of community-based projects. Specifically, we can explore the issues, actors, artifacts, and institutions affected by the issues, and the relations between them.

Above we presented the concepts of infrastructuring. Our goal in this work is to apply this concept to further the understanding of the underlying design process of community-based project and uncover the characteristics of the process. The theoretical framework articulated above serves as an analytical tool to reveal the inner workings of the tool library project.

3   Methodology

Our methodology approach is qualitative case study [31]. There is a shared understanding that the case study method has advantages in providing a holistic description of social phenomenon within a real-life and contemporary context.

In the process of data collection, we interviewed seven participants who were involved in the project to understand their collective design in the project. We also observed the projects by serving as a volunteer and participating in events, such as workshops. The site of the project as well as the working environment of participants was directly observed during the fieldwork. Moreover, documents related to the project, such as design files, policy files, agreements, annual reports, and online articles were also collected as evidence. Raw data, such as interviews and field notes, were converted into formatted write-ups and prepared for analysis.

The context of the case selected in this research is the city of Vancouver, which is located on the west coast of Canada. It is a dense city with citizens from diverse cultures and ethics. A large part of the population is immigrants, including Chinese, South Asians, Latin Americans, and so on. In 2011, the City Council approved the Greenest City 2020 Action Plan, which was developed to guide Vancouver to become the greenest city in the world by 2020. There are 10 goals outlined in this action plan: climate and renewables, green building, green transportation, zero waste, access to nature, clean water, local food, clean air, green economy, and lighter footprint. With respect to the goal of lighter footprint, the city will "develop a municipal sharing economy strategy" and "continue to expand the Greenest City Fund" [27:64].

Therefore, a variety of projects that are considered as building blocks to reach those goals have gained overwhelming support from the city (Fig. 1).

Fig. 1. The environment and interior of the Vancouver Tool Library

The Vancouver Tool Library is a non-profit community service cooperative in Vancouver. It was established in 2011. It provides tools for a variety of projects, such as everyday repair and gardening. As the library develops, its tool inventory is growing quickly. Currently, the Vancouver Tool Library offers over 2,000 tools to its 1,800 members. Members of Vancouver Tool Library can rent tools by paying a membership fee. In addition to tools, the Vancouver Tool Library provides diverse workshops, such as making wine racks, zippered pouch sewing, and sustainable home building. The goal of the Vancouver Tool Library project is to contribute to a more sustainable life style. It aims to enable its community to access a rich collection of tools without having to buy or rent them. It also helps individuals to save money and space that would otherwise be invested in tools. It has the benefit to the community of reducing waste. Furthermore, it connects neighbours and supports community building. The individuals who are running the Vancouver Tool Library are almost entirely volunteers. There is only one paid staff. Board of Directors, volunteers, and members keep Vancouver Tool Library moving forward. Currently, the Board of Directors consists of seven individuals who are responsible for strategic planning, budgeting, and volunteer recruitment. Coordinators were recently set up to help Directors with specific projects. Volunteers help manage the shop, maintain tools, and assist with workshops and other events. They believe that the library is an initiative that fosters the process of building vibrant neighbourhoods in the city.

4   Collective Design of the Vancouver Tool Library Project

In this section, we present the findings from studying the case Vancouver Tool Library project. By using the theory of infrastructuring in relation to the theoretical framework publics [16], we describe the project through its confronted issues and the emerged work of infrastructuring in the project. Again, our goal is to understand the collective design process and describe the characteristics of this process that can be supported by interaction designers.

4.1   Issues

From the data analysis, there are three critical issues that emerged in the collective design of Vancouver Tool Library project. They are *volunteering issues*, *cannot afford additional spaces*, and *lending tools as business*.

Volunteering Issues. The tool library is a volunteer-run cooperative. Except for its manager, the only paid staff, all the board members, coordinators and shop volunteers contribute their time and energy almost for free. Volunteers are waived their membership fee. However, mostly relying on its volunteers brings problems to the development of the tool library.

The time availability of volunteers varies. Balancing personal life and time contributed to the library is not easy, especially for those who have full-time jobs. When much time is asked to put into the tool library, the result is that many volunteers are burned out and quit their roles in the library. Therefore, finding the delicate balance between keeping the tool library running smoothly and not letting people burn out is very important. One interviewee commented that many of the prior board members were burned out because of too much work.

We had a lot of burn out within the board prior to our recent board been voted in. People were just too stressed, because they are doing both the strategic planning and taking on ground level projects. Being a volunteer position, that was just too much. (Gary)

Cannot Afford Additional Spaces. The second issue is that volunteers do not have sufficient money to afford a bigger space they need. As a library, the restricted space limits its capacity to store a larger amount of tools. As the tool coordinator expressed, they want to buy some tools but do not have space to fit all of them.

There are other tools we want to afford, but we have constraints on space. We don't have enough room to fit all the tools we may want to buy. (Paul)

In addition, the limited space makes it difficult for the volunteers to run workshops with a big group of participants or provide a workspace for members to work on their projects. One participant described his desire to have a larger space for people to do projects and run workshops.

It would be a dream to have a really large space where we can have people drop in and work on projects. But right now, you just don't have the space to house people's work. We can do workshops but we have very limited numbers of people that can do it. (David)

Lending Tools as Business. Lending tools is challenging per se. Different from books, tools have diverse shapes, functions, materials, and components. Maintaining a variety of tools requires much knowledge. Moreover, organizing and managing tools in an efficient way is not easy.

First, being a group that lends tools and encourages people to learn to use tools, volunteers face the challenge that tools may get broken intentionally or unintentionally. One participant described that not all members value the shared tools.

I have someone come in and say 'do you have this thickness planer? I got this wood. It is really dirty and I don't want to run it into my planer but I want to run it through your planer.' So, he is placing less value on our tools than his own personal tools. We encourage people who are new to the tools and who don't know tools to come in and just have a go, because we believe one way people learn is by doing. We want to support that. We also hope they use tools as intended. Because we have to repair that tool whether they were intentioned or not. Of course, tools get broken. Those challenges are just the nature of the business. (Paul)

The second challenge of being a tool library is about organizing and managing its tool inventory. For example, organizing tools in an efficient way so that volunteers can quickly find each tool is difficult.

In the physical tool inventory, when a new tool arrives, it is assigned with a code and labeled by Sharpie or by the code being carved into the tool. However, not all the tools are big enough to write a code on, for example the wrenches. There are also tools that come in a set. It is hard to really make sure each piece of it is returned. The following quote describes the participant's question about managing the small tools and those in sets (Fig. 2).

The wrenches are small and big and there are a lot of them. In theory, every single wrench should have an ID. There is another problem, that things are in a set, and a set has many different parts. So, when they come back, we get all our parts back. If we don't, how do we know and we end up with an incomplete set that doesn't actually meet the needs, but it was not obvious that it doesn't work. (Paul)

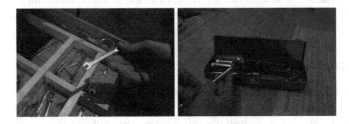

Fig. 2. The tools that have different size (left) and come in set (right).

Moreover, many codes are worn out or even disappear after a period of time. Almost all interviewees expressed worries about the coding system used in their tool management and tracking (Fig. 3).

The third challenge in lending tools relates to the digital system – myTurn – which was uniquely created for the tool library to track and manage tools. The digital system

Fig. 3. Codes on tools.

used for tracking tools is not synchronously updated. The asynchronous issue brings challenges to both the volunteers and the customers of the tool library. For example, participants described that sometimes tools listed as available in the online system may be under repair or otherwise not physically available.

Our inventory is extremely varied. Some tools are checked in but not. Because often the times, either the tool is in repair, or has been lost, that inventory online has not been updated. So, that is challenging. (David)

In addition, participants also expressed their expectation to have a more efficient way in using the digital system. Scanning, instead of manually inputting the code into the system, would be more appreciated.

If there is a way to scan a barcode, that would be easier. (David)

Ideally, we can just scan them and the system automatically does its thing. Right now, we have a manual system and we manually come up with ID. (Paul)

Another shortage of the digital system is that it lacks the financial record of renting tools.

Another one is myTurn. It has some limitations. MyTurn meets our basic needs. But there are definitely a lot of issues with the software. It is not good at recording the financial side of everything. (James)

Above we presented the issues confronted in the project of Vancouver Tool Library. The issues provide a "point of entry" [16:34] for articulating how different actors and artifacts and institutions are enrolled in the dynamic and complex collective design process in the Vancouver Tool Library project. In the following sections, we articulate the work of infrastructuring in contending with these issues.

4.2   The Work of Infrastructuring

In the above section, three significant issues in this project were described. In this section, we describe the work of infrastructuring emerged to contend with the issues. More precisely, the infrastructuring work emerged in studying this project includes: *infrastructuring the organization, infrastructuring the space, infrastructuring for workshop places, infrastructuring for more reliable relations, infrastructuring the tools, and infrastructuring the tool management system.* Below, we articulate each of the infrastructuring work in detail.

Infrastructuring the Organization. To avoid volunteers being burned out, positions of coordinators were created to reduce the workload of board members. With this organizational restructuring, many practical works of the board members can be split and shared. This change has helped relieve part of the volunteering issue of the tool library. As one participant commented, the restructuring also saves much of the manager's time so that he can focus more on other important tasks.

People were just too stressed... And that was where the restructuring happened for the past year where we created these coordinator positions and assigned them all the ground level projects. That freed off much time for the directors to focus on broader level strategies and making bigger pictures. It shifted a lot what our manager's position was, too. Before restructuring, our manager was quite all over the places. (Gary)

Infrastructuring the Space. In order to have more space for tools, shelves and sections were created to better organize them. It is also interesting to find that there is a section named "sick bay" to store the tools that need repair (Fig. 4).

Fig. 4. Shelves and sections created for organizing tools and the Sick Bay (right).

With the built shelves and clear sections, more tools can be included in the tool library. One participant also described that tools can be found more easily now.

We created the wall for all the clamps to make them very organized... Having a more organized shop has let us be more efficient. Because we organize in terms of our space, you can get them easily. (Paul)

While observing the space, two interesting and creative installations for storing tools were introduced by the participants. They are the pulley system and the French Cleat. These designs show the creativity of actors in using the resources (Fig. 5).

We made a pulley system for the lawn tool, which is only popular in summer. We also applied a system, which is quite adjustable, called French Cleat. You can add or remove one very easily. (Paul)

Fig. 5. The pulley system (left) and French Cleat system (right).

To create more space for tools and keep the inventory updated, actors of the tool library started doing a garage sale in spring. As one participant commented, the garage sale also brings more revenue for the tool library.

The other big change was every year now we do a garage sale where we get rid of old tools. We actually also make money from it and make space on our shelves. We had that these two years. (Paul)

Infrastructuring for Workshop Places. As discussed before, the tool library has limited space to hold all of its workshops. Volunteers then externalized the space resource to other partners, such as Wood Shop, Vancouver Hack Space, and Vancouver Public Library.

We are actively reaching out to different organizations and folks to come in. For example, the wood shop, they do workshops and also made customer products with salvaged material. They let us use their space to host workshops. (Gary)

As a participant observer, we took part in two workshops of the tool library. One was held in a meeting room of a branch of Vancouver Public Library. The other one was conducted in the loading bay of Vancouver Hack Space (Fig. 6).

Fig. 6. A workshop held in Vancouver Public Library (left) and in Vancouver Hack Space (right).

One interesting strategy the tool library adopted is that it uses its membership or physical tools as a "trade" to get the resources it needs. For example, to use the space of the Wood Shop for workshops, the tool library offers free organizational membership and waives the tool loan fees for tools borrowed by the Wood Shop.

Infrastructuring for More Reliable Relations. Many relations are very informal, such as partnerships with other organizations. These relationships are usually built on mutual benefits and friendship. In the collaborations, they help and learn from each other. However, sometimes, informal relations bring unreliability and unintelligibility. From data analysis, it was found that when actors identified an informal relation that often causes problems, they rebuilt the relation so that the problems were solved. In this way, an informal relation evolved into a more formal one. For example, as one participant described, there was only a verbal agreement between Vancouver Tool Library and the Wood Shop at the beginning. However, then they found they had to develop a Memorandum of Understanding (MOU) to clarify their collaboration. The MOU, including the responsibilities of Vancouver Tool Library and the space provider, specialized and clarifies the rules about their collaboration.

We hadn't really made a formal agreement, so it was not really communicated what we were expecting from this partnership. But to solve the problem, we came up with a kind of contract and we both agreed to, we both signed. (James)

Infrastructuring the Tools. In last year, volunteers made a change in its price for renting tools. Repricing the tools helps increase the revenue for the tool library. Moreover, the new charging rule encourages people to return the tools on time.

Recently just last summer, we changed the fees to $1 a day to encourage people to return the tools. So, we didn't need to buy many tools because they become more available. (Paul)

In addition to the price, physical tools were also modified. For example, one participant described that when a tool is often broken or hard to repair, he puts a note on the tool to remind people to use it carefully (Fig. 7).

We have a tool called a thickness planer. It is sharp and turns very fast. And they break very easily. To avoid the planer tool getting broken too often, we have notices on the tool saying please don't do this thing. (Paul)

Fig. 7. Note was put on the tool to remind people to use it carefully.

Infrastructuring the Tool Management System. Volunteers and the manager had to find other software to meet their financial needs since myTurn did not provide financial functions when it was integrated. That is the reason why they use the software program Vend for their finance and accounting.

Myturn meets our basic needs. But there are definitely a lot of issues with the software. It is not good at recording the financial side of everything. So we have the second software Vend to do financial tasks. (James)

To sum up, by applying the theoretical framework publics and the theory of infrastructuring, the underlying collective design of Vancouver Tool Library project is described. Specifically, it includes: *infrastructuring the organization, infrastructuring the space, infrastructuring the tools, infrastructuring for workshop places, infrastructuring for more reliable relations, and infrastructuring the tool management system.*

5   Discussion

In this part, we further discuss the findings from the case study of the Vancouver Tool Library project. We reflect on the infrastructuring work emerged in this project and analyze the characteristics of the collective design in Vancouver Tool Library project.

5.1   Creative and Resourceful

In many of the infrastructuring work presented above, publics who engage in the practices of designing could be described as creative and resourceful. In the design process, creativity and resourcefulness demonstrate in multiple ways.

First, publics use their creativity in developing vision for what the project could further be. For example, at first, the tool library was thought as a place for storing and sharing tools. Then, actors think about holding workshops to teach people how to use diverse tools. They also creatively started doing garage sales in order to save more space for new tools and keep the inventory updated. The actors are able to creatively generate new ideas or strategies in designing and shaping the project.

Second, creativity is also present in the practical ways publics are able to identify multiple artifacts and appropriate them for their own purposes. For example, French Cleat and the pulley system are creative designs that were made to help organize the tools more efficiently. The "sick bay" is also a creative design to store the broken tools. The creative thinking allows the publics to identify the elements or aspects in their infrastructure that can be changed to better deal with the issues they confronted.

Third, in addition to creativity, resourcefulness is present in the design process of Vancouver Tool Library project. In the work of infrastructuring, publics are aware of the different resources present in their attachments. For example, recycled wood and drawers are repurposed for making shelves. They also create new attachments to include the resources they did not previously have. For instance, workspace from other organizations are identified and integrated as places that can be used for workshops. Thus, publics adopt and appropriate the resources through their present and newly built attachments as their design resources.

In the design process, creativity and resourcefulness manifest in the multiple design strategies the actors used in dealing with the different issues. On the one hand, publics reduce the factors that cause the problems. For example, they get rid of old tools to save space to mitigate the issue of imitated space. On the other hand, publics increase their capacity to confront the result of the issues. For instance, they built the shelves so that more tools can be stored in the space. They also use space from others so that to augment the ability in contending with the issue of limited space.

5.2   Mutual Benefits as a Key Design Principle

In the Vancouver Tool Library project, mutual benefits are also found as a salient principle in the collective design process. The design process of the project is dependent on multiple social relations.

Throughout the project can be found mutual benefits as a critical principle in the work of infrastructuring. This is particularly obvious in creating new attachments. For instance, Wood Shop that provides its workspace as the place for the workshops was offered a free organizational membership of the tool library. Vancouver Hack Space, where we went for a workshop as a participant observer, could have more visitors and advertise its projects and space. Besides, volunteers who contribute their time working in the tool library can be waived their membership fee as well. Therefore, in the work of infrastructuring, the line between the service provider and consumer is seemingly blurring. All the actors and institutions involved in the project make contributions and gain benefits from each other.

Additionally, mutual benefits provide fertile ground for cultivating friendship that helps to strengthen and maintain the constituted relations in the design process. It thus consolidates the resources that can be used for future design act. Thus, a durable (although dynamic) infrastructure is formed in supporting the further design acts of publics.

Finally, in creating the mutual benefits, mutual respect is also found. Actors involved appreciate the understanding and respect between each other. For example, when tools get broken unintentionally, volunteers know that it happens to beginner users and they are willing to support and encourage them. When the mitre saw was broken in the workshop, participants, facilitators, and the volunteers all understood and accommodated that unexpected situation. The collective design process thus allows for trail and error. Individuals respect each other and benefit each other.

In summary, the collective design process creates mutual benefits and relies on this quality for following design acts. In creating the mutual benefits with all the actors and institutions involved, virtuous relations were built and strengthened which support the formation of the network of resources that can be used for publics' future design acts.

5.3   Sociotechnical Relations and Resources as Design Resources

The design resources involved in the design process are diverse. Sociotechnical relations and resources are understood to be resources for further design acts by publics who can adapt and appropriate them to respond to issues.

In the design process, publics see the social and material resources in the attachments as resources for further design acts. The capabilities of those social and technical resources are often what allow publics to see them as supports for design actions.

In addition, the informal relations built in the infrastructure enable publics to adjust or rebuild them in responding issues. When the informal relations cause problems such as lack of clarity and reliability, they were adjusted or reformed. For example, a MOU was created to clarify the obligations of both the tool library and Wood Shop. Therefore, the informal relations built in the design process allow publics to adapt them so that to act better in future design process.

To summarize, in the process of infrastructuring, publics see sociotechnical resources as well as relations as resources for further design acts.

6 Implication for Interaction Design

Scaffolded by the theory of infrastructuring, the work presented in the above sections present a detailed description of the design process in a community-based project. Based on these findings, in this section, we will propose some relevant design implications for interaction design in supporting the collective design of such projects.

6.1 Mapping the Network of Resources

One significant characteristic of collective design process in community-based project is that various social and material resources are adopted as design resources. In fact, not only artifacts, but also individuals and organizations in local areas can serve as resources for further design acts of publics. This characteristic suggests a design opportunity for interaction designers to support the publics in sorting and identifying the resources they could integrate into their future design process. This can happen in several ways. The most direct is to visualize the resources in their current relationships.

Today, there are various projects that deal with this direction. For instance, Kumu (refers to "source of wisdom" in Hawaiian) is a platform to allow people to map their relationships proposed by two brothers, Jeff and Ryna Mohr in Oahu and Silicon Valley: "Kumu is a powerful data visualization platform that helps you organize complex information into interactive relationship maps." The purpose of this platform is to create a context in which people can think. The starting point for this initiative was a simple motivation: "existing tools were overly academic and painful to use." As a response, Kumu was developed as a simple tool to use and no technical background is required.

The tools designed to support publics in the sorting and identification of resources in present infrastructure should also be simple and direct. Moreover, the threshold for accepting new tools is very low. Therefore, interaction designers have to carefully think about how to integrate the designed tool into the current built infrastructure. One recommendation could be thinking about assembling the tool with the artifacts that the actors are already using. For example, would it be possible for such a system to automatically collect information from the email threads or Facebook posts related to the projects and generate the network of resources?

6.2 Design Venues for Exchanges and Understandings

In the work of infrastructuring, publics not only identify resources that exist in their present infrastructure, but also integrate resources from newly created attachments, which are the new nodes that were not previously connected to their network. We have described how publics create the new attachments so that to access the resources desired for future design acts. These offer design opportunities for interaction designers in supporting the exchanges and understandings.

In terms of mutual benefits, a great example can be found is Swapsity. Swapsity is a social enterprise that supports online and offline bartering in Canada. Its members embrace the value of win-win exchanges and its online community gathers diverse resources including skills, services, and artifacts that are ready for exchanges. Marta

Nowinska, who is the founder of Swapsity, writes: "everyone has valuable gifts and inner creativity to unleash and share." The vision of Swapsity is to "help Canadians build a more collaborative and sustainable lifestyle through a peer-to-peer swapping community." In terms of the community-based projects, we encourage interaction designers to think about similar platforms that can be integrated by publics to exchange their resources with other necessaries.

In addition to online platforms, physical space could be created in neighbourhoods to support the actors in exchanges and understandings to connect with each other. A well-known example is the Malmö Living Lab in Sweden, which has been "working with participatory design approached and social innovation in the city of Malmö." The lab helps build a network of actors and organizations and connects them with neighbourhood residents. It facilitates continuous match-making process and emerging design opportunities. We propose that interaction designers who are interested in supporting community-rooted projects think about endeavouring to realize the physical living lab operated in his or her neighbourhood or city.

6.3   Design of Creative Social and Technical Resources

In this section, we emphasize the characteristics of creativeness and resourcefulness of the publics and discuss about how these characteristics can inspire interaction designers in supporting the design process of community-based projects.

In designing process, we have seen the multiple ways in which social and material resources are adopted and appropriated. How publics interpret and use their resources is very creative. It is hard to actually predict the context in which the designed artifacts would be used. When designing artifacts or systems to support the collective design process, how should interaction designers embrace the creativeness and resourcefulness of the publics?

Individuals' resourcefulness and creativeness were recognized and discussed in previous interaction design literature (e.g. [15, 22, 28, 30]). In these works, authors depict how people reuse, repair, and appropriate the artifacts around them. Particularly, in their paper, Wakkary and Tanenbaum named home dwellers as "everyday designers" to manifest people's capabilities in adapting the artifacts in their home [29]. In addition to home dwellers, Asad and Le Dantec studied the civic activities of communities [1]. They suggest a move away from designing artifacts as solutions and propose flexibility and process as two approaches to support civic activities. By design toward flexibility, they want to "cultivate more of a possibility space to encourage creativity and interpretation" [1:1701]. In terms of process, it refers to designs that "operate more like a platform than a single, deterministic service" [1:1701]. These works are inspirational; however, they merely tackle technological artifacts and do not speculate on how the social resources (e.g., actors and institutions) or a network of resources would support creativity for publics. We encourage interaction design researchers consider conducting studies on this direction.

7 Conclusion

The case study presented offer detailed evidence of the collective design process of a community-based project – Vancouver Tool Library. The work describes how publics identify and integrate diverse social and material resources in contending with the issues they confront. The theory of infrastructuring and the framework of publics applied in this study allowed for an account of the complexity and dynamism of the design process. Second, the case study conducted offer rich evidence in validating the effectiveness of the infrastructuring theory in relation to the framework of publics in describing the design process of project initiated in community context. Third, this work provides thoughtful evidence to further improve the theoretical framework in describing the design process of a community-based project. Finally, this study provides implications for interaction design.

For the future work, it would be valuable to continue this research and involve more actors who participated in the collective design process. In the Vancouver Tool Library project, most interviewees were current participants in the project. Data collected thus reflect the recent issues and the current publics, attachments, and infrastructuring work. Founders and actors in the initial design process of the projects are also very important. Although this research did not reach them, future work should study them so that to get a more holistic understanding about the design process of the project. In addition, this work only examined a community-based project in the city of Vancouver. It would be very worthwhile to study more community-initiated projects from other places with different social, political, and cultural backgrounds. This would allow for a more comprehensive view of how actors collectively design in order to tackle their shared issues and build their own idea of well-being. Third, since this work relied on in-depth interviews and short-term participant observations as the primary data source, it is hard to show a full picture of how the collective design of the project has evolved since it was initiated. In future studies, researchers could participate in the projects for a long term to reach more valuable findings. Through engaging in the process, researchers could explore more in-depth the design opportunities and challenges for guiding the future design process of community-based project. Expansive design knowledge would be produced.

Acknowledgments. We thank all our participants.

References

1. Asad, M., Le Dantec, C.A.: Illegitimate civic participation: supporting community activists on the ground. In: Proceedings of the 18th ACM Conference on Computer Supported Cooperative Work and Social Computing (CSCW 2015), pp. 1694–1703 (2015). https://doi.org/10.1145/2675133.2675156
2. Bjögvinsson, E., Ehn, P., Hillgren, P.-A.: Design things and design thinking: contemporary participatory design challenges. Des. Issues **28**(3), 101–116 (2012). https://doi.org/10.1162/DESI_a_00165

3. Björgvinsson, E., Ehn, P., Hillgren, P.-A.: Participatory design and "democratizing innovation". In: Proceedings of the 11th Biennial Participatory Design Conference (PDC 2010), pp. 41–50 (2010). https://doi.org/10.1145/1900441.1900448
4. Clement, A., McPhail, B., Smith, K.L., Ferenbok, J.: Probing, mocking and prototyping: participatory approaches to identity infrastructuring. In: Proceedings of the 12th Participatory Design Conference: Research Papers (PDC 2012), vol. 1, pp. 21–30 (2012). https://doi.org/10.1145/2347635.2347639
5. Le Dantec, C.A., DiSalvo, C.: Infrastructuring and the formation of publics in participatory design. Soc. Stud. Sci. **43**(2), 241–264 (2013). https://doi.org/10.1177/0306312712471581
6. Dewey, J.: The Public and Its Problems. Swallow, Denver (1927)
7. Edwards, P.N.: A Vast Machine: Computer Models, Climate Data, and the Politics of Global Warming. MIT Press, Cambridge (2010)
8. Edwards, P.N., Jackson, S.J., Bowker, G.C., Knobel, C.P.: Understanding infrastructure: dynamics, tensions, and design. MyScienceWork (2007). https://www.mysciencework.com/publication/show/f59d40ef08802cdb2da090cb6362cbb7. Accessed 2 Jan 2017
9. Ehn, P.: Participation in design things. In: Proceedings of the Tenth Anniversary Conference on Participatory Design 2008 (PDC 2008), pp. 92–101 (2008). http://dl.acm.org/citation.cfm?id=1795234.1795248. Accessed 6 Jan 2017
10. Gaver, W.: What should we expect from research through design? In: Proceedings of the SIGCHI Conference on Human Factors in Computing Systems (CHI 2012), pp. 937–946 (2012). https://doi.org/10.1145/2207676.2208538
11. Gaver, W., et al.: Energy babble: mixing environmentally-oriented internet content to engage community groups. In: Proceedings of the 33rd Annual ACM Conference on Human Factors in Computing Systems (CHI 2015), pp. 1115–1124 (2015). https://doi.org/10.1145/2702123.2702546
12. Karasti, H., Baker, K.S.: Infrastructuring for the long-term: ecological information management. In: 2004 Proceedings of the 37th Annual Hawaii International Conference on System Sciences, pp. 1–10 (2004). https://doi.org/10.1109/HICSS.2004.1265077
13. Karasti, H., Baker, K.S., Millerand, F.: Infrastructure time: long-term matters in collaborative development. Comput. Support. Coop. Work (CSCW) **19**(3–4), 377–415 (2010). https://doi.org/10.1007/s10606-010-9113-z
14. Karasti, H., Syrjänen, A.-L.: Artful infrastructuring in two cases of community PD. In: Proceedings of the Eighth Conference on Participatory Design: Artful Integration: Interweaving Media, Materials and Practices (PDC 2004), vol. 1, pp. 20–30 (2004). https://doi.org/10.1145/1011870.1011874
15. Kim, S., Paulos, E.: Practices in the creative reuse of e-waste. In: Proceedings of the SIGCHI Conference on Human Factors in Computing Systems (CHI 2011), pp. 2395–2404 (2011). https://doi.org/10.1145/1978942.1979292
16. Le Dantec, C.A.: Designing Publics. The MIT Press, Cambridge (2016)
17. Lim, Y., Kim, D., Jo, J., Woo, J.: Discovery-driven prototyping for user-driven creativity. IEEE Pervasive Comput. **12**(3), 74–80 (2013). https://doi.org/10.1109/MPRV.2012.57
18. Manzini, E.: Design, When Everybody Designs. MIT Press (2015). https://mitpress.mit.edu/books/design-when-everybody-designs. Accessed 23 Mar 2016
19. Marres, N.: The issues deserve more credit: pragmatist contributions to the study of public involvement in controversy. Soc. Stud. Sci. **37**(5), 759–780 (2007)
20. Neustaedter, C., Sengers, P.: Autobiographical design in HCI research: designing and learning through use-it-yourself. In: Proceedings of the Designing Interactive Systems Conference (DIS 2012), pp. 514–523 (2012). https://doi.org/10.1145/2317956.2318034
21. Pipek, V., Wulf, V.: Infrastructuring: toward an integrated perspective on the design and use of information technology. J. Assoc. Inf. Syst. **10**(5), 447–473 (2009)

22. Roedl, D., Bardzell, S., Bardzell, J.: Sustainable making? Balancing optimism and criticism in HCI discourse. ACM Trans. Comput.-Hum. Interact. **22**(3), 15:1–15:27 (2015). https://doi.org/10.1145/2699742

23. Star, S.L., Bowker, G.C.: How to infrastructure. In: Handbook of New Media: Social Shaping and Social Consequences of ICTs, Updated Student Edition, pp. 230–245. SAGE Publications Ltd., London (2010). http://sk.sagepub.com/reference/hdbk_newmedia/n13.xml . Accessed 20 July 2016

24. Star, S.L., Ruhleder, K.: Steps toward an ecology of infrastructure: design and access for large information spaces. Inf. Syst. Res. **7**(1), 111–134 (1996)

25. Suchman, L.: Located accountabilities in technology production. Scand. J. Inf. Syst. **14**(2), 91–105 (2002)

26. Tilson, D., Lyytinen, K., Sørensen, C.: Research commentary—digital infrastructures: the missing IS research agenda. Inf. Syst. Res. **21**(4), 748–759 (2010). https://doi.org/10.1287/isre.1100.0318

27. City of Vancouver: Greenest City Action Plan (2016). http://vancouver.ca/green-vancouver/greenest-city-action-plan.aspx. Accessed 21 Sept 2016

28. Wakkary, R., Desjardins, A., Hauser, S., Maestri, L.: A sustainable design fiction green practices. ACM Trans. Comput.-Hum. Interact. **20**(4), 23:1–23:34 (2013). https://doi.org/10.1145/2494265

29. Wakkary, R., Tanenbaum, K.: A sustainable identity: the creativity of an everyday designer. In: Proceedings of the SIGCHI Conference on Human Factors in Computing Systems (CHI 2009), pp. 365–374 (2009). https://doi.org/10.1145/1518701.1518761

30. Woodruff, A., Hasbrouck, J., Augustin, S.: A bright green perspective on sustainable choices. In: Proceedings of the SIGCHI Conference on Human Factors in Computing Systems (CHI 2008), pp. 313–322 (2008). https://doi.org/10.1145/1357054.1357109

31. Yin, R.K.: Case Study Research: Design and Methods. SAGE, Thousand Oaks (2009)

32. Zimmerman, J., Forlizzi, J., Evenson, S.: Research through design as a method for interaction design research in HCI. In: Proceedings of the SIGCHI Conference on Human Factors in Computing Systems (CHI 2007), pp. 493–502 (2007). https://doi.org/10.1145/1240624.1240704

Urban Interaction Design Supports Modular Design Practice for Urban Public Space

Huan Wang[1], Ming Yan[2], Han Xie[3], and Zhiyong Fu[4(✉)]

[1] Capital Normal University, Beijing 100048, China
rebeccawanghuan@sina.com
[2] Peking University, Beijing 100871, China
4039289@qq.com
[3] Yzscape Co. Ltd., Beijing 100084, China
Xiehan0914@outlook.com
[4] Tsinghua University, Beijing 100084, China
fuzhiyong@tsinghua.edu.cn

Abstract. Multiple-dimensional structured urban space directs to an inter-disciplinary considers on public space utilization. The people-users are con-sciously and unconsciously in the communicative activities with the city, where urban interactive design establishes cross-design accessibility in the virtual and physical public context. This paper introduces an approach that the Human-centered Design as a fundamental perspective and Interaction Design frames the program and motivates design elements for urban interaction design. Following a Smart Pavilion design practice for Baoding New City Plan in China. Partic-ularly conception of this design is the four modules creation of Information Block, Pavilion Block, Interior Block, Information Platform Block, and the attempt on organizing the modules to constitute three prototypes for different scenarios. People's real-time requirement, reflection, and emotion can be cap-tured by interfaces and delivered to the information platform towards a transfer qualitative symbols into data essentially design and improvement materials, and react to the Smart Pavilion to enable the Human Interactions in the 21st-century networked city.

Keywords: Urban interaction design · Human-centered design · Modular design · Public space

1 Background

In China facing complex problems from facilities, governance, and society, that results in city emphasize the interaction between people and the city itself seeking to urban public space regularly. Booming population, diverse functional requirements and urban quality standards lead to a single public space design encounter bottleneck. Though the public space refers to a place that is open and accessible to all citizens; prominent cities emerges a calling for the collaborative interdisciplinary-workshop on the relationship between built environment, economic development, and the social culture relations behind. Urban designers need to face the challenges:

© Springer Nature Switzerland AG 2019
P.-L. P. Rau (Ed.): HCII 2019, LNCS 11577, pp. 241–254, 2019.
https://doi.org/10.1007/978-3-030-22580-3_18

1- How to create a functional and extensible design for multiple-requirements of citizens?
2- How to highlight and tackle people's feedback and transfer it to advance design timely and accurately in urban public space?
3- How to react to citizens' reflection and emotion?
4- Can the urban public space link citizens' communication?

Urban is a hybrid subject where various sectors of society are seeking solutions, and among that, urban design particularly contributes to spatial practice because of its focus on the quality of urban space for citizens. However, what influences urban space refers to comprehensive factors, and who guides a sustainable urban space exists uncertain stakeholders' responsibilities. Since the information revolution era has begun, preliminary urban programs and practices have been asserting its powerful position owing to Human-Computer Intelligence developing rapidly in the smart city context. To face this era, China's urban design exploration started from smart designs for holding technologically attitudes to create and cultivate interactive interfaces of the city by using data as a communication language for planning, design, management, and prediction.

2   The City as an Urban Interaction Design Platform in Smart City Context

Urban interaction is a cross-disciplinary that combines spatial and technological factors to support design brings a creative approach and objects into citizens' surroundings. The Urban signifies the fundamentality on spatial aspects that affect human behaviors, emotion, and relationships, drawing on approaches from the social sciences. This space has become large and fluid, distributed and complex. It is filled with data streaming from various types of sources. "Interaction" refers to technology, particularly communication and networked technologies that convert the raw material of data into meaning that informs our decisions at scales that range from citywide solutions to grassroots hacking and tinkering.

From urban interaction design perspective, interactive design innovates the way we benefit from Smart City, actively adding the understanding for which facilities, devices, and apps that links city people and space. From the spatial environment perspective, is the practice of designing Smart City products or services, such as interactive digital products, environments, systems, and services, involving users actions and emotion into local shared space.

The public is involved in the urban interactive movement, and influences the city by the interactive activities that Individuals as creators, carriers, and sharers of data. Bottom-up approaches that towards improving a human-centered urban space have paved the way for citizens to become an element involved in the servicing-interactive processes associated with the making and remaking of cities. The human-computer interaction (HCI) and related fields, such as computer- supported cooperative work, cyber-physical system, interaction design, and urban computing or the Internet of Things, the rapid expanse of urban issues has fostered a parallel uptake of concepts from different disciplines such as ethnography and design, and shift from "interfaces" towards "interspaces". At one end of the spectrum, with the help of smart cities technology, interfaces of infrastructures, dashboards for networks and the central operation platform supports navigating design for sustainable development systematically.

3 Approach

For advance urban interaction design for human-centered cities, this paper state a converging approach as the public interaction practicing multiple-disciplinary collaborative process. Human-centered Design claims a human perspective and interactive design supports to direct the problem-solving conduct.

3.1 Human-Centered Design

As an approach to interactive system development, Human-centered design aims to make usable and useful system form a user-centered perspective. It focused on the users needing and requirement by applying human factors, usability knowledge, and techniques. Human-centered Design and Urban Design have a seeming similarity on design perspective of the human, while Human-centered Design has distinct empathize on engaging the user into the design activities, which as named the participatory design. In the design process, the human-centered design generally defines the problem, make prototype, test, and those processes together with the designer and the user, which supply the vacant urban space design designer. The real-world users of the urban space know what they are looking forward. It can be announced that the human-centered design bridge users and space from the bottom-up situation.

On account for citizens in urban public spaces in divers, the current design tends to appeal to more demanding needs due to periods for a multilevel usage of the limited urban area. For example, a square, as a pass way for office workers in the morning, a community space for the elderly in the afternoon, and a square dance venue in the evening. If it provides space for selling breakfast in the morning, showing broadcast news in the afternoon, and playing music in the evening, it will be very convenient for the crowds—however, this usage planning seeking solution relay on facilities and equipment advancing rather than space dividing. Thus, when the center of problem-solving returns to the actual needs of people, urban design is forced to cross the current discipline.

Human-centered design typically attempts at integrating technology and productive tools in order to alleviate problems with the centered focusing on human requirement and feeling, especially design as the dominant pattern facing a complex functional and aesthetic city requirement.

Interdisciplinary design collaboration proposes new ways of designing methodology. Outstandingly with disciplinary distinction, the human-centered design provides a starting point and the implementation proximity perspective following the urban interaction design. For example, on the 2014–2018 Challenging the City Scale project of European Human Cities (Humancities.eu) brings great repercussions to the urban community space by reshaping the urban space, fostering culture identification and activating street value. It aims to establish a co-design pattern with various city managers, planners, designers and users from a human-centered perspective. The deliveries include urban design, product design, visual design, network design, and civic events, among that 70.7% of the projects embraces practical design while 12% projects have the symptom of interactive design (Fig. 1).

Fig. 1. Unlimited-cities DIY project of Europe Human Cities

3.2 Data-Streamed Urban Interaction Design

Interaction Design, often abbreviated as IxD, is "the practice of designing interactive digital products, environments, systems, and services." (Cooper et al. 2011) It specifically inspires a creatively design thinking—generating alternatives, visualizing new possibilities, challenging inherent assumptions, and opening recognition to new information. Interaction design is useful in creating physical products and researching how users interact with the deliveries. Compared with industrial design and urban design, interaction designs focus on user behaviors form the synthesizing and imaging things potentially and explores the connection between the human and things forward reaching and planning users' requirement and calling for empathy and understanding of the users.

Urban Interaction Design (UrbanIxD) can be seen as being grounded in the traditions of society, technology, and arts. It explores the design processes involving the design of interfaces, living activities, and people-using that is happening in an urban context. While media architecture focuses primarily on the built environment, urban interactions tend to highlight the complex situations in multi-functional scopes. Urban stuck in the condition of complex requirements and issues, calling for an attempt to spatial reshape progress. Information technologies presents a multilevel interactive interface and technical possibilities, and construct a straight talking between the city users and city surroundings. Cites are being touched with sensors and interacted with mobile technologies that are generating a myriad of urban informatics experiences.

In particular, interactive design for public space as an approach delivers a human-centered design perspective as well as a broad range of understanding, definition, and narratives that fit into the toolkits of urban interaction design. Creative design conception emerges between the lines, in space where the designer used to set the boundary with experiences flourish and dramatic statements. While interactive urban design tends to emphasize the complicated situation in multi-functional spaces by building environment and individuals urban experience, data as a new communicating media vocabulary appears in front of urban designers and managers. Design base on reading data forms interactive feedback more than reading academic knowledge and living experience.

Standing in the middle of the urban design and interaction design, urban interaction design general adopting a traditional method of Mapping, Prototyping, DIY by Interaction Design [book]. Those methods are seemingly extracted from the traditional product, information, and urban design, while that embedded with electronics, software, sensors, and network connectivity techniques. In urban space, a flexible design process can help bridge the linkage between fields and advance a general and effective new design vocabulary that beyond sketching blueprint (Brynskov et al. 2014). The interaction deigns aims to embracing a reflective, collaborative approach to research and practice that embodies the trans-disciplinary position of urban interaction design.

3.3   An Initiative Interaction Design Model for Urban

This paper is an attempt to combine human-centered design and interaction design facing multiple-requirement of space. The human-centered design reminds a sustained process integrating users tracks. The interaction design presents design elements and philosophy systems to support innovation. Because the design process at this time integrates the physical and virtual space, the cyber-physical system that runs through the dimensions and elements is a surpassing substance, and it also effectively controls the virtual space (Brynskov et al. 2014). So another central control hub throughout should be proposed since the public design platform in the interaction design. Advanced research proposes a design platform as an application program interface (API) complex to relate urban life drove data in terms to establish resources of data flow.

On the input side, users' location, action, and emotion mean a useable description form the facilities and sensors in the public space. Location often comes from apps' feedback data, while it addresses with behavior mapping to reflect movement. The action is mainly divided to touch and speak; the former one enables connectivity between human mental object and technical operation system while the latter one has become an alternative interaction stream with the development of artificial intelligence in China. Emotion is the most untouchable and unidentifiable for design understanding. All surroundings can be heard, smelled, seen by people who tend to express their feeling by writing on the network website, apps, and platform. All the informative mental and behavioral states captured on design platform, which invokes the accessibility of users unconsciously and consciously engaged in public space, therefore facilitate a real-time definition of subjective construction.

On the other side, designers, managers, and administrators co-work based on the data directly, designers and professors research urban interaction design indirectly. When descript the public space and re-innovate space properties, urban design can have a synthetically situation definition that combines interactive users feedback more than a simplified spatial analysis. Product design, information design, and computer science are set to appropriate access to the urban design by data communicating method. At the same time, citizens are motivated and inspired to take action in the guided direction to contribute reflection, vision statements address their goals and a common cause that commit to their vision. Urban interaction design supports an urban design living-lab standing on the multi-disciplinary field (Fig. 2).

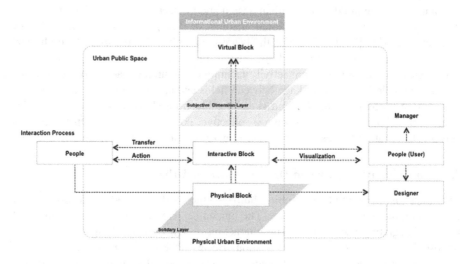

Fig. 2. Urban interaction design model

4 Design Practice—Smart Street Pavilion

4.1 Background

Baoding is China's National Historical and Cultural City and National Garden City, as well as the China's first innovation-driven development model city and WWF Low-carbon Pilot City. In April 2017, the State Council of the Communist Party of China decided to set up the Xiong'an New District of Hebei Province, which initiate the three divisions of Xiongxian, Rongcheng and Anxin that Baoding City involving. A new perspective developing program that aims to institute into a new urban plan that drives the development of Beijing-Tianjin-Hebei city's innovation drive for a future-leading urban space.

However, as Baoding generated in the third-tier cities, obviously urban spatial opportunities in the existing urban structure cannot be neglected: an uncompleted urban space open-system; insufficient and fragmentized urban public space without connectivity with the citizens; disorderly outdoor information interface floating over the city appearance (Fig. 3).

In this era and the development of the country, Baoding New City General Planning directs to launch out based on solving the existed urban space problems to create and innovate a human-centered public space with the technological support of smart

Fig. 3. Baoding map and street scenes

city and infrastructure construction objects. Drafting a vision statement for a innovative and interactive city, design concepts:

1- A modularized design meeting the contemporary mega polis well-being definition.
2- A flexible concrete available carrier for the historical and cultural city.
3- A real-time platform with citizens participating.
4- A multi-functional urban living-lab encouraging technology possibilities.

4.2   Function Definition

The urban public spaces used to be designed and planned for all city's resident and tourist groups, involving men, women, and children by professional expertise. The design incorporates various types of stakeholders who are designed and thought by architects, UI designers, IT designers, city managers, and residents together jointly conducted a brain-storming section to anchor the functional design positioning. The informal discussion workshop reveals the integrated proposing, and the dimension of the functional realization form division into urban informational and physical space, where has the service similarity center of city people. The function points included street scenes, retailing, information visualization, and so on.

At the same time, interdisciplinary cooperation unavoidable have a disciplinary background through the subject attributes to proposed function, which can be practiced according to the differentiation of the implementation approaches into several aspects, including Urban Design Elements for Usage, Urban Design Aspects for Space Quality and Interaction Design for Information Transfer. Urban interaction designer has penetrated the virtual and physical space involving the cross-directional practice (Fig. 4).

4.3   Modular Design

The next step is a practical modular design propose to make the design programming and development instruments accessible to these users so that rather than just suggesting improvements and new features, citizens can try to create their tracks and ideas to a better urban space.

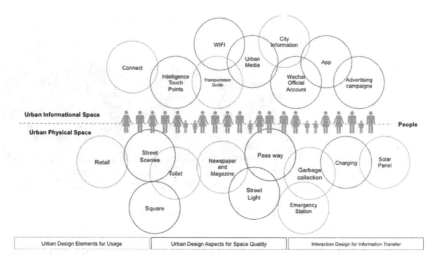

Fig. 4. Function definition mapping

As multiple infrastructures in the public space of the city, a basic **(A) Pavilion Block** to shelter from the rain and enhance the visual experience in the outdoor activities in the city is a fundamental block. Equipped with a large-span roof, the Pavilion builds fragmental walls that define consecutive spaces for possible space and a wooden bench to provide a piece of comfortable underarm equipment. What is improved this time is that the Smart Pavilion carries the solar panel roof to achieve the clean energy as much as possible.

Secondly, it is the **(B) Information Block** that is the response for interaction pattern, which integrates urban media and interactive interfaces into the infrastructure. The essential accessories include LED touch screen performance, audio, camera, voice recognition components, real-time execution of user commands and collection of users' feedback. Regarding the planning of circuit equipment, digital media related equipment such as WIFI transmission points, charging piles, and telephones are also deployed here to realize the smart city life experience.

Besides, an alternative section holds the **(C) Interior Block**, which aims to service space for indoor using attached on the pavilion frame. Working as a CAFÉ and a food-selling standing to service quick-making food and drinks can affect people into out-doors activities. Having toilet service is also a humanistic concern in the modern city. Newspaper and magazine borrowing service is facing the older adults who are inter-ested in the entity literature. This measure recommends introducing interflow of the population for bridging community communication. In some situations, the retailers can be replaced by auto retailers.

Finally, the **(D) Information Platform Block** is conducted out, which is a site established in the smart city central control system to acquire data and control entity objects through wireless devices remotely. The platform system includes a remote control system and connectivity to handheld devices, which enable a people to scale communicating on Apps, Facebook, Twitter, Wechat official account, and Sina Weibo, and the latter two created the most using interactive interfaces in China's current cities. When the public use the Wechat public account and the mobile terminal app to issue commands, accept and input information to the (A), (B), and (C) modular, thereby the design realizing the interaction between people and devices, and then bridge people in the city, such as finding city information, playing music and purchasing food. The generated data in these processes will be collected and stored by the platform system for the next stage on design reflection, design iteration enhancement, and research data foundation for urban interaction design (Fig. 5).

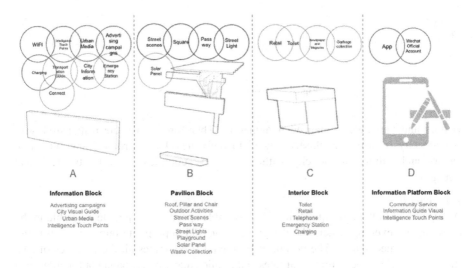

Fig. 5. Modular design

4.4   Prototype Generating and Interaction Design

A further attempt of this research is to organize the module for a suitable prototype to reach various urban living scenarios. According to the Baoding Urban Planning emphasized attention, firstly design needs meet the needs of transportation station, civic activity plazas, and civic parks square. The next generation of prototypes is similar to a human-centered function selection and integration process. Those modular provide possibilities for critical space usage, ultimately making the flexible design connectivity of architecture, hardware, and software design (Fig. 6).

Prototype I
It is a deepening adopting to the traffic station space proposal. Selects (A) Pavilion Block, (B) information Block, and (D) Information Platform Block. Users can access inquiry real-time traffic information, geographic location, weather, and tourism information through mobile screens interface. (D) Information Platform Block is a continuous design platform for information delivery. Along the street at Baoding, it is regularly to see the most people excess circulation rather than the amount of waiting. For passing-by viewing scenario, the Smart Pavilion as a street traffic booth attracts

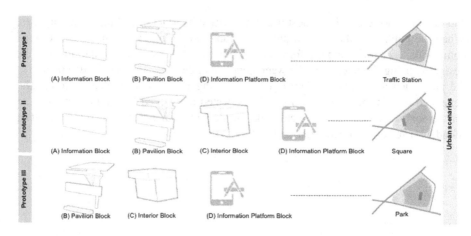

Fig. 6. Prototypes for city scenes

visitors and generates a glanced imagination. Therefore, it has the responsibility to provide city information closely related to daily travel and promote the spread of history and culture of the city with a relatively complete "smart city" technical function.

Prototype II

As a pavilion in the city square, it is an accessible space where people assemble in the morning and evening, where the design needs to add appropriate public infrastructure for affording necessities. The design of Prototype II combines all the modules of (A), (B), (C), and (D). The commercial sales and public education propaganda functions can be realized while meeting the outdoor activities of urban passers-by and attracting people to integrate into space. Interactive devices, such as the self-service interactive furniture and adjustable lights, allow surviving spaces to achieve a wide variety of functions at times of the day and to communicate with users.

Prototype III

Assemble the module (A), (C), and (D). Baoding City's urban public green space requires equipment for community activities and events. Therefore, the facilities placed inside the city park present a refreshing space for rest and help the simplistic sales function. Rest or stay hereabouts waiting for people to have a conversation with the people around and the activity space.

The three connected prototypes communicate on the design platform, which as the central management system to link the physical construction of the pavilion, information interfaces, and users' action and emotion. On the one hand, the city management through the information block and pavilion function practice management in the urban working sequence through media, function, and interface. On the other hand, people access and participate in the public space by touching, and speaking based on an operating system that technologically supported by interactive services. The key to the design is interactive virtual-physical design in urban public space to present—how the features interactively design from the public (Fig. 7).

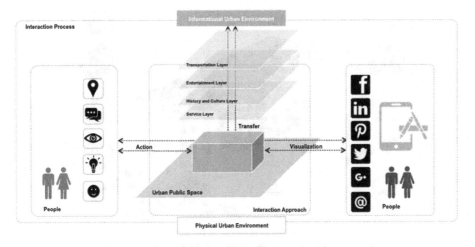

Fig. 7. Urban interaction design system of Smart Pavilion

Actually, the physical and digital contexts are similar. The appearance of digital objects reflects the intrinsic properties the physical analogs. These practices illustrate approaches enrich each other then making an exhaustive list of specific methodologies or techniques used in urban interaction design, that supports a further exploration in a virtual and physical space design context. Multi-disciplinary approaches enrich each other. As designers, the co-design team strives to craft interfaces, systems, and devices that enhance productivity, facilitate our actions, meet our needs, create value and even provide enjoyment.

4.5   Material and Components

At the fundamental concerning, the materials of the designed physical structure are advocating the low-price construction principle and environmental protection to be flexibly combined and re-designed.

Design applies Bamboo Steel as the pavilion frame constructional material, which comes from advanced bamboo industry in China. Particular designed steel connecting member to join components from the pillars bottom to cornice top. The enclosing wall sorts to use sesame ash granite for a permanent performance on the human-scale. The roof mostly made by Aluminum magnesium manganese alloy roofing board while partly covered by the solar panel to generate energy by itself. Water permeable brick covers the floor to support the water cycle in an urban context. The style of pavilion constructional aesthetic tends to a less decorative molding that to present functionalism (Fig. 8).

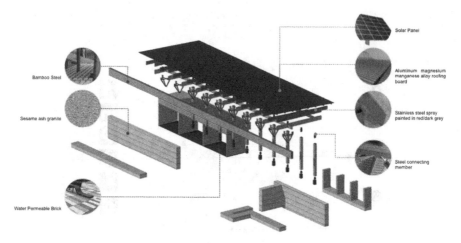

Fig. 8. Tangible material description

The improved design aspect is the focus of this practice. In order to achieve the design function planning of modular, the device and component supported by the ICT technology are used as the data terminal, which Includes: LED display. As a new type of outdoor media, LED integrates public information, corporate advertising, traffic guidance, multimedia display, information release, and human city interaction. Outdoors food court, which offers food and drink provision, can drive the activity of a region. WIFI, locally coverage the facility-centric wireless network. Hotspots are set up in densely populated areas to facilitate the daily necessities of facilities and attracting more users. Outdoor Charging Power Pedestal meets the creative and diverse demands of the ICT era. It will facilitate the modern life with the increasing the popularity of the types of equipment and make people stay longer (Fig. 9).

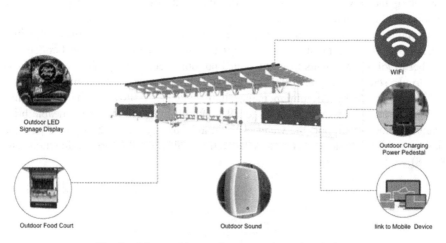

Fig. 9. Advanced interactive components description

5 Conclusion

It is practicing the urban interaction design approach, the Smart Pavilion design particular attempts four modular design blocks for extensive function in limited public space. A pavilion existed throughout virtual and physical dimensions for tackle qualitative users' actions and ideas in a digital form, which promotes the accuracy and timeliness of people's space interaction. Although it needs time on testing of citizens' engagement, it is affirmative considers that the interface has connected users with the city by information transmission.

The traditional urban design tends to follow the approach from the up-bottom perspective, resulting in the inherent professional direction of the disciplinary design deliveries in position with the industrial landscape of the manufacturing era, however, have to admit that it has touched the bottleneck. Urban Interaction design is an interdisciplinary co-design attempt. The project focuses on the objective is to articulate people vision to the designers and managers who actually directs the program and make users idea a substance. Human-computer interaction technique has the potential competitive advantage to stable and inspire innovative design and understanding the broader urban environment in which design operates, and to establish a particular system. The complex needs of the city sort into data streams, which are used to analyze and solve problems, and link people's actions and emotions with space design and planning management.

Urban interaction design processes accessibility existing conceptions of urban space design and citizens, demands by new and shared design vocabularies that bridging the connectivity that appears between systems and disciplines. The vocabularies extend physical aspects to virtual-physical linked approach and emphasize the platform procedure involving citizens reflection and action. Smart City Operating System enables user experience and software solution by data interaction, then the sights, resources, and opportunities converge on the urban interaction design platform.

The viewpoint that the Pubic has the capability of design and innovate city space, ICT allows individuals to participate in urban management through API. The interaction between people and cities has been inadvertently carried out silently. As smart cities operation system takes over the central urban management, data plays an essential role as a universal language actor. The interface is responsible for the communication platform for various disciplines and stakeholders. The design approach with people and functions as the core gradually becomes the interdisciplinary consensus of cooperation.

Acknowledgement. This paper is supported by Yzscape Co. Ltd. (http://www.yzscape.com/), Tsinghua University, and Capital Normal University. Authors are thankful to team members who provided expertise that greatly assisted the research.

References

Angotti, T., Doble, C., Horrigan, P. (eds.): Service-Learning in Design and Planning: Educating at the Boundaries. New Village Press, New York (2012)

Brynskov, M., et al.: Urban Interaction Design: Towards City Making. Schloss Neuhausen: UrbanIxD/Booksprints, Amsterdam (2014)

Buchanan, R.: Human dignity and human rights: thoughts on the principles of human-centered design. Des. Issues **17**(3), 35–39 (2001). https://doi.org/10.1162/074793601750357178

Cooper, A., Reimann, R., Cronin, D.: About Face 3: The Essentials of Interaction Design, p. 610. Wiley, Indianapolis (2007). ISBN 978-0-470-08411-3. Accessed 18 July 2011

Chan, D.: Sustainable communities for whom: cultural tactics in the pursuit of ecological sustainability. Asian Am. Policy Rev. **28**(1), 52–57 (2018)

Innovating for People: Handbook of Human-Centered Design Methods. LUMA Institute, LLC, Pittsburgh (2012)

Matheson, G.O., Pacione, C., Shultz, R.K., Klügl, M.: Leveraging human-centered design in chronic disease prevention. Am. J. Prev. Med. **48**(4), 472–479 (2015)

Mike, C.: Architect or Bee? South End Press, Brooklyn (1982)

Du, X., Su, L., Liu, J.: Developing sustainability curricula using the PBL method in a Chinese context. J. Clean. Prod. **61**, 80–88 (2013). https://doi.org/10.1016/j.jclepro.2013.01.012

Townsend, A.: Smart Cities. Big Data, Civic Hackers and the Quest for New Utopia (2013)

IBM: IBM Smarter City Solutions: Leadership and Innovation for Building Smarter Cities. Somers, New York (2011)

Batty, M., Axhausen, K.W., Giannotti, F., Pozdnoukhov, A., Bazzani, A., Wachowicz, M., et al.: Smart cities of the future. Eur. Phys. J. Spec. Top. **214**(1), 481–518 (2012)

Dobre, C., Xhafa, F.: Intelligent services for big data science. Future Gener. Comput. Syst. **37**, 267–281 (2014)

Rathore, M.M., Ahmad, A., Paul, A., Rho, S.: Urban planning and building smart cities based on the internet of things using big data analytics. Comput. Netw. **101**, 63–80 (2016)

Gohar, M., Muzammal, M., Rahman, A.U.: SMART TSS: defining transportation system behavior using big data analytics in smart cities. Sustain. Cities Soc. **41**, 114–119 (2018)

Kelley, D., Kelley, T.: Creative Confidence: Unleashing the Creative Potential Within Us All. Crown Business, New York (2013)

Zaffiro, G., Bracuto, M., Brynskov, M., Smyth, M.: A market analysis of urban interaction design. In: Stephanidis, C. (ed.) HCI 2015. CCIS, vol. 529, pp. 587–591. Springer, Cham (2015). https://doi.org/10.1007/978-3-319-21383-5_98

Zhou, Y., Jiang, N.: The research and co-creation model for urban interaction design and practices. In: Rau, P.-L.P. (ed.) CCD 2018. LNCS, vol. 10912, pp. 444–454. Springer, Cham (2018). https://doi.org/10.1007/978-3-319-92252-2_35

Yu, W., Jiang, X.: The third-type settlement: research of unified urban and rural living organisms and its interaction design. In: Marcus, A. (ed.) DUXU 2016. LNCS, vol. 9747, pp. 527–536. Springer, Cham (2016). https://doi.org/10.1007/978-3-319-40355-7_50

Jiang, T.: Cluster Comput. (2018). https://doi.org/10.1007/s10586-018-2194-z

Chang, T.W.: Supporting design learning with design puzzles. In: Van Leeuwen, J.P., Timmermans, H.J.P. (eds.) Recent Advances in Design and Decision Support Systems in Architecture and Urban Planning, pp. 293–307. Springer, Dordrecht (2004). https://doi.org/10.1007/1-4020-2409-6_19

On the road to quality urbanization, 25th June 2018. https://www.telegraph.co.uk/news/world/china-watch/business/urbanisation-in-china/

ET City Brain. https://www.alibabacloud.com/et/city

City Change Maker: A Design Innovation Workshop on Social Impact

Qing Xia and Zhiyong Fu[(✉)]

Tsinghua University, Beijing, China
xia-q18@mails.tsinghua.edu.cn,
fuzhiyong@tsinghua.edu.cn

Abstract. This paper presents a design innovation workshop, City Change Maker, aiming at solving city issues, including healthcare, education, transportation, city regeneration, cultural heritage, etc. The workshop selected multi-background students from Hong Kong and Macao to participate in a two-week social innovation design activity in Beijing. Through the workshop, we want to encourage the ambition of youth change maker to reform the city and design for good. Based on student project practices over the past three years, this paper reviews and discusses the goals, methods, content, and outcomes of the workshop. Through analysis and reflection on past activity data and organizational experience, this paper proposes a five-stage innovative education process, including perspective, integration, transition, outcome and impact, to help educators in the field of innovation and entrepreneurship plan similar design activities. The design approach of workshop emphasizes the city as a container of culture and the social impact as the output of the activity. The deliverables of the workshop are not only urban innovation concepts and design proposals, but also a multidisciplinary innovative education and training model.

Keywords: Education approach · Design workshop · Social impact ·
City culture

1 Background

In the global industrial integration, designer has begun to work in more industries than traditional fields and has gained a great interdisciplinary influence. In the practice of using design methods to solve social problems, many colleges and institutions have made pioneering attempts. University of Washington and Tsinghua University once launched a 7-week maker project World Lab in 2012 [1, 2], in which Chinese and American students jointly discussed how to solve global problems through technology and design. In China, the number of maker activities aiming at solving social issues has been rapidly rising, and design trials have begun to form ideas that affect society. The early action of using design to solve social problems was Design Now, a weekend workshop that initiated by Academy of Art and Design, Tsinghua University, which emphasized to solve current social problems through interdisciplinary design practices. Since then, in 2014, China has entered the era of the development of makers. The educational project, City Change Maker is born in the context of this era. Facing the

© Springer Nature Switzerland AG 2019
P.-L. P. Rau (Ed.): HCII 2019, LNCS 11577, pp. 255–269, 2019.
https://doi.org/10.1007/978-3-030-22580-3_19

circumstance of China's urbanization process wild developing, we hope to the encourage young people to become innovators, and the participants from different backgrounds can join together to solve the city problems and change the city (Fig. 1).

Fig. 1. Photos of workshop City Change Maker

From July 2016 to July 2018, we have held 3 times annual City Change Maker summer workshops [3], and have choose multi-background university students from Hong Kong and Macao to take participant in a 2-week workshop in Beijing. The workshop offers maker practice training and design thinking method as common knowledge. Students will be guided to organize teams based on same interest, explored the pain points of Beijing city through real field research. Several experts from academia and industry was invited to give the guidance and support to encourage the young to develop innovative product or service, and make a comprehensive evaluation during the final presentation. The purpose of this workshop is not only to solve the urban problems and reshape citizens' lifestyle, but also ignite the ambition of youth change maker to have the abilities to reform the city and design for good (Table 1).

Table 1. Brief information of workshop City Change Maker

Year	Student quantity	Output quantity	Topic			
			Urban community	Urban life	City space	Local culture
2016	85	16	1 Youth development 2 Aging	3 Education	4 Barrier free 5 Community regeneration	6 Culture and Creation
2017	51	7		1 Health 2 Food 3 Education	4 City regeneration	5 Culture and Creation 6 Cultural heritage
2018	73	10		1 Health 2 Agriculture 3 Education 4 Transportation	5 City regeneration	6 Cultural heritage 7 Sport Culture and Creation

During last 3 years, there are 207 students have participated in this project. They come from different academic backgrounds, and less than 6% were design students. In addition, Hong Kong and Macao are multicultural cities. Because of the different cultural and social systems, the problems encountered in urban life by their citizens are also different from those in the Mainland. We hope that the students from Hong Kong and Macao will be able to keep their diversity perspective when they visit Beijing, give different points of view into Beijing local projects, and develop a common methodology in individual cases. As of last year, in our three workshops, students have developed 14 design themes around urban culture in four directions, including urban community, urban life, urban space and local culture. On average, each team consists of six students, resulting in a total of 33 works (Table 2).

Table 2. Content of City Change Maker workshop

Year	2016		2017		2018	
Duration	12 Days		11 Days		12 Days	
Order	Content	Ratio	Content	Ratio	Content	Ratio
1	Orientation	1/24	Orientation	1/22	Orientation	- 0.5/24
2	Kick-off lecture	2/24	Campus tour	1/22	↑ Introduction & Challenge releasing	- 0.5/24
3	Challenge releasing	1/24	Introduction & Challenge releasing	1/22	Research method	1/24
4	Design thinking	1/24	Design thinking	1/22	↑ Field research	+ 2(4)/24
5	Design tools	1/24	↑ Field research	- 1/22	↓ Design thinking	+ 2/24
6	Business model	1/24	↑ User study	1/22	↑ Business model	1/24
7	Field research	1(3)/24	↑ Product design	- 0.5/22	Team work on prototype	1/24
8	User study	1/24	↓ Business model	- 0.5/22	↑ Phase report	1/24
9	Field research	1(3)/24	Conceptualization	1/22	↓ Campus tour	1/24
10	Culture experience	4/24	Preliminary prototype	1/22	↓ Culture experience	2/24
11	Open source coding	2/24	Phase report	1/22	Field research	+ 2(4)/24
12	Product design	1/24	↓ Culture experience	4/22	↑ Open source coding	2(3)/24
13	Field research	1(3)/24	Open source coding	+ 2(3)/22	Cultural translation	1/24
14	Product promotion	1/24	↑ Brand value	- 0.5/22	Prototype tools	1/24
15	Brand value	1/24	Crowdfunding	0.5/22	↑ Video producing	1/24
16	Video producing	1/24	Open source coding	+ 1(3)/22	Open source coding	1(3)/24
17	Team work	2/24	Product promotion	1/22	↑ Team work	+ 3/24
18	Presentation	1/24	↓ Video producing	1/22	Presentation	1/24
19			↓ Team work	- 1/22		
20			Presentation	1/22		

*Legend:

    Different classes or classes added from the previous year;
↑   The order is earlier than the previous year;
↓   The order is later than the previous year;
+   The course duration is longer than the previous year;
-    The course duration is shorter than the previous year.

The basic knowledge modules of workshop is divided into four fields: Design, Culture, Business and Technology. The main role of design fields is to provide an innovative process and problem-solving tools. The culture fields help students establish clear concepts and form appropriate evaluation criteria. The business fields help student to develop execution ability to run projects and spread the impact. The technical fields provide a rapid prototyping approach and help to present and validate solutions.

Depending on the purpose, outcomes and feedbacks of workshop, we adjust the syllabuses annually. There are five obvious changes in the syllabuses. (1) The proportion of research method and field research courses has increased and relevant classes have been scheduled at an early stage. We found that after fully understanding the local culture, students can discover more typical problems and lead to more unique and innovative solutions. (2) Cultural analysis class has been added in order to giving students more classes to understand and analyze urban culture. This class can help student learn to decode and transform cultural phenomena into design problems and enable student teams to carry out subsequent design processes or work more specifically. (3) The mid-term concept presentation and initial prototype show has been strengthened since 2017. In the mid-term of the workshop, the guidance on original concepts and expected solutions played a significant role in controlling the final results. (4) More time for team work, help participants to discuss and communicate in depth so that they can fully reach consensus and improve the final results. (5) Arrange timely evaluation of results in the workshop. In short-term activities, dynamic assessments and immediate suggestions help students quickly find research directions.

Through City Change Maker workshop, we hope to explore an education approach on design good for city issues, which can be widely applied and not limited to a specific city or participant background. In this way, students can quickly identify problems of the city, analyze problems and produce influential results.

2   Research Method

This paper conducts research on the educational activities of the workshop based on the grounded theory [4]. The first workshop in 2016 took the model of maker practice and regarded design thinking as a practical process. There are no theoretical assumptions and models in instructional design, so this research can begin with direct observation [5]. We collect the workshop data and use the feedback to adjust the classes every year to verify whether the teaching method contributes to the design practice of social impact. Grounded theory divides the analysis process into four stages: codes, concept, category and theory. Starting from the fragmentary data, this paper will summarize an educational vision and method for the cultivation of City Change Maker by progressive data combing. Through this project, we hope to cultivate makers with the ability to solve city problems, produce design proposals with a strong impact, improve the face of the city and affect the life philosophy of the residents. According to this purpose, we divide the workshop into five stages, namely perspective, integration, transition, outcome and impact. Each stage focuses on cultivating different abilities of students. The cooperation of five stages completes the growth journey of student's capacities. The growth journey was concatenated with different knowledge modules. To achieve the education purpose, we have arranged courses in four fields: Design, Culture, Business and Technology. Each field is subdivided into specific lecture or classes. The organizer needs to find and provide resources to support the teaching elements of workshops, namely educator, students, content, teaching method and tool, venue and more. According to four analysis stages of grounded theory, all activity data will be analyzed and collated in order to improve future education approach after the workshop (Fig. 2).

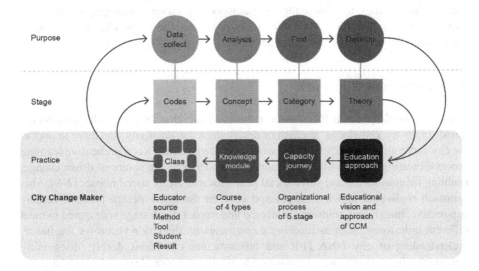

Fig. 2. Schematic diagram of research method based on Grounded Theory

In the data sorting stage, we mainly deal with four types of codes, which come from educators, curriculum content, students and activity output. (1) The educator's data mainly covers the educational background of the instructor, the design experience, the relevant experience on the specific topic, personal resources, reflection and feedback of activities. (2) Data of curriculum content includes the overall planning of the workshop, methods, tools, practice sites, etc. (3) Student data includes basic information of students, grouping, scores, self-evaluation and feedback about workshop. (4) Activity output data include phase results and ratings, final results and ratings, impact of design results and feedback, activity impact and feedback, etc.

Through code analysis and comparisons of similar elements, we have some interesting findings. For instance, the results of the expert's scoring of student projects show that the project of local culture promotion has gained a high degree of recognition, which is also reflected in the feedback of students. Compared to functional product or environmental design, students' project feedbacks are more positive on projects which focus on social impact. Students thought the subject or the theme was fresh and have more passion for them.

Therefore, compared to other professional workshops, our short-term urban related workshops, which themed on social influences and urban community culture, are more likely to trigger a sense of multidisciplinary student participation. City is a collection of citizens and their lives, and in a sense, the city is seen as a cultural container [6], more likely to resonate with participants.

Through the study of workshop data based on grounded theory, we try to summarize and draw up an educational approach. This approach can help organizers to create an innovative curriculum or workshop, especially activity for urban related innovation. Through this approach, event organizers can more smoothly setup design goals, promote students to discover problems, and guide them to develop concept with social influence, thus, to achieve the original workshop vision of changing the city with social innovation activities. After three years of testing, the method has become more mature and can contribute to similar activities.

3   Educational Approach

Our educational approach focusses on cultivating the change maker who possess the interdisciplinary knowledge, strength of design thinking, creativity, and drive to impact the city and community. Through the workshop, we designed a comprehensive learning process, creating opportunities for students to understand the nature of urban change, enabling them to locate and solve social problems and create social impact [7–9]. This approach is divided into five stages and covered the entire design process, namely perspective, integration, transition, outcome and impact. Each stage is designed to meet different milestones, such as reaching a consensus on the city's vision for the future, understanding of city DNA [10] and infrastructure conditions deeply, discovering important urban cultural life pain points, identifying the core ideas of the problem, and providing influential and sustainable solutions to ensure that the subsequent social impact can be expanded. It instructs the workshop organizer how to operate each specific stage, including the goal of this stage, what abilities that students should have, the knowledge modules and the duration, the methods and design tools that can be used, and the completion signs of this stage, etc. Teaching approach is also an iterative process that can be adjusted and optimized each time based on final feedback.

The five stages can be divided into two periods, the first four stages will fulfill during workshop and the stage Impact occurs after workshop. When students participate in the workshop, the organizers should integrate the resources of all parties to form a student's advanced journey, so that they can change from a visitor who knows nothing about a city to a change maker that produces a social innovation. After the workshop, the organizer should continue to contact the relevant subject institutions to help students promote and sustain the later application of results, make their innovative works have a lasting impact. In order to facilitate the application of the approach in practice, we will show more details of the stage in the Fig. 3. The purpose explains the tasks that each stage attempts to accomplish. The capacity of student shows the abilities that students can learn at this stage. The plan contains the knowledge modules and the estimated time of the stage. Tools contain commonly used design methods and toolkits. Organizers can selectively apply these tools depending on the length and focus of the project. The completion mark is the basis for judging whether a student has completed this stage of work. When students can meet the listed criteria, they can proceed to the next stage. Below, the paper will introduce the method, content and actual case of each stage.

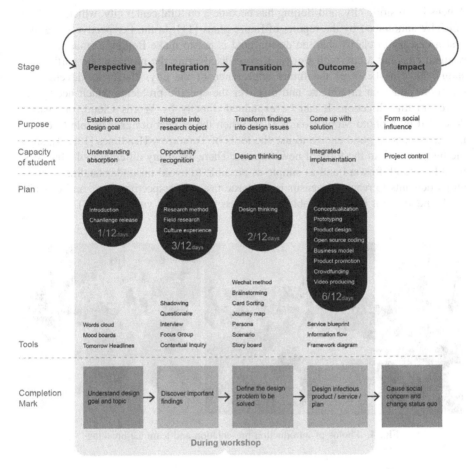

Fig. 3. Diagram of the education approach of design for social impact

3.1 Perspective

In the Perspective stage, the organizer needs to help the student team form a common design vision and goals. As an initial stage of the project, participants are encouraged to discover the city DNA, to fully understand the urban issues that need to be addressed and to find the appropriate way of action. This stage will introduce collaborators and issue challenge targets to help students fully understand and build action guides. The organizer will introduce the background of the event, considerations, implementation process and design methodology, and expected results. At the same time, instructors, mentors, students and volunteers will have opportunities to familiarize themselves with each other in order to form a team.

Before the participants directly feel the city and discover the problem, the stage should guide the participants to see the overall urban design direction. Every city has its own genes, for instance the New York is a financial city, Singapore is a safe city,

Athens is a historic city, and Beijing has become a cultural center city, which has been officially announced by the reports of future plans [11]. In the Perspective stage, it is first necessary to clarify that the design goal is not to make Beijing a smart city or a resilient city, but a city with stories. Before discovering the problem, the participants should have a sketch of the future appearance of the city, clarify its development direction, and then investigate and discover the specific problems which need to be solved in this direction. It can be explained directly by Words Cloud, or visually described by a photo Mood Boards [12]. When the project designer unable to clearly target, it is also a good choice to use the tools of Tomorrow Headlines [13, 14], show the future vision in the form of news reports. There are many different tools, but these must be straightforward and as simple as possible to avoid misunderstanding. Getting all participants to reach consensus is the basic task of Perspective stage, and it is also the foundation for building problem awareness and project vision (Fig. 4).

Fig. 4. Photos of introduction presentation and team ice-breaking

3.2 Integration

In integrating stage, our common approach is to give students a full understanding of the local situation through two levels of experience classes. First is a cultural journey dominated by immersive experience. Students do not need to observe a problem in a specific way, as long as they feel the overall cultural outlook of the city. We have arranged the famous monuments, gardens, old streets, specialty shops and other places in Beijing as a cultural experience classroom. Second is a deep field research that serves the subsequent design process. Before the field research [15], we will schedule a class to plan the investigation method for each topic, and contact the appropriate field survey site in advance, to enable students to target the problems faced by cities and residents. This stage focuses on developing students' opportunity recognition skills. Each team is asked to present 6 to 12 important findings for subsequent collation and selection.

At this stage, besides the student team, there are three other role interventions, local residents, agencies and mentors, to help students immerse themselves in local life or work from a cultural perspective. This stage should allow students to fully integrate into the research object and environment, so we usually choose characteristic field research sites to drop students into the actual situation in local context [16]. Mentors tend to bring participants to places with deep cultural characteristics in Beijing, such as old workers' settlements, historical hutongs, schools for children of migrant workers, and so on. It also means students and mentors are involved in community activities they may not be familiar with. It has both advantages and disadvantages in discovering urban problems. As a result, two additional roles have been added at this stage, namely, local residents and agencies. Local residents help introduce the real situation and take students to experience the local culture in depth. Agencies is usually a non-profit organization or NGO who interested in the subject, has maintained close contact with the local and carried out projects, as intermediaries and pioneers can objectively guide students, from the perspective of bystanders and researchers to explore the local cultural issues (Fig. 5).

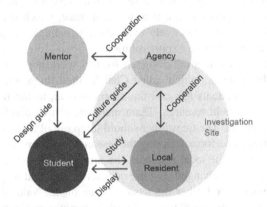

Fig. 5. Diagram of roles in step integrate

In a practice, the choice of local resident and agency is crucial because it determines the depth of the research. In 2018, one of cultural heritage project, the team of Huanzhuogege (A game to collect pigeon species of Beijing Hutong with mobile AR application) had a deep investigation in the old hutongs. They observed the original habit of residents and sat in the quadrangle to chat with the old Peking man as well as drinking tea, to experience the traditional lifestyle. The agent responsible for the docking of the research activities is the researcher of Hutong architecture. She chose Beijing's well-preserved Fayuan Temple neighborhood as research site, where she contacted local residents and shared issues identified in previous studies. In 2017, a partner of a food market in Beijing brought participants to the Wool Mill community in order to conduct a field survey on food topics. This community was where workers of a woolen mill had lived from the last century. The buildings and public space were aging and difficult to manage. The original public green space was privately circled by individual residents and vegetables were grown. In such context, agent communicate with community council directors, CSA (community-supported agriculture) volunteers, private growers and other residents to help students fully understand the claims of all stakeholders. The involvement of local residents and agency has had a huge impact on design research.

3.3 Transition

In Transition stage, we drive students to transform the research findings into design direction. This stage trains the student's capacity of design thinking that leads the solution from a local problem or citizen need. In this workshop, students will focus on solving one of the most representative problems due to factors such as activity time and design capabilities, which tend to be deeper than the big system, which attempts to cover all findings. Therefore, students have to choose the most characteristic finding, which can be interpreted from a new perspective, or undiscovered, or urgently solved. This phase is generally divided into two states to facilitate the collation of survey data, the analysis of data, the discovery of problems, and the selection of issues that need to be addressed. The first state is a semi-jump state, in which students often play the role of the interviewees to continue deducing the findings in research. The purpose of this process is to recall the memory of field research and expand the number of problems that can be studied. The second state is a full-jump state, which team members often use design analysis tools to objectively evaluate the findings, finally to choose one problem or one kind of issues to export solution.

In the first state, a new method designed for this workshop is often used to help students transfer the findings, which called Chat Method. In generally, it operates in such a way that some students ask and the others answer, to recall the memory and discuss the problems of field research. Team members can be divided into two parts: questioner and respondent. The questioner should jump out of the role of local resident who the students tried to perform as during the research and the respondent should give the answer as the way of the local resident. The numbers of two groups are not fixed and the roles also can be exchanged. For the questioner, it would be preferable to have well-prepared questions for further discussion based on the valuable findings of the field study. For respondents, maintaining the role's empathy position helps to respond more effectively. Before answering questions, the respondents should show their identity such as "I am Grandma Zhang of the first quadrangle in XXX Hutong" and answer questions in her capacity. This method is suitable for the early period, which can diversify the number of valuable questions. In the second state, the goal is to narrow down the problem pool and position the team on one problem. Many relatively mature design tools can be used to help students judge problems from the perspective of bystanders, such as card sorting, voted stickers or labels, etc. (Fig. 6).

Fig. 6. Photos of communicating with design tools

3.4 Outcome

The Outcome stage will take up half of the workshop period, students should develop the design results according to the survey, which can be a product, service, or action plan. In this stage, the tasks performed by the students are very similar to the traditional design and design evaluation process. Organizers help students fully consider and develop design projects by providing three types of classes: design, business and technology. At the same time, students need to report a number of results in this stage, presenting design concept, design prototype and high-fidelity models. With intensive assessment and feedback, students' works can be iterated multiple times in a short period of time, ensuring the maturity of the final results. In the final presentation, in addition to the high-fi prototype, each team will also display project poster and concept video. The poster is used by the guests to quickly grasp the project overview and communicate with the team members, the video is convenient to spread on social media and websites. When inviting final presentation reviewers, it is important to note that invitees' background should cover all topics, organizers also need to invite representatives from the media and investment, as well as government officials. Guests can make a full evaluation of the student project from all aspects, but also put forward the possibility of further development, in order to expand the social impact in the future. This stage mainly trains the students' integration realization ability.

It is suggested that the evaluation criteria of final works should be published at the beginning of workshop, and run through them all the times, as a consensus to guide the final design. Through the analysis of the final works, we find that the influential works usually have four features: social topic, narrative expression, co-participatory mechanism and transmissible carrier (Fig. 7).

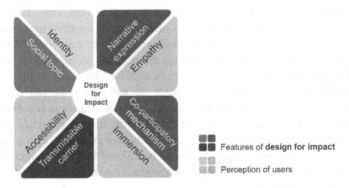

Fig. 7. Diagram of features of design for impact

The four features meet different users' cognitive needs and habits respectively [17, 18]. Social topic emphasizes that selected topic can evoke similar memories and experiences of the audience, or they can recognize the values conveyed by the work, so that it can catch the common feeling to deeply understand the connotation of the work. Narrative expression caters to the memory characteristics of the audience. Story cases are easier to be remembered and traced back than introductory content. At the same time, story-based content can touch and resonate the audience emotion directly. The purpose of co-participatory mechanism is to increase the richness of the user experience. Other features provide the audience with a passively perceived approach, and it is used to stimulate the audience's active behavior. Transmissible carrier is the decisive factor to the scope of impact. From the perspective of the audience, the ideas they can acquire are the basis for accepting and disseminating the concept of design works (Fig. 8).

Fig. 8. Photos of final presentation

3.5 Impact

This stage takes place after workshop. It was a time to promote the innovative achievements of the project and promote the social impact of the student's work. In the previous stages, we asked students to pay attention to the social impact of the work. In this stage, in addition to the transformation of final results, we also need to spread the concept of urban change and innovative design through project work. Because of the characteristics of short-term workshop, it is often difficult for team members to work together to improve and maintain the final achievement after the event. Therefore, it is an important task for the organizer to connect the appropriate cooperative partners for the team. These partners must be able to identify with the idea of the works, and be able to continuously promote or use it as a basis for subsequent project development, resulting in greater social impact of workshop. The connection between student teams and partners is not only reflected in the final presentation, we invited partners to participate in the project at the beginning, and they can even play as a team mentor. Such project results are more targeted and can be tailored to a more targeted solution. We hope the creations of this workshop could produce real effects on the urban lifestyle and even local culture industry.

In academic terms, at the end of each year's workshop, we will put forward a design action plan to discuss future research direction with our stakeholders. We hope the plans can provide references for urban innovation design in various fields. With our educational approach, student teams have created many works with social impact. A series of courses developed on the project has been using in QC Maker Education [19], the transportation solutions proposed at the event have been incorporated into the next step plan of the China Transportation Research Institute in Beijing. The urban regeneration project has been exhibited in public events, and we are pleased that the Beijing municipal government has introduced a policy to support urban regeneration rather than new construction after demolition, so student works will have a better prospect of application in the future.

4 Reflection and Discussion

As a unique design object, the city has a lot of issues need to be studied, no matter from the geographical range to the time range. Therefore, how to guide students to identify the characteristics and pain points of urban life is a topic worthy of study. This paper gives organizers three suggestions from the workshop practice, including emphasizing the citizen's lifestyle, taking the city as the culture container, and carrying out innovative design centering on cultural themes.

First of all, in the preparation of topic selection, organizers can start from the city's software, namely the city's culture. Because the culture is the embodiment of lifestyle, it can have more influence on urban communities and residents. In terms of culture, the design that focuses on solving everyday problems is often more difficult to land in the short term, and designs that focus on specific cultural issues are better disseminated. The second suggestion is to break down the elements of urban culture, just like peeling onions. Culture is a huge concept, in the short-term workshop, more suitable to focus on small and unique areas. During the preparatory phase, the project mentor needs to divide the cultural themes to lead the team to a more focused and targeted topic. Before the workshop, organizers can also send the subject content to members who have already signed up, allowing them to participate in learning and join with questions. Finally, it is best to choose a more distinctive problem, rather than a common problem of popularity. This is the general principle of most short-term design workshop. Accurate problem finding often helps to get good answers. Unique and clear questions always lead to corresponding good results. Therefore, it was necessary to spend more time to refine the problem, this iteration helps many teams to perform well in the final design.

Macroscopically, if the design for social impact is divided into two dimensions, one is how the output of design process achieves impact, and the other is how the design, as a social activity, makes greater impact. The fields of City Change Maker workshop touch on all aspects of urban life, from life, transportation, health to cultural activities, and design disciplines provides ideas and tools to systematically solve urban problems. During the workshop, our partners also changed their previous understanding of design, finding that design is not only a tool for visualization of ideas, but a means of pooling resources, tapping needs and making social innovations. Design can break people's inertial thinking mode, affect more stakeholders and have a greater impact in more areas, that is, what we call the concept of "big design", City Change Maker is also trying to break through the application of design routines, explore the role and value of "big design" to solve urban problems. However, because of the lack of understanding of design by the public and collaborators, there are still many difficulties and limitations in the promotion and implementation of the workshop.

The design practice cases and design methods presented in this paper are based on the following basic conditions: (1) The workshop time is compact, (2) The participants come from a multidisciplinary background, (3) The cross-cultural research and practice is carried out in unfamiliar urban communities, and (4) The demand for output emphasizes social influence. If the activity conditions are different, the applicability of the educational approach is also reduced. In addition, due to time and financial constraints, the target city studied in this paper is only Beijing, the students are only from Hong Kong and Macao, there is no other reference sample can be compared.

5 Conclusion

This paper introduces a short-term design innovation workshop, City Change Maker, aiming to solving city issues and change the city with social innovation methods. In the workshop, students from Hong Kong and Macao were invited to Beijing for a two-week design innovation training. With the project, we hope to develop students' capacity to identify and analysis the city issues to improve and enhance the quality of urban culture with innovative thinking and methods, and to train students became the change makers. This paper is a summary and reflection of the three-year workshop practice. Using grounded theory as an analytical approach, the authors propose educational approach that can be used for social innovation activities, and can promote the application of design thinking and practice in multidisciplinary teams. The approach is divided into five stages, namely perspective, integration, transition, outcome and impact. In Perspective stage, participants are led to fully understand the city DNA and build design consensus. In Integration stage, participants need to conduct field research and find real city problems that need to be solved. In Transition stage, participants should translate the results of field research into design issues. In Outcome stage, participants should prototype the ideas and propose an action plan. In Impact stage, the participants' results are released and the organizers and partners will help in disseminate and influence. In terms of practical content, we emphasize the city as a container of culture. At the research phase, student team needs to decompose and transform cultural issues into design problems. At the practice phase, the final results should be more social, communicative, participatory and experiential.

For the future research, based on the optimization of educational approach, we will combine the practical cases to focus on the design tools and presentation mode of the social influence of cultural projects.

Acknowledgement. City Change Maker is sponsored by the Hong Kong, Macao and Taiwan Office of Tsinghua University, and hosted by the Service Design Institute of Academy of Arts & Design, Tsinghua University and the Innovation & Entrepreneurship Education Alliance of China. The authors especially thank all the mentors, project partners, staffs and volunteers for their contribution to the workshop, and Ling Chyi Chan's help with paper writing.

References

1. World Lab. http://worldlab.cs.washington.edu/about/. Accessed 30 Jan 2019
2. Report of World Lab. http://www.washington.edu/news/2012/08/30/new-program-joins-computer-science-and-design-experts-at-uw-tsinghua-university/. Accessed 30 Jan 2019
3. Report of City Change Maker. http://servicedesign-tsinghua.com/index.php?g=&m=article&a=index&id=337&cid=14. Accessed 30 Jan 2019
4. Martin, P.Y., Turner, B.A.: Grounded theory and organizational research. J. Appl. Behav. Sci. **22**(2), 141 (1986)
5. Allan, G.: A critique of using grounded theory as a research method. Electron. J. Bus. Res. Methods **2**(1), 1–10 (2003)
6. Jiang, L., Li, P.Y., Fu, Y.Y.: City is the container of culture. Chin. Soc. Sci. Wkly. **6** (2017)
7. Latané, B.: The psychology of social impact. Am. Psychol. **36**(4), 343–356 (1981)
8. Jacobi, N., Chiappero-Martinetti, E.: Social innovation, individuals and societies: an empirical investigation of multi-layered effects. J. Soc. Entrep. **8**(3), 271–301 (2017)
9. Brown, T., Wyatt, J.: Design thinking for social innovation. Dev. Outreach **12**(1), 29–43 (2010)
10. Race, B.: We're turning our back on the city's design DNA. Indianap. Bus. J. **33**(40), 12A (2012)
11. Beijing City Master Plan (2016–2035). http://www.bjghw.gov.cn/web/ztgh/ztgh001.html/. Accessed 30 Jan 2019
12. Garner, S., McDonagh-Philp, D.: Problem interpretation and resolution via visual stimuli: the use of 'mood boards' in design education. Int. J. Art Des. Educ. **20**(1), 57–64 (2001)
13. Introduction Page of Tomorrow Headlines. http://www.servicedesigntools.org/tools/14. Accessed 30 Jan 2019
14. Introduction Page of Next Year's Headline. https://www.designmethodsfinder.com/methods/predict-next-years-headline. Accessed 30 Jan 2019
15. Burgess, R.G.: In the Field: An Introduction to Field Research, 4th edn. Routledge, New York (1990)
16. Vorkinn, M., Riese, H.: Environmental concern in a local context: the significance of place attachment. Environ. Behav. **33**(2), 249–263 (2001)
17. Rogoff, B.: Apprenticeship in Thinking: Cognitive Development in Social Context, 1st edn. Oxford University Press, New York (1990)
18. Neisser, U.: Cognitive Psychology, 1st edn. Psychology Press, New York (2014)
19. The Homepage of QC Maker Education. http://www.qcmaker.com/. Accessed 30 Jan 2019

A Comparison of Critical Time Interval Between Young and Old Subjects

Hongbo Zhang$^{(\boxtimes)}$

Department of Computer and Information Sciences, Virginia Military Institute,
Lexington, VA 24450, USA
zhangh@vmi.edu

Abstract. Earlier research showed that human quiet upright stance posture is intermittently controlled through both open and closed loop control mechanisms. Critical time interval (CTI), the duration describing the time interval between the intermittent control signals is essential to understand the switch frequency of between the open and closed loop control. Yet the value of CTI, in particular the differences between young and older adults remain insufficiently investigated and thus un-clarified. In this research, intermittent critical time interval (ICTI) method was proposed to evaluate the differences of CTI between young and older adults. Consistent to conventional CTI method, it was found that young adults have larger CTI than older adults. The results from the ICTI method have smaller variation and better consistency across participants compared to the conventional CTI method. It is suggested that the higher frequency of intermittent control signals among older adults could be an indicator of lack of confidence or capacity in maintaining quiet upright stance.

Keywords: Critical time interval · Quiet upright stance postural control · Aging

1 Introduction

Human postural control is critical for maintaining balance of posture, which is subjected to risks of falling due to gravity and other internal/external perturbations. Multiple factors contribute to postural control mainly including neuromuscular, vision, proprioception, and vestibular systems. All these factors are integrated together forming a control system including actuator and feedback and feed forward control signals (Zhang et al. 2016; Zhang et al. 2014; Lockhart and Ting 2007; Maurer et al. 2006; Peterka 2002). It was proposed that instead of continuously activating ankle and trunk muscles, these muscle groups only contract intermittently under both open and closed loop control for maintaining the postural stability (Asai et al. 2009; Collins and De Luca 1993; Gawthrop et al. 2011; Loram et al. 2011; Nomura et al. 2013; Suzuki et al. 2012). The time interval between the intermittent postural control signal bursting events, which is also the time taken shifting from open to closed loop control is defined as critical time interval (CTI) (Collins et al. 1995; Collins and De Luca 1993).

Though not thoroughly investigated, the impacts of aging on postural control, in particular the critical time interval of the intermittent postural controller have been

© Springer Nature Switzerland AG 2019
P.-L. P. Rau (Ed.): HCII 2019, LNCS 11577, pp. 270–278, 2019.
https://doi.org/10.1007/978-3-030-22580-3_20

studied by previous research. It was demonstrated that the open loop control time interval was 300–600 ms longer for older adults (Collins et al. 1995). Additionally, older adults have increased postural correction activities in the mediolateral plane with prolonged open loop control time interval (Mitchell et al. 1995). More specifically, the ankle muscle response latency was found 15–20 ms longer among older adults during balance recovery process (Mackey and Robinovitch 2006).

However, existing CTI quantification methods have produced conflicting results and not well clarified. While conventional CTI method yielded the results at a rather wide range of 0.33–1.67 s (Collins and De Luca 1993), yet a smaller range of critical time interval approximately 1.0 s, was demonstrated by other studies (Doyle et al. 2008; Peterka 2000). Meanwhile though some research demonstrated a CTI about 1.3– 1.6 s (Chiari et al. 2000; Newell et al. 1997), a much smaller approximately 0.5 s critical time interval has been identified by another study (Vieira et al. 2009). The lack of consensus for the critical time interval thus demands more research for investigating it. Hence, a further evaluation of the critical time interval differences between young and older adults is needed.

The objective of the study is thus to propose a new critical time interval (CTI) quantification method to quantify the differences of CTI between young and older adults. It is expected that the new CTI method can more consistently and accurately identify the effects of aging on the intermittent postural controller. The results of the study could also be useful for providing insights for postural control modeling studies.

2   Methods

2.1   Experimental Setup

32 participants, age and gender balanced, were recruited in this study. The details of the study is also given in the noted publication (Lin et al. 2008). All participants gave informed consent as approved by the Virginia Tech Institutional Review Board, and had no self-reported injuries, illness, musculoskeletal disorders, or falls in the year prior to the experiment. Participants were instructed to stand (without shoes) as still as possible on the force platform (AMTI OR6-7-1000, Massachusetts, USA) for three trials, with their feet together, arms by their sides, head upright, and eyes closed. Each trial lasted 75 s with at least one minute rest time interval from the next standing trial. The tri-axial ground reaction forces and moments from the force platform were sampled at 100 Hz. Raw signals were low-pass filtered (Butterworth, 5 Hz cut-off frequency, 4th order, zero lag), transformed to obtain center of pressure (COP) time series, and the first 10 s and the last 5 s were removed, resulting in 60 s COP data for use.

2.2   Critical Time Interval Methods

Conventional Critical Time Interval Method. The conventional critical time interval identification method demonstrated that the first minimum of the second order derivate of the diffusion coefficients corresponds to the CTI (Collins and De Luca 1993; Stamp

1997). The diffusion coefficients and its second order derivate are shown in Fig. 1. In Fig. 1 (bottom), it is evident that the second order derivate of the diffusion coefficients decreases starting from 0 s and reaches its first local minimum at around 1.0 s. Consistently, the time is also approximately equal to the time as the postural control switches from open-loop to closed-loop control, which is also the CTI (Fig. 1-top). As such, heuristically, the time window of the first local minimum of the second order derivate of the diffusion coefficients is determined as the critical time interval.

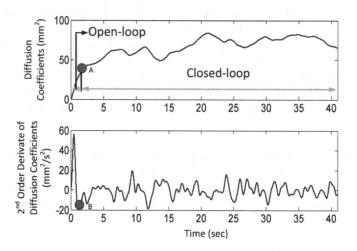

Fig. 1. Diffusion coefficients (top) and the second order derivate of the diffusion coefficients (bottom). Point A represents the distinction of open-loop control from closed-loop control. Point B is the first local minimum of the second order derivate of the diffusion coefficients.

More specifically, as shown in Fig. 1 (top), the critical time interval should be correspondent to the time interval when the increase rate of diffusion coefficient has slowly reached its minimum. It means that CTI should be approximately correspondent to the minimum of the changing rate. Mathematically, the second order derivate diffusion coefficients characterize the changing rate of the diffusion coefficients. Collins and De Luca 1993 proposed that the CTI is equal to the fist minimum of the second order derivate of the diffusion coefficients data. Likely based on a trial-and-error approach, they determined that the first local minimum of 2.5 s of the second order derivate of the diffusion coefficients data can yield the most confident CTI.

Intermittent Critical Time Interval Method. Upright stance is controlled intermittently. The intermittent control switches from open-loop to closed-loop can occur under the situation when the stability of the posture is threatened. More specifically, the intermittent contraction of the tibialis anterior muscle is evident when body sways away from the equilibrium positions during upright stance (Di Giulio et al. 2009). It was also suggested that the switching point is associated with local maximum (such as a local spike) of the posture (Bottaro et al. 2005). As such, identification of the local maxima can reveal the time intervals between the bursts of the intermittent postural control signals. For this aim, the Wavelet modulus maximum method was applied, because it is known able to extract the local maxima or singularities from a signal (Mallat and Hwang 1992).

Wavelet modulus maximum method searched the local region and identified local maxima from the wavelet power spectrum within a certain time and across a range of frequency band (Mallat and Hwang 1992). A representative output of the Wavelet modulus maximum is shown in Fig. 2. In Fig. 2, it is evident that the local maxima of the COP signal were extracted through the modulus maximum (MM). It also appears that MM is vertically aligned along the x-axis with the time interval between them approximately uniform. At a specific time, across the frequency of 0.5–1.1 Hz known associated with human quiet upright stance postural control (Singh et al. 2012; Thurner et al. 2000), MMs form a vertical line, namely Wavelet Modulus Maximum Line (MML). Since the MML represents the switching point between open-loop and closed-loop control, the time interval between the MMLs is equal to the CTI. The presence of MML is intermittent, as such the CTI is also named as intermittent CTI (ICTI) in distinction from the conventional CTI method.

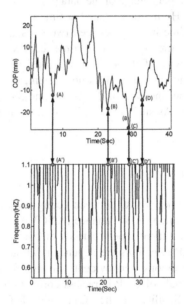

Fig. 2. Center of Pressure (COP, top) and Wavelet modulus maximum (Bottom). A, B, C, D represent the local maximum of the center of pressure. A', B', C', D' represent the Wavelet modulus maximum, which can corresponds to the positions of local maximum of the COP.

At specific time, MML method attempts to construct a vertical line from the discrete MM points across a range of frequency band. MML(f, t) was defined as a line consisting of the modulus maximum wavelet power spectrum points at time t across the frequency band from f_1 to f_2. This can be described by

$$MML(f,t) \overset{d}{=} \{MM(f,t), t = t_{\min}\ldots t_{\max}, f = f_1 \ldots f_2\} \tag{1}$$

s.t.

$$|t_{\max} - t_{\min}| \leq 2\Delta t_{MML}$$

where f is 0.5–1.1 Hz and t is between 0–40.96 s; and $MML(f,t)$ is a modulus maximum line consisting of modulus maximum $MM(f,t)$. Specifically, for time t, the modulus maximum line is restricted within a line searching time interval of $2\Delta t_{MML}$, start from $t - \Delta t_{MML}$ and end at $t + \Delta t_{MML}$.

As illustrated in Fig. 3, at a specific time t, the search scanned each frequency in the 0.5–1.1 Hz band (starting at the higher end) and marked the positions of the modulus maxima in the region of $[t - \Delta t_{MML}, t + \Delta t_{MML}]$. Within this region, the mean across identified modulus maxima at a given frequency was treated as one data point that belonged to the modulus maximum line at time t. This scanning and identification process was repeated for all times t in a trial 0 to 40.96 s and yielded a set of MMLs. To exclude the too short MMLs, the final MMLs also need to satisfy the length ratio of MML, which is equal to the percentage of the data points on a MML versus the total of data points across 0.5–1.1 Hz frequency band at time t.

CTI is defined as the time interval between two consequent MMLs. More specifically, CTI is equal to the differences of two consequent MMLs. ICTI is equal to the mean of CTIs. The sensitivity of the ICTI to the local searching region Δt_{MML} and length ratio of MML is shown in Fig. 4. Among them, 60% of length ratio yielded average level of CTI. Further increase of tMML beyond 390 ms did not benefit to the significant decrease of CTI. As such, 60% of length ratio and 390 ms of tMML were used in this study.

3 Statistical Analysis

The differences of critical time interval between young and older adults were analyzed through repeated measures analysis of variance (ANOVA). In ANOVA model, age is an independent variable and three repeated trials of conventional CTI and ICTI per subject in both ML and AP directions are dependent variables. No substantial departures from parametric assumptions were evident, and significance was concluded when $P < 0.05$. Three repeated trials of COP intraclass correlation coefficients (ICCs) were used to determine the reliability of the ICTI, with ICC < 0.4 (poor reliability), $0.4 \leq \text{ICC} \leq 0.75$ (fair to good reliability), and ICC > 0.75 (excellent reliability) (Chiari et al. 2000).

4 Results

The results of critical time interval from both conventional CTI and ICTI methods indicated young adult CTI is significantly larger than that of older adults in both mediolateral (ML) (<0.0001) and anteroposterior (AP) (<0.0001) directions. The

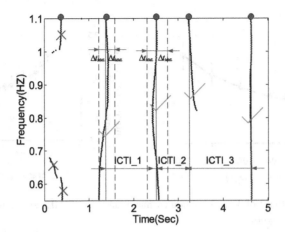

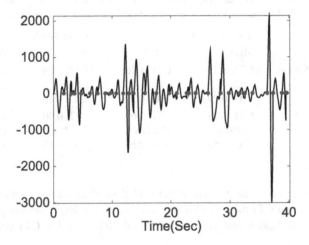

Fig. 3. Wavelet modulus maximum line (MML) identification process. Top: X represents the MMLs not able to meet the MML identification length ratio criterion. ∨ represents the qualified MML. CTI_1, CTI_2, and CTI_3 are the time intervals between MMLs. Δt_{MML} is the MML search interval. Bottom: An example of identified critical points.

results of the CTI and ICC for both young and older adults are summarized in the Table 1.

5   Discussion

In this research, a new CTI quantification method namely ICTI was created to quantify the critical time interval. In contrast to previous results (Collins et al. 1995), which showed that older adults have larger CTI, ICTI method however demonstrated the

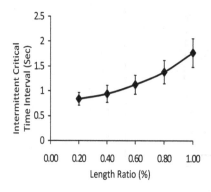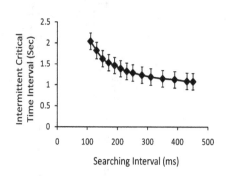

Fig. 4. The sensitivity of Wavelet modulus maximum line (MML) to length ratio (left) and searching interval (right).

Table 1. The results of critical time interval (CTI) and intraclass correlation coefficients (ICC) of young and older adults from both conventional CTI and ICTI methods

	Young Adults		Older Adults	
	ML	AP	ML	AP
Conventional Method (CTI)	CTI: 1.33 (0.38) s ICC: 0.27	CTI: 1.30 (0.41) s ICC: 0.58	CTI: 1.09 (0.38) s ICC: 0.16	CTI: 1.02 (0.39) s ICC: 0.06
New Method (ICTI)	CTI: 1.08 (0.19) s ICC: 0.53	CTI: 1.03 (0.14) s ICC: 0.65	CTI: 0.96 (0.17) s ICC: 0.67	CTI: 0.89 (0.12) s ICC: 0.70

opposite showing young adults have larger CTI than older adults. Consistent to ICTI results, conventional CTI method also showed that CTI is larger among young adults. The consistency indicates that older adults should have smaller CTI compared with young adults.

Though similar results yielded from both methods, the results from conventional CTI method have larger variation, which might explain the wide variation of CTI results obtained from conventional CTI methods in existing literatures. Conventional CTI method treated the first local minimum of the second order derivate of diffusion coefficients as its CTI making the method sensitive to noises embedded in the COP data. In distinction from the conventional CTI method, the ICTI method attempts to find the CTI in specific frequency range, 0.5–1.1 Hz. This frequency range is associated with postural control mechanisms and less likely containing high frequency noise (Singh et al. 2012).

The reduced critical time interval indicates increased frequency of postural control signal, which could be a result of lower extremity muscle weakness associated with aging frequently regarded as one major factor contributing to the compromised postural control among older adults (Daubney and Culham 1999; Pijnappels et al. 2008). Due to the lowered capacity of these postural control actuators, the lower extremity muscles need to adjust more frequently in order to maintain upright stance balance. Additionally, it is known that aging brain suffers from increased neuronal noises in the presence of structure, volumetric, and neurotransmitter changes (Bã et al. 2000; Boyke et al. 2008; Hedden and Gabrieli 2004; Raz et al. 2005). Thus it suspects that the aging brain might not able to generate appropriate postural control signals during quiet upright stance.

Compared to the conventional CTI method, the ICTI method is more reliable. Collins showed that the CTI ICC is between 0.04 and 0.62 (Collins and De Luca 1993). Similarly, ICCs from enhanced CTI method are in the range of 0.2–0.85 (Chiari et al. 2000). However, the ICTI method yielded the ICC all above 0.5 in both ML and AP directions and larger than conventional CTI method. Better reliability of the ICTI method may indicate the method is less likely affected by various postural control signal noises such as the neuromuscular, data collection, and environmental noises underlying the intermittent postural control signals.

Several drawbacks remain within this research. First, only limited frequency band 0.5–1.1 Hz was explored to identify CTI. Though this is a frequency band mostly likely associated with quiet upright stance postural control mechanisms, analysis of other frequency bands and its relationship with CTI could be useful. Second, the results demonstrated that older adults have smaller CTI, indicating the higher of postural control frequency, yet the specific underlying causes of this still remain to be identified.

References

Asai, Y., Tasaka, Y., Nomura, K., Nomura, T., Casadio, M., Morasso, P.: A model of postural control in quiet standing: robust compensation of delay-induced instability using intermittent activation of feedback control. PLoS ONE **4**, e6169 (2009)

Bã, L., Ginovart, N., Dixon, R.A., Wahlin, T.-B.R., Halldin, C., Farde, L.: Age-related cognitive deficits mediated by changes in the striatal dopamine system. Am. J. Psychiatry **157**, 635–637 (2000)

Bottaro, A., Casadio, M., Morasso, P.G., Sanguineti, V.: Body sway during quiet standing: is it the residual chattering of an intermittent stabilization process? Hum. Mov. Sci. **24**, 588–615 (2005)

Boyke, J., Driemeyer, J., Gaser, C., Büchel, C., May, A.: Training-induced brain structure changes in the elderly. J. Neurosci. **28**, 7031–7035 (2008)

Chiari, L., Cappello, A., Lenzi, D., Della, C.U.: An improved technique for the extraction of stochastic parameters from stabilograms. Gait Posture **12**, 225–234 (2000)

Collins, J., De Luca, C., Burrows, A., Lipsitz, L.: Age-related changes in open-loop and closed-loop postural control mechanisms. Exp. Brain Res. **104**, 480–492 (1995)

Collins, J.J., De Luca, C.J.: Open-loop and closed-loop control of posture: a random-walk analysis of center-of-pressure trajectories. Exp. Brain Res. **95**, 308–318 (1993)

Daubney, M.E., Culham, E.G.: Lower-extremity muscle force and balance performance in adults aged 65 years and older. Phys. Ther. **79**, 1177–1185 (1999)

Di Giulio, I., Maganaris, C.N., Baltzopoulos, V., Loram, I.D.: The proprioceptive and agonist roles of gastrocnemius, soleus and tibialis anterior muscles in maintaining human upright posture. J. Physiol. **587**, 2399–2416 (2009)

Doyle, R.J., Ragan, B.G., Rajendran, K., Rosengren, K.S., Hsiao-Wecksler, E.T.: Generalizability of stabilogram diffusion analysis of center of pressure measures. Gait Posture **27**, 223–230 (2008)

Gawthrop, P., Loram, I., Lakie, M., Gollee, H.: Intermittent control: a computational theory of human control. Biol. Cybern. **104**, 31–51 (2011)

Hedden, T., Gabrieli, J.D.: Insights into the ageing mind: a view from cognitive neuroscience. Nat. Rev. Neurosci. **5**, 87–96 (2004)

Lin, D., Seol, H., Nussbaum, M.A., Madigan, M.L.: Reliability of COP-based postural sway measures and age-related differences. Gait Posture **28**, 337–342 (2008)

Lockhart, D.B., Ting, L.H.: Optimal sensorimotor transformations for balance. Nat. Neurosci. **10**, 1329–1336 (2007)

Loram, I.D., Gollee, H., Lakie, M., Gawthrop, P.J.: Human control of an inverted pendulum: is continuous control necessary? Is intermittent control effective? Is intermittent control physiological? J. Physiol. **589**, 307–324 (2011)

Mackey, D.C., Robinovitch, S.N.: Mechanisms underlying age-related differences in ability to recover balance with the ankle strategy. Gait Posture **23**, 59–68 (2006)

Mallat, S., Hwang, W.L.: Singularity detection and processing with wavelets. IEEE Trans. Inf. Theory **38**, 617–643 (1992)

Maurer, C., Mergner, T., Peterka, R.: Multisensory control of human upright stance. Exp. Brain Res. **171**, 231–250 (2006)

Mitchell, S., Collin, J., De Luca, C., Burrows, A., Lipsitz, L.: Open-loop and closed-loop postural control mechanisms in Parkinson's disease: increased mediolateral activity during quiet standing. Neurosci. Lett. **197**, 133–136 (1995)

Newell, K., Slobounov, S., Slobounova, E., Molenaar, P.: Stochastic processes in postural center-of-pressure profiles. Exp. Brain Res. **113**, 158–164 (1997)

Nomura, T., Oshikawa, S., Suzuki, Y., Kiyono, K., Morasso, P.: Modeling human postural sway using an intermittent control and hemodynamic perturbations. Math. Biosci. **245**, 86–95 (2013)

Peterka, R.: Sensorimotor integration in human postural control. J. Neurophysiol. **88**, 1097–1118 (2002)

Peterka, R.J.: Postural control model interpretation of stabilogram diffusion analysis. Biol. Cybern. **82**, 335–343 (2000)

Pijnappels, M., Reeves, N.D., van Dieën, J.H.: Identification of elderly fallers by muscle strength measures. Eur. J. Appl. Physiol. **102**, 585–592 (2008)

Raz, N., Lindenberger, U., Rodrigue, K.M., Kennedy, K.M., Head, D., Williamson, A., et al.: Regional brain changes in aging healthy adults: general trends, individual differences and modifiers. Cereb. Cortex **15**, 1676–1689 (2005)

Singh, N.B., Taylor, W.R., Madigan, M.L., Nussbaum, M.A.: The spectral content of postural sway during quiet stance: influences of age, vision and somatosensory inputs. J. Electromyogr. Kinesiol. **22**, 131–136 (2012)

Stamp, A. (1997). http://isbweb.org/software/movanal/stamp/

Suzuki, Y., Nomura, T., Casadio, M., Morasso, P.: Intermittent control with ankle, hip, and mixed strategies during quiet standing: a theoretical proposal based on a double inverted pendulum model. J. Theor. Biol. **310**, 55–79 (2012)

Thurner, S., Mittermaier, C., Hanel, R., Ehrenberger, K.: Scaling-violation phenomena and fractality in the human posture control systems. arXiv preprint physics/0007067 (2000)

Vieira, Td.M.M., de Oliveira, L.F., Nadal, J.: An overview of age-related changes in postural control during quiet standing tasks using classical and modern stabilometric descriptors. J. Electromyogr. Kinesiol. **19**, e513–e519 (2009)

Zhang, H.B., Madigan, M.L., Nussbaum, M.A.: Use of wavelet coherence to assess two-joint coordination during quiet upright stance. J. Electromyogr. Kinesiol. **24**, 607–613 (2014)

Zhang, H.B., Madigan, M.L., Nussbaum, M.A.: Development of a sliding mode control model for quiet upright stance. Med. Eng. Phys. **38**, 204–208 (2016)

QianLi: A Modular System for Connecting Distant Family Members Through Tacit Interaction

Zhibin Zhou[1,2], Hao Jiang[1,2(✉)], Changyuan Yang[3], Jinglan Yang[2], Yong Yi Wendy Loy[4], and Lingyun Sun[1,2]

[1] Alibaba-Zhejiang University Joint Institute of Frontier Technologies, Hangzhou, China
jiang_hao@zju.edu.cn
[2] International Design Institute, Zhejiang University, Hangzhou, China
[3] Alibaba Group, Hangzhou, China
[4] Singapore University of Technology and Design, Singapore, Singapore

Abstract. Many families are now geographically separated for various reasons, while most of current communication technologies call for active participation and are intrusive. In this paper, we propose the concept of tacit interaction that supports nonintrusive communication. The concept is then applied to the design of the QianLi system comprising a central base and several modular devices that help distant family members to tacitly stay in touch without excessive intrusion. Such tacit interaction in the QianLi system is realized using artificial intelligence and the Internet of Things technology. When the user fulfils a predetermined condition, the QianLi system shows the corresponding customized reaction to other distant users. This paper also demonstrates the implementation methods, technical components, and interaction possibilities of the QianLi system. An evaluation reveals that our system assists users to share their lives with distant family members in a nonintrusive, customized and tacit way. In the future, QianLi may also serve as a potential research material that can be used to obtain more insights into tacit interaction in practical applications.

Keywords: Artificial intelligence · Internet of Things · Modular design · Tacit interaction · Nonintrusive communication

1 Introduction

Many families are separated, with family members being unable to see one another often, for various reasons. This paper terms such family members as distant family members. Distant family members can easily communicate with one another using current technologies that provide communication services, including text messaging and voice chatting. Although these services are convenient to use, we found that they require an accurate and timely response and active participation from both parties. Such communication methods also have a certain degree of intrusiveness into people's daily life because they drive users to view information notifications frequently, and even cause a form of psychological addiction [1], of which a prominent feature may be anxiety arising from a separation from communication devices [2].

© Springer Nature Switzerland AG 2019
P.-L. P. Rau (Ed.): HCII 2019, LNCS 11577, pp. 279–293, 2019.
https://doi.org/10.1007/978-3-030-22580-3_21

Existing research on nonintrusive communication and emerging techniques offer us new possibilities for connecting distant family members in a more natural and less intrusive way than current communication methods. Former studies on the emotion and information expression by actuators with limited degrees of freedom provided reasonable elements for constructing nonintrusive interaction, while artificial intelligence (AI) provided more interaction possibilities, such as emotion recognition and facial identification, and offered users a better experience when integrated with the Internet of Things (IoT) [3].

We therefore propose the form of tacit interaction that supports nonintrusive communication in a natural way, and develop QianLi on the basis of this form of interaction to connect distant family members. In our work, tacit interaction refers to ambiguous, simple, and periphery interaction that requires a certain degree of empathy but not demands timely responses. We apply the concept of tacit interaction to the QianLi system so that QianLi is developed as an AI and IoT (AIoT) system comprising a central base and several modular devices that connects distant family members without excessive intrusion while fully respecting the wishes of both parties. Because tacit interaction is not alike in different families, QianLi has a modular design that aims to connect distant families by providing customized communication channels. Adopting emerging AI and IoT technology, QianLi provides more diverse interaction possibilities between family members.

In this paper, we first define the concept of tacit interaction and provide design guidelines for this type of interaction. We then demonstrate the implementation methods, technical components, and interaction possibilities of the QianLi system. At last, we recruit several participants to create interactions between distant family members with the help of the system. The created design cases and the collected feedback demonstrate that our system can support the exploration of tacit interaction for connecting the distant family members.

The main contributions of the paper are as follows:

First, we propose the form of tacit interaction and develop the QianLi system as an implementation of the concept. The QianLi system applies AI and the IoT to connect distant family members, convey emotions or evoke precious memories in a tacit and nonintrusive way, and generate a feeling of "being together".

Second, we let the user decide how to map their input information to the reaction displayed on the other side, which makes QianLi a potential research material that allows users to contribute their preference in expressing such tacit interaction in a real-life scenario.

2   Related Work

2.1   Connecting Distant Family Members

Family activities, including celebrations, traditions, and patterned family interactions, are important in family lives and are called family rituals [4]. Petrelli et al. [5] constructed interactive machines for family Christmas rituals to reinforce the family's feeling for the annual celebration. Mynatt et al. [6] introduced the digital family portrait that provides qualitative visualizations of a family member's daily life and regarded the use of the portrait as a family ritual.

In recent years, studies have investigated distant family members who live separately owing to their jobs and other reasons [7]. Several design projects [8, 9] investigated the rituals of family members who live in different places. Chatting et al. [9] built playful tangible objects that help distant family members be involved in ritualized activities, such as drinking together or anticipation of time together, which constitute being a family [8].

However, Wolin et al. [4] proposed that all families struggle for finding a suitable role for rituals in their collective lives and their actual rituals vary greatly, which is consistent with the result of Family Rituals 2.0 [9], in which there are five different interactive machines for characteristics of different families.

Previous work on connecting family members with tangible objects [5] and phatic technologies [10, 11] led us to design networked things with tacit, nonintrusive, and natural interaction in this area. Former methods provide interesting devices for connecting distant families, but it seems more suitable for family members to have the opportunity to find their own way to express themselves because the actual solution for connecting families varies greatly across different families.

2.2 Nonintrusive Communication

Multiple communication services and technologies support a variety of social communication, but most communication methods, such as email, twitter, text messaging, and video chatting, are often accurate, and real-time. Such communications require us to express ourselves as accurately and timely as possible, which calls for active participation.

We classify the existing communication methods according to the complexity of the information, to what extent they work in real-time, and the demand for a response. Common communication methods are shown in terms of three dimensions (see Fig. 1). We generally consider a communication method that is simple, not instant, and does not require a response to be a type of nonintrusive communication.

Nonintrusive communication can be regarded as an attempt to design calm technology systems that inform but do not demand our focus, or attention [12]. Efforts have been made to accomplish such calm technology or nonintrusive communication. These studies explored one-way [13] and two-way [14] information channels as well as the interaction involving different information types, such as haptic [15] and light [16, 17].

The study of Olivera et al. [16] and García-Herranz et al. [18] showed new forms of interaction that restrictively express limited information based on the common context that conversational partners share and will possibly support intrusive forms of communication. However, such researches do not notice how people in daily activities reach tacit consensus for nonintrusive communication, which reminds us to leave more space to the users themselves to explore.

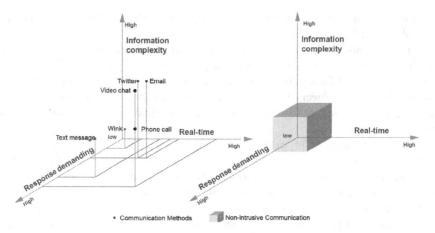

Fig. 1. Three-dimension space of communication methods and nonintrusive communication

3   Tacit Interaction

Compared with communication methods that call for the attention of users, less intrusive ways of communicating are more commonly used between people who are familiar with each other. Those who know each other often do not need two-way or accurate communication and only need, for example, facial expressions and gestures to achieve a tacit consensus and interact. Such interactions include the conversational and vocal ways of moving, engaging, and touching, and play an important role in structuring the forms of "being together" throughout life [19].

On the basis of those interactions achieving a tacit consensus and former research on nonintrusive communication, we propose the concept of tacit interaction that supports nonintrusive communication further.

Tacit interaction usually refers to ambiguous, simple, and periphery interaction that requires a certain degree of empathy but not demands timely responses. Several characteristics of tacit interaction are summarized and shown below.

No Response Required: Tacit interaction can be two-way but most tacit interaction often does not require an exact and immediate response, because the intention of such interaction is not to officially start a dialogue or communication. If an interaction is set to be real-time or must be responded to, then the receiver of the message will, to some extent, feel pressure of having to reply to the message.

Ambiguous: Tacit interaction cannot express and convey particularly accurate information, and is often used to express ambiguous information, such as complex feelings and different emotions. For example, it is difficult to accurately express information, such as the exact time and place of a meeting, through a simple gesture that is sufficient to express some emotions like joy or sad.

Simple: The information that tacit interaction conveys cannot be too complicated because excessive information may result in a cognitive load that is too high and even stress the user. For instance, an accident may occur if a user sends and receives messages while driving, but a quick glance at the indicator light on the dashboard usually does not increase the cognitive load.

Periphery: Both parties engaged in tacit interaction often realize such interaction by noticing something in their periphery of their attention. Indeed, most of these interactions are not deliberately prepared but simply express a type of thought inadvertently. The user may be disturbed by a pop-up notification when using a computer, but a vibrating alert of notification may not disrupt the user's concentration.

Empathy: Often, both parties of the interaction need to develop empathy with each other to better carry out tacit interaction. Playing the same song may generate different feelings in different users whose life experiences differ. On the contrary, the users may better understand the feeling of others if they have shared life experiences or memories related to the song.

It is difficult to establish tacit interaction because such interaction relies on previous consensus or similar prior experiences, and a lot of information expression methods that easily interferes with people are not suitable anymore. When designers want to design tacit interaction, they need to strike a balance between the possibility of users resonating and the possibility of annoying users. We thus propose several guidelines for the design of such interactions.

Scenario: Because tacit interaction is ambiguous, the lost detailed information needs to be reasoned and complemented by the receiver using contextual knowledge and information. Designers therefore consider engaging interactions in a scenario where it is easy to promote empathy among users or where a cultural or social consensus exists. As an example, a simple flashing light could mean anything, but if a light flashes in a specific scenario where both parties have reached a consensus in advance, such as a traffic scenario, its meaning may be clear.

Customized: Tacit interaction has much to do with the user's previous experiences and it is thus impossible to arouse a tacit feeling in the user by providing only one specific design to all users. It is more reasonable to give users the opportunity to customize such interaction according to their own ideas.

4 QianLi System

We intend to apply the concept of tacit interaction to the system for connecting distant family members because the distant family members are familiar with each other, which makes it easier to establish tacit interaction. Meanwhile, distant family members are in urgent need of nonintrusive communications rather than communication that can overload the user.

In Chinese, QianLi is the pronunciation of both "kilo miles away" and "hold your hands", which presents our sincere wish that QianLi can connect distant family members. In contrast with other systems of connecting distant families, the QianLi system lets users reserve the right to design their own expression because we assume that the interaction between family members differs from family to family.

To offer appropriate design space for users to explore tacit interaction, we look into unobtrusive ways of expression with limited information in previous research (see Table 1). We then take those reasonable expression methods as the expression elements of our system. We subsequently adopt user evaluations to verify whether users experience a satisfactory interaction if we provide them with space for exploration.

Table 1. Categories of expression with limited information

Category	Related findings
Light	The lighting has a strong expressive ability [20]. Sugano et al. [21] studied the relationship between static lighting and emotions and proposed the corresponding relationship between different colors of the light and emotions. Terada et al. [22] considered that the hue value of the light represents the basic emotional type, and the period and form of light change represents the intensity of the emotion
Sound	People may emotionally resonate based on various acoustic characteristics of the sound they hear (such as timbres, tones, etc.) [23]. Bartneck et al. [24] describes the relationship between emotions and musical parameters
Motion	Saerbeck et al. [25] studied the acceleration and radiance of the robot's motion to give the user different feelings. Tan et al. [26] studied the emotional expression ability of the shape-changing interface and found that the direction, speed, and magnitude of the interface can affect the user's emotional feelings
Vibration	Research has confirmed that vibration can be used for presenting complex information, such as monitoring of task processes [27], materialized representation of data [28]. Réhman and Liu [29] studied how to convey emotions with the telephone through the vibration

4.1   Expression with Limited Information

For there to be no intrusion, it is necessary to use limited and simple information or unobtrusive ways in the expression process. In fact, several researchers are studying how to use actuators with limited degrees of freedom can be used for the expression in mobile phones or wearable devices. We summarize these methods of expressing emotion or information, including the use of light, sound, motion, and vibration, in Table 1.

The above research and findings, especially the different methods of expression, provide us with the expression elements of the QianLi system. Although previous research has obtained some ground truth about emotional feelings and various expression (see Table 1), we leave the design space to the users to customize their own interactions because each family has its own ways of communication.

4.2   Description of QianLi

Our system has a minimalist design and fits well with various styles of interior design. It has simple shapes, such as a triangle and hexagon, all of which are formed using simple straight lines or arcs (see Fig. 2).

Fig. 2. Composition of the QianLi system

Central Base: The base consists of a Raspberry Pi and Movidius Neural Compute Stick [30] (NCS) (see Fig. 3). The NCS is used to deploy an AI application and the Raspberry Pi performs information processing and transmission between modules and QianLi platforms. To handle the amount of information, we tapped into Alibaba Cloud's server for data transmission.

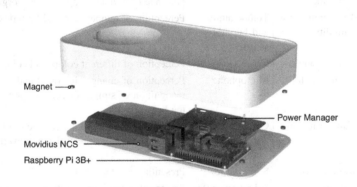

Fig. 3. Components of the central base.

Modules: We designed nine modules in total, comprising five input and four output modules. Each module consists of a NodeMcu [31], sensor or actuator, switch, and battery (see Fig. 4). The NodeMcu is used for wireless communication with the base and control of the sensor or actuator. All the input modules and output modules are shown in Table 2.

The camera module and sound module are empowered by AI technology and equipped with an NCS. The camera module has facial identity, facial emotion and object recognition abilities respectively afforded by different AI models, such as Inception model and FaceNet model [32]. The sound module can detect simple voice commands with the help of an NCS and AI models. To protect the user's privacy and to reduce the feeling of surveillance, no footage taken is recorded by these modules or the base. Users can customize the output depending on the voice, facial identity, facial emotion, or object detected. For instance, different output modules on the other side will be activated when the camera detects different people.

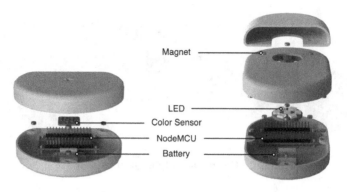

Magnet

LED
Color Sensor
NodeMCU
Battery

Fig. 4. Components of the modules.

Table 2. Summary of nine modules

Category	Module name	Sensor	Feature
Input modules	Passive infrared (PIR) module	PIR sensor	Perception of infrared radiation, that is, the presence of human beings or other organisms
	Temperature and humidity module	Temperature and humidity sensor	Perception of temperature and humidity
	Color module	Color sensor	Perception of different colors and color change
	Sound module	Microphone	Perception of changes in sound and recognition of simple speech recognition with the help of AI
	Camera module	Camera	Recognizing different objects, facial identity and facial emotions under the empowerment of AI
Output modules	Motion module	Servo motor	Presenting a rotary motion
	Vibration module	Vibration motor	Presenting vibrations of different frequencies and intervals
	Light module	RGB LED	Rendering lights of different colors
	Sound module	Microphone	Playing sound, music or voice

Interaction Possibilities: Distant family members would have individual sets of the QianLi system. Each communication is one way, with one set identified as the sender and the other as the receiver (see Fig. 5). Users can decide where QianLi is placed and how it is used. Users have the flexibility to mix and match the modules according to their preferences.

When one input module detects that a condition is fulfilled (e.g., a PIR sensor is triggered), it sends a signal to the central base and the QianLi platform (cloud server). The receiver base can then produce a customized output through a module, which could be the spinning of a rotation module or lighting up of a LED.

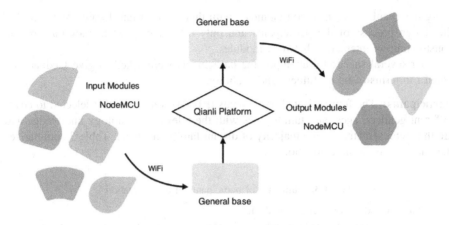

Fig. 5. Working process of the QianLi system

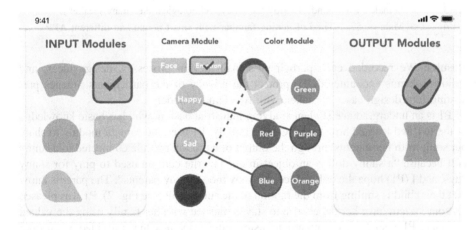

Fig. 6. Mobile application of customizing the mapping between input and output modules

Furthermore, the users themselves can decide how to present their output signal to enable actuators, such as those of an LED or rotation servo. For instance, the AI camera module can detect different faces and facial emotions, so that users can freely map their emotions to different colors of LED, rotation angles of servo, or vibration frequencies and durations (see Fig. 6).

4.3 Evaluation

To evaluate QianLi from the user's point of view, we recruited four participants who lived separately from their family to create tacit interaction they want for their family and received feedback for further development.

Procedure: Initially, participants were introduced to the system for around 15 min to ensure they knew how to set up the system. They were then invited to the formal trial of using the QianLi system to communicate with their own distant family. We recorded the design process of the participants and only offered help when they had trouble constructing an interaction between modules.

After several successful attempts, the participants were asked to give feedback on QianLi in terms of its usefulness and usability.

Participants: The four recruited participants (P1–P4) were carefully selected to cover different genders, ages, and familiarities with the relevant technology knowledge and are thus representative of the majority of distant family members. Table 3 summarizes the participants in the evaluation.

Table 3. Summary of participants in the evaluation

Number	Gender	Age	Brief introduction
1	Female	23	Industrial design students who is familiar with IoT technology
2	Male	25	Foreign students who is new to IoT but receptive to new tech
3	Female	46	Kind of enjoy the fancy technologies like smart speaker
4	Male	57	Tired of getting familiar with smart phone and different APP

Results: We recorded each participant's main design processes, design ideas, and major problems encountered. To protect the privacy of the participants, images presenting four design cases are taken with two female models.

P1 is an undergraduate student studying industrial design, who has basic knowledge of the IoT and learned how to use QianLi rapidly. P1 used the camera module to share her smile with her parents through the output of a motion module connected to a sunny doll because "a sunny doll is an object in our favorite cartoon used to pray for sunny days, and I (P1) hope the doll induces a happy mood in my parents". The parents know that their child is smiling from the motion of the sunny doll (see Fig. 7). P1 was pleased that our system gave her the chance to stay connected with her family using the valued memory. P1 also looked forward to using other modules that provided interesting feedback. P1 believed that more modules could be created to provide more possibilities such as odors. At the same time, she hoped for more control channels of the current outputs such as the flashing frequency or color change of lights.

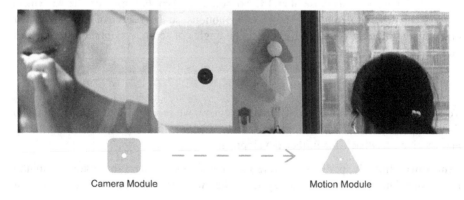

Camera Module   Motion Module

Fig. 7. Design case of P1

P2 is a foreign student whose family now lives in Spain. He is new to the IoT but receptive to new technology, and he thus smoothly became familiar with the system. In the design case of P2, a color sensor can be placed on the table to detect the color of fruit that he picks to eat. The corresponding LED will light up on his parents' side (see Fig. 8). This idea originated from his parents who has been always reminding him to eat fruit to obtain the required vitamins when he first came to China. Additionally, the different time zones between the two countries calls for an expression, such as that conveyed by lighting, to last longer. The parents can place a photograph of P2 under the light and see him when the light shines. P2 felt that expressions would be constrained when distant family members were in different time zones and hoped to record and replay interactions that have already occurred through the mobile app.

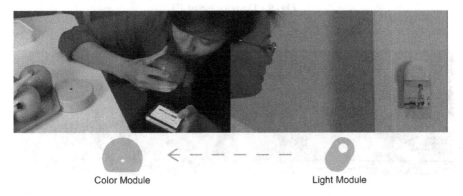

Color Module   Light Module

Fig. 8. Design case of P2

P3 is the mother of a 23-year-old girl and lives apart from her daughter because of work. P3 often uses a smart speaker and owns many smart home devices and she therefore learned how to use and set up the QianLi modules quickly. P3's proposal is shown in Fig. 9, where the sound module and vibration module are connected. When P3 uses a smart speaker or listens to music, the vibration module on the other side will shake and a toy bird will slide down a pole. P3 created this expression because she wanted to share her relaxing moments with her family and the motion of the funny toy bird makes her family laugh. P3 was highly appreciative of the system because she believed that being involved in the creation of the interaction with her children and husband allowed her to better express her love, and that the noninvasiveness would not bother her children. However, she wondered if the modules could be designed to connect to other IoT devices, like a smart speaker at home, so that she could play a song for her family even when she is absent.

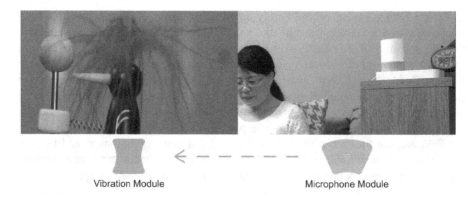

Vibration Module   Microphone Module

Fig. 9. Design case of P3

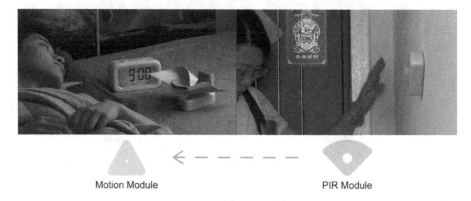

Motion Module   PIR Module

Fig. 10. Design case of P4

Figure 10 illustrates the design case of P4, showing a windmill turning on the other side when the child leaves the house or returns (i.e., the PIR sensor is placed near the door). The parents then know that the child is leaving for school or has returned from the motion of the windmill. This interaction involves a windmill, with P4 stating that "I taught my daughter how to make a windmill when she was a child, and the windmill is therefore the most representative symbol for us." P4 is not a fan of fancy technology and is tired of becoming familiar with smart phones and different applications. P4 spent much time getting familiar with the QianLi system with our help. P4 was happy to see the system helping him to connect with his daughter without using a mobile phone that is a little complex for him. P4 acknowledged the practicality of such system, but he felt that there were still difficulties in setting up the modules and hoped "that the children can help me set up the different modules or that I can get a customized interaction initialized when buying the modules".

5 Discussion

The evaluation showed that our system works well in providing a platform for customizable tacit interaction between family members. The interactions created by family members indeed conveyed emotions or evoked precious memories in a tacit and nonintrusive way, and generated a feeling of "being together". However, the interviews and records of the design process showed the shortcomings of the system and provided insights for improving the system.

First, QianLi is fully functional but not stable owing to time constraints in its design and it is still at the prototyping stage. The current QianLi system is not mature, and many deficiencies and defects need to be addressed to improve the ease of usage of the system; e.g., adding a way of recording and replaying the interaction. In addition, we are also considering expanding the functionality to connect with other IoT devices and improving all the modules with the usage of AI.

Second, hints and interesting interaction examples of how our modules can be used need to be provided because we found that participants were easily inspired by the designs of others or the provided examples to achieve interesting results. We also found that participants who were unfamiliar with IoT technology were reluctant to try the most complex AI input modules. Therefore, we may provide an interface that allows separated family members to set up modules for their parents.

Furthermore, we found that although participants were willing to associate their family memories and previous experiences with interaction designs, they used to present these special memories using additional objects. Previous studies found patterns of emotional expression, such as red being used for happiness and blue for unhappiness [21]. However, existing design cases have not paid much attention to emotional expression but rather sent a message in what can be considered a family ritual [4]. Perhaps it is because this is the first time that users have used QianLi and they only made simple attempts. However, it is also possible that we did not provide enough space for users to express their emotions. Therefore, we are considering providing different modules or more control channels of the current module to encourage exploration.

6 Conclusion

Inspired by the idea of nonintrusive communication, this paper proposes the concept of tacit interaction and presents an application, QianLi, a modular AIoT system comprising a base and several modular devices. Qianli is designed to connect distant family members by providing tacit interaction channels that can be customized by users. An evaluation demonstrated that users can indeed create their own way of nonintrusive communicating with their family tacitly with the help of the QianLi system. It also demonstrated that tacit interaction can make people feel connected in a nonintrusive way.

The modules of QianLi currently can only communicate within the system. However, we are interested in expanding the functionality to connect with other IoT devices and looking into the usage of AI to improve the functions and features of all the modules. In future work, we may explore other interactions that are created in the practical application of QianLi. So far, we have built a platform to invite participants to take part in the program. We hope to gain insights about tacit interaction from users' preferences in expressing themselves in addition to their attitudes and feelings towards the system.

Acknowledgements. This project is supported by the National Natural Science Foundation of China (No. 61672451), the National Basic Research Program (973) of China (No. 2015CB352503), Zhejiang Provincial Key Research and Development Plan of Zhejiang Province (No. 2019C03137), and the Alibaba-Zhejiang University Joint Institute of Frontier Technologies.

References

1. Social Media Obsession and Anxiety. https://adaa.org/social-media-obsession
2. Cheever, N.A., Rosen, L.D., Carrier, L.M., Chavez, A.: Out of sight is not out of mind: the impact of restricting wireless mobile device use on anxiety levels among low, moderate and high users. Comput. Hum. Behav. **37**, 290–297 (2014)
3. Serrano, M., Dang, H.N., Nguyen, H.M.Q.: Recent advances on artificial intelligence and internet of things convergence for human-centric applications: internet of things science. In: Proceedings of the 8th International Conference on the Internet of Things, p. 31. ACM, Santa Barbara (2018)
4. Wolin, S.J., Bennett, L.A.: Family rituals. Fam. Process **23**, 401–420 (1984)
5. Petrelli, D., Light, A.: Family rituals and the potential for interaction design: a study of Christmas. ACM Trans. Comput.-Hum. Interact. **21**, 1–29 (2014)
6. Mynatt, E.D., Rowan, J., Craighill, S., Jacobs, A.: Digital family portraits: supporting peace of mind for extended family members. In: Proceedings of the SIGCHI Conference on Human Factors in Computing Systems, pp. 333–340. ACM, Seattle (2001)
7. Chambers, D.: A Sociology of Family Life. Polity, New York (2012)
8. Kirk, D.S., Chatting, D., Yurman, P., Bichard, J.-A.: Ritual machines I & II: making technology at home. In: Proceedings of the 2016 CHI Conference on Human Factors in Computing Systems, pp. 2474–2486. ACM, San Jose (2016)
9. Chatting, D., Kirk, D.S., Durrant, A.C., Elsden, C., Yurman, P., Bichard, J.-A.: Making ritual machines: the mobile phone as a networked material for research products. In: Proceedings of the 2017 CHI Conference on Human Factors in Computing Systems, pp. 435–447. ACM, Denver (2017)
10. Gibbs, M.R., Vetere, F., Bunyan, M., Howard, S.: SynchroMate: a phatic technology for mediating intimacy. In: Proceedings of the 2005 Conference on Designing for User eXperience, p. 37. AIGA: American Institute of Graphic Arts, San Francisco (2005)
11. Hassenzahl, M., Heidecker, S., Eckoldt, K., Diefenbach, S., Hillmann, U.: All you need is love: current strategies of mediating intimate relationships through technology. ACM Trans. Comput.-Hum. Interact. **19**, 1–19 (2012)
12. Weiser, M., Brown, J.S.: Designing calm technology. PowerGrid J. **1**, 75–85 (1996)
13. Mankoff, J., Dey, A.K., Hsieh, G., Kientz, J., Lederer, S., Ames, M.: Heuristic evaluation of ambient displays. In: Proceedings of the SIGCHI Conference on Human Factors in Computing Systems, pp. 169–176. ACM, Ft. Lauderdale (2003)

14. Chang, A., Resner, B., Koerner, B., Wang, X., Ishii, H.: LumiTouch: an emotional communication device. In: CHI 2001 Extended Abstracts on Human Factors in Computing Systems, pp. 313–314. ACM, Seattle (2001)

15. Brave, S., Dahley, A.: inTouch: a medium for haptic interpersonal communication. In: CHI 1997 Extended Abstracts on Human Factors in Computing Systems, p. 363. ACM, Atlanta (1997)

16. Olivera, F., Rivas, A., Iturriaga, F.: Subtle Interaction for a Non Intrusive Communication. In: Urzaiz, G., Ochoa, S.F., Bravo, J., Chen, L.L., Oliveira, J. (eds.) Ubiquitous Computing and Ambient Intelligence. Context-Awareness and Context-Driven Interaction. LNCS, vol. 8276, pp. 215–222. Springer, Cham (2013). https://doi.org/10.1007/978-3-319-03176-7_28

17. Tollmar, K., Persson, J.: Understanding remote presence. In: Proceedings of the Second Nordic Conference on Human-Computer Interaction, pp. 41–50. ACM, Aarhus (2002)

18. García-Herranz, M., Olivera, F., Haya, P., Alamán, X.: Harnessing the interaction continuum for subtle assisted living. Sensors 12, 9829–9846 (2012)

19. Gratier, M., Greenfield, P.M., Isaac, A.: Tacit communicative style and cultural attunement in classroom interaction. Mind Culture Activity 16, 296–316 (2009)

20. Harrison, C., Horstman, J., Hsieh, G., Hudson, S.: Unlocking the expressivity of point lights. In: Proceedings of the SIGCHI Conference on Human Factors in Computing Systems, pp. 1683–1692. ACM, Austin (2012)

21. Sugano, S., Ogata, T.: Emergence of mind in robots for human interface-research methodology and robot model. Proceedings of IEEE International Conference on Robotics and Automation 1996, vol. 2, pp. 1191–1198. IEEE, Minneapolis (1996)

22. Terada, K., Yamauchi, A., Ito, A.: Artificial emotion expression for a robot by dynamic color change. In: 2012 IEEE RO-MAN, pp. 314–321. IEEE, Paris (2012)

23. Argyle, M.: Bodily Communication. Routledge, London (2013)

24. Bartneck, C.: Affective expressions of machines. In: Human Factors in Computing Systems: Chi Conference, pp. 189–190. ACM, Seattle (2001)

25. Saerbeck, M., Bartneck, C.: Perception of affect elicited by robot motion. In: Proceedings of the 5th ACM/IEEE International Conference on Human-Robot Interaction, pp. 53–60. IEEE Press, Osaka (2010)

26. Tan, H., Tiab, J., Šabanović, S., Hornbæk, K.: Happy moves, sad grooves: using theories of biological motion and affect to design shape-changing interfaces. In: Proceedings of the 2016 ACM Conference on Designing Interactive Systems, pp. 1282–1293. ACM, Brisbane (2016)

27. Cauchard, J.R., Cheng, J.L., Pietrzak, T., Landay, J.A.: ActiVibe: design and evaluation of vibrations for progress monitoring. In: Proceedings of the 2016 CHI Conference on Human Factors in Computing Systems, pp. 3261–3271. ACM, San Jose (2016)

28. Hogan, T., Hinrichs, U., Hornecker, E.: The visual and beyond: characterizing experiences with auditory, haptic and visual data representations. In: Proceedings of the 2017 Conference on Designing Interactive Systems, pp. 797–809. ACM, Edinburgh (2017)

29. Réhman, S.U., Liu, L.: Vibrotactile emotions on a mobile phone. In: SITIS'08. IEEE International Conference on Signal Image Technology and Internet Based Systems, pp. 239–243. IEEE, Bali (2008)

30. Intel® Neural Compute Stick 2. https://software.intel.com/en-us/neural-compute-stick

31. NodeMcu: Connect Things EASY. http://www.nodemcu.com/index_en.html

32. Schroff, F., Kalenichenko, D., Philbin, J.: FaceNet: a unified embedding for face recognition and clustering. In: Proceedings of the IEEE Conference on Computer Vision and Pattern Recognition, pp. 815–823. IEEE, Boston (2015)

Cross-Cultural Product and Service Design

The Vibrotactile Experience of the HOME Button on Smartphones

Jie Cai[1,2], Yan Ge[1,2(✉)], Xianghong Sun[1,2], Yubo Zhang[3], and Yanfang Liu[3]

[1] CAS Key Laboratory of Behavioral Science,
Institute of Psychology, Beijing, China
gey@psych.ac.cn
[2] Department of Psychology, University of Chinese Academy of Sciences,
Beijing, China
[3] Huawei Technologies Co., Ltd., Beijing, China
liuyanfang2@huawei.com

Abstract. The vibration of the virtual HOME button is very important for smartphone users. To understand the user experience of different vibration modes of the HOME button, we designed 2 experiments to study this issue. Study 1 compared 4 different HOME buttons that were experienced either in or out of visual sight. The results showed that the perceived intensity was the key factor related to the tactile experience of the HOME button regardless of the particular vibration mode. Study 2 explored the influence of vibration intensity on users' tactile experiences. The results showed that the frequency and amplitude of the vibration had a significant positive relationship with the overall evaluation of the tactile experience. More importantly, this effect was mediated by the perceived intensity. These results have implications for designing vibration modes that satisfy the needs of smartphone users.

Keywords: Perceived intensity · Frequency · Amplitude · HOME buttons

1 Introduction

Mobile phones are becoming part of everyday life, and their prevalence makes them ideal not only for communication but also for entertainment and games. As a means of communication, vibrotactile stimulation plays an important role in the use of mobile phones. For instance, mobile phone vibration engages people at different emotional levels and provides them with new ways of communicating and interacting (Liu 2010). Vibrations can be presented discretely to the user and can provide an alternative to auditory signals when interacting with a mobile handset in inhospitable environments (e.g., surrounded by the noise of traffic when walking on the street) (Qian et al. 2011). Fukumoto and Sugimura introduced Active Click using a vibrotactile signal, and their user evaluations showed that the tactile feedback reduced the touch panel operation time by approximately 5% in a silent environment and 15% in a noisy environment (Fukumoto and Sugimura 2001). Hoggan et al. demonstrated an improvement to not only onscreen typing but also button interactions by using different vibrotactile

© Springer Nature Switzerland AG 2019
P.-L. P. Rau (Ed.): HCII 2019, LNCS 11577, pp. 297–308, 2019.
https://doi.org/10.1007/978-3-030-22580-3_22

feedback for confirmation of different events (Hoggan et al. 2008). Brewster et al. used vibrotactile feedback to test users' performance, and they found text typing speed on a touchscreen to benefit significantly from tactile feedback in a quiet laboratory environment (Brewster et al. 2007). Therefore, vibrotactile stimulation has an invaluable role in the use of mobile phones.

With updates of mobile phones, the trend has been to replace the traditional physical button feedback with vibrotactile feedback. So what kind of vibrotactile stimulation can result in a better experience? Many studies have investigated the effect of vibrotactile stimulation on mobile phones. The most traditional and practical effect of vibrotactile stimulation for mobile phones has been improving their user interfaces. Nashel and Razzaque (2003) investigated different vibrotactile effects suitable for different contact events, such as pushing a button, crossing button edges, and lingering on a button (Nashel and Razzaque 2003). Hoggan et al. (2008) proved that vibrotactile feedback can boost accuracy and reduce completion time for text entry when the users were using a virtual keypad (Hall et al. 2008). Another use of vibrotactile stimulation is the delivery of information via vibrotactile signals in a mobile device. Li et al. (2008) developed a system called People-Tones, which can inform the user of the presence of friends nearby via vibrotactile cues from a mobile phone. A vibrotactile pattern was made by applying amplitude thresholding and bandpass filtering (Li et al. 2008). Kim and Kim (2007) proposed that users could be informed of the state of a car and the road by a vibrotactile signal in a mobile car racing game (Kim and Kim 2007). Brown and Kaaresoja (2006) developed tactons (tactile icons) to distinguish incoming calls, SMS and MMS by vibrotactile signals (Brown and Kaaresoja 2006). Kim and Tan used piezos to replace the dome structures of keys on a physical keyboard to simulate a flat, zero-travel keyboard with haptic feedback, and their study showed that users typed faster with local haptic keyclick feedback than with global feedback or no haptic feedback (Kim and Tan 2014). However, little research has explored the user experience of vibration. Koskinen et al. (2008) found that the rate of agreement of the keypad's vibra feedback with reality and comfort were higher than those of the keypad without tactile feedback (Koskinen et al. 2008). Therefore, it is necessary to explore users' vibrotactile experience on smart phones to improve the competitiveness of new phone designs.

The user experience of vibration is brought about by the motor, which is determined by its physical parameters. What factors could influence the user experience of vibrotactile stimulation? Some researchers have explored the effect of different physical parameters of vibration in many research fields. For example, the perceived intensity of vibration on a rigid steering wheel was determined using a method of magnitude estimation at seven frequencies (4 to 250 Hz) over a range of vibration magnitudes (0.1 to 1.58 m·s-2 r.m.s.). The comfort contours strongly depended on vibration magnitude, indicating that a frequency weighting for predicting sensation should be dependent on vibration magnitude (Griffin and Griffin 2017). Verrillo et al. (1969) studied the relationship between frequency and perceived intensity and found that it obeys a power law function (Verrillo et al. 1969). Terekhov and Hayward (2014) explored the relationship between the duration of a tactile stimulus and its perceived intensity. The results showed that in the case of a Gabor vibratory skin stimulation, the perceived intensity was negatively correlated with the temporal dimension of the envelope (Terekhov and Hayward 2014).

However, to the best of our knowledge, there has been no work investigating the key dimensions that influence the user experience of vibrotactile stimulation on the HOME button of mobile phones. In addition, there has been no work on the relationship between the users' tactile experience and the physical parameters of the HOME button of mobile phones. Therefore, to provide data relevant to the better design of the vibration characteristics of the HOME button, we designed the present experiment with two main aims. First, we wanted to find the key dimension that influences the users' tactile experience. Second, we investigated the relationship between the key dimension of tactile experience and the physical parameters.

2   Study 1

The aim of this study was to explore the effects of different vibration methods on user experience. Visual information was controlled in this experiment. Furthermore, we analyzed the impact of physical vibration parameters on the tactile experience.

2.1   Method

Participants. Twenty-six participants were recruited to complete this study. The average age was 23.3 years old (SD = 3.07), and there were 16 males and 10 females. All the participants were smartphone users, but they had never used test phones. The whole experiment lasted 90 min, and every participant received ¥60 as a reward after the experiment. The recruitment procedure and research protocol were approved by the Institutional Review Board of the Institute of Psychology, Chinese Academy of Science.

Design. A 2 (feedback method: tactile feedback with or without visual information) × 4 (vibration pattern: physical button, rotor motor, X-axis linear motor, Z-axis linear motor) within-subject experimental design was used in this study.

For the feedback method, in the condition with tactile feedback with visual information, participants executed tasks while looking at the test phone, whereas in the condition with tactile feedback without visual information, they executed tasks but could not see the test phone through an eye mask. To avoid an effect of the phone brand, the condition with tactile feedback without visual information was conducted in the first block. Then, the condition with visual information was conducted in the second block. In each block, users experienced 4 vibration patterns, which were incorporated into 4 different phones. The detailed parameters of the test phone are displayed in Table 1. The presentation order of these four vibration patterns in each block was randomly determined.

Table 1. Test phones used in the experiment

Phone	TM 1	TM 2	TM 3	TM 4
Vibration pattern	Physical button	Rotor motor	X-axis linear motor	Z-axis linear motor
Amplitude (g)	0.34	0.095	0.8	0.086
Frequency (Hz)	500	200	20	50
Duration (ms)	21.5	295	85	23

Materials. A Tactile Experience Questionnaire was designed to measure users' feelings when using the HOME button of mobile phones. The questionnaire contained 7 items that described the experience from different perspectives, including tactile authenticity, tactile comfort, perceived intensity, tactile timeliness, tactile duration, tactile location concentration, and tactile location proximity. The users needed to evaluate their experience on a 5-point Likert scale for each item. A higher score indicated a better experience. See Appendix for the detailed items. In addition, we set up a single 9-point item to assess the overall evaluation of the tactile experience. On this scale, 1 represented the worst feeling, 9 represented the best feeling, and every participant needed to choose one option that conformed to their feeling about the experience.

Procedure. First, all the participants signed confidentiality agreements before the experiment. Then, the instructions, including the experimental objective and experimental task, were explained by the experimenter. Third, all the participants executed the same experimental tasks on the test phones with different vibration patterns; each participant had two tasks. The first task was to press the test phone HOME button without constraint three times, and the second task was to press and hold the test phone HOME button for 2 s three times. Both of the tasks were performed using three hand positions, i.e., click by right hand thumb while the phone was in the right hand, click by right hand thumb while the phone was in the left hand, and click by right hand index finger while the phone was on the table. The three hand positions are displayed in Fig. 1. Finally, all the participants needed to evaluate their experience with the Tactile Experience Questionnaire and the additional item of overall evaluation of the tactile experience after two tasks. An open-ended question was provided to allow participants to evaluate the advantages and disadvantages of four kinds of vibration patterns.

Fig. 1. Hand gestures

Data Analysis. The data were analyzed using analysis of variance (ANOVAs) with repeated measures to examine the main effect of feedback method, vibration pattern, and the interaction effect of feedback method and vibration pattern. Then, linear regression was performed to investigate the influence of particular tactile experiences on the overall evaluation of the tactile experience. In the end, we used Spearman rank correlations to examine the relationships between tactile experience and vibration physical parameters. The physical button was not included in this part because the physical button did not use a vibration motor. The level of significance was set at $p < 0.05$ (two-tailed). All statistical analyses were performed using SPSS 21.0.

2.2   Results

1. Overall Evaluation of the Tactile Experience

The descriptive results of the overall evaluation of tactile experience in each condition are shown in Table 2. ANOVA with repeated measures showed that the main effect of feedback was significant. The mean overall evaluation of the tactile experience in the block with tactile feedback and visual information was 6.269 (SD = 0.218), which was higher than that in the block with tactile feedback and no visual information (mean = 5.702, SD = 0.241), $F = 14.783$, $p < 0.01$. In addition, the main effect of vibration pattern was also significant, $F = 5.555$, $p < 0.01$. The post hoc tests showed that the mean of the overall evaluation of the tactile experience of TM 2 was 6.615 (SD = 0.231), which was higher than that of TM 4 (mean = 5.096, SD = 0.365, $p < 0.01$) and TM 3 (mean = 5.769, SD = 0.399, $p < 0.05$). The mean of the overall evaluation of the tactile experience of TM 1 was 6.462 (SD = 0.327), which was higher than that of TM 4 (Mean = 5.096, SD = 0.365, $p < 0.01$). The interaction effect of feedback and vibration patterns was not significant.

Table 2. The descriptive statistics of the overall evaluation of tactile experience

Feedback method	Vibration pattern (M ± SD)			
	TM 1	TM 2	TM 3	TM 4
Tactile feedback without visual information	6.077 ± 1.719	6.423 ± 1.554	5.692 ± 2.035	4.615 ± 2.192
Tactile feedback with visual information	6.846 ± 1.782	6.808 ± 1.386	5.846 ± 2.185	5.577 ± 1.963

2. The Influential Factor on the Overall Evaluation of the Tactile Experience

To explore the effect of different dimensions of the tactile experience on the global user experience, linear regression was used to investigate the influence of each dimension. The results of the overall evaluation of the tactile experience showed that only perceived intensity had a significant effect on the overall evaluation of the tactile experience; the standardized regression coefficient was 0.688, $t = 4.641^{**}$, $F = 21.541^{**}$, $adj\ R^2 = 0.451$.

3. The Relationship Between the Tactile Experience and Vibration Physical Parameters

To investigate the relationship between the tactile experience and vibration physical parameters, we converted the vibration physical parameters into ordinal data for this analysis as the data did not conform to a normal distribution. Spearman rank correlations were used to explore the relationship between the tactile experience and vibration physical parameters. The correlation results showed that there was a significant positive correlation between perceived intensity and duration, $r = 0.266$, $p < 0.05$.

3 Study 2

Vibratory sensation is assumed to be a function of amplitude and vibration frequency, and the experience of intensity depends on vibration frequency, amplitude and energy of the vibration (Joel 1935). Additionally, study 1 found that perceived intensity had a significant positive correlation with vibration duration. However, we did not find a significant correlation between other subjective experiences and the objective parameters. One possible explanation was that the motor type was not the same in the four smartphones used in study 1. Thus, we controlled the motor type and adjust the vibration intensity through vibration physical parameters to investigate the relationship between tactile experience and vibration physical parameters in experiment 2.

3.1   Method

Participants. Twelve participants were recruited to complete this study. The average age was 24.2 years (SD = 2.47), and there were 4 males and 8 females. All participants were smartphone users, but they had never used test phones. The whole experiment lasted 30 min, and every participant received ¥25 as a reward after the experiment. The recruitment procedure and research protocol were approved by the Institutional Review Board of the Institute of Psychology, Chinese Academy of Science.

Design. A single factor completely randomized design was used in this study. The independent variable was vibration intensity with three levels: low, medium and high. The dependent variable was overall evaluation of the tactile experience. Twelve participants were randomly assigned to the three levels. The detailed parameters of the test phones are displayed in Table 3.

Table 3. Test phones used in the experiment

Vibration physical parameters	Vibration intensity		
	Low	Medium	High
Amplitude (g)	0.086	0.092	0.165
Frequency (Hz)	50	200	250
Duration (ms)	23	18.5	24.25

Materials. The questionnaire was the same as that used in study 1. To increase the ecological validity of the experiment, we used three vibration intensities of the same test phone to represent the three levels of intensity. The test phone was the TM 4, and the motor was the Z-axis linear motor.

Procedure. The procedure included only the condition of tactile feedback without visual information to avoid the impact of visual information. The users needed to operate the HOME button at three different vibration intensities. The order of these 3 conditions was counterbalanced using a Latin Square across participants.

Data Analysis. The data were analyzed using Pearson correlations to examine the relationship between the tactile experience and vibration physical parameters. One participant's data were excluded from the analysis as an outlier. The level of significance was set at $p < 0.05$ (two-tailed). All statistical analyses were performed using SPSS 21.0.

3.2 Results

1. The Relationship Between the Tactile Experience and Vibration Physical Parameters

Perceived intensity had a significant positive correlation with amplitude ($r = 0.726$, $p < 0.05$) and frequency ($r = 0.780$, $p < 0.05$). The overall evaluation of the tactile experience had a significant positive correlation with frequency ($r = 0.793$, $p < 0.05$) (Table 4).

Table 4. Correlations

	Amplitude	Frequency	Duration
Overall evaluation of the tactile experience	.495	.793**	−.233
Perceived intensity	.726*	.780**	.106

$*p < 0.05$ $**p < 0.01$ $***p < 0.001$

2. Mediation Analysis

To investigate the relationship among the physical parameters, perceived intensity, and overall evaluation of the tactile experience, we adopted a mediation analysis to explore the mediating effect of perceived intensity between amplitude, vibration frequency and duration and the overall evaluation of the tactile experience.

This research adopted a bootstrap method to examine the mediation effect. First, a * b was tested to determine whether it was significant, where a was the regression coefficient of the independent variable to the mediator variable, b was the regression coefficient of the mediator variable to the dependent variable. Second, if the result of a * b was significant, then c' should be tested to determine whether c' was significant; if c' was significant, it was implied that there was some other mediator or that c' was the regression coefficient of the independent variable to the dependent variable when the mediator variable was added. Third, if c' was significant, it was then necessary to judge the direction of a * b * c'; if a * b * c' > 0, it was implied that the direction of the missed mediator was the same as that in our model, and the missed mediator was called s complementary mediator. If a * b * c' < 0, it was implied that the direction of the missed mediator was contrary to the direction of the mediator in our model, and the missed mediator was called a competitive mediator (Chen 2010). The results were as follows (Table 5).

Table 5. Mediation effect table

	Effect	Boot SE	BootLLCI	BootULCI
Amplitude	40.8594	43.1832	17.9387	219.5323
Frequency	0.01	0.01	0.0006	0.0368
Duration	0.0702	0.4155	−0.3228	0.6568

Perceived intensity had a mediation effect between the amplitude and overall evaluation of the tactile experience (BootLLCI = 17.9387, BootULCI = 219.5323). Perceived intensity had a mediating effect between the frequency and overall evaluation of the tactile experience (BootLLCI = 0.0006, BootULCI = 0.0368). Then, c' was investigated as follows (Table 6):

Table 6. Regression coefficients

	Coefficient	SE	t	p	LLCI	ULCI
Amplitude	−13.879	14.0153	−0.9903	0.351	−46.2132	18.4553
Frequency	0.0073	0.006	1.2244	0.2556	−0.0065	0.0212
Duration	−0.2455	0.1114	−2.1941	0.0595	−0.5016	0.0126

The effect of amplitude on the overall evaluation of the tactile experience was not significant (LLCI = −46.2132, ULCI = 18.4553), and the effect of frequency on the overall evaluation of the tactile experience was not significant (LLCI = −0.0065, ULCI = 0.0212), implying that there were no other mediators in our model.

4   Discussion

The current study investigated the key dimension that influenced the user's experience of vibrotactile stimulation and explored the relationship between the subjective vibrotactile experience and the objective physical parameters of the HOME button on mobile phones. The results showed that the perceived intensity had a significant effect on the overall evaluation of tactile experience and that perceived intensity had a significant positive correlation with vibration duration on the HOME button. Moreover, perceived intensity had a mediation effect between the vibration amplitude and frequency and overall evaluation of the tactile experience.

Perceived intensity is the strength of a stimulus that a human user feels and is one of the most important properties to be taken into account in interface design (Ryu et al. 2010). The regression analysis revealed that perceived intensity was a linear function of tactile experience. In other words, when the perceived intensity was higher, the tactile experience was better. To the best of our knowledge, this is the first study to investigate the key dimension that influences tactile experience on the HOME button of mobile phones. In addition, we found a relationship between amplitude/frequency and perceived intensity in our study, which was in line with previous research conclusions (Verrillo and Gescheider 1992; Verrillo 1974; Verrillo and Capraro 1975). Nevertheless, Ryu et al. found that perceived intensity increased with amplitude depending on frequency. These exponents exhibited a U-shaped relation against frequency, with a minimum between 150 and 250 Hz for mobile devices (Ryu et al. 2010), and a chart can be defined the relates the frequency and amplitude of a vibration to its perceived intensity. These values can also be transformed to construct equal sensation contours, each of which represents a set of vibration frequencies and amplitudes that result in the same perceived intensity. These data are useful for the design of effective vibrotactile actuators. Unfortunately, we did not find a significant relationship between vibration duration and perceived intensity, which was the opposite of a previous study (Verrillo and Smith 1976). The reason for this discrepancy may be that the task was too simple. The participants were only required to push the HOME button three times in our study, so the response of the HOME button was rapid and transient, which led to this result.

Moreover, we found that there was a significant positive relationship between vibration frequency and overall evaluation of the tactile experience, which suggested that modification of the vibration frequency could improve users' experience. This was the first attempt to explore the relationship between the physical parameters and tactile experience as far as we know. Meanwhile, we found the mediation effect of perceived intensity between the physical parameters and user experience. This suggested that perceived intensity can be improved by increasing the amplitude and frequency, resulting in an improved user experience. We further explored the mechanism between these factors.

This study had some limitations. First, the participants were all young adults aged from 19 to 31 years. Previous studies have suggested that the user experience of vibrotactile stimulation in the elderly was different from that in young adults (Gescheider and Valetutti 1989; Cholewiak and Collins 1993). Studies with larger sample sizes and range of ages are needed to generalize the findings to a broader population. Second, we only tested the vibration of the HOME button in this study. Vibration can be used in many parts of the smartphone. In future studies, we can explore the vibrotactile experience of users' experience on other parts of the smartphone, for example, the vibrotactile experience of "SMS". Third, we investigated the relationship between three vibration physical parameters and perceived intensity. In fact, perceived intensity is related to many factors of vibration, such as amplitude, frequency, duration, contact area, contact force, contact site and so on (Verrillo and Gescheider 1992). Specifically, for vibration direction, there has been some evidence implicating the dependence of vibrotactile perceived intensity on vibration direction, but the quantitative effect of vibration direction has not yet been measured in terms of absolute measures, which is necessary for the optimal design of vibrotactile actuators and stimuli for mobile applications (Hwang et al. 2013). In this study, the kinds of parameters were limited, and we need to explore more physical parameters in future studies.

In summary, the findings of this paper can be used for many purposes in designing a vibrotactile HOME button for smartphones. For example, the designer of vibration actuators for smartphones often lacks information on the influential factors that are related to the vibrotactile experience. The present results indicated that the designers of vibration actuators should pay more attention to perceived intensity. Perceived intensity can be key to designing a satisfactory vibrotactile interface. In addition, the results of the mediation analysis showed that both amplitude and frequency had an indirect effect on the overall evaluation of the tactile experience through perceived intensity. This finding implies that amplitude and frequency may be adjusted to obtain a highly satisfactory vibration of the HOME button for smartphones. In future work, we are planning a series of follow-up studies to explore the psychophysical magnitude function between vibration physical parameters and user experience across all ages, and the experience should be extended to other operational scenarios on smart phones.

Acknowledgments. This study was partially supported by grants from the National Key Research and Development Plan (2017YFB0802800) and the Basic Project of National Science and Technology of China (No. 2009FY110100).

Appendix

Tactile Experience Questionnaire					
Vibration is very real	1	2	3	4	5
Vibration is very comfortable	1	2	3	4	5
Vibration intensity is very suitable	1	2	3	4	5
Vibration is very timely	1	2	3	4	5
Vibration location is centralized	1	2	3	4	5
Vibration duration is very suitable	1	2	3	4	5
Vibration location is close to touch location	1	2	3	4	5

1 = disagree completely, 2 = disagree, 3 = agree, 4 = very agree, 5 = agree completely

References

Brewster, S., Chohan, F., Brown, L.: Tactile feedback for mobile interactions. In: Proceedings of the SIGCHI Conference on Human Factors in Computing Systems, pp. 159–162. ACM, New York (2007). https://doi.org/10.1145/1240624.1240649

Brown, L.M., Kaaresoja, T.: Feel who's talking: using tactons for mobile phone alerts. In: CHI 2006 Extended Abstracts on Human Factors in Computing Systems, pp. 604–609. ACM, New York (2006). https://doi.org/10.1145/1125451.1125577

Zhao, X., Lynch Jr., J.G., Chen, Q.: Reconsidering Baron and Kenny: Myths and truths about mediation analysis. J. Consum. Res. **37**, 197–206 (2010). https://doi.org/10.1086/651257

Cholewiak, R.W., Collins, A.A.: A comparison of complex vibrotactile pattern perception on the OPTACON by young and old observers. J. Acoust. Soc. Am. **93**(4), 2361 (1993). https://doi.org/10.1121/1.406170

Fukumoto, M., Sugimura, T.: Active Click: tactile feedback for touch panels. In: CHI 2001 Extended Abstracts on Human Factors in Computing Systems, pp. 121–122. ACM, New York (2001). https://doi.org/10.1145/634067.634141

Gescheider, G.A., Valetutti Jr., A.: Vibrotactile forward masking in young and old subjects. J. Acoust. Soc. Am. **85**(S1), S64–S64 (1989). https://doi.org/10.1121/1.2027079

Griffin, M., Griffin, M.J.: Frequency dependence of perceived intensity of steering wheel vibration: effect of grip force. In: In Second Joint EuroHaptics Conference, 2007 and Symposium on Haptic Interfaces for Virtual Environment and Teleoperator Systems. World Haptics 2007, pp. 50–55 (2017). https://doi.org/10.1109/WHC.2007.58

Hall, M., Hoggan, E., Brewster, S.: T-Bars: towards tactile user interfaces for mobile touchscreens. In: Proceedings of the 10th International Conference on Human Computer Interaction with Mobile Devices and Services, pp. 411–414. ACM, New York (2008). https://doi.org/10.1145/1409240.1409301

Hoggan, E., Brewster, S.A., Hoggan, E., Brewster, S.A., Johnston, J.: Investigating the effectiveness of tactile feedback for mobile touchscreens. In: In Proceedings of the SIGCHI Conference on Human Factors in Computing Systems, pp. 1573–1582 (2008). https://doi.org/10.1145/1357054.1357300

Hwang, I., Seo, J.: Interactive racing game with graphic and haptic feedback. IEEE Trans. Haptics **6**, 352–362 (2013). https://doi.org/10.1109/TOH.2013.2

Joel, B.Y.W.: On the tactile perception of vibration. Psychol. Rev. **42**(3), 267–273 (1935)

Kim, J.R., Tan, H.Z.: A study of touch typing performance with keyclick feedback. In: 2014 IEEE Haptics Symposium (HAPTICS), pp. 227–233 (2014). https://doi.org/10.1109/HAPTICS.2014.6775459

Kim, S.-Y., Kim, K.-Y.: Interactive racing game with graphic and haptic feedback. In: Oakley, I., Brewster, S. (eds.) HAID 2007. LNCS, vol. 4813, pp. 69–77. Springer, Heidelberg (2007). https://doi.org/10.1007/978-3-540-76702-2_8

Koskinen, E., Kaaresoja, T., Laitinen, P.: Feel-good touch: finding the most pleasant tactile feedback for a mobile touch screen button. In: Proceedings of the 10th International Conference on Multimodal Interfaces, pp. 297–304 (2008)

Li, K.A., Sohn, T.Y., Huang, S., Griswold, W.G.: PeopleTones: a system for the detection and notification of buddy proximity on mobile phones. In: Proceedings of the 6th International Conference on Mobile Systems, Applications, and Services, pp. 160–173. ACM, New York (2008). https://doi.org/10.1145/1378600.1378619

Réhman, S., Liu, L.: *iFeeling*: vibrotactile rendering of human emotions on mobile phones. In: Jiang, X., Ma, M.Y., Chen, C.W. (eds.) WMMP 2008. LNCS, vol. 5960, pp. 1–20. Springer, Heidelberg (2010). https://doi.org/10.1007/978-3-642-12349-8_1

Nashel, A., Razzaque, S.: Tactile virtual buttons for mobile devices. In: CHI 2003 Extended Abstracts on Human Factors in Computing Systems, pp. 854–855. ACM, New York (2003). https://doi.org/10.1145/765891.766032

Qian, H., Kuber, R., Sears, A.: Towards developing perceivable tactile feedback for mobile devices. J. Hum. Comput. Stud. **69**(11), 705–719 (2011). https://doi.org/10.1016/j.ijhcs.2011.06.003

Ryu, J., Jung, J., Park, G., Choi, S.: Psychophysical model for vibrotactile rendering in mobile. Presence: Teleoperators Virtual Environ. **19**(4), 364–387 (2010)

Bochereau, S., Terekhov, A., Hayward, V.: Amplitude and duration interdependence in the perceived intensity of complex tactile signals. In: Auvray, M., Duriez, C. (eds.) EUROHAPTICS 2014. LNCS, vol. 8618, pp. 93–100. Springer, Heidelberg (2014). https://doi.org/10.1007/978-3-662-44193-0_13

Verrillo, R.T.: Vibrotactile intensity scaling at several body sites. In: Cutaneous Communication Systems and Devices, pp. 9–14 (1974)

Verrillo, R.T., Capraro, A.J.: Effect of stimulus frequency on subjective vibrotactile magnitude functions. Percept. Psychophys. **17**(1), 91–96 (1975)

Verrillo, R.T., Fraioli, A.J., Smith, R.L.: Sensation magnitude of vlbrotactUe stimuli. Percept. Psychophys. **6**(6), 366–372 (1969)

Verrillo, R.T., Gescheider, G.A.: Perception via the sense of touch. In: Tactile Aids for the Hearing Impaired, pp. 1–36 (1992)

Verrillo, R.T., Smith, R.L.: Effect of stimulus duration on vibrotactile sensation magnitude. Bull. Psychon. Soc. **8**(2), 112–114 (1976)

A Study of Japan's Welfare Beauty Service from Cultural Creative's Perspective

Chin-Lon Lin[1]([⊠]), Hui-Yun Yen[2]([⊠]), and Chun-Liang Chen[3]([⊠])

[1] Hungkuang University, Taichung, Taiwan
linpcl@sunrise.hk.edu.tw
[2] Department of Advertising, Chinese Culture University, Taipei, Taiwan
pccu.yhy@gmail.com
[3] Graduate School of Creative Industry Design,
National Taiwan University of Arts, New Taipei City, Taiwan
jun@ntua.edu.tw

Abstract. According to the National Development Council, Taiwan has one of the fastest growth rate of ageing and disabled population in the world. The two issues combined form a social problem that needs to be addressed immediately. Japan is the first country in Asia to reach "super-aged society", and its emphasis on aged and disabled population's social-wellness has often been the reference for other neighboring countries. Based on Japan's Constitution, all citizens are entitled to the rights of freedom, dignity, and pursuit of well and healthy life. The founder of Yamano Beauty College, Aiko Yamano, incorporated cosmetology and gerontology in 1998 and published a new ideology called "Biyo-Fukushi", or beauty-welfare. The core thinking, *five principles of beauty*, is manifested through an articulated home delivery system, "welfare beauty service", which aims to increase people's awareness and empathy towards the aged and disabled population, and achieve a common human desire of "ageing beautifully". This study begins with a research on Japan's historical development with social welfare, and later applies Lin's "form and ritual" analytical system to evaluate the cultural and creative aspect of welfare beauty service. The goal of this study is to redefine Japan's welfare beauty service to cater the ever-growing population of aged and disabled in Taiwan, and provide a solution to both long-term care and creative design market.

Keywords: Cultural innovation · Beauty welfare · Form and ritual

1 Introduction

According to the National Development Council, Taiwan has one of the fastest growth rate of ageing population in the world [29]. People with age 65 or older comprise 15% of the total national population in 2018, a number that's considered as "aged society" by the United Nations. This number is estimated to reach 41% by year 2060 along with Japan and South Korea. At the same time, Taiwan's disabled population has also grown from 263,557 in 1993 to 1,170,199 in 2016, which is equivalent to 4.94% of the population [27]. The two issues combined form various social problems that need to be addressed immediately.

© Springer Nature Switzerland AG 2019
P.-L. P. Rau (Ed.): HCII 2019, LNCS 11577, pp. 309–324, 2019.
https://doi.org/10.1007/978-3-030-22580-3_23

Japan is the first country in Asia to reach "super-aged society". Due to its geographical proximity and cultural similarities, Japan's emphasis on the aged and disabled population's social-wellness is often the reference for other neighboring countries. According to Nippon Research Institute's 2011 report, beauty services are one of the main recreations of the aged. Due to weak labor market, outflow of population in rural areas, and decrease in people's purchasing power, beauty salons are forced to move or close, causing the aged population difficulties to get access to beauty services. Based on Japan's Constitution, all citizens are entitled to the rights of freedom, dignity, and pursuit of well and healthy life [23]. When clients' constitutional right is restricted, there would eventually be no business activity. In the case of beauty industry, hairdressers would lose their clients due to life ageing, and customers would lose their access to beauty services due to distance and immobility. With this in mind, the founder of Yamano Beauty College, Aiko Yamano, incorporated cosmetology and gerontology in 1998 while she was hospitalized and unable to receive proper hair wash services, and published a new ideology called "Biyo-Fukushi", or beauty welfare. The ideology's core thinking, *five principles of beauty*, is manifested through an articulated home delivery system, "welfare beauty service", which aims to increase ageing and disabled awareness and empathy in the society, and achieve a common human desire of "ageing beautifully".

Ministry of Health of Welfare is the administration for aged and disable's equipment and services in Taiwan. Under its social welfare-oriented guidelines, only Non-Profit Organizations (NPO) are allowed to carry-out and/or distribute services and product in this industry [23]. This limitation has stalled the development and innovation of product and services. For an instance, "welfare-vehicle" is a professional bathing service from Japan which uses a van equipped with bathing tools and licensed personnel to give proper body cleaning to disabled people. The vehicle not only solves health and hygienic problems, it also contributes to the local communities by helping elders and disabled to live better. However, the Ministry of Welfare thinks that welfare vehicle service is not a necessity to regular families; Chen Deputy Director of Long-term Care Division, noted that unless the aged and disabled are in critical conditions, daily cleaning should be carried-out by family members or care-givers [3]. It is helpful for Taiwan government to take initiative in the development of public welfare, but the policies need to adhere more to people's actual needs.

Hairdressing is another beauty services that's common, or even necessary, in people's daily life. Hair washing is not only a process of hair and scalp cleansing, but also a therapeutic method to increase one's physical metabolism and blood circulation. One can also be spiritually and psychologically motivated by having an esthetically arranged hairstyle. With respective to Taiwan's current situation, the aged and disabled's hairdressing and cleaning are conducted by family member, or sometimes medically licensed care-givers, who are not professionally trained hair practitioners. Their emphasis are simply on the speed and efficiency of the work, and not the comfort during the process and the satisfaction after completion. In recent years, it is popular for hair professionals to provide free hair cutting and washing services to the local communities or the underprivileged, but these events are charitable and aperiodic. This act of charity only serves the purpose of improving the person or organization's public image, and not actually benefitting people's life.

Under current public regulations and social welfare functionality in Taiwan, innovative beauty services designed specifically for the aged and disabled population are not prevalence. With that in mind, the purposes of this study are: first, to provide the research on the formulation of Japan's beauty welfare ideology to further understand its historical development and implications with the aged and disabled population. Secondly, apply Lin's "form and ritual" model to evaluate cultural and creative aspect of welfare beauty service through "knowledge value-added" and "creativity value-added" perspectives, and later extended to customer relationship's "family value-added". The key to a prominent and sustainable business model in any given industry is when the customer relationship is transformed to friendship, or even a form of kinship. The goal of this study is to redefine Japan's welfare beauty service to better serve the ever-growing population of the aged and disabled in Taiwan, and provide a solution to both the long-term care and creative design market.

2 Literature Review

2.1 Cultural Innovation

Throughout the history, academics and scholars have approached the term "culture" with different perspectives, but the conception is the same. Merriam-Webster Dictionary defines "culture" as the characteristic features of everyday existence (such as diversions or a way of life) shared by people in a place or time. Han pointed out that Europeans have profound history in architecture, sculpture, and art, so they view culture as a form of art and a romantic way of living. Chinese are proud of their five thousand years long history, hence they see culture as an ethnical lifestyle and value [7]. Lee noted that "culture" is an aggregated reflection of living in everyday life [14]. Lin once said that "culture" is a way of living, "design" is a taste of life, and "creativity" is an emotional concurrence by a group of people [17]. In summary, scholars all agree that "culture" is equivalent to "life", and by combining culture to innovation, it implies a new thinking, service, or method to approach problems, improve standard of quality, and realize goals in life. Cultural innovation is also the concept of "reuse" of culture. It extends culture's functionality and value and creates new business opportunity by improving competence. Su noted that cultural innovation must be achieved through the act of reprocess and reuse [33]. In other word, the combination of culture and innovation represents a new form of living, service, or method, and the evolution of culture.

2.2 Welfare

The term "welfare" is often described as help given by the government or organizations to ones who need it in most languages, including Chinese. In comparison, the word means more than just that in Japanese culture; it means happiness and prosperity of the general public. Under the 25th Amendment of the Japanese Constitution, all citizens are entitled to the right to pursuit freedom, dignity, right, and proper life in a good state of health [34].

Japan has the fastest ageing rate and largest aged population in the world. The social issues arose from the aged and disabled have become the priority challenge of the government and private entities. As early as 1950s the Japanese government had joined Normalization movement which was initiated by Scandinavian countries, Denmark in particular, and issued "Disabilities Right Protection Act". This law allows disabled to return to the society and live at the comfort of their own home instead of institutions, giving the disabled more respect and freedom in their life [36]. Starting in 1963, the government began to focus on elders' physical and psychological wellness, and announced "Elderly Welfare Act" to provide elders various access to recreations and entertainments. It wasn't until the late 1980s that the ideology of "society formed by only healthy individuals is not normal" became popular, and based on this principle local government started to manifest their own policies on the aged population. Liu pointed out that 1994's "Golden Plan", a government policy that encouraged the notion of ageing actively and healthy, helped increase employment in the long-term care market and promote the development of welfare products that embody the concept of universal design [23]. The result of this expanded senior consumer market, and at the same time increased public's awareness for the elderly's healthcare. Entering into the 21st Century, elderly's psychological wellness has received extra attention from the government. In 1999, a policy on elders' health was established to emphasize on their human dignity and independency, and encourage them to actively participate in social events [22]. Huang noted that elders from the current era pay more attention to their appearances than before. Shiseido, a leading Japanese cosmetic company, used to target at female audience between the ages of 20–30; nowadays it chooses to host its beauty seminar at day-care centers or senior homes [8]. From the historical development and findings of Japan's aged and disabled population, it is clear that a "normal" way of life is no longer sufficient for today's ever-changing world, they need "customization" to cater to their specific needs in life.

2.3 Beauty Welfare

The Japanese word "biyo", or beauty services, has a wide range of coverage which includes make-up, hairdressing, manicure, styling, aroma therapy, massage...etc., and its idea is to improve one's wellness through external "decoration" and "reform" [5]. Beauty services are beneficial to an individual's physical and psychological condition, and not just to make someone look prettier. Certain beauty services revitalize the brain and body immune system, and provide better efficacy to the health in general. Proper maintenance of the appearance can prevent illness and prolong life. Toshikatsu Ota published the concept of "ageing happily" and suggested that people should grow old with good health no matter what [28]. Hiroshi Shibata described in his 2002 publication *80% of All Elders Should be Independent!* that the general perception of heath-and-age relationship is higher the age, lower the health; however, the ideal relationship between the two should be health remains high and steady in relation to age, and drops suddenly as it approaches death [31]. This theory is demonstrated by the solid line in Fig. 1.

The founder of Yamano Beauty College, Aiko Yamano, who was also a legendary beauty practitioner in Japan, merged cosmetology and gerontology in 1998 while she

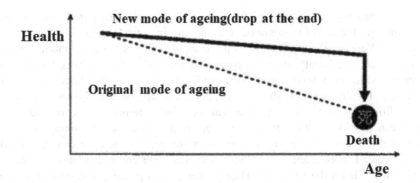

Fig. 1. Ideal ageing graph [31]

was hospitalized, and published a new ideology called "Biyo-Fukushi", or beauty-welfare. The term "beauty welfare" was acknowledged by the Ministry of Education as an official academic word. The ideology's core thinking, *five principles of beauty*, namely the enhancement of one's hair, make-up, appearance, spirit, and health to achieve wellness in health is manifested through an articulated home delivery service, "welfare beauty service", which aims to increase public awareness and empathy to the aged and disabled population, and achieve the desire of "ageing beautifully" and "staying young" [38].

The ideology of beauty welfare is centered around the aged and disabled population and based on the notion of normalization and national constitution. Under Japan's constitution everyone has the basic human right of "freedom" to the body, spirit, and economics in particular. Aiko Yamano pointed out that "freedom of body" refers to unrestriction of the body position when receiving or practicing beauty services. For instance, when giving haircut to a client who's lying in bed, the client's comfort and hygienic factors must be considered, as well as the practitioner's ability to move around freely. "Freedom of spirit" means the respect on the client and practitioner's belief and liking. If a hairdresser tried to manipulate the client's hair style preference with his/her personal liking, the client would be under pressure while receiving the haircut. In other words, it is another form of deprivation of one's constitutional freedom. "Freedom of economics" means people have the right to pursue their choice of career; for those who wish to practice welfare beauty service, or people who have needs in such service, should be granted the right [35].

2.4 Welfare Beauty Service

Welfare beauty service is not only a product for the aged and disabled population, but also an innovation in cultural creative industry. Unlike other industries, cultural creative industry's core value is intangible; its demand comes from consumers' understanding of a culture. Lin describes "culture" as a way of living, "design" as a taste of life, "creativity" as an emotional concurrence by a group of people, and "industry" as a mean or method to realize cultural creativity [17]. In other words, if "design" forms a particular lifestyle through creativity and industry, a hairdresser or beauty practitioner can help increasing the quality of life of the aged and disabled population and their family through the aid of professional training and innovative tools.

Japan's Yamano Beauty College is the leading organization in promoting welfare beauty service. The beauty service is created on the notion of *five principles of beauty* and delivered to one's home through the application of innovative hairdressing tools. The goal is for the aged and disabled population to age beautifully without the distraction from their physical, psychological, or other external factors. Before a hairdresser can provide welfare beauty service, he/she must take a training course on beauty welfare, and receive the license. Then the service must be carried out with special patented tools, namely Sui-Comb, a vacuum hair cutter that leaves no trace of the trimmed hair on the floor, and Happy Shampoo, a portable hair wash basin and shower head (Fig. 2). This service echoes Lin's quote "inspiration from culture, ideation with product, implementation for daily-life", and allows the innovation to be culturally creative [17].

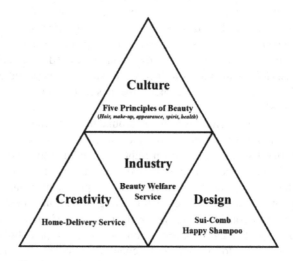

Fig. 2. Welfare beauty service's cultural creative value

2.5 "Form and Ritual" Design Model for Cultural Innovation

Lin and Lin described the purpose of having cultural innovation is to be "inspired from the past and represent into the present" [20]. The "form" of an object should be passed-on to remind people of the past, and based on the memory to provide a "ritual" that elevates skills in life. "Form and ritual" model (Fig. 3) is designed to achieve a living standard (life) with a group of people's living proclamation (culture); it focuses first on the cultural creative interface between one's living proclamation and taste (product), and then on the technological innovative interface between taste and living standard. Finally, feedbacks generated from their interaction give ideas to a product/service's practicality, functionality, and pleasure, and complete the process in branding.

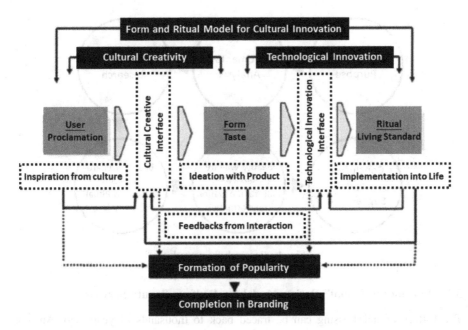

Fig. 3. Form and ritual design model for cultural innovation [20]

Kuo, Chang, and Sun, students from National Taiwan University of Arts, applied "form and ritual" model to product design and transformed Taiwan aborigine's drinking culture into a martini glass. The design concept uses Taiwan aboriginal culture's "twin-cup" Linnak, a wooden wine-drinking tool consisting of two cups, with one handle on each side, and transforms it into a vertically symmetrical pair of martini glasses connected together inversely to show the close relationship of the drinkers in a social scenario [20]. This design transformation has kept the connotations of "harmony" and "sharing" in aboriginal drinking culture, and represents them creatively in the present life.

3 Methodology

This study uses documentary analysis and descriptive research method to demonstrate welfare beauty service's cultural innovation transformation framework (Fig. 4). Document analysis is a form of qualitative research in which documents are reviewed, classified, described, and interpreted by the researcher to give voice and meaning around an assessment topic (Bowen 2009). It aims to understand the past and present and predict the future by collecting as much data as possible. Descriptive research is a method used to describe the characteristics of a population or phenomenon being studied with the researcher or others' opinions.

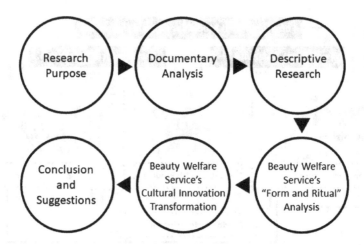

Fig. 4. Research framework

3.1 "Form and Ritual" Design Model for Welfare Beauty Service

The history of hairdressing can be traced back to thousands of years ago. Ancient Greek philosophers depicted hairdressing in their literatures and paintings [30]. Others have kept this "ritual" through teaching. Until the end of last century, mentorship had been the only method of teaching to pass-on hairdressing culture and keep the "memory" of hairdressing. However, factors such as differences in the curriculum, the mentor's teaching attitude, experience and knowledge in hairdressing, or even an unexpected injury or death of the mentor all contribute to the discontinuity of the culture and heritage. Form and ritual model allows welfare beauty service to convert such culture passed-on by predecessors into patented tools through Lin's knowledge and creative value-adding method, and finally achieve a desired living standard.

3.2 The Procedure of Value-Adding in Welfare Beauty Service

The procedure of value-adding is a process of analyzing and systemizing raw data, and converting it into meaningful knowledge which can be applied to design thinking [21]. The spread of knowledge allows a good design to become a recognizable and popular brand in the market. By combining cosmetology and gerontology, Yamano Aiko turned hairdressing culture into a knowledge that can be taught, and published *Five Principles of Beauty* as a guideline to carry it out in real life. Based on this ideology, a hairdresser expands his/her field of expertise from hair to care-giving and welfare through a series of value-adding. The process begins with "knowledge value-adding" stage in which a 4-days training course on senior welfare and long-term care is required to fulfill in order to be licensed to practice [5]. Next, in "creativity value-adding" stage, patented tools are applied to conduct hairdressing service outside of beauty salons. At the final stage, "wisdom", or know-how, of providing professional hairdressing services to the aged and disabled population at their home brings popularity and prosperity to the practitioner, and eventually becomes a new brand of service in the market (Fig. 5).

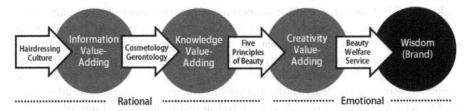

Fig. 5. Procedure of value adding in welfare beauty service

4   Research Findings and Discussion

4.1   Welfare Beauty Service Transformation Through "Form and Ritual" Design Model

Based on the analysis of "form and ritual" model, it indicates that Japan's welfare beauty service is not only a product of long-term care, but also cultural innovation. By thorough understanding of the culture and application of technologies, a beauty welfare practitioner can help people reaching their goal of "ageing beautifully". This achievement allows the customer relationship between the practitioner and client to become friendship, or even a form of kinship (Fig. 6).

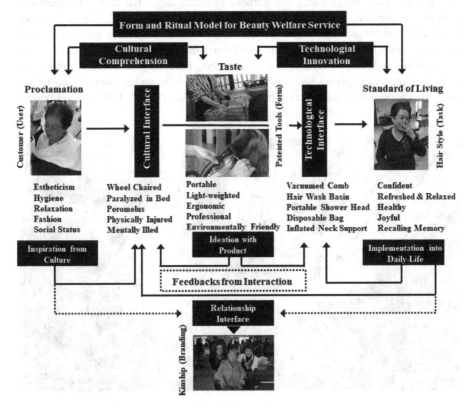

Fig. 6. Form and ritual analysis for welfare beauty service

In today's fast-changing world, customers not only hope to age beautifully, but also to maintain good hygiene, express personal taste in fashion, and pursue higher social status with proper appearance. In addition, hairdressing has become a method of relaxation and recreation for many people. As the aged and disabled population increases, more and more people lose their access to professional beauty services, hence the freedom to pursue happiness becomes restricted. In order to solve this problem, a home-visit beauty welfare practitioner must cater to the customer's physical and mental disabilities, or even the inadequacy of the environment, by applying technological innovations. Unlike conventional hairdressing tools, beauty welfare's special tools are the result of interaction between culture comprehension and technological innovation. The feedbacks of the two interfaces result in the transformation of conventional hairdressing tools, namely shampoo chair (basin and shower head), scissor, and comb, into patented "Happy Shampoo" and "Sui-Comb". In other words, these tools have preserved their traditional functionality and been creatively value-added to be more user-friendly.

Shampoo chair at salons are usually stationed and bulky, but with creative value-added it becomes portable and light-weighted. Although there are various product in the market, most of which are user-oriented, instead of customer, and missing the human touch of delivering soothing sensation that customers feel when having their hair washed and scalp massaged. For instance, a commonly seen method is to wash hair with water running down from an IV drip bag-like device above through a connected tubular hose. This design meets the purpose of "cleansing", but lacks the "pleasure" from shower pressure. It has "functionality", but missing "humanity". Happy Shampoo is a device that mimics the "form" of hair wash service at a beauty salon (Fig. 7). It uses a miniature motor pump to pump warm water from a container to the shower head and provides soothing sensation to the customers. Practitioners' posture remains the same, as if they were giving hair wash on a shampoo chair, and customers' satisfaction is elevated because the combination of hairdressing "form" and "skill" brought "ritual" to them that will last in their memory forever.

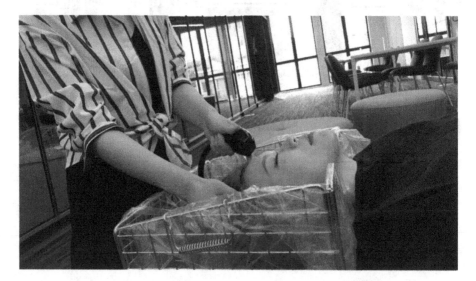

Fig. 7. "Happy Shampoo" portable hair wash basin and shower

Scissors and comb have existed in human history for thousands of years [1]. They are the basic tools of hairdressing, but from beauty welfare's stand point, they are "unfriendly" tools. Many elders and handicaps are relying on wheel chairs or lying in bed in life, and others may be living in spaces that are small and inadequate. Without the help of special tools, hairdressers are unable to provide services under these critical conditions. "Sui-comb" is a plastic fixture that's attached to a conventional vacuum cleaner to suck away trimmed hair during hair cutting (Fig. 8). Through this techno-logical innovation, practitioners can perform hair cut at any angle and under any condition, not afraid of contaminating the environment. When the service is completed, customers feel confident, clean, joyful, and young once again. By preserving the "skill" (form) of hairdressing, customer's experience (ritual) can be improved through cultural innovation.

Fig. 8. "Sui-comb" vacuumed hair comb

4.2   Welfare Beauty Service's Cultural Innovative Transformation

"If a product couldn't be implemented in daily-life, its creativity would be neglected; if a service couldn't touch the customers, its value would be reduced. The purpose of any designed product is to fulfill human's physical and psychological needs and improve the standard of living" [18]. In order for welfare beauty service to have more demand in daily-life, it needs to be recognized more than just a long-term care product, but also a culturally creative innovation. Through the analysis of Lin's "procedure value-adding" and "form and ritual model", this research demonstrates how hairdressing is trans-formed into a home delivery service through a process of professional training and application of patented tools (Fig. 9). This research also found out that the last stage of "value-adding" should be extended from "wisdom" to customer's "relationship value-adding", which change the business relationship between hairdresser and customer into friendship, or furthermore into kinship, and complete the business model. Noriko Onishi, Assistant Professor at Yamano College of Beauty, noted that many elders who has had the service before feel comforted in the heart because they are living alone most of the time, and they would call for the service without actual needs but just to seek companionship. During a beauty welfare seminar in Oyama Village, Shizuoka Prefecture, Ms. Miyashita from the Japanese Association of Social Welfare described how beauty service improves her living standard, and eases her symptoms from Alzheimer's disease [6]. Therefore, preserving hairdressing's tools (form) to recall pleasant memory from the past, and providing customers new experiences (ritual) to improve satisfaction, are the core value of welfare beauty service.

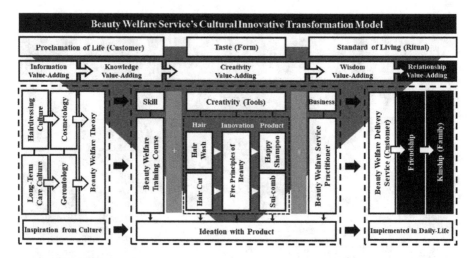

Fig. 9. Welfare beauty service's cultural innovative transformation model

5   Conclusion and Suggestions

Throughout different stages in life, people have different pursuits of living standard. During childhood, kids just want to play and have fun. As they grow older, their wish is to look good and fashionable to increase self-confidence and attract the opposite sex. When people enter their senior stage, they work hard to slow-down ageing and possibly finish the journey of life beautifully. All these wishes in life contribute to the formation of Yamano Aiko's *Five Principles of Beauty*. It is this proclamation that promotes cultural innovation through the preservation of tools (form) and improvement of skills (ritual). Various value are added along the process to bring culture to life, and transform customer relationship from business to friendship and even a form of kinship. This transformation guarantees the aged and disabled population's rights to pursue happiness in life, improves their self-confidence, increases their social participation, and lower social and family burden. To hairdressers, welfare beauty service prolongs their professional life expectancy through learning extra knowledge in senior welfare and long-term care, and achieve sustainability by growing old with the customers.

5.1 Long-Term Care Development in Japan and Taiwan

Due to geographic and cultural similarities, Japan's policies on long-term care and industry development have been the source of references for Taiwan. The main reason why beauty welfare theory and service are well-accepted and commonly applied in daily-life is because they are academic requirements in many beauty colleges' curriculum. Besides education, the formation of policies and differences in culture are two other factors that lead to the current development.

There are three main differences in the development of long-term care policy between Japan and Taiwan. First, the Japanese government started the planning when its population was relatively young and economy booming. Whereas Taiwan first launched its long-term care policy in 2007 when the society was already at an ageing stage; this leaves little room for any amendment. Secondly, Japan's long-term care policy was built on the foundation of the constitution; consequently people are entitled to their rights and protection. On the other hand, Taiwan's policy was formed under political pressure in democratic system. Finally, Japan's long-term care market is opened to private entities, this free market system has encouraged improvements and innovations in better product, services, and profitability. In contrast, Taiwanese government sees the long-term care market as part of its social-welfare network, and it only allows public entities and non-profit organization to participate in the operation. Hence, without competition from the market, development and innovations are hindered [23].

As early as 1980s, the Japanese government has made long-term care a requirement in the education system through legislation. For instance, during the two years curriculum at Yamano College of Aesthetics, a student must fulfill 60 h of gerontology and 30 h of *Five Principles of Beauty*. In addition, there's a 130 h of on-site training in nursing and senior care-giving. According to NPO Beauty Life, there were a total of 7217 Yamano graduates (1.45% of the total beauty practitioners in the market) who were registered as welfare beauty service practitioners between 2005 to 2015, and that's not including students from other schools or institutions [35]. Comparing this to Taiwan's development in long-term care education, only Taichung's Hungkuang University has Senior Hair Styling course in its college curriculum, the rest of the schools show little emphasis on the issue of ageing in their beauty education.

From a cultural perspective, Japanese people spend more time in their appearance more so than other Asians. According to Liu, studies show that Japanese's first impression of the people they meet comes from the person's appearance; they prefer a sleek and clean look [24]. Based on this preference, sales in wig, skin care, and plastic surgery have shown signs of rapid growth. Taiwan transformed from agricultural to a more wealthy industrial society in the 1960s, relatively late comparing to Japan, so the elders today still are more conservative in spending, and place less emphasis on their appearance. That being said, it is skeptical for the Taiwanese elders and their family members to believe that their physical and mental health could be improved through beauty services. With Taiwan's economic downturn and stagnant income, it is also questionable if the elders would on such service. These are some of the issues that will need to be addressed in the future.

5.2 Researcher's Suggestions

In order for Japan's welfare beauty service to be feasible in Taiwan's long-term care market, this research provides three suggestions:

- Taiwan's long-term care policy should be reevaluated. The reason why Japan's service and product are innovative is because of the free market system. Through market competitions and cross-industrial collaborations, improvements can be made and profit generated. In terms of government policies, Taiwan can try to open up its market and provide better investment opportunities to the world, and allow private profit organizations to participate in long-term care operation. Policy executions should be carried out in a more personalized and localized manner by working closely with the central government, and let innovations penetrate to every town and village in the country.
- Welfare beauty service's business model can be re-examined from different economic perspectives. Whether it's the service procedure, customer relationship, pricing strategy, or industry supply-chain, it should be more adaptive to different culture. Taiwan Beauty Association pointed out that Taiwan has the highest density of beauty salon in the world with total employment of 1.05 million people out of a mere 23 million national population. If Taiwanese beauty salons added welfare beauty service to its menu, it could utilize its current store network and quickly market the product. The mobility of welfare beauty service allows a beauty salon's to expand its business territory and prolong hairdressers' professional life expectancy.
- "Connecting to People" is a slogan from a cellule phone commercial, but it also points out the importance of "human" factor in a product design [39]. Sui-comb and Happy Shampoo are the key factors in welfare beauty service to transfer professional hair wash and cut from store to home. It will require further studies and discussion in the future to find out if they are both culturally and functionally ergonomic.

For citations of references, we prefer the use of square brackets and consecutive numbers. Citations using labels or the author/year convention are also acceptable. The following bibliography provides a sample reference list with entries for journal articles [1], an LNCS chapter [2], a book [3], proceedings without editors [4], as well as a URL [5].

References

1. Bellis, M.: Who invented scissors: ThoughtCo. (2017)
2. Chang, Y.H.: Cultural innovations under globalization. J. Nanjing For. Univ. 11–15 (2010)
3. Chen, J.S.: Only 60% of the home-visit bathing is subsidized. China Post (2018)

4. Chuang, G.Y., Lin, P.F.: The development of bathing services for the aged and disabled population. J. Long Term Care 279–295 (2005)
5. Japan Beauty Practitioner Law (1957)
6. Enjoying Fashionable and Happy Life, Shizuoka Prefecture (2006)
7. Han, P.T.: Culture and Cultural Creativity. Linking Books, Taipei (2014)
8. Huang, F.S.: Outlook on senior service industries and public service policy. Public Gov. Q. 21–32 (2016)
9. Inomura, Y.O.: The aged society and successful ageing. Nippon Rinsho **67**, 851–859 (2009)
10. Kreifeldt, J.: Toward a theory of man-tool system design applications to the consumer product area. In: Proceedings of the HFS 18th Annual Meeting, Hundsville, Alabama, pp. 301–309 (1974)
11. Kumano, H.O.: How the aged spend in Japan based on numbers (2016)
12. Kuo, C.C.: The Secret of Beauty Management. Weishin Management Consulting Co., Taipei (2015)
13. Law for the Development of Cultural and Creative Industries. Ministry of Culture (2010)
14. Lee, R.F.: In Search of Creative Minds. Book Life, Taipei (2008)
15. Lee, S.D.: Long-term care development and implementation. Taiwan Med. J. **46** (2010)
16. Liang, T.M.: Applying dynamic therapies to the aged population. Hungkuang Univ. Stud. Humanit. Soc. Sci. **11**, 85–107 (2009)
17. Lin, R.T.: Transforming Taipei into a world design city. Taipei Econ. Q. 14–21 (2011)
18. Lin, R.T.: Trend and development in creative industries–from creative design to marketing (2005)
19. Lin, R.T., Hsu, C.S.: The analysis of applying digital archive to cultural product design's value adding. Educ. Res. Resour. 39–63 (2012)
20. Lin, R.T., Lin, P.S.: The analysis of cultural innovations through form and ritual design model (2018)
21. Lin, R.T., Tu, L.J., Hsiao, M.T.: The application of digital archive in cultural creativity-using taiwan aboriginal totem in crafts and design. Collected Papers Arts Res. **6**, 27–44 (2006)
22. Lin, T.Y.: Marching to a long life society. Leisure Soc. Res. **6**, 57–67 (2012)
23. Liu, J.Y.: The needs analysis for the development of wellness and health promotion industry in Japan. Chang Gung J. Humanit. Soc. Sci. 301–345 (2015)
24. Liu, L.E.: The first impression is cleanliness. Business Today (2006)
25. Liu, Y.Y.: Home-visit bathing vehicle. Health World 30–33 (2013)
26. Farhad, M.: Electronic bidet seat is the luxury you won't want to live without. New York Times, New York (2015)
27. National Budget: Accountings and Statistics. Executive Yuan, R.O.C. (2017)
28. Oda, H.K.: A study on the concept of successful ageing. Tokushima Univ. J. Soc. Sci. **6**, 127–139 (1993)
29. Republic of China Population Forecast 2018–2065. National Development Committee (2018)
30. Sherrow, V.: Encyclopedia of Hair: A Cultural History. Greenwood Publishing Group, California (2011)
31. Shibata, H.: 80% of all elders should be independent! business publisher (2002)
32. Social Welfare Standard Dictionary (2015)
33. Su, H.T.: The cultural creative experience of an old hotel. J. Des. Sci. **14**(S), 237–256 (2011)
34. The Law of Beauty Practitioner. Ministry of Labor
35. Theory of Beauty Welfare. Yamano College (2016)

36. Tseng, S.Y.: From accessible design to universal design-the study of the development of the US and Japan in accessible environment. J. Des. **8**(2), 57–76 (2002)
37. Wei, Y.C.: Eat Less Exercise More. China Post (2018)
38. Yamano, M.: Gerontology. Tsushinsha, Tokyo (2015)
39. Yen, H.Y., Lin, C.L., Lin, R.T.: A study of design ergonomics to cultural ergonomics-from a design scholar's perspective (2018)

What Do Users like About Smart Bottle? Insights for Designers

Zhuo Poh[1], Chun Yong Chong[2], Pei-Lee Teh[1]([✉]),
Saramma Joseph[1], Shaun Lee Wen Huey[3],
Narayanan Ramakrishnan[4], and Rajendran Parthiban[4]

[1] School of Business, Monash University,
Subang Jaya, Selangor Darul Ehsan, Malaysia
{poh.zhuo,teh.pei.lee,saramma.joseph}@monash.edu
[2] School of Information Technology, Monash University Malaysia,
Subang Jaya, Selangor Darul Ehsan, Malaysia
chong.chunyong@monash.edu
[3] School of Pharmacy, Monash University Malaysia, Subang Jaya,
Selangor Darul Ehsan, Malaysia
shaun.lee@monash.edu
[4] School of Engineering, Monash University Malaysia, Subang Jaya,
Selangor Darul Ehsan, Malaysia
{ramakrishnan,rajendran.parthiban}@monash.edu

Abstract. Water plays a major role in our digestion, absorption, transportation and use of nutrients. Research has shown that inadequate water consumption can cause health risk of urinary stone disease, cancers, salivary gland functions, childhood and adolescent obesity and individuals' overall health. Therefore, daily adequate fluid intake is an important nutrition guideline for people of all age. However, achieving such daily habit is a considerable challenge in many people and there is little data assessing the compliance for fluid intake. Although smart bottles have been introduced in the market, the existing bottles merely focus on a single aspect (fluid intake monitoring). Other aspects (medical adherence and storage compartment) have been neglected in the design. Given that medication often needs to be taken with water, it is important to incorporate fluid and medication monitoring system in the smart bottle. This study aims to explore the young bottles users' needs and requirements of smart bottle through focus groups discussions as well as to propose a system design of smart bottle that integrates with the fluid intake monitoring system, medical adherence system and storage compartment. A sample of 14 young adults participated in the focus groups discussions. The results of focus groups discussions offer a fresh insight on three categories, namely, design, usage and technological features for smart bottle designers. A system design of a multi-functional smart bottle is also proposed. Research implications, limitations, and future research directions are also discussed.

Keywords: Smart bottle · Design · Medication · Young adults

© Springer Nature Switzerland AG 2019
P.-L. P. Rau (Ed.): HCII 2019, LNCS 11577, pp. 325–336, 2019.
https://doi.org/10.1007/978-3-030-22580-3_24

1   Introduction

Adequate water consumption is essential for health since water constitutes to approximately 60% of the human body [1]. Despite this, a recent survey has suggested that a large proportion of the population may are often mildly dehydrated [2]. Factors contributing to mild dehydration include (1) inadequate water consumption; (2) participation in exercise; and (3) environmental condition. While the National Research Council [3] recommends that adults consume approximately 2,500 mL of water daily [2], many people often do not drink enough water [4].

Research has shown that inadequate water consumption can cause health risk of urinary stone disease, cancers of the breast, colon and urinary tract, salivary gland functions, childhood and adolescent obesity and overall health in the older people [1, 2, 5]. Therefore, daily adequate fluid intake is an important nutrition guideline for everyone regardless of age. However, achieving such daily habit is a considerable challenge in many people and there is little data assessing the compliance for fluid intake.

Frost and Sullivan have recently projected that the smart healthcare market value to reach US$348.5 billion by 2025 [6]. The use of smart technology and mobile health applications have been shown to be beneficial in improving compliance and facilitate behavioral changes. Nevertheless, only very few studies [4, 7] have examined how increased fluid intake compliance can be achieved using smart bottles. Examples of smart bottles include the Hidrate Spark [8] and Ozmo Smart Bottle [9]. These smart bottles which handy, are made specifically targeting the young and healthy individuals and very little is known about how this technology can be incorporated to be used among the older adults.

This study aims to explore the perception among the young individuals regarding smart bottle through focus groups discussions. Information and data gathered will then be used to propose a system design of smart bottle that enables user to interact with the smart bottle, visualize text and graphical contents of the fluid intake monitoring system and yet was convenient and handy to use.

2   Literature Review

Many studies have been conducted to address the issue of inadequate water consumption using technology. Dong, Gallant and Biswas [10] in their work examined how a self-monitoring water bottle can be used to track the liquid intake of a user. In their system, the water bottle is attached with an elastic band, equipped with sensor and other electronics. Acceleration that the bottle experiences specifically during drinking events was captured by the band and sent through Bluetooth to a smartphone or notebook for tracking and data management. The system can attain up to 99% accuracy for detecting drinking event and up to 75% accuracy for intake volume estimation [10].

Another system that has been examined is the Hidrate Spark™ smart water bottle [11]. Borofsky et al. [11] conducted a pilot study to assess the accuracy of the fluid intake from the water bottle over 24-h period, which had a 97% accuracy. Another approach was the use of a mobile persuasion system, Playful Bottle system which uses the mobile phone to motivate healthy water intake [4]. In this system, users were encouraged and competed among each other on various games to promote liquid consumption. Results from their seven-week study showed that the games were effective for encouraging healthy water intake by users [4].

3   Research Method

3.1   Sample

This was a qualitative study where participants' views were obtained during focus groups discussions. This method was chosen as it is the most appropriate method to obtain a better understanding of a phenomenon and investigate individuals' decisions and priorities [12]. The study was approved by the Monash University Human Research Ethics Committee (MUHREC: Approval No: 17632). In this study, individuals aged 18 and above were invited to participate in one of the four focus groups conducted. All individuals were recruited through an advertisement which was posted around the university campus.

A focus group interview guide was developed by one of the investigators (PLT), reviewed and revised by the other researchers. The following categories were included in the interview guide: (1) the water drinking habits, (2) use of medications and supplements, (3) preference for smart technology and mobile health and (4) their preference for an ideal bottle.

3.2   Data Collection

The focus group was facilitated by one research assistant who guided the facilitation. The groups lasted approximately 60 min and were digitally recorded. Refreshments were served, and participants were awarded a good quality recycled Monash-tagged cloth bag as a token of appreciation for their time.

3.3   Data Analysis

All recordings were transcribed verbatim. Transcripts were entered into Microsoft Word (Microsoft Corporation, Redmond, Washington) to facilitate coding, grouping, sorting, and cross-referencing of the data. Textual data were categorized using directed qualitative content analysis techniques as described by Hsieh and Shannon [13]. In this method, transcriptions were read carefully, and data were clustered according to categories (e.g., design, usage and technological features). Several codes were developed for each category (see Table 2).

4   Results and Discussions

4.1   Results from Focus Group Discussions

A total of 14 participants comprising of nine males and five females were included in this study. The mean age of participants was 22 years old and all of them had completed their high school. Table 1 shows the profile of participants.

Table 1. Profile of participants.

	Items	Frequency (n = 14)	Percentage (100%)
Gender	Male	9	64.29%
	Female	5	35.71%
Age group	18–20	6	42.86%
	21–30	7	50.00%
	31–40	1	7.14%
Education	High school	9	64.29%
	Bachelor degree/professional qualification	1	7.14%
	Master/PhD	4	28.57%

Design

All 14 participants expressed their views on the design of water bottle. In terms of bottle size, most of the participants (64.29%) used bottles that can hold at least one liter of water, compared with 1.5 L and less than 1 L. Eighty-six percent of the participants suggested tall slim bottle shape and the remaining 14% of the participants recommended flat surfaced bottles.

There was a preference for non-slip grips, as the weight of the water bottle when filled, will not cause it to fall. Forty-three percent of the participants suggested curved design grip, 35.71% participants proposed rubber grip and 21.43% recommended bottle handle. For the material of the water bottle, there was a preference for plastic bottles as it is more durable and impact resistant compared to aluminum bottles. Ninety-three percent of the participants prefer a plastic bottle to other materials such as aluminum or metal. Durability of the bottle was one of the features that most of the participants valued. They preferred bottles that are sturdy and those that do not break, dent or are fragile. All the 14 participants would opt for a sturdy water bottle.

For cap designs, there was a preference for screw caps as it was more secure and leak proof. Ninety-three percent of the participants prefer screw caps, while none of the participants like flip top, and 7.14% likes a straw water bottle. Participants used different water bottle brands, namely Bros and Tupperware are relatively popular. Thirty-six percent of the participants owned a Bros water bottle, another 36% owned Tupperware water bottle, while the remaining of the participants, 28% of them were not sure of the brand of their water bottles.

The participants were also asked on their preferred position of an extra storage compartment on the water bottle. Fifty percent of the participants supported the idea of placing the storage compartment on the top of the bottle, 28.57% thinks that the compartment should be at the bottom of the bottle, while the rest (21.42%) thinks that it should be at the side of the bottle.

Usage

Additionally, participants discussed about their current usage of the water bottle and their medication or supplement intake. All the participants (100%) carried their water bottle around with them wherever they went so that they could have water by their side all the time. This is particularly common for people living in tropical climate such as Malaysia and Singapore.

Most participants who owned water bottles were in the habit of cleaning the water bottles. However, the frequency and the method of washing differed amongst the participants. A few of the participants washed it daily by just rinsing with water. Others would engage in heavy duty washing using a scrub or sponge with soap. Thirty-six percent of the participants washed their bottle daily, 42.86% of the participants washed their bottle weekly, and 14.29% of the participants washed their bottle monthly. Participants were also asked on their usage of storage compartment. All participants indicated that their water bottles did not have storage compartment. Some participants like the idea of storage compartment but some participants are concern of the increasing cost of bottle with storage compartment.

Majority of the participants (64.29%) did not take any medicine or supplement on a regular basis while the other 35.71% expressed that they took either medicine or supplements regularly. For all (100%) those that took medicine or supplements, they forgot to take their medicine occasionally.

Technological Features

In order to understand the user requirement of a smart water bottle, we asked participants to share their opinions on the ideal design of a smart water bottle that they would like. Global Positioning System (GPS) tracker on smart water bottle is one feature that many participants (50%) suggested. Participants reasoned that the GPS tracker will be useful as they have the tendency to lose their water bottle. Twenty-one percent of the participants suggested a water purification feature which will purify the water in the bottle so that the contained water will be safe to drink. Fourteen percent of the participants think that a reminder on the water bottle will be useful as they have experiences multiple occasion that they forgot to drink their water or take medication due to their busy schedule.

During the focus groups discussions, a prototype of water bottle, connected to a mobile application was shown to the participants (Fig. 1). Majority of the participants (92.86%) found the app to be user friendly and simple, but several (7.14%) participants thought that the app had too many pages. Participants also provided feedback to improve the app. Fifty-seven percent of the participants thought that the app should have more colors to look more attractive. Fourteen percent of the participants suggested the font to be larger, while 28.57% thought that there should be more options in the settings such as body measurements or lifestyle.

Participants also suggested several new ideas to improve the reminder feature. While many participants (78.57%) did not have additional comment on the improvement on reminder part, 7.14% had suggested to have a reminder on refilling water, another 7.14% proposed to connect the reminder through a wearable device (Fitbit), while the remaining 7.14% recommended to have an interactive screen or Artificial Intelligent such as Siri on the water bottle for communication. In regard to having medicine reminders, 71.43% of the participants viewed that it is impractical to be integrated with a water bottle. This was mainly because they were young adults and did not have the need to take medicine. However, 14.29% of the participants recommended the medicine reminder to be held on the app, 7.14% suggested on the water bottle and 7.14% suggested on both app and water bottle.

Table 2. The coding scheme

No	Categories	Subcategories	Codes	Examples of quotes
1	Design	Bottle volume/size	1.5 L (14.29%) 1 L (64.29%) Less than 1 L (21.43%)	I think I used 2 types one. For smaller type I use EPlas, for bigger type I use Tupperware. So, it's around 1 L, for the big one, the Tupperware. (Participant RN001)
		Bottle shape	Slim (85.71%) Flat surface (14.29%)	Uhh, maybe something slim, like not so tall. (Participant RN010)
		Bottle grip	Rubber grip (35.71%) Curved design grip (42.86%) Bottle handle (21.43%)	Oh the one that with rubber grip because it doesn't slip out and then like it fall onto ground and then it break. (Participant RN007)
		Bottle material	Plastic (92.86%) Aluminum (7.14%)	I like plastic ones because they usually have like cute designs than aluminum ones. (Participant RN006)
		Bottle durability	Sturdy (100%)	I think mine is quite sturdy ah, it's actually Tupperware, and you drop it and nothing will happen. (Participant RN001)
		Bottle cap	Screw caps (92.86%) Flip top (0%) Straw (7.14%)	I prefer screw cap. Yeah so that it's more secure uhm if it's a flipping up type thing it can the water pressure could be higher and then just breaks open. (Participant RN015)

(continued)

Table 2. (*continued*)

No	Categories	Subcategories	Codes	Examples of quotes
		Bottle brand	Bros (35.71%) Tupperware (35.71%) Not sure/unspecified (28.57%)	I bought it from *Popular* but I don't know the brand. Oh yeah Bros. It's just normal bottle I guess. (Participant RN006)
		Position of storage compartment/ enhancement	Top of bottle (50.00%) Side of bottle (28.57%) Bottom of bottle (21.42%)	On top of the bottle is fine I guess, you can see it and then if you put it on the side and then um you cannot really put it like…Supplements or medicines is fine but then other things I won't really use because like if you put cards and all and then if you lose it, then you will lose everything also. (Participant RN006)
2	Usage	Transport	Using/carrying bottle (100%)	I mostly carry them around. (Participant RN001)
		Cleaning the bottle	Daily (35.71%) Weekly (42.86%) Monthly (14.29%)	Casual wash then ya everyday la, but then I think like the hard wash that use the scrub and stuff only once a month. (Participant RN001)
		Storage compartment	Using (0%) Not using (0%) Do not have one (100%)	Yeah not necessary cause the price will increase as well. (Participant RN003)
		Regular intake of medicine/ supplement	Yes (35.71%) No (64.29%)	For the eye, for the digestive system, for asthma, ya. (Participant RN003)
		Forget to take medicine/ supplement	Sometimes forget (100%) for all that take medicine/ supplement Never forget (0%)	No, sometimes I really forget cause, if especially, okay because the vitamins is at home right, if it's, sometimes I forget in the morning if I wake up late. (Participant RN012)
3	Technological features	Proposed ideas	Water purification (21.43%) GPS tracker (50%) Reminder (14.29%) Self-cleaning (7.14%) Calendar on bottle (7.14%)	If you remind me to drink water, I guess it's a bit useful but most of my apps I don't use like I don't look at it so…The app that I had before actually you can like input like how much volume you drink and then like if you drink from like a cup, they know like the estimation of a cup size and all. (Participant RN006)

(*continued*)

Table 2. (*continued*)

No	Categories	Subcategories	Codes	Examples of quotes
		Mobile application usability	User friendly and simple (92.86%) Too many pages (7.14%)	I prefer swipe la. Let's say you have everything in one page it will be too wordy, unless like everything right is like a iPhone like ok like this tap for this go in another one like that (Participant RN003)
		Improvements to bottle/app	Better fonts or font sizes (14.29%) More colours (57.14%) More features in settings (28.57%)	Okay… now maybe… okay looking at it like that, the font size is good uhh maybe for older adults the font itself should be bold I think. I know this is bold so you either change the headings, bigger size and it would be useful if it's a bit bolder. Then the bottle itself could be a bit more…ahh better looking. Make it a bit more like techy, techy but uh attractive. (Participant RN014)
		Improvement on reminder	Reminder to refill water (7.14%) Screen on bottle or talk like Siri (7.14%) Fitbit connected (7.14%) No comment (78.57%)	Smart. AI. It is time to refill water. (Participant RN008)
		Reminder for medicine	On bottle (7.14%)	The reminder from phone is not so effective, but the reminder on the bottle itself could potentially be more effective. (Participant RN010)

Figure 1 shows some of the screenshots of the prototype of Android smartphone app. The first image is the homepage which shows the key information such as target water amount, water amount consumed and etc. The second page is the alarm and settings page in which the user can change their reminder settings and their age. This information is used to determine their heart rate and required water consumption. Users can select "user interface for the older adults" to have page view with bigger font size. The third page is the record of water consumption for a day.

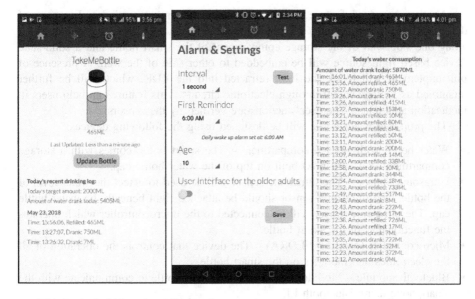

Fig. 1. Android-based mobile app that was showed in the focus groups discussions.

4.2 Proposed Design

The findings from the focus groups discussion gave useful insights on our proposed design of the smart bottle. In terms of the physical design of the water bottle, our proposed bottle follows most of the conventional water bottle design, which are slim and of decent height to contain approximately one liter of water. To design an ergonomically friendly grip for the water bottle, our proposed design will shape the middle part of the water bottle to be slimmer for better gripping. A handle will be added on the cap of the water bottle to enable users to hold the bottle, with a screw-on cap to ensure its leak-proof. The water bottle will be made with Bisphenol A (BPA) free plastic which is safe for drink consumption. A detachable storage compartment will be added on the top of the water bottle. The primary use for the storage compartment is to store either pills or supplements (or any other small items). Sensors will be built inside the storage compartment for monitoring system.

Regarding the functionality and features of the smart bottle, our proposed water bottle will have a GPS tracker to track the movement of the bottle. This tracking system uses GPS satellites and mobile phone triangulation to pinpoint the exact location of the water bottle in real time. Additionally, our proposed smart bottle has the water level tracking ability, integrating with the smartphone application. The water tracking could monitor user's drinking habits. In order to keep the user hydrated, our bottle will also incorporate a reminder system that alerts the user via smartphone and wearable device (e.g., Fitbit) to drink water from the bottle. The passing of water through the sensor, determines the water level in the bottle. This is the key indicator of the user's water consumption.

Another proposed feature is the medication/supplement reminder. For case of detecting the pill/supplement, a Light Dependent Resistor (LDR) will be embedded along one side wall of the storage compartment of the smart bottle and a solid-state device based light source will be embedded to other side of the wall. A presence of pill/supplement will block the light refracted into the LDR, which will be further quantified as voltage signal through electronic circuits. This feature can help users in medication adherence. The user's actions are verified by the sensors.

The proposed water bottle will be designed using the following devices:

- Water bottle with storage compartment – The smart bottle comes with a storage compartment (e.g., pill box) built on top of the water bottle cap.
- Ultrasonic Sensor – The ultrasonic sensor will be used to detect the water level of the bottle. The ultrasonic sensor should be attached right beneath the water bottle cap. The ultrasonic sensor will be connected to the microcontroller which operates the functionality of the smart bottle.
- Microcontroller (Adafruit FLORA) – The device that controls the operation of all the electronics and modules on the smart bottle.
- Bluetooth module – Module required for the smart bottle to communicate with the smartphone using Bluetooth LE.
- Light-emitting diode (LED) and Light Dependent Resistor (LDR) – The LED is used along with the LDR for detecting presence of capsule or tablets inside the storage compartment. If a capsule is inside the compartment, it will block out the light the LED is emitting and reducing the light intensity, thus increasing the resistance of the LDR. This method is used to detect the presence of the capsule inside the compartment.
- GPS tracker – A GPS tracker is installed to track the location of the water bottle. The information of the location of the water bottle will be sent to the phone. Users can use that information to track their water bottle in situation where they lose their water bottle.
- Rechargeable Battery – Since the water bottle will be carried around, therefore it requires power to function.
- Android-enabled smartphone – For this study, the smartphone application will run on the Android-enabled operating system.
- Fitness tracker/Smartwatch – An additional device that can track the user's activity which can be interpreted to dynamically set the user's water consumption target. It can also be used as a secondary reminder in situations where the user misses the reminder on their smartphone.

Figure 2 shows the conceptual workflow on how the proposed system will interface with multiple devices including water bottle, smartphone and wearable device (e.g., Fitbit). User could interact with the water bottle through the Android-based mobile application: (1) To receive alarm reminder; (2) To track their water consumption and medication adherence; (3) To track the location of the water bottle.

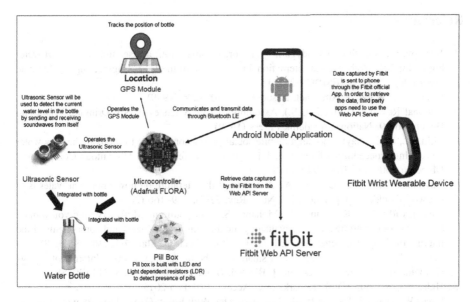

Fig. 2. Software architecture diagram

5   Conclusion

This study contributes to a better understanding of young adults' needs and requirements of a smart bottle design. From a practical viewpoint, this study highlights the key designs (e.g., detachable storage compartment), usage (e.g., medication/supplement reminder) and technological features (e.g., GPS tracker) for a multi-functional smart bottle among the young users. A system design of a smart water bottle is also proposed. This study has two research limitations. First, the sample size of the focus groups discussions was relatively small ($n = 14$) in this study. Future studies should increase the number of participants in their data collection. Second, the participants recruited in this study were young adults and the findings could differ with different age groups. This study should be extended with sample of older adults.

Acknowledgements. This research was supported by Monash University Malaysia's School of Business, School of Information Technology, School of Engineering, School of Pharmacy, Gerontechnology Laboratory, Health and Well-Being Cluster, Global Asia in the 21st Century (GA21) Platform. The authors wish to express their appreciation for all the volunteers who participated in the study. Special thanks are due to Dr. Hsien Hooi Lee and Mr. Sim Jing Yuan for their help in data collection.

References

1. Jovanov, E., Nallathimmareddygari, V., Pryor, J.: SmartStuff: a case study of a smart water bottle. In: 2016 38th Annual International Conference of the IEEE Engineering in Medicine and Biology Society (EMBC) (2016)
2. Kleiner, S.: Water. J. Am. Diet. Assoc. **99**(2), 200–206 (1999)
3. National Research Council (U.S.), Assembly of Life Sciences (U.S.): Drinking Water and Health, vol. 9. National Academies Press (1989)
4. Chiu, M., et al.: Playful bottle: a mobile social persuasion system to motivate healthy water intake. In: Proceedings of the 11th International Conference on Ubiquitous Computing - Ubicomp 2009, pp. 185–194 (2009)
5. Davidhizar, R., Dunn, C., Hart, A.: A review of the literature on how important water is to the world's elderly population. Int. Nurs. Rev. **51**(3), 159–166 (2004)
6. Sundaravadivel, P., Kougianos, E., Mohanty, S., Ganapathiraju, M.: Everything you wanted to know about smart health care: evaluating the different technologies and components of the internet of things for better health. IEEE Consum. Electron. Mag. **7**(1), 18–28 (2018)
7. Lee, N., Lee, T., Seo, D., Kim, S.: A smart water bottle for new seniors: Internet of Things (IoT) and health care services. Int. J. Bio-Sci. Bio-Technol. **7**(4), 305–314 (2015)
8. Hidrate Spark. https://hidratespark.com/. Accessed 01 Feb 2019
9. Smart Water Bottle | Smart Bottle That Integrates With Fitbit: Ozmo. https://www.ozmo.io/. Accessed 01 Feb 2019
10. Dong, B., Gallant, R., Biswas, S.: A self-monitoring water bottle for tracking liquid intake. In: 2014 IEEE Healthcare Innovation Conference (HIC) (2014)
11. Borofsky, M., Dauw, C., York, N., Terry, C., Lingeman, J.: Accuracy of daily fluid intake measurements using a "smart" water bottle. Urolithiasis **46**(4), 343–348 (2017)
12. Berg, B., Lune, H.: Qualitative Research Methods for the Social Sciences. Pearson Education Limited, London (2017)
13. Hsieh, H., Shannon, S.: Three approaches to qualitative content analysis. Qual. Health Res. **15**(9), 1277–1288 (2005)

Business Practice of Service Design in New Retail Era in China

Zhan Su[1(✉)] and Li Cui[2]

[1] Alibaba Group, Hangzhou, China
suzhan.sz@alibaba-inc.com
[2] Tsinghua University, Beijing, China

Abstract. This paper explores a model of experience-centered service design thinking based on real practice in order to provide practical solutions for systematic optimization in the New Retail Era in China. Service design consists of two parts, the understanding of service processes and the understanding of target users, and we proposed a five-stages thinking model to better summarize our experiences of how to organize the processes. We designed a flower purchase APP named Picky and applied it to an ordinary community in Haidian District, Beijing. HCI methods and the re-optimizing of the supply chain greatly improve the efficiency of traditional services, reduce the costs and improve the user experience. Within two months, we have collected 1200 users in this community and beyond. The experiences can be applied to strategically launch new services or optimize traditional services, and it will also be beneficial in establishing platform credibility and effective service mechanisms.

Keywords: Cross-cultural product and service design ·
User experience design · Design method

1 Introduction

China is a rapidly emerging market in Internet retail. The focus of current service design has shifted from effective production to streamlined consumption, and the evaluation of value has also changed from basic living to pursuing high-quality life [1]. With the improvement of the quality of life of Chinese residents, flowers have gradually become many people's daily like, however, the exorbitant prices keep some potential customers and flower likers, especially average-income users away.

This article takes a service design practice in flower retail industry as an example. We designed an online flower shopping product-Picky APP, along with the interview of more than 10 flower providers, channel merchants, consumers, and many other key players in the business. Through our service design and the re-shape of supply chain, we can provide high-quality flowers with an innovative and convenient service at a price of half or lower than the market price, meanwhile, keep a platform profit of more than 20%. The brand new online flowers purchase service rapidly wins the support and love of our consumers. In the course of follow-up service, we have accumulated more than 1,200 loyal customers, and the total sales amounted to 1 ton in 2 months. Through our practice, we rethink the relations between service design and business and

© Springer Nature Switzerland AG 2019
P.-L. P. Rau (Ed.): HCII 2019, LNCS 11577, pp. 337–353, 2019.
https://doi.org/10.1007/978-3-030-22580-3_25

integrate, analyze and optimize the production chains, supply chains, and sales. We combined two theories from design and business to finally design a thinking model, which can be practical in real service design in business environment.

Our practice shows that in China's existing business environment, there are still a large number of business services lacking of system-level optimization and reformation. Through the power of HCI, using service design methods, we can improve production and supply efficiency, reduce the costs and improve the experience, and then create more value for consumers and businesses, eliminate the waste of social resources.

2 Backgrounds

2.1 Internet Environment with Chinese Characteristics

According to the White Paper on China's Internet Economy of Ali Research Institute, China's Internet has three main characteristics, large but unique, rapidly developing and active for change [2].

In the past 15 years, the total annual growth rate of Chinese Internet users has reached 25%, ranking 1st in the world. Internet consumption has also grown at a compound annual growth rate of 32% in the past five years, leading the world's major countries. –Chinese Internet users are more likely to go online shopping and more often than those of developed countries, such as the United States. Meanwhile, China has a well-developed Internet infrastructure including cloud computing, big data, logistic and payment, which provide a sufficient environment for emerging services to grow and develop [2].

China has a vast territory with huge regional differences. The demand for services various in different industries, regions and social classes, showing a tendency of individualization and diversification. The desire for service and high-quality consumptions is growing rapidly in recent years, and there are a lot of innovative services in the Chinese Internet market [3].

2.2 Service Design

Service Design is a field of design emerged after 1991 and was first proposed by Dr. Michael Erlhoff of the School of Design at the Köln International School of Design [4]. This design area focused on the planning and management of enterprise service, and attached great importance to systematic approach and a customer-centric approach. Service design and business are inseparable and interdependent [5].

Business itself is a complex of services. In this complex, all the procedures and roles work together to achieve mutual benefit and win-win results, which jointly promote the vigorous development of society.

2.3   Retail and New Retail

Retail is the final stop of the supply chain, and all the procedures before it are the processes of adding value to the goods. Retail industry is more and more of vital importance in China's national economy [6].

Retail is the oldest and most typical commercial format. Service design in the retail industry is the most complex and comprehensive, which can be a good model for other businesses.

At the Ali Yunqi Conference in October 2016, Jack Ma, founder of Alibaba Group first proposed the concept of "New Retail" in his speech, "The next decade, or 20 years, there will be no e-commerce in China, only New Retail" [7].

The so-called "New Retail" means the companies are using technological methods such as big data, Artificial Intelligence to upgrade and reform the production, distribution, and sales processes and meanwhile, deeply integrate online services, offline experiences and modern logistic solutions. For short, New Retail, driven by big data, is to transform the existing retail industry through new technology in order to upgrade user experience [8]. New Retail brought about the connection and collaboration of consumer Internet and industry Internet [9].

2.4   Business Model

A business model is a theoretical tool that contains a large number of business elements and the relationships between them, and can describe the business model of a particular company.

Harvard Business School professor Christensen, and SAP co-CEO Kagermann mentioned that successful companies should have business model that can be broken down into four elements: a customer value proposition that fulfills an important job for the customer in a better way than competitors' offerings do; a profit formula that lays out how the company makes money delivering the value proposition; and the key resources and key processes needed to deliver that proposition. Game-changing opportunities deliver radically new customer value propositions. They fulfill a job to be done in a dramatically better way, solve a problem that's never been solved before, or serve an entirely unaddressed customer base [10].

Business is a complex of services. Through our study and thinking of the business logic, combined with the principles and methods of service design, we found out the differences and connections between the two, and generate relevant insights that can be used to optimize the service design thinking methods and help designers quickly and systematically build business thinking logic.

3   Service Design Thinking Model

In the traditional service design thinking process, we can use a variety of thinking tools, such as: user journey map, user cases, touchpoints matrix, story board, blueprint, character profiles, experience prototype, service prototype, personas, issue cards, etc. [11, 12]. These are useful tools or thinking methods used in different stages of the service design, however, we are still lack of a whole thinking model for overall understanding in service design.

Combining Christensen's thinking about business models with the methods and practices of service design, we propose a thinking model of service design. Our thinking about service design is divided into two modules: service understanding and target users understanding. Among them, we divide service understanding into three levels: macro, meso and micro. Target user understanding is divided into two perspectives: user perspective and expert perspective. Every stage of the thinking above needs to be quickly verified and tested.

We try to demonstrate the thinking model through our business practice of Picky, a flower retail service, through which we can build a holistic service perception and thus it is a lot easier to optimize user experience and integrate the whole process (Fig. 1).

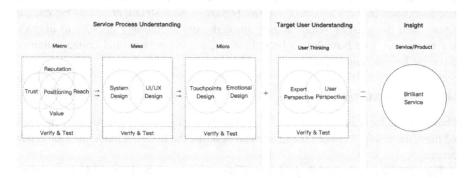

Fig. 1. Thinking model of service design

3.1   Service Process Understanding

We divide the service design understanding into three levels: macro level, meso level and micro level. The macro level is mainly completed by the "Hierarchical model of service demand" (will explain below), through which we can quickly understand a service from the macro perspective. The meso level is divided into the system layer and the front-end layer. The system frameworks for the whole service, which refers to the background system for building the service, such as the warehouse system (WMS), logistics system (TMS), customer management system, etc. Front-end layer: mainly designed for interaction and vision, the front-end solution based on complex system support and will be presented directly to consumers. The micro level was divided into touchpoints design and emotional design. By analyzing service and customer touchpoints, we can design accurately. By emotional design, we can understand the scene and context in order to provide specialized and proper design. Through the combination of the two, we can have a clear understanding of the whole micro level. To sum up, the three levels thinking model help us understand the service.

Macro Level. On the macro level of thinking, we explored and constructed a five-step hierarchical model of service requirements:

When we think about a service, the first thing is positioning, how we provide services to whom; the second step is to think about what is the unique value that our service can provide for the users; third step is to consider how to reach target users and how to interact with the users; then fourth, find out how to win the trust of users and let them approve our service; finally, think about how we can get social reputation by the autonomously recommend and spread of our loyal users (Fig. 2).

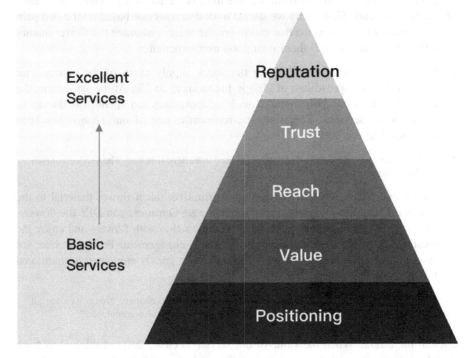

Fig. 2. Five-step hierarchical model of service requirements

Positioning. Positioning is to identify a company or product image and status in the eyes of customers or consumers [13]. Before we start to all the services, first of all, we need to think about the positioning and determine who are our target users, what kind of requirements of them have not been met and what kind of services we can provide.

China is an acquaintance society [14] in which mothers are generally assumed to take more divisions in family social contact and procurement, prefer sharing and communication, and interact with neighbors more frequently. At the same time, this group is relatively more concentrated and with strong consumption ability. Therefore, this group of people is targeted in our design practice. In the case, we positioned our product to provide better flower purchasing experiences for the mother group in modern communities in China's first-tier cities.

Value. When our service is well positioned, then the value of the service will be the next question that needs to be considered. Why these users want to use our service, what value our service brings to them, and what kind of need was satisfied. The thinking of this module will determine whether consumers will choose your service, and through this we can guarantee users satisfaction through the enhancement of commodity value and the experience value.

We conducted user interviews in the communities mother group and we found a common feature of this group, the improvement of the quality of life and the pursuit of beauty.

Flowers are popular among them, but the high price and bad purchase experience restrain their demand. That's why we decide to design a service based on the two pain points to create a flower service that can lower the price, guarantee the flower quality and at the same time provide them with good user experience.

(1) Commodity Value: By optimizing the entire supply chain of the process, we reduced the widespread loss of 20% in the industry to 2%. At the same time, the price of flowers has been reduced to 1/3. Consumers can spend less money to obtain better services. Therefore, the repurchase rate of our service has been maintained above 80%.

.... "The flowers are really fresh and cheap! So hard to believe it is true. The service is much better than other platforms."

(2) Experience Value: We provide the most primitive, uncut flower material to the customers and provide useful tools as a package. Our users can DIY the flowers, which allows them to fully involve in the interaction with flowers and enjoy the creation of flower art, then enhance the user's engagement. From our side, we save a lot of labor cost and reduce flower damage greatly compared to traditional flower shops.

.... "Yesterday I shared a picture of my DIY flowers in my community group, they are all excited, can you deliver it to other provinces? Price increment is also acceptable!"

Reach to the Users. When the value of our service is clear, the next thing is to think about how to reach more target audience. To marketing "Picky App", we built and maintained several WeChat (The most popular IM App in China) groups to connect with our potential users, and these groups are self-organized and grow bigger day by day though our campaign programs and the invitation of loyal users. This direct connection can ensure that our service reach to the target users.

Trust. As a service, even if it brings value, users still need to consider whether the service is secure and reliable to decide whether they can rely on it in the long-term. So we need to convince our customers that our service is safe and trustworthy, and we are making all effort in building trust in designing our service.

(1) Technical Level: We designed an APP, which is stable with rapid feedback. At the same time, our products are built in WeChat's App, which has passed the technical review of the third party (WeChat) to ensure the security of the program and the legality of the service and information acquisition.

(2) Experience Level: We designed the brand name of the project "花品集" ("Flower Collection" in English) and a special logo. At the same time, we also designed and organized the website and WeChat App. Through these comprehensive design, we successfully gained user recognition.

(3) Feedback Level: We set up a hotline and customer service channel in the WeChat App and solve customer problems in a timely manner, in order to build trust through patient feedbacks.

.... "Thank you for making life so wonderful, with the company of flowers, I feel passionate for work. I choose to use your platform from all the platforms and I will definitely recommend it to my friends."

Reputation. Through the design of each of the above modules, our products have gained the trust of users. A deeper level of service design is the word of mouth, in other word, reputation. We need to think about how to let users do marketing for us voluntarily.

We believe that if our service solution is more efficient, providing better experience and at the same time with a lower price, then it has met the requirements of spreading out by the word of mouth. We designed some promotion plans that can help our users more eager to spread, such as group purchasing (invite your friend to buy together), purchase more get more discount, free gift for inviting, free delivery, etc., to encourage user's sharing behavior, and organizing offline floral activities regularly to attract more users and stimulate their will to share.

...."I have organized many young mothers in our community to buy together, should let more people enjoy this good service!"

Through the thinking of these five levels of service processes, we are able to fully understand the service process from a relatively macro perspective and establish a macro thinking model.

Meso Level. Many of the design methods are focusing on at the meso-level, such as storyboards, service design blueprints, etc. Meso-level service design includes system-level thinking, front-end interaction and design-level thinking. Through the system level to design all processes and interactions, the front-end level to complete the interaction of relationships and the delivery of services.

The meso-level design can be divided into two modules, one is system design, focus on the system-level logical framework for building a service, the other one is front-end design, mainly focus on the communication with customers through user interface and provides service content to customers through interaction.

System Design. We build a system-level logical framework for services in this module. Take Picky App as an example, the service is to sell flowers to the user. In this "selling" process, multiple systems are required to be thought parallel, such as logistics systems, store management systems, store cashier systems, APP systems, and user & order management systems. Three key processes can be abstracted in these systems: commodity flow, capital flow and logistics. These systems and processes manage complex commercial processes in a digital way.

(1) Core Players: The core players can be divided into suppliers, distributors, logistics providers, sellers, couriers and customers. The system module involves all the core players in the service, as well as the interactions, interests, and divisions between different roles. We need to make sure that all participants in the entire

service system are satisfied in order to make the entire system healthy, effective and sustainable. Usually, we use the Stakeholders approach to analyze.

A seemingly simple flower sales service actually involves all the above module systems. Any one of them is a separate service module. The service between module and module seems to be independent, but actually, it is crucial for user experience design. And it is also the breakthrough point of our service innovation. Through the combing of the whole process, we changed the order of the processes, pre-installed the user purchase process, and we received the orders before restocking and delivery. This purchasing mode can greatly reduce the flower damage by 20%–30% compared with the traditional flower shops. Since we reduced the natural loss and the cost of inventory, so the price will be greatly reduced. After test and verify, we found that almost all the consumers are willing use the pre-paid mode.

Front-end Design. The design of the front end mainly includes the interface and interaction design. Through the understanding of the functions and the system levels, we display the functions to the consumers through the interface, so that the consumers can enjoy our service through the operation on the interface. The design of the front end is closely related to the background function. We manage the complex tasks efficiently through the background system and make the front-end solution simplest, through which users can purchase the flowers they want with only 2 clicks (Fig. 3).

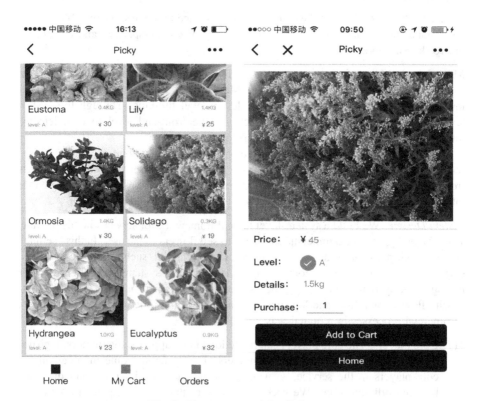

Fig. 3. Home page and detailed page

Through the meso-level service design and thinking, we can systematically understand the service. We complete the extremely complicated management, calculation, and make the operation extremely simple and efficient on the front end. The right to make a decision easily is always available for the consumers. Users are able to provide extremely complex service requirements to our system without knowing it and get an excellent service experience (Fig. 4).

Fig. 4. Automatic flowers cabinet

Micro Level. Micro perspective means that after the service has been basically structured, we need to think about how to improve the micro touchpoints and nodes in the service process and try to establish emotional relations with our consumers. It is also an important stage to fight the competitors with unique and perfect service. Similarly, micro service design also has tools to assist, such as service touchpoints, user experience maps and so on.

In the thinking of micro perspective service design, here come the two topics:

(1) User Touchpoints: It is the touchpoints where our service interacts with the customers. In the software interaction, it is necessary to meet the expectations of the user, in line with the user's psychology at that time and meanwhile to ensure efficient, accurate, fault-tolerant and timely reminders. In the abstract service, we should design and control the emotions generated in the service scene. For example, our off-line flower picking point is near the residential area. The flowers reserved by the user will be placed in the specific community. The user only needs to scan the code to take it away. In the process, the user only needs to follow the steps: Be informed where is the flowers pick up point - freely choose a time - scan the code - get the flower.

(2) Emotional Design: American cognitive psychologist Donald Norman in 2002 put forward the "emotional" concept of product design, the emotions are divided into three levels: instinct, behavior and reflection [15]. Our design should have ways to emotionally interact with the users, making the product no longer feedback indifferently and cold, but with personalized features to establish an emotional connection with the users. For example, if the shopping cart is vacant for a long time, it will prompt: "I am hungry, get some flowers for me." Personalize a software can create a better emotional relations between product and users.

3.2   Target User Understanding

User Perspective. In order to make users feel the charm of your service, we need to think about our service from the perspective of users. As the founder of 7-eleven said: "The seller should not start from the perspective of "think for the customer", but "think in the shoe of customers" [16]. Through the user's perspective, we can feel that the expectation of the users is not only getting the product (flowers), but to participate in the process of making flowers and their house more beautiful. So, according to the corresponding scene, we create a new purchase experience for them by allowing the users participate in the DIY parts that they are interested in.

Expert Perspective. Japanese famous designer Sato Keishi believes that inspiration and creativity are always hidden in daily life. When we observe life, we have two identities. One is as the ordinary self, and the other is to observe the former self as a designer [16]. Similarly, when we are designing services, we must not only use user perspective but also use an expert perspective. See yourself as a user through a professional perspective will allow you to come up with professional solutions that exceed ordinary users' expectations.

Verify and Test. Through the above-mentioned various dimensions and levels of thinking, we have formed preliminary conclusions and insights, however, we still need to be verified in a smart way. Eric Ries proposed the MVP (Minimum Variable Product) method in his book Lean Startup, which can be used in the verification and test in field of service design. By designing a simplest and functional model, direct feedbacks can be obtained quickly and easily which can help reduce the uncertainty that accompanies most of the commercialized projects, getting a quick verification from the market [17]. This method has been used repeatedly for verification during our design process.

Verification and testing is throughout the entire process, we can effectively use this method to calibrate our services and use the lowest cost to try and find fault, in order to build our services faster and better.

Conclusion. Through the two perspectives, we have a more comprehensive understanding and insight into product and service, and we get a practical service design and implementation solution through in-depth thinking. Through our thinking model, designers can fully understand the services we design and the real needs of our users. The strategic thinking model we established will be useful in guiding and optimizing service design, and help service designers maintain the ability to innovate in services.

4 Field Investigations

The research method is guided by service design, user-centered design and data-driven design. We used usability testing, user interviews and other research methods. At the same time, the minimum available selection in the business is used for testing (MVP test) to obtain a large amount of data and feedback.

4.1 Recruitment

Before the Launch of the Product. We recruited 10 users as our seed users. Our target is the mother group in the community of China's first-tier city (Beijing). They have the common characteristics, aged 25–45, and have stable jobs. They have their own real estate or a fixed residence, and the monthly income is about 10,000 RMB. They have requirements for quality of life, who like communication and sharing.

User 1: Ms. Wang

Wang lives in a residential area in the western suburbs of Beijing. It is about 20 km away from our flower pick up point. She knows our flower service through the recommendation of a friend. After trying to order, she found that she exceeded her expectations and became a heavy user of our service. Her job is to be a college teacher in Haidian District. She has 2 children. She is an opinion leader in the community. She is the owner of their community WeChat group. She likes our service very much and recommended our service to the mothers in the group. Under her recommendation, we added more than 100 users in one day.

During the Launch of the Product. Our products and services started to be launched and promoted. During the promotion process, we randomly selected about 10 typical users as our research customers in the launch, which are also young mothers in Beijing residential community. They are very familiar with our services and they generally have the habit of buying flowers.

User 2: Ms. Xu

Ms. Xu is a teacher of the No. 22 Middle School in Beijing. She started to order flowers from our platform through the recommendation of her friend. After several attempts, she liked the service and recommended to colleagues around her. They created a new group to voluntarily help neighbor receive and distribute flowers, the group purchased more than 100 kg of flowers at a time in a single purchase (Figs. 5 and 6).

Fig. 5. Our off-line flower pick-up point

Fig. 6. Customer feedbacks

4.2 Semi-structured Interviews

User C:

"I am a white-collar woman, living alone, who likes to have a quality of life. In the past, I mainly went to the flower shop or online to buy flowers, but the flowers purchased online are usually not fresh. The longer-used service is "Hua Jia" and "Hua Dian Shi Jian". Their service is characterized by year package. The cost of one-year service is a fixed fee, but we can't choose the flowers that we want. These platforms send flowers to me every month. The average cost of a bunch of flowers is about 40 yuan or so, but the amount of flowers is relatively small, about 5–7. Many times, the flowers are dehydrated when they are delivered here, and the quality of the flowers is not good. Now I often buy flowers in Picky App, I feel that the flowers are very fresh, the quality is very high, I enjoy the process of cutting flowers and putting it into the vase, and the price is also favorable, the weight is about 2–3 times more than other platform. I like Picky App very much."

User D:

"I owned a restaurant, hoping to make the restaurant more tasteful and enhance the dining experience of our customers. In the past, fake flowers were used on the table, mainly considering the cost. But personally, I love fresh flowers. I started to know Picky App from a neighbors' recommendation. I tried to buy it once, and the quality of the flower is really good. Now we have real flowers in our restaurants, and also in my house. Although it is pre-paid, we cannot see and touch the flowers, but after several attempts, I am very satisfied with the expected service. And the process of buying flowers is really simple."

4.3 Testing Data

Our service has been officially launched for 2 months, and we have obtained a lot of valuable data in two months (Fig. 7).

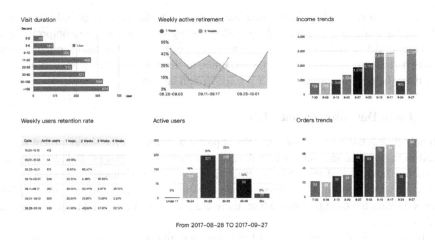

From 2017–08–28 TO 2017–09–27

Fig. 7. Testing data

User's Stay Time. More than 566 people stayed in the APP for more than 50–100 s, accounted for 19.3% of the total number. There are 614 people over 100 s, accounted for 21% of the total. The data shows that although our product operations are really simple, users are still happy to enjoy the pictures and choose flowers.

Monthly Active Retention. The data shows that our active users will still be close to 40% after three weeks (the reason for the peak is that we open it regularly every week). This shows that users stuck to our services, and 40% of the users still willing to use our service after one month.

Purchase Volume. We did not initiate publicity. New users come here relying on word-of-mouth communication, and our weekly sales volume increased by an average of 26%.

Basic Data of User Groups. Users aged 25–49 accounted for 74% of our core users, and 75% of the total user group are female.

Through the analysis of the above data, we can find that the user group is highly consistent with the target that group we originally positioned. Our service has also been recognized and sustained by the users and it has a certain word-of-mouth effect.

5 Discussion and Implications for Design

We established our product service through PICKY and formed a relatively complete service loop. Through a systematic thinking and practical design execution, we have collected insights of the relationship between service design and business practice. In the future, we can further apply them into other business or industry fields, and enhance user experience through the power of HCI.

5.1 Break the Barriers of Industries

Service design is closely related to business, but due to the barriers of industries, it is difficult for designers to have a deep understanding of business. The comprehensive thinking model combines the relevant knowledge of business and also service design, builds a strategic perspective for the designer to think thoroughly with various perspectives, helping designers build a service design strategy.

5.2 Retail Digitalization and HCI

China's new retail environment actually represents a trend in the development of the retail industry: business started to link to each other with a trend of digitalization, the consumer Internet and industrial Internet fully integrated, technology changed traditional business model of traditional industries and even consumers' consumption habits. During the changing procedure, there are a lot of services need to be re-planned and designed.

In the future, all the commercial links will be digitalized and flexible, iterate in the direction of faster, cheaper and better. Users' consumption habits and shopping habits will change according to the changes of business rules. Prepaid will become a leading trend, through which we can release the pressure of the supply chain. Through accurate forecasting, we can eliminate the uncertainty of services and improve efficiency and achieve development (Fig. 8).

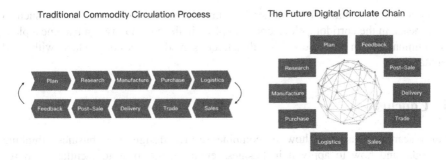

Fig. 8. The change of commodity circulate chain

In the case of Picky, our users choose to trust us and pre-paid before the product been received, thus changing the traditional sales model. Based on this, we can precisely control the quantity of products supply and choose the proper transportation mode, thus reducing the time and waste of each process, provide best experience for our users at the best price.

Practice showed that through HCI technology and methods, combined with inter-disciplinary knowledge, we could quickly understand the needs and trends and establish an innovative and efficient service system. Finally, we can reduce the collaboration costs, shorten the supply cycle, optimize user experience, and reduce the waste of resources.

5.3 Create Value for the Users

Excellent service systems are extremely complex, requiring user-oriented spread and expansion, horizontally across multiple industries, and vertically deep into multiple levels. As a service designer, we need comprehensive knowledge and practical exploration capabilities to build a comprehensive and holistic strategy in order to guide and optimize the service design. We need to see the complexity from simple, see simple from complexity, and we need to have the skills and methods to identify different insights. Of course, regardless of any skill or method, we need to follow a gold principle: Design should be user-oriented, create value for the users is of vital importance.

5.4 Consumption Characters of Chinese Society

Community is the basic cell that constitutes the life of Chinese residents. The consumption behavior of Chinese residents in the community has many characteristics. For example, the purchasing behaviors of a community groups have some rules to follow. Through our analysis of service data, we can find that the repurchase period of flowers products is 1–2 weeks (flowers are generally faded after 2 weeks) and users need to continue to repurchase to maintain a quality life experience. Through the accumulation of future data, it is easier for us to provide more accurate effective service solutions to our users.

In addition, community consumers' communication scenarios are various, such as after meals, in the corridors, elevators. Any place in the community can become a place to communicate. In this case, users will actively spread services or products with good reputations.

6 Conclusions

Our research focuses on how to combine service design with business thinking methods, and how to apply it in business environment so as to facilitate resource optimization and to establish a more effective and healthier service model. In real business practice, we managed to design a product together with our users and launched the APP successfully. Within only 2 months, the service expanded to more than 20 communities, with more than 1,200 customers.

Through the practice, we validated the macro-thinking model of full-link analysis, and through link optimization we improved the efficiency and convenience of the business model. To summarize, the purpose of this paper is to make business more efficient through service design and to make services more sustainable by improving business efficiency. We explored the relationship and boundary between services and business, and attempted to integrate knowledge across industries and across disciplines. By doing this, we came up with the thinking model, and provided designers with a new way to understand services.

References

1. Polai, A., Lovlie, L., Reasons, B.: Service Design and Innovation Practice, p. 20. Tsinghua University Press, Beijing (2015)
2. Ali Research Institute: China Internet Economy White Paper: Interpreting China's Internet Features (2017)
3. Huang, J., Li, J.: The characteristics measurement and development of china's consumption upgrade. China Bus. Mark. (2018)
4. Xin, D.: Rise, innovation and development: "service design" in the background of contemporary globalization. Beauty Times (2011)
5. Gu, G.: A summary and views of the retailers returning to the essence of business. Commer. Times, 20–22 (2015)
6. Lu, Q.: Home depot retail strategy analysis. change to create miracles. Mark. Mod. (2007)
7. Gao, H.: New retail drives new logistics. Ali Research Institute (2018). http://www.aliresearch.com/blog/article/detail/id/21527.html
8. Zhao, M.: How to attract users and make them stay: two thoughts on the transformation of operators' channels. China Telecom **12**, 36–39 (2017)
9. Gao, H.: 2017, new retail is on the way. Ali Research Institute (2018). http://www.aliresearch.com/blog/article/detail/id/21413.html
10. Johnson, M.W., Christensen, C.M., Kagermann, H.: Reinventing your business model. Harvard Bus. Rev. **87**, 52–60 (2008)
11. Vertelney, L., Curtis, G.: Storyboards and sketch prototypes for rapid interface visualization. In: CHI Tutorial (1990)

12. Service Design Tools. Communication Methods Supporting Design Processes. http://www.servicedesigntools.org/tools/108
13. Li, F.: The three steps of marketing positioning method: from product positioning to the marketing positioning. Mark. Mod. **10**, 17–18 (2003)
14. Fei, X.: Rural development in China: Prospect and Retrospect. University of Chicago Press, Chicago (1989)
15. Norman, D.A.: Design Psychology 3. Emotional Design. CITIC Press, Beijing (2012)
16. Suzuki, M., Gu, X.: Retail Psychology War: Don't Think for the Customer, But Think in the Shoe of Customers, p. 85. Jiangsu Literature and Art Publishing House (2015)
17. Moogk, D.R.: Minimum viable product and the importance of experimentation in technology startups. Technol. Innov. Manag. Rev. **2**(3) (2012)

Attempts to Leverage Interaction Design to Mimic Emotional Care and Empathy-Based Feedback on Smart Speakers

Yanyan Sun[⊠], Ting Wang, Xiang Ge, Jianping Qi, Min Zhao,
Liming Zou, Dan Li, Shiyan Li, and Daisong Guan

Baidu AI Interaction Design Lab, Beijing, China
sunyanyan@baidu.com

Abstract. Noticing that many existing smart speakers in China are lack of good emotion experience, we explore Chinese users' expectation about smart speakers through user research. Along with the increasing development of AI technologies, we found in our recent user experience studies that AI technologies could enable smart devices various human-like capabilities such as "speak", "see", and "body language", which naturally provide users psychological perception that the smart devices have human characteristic during the interaction process. There are two major contributions in this paper. Firstly, we investigate and summarize the emotional care and empathy-based feedback in interpersonal communication, especially in the Chinese culture context. We surveyed some professional psychological counselors and observed their interactions with other individuals at the emotional connection level. In general, the feedback strategies from psychological counselors tend to make people comfortable and help counselors establish good relationships with others. Desk studies on networking skills and interpersonal communication followed then to summarize the characters and patterns of good communications in our daily life. Patterns and rules found in these investigations are transferred into emotion interaction design. For example, an expression of empathy by adding a certain tone in the voice of smart speakers. Secondly, we demonstrate how to leverage interaction design to mimic or enable emotional care and empathy-based feedback on smart speakers. We further validate our designs through two major user experiments.

Keywords: HCI · Smart speakers · Interpersonal communication ·
Emotional interaction · Tone of voice · Emotional interaction strategy design

1 Introduction

In the last season of 2018, the amount of smart speakers sold in China surged. According to the quarterly research published on November 2018 from Strategy Analytics, global smart speaker shipments grew an astonishing 197% year-over-year to reach a record 22.7 million units in Q3 2018 putting the market on track to surpass 100 million units in use during the final quarter of the year. And in China's Baidu was the biggest mover in the quarter increasing its share from just 1% in Q2 2018 to 8% in Q3 2018. Baidu has joined Alibaba and Xiaomi in a three-way battle for leadership of the

© Springer Nature Switzerland AG 2019
P.-L. P. Rau (Ed.): HCII 2019, LNCS 11577, pp. 354–369, 2019.
https://doi.org/10.1007/978-3-030-22580-3_26

fledging smart speaker market in China [1]. Designers now are facing a rapidly growing group of Chinese users who own smart speakers while noticing that many existing smart speakers in China are lack of good emotion interaction experience.

However, from the perspective of the user, is the emotional interaction experience of smart speakers necessary?

The *Emotional Design* [2] proposed by Dr. Norman has demonstrated that emotional experience provided by a product is essential and could be even more attractive than the offered functional experience to users. Pure reason doesn't always suffice. Successful design now means going far beyond understanding the "cognitive load" or "steps of a task"–Karen Holtzblatt and Hugh Beyer have revealed in the *Contextual Design* [3]. It means that designers must understand a much wider life context than they ever had to before including various activities of users, and among all the activities, a lot of information is conveyed through non-verbal, especially emotional information which Albert Mehrabian's studies suggested that we overwhelmingly deduce our feelings, attitudes, and beliefs about what someone says not by the actual words spoken, but by the speaker's body language and tone of voice [4, 5].

Nonetheless, Rosalind Picard pointed out in the *Affective Computing*, emotion has a critical role in cognition and in human-computer interaction, it do not need to be put into every thing that computes. An affective computer still needs to have logical reasoning abilities. Designers should not go overboard trying to make computers and other smart devices such as a printer affective [6].

In this paper we will explore users' need for emotion interaction of smart speakers, and attempt to leverage interaction design to mimic or enable emotional care and empathy-based feedback on smart speakers.

2 Do Smart Speakers Need to Mimic Emotional Care and Empathy-Based Feedback? User Research and Discoveries

2.1 Observation from Previous User Researches and Surveys

What emotions or emotional responses will smart devices like a robot or a smart speaker to have? Norman writes in *Emotional Design*, the answer depends upon the sort of robot we are thinking about, the tasks it is to perform, the nature of the environment, and what its social life is like. Does it interact with other robots or people? If so, it will need to expression its own emotional state as well as to assess the emotions of people it interacts with [2].

Smart speakers are mainly used in home scenario according to our previous user investigation, and people interact with smart speakers, it will need to expression its own emotional state as well as to assess the emotions of people it interacts with as well.

From our observation of previous user researches and surveys on smart speakers, AI technologies could enable smart devices various human-like capabilities such as "speak", "see", and "body language", which naturally provide users psychological perception that the smart devices have human characteristic during the interaction process.

2.2   User Research on Emotional Experience User Needs

In order to find out whether there is a common phenomenon of that Chinese users are expecting an emotional interaction on smart speakers, and to find out how important to Chinese users to have emotional experience in their interacting with smart speakers, we have carried out a special research on the emotional interaction user needs of smart speakers.

Subject of Research, Method and Assessment Tool

Subject of Research:

Total 776 users. Male to female ratio 4:6 with balanced demographic variables such as age, occupation, and place of residence.

Method:

Questionnaire Assessment.

Assessment Tool:

The Likert Scale. From 1 to 5, the higher the score is, the more important the user evaluates.

The Research Process

Firstly, we collect the descriptions that users would apply to describe their interaction experience with the smart speakers through the user log and interviews. In the following brainstorming session, theses collected descriptions have been refined and then printed in cards for classification. Users use the classified cards to evaluate the importance of descriptions.

The classification of these words follows the three levels – Visceral, Behavioral and Reflective – of Norman's emotional experience.

Descriptions corresponding to the visceral layer are " Engaging ID Design", "Charming Voice", "Enjoyable Touch Feeling" and so on.

Descriptions corresponding to the behavior layer are "Easy to use", "Enjoyable Surprise" and so on.

Descriptions corresponding to the reflective layer are "Sense of Humor", "Ability of Empathy", "Ability of Caring " and so on.

Found of this Research

Emotional experience is as important as functional experience.

The more experienced with the smart speaker a user is, the more important he/she thinks the emotional experience provided by smart speakers is.

Result shows that, compared with users who interact with smart speakers less than 1 time everyday, users frequently interact with smart speakers (5 times or more everyday) have higher evaluation about the descriptions representing emotional experiences more, such as "ability of empathy". See Table 1.

Result also shows that users who are have rich experience with smart products values the emotional experience more when compared with users have little experience with smart speakers. See Table 2.

Table 1. The relationship between usage frequency of smart speakers and user expectation of emotional interaction experience

	Less than 1 time per week	Less than 1 time per day	1–2 times per day	3–5 times per day	More than 5 times per day
Engaging ID design	4.01	3.99	4.15	4.14	4.22
Charming voice	4.23	4.17	4.41	4.50	4.49
Pleasant touch feeling	3.75	3.65	3.91	3.80	4.05
Ease to use	4.15	4.14	4.37	4.39	4.43
Enjoyable surprise	3.56	3.66	3.91	4.00	4.35
Sense of humor	3.96	3.89	4.13	4.16	4.41
Ability of empathy	3.76	3.71	3.93	4.06	4.30
Ability of caring	3.80	3.88	4.06	4.13	4.14

*Based on a Likert Scale. From 1 to 5, the higher the score is, the more important the user evaluates.

Table 2. The relationship between smart product experience and user evaluation of the importance of emotional interaction experience

	Inexperienced	Little experience	Experienced	Rich experience
Enjoyable ID design	3.97	4.01	4.05	4.21
Enjoyable voice	4.27	4.23	4.33	4.45
Enjoyable touch feeling	3.90	3.74	3.84	3.82
Ease of use	4.23	4.23	4.25	4.38
Enjoyable surprise	3.83	3.61	3.90	3.97
Sense of Humor	3.80	3.96	4.06	4.20
Ability of empathy	3.53	3.69	3.95	4.02
Ability of caring	3.67	3.87	3.98	4.17

*Based on a Likert Scale. From 1 to 5, the higher the score is, the more important the user evaluates.

3 How to Leverage Design to Mimic Emotional Care and Empathy-Based Feedback on Smart Speakers

3.1 Studies on How Human Responds to Emotions

How Professional Counselors Respond to Emotions

We visited three professional counselors in Beijing to learn how they respond to visitors who come to the consultation with emotions. And professional counselors have their strategies when interact with visitors with emotions.

Listed below are typical strategies they will apply during the counseling.

Tone of Voice.

It's the most timely and efficient way to empathy.

"When facing sad visitors, the speed of speech should be slow, the tone of the voice should be sounded low."

"The speech speed should not be too fast and too slow when talk to a sad visitor, you should maintain a moderate rate of speech, and keep the tone similar to the visitor; in the face of different emotions, the tone of the voice should be frequency modulated, and visit On a frequency."

Identify Emotions.

"I guess you are a little sad now.""Are you sad now?" "Sounds like / I guess / there is a point that you are sad."

Accept Emotions

"That happens." "It's very common to feel that way."

Venting Emotions

Be a good listener."I'm willing to hear about it."

Behavior feedback. "I can hear you crying more heavily, are you thinking of things make you feel more sad?"

"If you want to talk about it, you can talk about it. If you don't want to talk about it, it's ok, I will be here."

Offering Help

Solve problems or change perceptions.

Provide a variety of forms to divert attention, such as: watching videos, sports, sandbags, etc.

Classic Interpersonal Communication Theories

Mehrabian comes to two main conclusions in his studies of interpersonal communications [7]:

Firstly, there are basically three elements in any face-to-face communication: Words, Tone of voice, and Nonverbal behaviors. Words are what literally being said. The spoken word is part of the verbal communication in this and the intonation and body language are both part of the non-verbal communication. Tone of voice, also known as intonation, is how something is said (use of voice). Intonation is the vocal factor and body language the vocal factor. Nonverbal behaviors, also known as body language (Visual), which are posture, facial expressions and gestures someone uses. Secondly, the non-verbal elements are particularly important for communicating feelings and attitude, especially when they are inconsistent, i.e. if words disagree with the tone of voice and nonverbal behaviors, people tend to believe the tonality and nonverbal behaviors.

Secondly, the non-verbal elements are particularly important for communicating feelings and attitude, especially when they are inconsistent, i.e. if words disagree with the tone of voice and nonverbal behaviors, people tend to believe the tonality and nonverbal behaviors.

Classic Social Skills Theories

Definitions of social skill developed over time [8]:

Phillips (1978) noted that "knowing how to behavior in a variety of situation" is part of social skills.

Later, Ellis (1980) pointed out that "By social skills I refer to sequences of individual behavior which are integrated in some way with the behavior of one or more others and which measure up to some pre-determined criterion or criteria." Other definitions, while focusing upon behavior, have included the concept of positive or negative reactions by other person as an element of skilled behavior.

Another definition by Becker et al. (1987) highlighted the fact that "to perform skillfully, the individual must be able to identify the emotions or intent expressed by the other person and make sophisticated judgments about the form and timing of the appropriate response".

Michelson et al. (1983) identified six elements to constitute the core concept of social skills, namely that they (1) are learned; (2) are composed of specific verbal and non-verbal behaviors; (3) entail appropriate initiations and responses; (4) maximize available rewards from others; (5) require appropriate timing and control of specific behaviors; (6) are influenced by prevailing contextual factors.

And the definition adopted by Owen D.W. Hargie is that social skill is the process whereby the individual implement a set of goal-directed, interrelated, situationally appropriate social behaviors which are learned and controlled. This definition emphasizes six main features of social skills.

3.2   Leverage Interaction Design to Mimic Emotional Care

Now we know that the tone of voice played the first key role in interpersonal communications, it is more important than the meaning of the actual spoken words. Thus for a smart speaker, the tone of voice needs to be designed to mimic the empathy when interacts with users with emotions.

At present, the voice interaction between Smart Speaker and user in the Chinese market mainly focuses on the voice recognition then giving feedback process. No matter the user interact with the speakers with emotions or not, the smart speakers will only fulfill the instruction inputted by the user. Currently almost all TTS voice smart speakers applied is synthetic and sound happy.

The Tone of Voice Design for Smart Speakers

The tone of the voice of the smart speaker needs to be adjusted according to the user's emotional state. For example, when the smart speaker detected that the user is in a sad mood, it is not very suitable to give the user feedbacks with a happy voice, the smart speaker should give feedbacks with a sad tone too for sad users.

The tone of voice of smart speakers can be designed at least 3 kinds:

One is opposite to the user's tone of voice.

One is same to the user's tone of voice.

And one is emotionless.

Mimic Emotional Care and Empathy-Based Feedback on Smart Speakers

An affective computer should not be built with only affective abilities, which would lead to infantile behavior at best. An affective computer still needs to have logical reasoning abilities [6].

Also, goal oriented is one of the most important interpersonal communication rules [8]. A smart speaker should not only respond to users' emotion, it should provide proper functional feedback to mimic empathy: sometimes they respond to users' emotion first, sometimes they fulfill what users' instruct them to do first, and some times they offer recommendations first. However, respond to users' emotion and give functional feedbacks, which step should the smart speaker do first? We need to mimic empathy-based feedback strategies for smart speakers.

User's Instruction and Emotion Status - Criteria for Feedback Strategy Choosing

The mimic of empathy-based feedback strategies help the smart speaker to decide that it should respond to user's emotion or fulfill user's instruction first. Face emotion recognition technology can recognize user's emotion, and NLP technology can distinguish user's intent.

Although human is very expressive, our natural emotions can be distinguished up into 27 distinct categories of emotions [9], computers can currently discriminate about six different facial expressions and up to eight different vocal expressions under certain conditions. And we found that happy, neutral, sad and angry emotions are most common emotions occurred during the Chinese users' interacting with smart speakers. Ability to respond to these common emotions can satisfy current user needs.

Summarized from our previous researches on smart speakers, there are 4 possible situations of user's instruction and emotion status the smart speakers face, see Table 3:

Table 3. Scenes of emotional interaction needs of smart speakers

	Instruction to smart speakers	Emotion towards
Situation 1	Clear	Emotion towards the Smart Speaker
Situation 2	Clear	Emotion not towards the Smart Speaker
Situation 3	Fuzzy	Emotion towards the Smart Speaker
Situation 4	Fuzzy	Emotion not towards the Smart Speaker

Situation 1

User conducts a clear instruction with emotion towards the smart speaker. E.g., "(Angrily) Set a clock for tomorrow 6:00 am." This usually happened after multiple times of failure of recognition of user's instruction due to reasons such as heavy accent or background noise.

Situation 2

User conducts a clear instruction with emotion not towards the smart speaker. E.g., "(Sad and anxious) Please find me a vet lives nearby."

Situation 3

User conducts a fuzzy instruction with emotion. E.g., "(Sad and anxious) My puppy's eyes look red and swollen."

Situation 4

User conducts a fuzzy instruction with emotion. E.g., "(Sad) I'm tied!"

Feedback Strategies

Social skill is the process whereby the individual implement a set of goal-directed, interrelated, situationally appropriate social behaviors which are learned and controlled.

Smart speakers will need at least 6 different feedback strategies including the one (task fulfillment only) that many existing smart speakers in Chinese market have to mimic the social skills to interact with users with emotion in the first round of HCI, see Table 4:

Table 4. Smart speakers feedback strategy design

Feedback strategy	Examples
Respond to emotion only	You look angry, would you like to talk about it?
Task recommendation only	Would you like me to play a song for you?
Response to emotion first then task recommendation	Are you not feeling well? Would you like me to play a song for you?
Instruction fulfillment first then respond to emotions	Alarm has been set for tomorrow 6:00 am. Don't worry you'll make it
Respond to emotions first then instruction fulfillment	Don't worry you'll make it. Alarm has been set for tomorrow 6:00 am
Task fulfillment only	Alarm has been set for tomorrow 6:00 am

4 User Experiments of Emotional Interaction to Mimic Emotional Care on Smart Speakers

4.1 User Experiment of Voice of Tone Design

Smart speakers will need to determine its own feedback voice tone according to the emotion state of the user. Taking the sad users as an example, we have studied through experiments to find out two answers: Firstly, we want to find out whether the user wants the smart speaker to respond to them in a voice with tone. Secondly, what kind of tone of voice the sad users will prefer. The method is an inter-group experiment:

The independent variable is the three replies with exactly the same literally content, but with different tone of voice. The dependent variable is the preference of interest in tones by using the 7-point scale. The higher the score is, the more likeness there is. There are two control factors, one is the literally content of the speech, the three segments of audio use the same content; the second is the sequential effect, using a completely random method to balance the ordering effect of the audio.

Experiment Design

The experiment was carried out using the Wizard of Oz.

Pre-prepared experiment materials included are 3 listed below:

A piece of emotionally neutral music [10] to make sure the user begins the experimental interaction with the smart speaker verified through EEG data.

A piece of video that can induces sad emotion on more than 90% of the users supported by EEG data.

3 audios with exactly the same literally contents but with different tone of voice. Because the current TTS technology can not synthesize the emotional tone of voices, we asked a professional actor to record the audios to make sure there are 3 obviously perceptible different voice tone in them.

The experiment is executed in 4 steps. The first step is to play the neutral music to the user to make sure the user begin the experiment with a relatively neutral emotion. The second step is to induce the user's sadness by showing him or her the sad story video. The third step is to instruct the user to interact with the smart speaker when the user is in sad emotion read from the EEG and face reading data, and let the user to experience one feedback strategy. In the fourth step, ask the user to fill in the assessment questionnaire about the user's emotional state and the preference of the speaker's tone.

Result

Core discovery:

When users are in sad mood, their favorite choice of voice tone on smart speakers is tone similar to theirs: a sad tone.

All users participated in the experiment can perceive the 3 given audios have 3 voice of tone, one is happy, one is sad, and one is neutral. And 62% of the users in the experiment, when they are sad, they expect the smart speaker can give them feedbacks with a sad tone.

Table 5. Sad users' preference for 3 different smart speaker voices tones - within group

Tone of the voice	Preference proportion
Opposite to the user's	20%
Emotionless	18%
Same to the user's	62%

*N = 34

4.2 User Experiment of Feedback Strategies Design

Core Goal of the Experiment

What kind of emotional feedback strategies should the smart speaker provide in the first round of HCI dialogue when facing sad users?

The smart speaker may encounter 3 scenarios with sad users in this experiment:

Scenario A, the user input a clear command with an emotion that does not toward the speaker: the user will feel sad after watching the sad video and will be instructed to talk to the smart speaker "I don't feel well, can you play me a music?"

Scenario B, the user input an unclear command with an emotion that does not toward the speaker: the user will feel sad after watching the sad video and will be instructed to talk to the smart speaker "I just watched a video."

Scenario C, the user with a sad emotion that does not toward the speaker and will be instructed to expresses emotions to the smart speaker: the user will feel sad after watching the sad video and instructed to talk to the smart speaker "I don't feel well."

The smart speaker will give the listed 6 kinds of feedbacks randomly:

Feedback 1, Only respond to emotions. "What makes you not feeling good?"

Feedback 2, Respond to emotions first, then recommend tasks. "What makes you not feeling good? Would you like me to play a song for you?"

Feedback 3, Respond to emotions first, then recommend tasks. "What makes you not feeling good? Let me play a song for you. (Then the smart speaker plays the song.)"

Feedback 4, Fulfill the task first, then respond to emotions. "Let me play a song for you. (Then the smart speaker plays the song.) Hope you will feel better."

Feedback 5, Respond to emotions first, then fulfill tasks. "Hope you will feel better. Let me play a song for you. (Then the smart speaker plays the song.)"

Feedback 6, Only fulfill tasks. "Let me play a song for you. (Then the smart speaker plays the song.)"

Currently Feedback 6 is the most common way of feedback that smart speakers have in Chinese market.

Independent variables:

The 6 different feedbacks.

Dependent variables:

A subjective questionnaire on the degree of the user's aroused sad emotion, and a subjective questionnaire on the user's preference of given feedback.

Controlling factors:

Keep the content of the verbal tricks of feedbacks all the same.

Recommended tasks: four scenarios, using the same recommended task Sequential effect: the sequential effect of balancing coping styles with a completely random method.

Experiment method:

The Wizard of Oz.

The main tester will execute the feedback strategy accordingly to simulate the real HCI dialogue.

Experiment for Scenario A

The user will order a clear instruction with an emotion that does not toward the speaker: the user will feel sad after watching the sad video and will be instructed to talk to the smart speaker "I don't feel well, can you play me a music?"

The 3 feedbacks given via the Wizard of OZ on the smart speaker in random order are:

A1. "Let me play a song for you. (Then the smart speaker plays the song.) Hope you will feel better."

A2. "Hope you will feel better. Let me play a song for you. (Then the smart speaker plays the song.)"

A3. "Let me play a song for you. (Then the smart speaker plays the song.)"

The most favorite feedback strategy has been found upon scenario A is feedback strategy A2. See Table 5.

However, considering the effect of alleviating sadness, all three strategies can significantly alleviate the user's sadness. Strategy A2 has been proved the best one, and Strategy A2 is significantly better than Strategy A1. See Table 5.

In scenario A, Strategy A1 is more preferred than Strategy A2, but there is no significant difference between the two. Both A1 and A2 are significantly more preferred than Strategy A3. See Table 6.

Table 6. Comparison of 3 feedback strategies in scenario A- between groups

	Degree of sadness before experimental HCI	Degree of sadness after experimental HCI	Difference
Strategy A1	4.80	3.30	1.60
Strategy A2	5.30	2.50	2.70
Strategy A3	4.90	2.50	2.40

(N1 = 23, N2 =19, N3 = 22)

Reasons for preference of Strategy A1. Users have different preference of 3 Strategies in scenario A:

Table 7. Users' preference of 3 strategies in scenario A- within groups

Strategy	AI	A2	A3
Preference	53%	45%	2%

(N = 64)

A strong sense of companionship. Listed below are some of the user comments:

"I feel that the smart speaker has been paying attention to my emotions and offering its accompany by suggesting me to listen to the song."

"Timing is more close to real life situation. Before listening the music, I can't really be happy just because the smart speaker told me so. It makes much more sense the smart speaker said so after I listening the music."

Reasons for none preference of Strategy A1:

The verbal tricks are superfluous. Listed below are some of the user comments:

"After listening to the song, my sadness has been eased already, so there is no need to say something like the smart speaker wants me to feel better."

Reasons for preference of Strategy A2:

A timely sense of caring. Listed below are some of the user comments:

"Your sadness can be quickly eased through the comfort."

"In daily life, this is usually what people do, you comfort others first."

Reasons for none preference of Strategy A2:

The verbal tricks sound in sincere. Listed below are some of the user comments:

"It feels more sincere to say 'I hope you could feel better' after I actually listen to the music."

Reasons for preference of Strategy A3:

A smart speaker is still a machine, and a machine only needs to complete the instructed orders.

Reasons for none preference of Strategy A2:

Lack of emotion response.

Experiment for Scenario B

The user will order a fuzzy instruction with an emotion that does not toward the speaker: the user will feel sad after watching the sad video and will be instructed to talk to the smart speaker "I watched a video."

The 2 feedbacks given via the Wizard of OZ on the smart speaker in random order are:

B1. "Are you feeling unwell? Would you like me to play a song for you?"

B2. "Are you feeling unwell?"

Result shows that responding to user emotions can significantly help users to alleviate sadness, but music recommendation has no additive effect. See Table 8.

Table 8. Comparison of 2 strategies in scenario B- between groups

	Degree of sadness before experimental HCI	Degree of sadness after experimental HCI	Difference
Strategy B1	4.50	3.70	0.80
Strategy B2	5.20	4.40	0.80

(N1 = 22, N2 = 22)

In scenario B, Strategy B1 is more preferred than Strategy B2. See Table 9.

Table 9. Users' preference of 2 strategies - within groups

Strategy	BI	B2
Preference	77%	23%

(N = 44)

Reasons for preference of Strategy B1:

A sense of being caring and considerate by recommending music. Listed below are some of the user comments:

"I feel that this smart speaker is being caring. It looks that it's trying to help me to alleviate my sadness by diverting my attention to my sadness by recommending music."

Reasons for none preference of Strategy B1:

The recommendation is so limited.

The experiment is executed by the Wizard of Oz with controlled variables, the recommendation of music is the only recommended task.

Reasons for preference of Strategy B2:

Being smart. Listed below are some of the user comments:

"It looks like that the smart speaker can recognize my emotions!"

Reasons for none preference of Strategy B2:

It's not enough to just recognize the emotion. Listed below are some of the user comments:

"Only talk about the negative emotion may strengthen my sadness, and when it comes to negative emotions, only talk about it will make me feel more sad."

"I don't know how to keep the conversation going when the smart speaker tried to talk about my feelings."

Experiment for Scenario C

The user will just express his or her emotion to the speaker: the user will feel sad after watching the sad video and will be instructed to talk to the smart speaker "I don't feel well." Or "I feel sad." And so on.

The 2 feedbacks given via the Wizard of OZ on the smart speaker in random order are:

C1. "Are you feeling unwell?"

C2. "Are you feeling unwell? Would you like me to play a song for you? (Then the smart speaker plays the song.)"

Result shows that responding to user emotions can significantly help users to alleviate sadness, but music recommendation has no additive effect. See Table 10.

Table 10. Comparison of 2 strategies - between groups

	Degree of sadness before experimental HCI	Degree of sadness after experimental HCI	Difference
Strategy C1	5.30	4.80	0.50
Strategy C2	5.40	4.50	0.90

(N1 = 35, N2 = 29)

In scenario C, Strategy C1 is more preferred than Strategy C2. See Table 11.

Table 11. User preference of 2 strategies - within groups

Strategy	CI	C2
Preference	62%	38%

(N = 64)

Reasons for preference of Strategy C1:

A sense of being caring and considerate by recommending music. Listed below are some of the user comments:

"I feel that this smart speaker is trying to alleviate my sadness by diverting my attention to my sadness by recommending music."

Reasons for none preference of Strategy C1:

Being interrupted. The recommendation is so limited. Listed below are some of the user comments:

"I am immersed in my sadness mood, and I don't want to be diverted to something else like a song so quickly. It was a bit awkward for me to be recommended by a smart speaker of a song."

5   Discussion

5.1   Insufficiency of the Research, Design and Experiments

Insufficiency of the Design

The turn-on mechanism for the smart speaker to mimic emotional care is not been designed. The trigger to give emotion care could be time, the kind of instructions given by the user, the degree of the users' emotion, and the user profiles.

The interaction design of this case to mimic emotion care only considered the emotional interaction feedback state design of the first round HCI between the smart speaker and the user. However, in real life, the number of HCI round may be more than 1 time each day; The time of the first round of HCI between the user and the smart speaker is unknown, some of them may occur in the early morning, and some may occur in the middle of the night. A smart speaker does not always respond to users' emotion, it needs a rule of social time so it can respond to the user in a timely good manner.

In real life, instructions given by users various, it could be a very simple task, such as setting an alarm clock, or it could be a very complicated task, such as information search. Does smart speaker need to respond to user's emotion every time no matter the given instruction is?

Factors such as user's gender and personality may affect the user's preference for the emotional feedback too.

Insufficiency of Experiments

Experiment Was Only Carried on Sad Users

In order to let the user accept the experiment in an effective emotion, and the sadness is the easiest emotion to be successfully induced than happiness and anger, the experiment only carries out research on the emotion of "sadness".

Presentation of Experimental Strategy is Limited

Because most existing smart speakers in Chinese market do not have good emotional interaction abilities, the experiment adopts the Wizard of Oz method, and only pays attention to the initial exploration of the expression way of "speech".

However, many existing smart speakers have screen to display an avatar to make facial expressions, and facial expression could enrich the feedback state of the smart speaker to mimic emotional care. Also, the hardware of the smart speaker can be considered to enrich the feedback state of the smart speakers such as light and light motion design.

The Recommended Task in the Experimental of Feedback Strategy is limited

The experiment was conducted with the Wizard of Oz, and by considering the control of variables, the strategy of recommending the task only has been played to users as a recommended music.

Insufficient findings

We observed during the experiments that it seems that people with different personalities may have different feedback strategy preferences for HCI's first round of emotional interaction with smart speakers.

Each user was required to fill out the Big Five Personality Scale after the experiment, but the results shows no clear clue of the significant relationship between personality and strategy preference.

5.2   Future Design and Research Goals

We observed during the experiments that when watch of the same piece of video to arouse the sad emotion, some users think that the degree of sadness is deep, and some of them think the degree are very low. Different degree of sadness may affect the user's preference for the feedback strategy of the first round HCI of emotional feedback son smart speakers.

Both in interpersonal communication theories and real life, the emotional state, degree and the timing are key factors that make people to decide whether to initiate interpersonal communication or not. In the emotional interaction between smart speakers and users, these factors need to be considered and designed too. There are lot of factors can be considered too, and we need to find out more through more studies and research on interpersonal communication and social skills.

Also, the multiple channels have different communication effects, for example, people with intense angry emotion may not listen to others very well while they can still get information trough look.

It is necessary to further our study about the different channels such as the sound channel and the screen channel from the perspective of human factors to make the mimic of emotion care and empathy-based feedback on smart speakers more natural and more effective.

References

1. Global Smart Speaker Vendor & OS Shipment and Installed Base Market Share by Region: Q3 (2018). https://www.strategyanalytics.com/access-services/devices/connected-home/smart-speakers-and-screens/market-data/report-detail/global-smart-speaker-vendor-os-shipment-and-installed-base-market-share-by-region-q3-2018. Accessed 09 Nov 2018
2. Norman, D.A.: Emotional Design. Basic Books, New York (2004)
3. Holtzblatt, K., Beyer, H.: Contextual Design, Design For Life, 2nd edn. Elsevier, Singapore (2018)
4. Mehrabian, A., Wiener, M.: Decoding of inconsistent communications. J. Pers. Soc. Psychol. **6**(1), 109–114 (1967)

5. Russell, J.A., Mehrabian, A.: Evidence for a three-factor theory of emotions. J. Res. Pers. **11** (3), 273–294 (1977)
6. Picard, R.: Affective Computing, Reprint edition. The MIT Press (2000)
7. Mehrabian, A., Epstein, N.: A measure of emotional empathy. J. Pers. USA, First published (1972)
8. Hargie, O. (ed.): The Handbook of Social Skills, 3rd edn. Routledge, London (2006)
9. Cowen, A.S., Keltner, D.: Self-report captures 27 distinct categories of emotion bridged by continuous gradients. In: PNAS, USA (2017)
10. Su, D., Picard, R., Liu, Y.: AMAI: adaptive music for affect improvement. In: Proceedings of the 44th International Computer Music Conference (ICMC), Daegu, Korea (2018)

A Feasibility Study on the Transformation and Sustainable Development of "Disposable Tableware" in Taiwan Night Market

Yikang Sun[1(✉)] and Szuyao Lin[2]

[1] School of Fine Arts, Nanjing Normal University,
Nanjing, People's Republic of China
sunyikang120110@hotmail.com
[2] Graduate School of Creative Industry Design,
National Taiwan University of Arts, New Taipei City, Taiwan
cynszlin@gmail.com

Abstract. Taiwan's night markets have a long history and are well-known overseas. Visiting a night market is one of the essential trips for foreign tourists who come to Taiwan. For short-stay travelers, the night market gives them a variety of typical Taiwanese cuisine experiences in a short period of time and the feeling of Taiwanese culture full of warm hospitality. For locals, the night market is an important part of daily life. Besides enjoying food inside the shops, many people prefer to eat while walking, or take food back home. As a result, a lot of lunch boxes and utensils are used and unfortunately, much of this cutlery such as disposable chopsticks, foam bowls, and other disposable table-ware is difficult to degrade and not environmentally friendly. Nowadays, there are more than 400-night markets in Taiwan and it is easy to imagine how much garbage will be produced even if only a quarter of these are open every day. If we fail to handle this waste problem properly, the environment will bear a heavy burden. This study will trace the history of Taiwan's night markets, look for potential cultural factors, and analyze the impact of consumer behavior and eating habits on the design of tableware. It is expected to establish a sustainable development system to reduce and gradually eliminate "Disposable Tableware" in the future. Based on this, we will further enhance the night market experience of both Taiwanese people and tourists and explore the connotation of night market culture with the core of "Eating-together", "Sharing" and "Interaction". Through Value-added culture, it is possible to convert such new tableware into a special "cultural product" that becomes a potential derivative of the night market culture.

Keywords: Taiwan night market culture · Disposable tableware · Sustainable development · Reducing plastic · Low-carbon

1 Introduction

Typical Taiwanese snacks are found everywhere, but Taiwan's night markets, in particular, are the places where these snacks can be found in abundance. Trying out these snacks, tourists will be able to learn about different specialties, cultures, and

© Springer Nature Switzerland AG 2019
P.-L. P. Rau (Ed.): HCII 2019, LNCS 11577, pp. 370–381, 2019.
https://doi.org/10.1007/978-3-030-22580-3_27

people from different areas, adding a whole new perspective to traveling since each night market has its own traditions and characteristics. Shilin Night Market is the largest and one of the most famous night markets in Northern Taiwan, located in capital city of Taipei. The daytime Shilin Market was formally established in this area in 1909, and the market was inaugurated in 1913; now it is famous for its various eateries selling authentic Taiwanese snacks. In Taiwan, the best nightlife is found in food markets and these magnificent markets add rich flavors to Taiwan's nightlife. The country has a penchant for snacking and there is a strong desire amongst the people to eat with friends all night long. For overseas visitor swishing to get a real Taiwanese experience, skipping the convenience stores and heading out on the town for a night market snacking excursion is essential. In recent years, many of the night markets have become popular tourist destinations among sightseeing foreign travelers. In addition to food, night markets feature various forms of entertainment and a lot of shopping. Across their centuries-old history, the "Memory" and "Technique" in the Taiwan night markets have become special cultural factors.

At present, when people go to the night market to taste the food, consumption is roughly divided into two modes: "inside use" (which means eat in the store) and "outside" (meaning to take away the food and eat while walking). The first case will tend to reduce the use of unfriendly tableware by use of reusable tableware but some stores will also provide disposable tableware to allay any concerns that the tableware provided by the store may be unsanitary. However, the author believes that those disposable tableware may be even more unsanitary.

When people choose to take away their food, the store can only provide "disposable tableware" to consumers: disposable chopsticks, cartons, paper bowls, plastic bags, etc. Many people also like to eat while walking through the night market and at the entrances and exits of the night market, managers usually place several large trash cans which may or may not be segregated for recycling. We can't help but ask, after the end of the night market business, are there any staff to sort the garbage in the trash can? If there is, then you need to give them applause. But I am afraid the actual situation is no. In this way, the seriousness of the problem is even more dramatic. However, when people enjoy food, do they realize that the tableware used is not environmentally friendly? In addition, some tableware such as foam bowls give off many substances that are detrimental to the body when burned (Figs. 1 and 2).

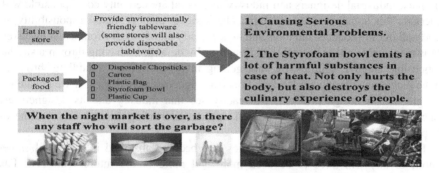

Fig. 1. The cost behind the deliciousness - Serious environmental problems

Fig. 2. Garbage brings fatal danger to other creatures

2   Literature Review

2.1   Green Design

In recent years, as people's awareness of environmental protection has increased, people's attention to and review of environmental issues have been repeatedly mentioned. Stephen P. Bayley, the former director of the Design Museum, said: "Green Design is a foolish idea, something created for and by journalists [1]." However, no matter what people think about "green design," environmental problems have become more serious. Environmentally Sustainable design (also called environmentally conscious design, eco design etc.) is the philosophy of designing physical objects, the built environment, and services to comply with the principles of ecological sustainability [7].

Food, shelter, and clothing: that is the way we have always described mankind's basic needs. With increasing sophistication we have added tools and machines to our list because they enable us to produce the other three items. But man has more basic needs than food, shelter, and clothing. We have taken clean air and pure water for granted for the first ten million years or so, but now this picture has changed drastically. While the reasons for our poisoned air and polluted streams and lakes are fairly complex, industrial designers and industry in general are certainly co-responsible with others for this appalling state of affairs. The designer-planner shares responsibility for nearly all of our products and tools and hence nearly all of our environmental mistakes. He is responsible either through bad design or by default: by having thrown away his responsible creative abilities, by "not getting involved," or by "muddling through." Three diagrams will explain the lack of social engagement in design. If we equate the triangle with a design problem, we readily see that industry and its designers are concerned only with the tiny top portion, without addressing themselves to real needs [9, pp. 56–57] (Fig. 3).

Biodegradable materials (i.e., plastics that become absorbed into the soil, water runoff, or air) will have to be used more and more in the future. The Tetra-Pak Company in Sweden, responsible for the distribution of seven billion milk, cream, and

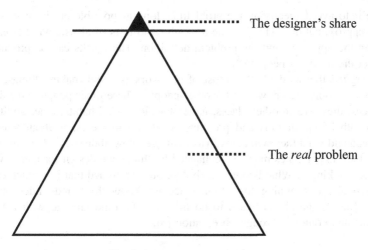

The designer's share

The *real* problem

Fig. 3. The design problem [8]

other packages a year, is now working on an ideal self—destructing package. A new process, developed in 1970 in collaboration with the Institute for Polymer Technology in Stockholm, accelerates the decomposition rate of polyethylene plastics. Thus, packages decompose much more rapidly after they have been discarded without affecting their strength and other properties while still in use. A new disposable, self-destructive beer bottle called Rigello has been on the market since 1977. Many more than just these few early Swedish solutions will need to be introduced to save us from product pollution [9, p. 95].

Ecology and the environmental equilibrium are the basic underpinnings of all life on earth; there can be neither human life nor human culture without it. Design is concerned with the development of products, tools, machines, artefacts and other devices, and this activity has a profound and direct influence on ecology. The design response must be positive and unifying. Design must be the bridge between human needs, culture and ecology. This can be clearly demonstrated. The creation and manufacture of any product—both during its period of active use and its existence afterwards—fall into at least six separate cycles, each of which has the potential for ecological harm [10].

2.2 Emotional Design

The relationship between products and people is equally important too. Norman argued that the solution is human-centered design (HCD), an approach that puts human needs, capabilities, and behavior first, then designs to accommodate those. Human-centered design is a design philosophy which starts with a good understanding of people and the needs that the design is intended to meet. This understanding comes about primarily through observation, for people themselves are often unaware of their true needs, even unaware of the difficulties they are encountering. Defining the specification of the product is one of the most difficult parts of the design, so much so that the HCD principle is to avoid specifying the problem as long as possible but instead to iterate repeated approximations. This is done through rapid tests of ideas, and after each test modifying the approach and the problem definition. The results can be products that truly meet the needs of people [8].

Suri argued that as designers, most of our work is about making things, not for ourselves or people we know, but for other people. These other people have different experiences; they live in other places, have other ideas and habits, other abilities and concerns, other expectations and preferences. How can we learn about what other people need and what they will enjoy? How can we know about what they currently do and how their experiences might be enhanced by things we design for them? We also need to be Looking at What People Really Do. Suri continued that it is much easier to get excited about designing for people once we know them and understand their situation. One of the classic ways to do this is to become familiar with a few key individuals and contexts through observation [3].

2.3   Culture Creative

In today's competitive market, "Innovation" serves as a competitive advantage allowing companies to dominate particular market segments. With respect to corporate design strategy, innovation is not only the key to expanding market share, but also the key to increasing commercial gains [2]. With the transformation and shifting of the industrial structure, the current goals are "improving value" through design, adding value to industry through cultural creativity, and enhancing the "added value" of products [6].

The purpose of design is to improve the quality of life of human beings and to enhance the cultural level of society. Designers must master the pulse of social culture as a design reference and reflect on design. Future designs must return to the perspective of humanistic aesthetics. Technology is only a technical aid and cannot be used to dominate design. The future design is the integration of art, culture and science to solve social problems and reposition human life forms. In particular, the digital technology world of the 21st century is based on "humanity" and the design of "culture" is more important, the so-called cultural creative design. This paper aims to explore how to convert "culture" into "creative" and value-added products "design": that is, how "cultural creativity" is "value-added design" [5].

3   Research Methods

Visiting night markets, observing the behavior patterns of consumers, recording the tableware needed for different foods, and finding areas where the environmental friendliness can be improved. At the same time, understanding how other countries deal with similar problems and tapping into the parts that can be used for reference. Finally, studying existing policies and regulations as a basis for further design and exploration (Fig. 4).

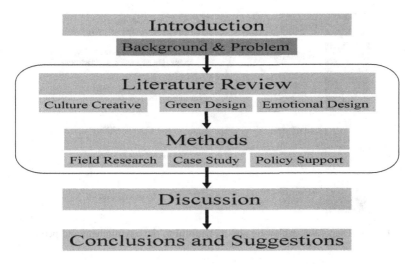

Fig. 4. Research process

3.1 Field Research

Taiwan has more than 400-night markets. The author uses Taiwan's leisure time to study and visit several night markets, such as NingXia Night Market, Nanjichang Night Market, Raohe St. Night Market, Huaxi St. Tourist Night Market, Yansan Night Market, Nanya Night Market, Taitung Tourism Night Market, Keelung Temple Night Market, HuaYuan Night Market, Dadong Night Market and so on.

Through the visit, typical night market foods and tableware used for take away food was collected. It is not difficult to see that this tableware is not friendly to the environment. Some even poses certain dangers, such as bamboo sticks. In addition, some stores offer disposable tableware to consumers while also providing environmentally-friendly tableware (Figs. 5 and 6).

Night Market Dishes	Disposable Tableware to be used
Coffin Board	Paper Bag, and Disposable Chopsticks
Ta-a Noodles	Carton, and Disposable Chopsticks
Oyster Omelette or Vermicelli	Styrofoam or Paper Bowl, and Disposable Chopsticks
Minced Pork Rice	Styrofoam or Paper Bowl, and Disposable Chopsticks
Bubble Tea	Plastic Cup and Straw
Stinky Tofu	Paper Bag, and Bamboo Stick
Taiwanese Meatball or Sausages	Paper Bag, and Bamboo Stick
Green Onion Pancake	Paper Bag, and Plastic Bag
Shaved Ice	Carton, and Plastic Spoon
Taiwanese Spring Roll	Plastic wrap and Bag
Popcorn Chicken	Paper Bag, and Bamboo Stick

Fig. 5. Some typical night market foods and tableware used

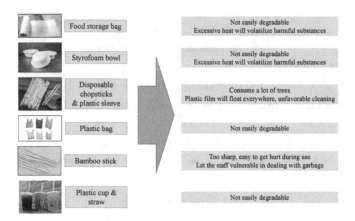

Fig. 6. Disposable tableware and its harmful to the environment and people

3.2   Case Study: Some Attempts in Taiwan, Korea, and India

Taiwan. In recent years, with the improvement of national environmental awareness, many night markets in Taiwan have also reduced the harm caused by disposable tableware through some simple measures.

In order to encourage people to bring their own tableware, some night markets have set up special areas with cleaning supplies for the public to clean their tableware. There are also some night markets which offer large dishwashers for the convenience of the store. Of course, if we start to improve from source, it is better. For example, some stores have begun piloting the elimination of disposable tableware. At the same time, they post notices in eye-catching places to tell people that the tableware provided has been disinfected and can be used with confidence. In addition, more and more people will bring their own tableware. However, for foreign tourists, it may be a little difficult to bring their own utensils. They depend on the store to provide environmentally friendly tableware.

An Uruguayan mixed-race girl, nicknamed Goldfish Brain uploaded a 4 min video on YouTube to promote her environmental philosophy. She said: "I feel that environmental protection is a satisfied attitude. I don't take extra things, like plastic bags or cups, but make good use of my existing items." When she goes out, she will carry eco-friendly cups, environmentally-friendly cutlery sets and folding bowls. In addition, she will carry a variety of environmentally friendly straws, including bamboo straws, glass straws, and stainless steel, so that she can introduce them to different stores. Most Taiwanese people and foreign tourists do not bring their own environmentally friendly tableware. She, on the other hand, will prepare a green bag for her mother to carry food purchases home. Initially, her mother forgot it every time, and continued to bring home plastic bags from the market. However, as time passed, her mother was also fell into the habit, reducing the use of plastic bags (Fig. 7).

Korea. Tong Market (통인시장) in Seoul, South Korea, is a traditional market and located near to the Royal Palace and the MRT station. As a result, it is visited by many

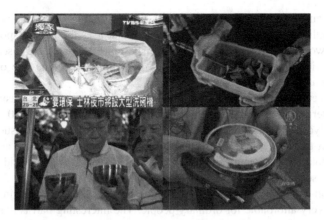

Fig. 7. Some improvement measures in Taiwan night market

foreign tourists. The market consists of about 75 storefronts, with restaurants and stalls selling mostly food, as well as fresh produce, clothes and daily goods. In order to revitalize the traditional market, market managers have come up with a great idea.

Visitors can exchange Korean won for traditional copper coins and then play at the market. The market also provides a lunch box (unfortunately not environmentally friendly) and, visitors can take the copper coins to different stores, following the prompts to buy different foods (approximately 2–3 coins can buy a food). Visitors can choose to eat while walking, or return to the tourist service center in the middle of the market Where a dining area and reusable cutlery are provided. In my view, this idea of a lunch box for everyone is worth learning as this will at least reduce the amount of such tableware used. However, some foods such as seafood soups and other liquid foods may require a bowl (Fig. 8).

Fig. 8. A method worth learning from Tong Market, Seoul, Korea

India. The same situation exists in India too. India currently has a total population of about 1.31 billion people and is also the country that uses the most disposable tableware in the world. On average, 120 billion disposable tableware are discarded every year. The environmental pollution caused by garbage has become one of the major social problems in India.

Indian inventor Narayan Peesapaty aimed to reduce the amount of plastic tableware discarded after single use and which polluted the environment. In 2010, he founded Bakey's in Hyderabad, Central India, using various natural ingredients such as millet, rice, and flour to make edible spoons and chopsticks which can be eaten after the meal is finished. Bakey's tableware can be stored for three years before use and contains no preservatives so after use, it will decompose on its own in about 4 or 5 days if not eaten. This set of edible tableware not only does not pollute the environment, but the price is also very affordable for ordinary people. The interesting part is that this spoon doesn't get soggy even in hot food and water and remains edible for up to 3 years. Narayan said in an interview with the Deccan Chronicle: "I know that my main competitor is a cheap plastic spoon. My spoon is 2 rupees each (about NT$ 1), but I am trying to lower the price to 1.5 rupees, or even 1 Rupee. If demand increases, prices will fall even more. I'm looking forward to replacing plastic tableware with our products in small restaurants and railway restaurants in the future."

This is currently the most desirable way to find other alternatives. For me, why not take such a fun tableware home? This is also a focus of future research in this study. A tableware with a strong Taiwanese culture, would encourage every visitor interested in Taiwan to bring it back to their home country, allowing the tableware to sublimate into a gift and cultural product (Fig. 9).

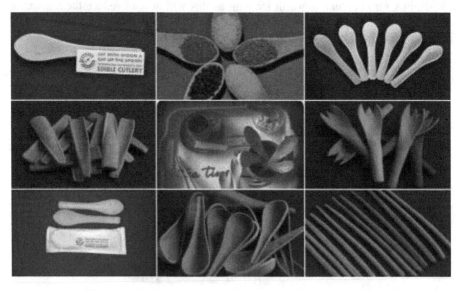

Fig. 9. Edible tableware invention by Naran Peesapaty, India

3.3   Policy Support

Environmental issues are not limited to impassioned "slogans", nor can they rely entirely on people's "consciousness." In this study, the promotion of "environmental tableware" will undoubtedly bring about a lot of behavioral changes but whether the cost of such tableware should be borne by the store or the consumer is worth further discussion and it may be necessary to have a policy at the national level. At present, many countries including Taiwan have formulated corresponding policies and regulations - for example, many countries no longer offer plastic bags for free, which encourages people to use reusable bags, including those made of environmentally friendly materials (such as tote bags).

Only policy support can avoid many problems in the process of implementation. An example worth studying is the Environmental Protection Administration of ROC promotion of a 2 years project in Hsiao Liouciou Island named "Plastic-free, Low-carbon Island Demonstration Project". The project consists of five components. (1) Reduce plastic & forced waste sorting from source. (2) Resource recovery & reduction of waste. (3) Properly treat sewage & improve air quality. (4) Landscaping and high-quality drinking water. (5) Eco-friendly hotel & reduction of carbon emissions and waste. The scope of this project is very large, and some of these measures are clearly able to provide a lot of input to this study.

4   Discussion

This study traces the history of Taiwan's night markets, looks for potential cultural factors, and analyzes the impact of consumer behavior and eating habits on tableware design. It is expected that a sustainable development system will be established in the future to reduce and gradually eliminate "disposable tableware". Through this system, it is expected to further enhance the night market experience of the public and tourists, with Eating-together, Sharing, and Interaction as the entry point. Design to experience the special cultural connotations of Taiwan's night market. In turn, through the appreciation of culture, this tableware has transformed into a special cultural product, which has become a potential derivative of the night market culture.

Through observation, people are actually aware of the problems in the tableware currently used, and they also understand that they have already placed a burden on the environment. The authors found that more and more people are carrying their own tableware to night markets. Some stores will also call for the government to introduce measures, such as the appropriate reduction of the use of plastic bags.

Although the style of Eastern and Western cuisines is different in the way of dining, I think it is possible to learn from the Western buffet diet. The environmentally friendly tableware should be a group consisting of a bowl and a pair of chopsticks. But if you just replace the bowl and chopsticks with environmentally friendly materials, it does not seem to be the ultimate goal of this study. In this way, the cost of this set of tableware will eventually be passed on to the consumer (even if the store bears the cost of tableware, it will increase the price of the food).

In the future, the following three points should be at the core of the concept and design of this set of equipment: Eating-together, Sharing, and Interaction.

Eating-together. Chinese & Taiwanese cuisine is different from Western food, and everyone likes to sit and enjoy it together. Generally, people will go to the night markets together since people like to share food. Because the night market food sometimes comes in large portions, the advantage is that you can eat a variety of foods without consuming enough of any one to make yourself full.

Sharing. For foreigners, the Taiwan night market is usually recommended by the Internet and friends. The word of mouth between friends allows food experiences to spread. This is the spirit of sharing. In addition, in the process of tasting food and sharing experiences amongst friends, mutual emotions and friendships increase.

Interaction. Visiting the night market is a process of fully experiencing Taiwan's local culture. In the night market, there are not only a variety of foods, but also many other activities to experience, such as some traditional games. For people, whether it is tasting food or gaming experience, it is an interactive experience. In this study, the design of tableware also needs to consider the details of the interaction process, such as that the tableware should be stable, and even have a temporary cover to protect it from the elements and contamination (Fig. 10).

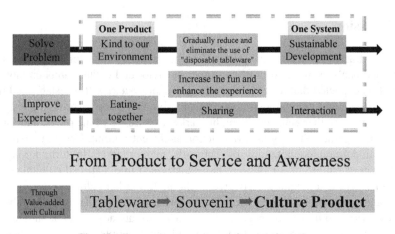

Fig. 10. Research purposes and future conception

5   Conclusions and Suggestions

This study is still in progress and no model of a product has yet been proposed. According to the previous research and discussion, I expect to find some potential entry points and be able to translate these into the basic concepts of design in the future. At this stage, it is obviously impossible to completely eliminate the use of disposable tableware as the store and consumers are not fully prepared.

Taiwan is a multi-cultural society with a variety of inputs from Southern China, significant East Asian influences including Japanese and such Western influences as American, Spanish and Dutch. Over time, Taiwan gradually developed its own distinctive culture [4] and the night market is a representative of the Taiwanese lifestyle. The tableware of the future should also have strong Taiwanese cultural elements. In this way, through the cultural value-addition, this tableware becomes a gift and eventually a cultural commodity. Whether it is for locals or foreigners, I hope that this product is not only a traditional tableware but also a cultural product. Whenever you see it, you can feel the culture and characteristics of Taiwan.

At the policy level, the government has also formulated many regulations and policies. In the author's opinion, it may be possible to promote these in certain areas first and receive timely feedback from consumers and industry. This may be more secure than laying it out without any experimentation.

Finally, it is important to experience the culture of Taiwan in the process of enjoying the food but more importantly, to be kind to our environment and protect the planet we live on.

Acknowledgments. The authors gratefully acknowledge the support for this research provided by Nanjing Normal University, under Grants YXXT18_017 (Doctoral Dissertation Excellent Topic Funding Program), and a project funded by the key academic program (Design) of Nanjing Normal University. The authors also wish to thank those who contributed to the research.

References

1. Bayley, S.: On green design. Design, 52 p. (1991)
2. Hsu, C., Chang, S., Lin, R.: A design strategy for turning local culture into global market products. Int. J. Affect. Eng. **12**(2), 275–283 (2013)
3. Koskinen, I., Battarbee, K., Mattelmäki, T.: Empathic Design: User Experience in Product Design, pp. 52–54. IT Press, Helsinki (2003)
4. Lin, R.: Transforming Taiwan aboriginal cultural features into modern product design: a case study of a cross-cultural product design model. Int. J. Des. **1**, 45–53 (2007)
5. Lin, R.: Cultural creativity added design value. Art Apprec. **2**, 1–9 (2005)
6. Lin, R., Lin, P.H.: A study of integrating culture and aesthetics to promote cultural and creative industries. J. Natl. Taiwan College Arts **5**(2), 81–106 (2009)
7. McLennan, J.: The Philosophy of Sustainable Design. Ecotone, Kansas City (2004)
8. Norman, D.A.: The Design of Everyday Things, pp. 8–9. Basic Books, New York (2013)
9. Papanek, V.: Design for the Real World: Human Ecology and Social Change. Thames & Hudson, London (1984)
10. Papanek, V.: The Green Imperative: Natural Design for the Real World, p. 29. Thames & Hudson, London (1995)

Elderly-Oriented Design for the Instrument Panel and Central Console of Intelligent Passengercars

Hao Yang[1]([✉]), Ying Zhao[2,3]([✉]), and Sida Hou[1]

[1] North China University of Technology, Beijing, China
hao-yang12@ncut.edu.cn
[2] Guangdong University of Technology, Guangdong, China
[3] Beijing Institute of Graphic Communication, Beijing, China

Abstract. Based on the elder drivers' perceptual experience, this paper makes a study on the design of human-machine interface of intelligent passenger cars. The study focuseson finding the interior structure which conforms with users' behavioral habits under the background of driving assistance technologies. By means of System Usability Sale (SUS), elder users' perceptual data are collected and the most suited interior structure ($p < 0.001$) will be clarified according to the Analysis of Variance (ANOVA) of the SUS scores. The cross-section shape of the instrument also influenced the in-vehicle interactive performance. Based on Analytic Hierarchy Process (AHP), the shape of upright is given the highest weight. In order to make designs for central console, arc-cotangent function is used to calculate the tilt angle of the line connecting the upper edge of the instrument panel and the transmission lever, and it can be known that a tilt angle of about 48° is preferred by senior people. Following the basic in-vehicle dimension parameters, an instrument panel and central console design is proposed.

Keywords: Senior people · Intelligent car · Instrument panel ·
Central console · Sensory information · Perceptual evaluation

1 Introduction

Contemporarily, with Chinese cars entering families widely, consumers' attitude towards consumption is also changing gradually. They no longer pursue mechanical properties and functions only, but the design quality and user experience of passenger cars also start to influence consumers' choice. Interior design, as the most intimate part of passenger car design, will naturally attract consumers' attention, especially those in the senior-middle and old age. The success of interior design will directly affect consumers' driving experience and interactive performance.

There have been more and more intelligent cars. Almost all of the new types of passenger cars have some intelligent functions. In an aging society, this may bring about problems of learnability and the degree of acceptance. Senior people's ability in moving their limbs is different from the young group. So it is necessary to clarify what kind of style and interior structure are more suited for them.

© Springer Nature Switzerland AG 2019
P.-L. P. Rau (Ed.): HCII 2019, LNCS 11577, pp. 382–393, 2019.
https://doi.org/10.1007/978-3-030-22580-3_28

Generally, automotive interior includes instrument panel (or dashboard), central console, door trim panel and seats. Hundreds of independent components constitute different subsystems of a car's interior. Each subsystem bears part of the functions, while among them the most important one is the dashboard system as well as the central console, which carries the most critical driving and operating functions in the interior. The carrier of operation and interaction is structure and modeling. Thus it is meaningful for drivers' interactive performance to make a study on the structural and style design of the two subsystems [1].

New driving assistance technologies and automatic driving technologies will change the driving mode of future passenger cars. The style design of the dashboard system and central console may change a lot under the new driving modes. New designs will evolve towards driving convenience and commodious interior space, driver-passenger interaction, privacy of space, personalized customization, health, environmental protection and high expectations. Based on the drivers' perceptual experience, this paper makes a study on the style design of the dashboard system and central console of intelligent passenger cars.

2 Background

The contemporary pre-elderly in China were born in the era of the 1950s to 1960s. The special historical background and the physiological change brought about by age make this generation have a series of driving psychological characteristics, such as pride, a heavy mental burden and the decline of cognitive functions [2]. In the near future when smart cars play a more and more important role, it is useful to find points that conform with the elderly's psychological characteristics by design.

Psychology of pride. Because of the rich experience in driving, senior drivers always hold an overestimate to their driving abilities while ignore operating according to rules. Some inappropriate behaviors may happen such as turning without turn signals, driving on the wrong side of the road, overtaking, changing lanes at will or talking with passengers in the car, etc. If something emergent happens, senior people will not react in time, which is likely to cause traffic accidents. Some driver assistance systems and alarm devices are needed to compensate for senior drivers' pride for their driving experience.

Excessive psychological burden. The physical activities of the elderly are easily inhibited by negative emotions, resulting in inattention and a decline in self-control, which have an impact on the response and accuracy of thinking and action. Driving with emotions often leads to incorrect steering wheel operation, heavy throttling, untimely braking control and misjudgement of emergencies. And driver assistance systems can make up for these problems.

Besides, senior people present a decline in cognitive functions. Thus it is necessary to consider the size of screens, control units and other elements of the human-machine interface (HMI) in design. With the rise of smart cars, new technologies, devices and abundant non-driving operations in entertainment system compensate for the decline and their negative psychology, such as advanced driver assistance systems (ADAS), head up display (HUD), in-vehicle advanced reality (AR), gesture recognition and high definition (HD) screens in the area of the front passenger seat. But new interactive technologies make senior people feel hard to learn [3] and put forward new requirements for interior design of intelligent cars. In order to present these information interactive systems on the instrument panel and the central console, the shape and structure, which exert an influence on interactive performance and can be seen as the core factor of the instrument system, needs to be considered. And the key of design is the proportional relationship of interior spatial layout.

3   Methods and Results

3.1   Study of Interior Design Language

The structure of automobiles interior is basically T-shaped. It is mainly because of the basic frame formed naturally by the vertical-placed shifting device of transmission gears and the steel beams that support the instrument panel. Automotive interior can be mainly divided into two types: wraparound structure and driver orientation structure. And in the dimension of symmetry, the symmetrical and asymmetrical structure will bring about different interactive performance of the drivers, and their cognitive efficiency will also be diverse.

In this way, there are four kinds of basic structures: symmetrical wraparound structure (such as Nissan Qashqai), asymmetrical wraparound structure (such as Mercedes Benz W222), symmetrical driver orientation structure (such as Ferrari 812) and asymmetrical driver orientation structure (such as Porsche 928).

Sensibility is people's psychological feelings or images of things or phenomena [4]. In the process of user's subjective perception evaluation of products, the processing of sensory information will be based on the inherent psychological model of different users. The level and content of perceptual demands for product quality described by sensory information become more diversified with the rapid development of science and technology and the change of consumption concept, which is more suitable for researches of user experience that are difficult to apply objective measurement methods [5]. This study collects senior drivers' sensory evaluation and quantifies the 4 design languages with the System Usability Scale (SUS). A large sample study shows that SUS is effective and the reliability coefficient of SUS is 0.91, which shows an excellent and reliable internal consistency [6]. When the participants finish a series of tasks, they can quickly score the items in the SUS scale. Then it is needed to transform the scores of each item. For the odd numbered items, the converted values are calculated by "the original score minus 1" and for the even numbered items, "5 minus the original score" is used. By adding up the converted scores of all the items and multiplying the summation by 2.5, the SUS score can be obtained. Each kind of interior structure is scored by SUS to calculate the usability of the four structures. The significance of the differences is judged by analysis of variance (ANOVA). The SUS questionnaires were distributed to senior drivers aged 50–65 and with automobile driving experiences. A total of 158 valid questionnaires were collected, of which 96 were males and 62 were females. The statistical results are shown in Table 1. The results show that the four structures have significant differences in system availability ($F = 12.26$, $p < 0.001$), which is in line with consumers' preferences. And among them, asymmetrical driver orientation structure presents the highest score, which means the subjects prefer this structure most.

Table 1. Results of SUS of instrument panel structure

	Symmetrical wraparound structure	Asymmetrical wraparound structure	Symmetrical driver orientation structure	Asymmetrical driver orientation structure
Mean	81.778	79.241	83.886	84.652
Std. Deviation	9.501	6.790	9.898	8.305

The interior is mainly constructed by the instrument panel. In addition to the structure, the cross-section shape of the instrument panel plays an important role in the shape style and information recognition of the whole interior. Besides, there are air conditioning outlets, glove boxes and a few controllers on the panel. The layout of them also affects the user's interactive experience.

The cross-section shape of the instrument panel is generally divided into three types: upright, layered, and sporty. The panel with an upright cross-section often appears in SUVs. The cross-section is straighter and more vertical, which presents all the information directly to the driver. The layered cross-section means that if the volume of the instrument panel is too large in the vertical direction, it can be processed by dividing the shape with more layers, separating the entirety with different colors and so on to make a design. The sporty cross-section also layers the shape of the instrument panel, but it shows a strong sense of speed. The upper level of the panel is more protruding than the lower level, so the posture is very vivid.

To evaluate the design of vehicles, Technology Acceptance Model (TAM) can achieve effective results [7, 8]. Based on TAM, we use *usability, ease of use, compatibility* and *perceived risk* as main indexes to set up an analytic hierarchy process (AHP) model (Fig. 1) to evaluate the three kinds of cross-section shapes and find out the one with the best interactive performance.

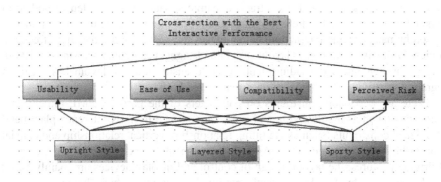

Fig. 1. AHP model for the evaluation of cross-section shape

The evaluation is made by 4 professional designers in the automotive industry who know the interior design of intelligent cars well. Using the software Yaahp 10.3, total order weight values of every evaluator's judgment matrix are generated. C.I. Values of all their judgment matrices are less than 0.1, passing the consistency test. After dealing with the 4 experts' total order weight, the group-decision results are listed as Table 2:

Table 2. Results of AHP for the evaluation of cross-section shape

	Usability	Ease of use	Compatibility	Perceived risk	Weight of total order	Total order sorting
	0.2321	0.1080	0.4782	0.1817		
Upright	0.3874	0.2970	0.5278	0.5396	0.4822	1
Layered	0.1692	0.1634	0.1369	0.1571	0.1522	3
Sporty	0.4434	0.5396	0.3325	0.2493	0.3655	2

From the results, it can be seen that the upright cross-section won the highest weight (W = 0.4822) among the three kinds of shapes. Among the 4 indexes, the weight of *compatibility* is highest (W = 0.4782). It means *compatibility* plays the most important role in interactive performance. And among the shapes, compatibility of the upright shape performs best (W = 0.5278). The results show that for elder drivers, the driving experience of intelligent cars may be improved if the cross-section is *upright*.

3.2   Design of the Spatial Layout of the Central Console

Human-Machine Relationship Analysis. Besides the style of the instrument panel, the structure of spatial layout also affects human-machine interaction. In intelligent cars, there are more non-driving interactive behaviors and searching behaviors. Thus the analysis for HMI should be more detailed. Especially for the elderly, a reasonable space layout helps to ease their heavy psychological burden. The structures of spatial layout can be devided into dynamic ones and static ones. If the relationship among different elements is fixed, it is a static spatial layout. Like the central console is always on the central axis of the interior and under the windshield. It will not be laid out as an aircraft or tank cockpit. On the contrary, dynamic spatial layout is often embodied in some parts which do not require too much about function and structure. Its parameters rely on human-machine interaction, which makes the spatial layout has more freedom. In view of the dynamic spatial layout structure, designers can obtain satisfactory layout scheme through interactive adjustment, so as to ensure that the layout has a certain degree of creativity and openness on a reasonable basis.

There are two main constraints on parameters of the parts of HMI: dimensional constraints (such as the deviation and angle of a surface from its reference plane) and topological constraints (such as the fitting relationship, vertical relationship and coaxial relationship of two surfaces, etc.). Among them, the amenity design of HMI, the check of driving postures, the layout design of control and display devices are mainly based on the size of human bodies and interior key points, which belong to static measurement. And the parameters such as the tilt angle of the instrument panel, the spatial relationship between the transmission lever and the instrument panel, which can be judged by the perceived comfort degree in the process of interaction, belong to the dynamic measurement. If the height of the surface on which the transmission lever locates is low while the upper edge of the instrument panel is too higher, a longer moving route of hand will be formed and the misoperation rate will be increased. The joints movements involved in driving postures are shown in Fig. 2. In driving tasks, the angle of A3 generally changes greatly, which makes against to the elderly whose limb functions decline to some extent. Therefore, it is necessary to locate the appropriate position of A3 that is suitable for the elderly.

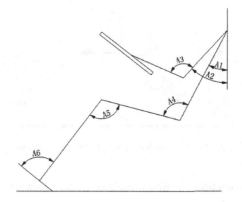

Fig. 2. Movement of joints under sitting posture

Existing researches always focus on traditional HMI such as seats, steering wheels, pedals and doors, while ignoring information exchange media such as central console, central monitor and so on. In this study, we collected the most comfortable spatial position of the hand and elbow joints when the elderly subjects operated the transmission lever at the datum point, along with the appropriate height of the instrument panel, and signed it with color tape in the vehicle. The relative position of the panel on which the lever is located is calculated by the arc-cotangent function, and the inclination angle of the transition surface between the instrument panel and the central console is estimated to achieve the central console design.

Design of the Spatial Layout. Taking the seating reference point (SgRP) as the datum point, researchers collected data of 158 drivers of intelligent car. Field assistance is provided by the specialist on the front passenger seat. Adjusting the seat to the position of SgRP, the driver was asked to find the most comfortable spatial position of his/her right hand and elbow and signed it in the space by color tape. The collected data include:

$X1$: the distance from the right hand to the ground (mm);
$X2$: the distance from the top of the transmission lever to the panel on which the lever locates (mm);

X3: the distance from the panel on which the lever is located to the ground (mm), and *X3* = *X1* − *X2*;

X4: the appropriate height of the upper edge of the instrument panel (mm);

X5: the horizontal distance from the right hand to the point, which locates against the top of transmission lever, on the upper edge of the instrument panel (mm).

In this position, three key points are signed in Fig. 3. Point A is the top of the transmission lever of a passenger car. Point B is on the upper edge of the instrument panel and it is located on the same line as Point A on the Y axis. And Point C is the SgRP.

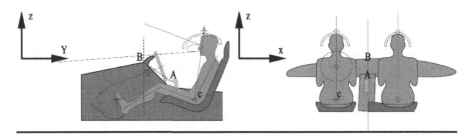

Fig. 3. Human-machine relationship and key points

By arc-cotangent function, the tilting angle of the line between Point A and Point B can be obtained as Eq. (1):

$$y = \text{arccot}(\frac{X4 - X3}{X5}) \tag{1}$$

After transforming *y* into angle value (θ), the results are listed in Table 3. The mean value of ∠θ is less than 48°, and the value of *X3* is about 532 mm. So in order to make the form of the central console consistent with the instrument panel, it is reasonable to design three surfaces in a mellow form: an inclined transition surface (Surface α), the instrument panel (Surface β) and the panel on which the transmission lever locates (Surface δ). Surface α should connect with Surface β smoothly and naturally. And Surface δ should be about 532 mm's high to shorten the hand moving path.

The part that consists of Surface α and Surface δ, which starts from the upper edge of the instrument panel and stretches to the tail of the T-structure, can be used to place the central screen and the transmission lever. It can improve the degree of senior drivers' comfort to some extent.

Table 3. Key dimensions suitable for elderly drivers

Variables	Mean	Std. Deviation	Minimum	Maximum
θ (°)	47.751	1.618	42.982	52.895
X1 (mm)	622.55	16.111	586	668
X2 (mm)	90.58	4.532	81	103
X3 (mm)	531.975	16.624	491	578
X4 (mm)	912.35	12.217	879	948
X5 (mm)	418.41	10.964	391	453

4 Discussion

4.1 Platform Thinking and Perceptual Compensation

For the interior design for elderly drivers, their perceptual performance needs to be taken into consideration. In the process of driving, operations related to visual resource consumption mainly includes information inputting and display observing. For solving the problem of senior drivers' occupancy rate of visual attention resource, platform thinking can play an important role especially in instrument panel design of intelligent cars [9]. The panel carries most of the interior controlling devices, so the whole instrument panel system can be seemed as a platform. The essential components such as instruments, transmission lever, steering wheel and auxiliary devices, are all products on this platform. For the elderly, the too much information display needs to be organized flexibly to compensate for the weakening of their psychological functions while not taking up their cognitive resource excessively. An effective solution is to make users selectively install some intelligent devices on the instrument panel according to their own needs, such as ADAS, HUD, AR display, gesture recognition and HD screens in the area of the front passenger seat [10]. Therefore, the panel needs to be concise enough to embody inclusive semanteme in design, so that users can install auxiliary functions on demand.

The main manifestations of the aging mental functions are slowing thinking activities, declining memory and understanding abilities, weakening abilities to learn new things and adapt to new environment [11]. Because of the complexity of human body structure, all basic movements need to be perfectly coordinated through the brain, eyes, nervous system, hands and feet. For the elderly, compared with their adulthood the ability to cooperate with other parts of the human body will be much worse, which will lead to a decline in response ability [12]. To compensate for this, the rapid development of image recognition technologies and ADAS has brought great opportunities. And relying on the Internet technologies, intelligent in-vehicle information system is becoming more and more mature and has been widely used, which provides a guarantee for the elderly to set up their own instrument panel platform. In this study, we made an analysis for the auxiliary functions based on platform thinking. By means of AHP, the functions and devices that can be installed on the instrument panel are sorted to provide a reference to the design work.

According to the design language obtained from the above research, the basic structure of instrument panel is drawn (Fig. 4) to present an asymmetrical driver orientation structure with an upright cross-section shape. This design ensures the five auxiliary devices can be placed on the panel and the in-vehicle information can be presented intuitively.

Fig. 4. Sketches of basic structure of instrument panel

After constructing the AHP model shown in Fig. 5, the 4 experienced professional designers are invited again to evaluate the weight value, with reference to the sketch. The importance of the five auxiliary functions under different indexes is evaluated.

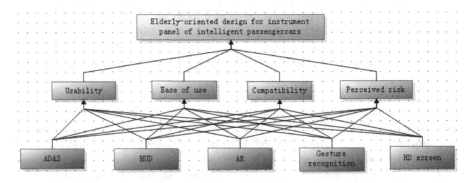

Fig. 5. AHP model for the evaluation of auxiliary functions

C.I. Values of all their judgment matrices are less than 0.1, passing the consistency test. The group-decision results are listed as Table 4.

From the results it can be seen that the weight of HUD is the highest (W = 0.3024). It means for senior people, HUD can compensate for their mental functions best. And on the aspects of *usability* and *compatibility*, HUD performs better. On the contrary, there are some deficiencies in other auxiliary functions. Especially for AR and gesture recognition, the weight values of *ease of use*, *compatibility* and *perceived risk* are all much lower than the others. So in order to improve elder drivers' experience in intelligent passengercars, it is reasonable to give priority to HUD devices. ADAS and HD entertainment screens in the area of the front passenger seat also have advantages and feasibility in some aspects. However, AR and gesture recognition cannot be trusted by experts, and could be ignored in platform design.

Table 4. Results of AHP for the evaluation of auxiliary functions

	Usability	Ease of use	Compatibility	Perceived risk	Weight of total order	Total order sorting
	0.1428	0.0825	0.2942	0.4805		
ADAS	0.1350	0.4060	0.1837	0.3271	0.2640	2
HUD	0.3365	0.0981	0.4321	0.2479	0.3024	1
AR	0.2550	0.0806	0.1794	0.0799	0.1342	4
Gesture recognition	0.1932	0.1374	0.0763	0.0972	0.1081	5
HD screen	0.0802	0.2778	0.1284	0.2479	0.1913	3

4.2 Design Proposals

Based on the above analysis, the interior design of intelligent passenger cars suitable for senior drivers is presented (Fig. 6). Following the research achievements, the design proposal has an asymmetrical driver orientation structure. Under such a structure, each component is encircled around the driver. The driver spends the least psychological resources in the process of obtaining information, and can quickly complete the required operation to compensate for the decline of their psychological functions. Besides, this kind of structure can produce a sense of security to the elderly, and also meet the psychological needs of them.

According to the results of Table 2, the cross-section shape of the instrument panel is upright. In this way a modeling language with strong usability and compatibility is formed. Down the instrument panel, a transition surface smoothly connects the dashboard and the central console. According to the result of arc-cotangent function, the tilt angle of this transition surface is approaching 48° and the position of the panel on which the transmission lever locates is elevated to a height about 532 mm from the interior ground. The overall appearance of the instrument panel and the central console shows a strong wholeness.

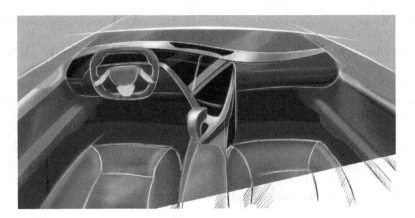

Fig. 6. A design proposal of instrument panel and central console

Ensuring the instrument panel works as a platform, there is enough space for users to install auxiliary functions on it according to their specific needs. In terms of color, warm grey is used. Elderly people prefer warm colors, which can reduce their aloneness and bring about a warm and intimate feeling to people [12]. The tendency of warm grey can play a better role in decorative color separation. Because the color conflict will not be very strong as well as making things harmonious.

5   Conclusion

Under the background of aging population, researchers from many countries have launched studies on driving behaviors for the elderly. With the popularization of Level 3 self-driving technology, methods to make intelligent car design conform to the physiological and psychological characteristics of the elderly is an important basis for carrying out the studies. Driving is a complex behavior. Analyzing the perceptual evaluation from elderly drivers in the context of intelligent vehicles is an important method to make the interior design reasonable and effective.

With the integration of a large number of intelligent driving assistance systems, automotive interior decoration becomes more complex. This research focuses on the instrument panel and the central console, which are the main carriers of in-vehicle information system. It analyzes the perceptual evaluation of the elderly drivers from the aspects of structure, cross-section shape, spatial layout, inclination angle and the height of the central console. And platform thinking is used to sort the auxiliary functions. According to the conclusions of the study, the output proposal could be feasible to some extent.

In the study of next phase, based on the conclusions of this study, the entity model of the design proposal could be built. Driving simulators can be used to collect the response time, operation completing time and EEG data of the elderly during driving and non-driving tasks. And the interior design of intelligent cars suitable for the elderly can be improved.

Acknowledgments. Our thanks to Scientific Research Foundation of North China University of Technology (NCUT11201601), Yuyou Talent Support Program of North China University of Technology (107051360018XN012/018), Beijing Social Science Foundation (18YTC040), and Scientific Research Project of Beijing Educational Committee (KM201910015002) for funding us to do this research.

References

1. Tan, H., Li, W., Tan, Z.: 3D gesture interaction product design of vehicle information system. Packag. Eng. **36**(18), 45–48+53 (2015)
2. Liu, L.: Traffic characteristics analysis and traffic safety countermeasures for elder motor vehicle drivers. Legal Syst. Soc. (21), 176–177 (2017)
3. Yang, J., Coughlin, J.F.: In-vehicle technology for self-driving cars: advantages and challenges for aging drivers. Int. J. Automot. Technol. **15**(2), 333–340 (2014)
4. Nagamachi, M.: Kansei engineering: a new ergonomic consumer oriented technology for product development. Int. J. Ind. Ergon. **35**(11), 3–11 (1995)
5. Zhou, H., Jiao, Y.: Research on appraisement new product alternatives based on semantic sensory information. Ind. Eng. Manag. **19**(06), 110–116 (2014)
6. Lewis, J.R., Sauro, J.: The factor structure of the system usability scale. In: Kurosu, M. (ed.) HCD 2009. LNCS, vol. 5619, pp. 94–103. Springer, Heidelberg (2009). https://doi.org/10.1007/978-3-642-02806-9_12
7. Hu, L., Tang, Y., Mao, Y.: Influencing factors of the acceptance of small electric car based on TAM. Sci. Technol. Manag. Res. (05), 122–125+130 (2015)
8. Yang, H., Yan, Y., Hu, Y.: Study on prototype design of elderly-oriented scooters based on driving operation behavioral analysis. J. Mach. Des. **35**(06), 105–112 (2018)
9. Wang, Y., Zhang, W., Wu, S.: In-vehicle information system and driving safety. Sci. Technol. Rev. **27**(13), 105–110 (2009)
10. Wang, B.: Research on styling design of instrument panel system in future vehicle. Huazhong University of Science & Technology (2016)
11. Wu, J.: Electric vehicle design for the elderly. Kunming University of Science & Technology (2017)
12. Dai, Y.: Research on the design of travel tools for the elderly. North China University of Technology (2018)

Luxury Industry's Chinese User Experience Design

Wei Yu[(⊠)] and Wenxue Zhai

School of Art Design and Media,
East China University of Science and Technology, Shanghai, China
weiyu@ecust.edu.cn

Abstract. The Chinese consumer market has gradually become an abattoir for well-known foreign luxury brands. Different brands are competing as they adopted all kinds of ways to attract the Chinese millennial. However, the differences in lifestyles and cultures of China and the Western countries have created disparities in the users' behavior habits, so foreign brands cannot reproduce the design from the experience of the users in their motherland but should consider the difference in two cultures. This article explores the difficulties from cultural differences to the experience design of foreign luxury brands in China and provides corresponding solutions to give foreign luxury brands some reference and help them to create interactions for Chinese consumers. Shopping would be easy and enjoyable with a full-process service experience which increases the market share in China.

Keywords: Luxury brands · Millennials · Chinese and Western culture ·
Difference-complementary · User experience

1 Introduction

The luxury is a category of goods that exceed the basic needs of survival and development of people [1]. They are usually scarce and expensive. Different from other products, the luxury is not necessary. It can neither create practical value, nor provide basic functional needs for human daily life. It is the result of the spiritual needs after the prosperity of material civilization. With the continuous rise of China's economy and the growth of China's "millennial", more and more luxury companies are aware of the importance of entering the market of China. Using various modern technologies, building service platform with quality, and adopting customer-friendly policies to provide a high level and personalized digital luxury service for Chinese users, and by doing this, they can take a preemptive opportunity in China. The Swiss Richemont and the Kering have all launched and taken actions in China.

© Springer Nature Switzerland AG 2019
P.-L. P. Rau (Ed.): HCII 2019, LNCS 11577, pp. 394–403, 2019.
https://doi.org/10.1007/978-3-030-22580-3_29

2 Characteristics and Behaviors of Chinese Consumers

In China, the consumer groups of luxury goods are becoming younger, and the "millennials" have now become the new major consumers. The millennial generation in China refers to a generation born between 1982 and 2000. From birth to adulthood, they are in the period of rapid development of the Chinese economy, and the economic conditions of family prosperity make them have more personalized consumption habits than the previous generation [2]. As millennials are mostly only children and loved by their elders, they can more directly transfer the purchasing power from their parents and even their ancestors, their spending power is strong, and they will even consume ahead of time. In general, the millennial consumer behavior has three main characteristics.

2.1 Pursuit of High Quality

The first is to pursue high quality products and focus on the excellent experience of the entire consumption process. Since the 21st century, China's economy has developed at a high speed. The millennials who have grown up at this time have not experienced the material shortages and hardships experienced by their parents and ancestors, they also don't have heavy academic loans, and many parents buy them real estate. Therefore, China's millennials are "free consumers" who can spend a greater proportion of their income on consumption. They have a higher level of disposable economy and enjoy a more urban and modern life. In addition, most of them are well-educated, have a high aesthetic value, as well as a clear understanding of the product and a strong sense of autonomy. They are hard to be fooled by appearances and will pay more attention to the true value of the products. They are highly eager to live a better life rather than just satisfying their basic needs. Therefore, when making consumption, they are more carefully to select and more willing to pay for quality. And they are more focused on the consumer experience, more concerned about the convenience of consumption and a smooth digital experience and expect to turn consumption in the digital economy into "social activity."

2.2 Pursuit of Personalization

The second characteristic is the pursuit of personalized products. The millennial generation of China is affected by the global environment and multiculturalism in the process of growth. They have active thinking, pay more attention to the aesthetics of new things and do not like to be like people, whether in terms of consumption and self-expression, they are pursuing uniqueness. They dare to innovate and dare to transcend themselves. They are keen to innovate the use and form of various products. For luxury goods, they not only value their aesthetic attributes, but also pursue a unique experience of multiple integrations such as fashion, personality and cultural connotation. Brands with artistic, cool, extravagant, cultural and other qualities can help them to show their taste and personality, which is more popular with them.

2.3 Rapid Consumption

The third characteristic is the rapid consumption. Millennials are the Internet generation, and there are more and more channels for discoveries of luxury goods, information gathering, shopping, payment, delivery methods, and after-sales activities for
them to choose, and the speed is getting faster and faster. Most of them get product
information through various online platforms and online social media. Shopping is no
longer limited to offline stores, and there are endless ways to buy online brands such as
online official malls, WeChat brand public accounts, WeChat mini programs and third-
party social media. The network has shifted most of their attention, especially in some
mobile super applications like WeChat and Weibo. Compared with their parents, they
are less influenced by traditional advertising, more willing to believe in promotion on
social platforms and are more willing to explore and discover good products and share
them with friends. Social shopping is becoming more and more popular in the Chinese
luxury goods industry. The millennial generation has a fast pace of life. For them, the
products must be the latest and the most fashionable, and the purchase speed should be
faster and more convenient. Any unsmooth shopping experience will cause the loss of
millennials.

3 Difficulties and Challenges Faced by Luxury Brands
   in China

For a foreign luxury brand, it is difficult to bring the best experience to Chinese
customers. The differences regarding political, economic and cultural factors will bring
different degrees of challenges. The most important factor should be the culture. The
cultural differences warn foreign luxury brands that it's not feasible in China if they
copy the design forms for other countries.

The differences between Chinese and Western cultures are not only manifested in
the external aspects of language, diet, customs, but also in the internal aspects of
people's values, ways of thinking, and behavioral habits [3]. In general, the differences
between the Chinese and Western cultures are mainly in three aspects: One is the
difference in superficial material culture at the respect of daily lives; the other is the
difference in behavioral culture at the social level; and the third is the difference in
ideological culture.

3.1 Superficial Material Culture

The superficial material culture refers to the summation of the material production
activities and the physical achievements of people. It is a culture with material that can
be concretely perceived. It contains a wide range of ways of clothing, eating, residence
and transportation. It is the foundation of all cultural elements and mainly to meet
people's basic needs of life - wearing, food and the shelter, which can directly reflect
the level of development of the national social productivity [4]. In general, solid culture
can be divided into two parts: production modes and lifestyle. Due to the different
geographical conditions, scientific and technological conditions in each country, the

production modes would be in different degrees. This article focuses on the impact of different lifestyles in Chinese and Western countries on foreign luxury brands, especially the differences in technological platforms.

In recent years, the daily life style of the Chinese people has been deeply affected by the development of science and technology, especially the emergence of mobile phone, mobile applications and high-speed networks, which has gradually cultivated some habits different from the past. In China, to a large group of people, especially after 90s and 00s, mobile devices such as mobile phones have become an indispensable part of their lives. There are various types of applications on mobile phones, which involve all aspects of life. By browsing news applications, they can quickly know the most important events happening on the day, and they can comment and express their opinions as well. Through communication applications, they can instantly chat with friends, and intelligently make friends quickly. Through shopping applications, shopping becomes more convenient. You can go around and search products that are more suitable; in addition, mobile apps can help you pay for products more easily, and send email, rent apartments or apply for jobs more quickly. Luxury brands need to understand the current lifestyles of Chinese consumers and explore the opportunities, so that they can bring a pleasant experience to their whole consumption process. Otherwise, if any small process is missing or is contradict with daily lifestyle of people, it will cause the loss of a large number of users.

3.2 Behavioral-Level Culture

The behavioral-level culture at the social level refers to the behavioral norms and behaviors formed in people's daily activities [5]. It includes various rules and regulations, ethics, customs and behavioral habits. It is a behavior of a group, not a result of one person, and it is obvious that China and the West are significantly different in terms of laws and regulations, ethics and customs. In terms of ethics, when dealing with people, the Chinese obey the concept of "benevolence" and "ritual" in Confucianism. Among them, "benevolence" is not only the standard to be achieved by individual personality, but also the basic norm in dealing with interpersonal relationships; and "ritual" is a moral norm of daily behavior. The "ritual" is the external manifestation of "benevolence", and "benevolence" is the inner spirit of "ritual". Only by combining "benevolence" and "ritual" can we truly realize the harmony of interpersonal relationship and even social relations. Chinese consumers are hoping to be respected by brands during the process of consumption, and they should be provided with quality services to feel "benevolence" and "ritual".

3.3 Ideological Culture

The ideological culture, at the level of consciousness, refers to an ideology produced by human beings in material production activities. It uses words, language, music, dance, etc. as the medium of communication, including philosophy, religion, literature, art, science and technology, etc. The core content is also the level that best reflects the cultural differences between the East and the West. China has a cultural history of more than 5,000 years. Under the influence of this profound cultural heritage, China has formed certain values and has been inherited and developed, affecting people's daily behavior. Taking Confucian culture as the leading factor, the integration of the overall culture of Buddhism and Taoism has had a profound impact on the way of thinking of the Chinese nation, and this influence is sustainable. So far, in modern times, most people's minds are still influenced by the traditional culture of "Nature and man in one" and "the doctrine of the Mean". When looking at things, they pay attention to the whole and do not partially describe the total. They like to analyze things with dialectical thinking, and advocate that all things and activities must be carefully grasped, and everything should be moderate. Chinese people and this kind of value is difficult to change in a short time, so luxury brands should pay attention to the moderation in China. Over-design, over-packaging, over-marketing, etc. are not desirable. They should focus on giving consumers a modest overall experience.

4   Strategies that Foreign Luxury Brands Can Adopt

For the difficulties mentioned in the previous article, foreign luxury brands can consider creating a better customer experience for Chinese consumers in the following aspects:

4.1   Dig Deeply into the Aesthetic Form of China's Mainland

For a period of time, many foreign brands have released some specific limited-edition products in order to narrow the emotional distance with Chinese consumers during traditional Chinese festivals such as the Spring Festival and Chinese Valentine's Day. However, many times, these products have not received good market response, but have caused strong dissatisfaction from consumers. This is because many luxury brands have launched products that are very rigid, and the products that Chinese consumers want to integrate Chinese culture are not simply to build Chinese elements on products. Luxury brands should conduct in-depth research on the aesthetic form of China and find a suitable style to integrate with their own products.

The popular aesthetic forms in China are mainly divided into three types: the traditional aesthetic form unique to the Chinese nation, the Western aesthetic form that has been localized and the aesthetic form that is appreciated by both China and the West. The aesthetic form accepted by both China and the West is universal and popular, and it is difficult to meet the preferences of Chinese luxury consumers. The root cause of the popularization of the localized Western aesthetic form is the full exploration of the traditional Chinese aesthetic form. This article only studies the first form here.

There are many kinds of traditional aesthetic forms unique to the Chinese nation, including "neutralization", "spirit" and "artistic conception".

Neutralization is the most primitive aesthetic form and the foundation of Chinese traditional cultural spirit. It has been running through the development of ancient Chinese aesthetics. The aesthetic characteristics of neutrality first emphasize moderateness, not only in the moderate form of matter, but also in the gentleness of emotion and the harmony between personality and spirit [6]. The second feature of neutrality is the unification of multiple aesthetic factors. As a kind of spiritual consciousness, aesthetics has many forms, and the beauty of neutralization is the unity of aesthetic diversity, which is embodied in the harmonious beauty of the combination of elegance and strength. The highest level of neutrality is the harmony between man and nature, which is the soul of Chinese traditional philosophical thinking and aesthetic culture. The "Yin and Yang" and "Heaven and Man" emphasized by Taoism and the concept of "neutralization" proposed by Confucianism are all explaining this point. "Moderate" is the fundamental state of the world, and "harmony" is the ultimate destination of the world. When the "neutralization" realm is reached, the world is in harmony and everything is flourishing. The aesthetic form of neutrality requires that the design of luxury goods should be subtle and achieve a harmonious unity of various aesthetic factors.

Spirit is developed based on neutrality, and it is an aesthetic realm created by people in the aesthetic activities with the spirit of life and of freedom. Spirit emphasizes the vitality of life and the charm of nature. It requires the aesthetic object not only to have vitality, but also to have the rhythm generated by the release and convergence, the tension and relaxation, the movement and the static and the virtual and the reality. The outside is not a blunt patchwork of various pieces of debris, but an organic whole with flesh and blood and vitality, which is inseparable. Spirit's aesthetic form requires the design of luxury goods to avoid the simple patchwork of various elements and to give the product vitality and rhythm.

Artistic conception is the aesthetic form of the highest realm, and its most fundamental aesthetic connotation is the unity of subject and object [7]. The unity of the subject and the object refers to the unity of the subject (including the person's emotion, will and cognition) and the aesthetic object as the object in the mind. Artistic conception has the characteristics of blending scenes, combining virtual and real, and endless rhyme. Among them, rhyme refers to the endless aesthetic effects contained in the artistic conception, including emotion, reason, meaning, taste and taste. The aesthetic form of artistic conception warns luxury brands that the consumer's buying behavior does not mean the termination of the product aesthetic process, and only products that can bring endless aesthetic feelings to users can truly attract customers.

Only by deepening the exploration of the Chinese form that Chinese consumers like, the brand can create high-quality products, which is the basis for ensuring a good experience for consumers.

4.2 Select the Appropriate Sales Methods

Millennials have obvious characteristics. They are used to browsing information quickly, like to express their personal opinions, attach importance to sensory experience, and are younger, livelier and more passionate about socializing, which means that traditional offline marketing is difficult to break down the communication barriers between users and brands. Online channels are very important if foreign luxury goods want to win the favor of Chinese millennials. Thanks to the rapid development of online shopping and mobile e-commerce, retail industry in China is undergoing earth-shaking changes. Mobile phones have gradually become the main way for people to shop online and browse the web because of its convenience. Especially in the millennial generation, the mobile phone and the Internet are more popular. Millennials tend to make friends, shop, learn and communicate online, and mobile apps are a toolkit for them in their daily lives.

Millennials are accustomed to shopping online, and they hope that this online shopping experience can be efficient and personalized. Brands that truly understand the changes of consumer demand and are responsive to meeting their needs are likely to succeed. Therefore, for the experience design of Chinese users, Weibo, WeChat public accounts and mini programs are platforms that luxury brands should pay close attention to. The emergence of mini programs has opened up new opportunities for luxury brands' retail platforms, which opens up the boundaries between online and offline, linking social and business behavior. Brands can use mini programs to build their brand's official malls, through a variety of product capabilities of mini programs to complete a series of business goals such as brand awareness, user precipitation, efficient conversion and attracting fans. The luxury industry's use of mainstream tools commonly used by Chinese users such as mini programs can bring basic convenience to Chinese customers.

It should be noted that although the digital retail channel is very important, it is not the only choice for millennials, the experience in the store is also important to them. Offline activities are an important means for luxury brands to interact with users and build brand image. Foreign luxury brands should combine offline high-end experience with online youth marketing, Foreign luxury brands should combine online sales channels with offline experience and make use of the rapidly rising online channels to better promote and drain offline events.

4.3 Adopt Younger Marketing Approaches

Compared with traditional marketing methods, they prefer the promotion of social networks (such as Weibo, WeChat, Tmall, JD.com) and short video platforms (such as Douyin and Miaopai), and the network community consisting of Chinese stars and popular bloggers also has considerable influence on them. They like to show themselves online through WeChat moments, posts, blogs and status, share their daily life with friends, and enjoy using their mobile phones to learn about their favorite brands on social media platforms. In response to this, luxury brands can adopt some young marketing methods, such as scene marketing, social marketing, celebrity marketing and cross-border marketing, to provide consumers with two-way dialogue opportunities, which will attract more millennials and gain their loyalty to the brand.

Scene marketing refers to the marketing behavior that a brand performs in the process of constructing a specific scene to attract and stimulate customer's desire to purchase [8]. To achieve its value, brands must have specific scenes. Luxury brands can build virtual scenes through the network based on current technology, or they can use real-life scenes to conduct marketing activities. The emergence of the Internet has shifted the attention of customers from traditional shopping malls and offline stores to the Internet. From the perspective of scene marketing, it is easier for technology to realize the construction of some virtual scenes, and with some scenes of advertising, not only can bring a stronger visual experience, but also make people feel the noble sense of luxury itself. The real scene marketing not only helps to shape the brand image, but also helps to deeply explore the real needs of customers. The combination of the two kinds of scene marketing makes the effect of the scene marketing of the product obvious and stimulates the purchase desire of the customer to a greater extent.

The worship of celebrities is a very common phenomenon in modern society, especially for millennials, most of them have their own idols, and they are more likely to accept products recommended by their idols. In recent years, it is common for the current popular celebrities to endorse the brand, and the celebrity endorsement is conducive to improving the high-quality image of brands. Celebrity marketing allows customers to establish an emotional connection with the brand, that is, customers will associate with the brand when they see celebrities, which will lead to sales increase. However, not all celebrity endorsements can promote brand sales. Many brands use celebrities who are inconsistent with their product positioning, failing to meet the consumer's psychological expectations and achieving the opposite effect. Luxury brands should consider the purpose of marketing when choosing celebrity endorsements. When choosing a celebrity endorsement, luxury brands should consider the purpose of marketing, identify celebrities that match their own brand tonality and have their own label attributes, so that consumers can gradually understand the characteristics of this product.

Contacting consumers through traditional methods requires a lot of money, but it does not achieve the desired results. With social platforms such as WeChat and Weibo with strong user groups and social attributes, luxury brands can market and promote to consumers who are difficult to reach under the premise of controlling costs, resulting in a fissile effect. In addition, social marketing can quickly narrow the gap between millennials and luxury goods, through modern technology, it spreads fashionable and interesting content to consumers and promotes their sharing with friends, thus achieving the radiant diffusion effect in the circle.

Millennials are a generation that emphasizes individuality, and cross-border marketing is a good way for them. The combination of luxury brands and home, design, food and other fields can radiate their brand concept to all aspects of consumer life, increase the exposure of the brand itself, and let consumers feel the unique tonality of the brand.

In addition to the several marketing methods mentioned above, there are many other methods. Luxury brands should find a marketing method which is conducive to the development of brands in China based on their product positioning and the characteristics of Chinese consumers.

4.4 Deepen the Brand Experience

The essence of a brand is experience and perception and create value and meaning. From the perspective of strategy, strategy and execution, brand marketing, from the perspective of online and offline, the essence of brand marketing is to consider building, implementing and communicating the brand experience, which is especially true for luxury goods. The value of luxury goods lies in the symbolic meaning of social identity on the one hand and the extraordinary and innovative experience on the other. This experience comes from two levels: one is the characteristic experience of the product and the emotional experience of the brand. For the brand, how to tell the brand story and cause the emotional resonance of the consumer is the most crucial. The second is the all-round experience of consumption. In the current experience of the economy, consumer demand has gradually become more experiential, emotional and personalized. More and more individualized product services and a good consumer experience can satisfy the psychological needs of consumers.

5 Gucci's Experience Design in China

Among the many luxury brands, Gucci is a representative of Chinese millennial generation and has achieved great success in China, which caters to the preferences of Chinese millennials in terms of product design, brand image and marketing strategy.

First of all, Gucci uses a lot of literary retro patterns and elements to make the product full of literary tones. So, for consumers, their products not only include Gucci's brand added value, but also include cultural added value. In the Spring Festival of 2018, Gucci's creative director was inspired by his dog. In order to cater to the preferences of Chinese consumers, with the theme of Chinese traditional zodiac, a series of special items for the Year of the Dog were designed for sale in Chinese boutiques and online and received high praise from consumers. The pattern adopted by Gucci is not the traditional Chinese zodiac animal image, but the animal image with Gucci's aesthetic characteristics. While maintaining the brand's characteristics, it has ingeniously integrated Chinese culture, avoiding the design misunderstanding that traditional luxury brands have combined traditional Chinese images with products. In the spring and summer of 2018 series, Gucci also incorporates many elements of Chinese style. The localization of design has aroused the resonance of Chinese consumers.

In terms of shopping channels, Gucci has started online purchasing services in China's official website since 2017 and has started to cooperate with third-party sales platforms. This younger shopping method has greatly increased its turnover in China. In terms of marketing, in addition to adopting some more traditional marketing methods, Gucci also adopted some younger ways such as digital marketing. Due to the popularity of social software in Chinese people's daily lives, Gucci collaborated with Meitu camera, a popular selfie app in China, and launched the "self-promotion" campaign, in which users can upload their own selfies and add Gucci patterns to generate their own dynamic expressions and share them with friends. Although it is common for luxury brands to launch such marketing campaigns, driven by Gucci's unique aesthetics, this event is still popular with young Chinese consumers. The dynamic imagery enhances interactivity and the consumer's sense of experience, making the event more in line with the attributes of their preferred social media.

Gucci has also collaborated with fashion blogger gogoboi, and gogoboi commented on the limited-edition products to be released in plain text, bringing the readers closer to luxury. The main content of his blog is to teach readers to unlock a new Gucci gameplay - how to get a free GUCCI: Download the official GUCCI app, upload a selfie in plain clothes, choose your favorite GUCCI logo such as GUCCI's most representative bees, butterflies, flowers and mythical characters to customize a limited-edition shirt, and finally share in WeChat moments. This "clothing" is suitable for sharing in WeChat moments, which meets the psychological needs of some consumers [9].

Whether in product design, offline store experience, shopping methods and marketing, Gucci relies on the characteristics and behavioral characteristics of Chinese consumers. Its success in China also proves the importance of marketing that luxury brands tap into China's local aesthetic form and youthfulness.

6 Summary

The changes in Chinese consumer iterations, commodity consumption and information consumption channels promote the online sales of luxury goods. The core of the luxury goods industry is not simply high-end customized products but includes business and other comprehensive service design and experience values such as product design, store construction, customer experience, marketing interaction, and membership. The essence of luxury goods is gradually shifting from being an entity to a feeling of experience of luxury. As the behavior of luxury consumer's changes, the market needs a more differentiated and more personalized connotation. The product of luxury brands must not only consider economic and technological aspects, but also accurately estimate the differences between Chinese and Western from a perspective of culture and try to understand the cultural psychology of Chinese customers, integrating them correctly to give the whole experience with eastern culture and modern humanistic feelings. By doing this, it is more likely to take the lead in the Chinese market.

References

1. Memushi, A.: Conspicuous consumption of luxury goods: literature review of theoretical and empirical evidences. Int. J. Sci. Eng. Res. 4(12), 250–255 (2013)
2. Hou, X., Li, Y., Tu, Y.: Work values of Chinese millennial generation: structure, measurement and effects on employee performance. Acta Psychologica Sinica 46(6), 823–840 (2014)
3. Ralston, D.A., et al.: The impact of natural culture and economic ideology on managerial work values: a study of the United States, Russia, Japan, and China. J. Int. Bus. Stud. 28(1), 177–207 (1997)
4. Ding, S., Saunders, R.A.: Talking up China: an analysis of China's rising cultural power and global promotion of the Chinese language. East Asia 23(2), 3–33 (2006)
5. Lu, J., et al.: Comparison of mobile shopping continuance intention between China and USA from an espoused cultural perspective. Comput. Hum. Behav. 75, 130–146 (2017)
6. Kang, L.: Subjectivity, Marxism, and culture theory in China. Soc. Text (31/32), 114–140 (1992)
7. Zhang, B.: Brief analysis for the aesthetic form of Chinese garden art. In: Applied Mechanics & Materials (2014)
8. Svensson, P.: Setting the Marketing Scene: Reality Production in Everyday Marketing Work. Lund Business Press, Lund (2004)
9. Gucci's alternative approach in China: cooperating with KOL rather than Tmall. http://www.sohu.com/a/211572231_114778

A Digital Pathway to Having Authentic Food and Cultural Experiences While Traveling in a Foreign Country

Yue Yuan[✉]

Department of Interaction Design, School of Visual Arts, 136 West 21st Street,
New York City, USA
yuelilianyuan@gmail.com

Abstract. Food is important and essential to understanding and appreciating the culture, heritage, and people of a region. Recipes and cooking techniques are passed down from generation to generation. Some dishes tell the story of a nation, while others are specific to a region. However, unfamiliar geography, language, and customs may make it difficult for tourists to find and enjoy truly authentic local cuisine.

In this paper, I present a solution: a platform I designed called Locavores. It connects tourists wanting authentic food and cultural experiences with locals who also want to learn about different cultures. Together, they meet, share a meal, and exchange information about each other's culture, and maybe make a new friend.

Keywords: Mobile application · Food · Cultural experience · Travel ·
Cross-culture design · Experience design · User-centered design ·
Design thinking · Human-computer interaction

1 Problems

1.1 Background

Food experiences have become important in tourism. According to the U.S Travel Association, tourists spent $258 billion on food and drink in 2017. Local cuisine is an essential part of a travel experience. Eating authentic food is one way to understand a culture, heritage, and people of a region. For example, each geographic region in China has a distinct cuisine. Fish can be cooked in various ways to represent different regions. Shanghai Smoked Fish is a must-have traditional Shanghainese dish for Chinese New Year. Squirrel-shaped Mandarin Fish is a typical Suzhou cuisine known for more than 200 years. Sichuan Boiled Fish originates in Chongqing.

Tourists who are foodies spend more than half of their budget on food- and beverage-related activities while traveling, based on a 2016 research report from the World Food Travel Association.

© Springer Nature Switzerland AG 2019
P.-L. P. Rau (Ed.): HCII 2019, LNCS 11577, pp. 404–420, 2019.
https://doi.org/10.1007/978-3-030-22580-3_30

1.2   Research and Problems

I surveyed 232 tourists who were foodies and had traveled to foreign countries[1]; 85% of them sought to experience the tradition and culture of the places they visited through eating authentic local food. More than 80% believed that truly regional cuisine meant a dish originated from that region, or kept a traditional cooking way, or represented local culture or custom.

I then designed and executed user interviews with 20 foodies[2] who were American and had traveled to foreign countries, to understand their behaviors, concerns, and needs further. After these interviews, I learned that some of them had participated in local food tours or gone shopping in local gourmet stores. They loved to have new and unique food experiences and wanted to gain a better sense of local culture and traditions through tasting local food.

However, interviews also helped me identify major problems that the interviewees encountered while traveling to a foreign country. Unfamiliar geography, language, and customs might make it difficult for them to find and enjoy local cuisine because the interviewees were not familiar with a region in a foreign country, and it was difficult for them to find good local foods without guidance. Many interviewees were not able to communicate well with locals due to language and cultural barriers, so not only did they not understand menus, but they also did not know the culture and customs that accompany the food. Therefore, even if they went to places that were local and authentic, they did not know what and how to order. Sometimes, many small but amazing local restaurants were hidden away and difficult for them to find, especially in rural regions.

1.3   Market Research

There are some solutions related to food and tourism on the market such as TripAdvisor, Yelp, Foursquare, and Cool Cousin. However, none of them offer real connections to locals, bring people together to share cultures, make traditional regional cuisines accessible for tourists who cannot speak the local language, or facilitate access to local restaurants that cannot be found online.

Airbnb Experiences has some aptitude for connecting tourists with locals but, it has numerous limitations. For example, Airbnb Experiences food tours in China are limited to English- and Chinese-speaking tourists, most of them do not provide a choice of "one-on-one" meal sharing, and the price of most food tours is more than triple the price of an average meal.

There is no affordable way to learn about regional cuisines and build knowledge about local culture while traveling.

---

[1] Online survey about traveling abroad conducted by the author in 2017.

[2] Remote user interviews with 20 American travelers whose ages are from 22 to 65 years old and who had previous experience traveling to foreign countries.

2 Solution

2.1 Overview

The solution is a platform I designed called Locavores, which is an app that connects tourists who want to have authentic food and cultural experiences with locals who also want to learn about different cultures by sharing a meal together.

Through Locavores, a tourist can learn about must-eat local cuisines based on a specific region and the dishes most popular with locals.

Locavores allows a tourist to set his/her preferred language, dates and times of travel, and to access reviews. When local people and tourist preferences are matched, the tourist can choose whether he/she wants a one-on-one meal-sharing experience with a local or whether to share food with a group of other tourists and a local.

Locavores offers real connections with locals, helps food tourists find hidden places, and brings both together to share culture while socializing. Both the tourist and the local enjoy the experience and make new friends.

2.2 System Design

The table below shows the design for the whole system showing why and how tourists and locals use Locavores.

	Aspire	Learn	Connect	Meet	Share
Travelers	To better understand a different culture by experiencing authentic local cuisines	To learn about regional cuisines and where to eat	To connect a local based on matching food, time, and language preferences	To meet with a local and pay a small but appropriate amount of money to have a unique food and cultural experience	To exchange cultural experiences and to acquire deeper understanding of differences
	Aspire	Recommend	Connect	Meet	Share
Locals	To better understand different cultures	To connect tourists from all around the world by recommending authentic regional cuisines and where they are located	To connect tourists based on matching food, time, and language preferences	To meet with tourists and receive a fair fee for facilitating a food and cultural experience	To exchange cultural experiences and to acquire deeper understanding of differences

2.3 Persona

Based on research findings from the user interviews, I have created two user personas. One persona is named Jessica. She is a New Yorker who cannot speak Mandarin. She wants to experience authentic food and learn about Shanghai's culture when she is traveling there. She wants to connect with locals who can help her find truly Shanghainese food.

Another persona is Fang. She is from Shanghai who knows where to eat traditional local cuisine. She also wants to improve her English and learn about different cultures by connecting with tourists.

2.4 Use Scenario

Jessica travels to Shanghai, China, for two weeks. She discovers the Locavores app. Jessica hits the "Locating Current Location" button, finds a range of local cuisines, and learns of the top five dishes that locals recommend. This gives Jessica a sense of what locals like to eat on most days.

She is interested in a dish called Four Happiness Kao Fu, which she has never seen before. Four Happiness Koa Fu is recommended as a typical everyday dish and rated as "Do not miss!" Jessica hits the "Find Locals" button to locate people who want to share Four Happiness Koa Fu and know where to find it. Jessica taps the "Filter" button to set the language and the days and times she prefers to eat. She sees locals who match her preferences. Jessica then scans a brief description of the food experience that is provided by these locals. Jessica likes what Fang describes and scans Fang's profile and reviews feedback from other tourists. She views photos of a restaurant that has a long history in Shanghai, which appeals to her.

Finally, Jessica hits the "Connect" button and chooses a one-on-one food experience with Fang. Once Fang accepts, Locavores shows the upcoming connection between them. Jessica meets Fang in Shanghai.

They stroll together to the restaurant from a nearby meeting place, and Fang shows her neighborhoods and restaurants that Jessica would never have found on her own. Fang gives valuable tips about traveling in the area, and they share their cultures while enjoying local cuisine.

After they part ways, Jessica taps "Positive Feedback" for Fang, and indicates that she'd like to connect with her again on her next Shanghai trip. She recommends that her friend who is going to visit Shanghai soon connect with Fang for local culture and food.

2.5 User Interface Design and User Testing

I created a key user interface design (see Figs. 1 and 2) and recruited 12 tourists who had sought authentic food experience while traveling abroad for user testing. I asked if they thought the design would help them easily discover and experience authentic local cuisine and culture. I also identified possible usability issues and potential primary users' needs.

Fig. 1. Viewing matched local people

Fig. 2. Viewing a local's profile

After conducting the user tests, I learned what mainly concerned them and what was not clear in my design. Almost all interviewees thought that they would get a better food and cultural experience by using Locavores, and would gain information they could not get on their own.

First of all, I learned that most interviewees felt more comfortable if there was a money exchange on the Locavores platform because they believed that a local person would spend time more readily and share knowledge with them. It was not obvious in my design. Some of them had paid about $60–$80 per person to get help from a local guide when they visited some foreign countries. They also wanted to know who would be paying for the meal, or how they would be splitting payment for the meal.

Secondly, understanding the motivation of a local person for sharing was important to the interviewees. They wanted to know if a local person wanted to have a free meal, practice a second language, or had some other motivation.

Thirdly, they liked being able to read feedback from other tourists, which gave them insight about the person they were going to meet.

2.6   Updated User Interface Design

I updated user interface based on feedback and created two sets of key designs that were used for local people and tourists.

Key User Interface Design for Local People

Recommending a Typical Local Cuisine. A local person can select existing local dishes recommended by other locals or add a new dish that could represent the region (See Fig. 3).

Fig. 3. Recommending a typical local cuisine

Adding Reasons for Recommendation. A local person adds tags or selects existing tags for the dish to explain why he/she thinks this dish is typical. Tags will help tourists better understand the differences between regional dishes (See Fig. 4).

Recommending a Restaurant. The local person recommends a local restaurant that serves local cuisine by choosing particular reasons; for example, a certain of history or stories behind it. Some restaurants are well-known by neighbors because the process of

Fig. 4. Adding reasons for recommendation   **Fig. 5.** Recommending a restaurant

cooking a certain dish is unique. These reasons give tourists a good sense of the unique features of the restaurant (See Fig. 5).

Describing a Restaurant with Details. While food is essential, dining at a restaurant is not just about the meal itself, but also about the experience. The atmosphere or ambiance of a restaurant influences a diner's experience. Therefore, Locavores allows a local to upload a photo or take a picture of the recommended restaurant so that tourists can seethe atmosphere of the restaurant (See Fig. 6).

Describing an Experience. The local summarizes what kind of food experience he/she will bring to tourists, which is a great way for him/her to promote his/her "brand" and convey some outstanding or unique points of the experience (See Fig. 7).

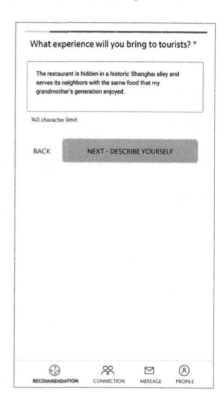

Fig. 6. Describing a restaurant with details   **Fig. 7.** Describing an experience

Describing Self. In this step, Locavores asks the local to describe why he/she wants to connect with tourists and share a meal together. Describing his/her motivation helps tourists learn about him/her, so they can more easily make a decision about whether or not to meet with him/her (See Fig. 8).

Setting Up Method of Payment. The local needs to set up methods of payment to get a fee from participants. Once finished, he/she can choose his/her availability and preference, and then publish the food experiences he/she is available for on the Locavores platform. The platform will automatically notify him/her if there are requests from tourists who match his/her settings. Then, he/she can decide to accept or deny the requests (See Fig. 9).

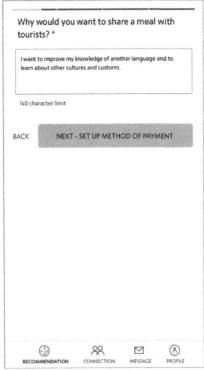

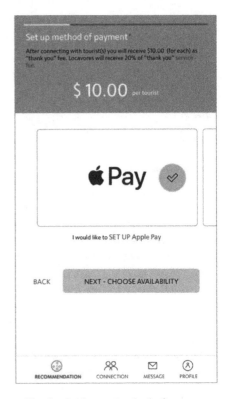

Fig. 8. Describing self   **Fig. 9.** Setting up method of payment

Key User Interface Design for Tourists

Inputting a Destination. A tourist uses Locavores to input which country or city he/she will travel to, or uses the "Locate Me" function to show his/her current location based on GPS detection. With its user-friendly interface, the tourist can quickly understand how the app works and how much he/she might pay for connecting with a local person before making a final decision (See Fig. 10).

Learning About Typical Local Cuisines. The tourist can quickly learn about local cuisine that represents the selected region and the top five dishes that locals recommend —labeled as "Do Not Miss"—which provides the tourist a sense of what locals like to eat on most days (See Fig. 11).

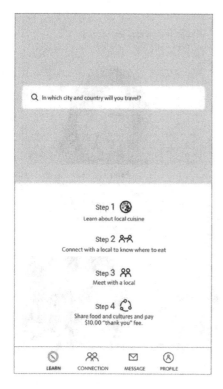

Fig. 10. Inputting a destination

Fig. 11. Learning about typical local cuisines

Viewing Details about a Regional Dish. The tourist taps on the photo of the recommended dish to view further details. The details include a summary, the number of recommendations from local people, and the type of food, using an icon (e.g., vegetable, meat, or seafood). The tourist learns about how popular the dish is with locals. Hitting the "Next–Find Locals to Learn Where to Eat" button allows the tourist to view a list of local people who know good places to have the dish (See Fig. 12).

Viewing Locals. The tourist can view a list of locals who have recommended places to eat and a brief description of the food experience that each will bring. On the top of the screen, the tourist can know how much he/she would pay to meet up with a local to learn about local food, tips, customs, and culture (See Fig. 13).

Fig. 12. Viewing details about a regional dish

Fig. 13. Viewing locals

Filtering Locals to Match Personal Preference. After tapping the "Filter" function, the screen shows options for languages, days and times, and distances. The tourist can set his/her preference to narrow down locals who match his/her choice (See Fig. 14).

Viewing a Local's Profile. The tourist learns more about the local person by viewing his/her/her profile, which includes their motivation for sharing food experiences with tourists and feedback from other tourists who have met with them. It helps the tourist

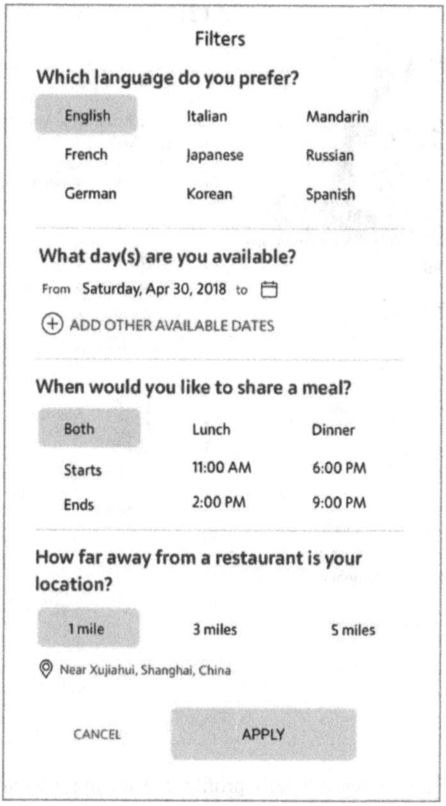

Fig. 14. Filtering locals to match personal preference

make a decision about meeting and sharing a meal, as well as having some cultural exchange, with the local. The tourist also can choose if s/he would have a one-on-one meal experience with the local or join in a group with other tourists. Some tourists might prefer to have more time to have a conversation with the local, while some might prefer to stay with a group when they first visit a foreign country to feel safer (See Fig. 15.1 and 2).

(1)   **(2)**

Fig. 15. 1. Viewing a local's profile 2. Viewing a local's profile

Setting Up Methods of Payment. After the tourist hits the "Connect" button, he/she must choose his/her payment method if he/she is a first-time user. The fee will be automatically charged after he/she meets with the local at the appointed place (See Fig. 16).

Viewing Upcoming Connection. The tourist views upcoming connection between him/her and the local, including date and time, location, contact of the local person, and a selected must-eat local dish. At this point, the tourist can use the "Send a Message" function to connect with the local if he/she wants to determine ahead of time how they will pay for or split the price of the meal (See Fig. 17).

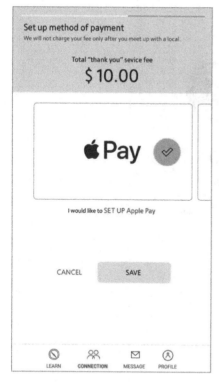

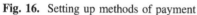

Fig. 16. Setting up methods of payment

Fig. 17. Viewing upcoming connection

Confirming Payment at Meeting. Once the tourist meets with the local, the Locavores app automatically asks the tourist to confirm the in-person connection, which is authenticated based on GPS detection and matched date and time, and then to pay. After the tourist confirms the payment, Locavores will automatically transfer money to the local, minus the Locavores service fee (See Fig. 18).

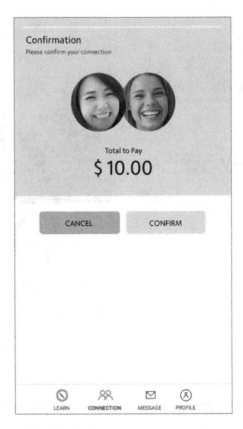

Fig. 18. Confirming payment at meeting

3 Evaluation

I conducted user testing to learn if my solution, the Locavores app, could enhance food experiences for travelers when they went abroad, how feasible it was for tourists to meet with locals, and how much tourists were willing to pay for locals' knowledge. I interviewed 26 American travelers, ages 25 to 60, with average annual income of $65,000. Every interviewee had travel experience in countries where they did not speak the local language(s).

Almost all interviewees thought that they would get more insight and a better food experience by using Locavores. Some people noted that Locavores begins with the food they want to try, then narrows their choices of local to meet and share a meal. They felt this was a great idea because, in this specific context, food was the primary factor for their decision. They wanted to eat special foods that represent a local area while traveling in a foreign country.

On average, interviewees expressed more than 85% probability of connecting with a local and sharing a meal, because they believed that if they were in Shanghai, China, and were not familiar with the culture at all, they would want somebody who knew the region well to help them.

Most of them were willing to pay at least $20 for a one-time meeting with locals because they said that local people would help them better learn about a foreign country. Most of them said they had learned about China on the internet. They believed that it would be more authentic if they could meet with local people and learn from them in person. Admittedly, there is a good bit of market research to do to understand what the app should charge in different countries and local markets.

Some interviewees mentioned safety. Most of them preferred meet for lunch with a local people because it was daytime and safer. I followed up by asking if they would feel safer if the app allowed them to share a real-time GPS location with their family or friends. The interviewees believed that it could make them feel safe while meeting up with a stranger.

Besides online user testing, I did six experiments of cultural exchange through sharing a meal in New York City, the USA. I wanted to see personally what the possibilities were for strangers to connect based on sharing cultures and cuisines. I created events about introducing Shanghai traditional cuisines, related custom and sharing a meal in New York City and published the events online, which included information about brief introduction of me, typical Shanghainese food, date and time and addresses. After people selected events and confirmed with me about dates and locations for meetup online based on their personal preference, I hosted food experiences and met with them with a different background offline in New York City. I introduced traditional Shanghai cuisines, customs, and culture while sharing a meal with participants. We talked about personal experiences and cultures and learned from each other while eating Shanghainese dishes. I still keep in touch with some of them, so this kind of exchange can create connections between people.

4   Conclusion

The problem I was hoping to solve was that there is no viable and affordable way to learn about regional cuisines and build knowledge about local culture when traveling. Overall, I have received positive feedback by testing my solution in different ways. The app I designed, Locavores, brings unique value to tourists in the following ways:

- **Flexibility:** Locavores allows tourists to choose to connect in person with a local or to join a group, based on their personal preference.
- **Affordability:** Tourists spend a small but appropriate amount of money acquiring information that they cannot get on their own or from websites.
- **Accessibility:** Locavores helps tourists easily access places, including hidden and remote places.
- **Learning:** Locavores helps tourists acquire a deeper and richer cultural experience.

Acknowledgements. The author thanks Eric Forman, faculty and Head of Innovation, from the School of Visual Arts' Interaction Design Program, and Nitzan Hermon, researcher and strategist, Future-of Agency, for their advice and help.

References

1. China Tourism: 2016 Statistics and 2017 Economic Predictions. World Tourism Alliance, CNTA. http://www.wta-web.org/eng/sjzx_4026/lytjgb_4027/201710/t20171013_842558.shtml. Accessed 13 Oct 2017
2. Future Shines Bright for Food & Beverage Tourism Says World Largest Industry Research Study. World Food Travel Association. https://www.prnewswire.com/news-releases/future-shines-bright-for-food–beverage-tourism-says-worlds-largest-industry-research-study-300303057.html. Accessed 26 Jul 2016
3. Second Global Report on Gastronomy Tourism. World Tourism Organization, Affiliate Members Report, vol. 16 (2017). http://cf.cdn.unwto.org/sites/all/files/pdf/gastronomy_report_web.pdf
4. What Is Food Tourism? World Food Travel Association (2018). https://www.worldfoodtravel.org/cpages/what-is-food-tourism

Does Heat Matter in Phone Usage? Antecedents and Consequences of Mobile Thermal Satisfaction

Andong Zhang, Pei-Luen Patrick Rau[✉], Zhaoyi Ma, Qin Gao, and Lili Dong

Tsinghua University, Beijing 100084, China
rpl@mail.tsinghua.edu.cn

Abstract. Overheated phones lead to uncomfortable user experience and degrade the reputation of the phone brand. This paper focused on the antecedents and consequences of mobile thermal satisfaction. The paper proposed the top influencing factors that affect the thermal satisfaction of mobile phones and emphasized the importance of mobile thermal performance in user experience and purchasing decision. A two-phase study was conducted. In phase I, 10 experts in human–computer interaction and phone engineering participated in a focus group study to obtain influencing factors of mobile thermal satisfaction. The experts highlighted the importance of thermal performance by ranking it with other key performance indexes of mobile phones. In phase II, 82 experienced phone users with gaming experience were interviewed on their thermal experience during daily phone usage. The user interviews provided key insights into how thermal satisfaction influenced user experience and indicated that thermal performance played an important role in purchasing decision of mobile phones.

Keywords: Thermal satisfaction · Mobile phones · User experience

1 Introduction

With the development of smartphones and phone applications such as phone games, people are using phones more frequently compared to traditional phone call usage. In addition, the power consumption of mobile phones has increased dramatically leading to their higher surface temperature. Overheated phones can result in uncomfortable user experience and degrade the reputation of the phone brand [1]. Therefore, users' thermal satisfaction is a pressing concern for mobile phone manufacturers. This study is aimed at measuring thermal satisfaction from a comprehensive perspective, including both physiological and psychological factors and emphasizing the importance of thermal performance in phone usage.

According to international safety standards [2], the surface temperature of handheld devices should be below 48 °C to avoid safety hazards, such as skin burns and battery damage. Studies on human temperature perception suggested that the comfortable thermal threshold of users is from 28 °C to 40 °C in general [3, 4]. Experiments using

© Springer Nature Switzerland AG 2019
P.-L. P. Rau (Ed.): HCII 2019, LNCS 11577, pp. 421–431, 2019.
https://doi.org/10.1007/978-3-030-22580-3_31

simulators were carried out to examine the underlying characteristics of human thermal perception, such as the changing speed of temperature and gesture [3–5]. However, experimental studies have limitations because the controlled environment cannot simulate usage scenarios completely. Therefore, unstudied questions still remain on how people perceive and evaluate mobile thermal performance when they are engaged in daily phone tasks.

This study proposed to generate the influential factors from different perspectives and obtain a deeper understanding of users' thermal experience of mobile phones. A two-phase study was conducted to achieve these objectives. In the first phase, we organized a focus group including experts in user experience and phone engineers to build the framework of thermal satisfaction and obtain the key influencing factors. In the second phase, an in-depth interview was carried out based on the results of phase I to further explore the user experience related to the thermal performance of mobile phones.

2 Focus Group Study

2.1 Methodology

In order to obtain representative opinions from different perspectives, 10 experts from different fields, i.e., five experts in human–computer interaction and five experts in mobile engineering were invited to a focus group study.

The focus group discussion concentrated on the influencing factors of mobile thermal satisfaction and the importance of mobile thermal performance during phone usage.

The experts used a brain storming method to generate as many influencing factors of thermal satisfaction as possible. These influencing factors were then summarized, classified, and ranked by their importance to finally compile a list of 10 influencing factors. A similar methodology was used during the discussion regarding the importance of thermal performance. The experts summarized key performance indexes of mobile phones including thermal performance and ranked these indexes by their influence on overall user experience.

2.2 Influencing Factors of Mobile Thermal Satisfaction

Satisfaction is a mental state, which refers to a subjective evaluation of quality of a product. In this study, mobile thermal satisfaction is defined as users' subjective evaluation of mobile thermal performance. Further discussion was based on the unified definition. Experts explored the influencing factors from three perspectives, phone, user and environment. Ten influencing factors were summarized according to experts' discussion.

Temperature. Temperature of phone surface is indicated to influence users' thermal perception and thermal satisfaction directly. Previous studies also pointed out that the thermal perception should be influenced not only by the current surface temperature but also by the changing speed of temperature [6].

Phone Usage. Phone usage refers to both the using time of mobile phones and the task content. Being exposed to over-heated for long time is supposed to increase users' dissatisfaction. In addition, task content is considered as an indirect factor of thermal satisfactory during phone usage because high-engagement task, like phone games, might decrease users' awareness of environment and thermal sensation.

Physical Design. Physical design refers to the hardware design of mobile phones, including the material of phone shell, the location and size of CPU (heated part of mobile phones). According to experts, material will influence the tactile feeling as well as the heat dissipation of mobile phones.

Environment (Physical). Thermal satisfaction is regarded as a kind of local thermal sensation and might be influenced by the overall thermal sensation, which is decided by the environmental factors [7]. According to previous studies on thermal comfort, temperature, humidity and illumination were indicated to influence environmental thermal comfort simultaneously which would indirectly influence users' thermal satisfaction of mobile phones [8].

System Performance. As phone heating is the result of over-loaded CPU and power-consumption, it is sometimes accompanied by system slowdown and other reliability problems. Although system performance has nothing to do with the thermal perception, it will influence user experience and satisfaction. Considering users may ascribe decreased system performance on phone heating, system performance is summarized as one of influencing factors of thermal satisfaction.

Mood. Mood is also suggested to be included as an indirect influencing factor. Given an example, Sam just finished a game on phone and got a little annoyed with the failure. Then he felt the over-heated phone shell, it is understandable that Sam would be more dissatisfied with the thermal performance of his mobile phone than usual as he was already in a poor mood.

Gesture. Gestures refers to the way users hold their mobile phones and gesture decide the contact region on hands during phone usage. It has been proved that thermal sensation of different region on human bodies are different [9, 10]. Therefore, the way people holding their phones will influence the thermal sensation and thermal satisfaction. Moreover, when people are playing mobile games, they are not holding the phones still. Green studied dynamic tactile simulation in 2009 and suggested dynamic contact could inhibit nociceptive and thermal sensation on the hands [11].

Individual Difference. Individual differences including gender, age and other individual characteristics were found in previous studies on thermal comfort [12]. It can be deduced that individuals also have differences in thermal sensation and thermal endurance of mobile devices.

Brand Effect. As mobile phones are products, they are unavoidably influenced by brand reputation. Good brand reputation may influence users' attitude towards phone heating phenomenon, and decrease their dissatisfaction when the heating is in an acceptable range.

Culture. Culture is a core concept of anthropology and contains a series of phenomena that are transmitted through the sociology department in human society. In Hanley's iceberg theory [13], culture will influence people's internal drive, social motivation, values etc., including users' behavior and decision-making. Therefore, cultural factors should be included as one of indirect influencing factors (Table 1).

Table 1. Ranking results of influencing factors

Influencing factors	Experts scores										Average score	Rank
	1	2	3	4	5	6	7	8	9	10		
Temperature	10	10	10	10	10	10	10	10	10	9	9.9	1
Phone usage	6	7	6	5	7	8	8	9	8	8	7.2	4
Physical design	7	8	5	8	8	7	9	8	9	7	7.6	2
Environment	8	9	7	7	9	9	7	3	4	10	7.3	3
System performance	5	3	4	9	3	6	5	7	7	6	5.5	6
Mood	9	6	8	8	2	4	6	6	5	3	5.7	5
Gesture	1	4	9	3	5	5	4	5	3	5	4.4	7
Individual difference	4	5	2	4	6	3	3	4	6	4	4.1	8
Brand effect	3	1	3	1	4	2	1	2	2	1	2	9
Culture	2	2	1	2	1	1	2	1	1	2	1.5	10

Experts were asked to rank the ten influencing factors by importance individually. For the convenience of calculation, the importance of each factor would be scored continuously according to the ranking order of each expert, the most important item scored 10 and the least important one scored 1. The importance scores were shown in the following table. By calculating the mean of importance scores given by ten experts, we can obtain the top influencing factors: temperature, physical design, environment and phone usage. According to the definition and description of influencing factors, ten influencing factors were categorized from three perspectives, phone, user and environment, as shown in Fig. 1.

2.3 Performance Indexes of Overall User Experience

Six key performance indexes were summarized to evaluate the overall user experience of mobile phones: interactive experience, battery, screen, display quality, sound quality, and thermal performance. Interactive experience constitutes both the hardware features and software features related to the interaction.

Experts were asked to rank the six performance indexes by importance individually. For the convenience of calculation, the importance of each index would be scored continuously according to the ranking order of each expert. The most important item was scored 6 and the least important one was scored 1. Experts unanimously agreed that interactive experience should be the top influencing factor in the overall user experience. However, thermal performance did not rank high in the overall performance indexes and experts' attitude toward thermal performance varied differently. The

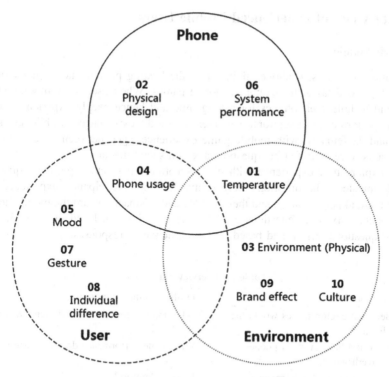

Fig. 1. Influencing factors of mobile thermal satisfaction

differences can be explained by their different mobile experience. Although experts are also mobile phone users at the same time, we still need to investigate more ordinary mobile users in order to understand the impact of thermal performance on overall user experience (Table 2).

Table 2. Ranking results of performance indexes

Performance indexes	Experts scores										Average scores	Rank
	1	2	3	4	5	6	7	8	9	10		
Interactive experience	6	5	6	6	6	6	6	6	6	6	5.9	1
Battery	4	2	5	4	2	5	5	5	5	1	3.8	3
Screen	2	1	2	3	3	3	2	4	2	5	2.7	4
Display quality	5	6	3	5	5	4	4	2	4	4	4.2	2
Sound quality	1	3	1	1	4	2	1	1	1	3	1.8	6
Thermal performance	3	4	4	2	1	1	3	3	3	2	2.6	5

3   Interviews of experienced Mobile Users

3.1   Methodology

According to experts in phone engineering, the heating phenomenon usually occurs during high-load tasks, for example, mobile games. When users play mobile games, they tend to hold their phones for a long time and hence deeply experience mobile thermal performance. Therefore, we interviewed 82 experienced mobile users (40 males and 42 females) with mobile game experience, aged between 18 and 25. The participants were recruited via questionnaires on social media.

To explore user experience with phone heating, open and explorative questions were formulated. The questions were primarily about participants' experience with mobile thermal performance, and their attitude and feedback toward the mobile heating phenomenon. Six basic questions used for the interview are listed in Table 3. More detailed questions were asked based on the participants' responses.

Table 3. Interview questions

Six basic questions	Further detailed questions
1. Under what circumstances would the phone be hot?	What kind of mobile tasks? When? Where?
2. What would happen when phones become overheated?	Will phone performance decrease with heat?
3. Did mobile thermal performance influence your user experience?	Mood? Comfort?
4. Did you complain about mobile thermal performance?	Did you complain to your friends, on the SNS, or to the mobile manufacturer?
5. Did you worry about the phone safety when it was overheated?	What kind of worries? Why? What would you do?
6. Would phone thermal performance influence your consuming behavior?	What else would influence your consuming behavior?

3.2   Interview Findings

Mobile Thermal Experience. Most (89%) participants reported phone heat during their usage. Consistent with the views of experts in the focus group study, experienced users related phone heating to the phone tasks closely. Playing games, charging, and watching videos were the most mentioned phone tasks among these participants. Two participants mentioned their phones sometimes simply got overheated without any reason. In addition to phone tasks, 24% (20 of 82) participants reported that the phone would get overheated more easily and frequently in summer. Five participants also mentioned other environmental factors such as direct sunshine and temperature (Table 4).

Table 4. Reported phone task when phone is hot

Reported mobile task when phone is hot	N	%
Playing games	62	76
Watching videos	18	22
Charging	41	50
Multi-task switching	4	5
Phone calling	3	4

Perceived Impacts of Thermal Performance. More than half of the participants (52%) mentioned that phone heating would cause negative mood, including irritability, anxiety, worry and distraction. Thirty-one participants of the total 82 (38%) pointed out that phone heating would decrease their thermal comfort on hands. Sweating and thermal pain were two main reasons for their lower comfort. In addition to the direct influence of phone heating, 29% (24 of 82) participants mentioned that phone reliability would decrease when phone got overheated. They ascribed the decreased reliability, such as system slowdown, quick power consumption, auto power-down, and other failures to bad thermal performance. Some participants claimed they did not worry about mobile thermal performance unless it was accompanied with decreased phone reliability.

User Complaints on Overheated Phones. The majority of participants (78%) would complain about the unsatisfied mobile thermal performance. However, most of them choose to keep the complaints only to friends; only seven of them would complain on social media. Only two participants claimed they had experience of reporting the thermal-related mobile problem to an official. Eighteen mobile users did not show intention of complaining because they thought it was common for mobile phones to get hot and the thermal performance of their phones was in an acceptable range. The interview results showed that only a few people would show their dissatisfaction on mobile thermal performance to the public, which may lead to a gap between the users' attitude toward mobile thermal performance and what phone manufacturers believed (Table 5).

Table 5. Reported thermal-related complaining behaviors

Reported thermal-related complaining behaviors	N	%
Complain to friends	46	56
Complain on SNS	7	9
Complain to mobile manufactures	2	2
Do not complain	18	22

Quality Worries. Fifty-three participants of the total 82 (65%) mentioned they were worried about the quality of mobile phones when faced with overheated phones. Decreased performance, shortened phone life, and safety concerns were users' major worries. Twenty-seven participants of the total 82 (33%) mentioned phone explosion when charging and expressed their worries about overheated phones. One of the participants mentioned his intensity of quality worries depended on the phone brand. Sixty-two participants of the total 82 (76%) would stop using phones when phone got overheated. Some participants would adopt certain measures to reduce the phone temperature, such as shutting down the phone, removing the phone case, and changing the environment temperature. Although most participants agreed that an explosion is an accidental event, they still could not stop worrying about the phone quality when their phone got overheated and adopted measures to cool down the phone. Some users mentioned that they would be more worried and more sensitive to mobile thermal performance if mobile phone brand had a history of explosion.

Impacts on Purchasing. Twenty-two participants of the total 82 (27%) would consider thermal performance in the first place and search for related information during purchase survey. Thirty-two participants of the total 82 (39%) mentioned they would consider thermal performance when other key performance indexes were similar. The rest of the participants (34%) mentioned they did not pay much attention to thermal performance in their experience. From another perspective, for 54 participants who reported unsatisfied thermal experience with their current mobile phones, 70% (38 of 54) of them mentioned the thermal performance would influence their repurchasing decision. In addition to thermal performance, users mentioned other influencing factors on phone purchasing, such as system performance, physical design, battery, image quality, sound quality, brand image, prize, and after-sale service. The influencing factors and the word frequencies are summarized in Table 6.

Table 6. Influencing factors of purchase

Category	Influencing factors of purchase	N	%
System performance	System configuration	38	46
	Smooth	17	21
	Memory	13	16
	Photography	8	10
	Reliability	1	1
	Phone life	1	1
Physical design	Appearance	9	11
	Screen	2	2
	Size	2	2
	Weight	1	1
Battery	Battery life	12	15
	Charging speed	1	1
Image quality	Image quality	6	7
Sound quality	Sound quality	1	1
Brand image	Brand	10	12
	Reputation	4	5
Prize	Prize-quality ratio	7	9
	Prize	7	9
After-sale service	After-sale service	1	1

4 Discussion

Based on the result of focus group study, 10 influencing factors of mobile thermal satisfaction are summarized below. In addition, the temperature of phone surface, physical design, environment, and phone usage are supposed to play important roles in mobile thermal satisfaction. From the in-depth interview, users discussed regarding their thermal experience, including the phone task, using time, and the environmental factors when they faced overheated phones. From the users' perspective, they focus more on direct feeling on body and brain, like sweating, thermal pain, decreased mood, and distraction from the task. In addition, many users regarded the phenomenon of system slowdown as a result of phone heating when they occurred together. Therefore, their satisfaction is closely related to system performance when the phone is hot. The brand effect was mentioned by some users when they discussed phone safety and users' worries. Gesture, individual differences, and culture were not mentioned by participants as they were indirect factors and sometimes difficult for ordinary users to determine.

In addition to discomfort and negative mood reported by users, thermal performance may cause users' concerns about phone quality and safety when the phone is overheated. Although some users understand that explosion is an accidental event, most still expressed worries about the overheated phone and phone charging, especially the brands with a bad history. As a result, most users would avoid continuing using overheated mobile phones and some of them would try some measures to help phones cool down. However, the interruption will decrease mobile user experience as well. To summarize, poor thermal performance will cause

- Discomfort (sweating and thermal pain)
- Negative mood (annoyed, anxious, distraction)
- Safety worries
- Interrupted user experience.

Most of the participants experienced unsatisfied mobile thermal performance, but not many of them would deliver the complaints to phone manufacturers. They just voted on foot and reduced trust on this brand. This may explain why phone engineering considers thermal comfort as important as other key performance indexes in the focus group study (fifth of six indexes). There exists a gap between users' and phone manufacturers' opinions toward thermal performance because phone companies only receive a small percentage of complaints. When users make a purchasing decision, they may not consider thermal performance as the primary factor. However, when they use the phone, they will experience thermal performance more directly. Bad thermal performance will have negative effects on the brand image and influence users' repurchasing decisions. Therefore, phone manufacturers should pay more attention to mobile thermal performance to improve overall mobile user experience and mobile sales. In summary, a graphical representation of antecedents and consequences of mobile thermal satisfaction is presented below showing the influencing factors of thermal satisfaction and its impact on user behaviors (Fig. 2).

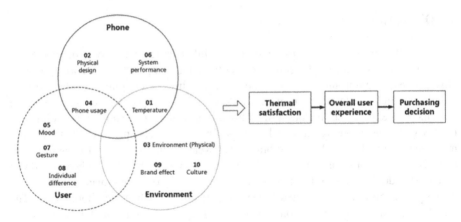

Fig. 2. Antecedents and consequences of mobile thermal satisfaction

5 Conclusion

This study proposed to explore the antecedents and consequences of thermal satisfaction during mobile phone usage. First, 10 influencing factors were summarized and ranked by importance according to experts' discussion. Temperature, physical design, phone usage, and environment were the top four factors in mobile thermal satisfaction. The evidence from in-depth interviews also suggested many users regarded decreased system performance as a result of phone heating. Therefore, phone engineers should pay more attention to system performance as well as temperature and physical design to improve mobile thermal satisfaction. In addition, the study discussed the importance of mobile thermal satisfaction from the perspectives of both experts and experienced phone users. The results of focus group study and in-depth interviews indicated that phone users cared more about mobile thermal performance than phone manufacturers believed. According to users, bad thermal performance will result in discomfort, negative mood, safety worries, and influence user experience. Furthermore, thermal satisfaction is suggested to influence users' purchasing and repurchasing decisions. In conclusion, this research emphasized the importance of thermal satisfaction in overall mobile user experience and users' purchasing decision.

One of the limitations of this interview study was that only subjective results were collected and the bias caused by self-reported measures could not be eliminated. However, as thermal satisfaction is a subjective feeling, it is acceptable that only interviews were included in this study. Another limitation is the sampling of interviewees, which were not representative enough, as most of the participants were young, college students.

References

1. Mankowski, P.J., Kanevsky, J., Bakirtzian, P., Cugno, S.: Cellular phone collateral damage: a review of burns associated with lithium battery powered mobile devices. Burns **42**(4), 61–64 (2016)
2. International Electrotechnical Commission: Audio/Video, Information and Communication Technology Equipment, 3rd edn. International Electrotechnical Commission, Geneva (2014)
3. Jones, L.A., Berris, M.: The psychophysics of temperature perception and thermal-interface design. In: Proceedings of 10th Symposium on Haptic Interfaces for Virtual Environment and Teleoperator Systems, HAPTICS, pp. 137–142. IEEE, Orlando (2002)
4. Wilson, G., Halvey, M., Brewster, S.A., Hughes, S.: Some like it hot: thermal feedback for mobile devices. In: 2011 SIGCHI Conference on Human Factors in Computing Systems, pp. 2555–2564. ACM, Vancouver (2011)
5. Craenendonck, V.S., Lauriks, L., Vuye, C., Kampen, J.K.: A review of human thermal comfort experiments in controlled and semi-controlled environments. Renew. Sustain. Energy Rev. **82**, 3365–3378 (2017)
6. Claus, D., Hilz, M.J., Hummer, I., Neundorfer, B.: Methods of measurement of thermal thresholds. Acta Neurol. Scand. **76**(4), 288–296 (2010)
7. Fang, Z., Liu, H., Li, B., Tan, M., Olaide, O.M.: Experimental investigation on thermal comfort model between local thermal sensation and overall thermal sensation. Energy Build. **158**, 1286–1295 (2018)
8. ANSI/ASHRAE: Thermal Environmental Conditions for Human Occupancy, 2nd edn. ASHRAE, Atlanta (2017)
9. Hagander, L.G., Midani, H.A., Kuskowski, M.A., Parry, G.J.G.: Quantitative sensory testing: effect of site and skin temperature on thermal thresholds. Clin. Neurophysiol. Off. J. Int. Fed. Clin. Neurophysiol. **111**(1), 17–22 (2000)
10. Ciuha, U., Mekjavic, I.B.: Thermal comfort zone of the hands, feet and head in males and females. Physiol. Behav. **179**, 427–433 (2017)
11. Green, B.G.: Temperature perception on the hand during static versus dynamic contact with a surface. Atten. Percept. Psychophys. **71**(5), 1185–1196 (2009)
12. Wang, Z., et al.: Individual difference in thermal comfort: a literature review. Build. Environ. **138**, 181–193 (2018)
13. Hanley, J.H.: Beyond the tip of the iceberg: five stages toward cultural competence. Reach. Today's Youth **3**(2), 9–12 (1999)

Intercultural Learning

How Learners with Different Cognitive Styles Read Learning Materials with Text and Pictures: A Gaze Analysis

Koh Kakusho[1(✉)], Fumiaki Takase[1], Masayuki Murakami[2],
Weijane Lin[3], and Hsiu-Ping Yueh[3]

[1] Kwansei Gakuin University, 2-1 Gakuen, Sanda 669-1337, Japan
kakusho@kwansei.ac.jp
[2] Kyoto University of Foreign Studies, 6 Saiinkasamecho,
Ukyo-ku, Kyoto 615-8558, Japan
masayuki@murakami-lab.org
[3] National Taiwan University,
No. 1, Sec. 4, Roosevelt Road, Taipei 10617, Taiwan
{vjlin, yueh}@ntu.edu.tw

Abstract. This paper describes the pilot study that attempts to analyze the difference in learners' behavior of reading multimedia learning materials by our program. Learners with different cognitive styles characterized as *verbalizers* and *visualizers* were assigned to read the materials about cooking science with their eye movement recorded, and analyzed. An alternative strategy of visualization to integrate the instructional message with the temporal and spatial data in a single diagram is attempted and testified in this pilot study. As the result, it is observed that the gaze of the verbalizers mainly moves back and forth among the paragraph areas constituted mainly by text of each page whereas the visualizers frequently check pictures referenced by some text, yet figure legends are more read by verbalizers. Preliminary findings from the pilot study provide data presentation and interpretation in better granularity, and support that learners' cognitive styles affect their decisions of orders, emphasis, and repetition to read text and pictures.

Keywords: Gaze analysis · Eye movement · Cognitive styles ·
Multimedia learning materials

1 Introduction

With widespread of IT technologies in our daily lives, resourceful learning environment with multimedia instruction and learning materials becomes common for instructors and learners to access. In this learner-controlled multimedia learning environment, how learners' decisions and preferences of information seeking and processing influence their learning, has been a critical yet controversial issue in the field of educational psychology [1–3]. In addition to the relationship between students' preferences and capabilities, instructors specifically concerned whether and how the instructional program should be accommodated to learners' preferences. However,

P.-L. P. Rau (Ed.): HCII 2019, LNCS 11577, pp. 435–445, 2019.
https://doi.org/10.1007/978-3-030-22580-3_32

relatively few studies have been conducted to resolve the problems [4]. Also a lack of objective and clear data has been criticized because most of previous studies adopted indirect self-reported measurement instead of direct observational method like eye-tracking [5]. For a few studies [5, 6], which attempt to directly examine verbal and visual learners' eye movements in the context of multimedia learning with pictorial and textual stimuli, they reported real challenges in generalizability due to limited granularity of existing eye trackers and rather smaller sample size. A major cause to their challenges results from the fact that cognitive styles of verbalizer-visualizer are dimensional, not in dichotomy, meaning that most people display both styles to some extent [2, 6]. Based on this premise, it is understood that exploring the reading interaction between learners' cognitive style, learning preference and performance in details will call for instruments with better granularity to not only record but also present fine-grained differentiation in their reading behaviors. Our study therefore attempts to analyze the data obtained by eye-tracking systems in terms of area of interests (AOIs) by our program developed in house.

In addition to the individual trait of cognitive style, learners' preferences in choosing text or pictures in instructional texts also influence their learning performance [7]. While the research results are inconsistent on the causal relationship between cognitive styles and preferences, it is supported that a combination of text and pictures support learning based on the dual-coding theory [8, 9]. To approach the unanswered questions of the advantages of instructional text and pictures for verbalizers and visualizers, further empirical investigation of learners' cognitive styles and multimedia messages design will be necessary. Therefore, this study focuses on learners' cognitive styles on verbalizer-visualizer dimension, and provides reading materials in multiple media formats including text, pictures and figure legends to investigate learners' reading interaction with different representations.

Motivated by the aforementioned issues, this study intends to explore the interaction between visualizer-verbalizer learners and text-picture materials by direct observation of the learners' gaze behaviors and eye movement. The observed gaze behaviors will be recorded for comparison between verbalizers and visualizers. In addition to the general yet fractional presentation of eye-tracking data in fixations and saccades, an alternative strategy of visualization to integrate the instructional message with the temporal and spatial data in a single diagram is attempted. In the remainder of this article, the research design including the measurement, instrument, and materials will be reported in Sect. 2. Preliminary findings of the pilot study will be presented in Sect. 3. Finally, the conclusion and future works will be discussed in Sect. 4.

2 Research Design

2.1 Cognitive Styles

This study investigates the reading interaction of learners of verbalizer-visualizer cognitive styles with multimedia message in textual, graphical and annotated illustrational formats. This study followed the quasi-experiment methodology for the research design, and a between-group experiment was conducted. College students were invited to participate in the user experiment to read a scientific text of chemical reactions and recipes about daily cooking. Scientific text was selected in this study because the intentional use of text and pictures to facilitate comprehension and learning is common in scientific text, and the material of a rather general topic of daily cooking was designed in order to avoid interference with learners' prior knowledge and intelligence. A total number of 16 valid sample was collected and analyzed for this pilot study to testify the algorithm of the proposed analyzer program.

Table 1. Example questions of SOPS.

認知風格量表 Style of Processing Scale

項目 Items	總是如此 Always True	經常如此 Usually True	很少如此 Usually False	從來如此 Always False
1.我喜歡做需要用到文字的事情 I enjoy doing work that requires the use of word (W)	1	2	3	4
2.回想以前事情的時候，我的心裡常常浮出現那時候的畫面 There are some special times in my life that I like to relive by mentally "picturing" just how everything looked (P)	1	2	3	4
3.我常常沒辦法找到合適的字來表示自己的意思 I can never seem to find the right word when I need it (W)	1	2	3	4
4.我看很多書 I do a lot of reading (W)	1	2	3	4
5.學習新的事情時，我比較喜歡直接看別人怎麼做，而不是看文字說明 When I'm trying to learn something new, I'd rather watch a demonstration than read how to do it (P)	1	2	3	4
6.我覺得我常常使用錯誤的文字表達 I think I often use words in the wrong way (W)	1	2	3	4
7.我喜歡認識新的字 I enjoy learning new words (W)	1	2	3	4
8. 如果可以自己買想要的東西，我喜歡想像要怎麼布置我的房間或房子 I like to picture how I could fix up my apartment or a room if I could buy anything I wanted (P)				
9.我常常寫筆記 I often make written notes to myself (W)	1	2	3	4
10. 我喜歡想像各種事情 I like to daydream (P)				
11.跟只有文字的說明比起來，我比較喜歡有圖片的說明 I generally prefer to use a diagram rather than a written set of instructions (P)	1	2	3	4
12.我喜歡畫畫 I like to "doodle" (P)	1	2	3	4
14.用認識一個人的時候，我很容易記得他的樣子，但是不太會記得太多關於他的事 After I meet someone for the first time, I can usually remember what they look like, but not much about them (P)	1	2	3	4
15.我喜歡找出各種相同意思的詞彙 I like to think of synonyms for words (W)	1	2	3	4

2.2   Instruments and Procedures

Previous studies on cognitive style were inconsistent in distinguishing the structure of verbalizer and visualizer. Some studies identified verbalizer and visualizer as different factors with different scales, and some defined verbalizer-visualizer as continuous on a single scale. For the belief that the verbalizer-visualizer cognitive style is dimensional in nature, this study viewed the distinction as a one-scale dimension [3], with verbal and visual cognitive style at either end. The Style of Processing Scale (SOPS) developed by Childers, Houston & Heckler in 1985 [9] is adopted accordingly to measure and determine the participants' cognitive styles. SOPS is a modified instrument from the original 6-itemed Visualizer-Verbalizer Questionnaire (VVQ) [10]. SOPS employs 16 more items in addition to 6 items of the VVQ and changes the response, which is originally binary, to a continuous scale for the same extent. The scale was scored to give a single overall score, where verbal and visual styles are in opposition [9]. The total of 22 questions of SOPS inquires the participants about their typical behaviors when carrying out different mental tasks, among which 11 items are related to verbal processing and 11 are related to visual processing. The inventory of SOPS was translated into Chinese as shown in Table 1, and administered online before the user experiment. According to the participants' scores of SOPS, all 16 participants were distinguished as 8 verbalizers and 8 visualizers with the calculation of relative tendency by the median [9].

The two groups of participants were then randomly assigned to read two types of reading materials with different text-picture layouts. As shown in Fig. 1, layout in Fig. 1(a) consists of explanatory illustrations and pictures as additional remark to the text above. Layout in (b) consists of annotated illustrations located next to the corresponding text, and with supplemental figure legends under the pictures. Layout in (c) consists of procedural presentation of text and a corresponding picture.

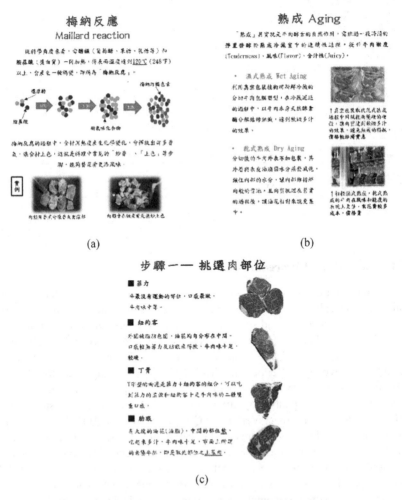

(a)

(b)

(c)

Fig. 1. Pages of the learning materials used for the experiment.

2.3   Obtaining Gaze Data

Each participant was required to read through the learning materials and their eye movement was observed and recorded by Tobii EyeX Controller, a screen-based eye-tracker with the sampling rate of 50 Hz. This eye-tracker was attached to the computer screen in front of the participants when they read the materials on the screen. Figure 2 illustrates examples of those gaze data for two different participants characterized as the verbalizers and the visualizers respectively for the layout in Fig. 1(b). Each fixation point is shown by the circle with the diameter corresponding to the amount of time while the point is being gazed by the participant. With the raw data of eye movement obtained by the eye-tracker, we further specified the region of interests (ROIs) and extracted the period of fixation based on the ROIs for purposeful analyses by our program afterwards.

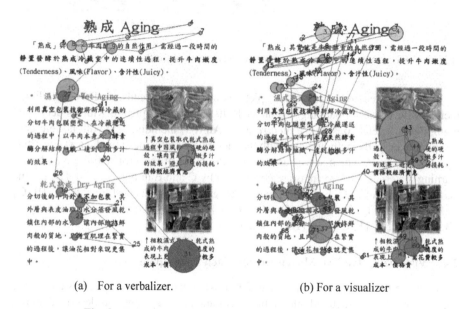

(a)   For a verbalizer.   (b) For a visualizer

Fig. 2.   Examples of fixation points for the layout in Fig. 1(b).

Each ROI corresponds to a single element of the description in the learning materials. Figure 3 illustrates the ROIs specified for the page with the layout in Fig. 1 (b) by rectangular regions labeled in alphabetical order with A, B and so on. Each ROI includes one of the three kinds of description: text, pictures and figure legends, which are shown in Fig. 3 respectively as a dark shade, light shade and no shade applied to the corresponding region.

Among these descriptions, some text refers to pictures, and some pictures are accompanied with figure legends. To be more specific, text in B and D refers to pictures in C and E respectively in Fig. 4(a). Text in C and F refers to pictures in D and G respectively in (b). Furthermore, pictures in D and G are accompanied with figure legends in E and H respectively. Text in B, D, F and H refers to pictures in C, E, G and I respectively in (c).

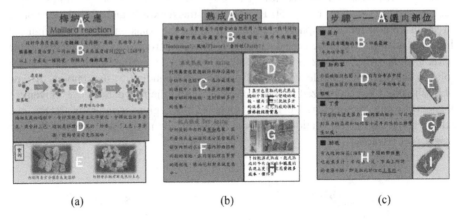

(a)   (b)   (c)

Fig. 3. ROIs of texts, pictures and figure legends specified for the analysis by our program.

With these relations among text, pictures and figure legends, an ROI including a picture with no accompanying legend or ROIs including a picture with its accompanying figure legend constitute a *picture area*. An ROI including text with no reference to a picture or ROIs including text with the picture area referenced by the text constitute a *paragraph area*, which serves as a step in the order of the explanation given by the learning materials. Picture areas are constituted by C and E in Fig. 3(a), by {D, E} and {G, H} in (b), and by C, E, G and I in (c). Paragraph areas are constituted by A, {B, C} and {D, E} in Fig. 3(a), by A, B, {C, {D, E}} and {F, {G, H}} in (b), and by A, {B, C}, {D, E}, {F, G} and {H, I} in (c).

2.4   Visualizing the Eye Movement for Each Participant

To visualize the eye movement over different ROIs including text, pictures and figure legends, which are structured into picture areas and paragraph areas as described above, the periods while fixation points of the gaze kept staying in the same ROI were drawn by diagrams. Figure 4 shows examples of the diagrams for the gaze of eight participants characterized as verbalizers and those as visualizers for the page in Fig. 1(b) with explanatory illustrations and pictures as additional remark to the text. In each diagram, horizontal lines along with one of the four rows correspond to the periods while the fixation points of the gaze were staying in the paragraph area that serves as the step in the order corresponding to the row among the four paragraph areas in the page. The parts colored in black, gray and white within the same period respectively correspond to the period for the fixation points to stay in the ROIs including text, pictures and figure legends constituting the paragraph area (see Fig. 5).

The results in Fig. 5 show that some learners did not read through the page from the top to the bottom. They sometimes omitted to check the picture referenced by text and to read the figure legend accompanied by a picture after reading the text and the picture. The tendency of these behaviors differed with the learners, and there seemed to be some difference in these tendency between those who characterized as the verbalizers and visualizers, although the difference was not so clear.

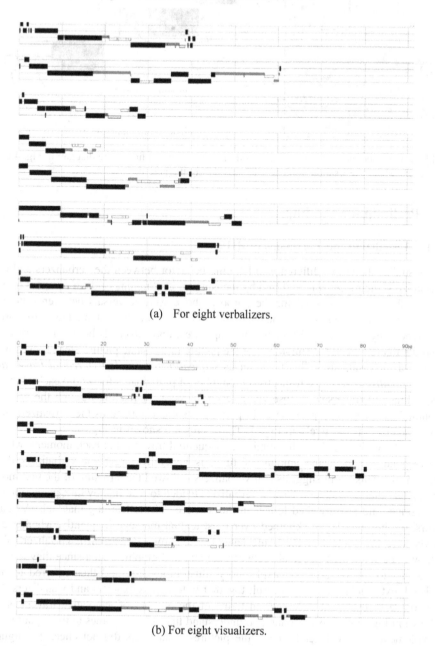

(a)   For eight verbalizers.

(b) For eight visualizers.

Fig. 4. Periods with fixation points in different ROIs with text, pictures and figure legends in each paragraph area for Fig. 1(b).

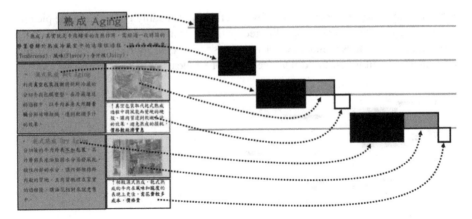

Fig. 5. Correspondence between the period of each horizontal line in the diagram in Fig. 4 and the ROIs where the fixation points are located during the period.

3 Preliminary Findings

3.1 Visualizing the Traversals of ROIs

To visualize the above difference in learning behavior between the verbalizers and the visualizers, their gaze was analyzed by focusing on its different kinds of traversal of the ROIs. What we considered for the purpose above were traversals between different paragraphs sequenced in the same page, traversals between the text and the picture area referenced by the text in the same paragraph area, and traversals between the picture and the figure legend for annotation of the picture in the same picture area. These three kinds of traversals are called hereafter as *sequential traversals*, *referential traversals* and *annotative traversals*, respectively. Number of participants for whom each of these three kinds of traversals is observed at each moment for reading through the page is counted over each group of the eight participants characterized as the verbalizers and the visualizers respectively in Fig. 4. The results are shown in Fig. 6.

As shown in Fig. 6(a), the number of sequential traversals at each moment, which corresponds to the same amount of time, is generally larger for verbalizers than visualizers. This result suggests that verbalizers followed the structure of the text more frequently than visualizers. That is, verbalizers tended to read line by line, paragraph by paragraph, and also dwelled longer in the text area of the learning materials. Visualizers, on the other hand, skimmed over most textual message frequently, whether the texts were the context or the figure legends. As shown in Fig. 6(b), visualizers also show more referential traversals between the text and graphical area since they tended to attend to the pictures and explanatory illustrations first and then referred to the related text quickly. From this result together with that verbalizers and visualizers did not possess significant difference in terms of the number of annotative traversals as shown in Fig. 6(c), it is reasonable to understand that when it comes to the layout with supplemental figure legends under the pictures, visualizers did not check the figure legends accompanying with each picture so frequently as the verbalizers do. By the

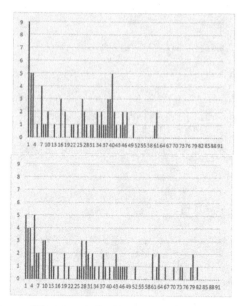

(a) Sequential traversals (Left:Verbalizers, Right:Visualizers).

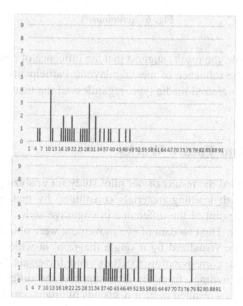

(b) Referential traversals (Left:Verbalizers, Right:Visualizers).

Fig. 6. Number of the participants with the traversal of gaze between the ROIs of different types at each moment for reading through the page in Fig. 1(b).

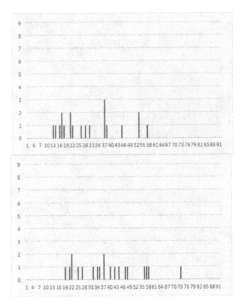

(c) Annotative traversals (Left:Verbalizers, Right:Visualizers).

Fig. 6. (*continued*)

number of the traversals, the results suggest that the influence of participants' cognitive style could override the influence of message layout. Participants' attention was intuitively drawn to their preferred media type, regardless of the text-graphic layout of the learning materials.

4   Conclusions and Future Works

This article has presented the results of our pilot study for analyzing gaze behaviors of learners reading through learning materials constituted by text, pictures and figure legends from the viewpoint of the difference in cognitive styles characterized as *verbalizers* and *visualizers*. The raw data of eye movement were obtained by eye-tracking devices. Those data are visualized by a single diagram, in which fixation points are integrated into periods corresponding to ROIs, and traversals between them were analyzed. Preliminary findings from the data supports the differences in verbalizer-visualizer cognitive styles resulted in their decisions of orders, emphasis, and repetition to read text and pictures. Verbalizers draw their attention to and read more frequently the text and figure legends than visualizers in layouts with explanatory and annotated illustrations. To verify the tendency of the gaze behaviors above as one of our future steps, further analysis will incorporate larger number of participants and investigate learners' reading performance to empirically access the causal relationship among cognitive styles, learning preferences and the learning performance. In addition, different layouts of message design that assemble scientific text in real world are also considered in our future work to investigate learners' performance in genuine contexts with better generalizability.

References

1. Cassidy, S.: Learning styles: an overview of theories, models, and measures. Educ. Psychol. **24**, 419–444 (2004)
2. Kirschner, P.A., van Merriënboer, J.J.: Do learners really know best? Urban legends in education. Educ. Psychol. **48**(3), 169–183 (2013)
3. Mayer, R.E., Massa, L.: Three facets of visual and verbal learners: cognitive ability, cognitive style, and learning preference. J. Educ. Psychol. **95**(4), 833 (2003)
4. Höffler, T.N., Prechtl, H., Nerdel, C.: The influence of visual cognitive style when learning from instructional animations and static pictures. Learn. Individ. Differ. **20**(5), 479–483 (2010)
5. Mehigan, T.J., Barry, M., Kehoe, A., Pitt, I.: Using eye tracking technology to identify visual and verbal learners. In: IEEE International Conference on Multimedia and Expo (IEEE ICME 2011), pp. 1–6 (2011)
6. Koć-Januchta, M., Höffler, T., Thoma, G.-B., Prechtl, H., Leutner, D.: Visualizers versus verbalizers: effects of cognitive style on learning with texts and pictures–an eye-tracking study. Comput. Hum. Behav. **68**, 170–179 (2017)
7. Clark, J.M., Paivio, A.: Dual coding theory and education. Educ. Psychol. Rev. **3**(3), 149–210 (1991)
8. Clark, R.E., Feldon, D.F., Mayer, R.E.: The Cambridge Handbook of Multimedia Learning (2005)
9. Childers, T.L.: Measurement of individual differences in visual versus verbal information processing. J. Consum. Res. **12**(2), 125–134 (1985)
10. Richardson, A.: Verbalizer-visualizer: a cognitive style dimension. J. Ment. Imag. **1**(1), 109–125 (1977)

The Classification of Different Situations in a Lecture Based on Students' Observed Postures

Yuki Kotakehara[1(✉)], Koh Kakusho[1], Satoshi Nishiguchi[2], Masaaki Iiyama[3], and Masayuki Murakami[4]

[1] Kwansei Gakuin University, 2-1 Gakuen, Sanda 669-1337, Japan
{yuki-kotakehara,kakusho}@kwansei.ac.jp
[2] Osaka Institute of Technology, 1-79-1 Kitayama, Hirakata 573-0196, Japan
satoshi.nishiguchi@oit.ac.jp
[3] Kyoto University, Yoshidahonmachi, Sakyo-ku, Kyoto 606-8501, Japan
iiyama@mm.media.kyoto-u.ac.jp
[4] Kyoto University of Foreign Studies, 6 Saiinkasamecho, Ukyo-ku,
Kyoto 615-8558, Japan
masayuki@murakami-lab.org

Abstract. This paper discusses the possibility of identifying different situations related to the students during a lecture from its video by classifying the situations that happen in the lecture based on the similarity in the posture of each student. The recognized situations can be used as indexes for the instructor to watch the video to further improve the lecture. Although it has been shown in a previous work that there are some relations between the postures taken by the students and their understanding of the lecture, it is not clear what types of situations actually happen during the lectures, and the postures taken by the students differ even when they are in the same situations. To deal with these problems, the representative postures of each student in different situations are first obtained by clustering the postures actually taken by the student, and then different situations of the class are obtained by clustering the combinations of representative postures of all the students under the assumptions that similar postures are taken by each student and similar combinations of those postures are observed for the whole group of students when they are in the same situation.

Keywords: Lecture situation · Student posture · Clustering

1 Introduction

Recently, in the field of higher education, it has been often suggested to record the lectures on videos to review them for *Faculty Development* (FD) [1–3]. However, the instructors cannot easily select the scenes to be watched, and it is very time-consuming for them to review their lectures by watching the whole video. To reduce the heavy workload of watching the lecture videos, previous works have proposed to recognize various situations related to the instructor and the students for indexing the videos [4–9].

P.-L. P. Rau (Ed.): HCII 2019, LNCS 11577, pp. 446–457, 2019.
https://doi.org/10.1007/978-3-030-22580-3_33

Those previous works can be classified into two types: those that consider mainly the situations related to the instructor [4–7], and those that focus on the students [8, 9]. The previous works of the first type discuss how to recognize the instructor's behaviors, which include writing on the blackboard, presenting slides, talking to the students and so on. Those of the second type focus mainly on students' behaviors because it has been pointed out that there is a relation between students' behaviors and their interest during the lectures. That is, students' behavior of looking ahead often reflects their interest in the lecture [10].

Additionally, recent work has analyzed the relation between the postures taken by the students during a lecture, and as the result, it has been shown that different behaviors such as dozing off and looking away as well as looking ahead can be used as useful clues to estimate the students' understanding of the lecture [11]. Based on these results, this article discusses how to recognize combinations of those behaviors of the whole group of the students in the classroom during a lecture as the situation of the lecture. To this aim, it is necessary to clarify what kinds of situations can be observed in the lecture, because the situations of lectures related to the behaviors of the whole group of the students are not so well organized as those of the instructors, who gives the lectures with the specific purpose of giving clear explanations using slides and whiteboards. Moreover, whereas most students look ahead when they are paying attention to the lectures, the postures taken by the students while they are dozing off or looking away might be different for different students.

In our work, we classify different types of situations from the combinations of the behaviors observed for the whole group of the students at different moments of the lectures. To cope with individual differences in the postures for the same behavior in this classification, we assume that the same posture taken by the same student implies the same behavior of the student, and classify different behaviors of each student based on the similarity between the postures actually observed for the student. More precisely, first we obtain representative postures for each student by clustering his/her postures observed at each moment of the lecture. Then, we describe specific situations at each moment of the lecture combining the representative postures of all students attending the lecture. Finally, those situations are again clustered based on the similarity in the combination of the representative postures, and different situations related to the students during the lecture are recognized.

In Sect. 2, we will provide a more detailed explanation of the procedure used in this study. In Sect. 3, we will present the results of an experiment conducted by one of the authors in his university to evaluate the procedure described above. Finally, in Sect. 4, we will summarize the main points of this article and discuss possible future steps for our research.

2 The Classification of Students' Situations by Clustering Their Postures

2.1   The Identification of Representative Postures for Each Student

The posture of each student observed in each frame of the lecture video can be obtained by conventional human image processing techniques for pose estimation. The obtained posture is described by the two-dimensional (2D) coordinates of all the observable feature points of the student's body. Let $x_i(t)$ denote the posture of i-th student denoted by S_i observed in t-th frame denoted by F_t of the lecture video ($i = 1, \cdots, N$; $t = 1, \cdots, T$), where N and T denote the number of the students observed in the lecture video and that of the frames constituting the video, respectively. The posture $x_i(t)$ is a $2J$ dimensional vector, where J denotes the number of feature points, mainly the joints, of a student's body. In this article, this vector is named the *observed posture* of student S_i at frame F_t. Since each observed posture describes only 2D positions in the image frame for the feature points of each student, and therefore does not include any information concerning depth, the observed posture changes according to the geometric relation between the student and the camera used to take the lecture video, even when the same posture and the same student are involved. However, it is possible to keep this geometric relation unchanged by fixing the camera in the classroom, given that each student sits in the same seat throughout the lecture. Under this condition, the difference in observed posture $x_i(t)$ reflects the difference in actual 3D posture of student S_i.

The set of all the observed postures in each video frame obtained for student S_i is denoted by $O_i = \{x_i(1), \cdots, x_i(T)\}$. Assuming that each student should take similar postures for the same behavior, the clusters denoted by $C_i = \left\{ C_i^1, \cdots, C_i^{K(i)} \right\}$, in which $K(i)$ denotes the number of the clusters, are obtained by grouping all the postures included in O_i, which should correspond to the number of different postures actually taken by student S_i, and thus differs from one student to another (see Fig. 1). Since the observed postures $\left\{ x_i(t) | x_i(t) \in C_i^{k(i)}, C_i^{k(i)} \in C_i \right\}$, which are all classified into the same cluster $C_i^{k(i)}$, are similar to each other, those postures are regarded as representing the same posture taken by student S_i for the same behavior. The representative postures are defined to indicate these observed postures taken for the same behavior by each student. The $k(i)$-th *representative posture* $X_i^{k(i)}$ of student S_i is defined by the centroid of $C_i^{k(i)}$ as follows:

$$X_i^{k(i)} = \frac{1}{|C_i^{k(i)}|} \sum_{x_i(t) \in C_i^{k(i)}} x_i(t) \tag{1}$$

where all the representative postures of student S_i are given by the set $X_i = \left\{ X_i^1, \cdots, X_i^{K(i)} \right\}$.

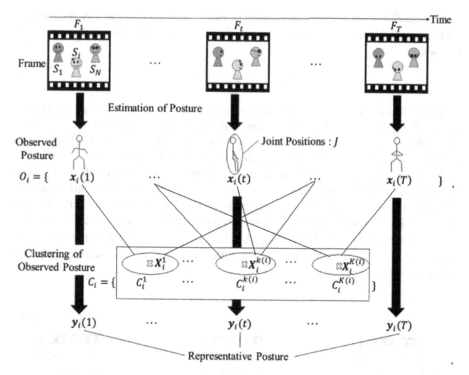

Fig. 1. Representative postures obtained by clustering observed postures.

To describe the behavior associated to an observed posture for each student at any frame, the observed posture is substituted by the representative posture that is more similar to that observed among all the representative postures of the student. Let $y_i(t)$ denote the representative posture to substitute observed posture $x_i(t)$ of student S_i in frame F_t. This representative posture is given as that with the minimal Euclidian distance from $x_i(t)$ in X_i as follows:

$$y_i(t) = \underset{X_i^{k(i)} \in X_i}{\mathrm{argmin}} \left\| x_i(t) - X_i^{k(i)} \right\| \tag{2}$$

2.2 The Classification of Different Situations in the Whole Group of Students

As a result of the procedure described in Sect 2.1, representative postures $y_1(t), \cdots, y_N(t)$ of all the students $S_1, \cdots, S_N$ are obtained for each frame F_t. Since any observed posture is described as a $2J$ dimensional vector, any of the N representative postures are also described as a $2J$ dimensional vector. These N representative postures are employed to describe the situation of the whole group of students in each frame. The situation of the whole group of students in frame F_t is denoted by $y(t)$, which is called here *combined representative posture*, and it is defined as the $2JN$ dimensional vector, whose elements are constituted by those of the N representative postures as follows:

$$y(t) = [y_1(t) \cdots y_N(t)] \tag{3}$$

Let R denote the set of the combined representative posture $y(t)$ for all the frames, where $R = \{y(1), \cdots, y(T)\}$. Since the frames in which each student takes the observable postures to be substituted by the same representative posture of his/her own should be regarded as the frames with the same behavior for the whole group of the students, the frames with similar combined representative postures can be regarded as the frames representing the same situation for the whole group of students. Based on this idea, the sets of all combined representative postures R are classified into the clusters, each including similar combined representative postures (see Fig. 2). The resultant set of clusters is denoted by $D = \{D^1, \cdots, D^L\}$, where L is the number of clusters corresponding to the number of different situations that actually occurred during the observed lecture.

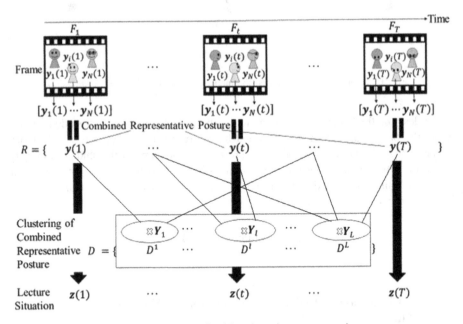

Fig. 2. Lecture situations obtained by clustering representative postures.

If the situation for each frame needs to be further recognized among its possible variations obtained as D described above, the situation to be recognized for frame F_t

can be obtained by replacing combined representative posture $y(t)$ with the centroid of the cluster including $y(t)$. Let Y_l denote the centroid of cluster D^l $(l = 1, \cdots, L)$, which is defined as follows:

$$Y_l = \frac{1}{|D^l|} \sum_{y(t) \in D^l} y(t) \tag{4}$$

where $Y = \{Y_1, \cdots, Y_L\}$ describes different situations of the whole group of the students. Thus, the situation of the whole group of students in frame F_t can be recognized by finding $z(t)$, which denotes the element with the minimal Euclidean distance from $y(t)$ among Y:

$$z(t) = \underset{Y_l \in Y}{\operatorname{argmin}} \|y(t) - Y_l\| \tag{5}$$

Since Y is not given in advance but is obtained based on the similarity between the students' postures, in order to identify the situations in which the students are involved, we do not need to know in advance neither what kinds of situations possibly happen during the lecture nor what postures are actually taken by each student in each situation.

3 Experimental Results

3.1 Students' Observed Postures

We run an experiment to evaluate whether the method described in Sect. 2 can be successfully used to identify situations that are useful for instructors to review and improve their lectures. We recorded the seminar supervised by one of the authors of this article by fixing a camera in the classroom after obtaining students' approval. The recorded video consisted of 2771 frames ($T = 2771$) and lasted 90 min. The results of pose estimation for the students appearing in the video included the postures of 13 students out of all those who attended the seminar for each frame ($N = 13$). OpenPose [12] was employed to pose estimations. Postures of all the other students could not be obtained due to occlusions among the students. The observed posture for a student for each frame is described as a 24-dimensional vector, which consists of 2D coordinates in the image frame for 12 feature points, including the nose, neck, shoulders, elbows, wrists, eyes, and ears ($J = 12$). Figure 3 illustrates the observed postures for the 13 students in a frame of the lecture video. Different lines indicate different pairs of feature points adjacent to each other. The face of each student is hidden in the image for privacy protection.

Fig. 3. An example of the observed postures.

3.2   Representative Postures Obtained for Each Student

The observed postures obtained for each student in all frames were classified into clusters of similar postures. The *k-means* method [13] was employed for clustering. Since this method requires that the number of clusters $K(i)$ is specified, we tried different values for $K(i)$ in order to find the appropriate number for the clusters. As a result, clusters including the observed postures that can be interpreted as meaningful behaviors were obtained for $K(i) = 2$–8.

Figures 4 and 5 show examples of the observed postures included in each of the three clusters obtained for two different students when $K(i) = 3$. The observed postures in this example can be interpreted as the behaviors of *looking ahead*, *taking notes*, and *looking away*. However, the observed postures included in the clusters corresponding to the same behavior for different students are not necessarily similar in terms of their geometric shapes. This result implies that the observed postures taken by different students during the same lecture may have a similar variation of their behavior, whereas the geometric shapes of the observed postures that can be interpreted as the same behavior often include individual difference. Nevertheless, our method allows us to extract meaningful behaviors that occur during the lecture while tolerating individual differences in the observed postures by merely clustering the observed postures of each student.

(a) Examples of observed postures for looking ahead.

(b) Examples of observed postures for taking notes.

(c) Examples of observed postures for looking away.

Fig. 4. The representative postures of student A.

3.3   Obtaining the Situations of the Whole Group of Students

The representative postures of each student were obtained as the centroids of the clusters of the observed postures obtained in Sect 3.2 to replace the observed postures of the student in each frame with one of those representative postures and form the combined representative postures for the whole group of students in the frame. By clustering the combined representative postures in all frames, different situations of the group of students during the lecture were obtained. The *k-means* method was employed again for clustering. Since the number of clusters L is unknown, we tried different values also for L. As a result, most clusters could be interpreted as meaningful situations for the whole group of students for $L = 4$.

Figures 6 and 7 show examples of frames classified into different clusters. In each figure, the representative posture of each student is shown at the position of the student in the image frame. Figure 6 shows examples of situations that can be given a meaningful interpretation, whereas the situations depicted in Fig. 7 cannot be interpreted meaningfully. For example, the situations illustrated in Fig. 6 can be interpreted respectively as (a) *paying attention to the lecture*, (b) *taking notes*, and (c) *looking*

(a) Examples of observed postures for looking ahead.

(b) Example of observed postures for taking notes.

(c) Examples of observed postures for looking away.

Fig. 5. The representative postures of student B.

away, because almost all students show the same behavior although the geometric shapes of the representative postures are different. On the other hand, the examples in Fig. 7 are not easily interpreted in a meaningful way for the whole group, because some students are paying attention to the lecture while others are taking notes.

From the examples reported above, it can be said that our method is fairly useful in obtaining meaningful situations of the students regardless of their individual differences in posture, but still needs further improvement. One of the reasons why the situations in Fig. 7 cannot be interpreted univocally is that the students begin and finish taking notes in different moments. To deal with the asynchrony of the behaviors, it is necessary to make our clustering method tolerant for a slight temporal difference.

(a) Sample situations to be interpreted as *looking ahead*.

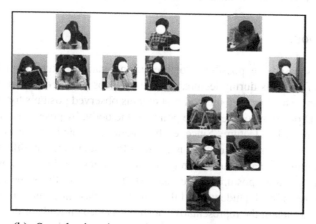

(b) Sample situations to be interpreted as *taking notes*.

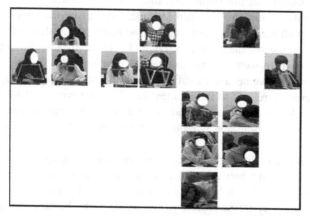

(c) Sample situations to be interpreted as *looking away*.

Fig. 6. Examples of situations that have meaningful interpretations.

Fig. 7. Examples of situations that are difficult to interpret meaningfully.

4   Conclusions

This article discussed the possibility of identifying various situations related to the whole group of students during lectures from the videos obtained with a fixed camera in the classroom. The proposed method first obtains observed postures for each student, described as 2D positions of the feature points of the body, by pose estimation for each frame of the recorded lecture. Since each student is seated at the same location throughout the lecture and the camera is fixed in the classroom, the differences in the observed postures of each student reflect the changes in his/her posture. Thus, assuming that the same posture of the same student reflects the same behavior, the observed postures of each student in all the frames are classified into clusters based on their similarity to obtain the representative postures as the centroids of the clusters. The representative postures of all students in each frame are used to form the combined representative postures in the frame, and different situations of the whole group of students during the lecture are obtained by further clustering the combined representative postures in all the frames. Applying this method to the analysis of the video of a seminar, most of the obtained clusters could be given meaningful interpretations, although some of them were difficult to interpret meaningfully.

In future research, we need to modify the method so that the clustering can tolerate individual differences related to the moment in which the posture changes. Although the most straightforward solution would be to reduce the temporal resolution of the video frames, further discussion is required to understand how to address this issue properly.

It is also important to consider the different relevance of different feature points for evaluating the similarity between different postures based on their positions. For example, the position of each hand is not as relevant as the position of the head for evaluating the similarity in the posture of the whole body, because the hands tend to take more different positions than the head for the same behavior including paying attention, taking notes, and looking away. Thus, it becomes necessary for the clustering to give different weights to different feature points or to normalize the distance between the feature points for evaluating the difference in posture.

References

1. Minoh, M., Nishiguchi, S.: Environmental media – in the case of lecture archiving system. In: Palade, V., Howlett, R.J., Jain, L. (eds.) KES 2003. LNCS (LNAI), vol. 2774, pp. 1070–1076. Springer, Heidelberg (2003). https://doi.org/10.1007/978-3-540-45226-3_146
2. Coursera. https://www.coursera.org. Accessed 10 Dec 2018
3. edX. https://www.edx.org. Accessed 10 Dec 2018
4. Onishi, M., Fukunaga, K.: Shooting the lecture scene using computer-controlled cameras based on situation understanding and evaluation of video images. In: International Conference on Pattern Recognition (ICPR), Cambridge, pp. 781–784. IEEE (2004)
5. Shimada, A., Suganuma, A., Taniguchi, R.: Automatic camera control system for a distant lecture based on estimation of teacher's behavior. In: IASTED International Conference on Computers and Advanced Technology in Education, pp. 106–111 (2004)
6. Yousaf, M.H., Azhar, K., Sial, H.A.: A novel vision based approach for instructor's performance and behavior analysis. In: International Conference on Communications, Signal Processing, and their Applications (ICCSPA), Sharjah, pp. 1–6. IEEE (2015)
7. Lin, Y.-T., Tsai, H.-Y., Chang, C.-H., Lee, G.C.: Learning-focused structuring for blackboard lecture videos. In: Fourth International Conference on Semantic Computing, Pittsburgh, pp. 149–155. IEEE (2010)
8. Narayanan, S.A., Prasanth, M., Mohan, P., Kaimal, M.R., Bijlani, K.: Attention analysis in e-learning environment using a simple web camera. In: International Conference on Technology Enhanced Education (ICTEE), Kerala, pp. 1–4. IEEE (2012)
9. Yongyi, C.: Construction of a course video resource system based on students' visual attention. In: International Conference on E-Business and E-Government, Guangzhou, pp. 3840–3844. IEEE (2010)
10. Murakami, M., Kakusho, K., Minoh, M.: Analysis of students' eye movement in relation to contents of multimedia lecture. In: World Conference on E-Learning in Corporate, Government, Healthcare, and Higher Education (E-Learn), pp. 1965–1968 (2002)
11. Mukunoki, M., Yoshitsugu, K., Minoh, M.: Students' posture sequence estimation using spatio-temporal constraints. In: Greco, S., Bouchon-Meunier, B., Coletti, G., Fedrizzi, M., Matarazzo, B., Yager, R.R. (eds.) IPMU 2012. CCIS, vol. 298, pp. 415–424. Springer, Heidelberg (2012). https://doi.org/10.1007/978-3-642-31715-6_44
12. Cao, Z., Simon, T., Wei, S.-E., Sheikh, Y.: Realtime multi-person 2D pose estimation using part affinity fields. In: Conference on Computer Vision and Pattern Recognition (CVPR), Honolulu, pp. 1302–1310. IEEE (2017)
13. MacQueen, J.B.: Some methods for classification and analysis of multivariate observations. In: Proceedings of 5th Berkley Symposium on Mathematical Statistics and Probability, vol. 1, pp. 281–297 (1967)

Design of an Online Education Evaluation System Based on Multimodal Data of Learners

Qijia Peng[1(✉)], Nan Qie[2], Liang Yuan[3], Yue Chen[2], and Qin Gao[2]

[1] Graduate School of Comprehensive Human Sciences, University of Tsukuba, 1-1-1 Tennodai, Tsukuba, Ibaraki 305-8577, Japan
pengqj92@hotmail.com
[2] Institute of Human Factors and Ergonomics, Department of Industrial Engineering, Tsinghua University, Haidian District, Beijing 100084, People's Republic of China
[3] Graduate School of System and Information Engineering, University of Tsukuba, 1-1-1 Tennodai, Tsukuba, Ibaraki 305-8577, Japan

Abstract. Online education breaks the time and space constraints of learning, but it also presents some new challenges for the teachers: less interaction between instructors and learners, and loss of real-time feedback of teaching effects. Our study aims to fill these gaps by designing a tool for instructors that shows how learners' status change along the lecture video timeline. The study uses multimodal data consist of facial expressions and timeline-anchored comments and labels the data with two learning status dimensions (difficulty and interestingness). To acquire training dataset, 20 teaching video clips are selected, and 15 volunteers are invited to watch the videos to collect their facial expressions and subjective learning status ratings. Then we build a fusion model with results from a CNN (Convolutional Neural Network) model and a LSTM (Long Short-Term Memory) model, and design an effective interface to present feedbacks from the model. After evaluation of the model, we put forward some possible improvements and future prospects for this design.

Keywords: Online education · Multimodal data · Deep learning

1 Introduction

Online courses break the constraints of time and space and share high-quality educational resources through the Internet. Compared with face-to-face learning in classrooms, online learning enriches learners' interactions with learning materials such as lecture videos but decreases social interactions. Especially, a massive open online course (MOOC) usually involves several instructors and thousands of learners. From instructors' perspectives, it is hard to gather and analyze the large scale of learning data from all the students effectively and efficiently. Instructors cannot get feedbacks during lectures as they can in classrooms. They also experience overwhelming information from different sources and feel difficult to fully use it to improve instruction [1]. As a result, learners less interact with instructors and perceive less teaching presence,

© Springer Nature Switzerland AG 2019
P.-L. P. Rau (Ed.): HCII 2019, LNCS 11577, pp. 458–468, 2019.
https://doi.org/10.1007/978-3-030-22580-3_34

i.e., perceived level of effective instruction and guidance from instructors [2, 3] and is found to promote effective learning, performance and satisfaction [4, 5].

To help instructors analyze learning data and further promote learners' teaching presence, educational systems have adopted learning analytics and educational data mining. Most previous research focused on a course level analysis, such as to predict performance, predict dropout, enhance social interactions, and recommend resources [6]. To improve instruction, instructors need more detailed information in a lecture video level, i.e., learners' feedback along with the video timeline, so that they can improve their instructions of different knowledge points. Several studies designed tools to analyze learners' cognitive load and engagement in a lecture video by video clickstream [7–9]. The overall clickstream pattern of a video could well predict the possibility of dropout, but it remained hard to interpret learners' feelings by the click data at a specific video timepoint.

To get learners' feedbacks in fine granularity, researchers could choose some alternative data sources changing along with the video timeline. Physiological signals such as facial expressions and eye gazing, change during lecture learning and can well reflect learners' mental states such as cognitive load and engagement. However, most physiological data are hard to collect in online learning contexts and therefore are adopted by few studies [10]. Some research collected data through web cameras on learners' devices [11–13]. They aimed to design adaptive learning systems for learners but not to show how learners' states change along with the lecture video for instructors.

Besides physiological data, contents generated by learners can also reflect learners' engagement. Most previous research [14, 15] analyzed forum discussion data, which showed a course level of learners' feedbacks. To show a video level of feedbacks, a better data source is timeline-anchored commenting, which has been incorporated in many studies to promote discussions during learning lecture videos [16–21]. Learners can post a comment or an annotation specific to a playback time of the video, and later viewers will see these comments when the video plays to that exact time point. Timeline-anchored commenting can expose learners with more discussions specific to timepoints and further promote learning [17, 18, 20, 22, 23]. We found one study attempted to analyze these timeline-anchored comments and design a visualization tool for instructors [24, 25]. This tool showed how learners' emotion valence, the relevance of discussions, and the topics changed along the video timeline. But it missed learners' perceived difficulty or workload and learners' interest or engagement, which instructors are highly interested in [26, 27].

Therefore, our study aims to fill these gaps and design a system for instructors that shows how learners' perceived learning status change along the lecture video timeline. In addition, most studies only analyzed data from a single data source despite the diversity of sources according to two recent review papers about learning analytic tools [10, 28]. To provide instructors with a more comprehensive view, this study attempts to build a tool to analyze data from different data sources, i.e., facial expressions and timeline-anchored comments, with multimodal methods.

2 Method

In order to construct the system, we design a data collection platform, collect data from a sample group of students, preprocess the data, and train an artificial neural network model based on those data.

2.1 Data Collection

Before we train the model and build the feedback system, basic work such as choosing evaluation dimensions, collecting training data and data formatting should be done.

Learning Status Dimensions
First, we determine proper dimensions to evaluate learning status. In order to give structural feedback to the teachers, the dimensions should be real-time, relevant to facial expressions and comments, easy to understand and evaluate, and instructive to teaching improvement.

According to the review of Student Rating of Teaching [26, 27], we choose two dimensions: "difficulty/workload" and "level of interest". We use "Difficult/Easy" and "Interesting/Boring" as the name of these two dimensions in the following study.

Data Collection Platform
We need both facial expressions and comments as training dataset, and watchers' emotion feedback ratings (on difficulty and interestingness) as label dataset. Thus, we build an online experiment platform based on HTML/JavaScript. Participants watch some selected video clips on the platform, and their facial expressions and ratings will be recorded.

First, we choose video clips from documentaries, speeches and public classes on a Chinese video sharing website "Bilibili". This website has both good quantity and quality of educational videos and is famous for the "Danmaku" (a type of timeline-anchored comments) culture in China. The proper video clip should be easy to trigger emotions about difficulty or interestingness and rich in watchers' comments. 20 video clips (in Chinese or English) are finally selected by the researchers after rated separately on both dimensions. The topic of the teaching videos includes physics, math, language and history. Each video clip contains only one specific topic and lasts for around 1 min, which makes it possible for the emotion feedback ratings to reflect watchers' learning status. Timeline-anchored comments of those video clips are also collected respectively for the study.

The webpage of the platform collects facial expressions during the participants watching the video by using the camera on the PC (MediaStream interface on Chrome browser), saving as webm format videos (24 fps) (See Fig. 1). The webpage starts recording when the video clip starts to play, and end recording when the video is played. The emotion ratings towards the video are collected by two sliders on the webpage (range from −1 to 1, step 0.1), and the sliders will show after finishing watching the video (See Fig. 2).

• Record test

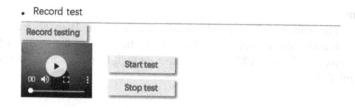

• Record

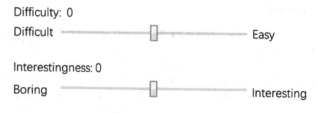

Fig. 1. Facial expressions record interface.

For this video, I think

Difficulty: 0
Difficult ———————————□———————— Easy

Interestingness: 0
Boring ——————————□———————— Interesting

Download

Fig. 2. Learning status rating interface

Participants

Fifteen university students (7 man and 8 woman), aging from 21 to 27, recruited from Tsinghua University and University of Tsukuba participated in the study. All participants are native speakers of Chinese, and have enough English ability to understand videos in English.

2.2   Data Preprocessing

Before the comprehensive fusion training of the multimodal data, we first preprocessed data of facial expressions and comments separately.

For facial expression data, we use interface from opencv in python to detect and extract facial expressions from the recorded videos. We choose one facial expression (screenshot in the video) per second and extract facial expressions by a well-trained universal model (haarcascade_frontalface_default) from opencv. All facial expressions pictures are set in 128px * 128px * 1 channel after resizing and grayscale processing. For each video of each participant we choose 20 pictures to analyze and labeled with his/her emotional ratings in two dimensions (difficulty and interestingness).

For timeline-anchored comments ("Danmaku" in this study), we have to extract those topic-related comments and screen out the irrelevant, meaningless comments such as greetings, internet memes, repeating words and emoticons. Moreover, in "Danmaku" culture, contents tend to be cute and popular, which also makes it not suitable for training in universal emotional analysis model directly. Thus, we set up both stop word list and "word meaning transfer" list. After screening the irrelevant contents, we calculate the emotional tendency classification and its possibility and confidence for each "Danmaku" comment by the interface provided by Baidu NLP. Then we choose those comments with confidence >0.1 and split the sentence into words by interface from Jieba Chinese text segmentation. Each word is then transferred to a word vector by genism and unified in length. Finally, we get 899 valid Danmaku comments in total and label them with the average emotional ratings in two dimensions (difficulty and interestingness) of the videos accordingly.

Moreover, the subjective evaluation of "Difficulty" and "Interestingness", which will be used as label in the training process, is convert to a classification factor ($-1/1$) according to the emotional ratings (positive/negative).

2.3   Model Training

We choose randomly from the preprocessed dataset into the training set, which contains facial expressions of 12 participants and 750 Danmaku comments.

The fusion model is based on Stacked Generalization [29]. We use a 4-level Long Short-Term Memory Network (LSTM) model to classify the data from comments, and a 5-level Convolutional Neural Network (CNN) model with an MSE loss function to train the data of facial expressions. In the fusion level, those two models are integrated by a 2-level Stacked Generalization-based ensemble model, which outputs the final classification of the learning status. Those three models are trained separately.

Figure 3 summarizes the structure and process of the model. A Danmaku comment labeled by the video's average rating enters the LSTM model and it outputs a predicted classification. A facial expression labeled by the according rating enters the CNN model and it outputs a predicted classification. Then Danmaku comment and facial expressions which are from the same person watching the same video will then enter the fusion level, and the model will output the final predicted classification.

Considering that information in Danmaku comments cannot easily reflect feelings about "Difficulty", we use only facial expression data with CNN model in "Difficulty" dimension.

3   Model Evaluation

We have facial expression data from 3 participants and 149 Danmaku comments in the test set. Accuracy, precision, recall and F-measure are calculated separately according to the results from the test set (see Table 1).

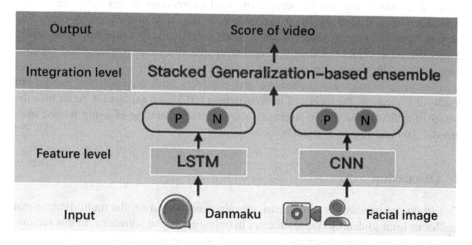

Fig. 3. The fusion model including an LSTM model and an CNN model.

The accuracy of this model for interestingness is 62.4%, and for difficulty is 58.4%, which is higher than a random classification (50%). Considering the sample size of training dataset, the results of accuracy is acceptable and bigger size of training set is necessary for the improvement of the model's accuracy.

The precision for interestingness is 65.2% for positive feedback and 61.2% for negative feedback, and for difficulty is 74.4% for positive and 36.5% for negative. The precision is better when detecting "interesting", "boring" and "difficult", but not good in "easy".

The recall is only 42.9% for "interesting" and 51.1% for "difficult", but better performance on "boring" (79.7%) and "easy" (61.5%). The reason might lie in the habits of facial expression from the watchers. Comparing with "boring" and "easy", "interesting" and "difficult" are more likely to provoke larger facial expression changes, and thus the model tends to relate rich expressions to interesting and difficult learning

Table 1. Accuracy, precision, recall and F-measure of the model.

		Interestingness	Difficulty
Accuracy		0.624	0.584
Precision	Positive	0.652	0.744
	Negative	0.612	0.365
	Average	0.632	0.555
Recall	Positive	0.429	0.615
	Negative	0.797	0.511
	Average	0.613	0.563
F-measure	Positive	0.517	0.674
	Negative	0.692	0.426
	Average	0.605	0.550

status. But considering that the sample of facial expressions in this study are chosen randomly within around 60 s, rich expressions in limit time could possibly diluted by large number of plain expressions, which leads to a relatively worse results on recall. A possible improvement method is to find more effective emotion trigger and improve time accuracy for expression detection.

F-measure is more comprehensive and considers both precision and recall. For results of F-measure, the model of interestingness (60.5% on average) is better than the model of difficulty (55.0% on average), showing the advantage of using related multimodal data and fusion of models.

4   Discussion

This study put forward a comprehensive evaluation method for the multi-dimensional feedbacks from students to the instructors in online education situations. In this section, we discuss about the contribution of this model based on facial expressions and comments in theoretical aspects, and the future prospects for implementation of the system in practical aspects.

4.1   Theoretical Contribution

In theoretical aspect, the methodology of this study can be used to establish links of more learning status with facial expressions and comments. Recent researches and products are already able to recognize general emotions (such as happy, angry, etc.) with facial expressions, but in online education situations, learning status may not be always associated with general emotions. In the context of online learning, this study presents a possible method to detect more learning related status, such as concentration and distraction, by analyzing facial expressions labeled with learners' status. Also, the timeliness provided by timeline-anchored comments may also help detecting real-time learning status by emotional recognition of the comments.

Moreover, this study provides another way to recognize emotions from comments like "Danmaku" in the future. Comments in "Danmaku" are more like memes on the internet, and thus have special language style and are quite different from the language in everyday life. The vague range of the meaning and the lack of context make it difficult for traditional method (such as TF-IDF and word2vec) to handle. However, in online education situations, this study provides a platform where learning status related emotions can be detected, and thus make it easier to label those timeline-anchored comments even if we don't know their exact meanings.

4.2 Practical Contribution

In practical aspect, this model and system can help reduce teaching pressure of instructors facing hundreds of students at the same time when teaching on the internet. An experienced teacher can handle the students' learning status so that he/she may improve or adjust teaching strategy, but in online real-time teaching situations the instructors require more feedbacks from the students. This study provides a practical method to show comprehensive and real-time feedbacks, with data obtained from common channels: facial expressions from live camera, and real-time comments from Danmaku or chatting room.

To illustrate the feasibility of this idea, we design an interface to clearly present all the data generated from the model (see Fig. 4). The upper part shows the education video, and the lower part shows the trends of emotions on a line chart with an axis of timeline.

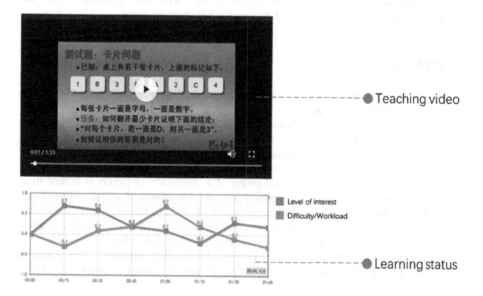

Fig. 4. Feedback interface of learning status

Based on the multimodal data collected from the video watchers, the chart shows the confidence of the emotional classification from the fusion model at a frequency of once per 15 s. When the number is positive, the more it closes to 1, the more likely the watcher feels interesting/easy about the video content; when the number is negative, the more it closes to −1, the more likely the watcher feels boring/difficult. This feedback might help the instructors to judge whether their students are in a good learning status.

Moreover, the feedbacks are also anchored with time. Click the data point on the chart, and the upper video will skip to the time accordingly. This would help the instructors to focus on the exact time that really matters on students' learning status.

5 Conclusion

In this study we collect the multimodal data including facial expressions and comment text when the students watch teaching videos online and label them with two dimensions (interestingness, difficulty) in the subjective learning status. Then after pre-processing such as face recognition from video screenshots and normalization of comment text, we build a fusion model with artificial neural network methods to calculate the real-time learning status in the two dimensions. The study also designs a result display interface, showing the results from the model and interactive functions that are easy for instructors to check the real-time teaching effect.

Our system can give objective, specific timeline-based feedback to instructors, which overcomes the shortages of previous feedback methods. Moreover, we put forward a possible approach to link multiple learning status with facial expressions and recognition of learning status related comments based on the method of our study.

References

1. Bill & Melinda Gates Foundation: Teachers Know Best: Making Data Work for Teachers and Students. Bill & Melinda Gates Foundation (2015)
2. Garrison, D.R., Arbaugh, J.B.: Researching the community of inquiry framework: review, issues, and future directions. Internet High. Educ. 10, 157–172 (2007)
3. Picciano, A.G.: Beyond student perceptions: issues of interaction, presence, and performance in an online course. J. Asynchronous Learn. Netw. 6, 21–40 (2002)
4. Akyol, Z., Garrison, D.R.: The development of a community of inquiry over time in an online course: understanding the progression and integration of social, cognitive and teaching presence. J. Asynchronous Learn. Netw. 12, 3–22 (2008)
5. Ke, F., Kwak, D.: Online learning across ethnicity and age: a study on learning interaction participation, perception, and learning satisfaction. Comput. Educ. 61, 43–51 (2013)
6. Papamitsiou, Z., Economides, A.A.: Learning analytics and educational data mining in practice: a systematic literature review of empirical evidence. J. Educ. Technol. Soc. 17, 49–64 (2014)

7. Kim, J., Guo, P.J., Cai, C.J., Li, S.-W.(D.), Gajos, K.Z., Miller, R.C.: Data-driven interaction techniques for improving navigation of educational videos. In: Proceedings of the 27th Annual ACM Symposium on User Interface Software and Technology, pp. 563–572. ACM, New York (2014)

8. Shi, C., Fu, S., Chen, Q., Qu, H.: VisMOOC: visualizing video clickstream data from massive open online courses. In: 2014 IEEE Conference on Visual Analytics Science and Technology (VAST), pp. 277–278 (2014)

9. Sinha, T., Jermann, P., Li, N., Dillenbourg, P.: Your click decides your fate: inferring information processing and attrition behavior from MOOC video clickstream interactions (2014). arXiv:1407.7131

10. Vieira, C., Parsons, P., Byrd, V.: Visual learning analytics of educational data: a systematic literature review and research agenda. Comput. Educ. **122**, 119–135 (2018)

11. Pham, P., Wang, J.: Predicting learners' emotions in mobile MOOC learning via a multimodal intelligent tutor. In: Nkambou, R., Azevedo, R., Vassileva, J. (eds.) ITS 2018. LNCS, vol. 10858, pp. 150–159. Springer, Cham (2018). https://doi.org/10.1007/978-3-319-91464-0_15

12. Pham, P., Wang, J.: Adaptive review for mobile MOOC learning via multimodal physiological signal sensing - a longitudinal Study. In: Proceedings of the 20th ACM International Conference on Multimodal Interaction, pp. 63–72. ACM, New York (2018)

13. Soltani, M., Zarzour, H., Babahenini, M.C.: Facial emotion detection in massive open online courses. In: Rocha, Á., Adeli, H., Reis, L.P., Costanzo, S. (eds.) WorldCIST 2018. AISC, vol. 745, pp. 277–286. Springer, Cham (2018). https://doi.org/10.1007/978-3-319-77703-0_28

14. Chen, B., Chang, Y.-H., Ouyang, F., Zhou, W.: Fostering student engagement in online discussion through social learning analytics. Internet High. Educ. **31**, 21–30 (2018)

15. Gillani, N., Eynon, R.: Communication patterns in massively open online courses. Internet High. Educ. **23**, 18–26 (2014)

16. Chen, Y., Gao, Q., Yuan, Q.: DanMOOC: enhancing content and social interaction in MOOCs with synchronized commenting. In: Rau, P.-L.P. (ed.) CCD 2017. LNCS, vol. 10281, pp. 509–520. Springer, Cham (2017). https://doi.org/10.1007/978-3-319-57931-3_40

17. Chen, Y., Gao, Q., Yuan, Q., Tang, Y.: Facilitating students' interaction in MOOCs through timeline-anchored discussion. Int. J. Hum.-Comput. Interact. (2019, accepted)

18. Lee, Y.-C., Lin, W.-C., Cherng, F.-Y., Wang, H.-C., Sung, C.-Y., King, J.-T.: Using time-anchored peer comments to enhance social interaction in online educational videos. In: Proceedings of the 33rd Annual ACM Conference on Human Factors in Computing Systems, pp. 689–698. ACM, New York (2015)

19. Leng, J., Zhu, J., Wang, X., Gu, X.: Identifying the potential of Danmaku video from Eye Gaze Data. In: IEEE 16th International Conference on Advanced Learning Technologies 2016 (ICALT), pp. 288–292. IEEE (2016)

20. Yao, Y., Bort, J., Huang, Y.: Understanding Danmaku's potential in online video learning. In: Proceedings of the 2017 CHI Conference Extended Abstracts on Human Factors in Computing Systems, pp. 3034–3040. ACM, New York (2017)

21. Yousef, A.M.F., Chatti, M.A., Schroeder, U., Wosnitza, M.: A usability evaluation of a blended MOOC environment: an experimental case study. Int. Rev. Res. Open Distrib. Learn. **16** (2015)

22. Chen, Y., Gao, Q., Rau, P.-L.P.: Understanding gratifications of watching Danmaku videos – videos with overlaid comments. In: Rau, P.-L.P. (ed.) CCD 2015. LNCS, vol. 9180, pp. 153–163. Springer, Cham (2015). https://doi.org/10.1007/978-3-319-20907-4_14

23. Chen, Y., Gao, Q., Rau, P.-L.P.: Watching a movie alone yet together: understanding reasons for watching Danmaku videos. Int. J. Hum.-Comput. Interact. **33**, 731–743 (2017)

24. Sung, C.-Y., Huang, X.-Y., Shen, Y., Cherng, F.-Y., Lin, W.-C., Wang, H.-C.: ToPIN: a visual analysis tool for time-anchored comments in online educational videos. In: Proceedings of the 2016 CHI Conference Extended Abstracts on Human Factors in Computing Systems, pp. 2185–2191. ACM, New York (2016)
25. Sung, C.-Y., et al.: Exploring online learners' interactive dynamics by visually analyzing their time-anchored comments. Comput. Graph. Forum. **36**(7), 145–155 (2017)
26. Spooren, P., Brockx, B., Mortelmans, D.: On the validity of student evaluation of teaching: the state of the art. Rev. Educ. Res. **83**, 598–642 (2013)
27. Zabaleta, F.: The use and misuse of student evaluations of teaching. Teach. High. Educ. **12**, 55–76 (2007)
28. Mangaroska, K., Giannakos, M.N.: Learning analytics for learning design: a systematic literature review of analytics-driven design to enhance learning. IEEE Trans. Learn. Technol. 1 (2018)
29. Wolpert, D.H.: Stacked generalization. Neural Netw. **5**, 241–259 (1992)

Integrating Multimodal Learning Analytics and Inclusive Learning Support Systems for People of All Ages

Kaori Tamura[1], Min Lu[1], Shin'ichi Konomi[1(✉)], Kohei Hatano[1],
Miyuki Inaba[1], Misato Oi[2], Tsuyoshi Okamoto[1], Fumiya Okubo[3],
Atsushi Shimada[4], Jingyun Wang[5], Masanori Yamada[1],
and Yuki Yamada[1]

[1] Faculty of Arts and Science, Kyushu University, 744, Motooka,
Nishi-Ku, Fukuoka 819-0395, Japan
{tamurak, lu}@artsci.kyushu-u.ac.jp, konomi@acm.org
[2] Innovation Center for Educational Resource, Kyushu University, 744,
Motooka, Nishi-Ku, Fukuoka 819-0395, Japan
[3] Faculty of Business Administration, Takachiho University, 19-1, 2, Omiya,
Suginami-Ku, Tokyo 168-8508, Japan
[4] Faculty of Information Science and Electrical Engineering, Kyushu University,
744, Motooka,Nishi-Ku, Fukuoka 819-0395, Japan
[5] Research Institute for Information Technology, Kyushu University, 744,
Motooka, Nishi-Ku, Fukuoka 819-0395, Japan

Abstract. Extended learning environments involving system to collect data for learning analytics and to support learners will be useful for all-age education. As the first steps towards to build new learning environments, we developed a system for multimodal learning analytics using eye-tracker and EEG measurement, and inclusive user interface design for elderly learners by dual-tablet system. Multimodal learning analytics system can be supportive to extract where and how learners with varied backgrounds feel difficulty in learning process. The eye-tracker can retrieve information where the learners paid attention. EEG signals will provide clues to estimate their mental states during gazes in learning. We developed simultaneous measurement system of these multimodal responses and are trying to integrate the information to explore learning problems. A dual-tablet user interface with simplified visual layers and more intuitive operations was designed aiming to reduce the physical and mental loads of elderly learners. A prototype was developed based on a cross-platform framework, which is being refined by iterative formative evaluations participated by elderlies, in order to improve the usability of the interface design. We propose a system architecture applying the multimodal learning analytics and the user-friendly design for elderly learners, which couples learning analytics "in the wild" environment and learning analytics in controlled lab environments.

Keywords: All-age learning · Learning support systems · Learning analytics · Multimodal sensing · Inclusive design

P.-L. P. Rau (Ed.): HCII 2019, LNCS 11577, pp. 469–481, 2019.
https://doi.org/10.1007/978-3-030-22580-3_35

1 Introduction

There is an increasing need to develop learning environments for people of all ages as the average life expectancy in many countries increases. In addition, the advances and the pervasiveness of smart technologies are arguably changing what people should learn to live meaningfully as valuable participants of our society, which can deeply influence the design and development of the technology-enhanced learning environments of the future. Such environments may potentially enhance multigenerational co-creation and social activities of older adults [1].

In this paper, we present our approach and first steps towards building technology-enhanced learning environments for adults of all ages. Our approach exploits learning analytics, which involves measurement, collection, analysis and reporting of data about learners and their contexts to optimize learning environments. Although learning analytics are often intended for online learning environments such as MOOCs, they are increasingly used in hybrid learning environments such as university courses combining physically-based classrooms and digital learning tools.

Learning analytics-based hybrid learning environments can be extremely useful for supporting learners of all ages, as they can combine online, offline and in situ learning to acquire different kinds of knowledge and skills. Most of the conventional learning analytics systems, however, are inherently limited in supporting people of all ages. We thus aim at improving the usability of learning systems for all ages, enriching learning data, and providing relevant feedback to learners and instructors.

Figure 1 shows a system architecture of a learning analytics-based hybrid learning environment for university students. The system allows learners and instructors to use course management tools, e-portfolio tools, and learning material management tools via the web-based user interface. These tools generate exhaust data that are stored as learning records in the database. Learning analytics tools processes and visualizes learning records to provide feedback to learners and instructors (e.g., by displaying descriptive statistics of the usage of learning materials).

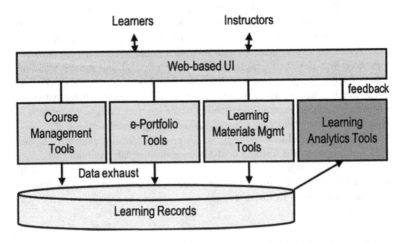

Fig. 1. System architecture of a learning analytics-based hybrid learning environment

Systems based on this architecture could not support diverse users of all ages without accurately detecting and resolving a wide range of learning problems, and making their user interfaces very friendly to non-tech savvy people. In order to extended learning analytics-based hybrid learning environments for adults of all ages, we propose a novel platform based on (1) *multimodal learning analytics* using eye-tracker and EEG measurement, which can be used to detect and resolve learning problems with accuracy based on 'honest' signals, and (2) *easy-to-use user interface design for non-tech savvy older adults*, which exploits the ubiquity of tablet computers to enhance physical affordance of information. Firstly, our *multimodal learning analytics environment* can support the process to identify a text, image, etc. in a learning material that various learners perceive difficult to understand, and examine different mental states related to such perceived difficulty. Eye-tracker can be used to identify the pieces of information that the learners pay attention to. EEG signals provide clues to estimate learners' mental states that eye trackers cannot uncover. Thus, we have developed a system to measure eye-tracking and EEG signals to support the process of narrowing down what hampers learning, based on multimodal signals. Secondly, we have developed a prototype of a cross-platform, dual-tablet user interface that enhances the physical affordance of information and supports intuitive operations. We expect that the user interface we propose would reduce the physical and mental loads of older adults in using learning analytics-based systems. We conduct iterative formative evaluation of the prototype focusing on the usability improvements for older adults. Furthermore, we discuss how these developments can be integrated to realize a novel learning support environment for adults of all ages.

2 Multimodal Sensing to Improve Educational Design

2.1 Background and Hypothesis

In order to develop learning environment for people of all ages, design of educational material is an important factor. Conventional materials might not be appropriate for every learner with different background. Extracting where such learners feel difficult in conventional materials is very useful to improve education design. High-frequency physiological data during learning process could provide more information about their mental state including difficulty feelings. In this study, we introduced a simultaneous measurement of eye gaze data and electroencephalogram signals during the self-learning process in our learning support system.

Eye tracking system could provide information on where learners paid attention in a material during learning process. In the field of educational science, eye-tracking has been widely used to evaluate and improve visual design of computer-based learning [2]. Common metrics of eye tracking data include spatial parameters which indicate where the learners focused. Several studies have shown that eye learning performance or abilities engaged in eye movements where and how long focused on an educational material [3–5]. These pieces of eye-tracking literature supported that eye-tracking data could be effective to extract points, which are difficult to understand for learners with less background knowledge.

Eye gaze data can indicate regions oriented attention, but there can be several candidate reasons why learners paid attention: interest, difficulty, organizing, and so on [6]. To understand the reason why the specific points were focused on, another type of physiological measurement is necessary. EEG can be measured simultaneously with eye gaze data. Integration of EEG and eye gaze measurement can be used to assess learners' emotion and motivation during eye fixations, and determine where they felt difficult to understand.

Our investigation is based on the following hypothesis:

H1. When learners had difficulties to understand descriptions of a textbook, they gazed at the points longer than where they could understand. However, gaze data includes responses involved in other cognitive processes.

H2. EEG signals reflect mental state during the gaze fixation, and the signals can be used to estimate the cognitive process during fixation.

2.2   Methods

System Overview. In this system, eye-tracking, EEG, and computer-based learning were integrated and their events were synchronized. When a participant started the learning task, eye tracking system started to measure eye gaze data and insert a start event to the EEG measurement system. Click events to advance or backward pages displayed on the screen were synchronized to EEG measurement system and eye tracking system. The learning task and automatic manipulation of the eye-tracking system were controlled by independently developed programs in Psychtoolbox [7] and Tobii pro SDK in Matlab [8]. The EEG measurement was controlled by cognionics data acquisition software suite (Cognionics Inc., San Diego, US). EEG signals and inserted events were sent from EEG headset to the data acquisition software on PC via Bluetooth.

Experiment Design. The current experiment was approved by the ethical committee of Kyushu University. All procedures were performed in accordance with approved guidelines of the ethical committee of Kyushu University. All participants gave written informed consent in accordance with the Declaration of Helsinki before participating.

Participants performed a self-paced learning task in a dark room. They read two types of learning materials: "Correlation and Statistical testing" and "Principal component analysis and Factor analysis". These learning materials were designed for Information Science course in Kyushu University, which include text, images, and equations. We recruited 19 participants who had little knowledge of information science and statistics and confirmed their experience of learning related knowledge of the contents presented in our experiment. The participants followed the same sequence of tasks.

The learning materials were presented in a full-screen LCD display and participants could advance or backward pages by clicking. They were asked to response difficulty and interest levels from 0 (easy, no interest) to 10 (difficult, interest) on an interactive slider scale after red each page (Fig. 2). Following the reading of one set of material, they took a quiz to confirm their understanding of the contents.

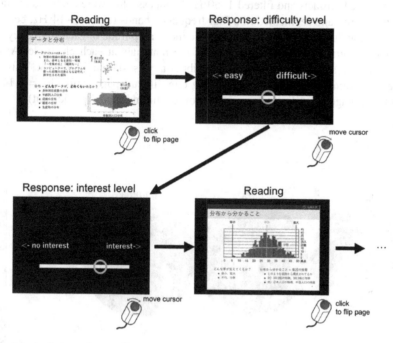

Fig. 2. Manipulation of page flipping and evaluation of difficulty and interest levels of each page during the experiment (Color figure online)

The experimenter monitored the experiment systems and measured signals outside the dark room.

Eye Tracking Measurement. During learning and quiz, eye movements were recorded with a 150-Hz remote eye tracking system (Tobii Pro Spectrum 150 Hz, Tobii AB, Stockholm, Sweden), which was mounted on the LCD display. The system was calibrated before each beginning of the learnings and quizzes. The distance from display to eyes was kept 57 cm.

EEG Measurement. EEG was performed across 19 channels with active electrodes (Flex sensors or Drypad sensors, Cognionics Inc.) according to the International 10–20 system. The reference electrode was placed on A1, i.e., left earlobe, and the ground electrodes were placed on near Fp1 and Fp2, i.e., left and right prefrontal sites. Electrode impedances were kept under 500 kΩ. EEGs were recorded using a Quick-20 (Cognionics Inc.) amplified at by a gain of 3, and digitalized at a sampling rate of 500 Hz.

2.3   Preliminary Results and Discussion

In this manuscript, we will display preliminary results from EEG analysis only. EEG signals removed artifacts and filtered 1–50 Hz bandpass filter were analyzed using fast fourier transform, and segmented into four frequency bands (alpha: 8–14 Hz, beta: 14–30 Hz, gamma: 30–50 Hz). We calculated the mean amplitude of each frequency band during the learning process in each page of the materials at each electrode. A topographic map of averaged EEG scalp distribution was shown in Fig. 3. This map indicated individual response during reading one difficult page (difficulty = 6.14, the most difficult page according to the evaluation of the individual participant).

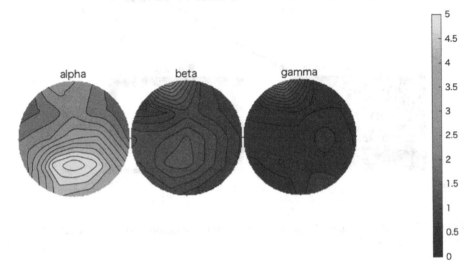

Fig. 3. An example of EEG topographic map during reading a difficult page (Each circle represents scalp topography of a common participant. Color bar indicates amplitude of each frequency band [micro-V].) (Color figure online)

The results indicated an increase of alpha amplitudes at parietal sites when the learner felt difficult in the learning process. It has been suggested that alpha activities at parietal involved in mental fatigue, drowsiness, and low vigilance levels [9]. Therefore, we can estimate that the learner was tired and could not keep his concentration on learning when he felt difficult. In this case, the page should be improved to enhance the motivation of beginners, for example, add more attractive figures.

2.4   Future Study

We developed the system to measure multimodal data and detected specific EEG responses correlated to difficulty feeling in learning. The next step is to extract points where the learners paid attention from eye gaze data, and integrate EEG signals and difficulty evaluations. This multimodal measurement can obtain information about learners' mental states and cognitive load levels directly and objectively.

3 User Interface Design for Elderly Learners

3.1 Purposes and Problems

For the development of the learning-support system for all age, we focused on elderly learners as an initial step. We started with extending the existing e-learning system, which has been designed for university students, to provide learning content and functions for the elderly learners. Our first goal is to redesign the user interface (UI) of the new system for the elderly users who have very basic skills of operating personal computers and/or smartphones.

The conventional e-learning system are usually too complicated for elderly users. In a lecture oriented to the elderlies using the existing e-learning platform of Kyushu University, we found the participants often meet problems in operating with the web-based UI, even if most of them have the experience of operating digital devices like PCs or smartphones. The limitations and preferences of the elderly users must be considered in the UI design, which should consider reducing both the physical and mental loads of the users. Otherwise, tiredness, confusion or frustration caused by the interface will hinder the elderly users.

Physical Limitations. The aging of body can prevent the elderly users from achieving smooth operation experience. For example, the diminution of vision brings difficulties of reading long text in small font size or identify symbols from the background with low contrast colors [10], and the dry skin of fingers makes occasional loss of responses when using touch screens.

Mental Limitations. With the decline of cognitive capacities, elderly users would prefer simple and intuitive logic way of information presentation [11]. It is easy to get frustrated when facing unexpected situations or inconsistent information display [12].

Preference. The preference of user interface of the elderly users can be connected with their previous experience and lifestyles. The UI design metaphors widely applied in the information systems can still be unfamiliar to the elderly users [13].

3.2 Dual-Tablet Interface Design

We propose a dual-tablet interface, which has a main screen to display and operate the main content (usually a page of the slide), and a secondary screen to deal with the supplementary information (e.g. page previews and progress) and operations (e.g. text input), as shown in Fig. 4. The interface is designed to reduce the layers of operations and fix the main visual representation (i.e. the page of slide), in order to avoid the frequent view changing and reduce the annoying overlaps of main content.

We want to at first implement the basic functions of reading learning materials, which contains the display of the slide pages, page control, bookmark, marker input, memo input and edit, etc. We modified the visual design from the web-based interface of the existing e-learning system in the following aspects:

- Move the buttons out of the view of the page, fix the buttons' positions and removed the auto-hide effect;

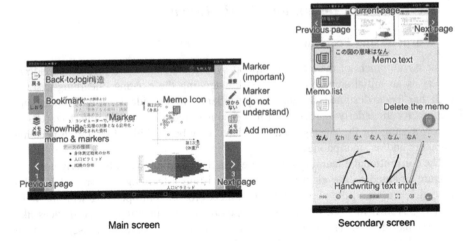

Main screen   Secondary screen

Fig. 4. Dual-tablet interface designed for elderly users of e-learning system

- Use one button for only one position, and remove the second-level menu of the buttons;
- Enlarge the sizes of the buttons and always show the text of their functions;
- Use distinct color changes of the buttons when they are pushed.

The operations are modified from the mouse-keyboard input to finger/touch pen input to adopt the touch screen interface. However, we disabled most of the gesture operations on the main content to avoid misoperations that can frustrate the users. We also estimate the handwriting input as the main text input method.

The dual-tablet interface requires some special designs to make users clear with the correspondence of the UI components between the two devices. For example, the original web-based interface uses the same icon for different memos on the page. In the new interface, we use a coloring sequence to show more obviously that which memo on the main screen is selected and being edit on the secondary screen.

3.3   Prototype Development

To realize the data synchronization for the operations of the dual-tablet interface, we implemented a server to transmit the data between the two devices through WebSocket [14]. The latency can be a vulnerable point of this solution comparing to the direct connections between the two devices, such as Wi-Fi or Bluetooth. However, this solution can be applied to the client devices of different hardware/software platforms, so that can be easily extended to, for example, PC-tablet or tablet-smartphone interfaces. The frontend is developed with Ionic Framework (Version 3.9.2), also purposed to achieve the cross-platform expandability. For the experiments, we deployed the server on Amazon Web Services (AWS) and the clients on HUAWEI MediaPad M3 Lite 10 with Android 7.0. The structure of the prototype is shown as Fig. 5.

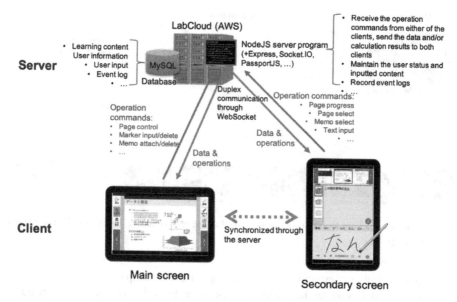

Fig. 5. Structure of the dual-tablet user interface prototype

3.4 Preliminary Experiment and Discussion

For the evaluation of the new touch screen UI by the target users, a preliminary experiment was carried out on October 2018. Eight participants (2 females and 6 males, aged from 63 to 71) took part in the experiment. Seven of them have experience of using smartphones, and six of them have used tablets before. The participants were divided into two groups equally. After a brief introduction of prototype's functions, each participant was asked to read the learning material (a 15-page slide about data visualization) with the prototype in around 20 min, and tried to use the prototype's marker and memo functions. During the experiment, video records of each participant's hand movement and operations on the tablets were taken. The event logs of the participants' operations were also recorded in the server. After the experiment, the participants were asked about their understanding of the interface and opinions to the usability of the prototype. Open discussions were also conducted for more feedbacks. The participants followed the same sequence of tasks.

As a prototype still under development, we expected that the users may have difficulties in operating it. And the result of questionnaires shows the evaluation of the prototype's usability is still not good enough. However, the participants were still positive to say that the meanings of UI components like buttons and their functions were easy to understand. The main problem is the operations that can make them confused or frustrated. The recorded videos were analyzed with the operation logs to find out the cases and situations that the participants misoperated or got confused (as shown in Fig. 6). The preliminary findings from the experiment are as follows.

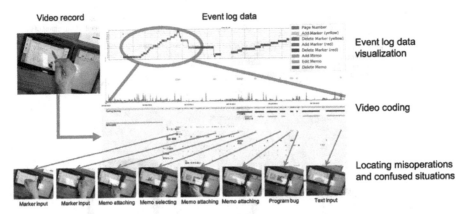

Fig. 6. Analyzing event log data and video record of the experiment to locate problems engaged by the participants

1. Counter-intuitive operations were confusing for the participants
   In the original browser interface, the operation to add a marker to the page is dragging a rectangle with the mouse cursor. When applying the same operation in the touch screen interface, the participants tended to draw a straight line with the touch pen, expecting a colored bar to appear, but the result would be a thin line that can hardly be seen, which could be frustrating. Even if we explained the way of drawing a rectangle, some participants still repeated the incorrect operations.
2. Some gestures are difficult for elderly users, but other gestures were acceptable
   We applied long press gesture for the operations such as adding a new memo icon on the page, or deleting the pressed existing marker or memo. This design was on purpose to avoid misoperations such as deleting something with an accidental tap. However, the most participants got confused of, for example, how long they should keep pressing, should they press and move, should they long press the button or the icon, and so on. On the other hand, some of the participants tried to zoom in the page with pinch gesture when they feel the size of some text is too small to read, as they declared that they often do so with smartphones.
3. Hand-writing text input is not always appropriate
   Although we estimated hand-writing text input would be easily accepted by most of the users, some of the participants complained that they wanted to use the soft keyboards as they usually used in smartphones. At the same time some participants expected more intuitive hand-writing or drawing, which means they would not need to convert the drawings to digital text.
       In general, we should not just give the users what we think is good for them. The characteristics of "elderly users" can be vary and changing by time.

3.5   Future Study

We are conducting iterative formative evaluations on the prototype to improve the inclusive interface design. Thus, more experiment with inclusive participants will be conducted, and the data collected in the experiments need further analysis. In the future experiments and evaluations, we want to collect more objective data such as more detailed logs, eye tracking data, and so on, for the more accurate evaluation. We are going to integrate the new user interface with the experimental learning support system to provide learning materials and functions for older adults.

4   An Architecture for Supporting Learners of All Ages

Next, we propose a system architecture that couples learning analytics "in the wild" and learning analytics in controlled lab environments, and discuss how our multimodal learning analytics and user interface prototype can fit in this architecture to realize a novel learning support environment for all ages.

As shown in Fig. 7, existing learning analytics architecture in Fig. 1 can be extended to support learners of all ages. Clearly, the user-friendly UI for all ages is a critical building block in this architecture, which provides easy access to and intuitive interactions with course management, e-portfolio, learning material management mechanisms. Their exhaust data flow into the learning database, thereby enabling learning analytics to provide learners and instructors with actionable information based on machine learning-based models. In this process, we can exploit data from auxiliary sensors such as embedded accelerometers, magnetometers, gyro sensors, and cameras as well as inexpensive eye trackers and Wi-Fi/Bluetooth devices. The data from auxiliary sensors can be used to improve the accuracy and granularity of the information that is fed back to the learners and instructors through the learning analytics tools. The knowledge base for supporting learners allows for accumulation and retrieval of relevant information for the improvement of content, layout, and structures of learning materials as well as the support of learners' motivation and social contexts.

To provide useful and actionable feedback to learners and instructors, we analyze learners at a finer level in the LA Lab, a controlled sensor-armed lab environment for conducting in-depth learning analytics so as to update the machine learning-based models and the knowledge base of the LA "in the wild."

In the LA Lab, multimodal sensors including EEG and eye trackers collect rich and detailed signals from learners who agreed to participate in experiential learning sessions. In addition to the learning data from the learning support system they use, the LA Lab system generates fine-grained learning data that enables in-depth learning analytics tools for experts including learning scientists, instructional designers, and cognitive scientists. These experts can also record structured and unstructured information in the knowledge base. In addition, they could potentially suggest desirable data to collect via the tools and the sensors so as to improve the usefulness of the overall system. Juxtaposed to Experts in Fig. 7 is the machine learning component (Machine Learning) that generates and updates the machine learning-based models (ML-based Models) for predicting relevant items in the knowledge base by using the learning data only.

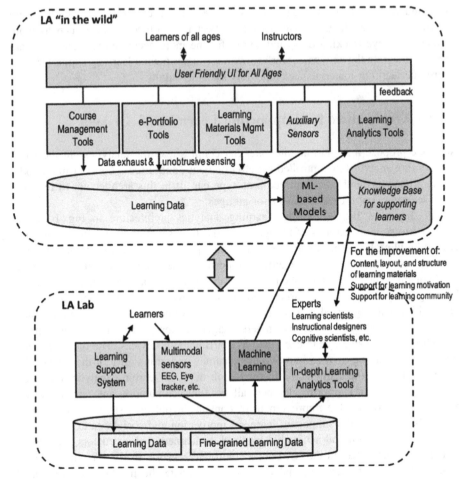

Fig. 7. Coupled architecture for supporting learners of all ages

5   Conclusion

We have presented our approach and first steps towards building technology-enhanced learning environments for adults of all ages. Our approach exploits learning analytics in hybrid learning environments and combines the lab-based in-depth learning analytics tools and the mechanisms for providing relevant and actionable feedback "in the wild." We have developed a system to measure eye-tracking and EEG signals to support the process of narrowing down what hampers learning, based on multimodal signals. We have also developed a prototype of a dual-tablet user interface that enhances the physical affordance of information and supports intuitive operations.

At this moment, our research efforts focus on the kinds of practical learning that can lead to increased opportunities for social participation. They include acquisition of the skills to use digital technologies and/or data. We are also interested in supporting people to learn caregiving skills. Learning such skills would require acquisition of tacit knowledge and embodied skills, and thus supporting it would create exciting sets of challenges to tackle in the future. Moreover, automating feedback to learners and instructors as much as possible would improve the scalability and deployability of the proposed environment.

Acknowledgement. This work was supported by JST Mirai Grant Number 17-171024547, Japan.

References

1. Konomi, S., et al.: Towards supporting multigenerational co-creation and social activities: extending learning analytics platforms and beyond. In: Streitz, N., Konomi, S. (eds.) DAPI 2018. LNCS, vol. 10922, pp. 82–91. Springer, Cham (2018). https://doi.org/10.1007/978-3-319-91131-1_6
2. Jarodzka, H., Holmqvist, K., Gruber, H.: Eye tracking in educational science: theoretical frameworks and research agendas. J. Eye Mov. Res. **10**(1) (2017)
3. Jian, Y.-C., Ko, H.-W.: Influences of text difficulty and reading ability on learning illustrated science texts for children: an eye movement study. Comput. Educ. **113**, 263–279 (2017)
4. Hu, Y., Wu, B., Gu, X.: An eye tracking study of high- and low-performing students in solving interactive and analytical problems. Educ. Technol. Soc. **20**, 300–311 (2017)
5. Gegenfurtner, A., Lehtinen, E., Säljö, R.: Expertise differences in the comprehension of visualizations: a meta-analysis of eye-tracking research in professional domains (2011). https://doi.org/10.1007/s10648-011-9174-7
6. Alemdag, E., Cagiltay, K.: A systematic review of eye tracking research on multimedia learning. Comput. Educ. **125**, 413–428 (2018)
7. Kleiner, M., Brainard, D., Pelli, D., Ingling, A., Murray, R., Broussard, C.: What's new in psychtoolbox-3. Perception **36**, 1–16 (2007)
8. Tobii Pro .http://developer.tobiipro.com Accessed 30 Nov 2018
9. Borghini, G., Astolfi, L., Vecchiato, G., Mattia, D., Babiloni, F.: Measuring neurophysiological signals in aircraft pilots and car drivers for the assessment of mental workload, fatigue and drowsiness (2014). https://www.sciencedirect.com/science/article/pii/via%3Dihub
10. Morris, J.M.: User-Interface design for older adults. Interact. Comput. **6**, 373–393 (1994)
11. Al-Razgan, M.S., Al-Khalifa, H.S., Al-Shahrani, M.D., AlAjmi, H.H.: Touch-based mobile phone interface guidelines and design recommendations for elderly people: a survey of the literature. In: Huang, T., Zeng, Z., Li, C., Leung, C.S. (eds.) ICONIP 2012. LNCS, vol. 7666, pp. 568–574. Springer, Heidelberg (2012). https://doi.org/10.1007/978-3-642-34478-7_69
12. Hawthorn, D.: Possible implications of aging for interface designers. Interact. Comput. **12**, 507–528 (2000)
13. Leung, R., McGrenere, J., Graf, P.: Age-related differences in the initial usability of mobile device icons. Behav. Inf. Technol. **30**, 629–642 (2011)
14. Pimentel, V., Nickerson, B.G.: Communicating and displaying real-time data with websocket. IEEE Internet Comput. **16**, 45–53 (2012)

Collaborate or Compete? How Will Multiplayers' Interaction Affect Their Learning Performance in Serious Games

Jui-Ying Wang, Weijane Lin[✉], and Hsiu-Ping Yueh

National Taiwan University, Taipei, Taiwan
vjlin@ntu.edu.tw

Abstract. Serious games have received much attention in the field of education because of its interactive and complex learning environment which involves many people, contexts, academic knowledge and learning outcomes. It is a topic of concern that how cooperative and competitive peer relationship would affects users' learning performance. This study aimed to design an online multiplayer serious game to explore the difference in learning outcomes among learners in one-on-one competition, one-on-one collaboration, and solo play. The preliminary findings suggested that participants performed better and were more satisfied within multiple player interaction modes, whether it be with collaborative partners or competitive opponents. The results of participants' flow state also supported that the existence of peers affected participants' learning experiences positively. Based on the findings of the study, practical suggestions for libraries and museums to introduce serious games to the fields were provided.

Keywords: Serious game · Cooperative learning · Collaborative learning

1 Introduction

Games have become prevalent in education for its potential to provide a motivational and meaningful learning systems that tailor learner interactions with instructional materials and tasks. In a typical game design, the user's success depends on overcoming various challenges in the games which offer a highly self-directed and immersive experiences [1]. By allowing learners to explore and experience the context, learners can be more engaged [2]. Compared to traditional instructional media, previous study [3] supported that games led to higher involvement, higher motivation and higher entertainment. Serious games were defined as the combination of the educational purposes with the form of game-based learning. Serious games could accommodate the complex dynamic interactions of multiple people, contexts, subject knowledge and learning outcomes in the educational environment [1], and grant enjoyable opportunities for formal and informal learning environment. The process of playing games often involves problem solving, reading comprehension, and social skills [3], more educational studies conducted in informal learning environment, such as libraries and museums, have paid attention to serious games for information literacy

© Springer Nature Switzerland AG 2019
P.-L. P. Rau (Ed.): HCII 2019, LNCS 11577, pp. 482–491, 2019.
https://doi.org/10.1007/978-3-030-22580-3_36

education to motivate and enhance patrons' problem identification skill, thinking skill, analysis skill, expression skill and ability to communicate [4].

Serious games are used in a wide variety of occasions. Michael and Chen divides serious games into eight categories according to the market: educational games, business games, medical games, government games, political games, military games, religious games, and art games [5]. Regarding the character design of serious games, Bonsignore, Hansen, Kraus, Visconti and Fraistat pointed out that there are three important roles in the immersive serious game, the protagonist-by-proxy, the protagonist-mentor and the antagonist. The protagonist-by-proxy is the avatar that the learner himself manipulates in the game or other characters which have similar skill. The design of protagonist-by-proxy needs to be similar to the learner's age to simulate the efficient information search and solution that the player can emulate. The protagonist-mentor provides learner with training and advice. In the serious game of information literacy, the protagonist-mentor often appears as a librarian. The antagonist, on the other hand, can cause conflicts and promote user participation.

However, when learners interact with one another together in the game-based learning environment, the interaction could be complicated with a variety of connections and relationships occurred. Cooperation and competition, for example, were explored by previous studies as they were typical in many games, yet sometimes counteracted with each other in terms of motivation and learning. Cooperative learning is considered to minimize the unpleasantness of group work and improve learning outcomes and satisfaction in both formal and informal educational situation [6]. While competitive learning is considered to enhance learning outcomes by competing with each other [7], yet it also causes negative effects such as disruption of relationships and anxiety [8]. Competition and collaboration are both common motivational factors for business multiplayer games and online games [9], but the impact of competition and collaboration on learning motivation, learning participation and learning effectiveness in serious games are not consistent in past research works.

In addition, the current empirical research on the impact of collaboration or competitive interaction on learning outcomes is limited to serious games without simulations, virtual characters, and tasks. Most of the empirical studies were conducted in formal education contexts, and there is a lack of in-game communication channel. While the simulation scenario is helpful to promote learners' engagement [2] and learners' emotions and motivations could largely differ in formal and informal education, empirical studies would be necessary to investigate the impact of collaboration and competition on learning in a simulation games with learning tasks.

Motivated by the aforementioned issues, this study intends to explore the elements of collaboration and competition in a multi-player serious game. An online game-based learning environment and materials were designed and developed for college students to understand the topic of citrus fruits, and participants' interaction behaviors and performance were recorded and analyzed.

484 J.-Y. Wang et al.

2 Research Design

This study compared the impact of different forms of learning on learning outcomes. A quasi-experimental design was adopted. Twenty-four college students were recruited to participate in the study. And they were randomly assigned into three groups with 8 valid samples in each group. From the review of the related studies, it was hypothesized that the game could train users to find, use and judge information. Helpful elements such as virtual characters, backgrounds and plots, tasks in games were therefore introduced and designed in this study to carry out practical operations and exercises.

2.1 Game Design and Development – The Citrus

For the instructional purpose to develop college students' awareness and literacy about the library special collection, the topics of plant taxonomy that related to a series of special collection called "Tanaka Collection [10]" was selected for the serious game. The learning progression that outlined the sequence of the sequence of the instruction was defined with reference to the literature, librarians, and subject matter experts with a background in botany. Tanaka Collection consisted of 3,856 titles of books, journals, magazine, and pamphlets written in more than 15 languages, which could be viewed as a major library in the world in the area of botany studies. This collection was made by Prof. Tyôzaburô Tanaka during his term of the first University Librarian of Taihoku Imperial University, the predecessor of National Taiwan University. The Collection itself stood for an exceptional case of colonialism and modernity, which was believed to benefit Taiwanese students to develop cultural legacy. Based on the historical importance of the collection and the rich contextual resources provided in the literature of this collection, the game was set in historic time period of 1928–1945 when Prof. Tanaka was a professor at the Department of Horticultural of the College of Science, Thaihoku Imperial University. Players were asked to visit the simulated setting of Shilin Horticultural Experimental Branch, where Prof. Tanaka often conducted his field research, and use the botanical concepts to help Prof. Tanaka identify certain citrus fruits.

Players joined the game by their avatars to play the game alone, or to interact with others under different social contexts: the one-on-one collaborative learning and one-on-one competitive learning modes. The protagonist-by-proxy character design proposed by Bonsignore et al. [11] was adopted because it prompted the learners to engage in the role and naturally develop a collaborative or competitive relationship. Gaming tasks and challenges included the readings of the literature collection, and citrus species classification. The educational purpose of this serious game is to enhance learners' understanding of citrus species, the use of literature, and the value of library special collections.

The game was implemented by Unity®. According to the designed roles and relationships between learners, three modes of interaction were developed: "Individualistic", "One-on-One collaborative" and "One-on-One Competitive" delivered in identical story theme and learning task in terms of information quantity and difficulty. The task is to observe the appearance of the plant, including the shape of trees, fruit and leaf in order to classify 3 types of different citrus fruits including Tankan, Ponkan, and Citrus Unshiu with the literature at their hands. The game design contains immersive background settings and contexts, including modern citrus exhibition scenes and the real citrus garden in the 1920s. In the citrus garden user can choose to take a closer look at the tree, the fruit, and the leaf. Also they could cut off the fruit to see the sectional view as shown in Fig. 1.

Fig. 1. Users can choose to observe the citrus fruits by different points of view

Participants were assigned to play the two virtual characters of Mei and Satoshi to interact with Pr. Tanaka in the game, as shown in Fig. 2. With critical information highlighted for the learners, participants needed to read the literature, determine which type of observations to perform, observe and compare the types of features to classify them (see Fig. 3). The game supported different level of investigation from the basic watch-and-remember, to more complicated judging tasks such as cross-referencing all available resources to the observation and problem-solving.

Fig. 2. Users played the virtual roles to interact with the leading character Pr. Tanaka

A between-subject experiment was conducted. Participants were randomly assigned into three groups of interaction modes of individual, collaborative and competitive, with their learning outcomes, interactions and behaviors recorded for analysis. For "One-on-One collaborative" and "One-on-One Competitive" groups, to enable participants' conversation with each other, a chatbot was implemented by the social networking site Slack and Flow XO settings. The chatbot played the virtual character of "Mystery Citrus" in the game for participants to talk with and ask questions to (see Fig. 4).

Fig. 3. Handbook of literature (left); A closer and sectional view of the citrus fruits

Fig. 4. The Mystery Citrus in the game (left) and in the chat room (right) for context extension.

2.2 Interaction Modes

According to the designed roles and relationships between learners, three modes of interaction were developed: Group 1 (Individualistic), Group 2 (One-on-One collaborative) and Group 3 (One-on-One Competitive). Group 1 (Individual) participants were assigned to play the role Mei who meet Pr. Tanaka and his student Satoshi from the past, and need to observe the fruit trees and reading the literature at the same time herself to classify the citrus. Participants were given a tablet and a printed handbook of literature, as shown in Fig. 5 to complete the game challenges.

For Group 2 (Collaborative) participants, they were assigned to play the role of Mei (A) and Satoshi(B) who were located in two different physical space. They work together online to complete the game tasks of classifying citrus fruits. The character Mei(A) is responsible for explore the field by observing the trees, fruits and leaves, while Satoshi(B) is responsible for reading the handbook of literature. Two participants and the chat robot (Mystery Citrus) communicate with one another by text through online chat rooms to classify citrus species as shown in Fig. 6.

Group 3 (Competitive) participants were assigned to play the same character of Mei (A) and Satoshi(B), but they compete for limited resources and hints provided by the chatbot (Mystery Citrus) online. There are 9 items of literature in total, 4 are in Chinese

Fig. 5. Individualistic version experiment setting

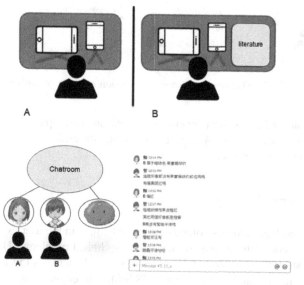

Fig. 6. One-on-one collaborative version experiment setting

and 5 are in Japanese, each of which can only be used by one person. Through the competition of resources, the two participants must explore the citrus garden faster than the other party and judge the required documents earlier. Figure 7 show how the users could get the resources in electronic forms through the online chatroom.

2.3   Instruments and Procedures

A questionnaire to investigate participants' prior experiences and knowledge toward the collections was developed and distributed during the recruitment. Volunteers with similar background were sampled, and randomly assigned into three groups of different interaction modes. Formative assessment in quiz type were integrated in the game tasks to understand participants' learning performance. Their interaction behaviors during the experiment were observed and screen-recorded. After they completed the game, the participants were asked to fill in a questionnaire of game attitude on a semantic

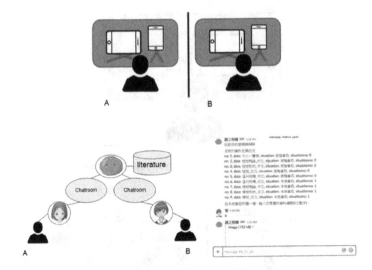

Fig. 7. One-on-one competitive version experiment setting

differential scale and a post-test inventory to measure participants' flow experiences. The instrument consisted of 14 aspects to investigate critical factors that influence users' engagement in a game.

3 Preliminary Findings

There were 27 college students volunteered to participate in the user experiment. Three of them did not complete the experiment due to technical problems. The valid sample of 24 college students consisted of 11 males (45.8%), 13 females (54.2%). 15 of them majored in liberal arts and social science (58.3%), 7 in engineering (29.2%) and 2 in agriculture (8.3%). And they were randomly assigned into three groups with 8 valid samples in each group.

3.1 Learning Performance of Different Groups

To understand whether the design of collaboration and competition will affect the learning outcome, we compared the learning outcomes of the three groups by the number of correct answers: Group 1(Individualistic), Group 2(Collaborative), and Group 3 (Competitive).

The three groups were significantly different in their learning outcomes. As shown in Table 1, both the one-on-one collaborative learning outcomes and one-on-one competitive learning outcomes were significantly greater than the individual learning outcomes, while the one-on-one collaborative and one-on-one competitive learning results were not significant (Group 2 > Group 1**, Group 3 > Group 1*, Group 2 > Group 3). The possible reasons why collaborative learning is better than individual learning is because of distinguishing the important parts of literatures during the discussion, and the Group-to-individual transfer. In addition, due to the need of communication and confirmation, or the internal reasons for solving the problem, the participants will spend more time in learning and have complicated learning behavior, so they can achieve better learning results. For example, Group 2 (Collaborative) participants seemed more open-minded than Group 3 (Competitive) participants. They reported that because of the discussion, all the information was double checked, which increased their exposures and rehearsals of the information.

Table 1. Comparison of the learning performance among the three groups

	SS	df	MS	F	P-value	Post hoc
Within group	25.33	2	12.67	12.09	0.0003	Group 2 > Group 1** Group 3 > Group 1*
Between groups	22.00	21	1.05			
Total	47.33	23				

On the other hand, participants who play the game together tended to feel more satisfied toward the game experiences (Group 2 > Group 1, Group 3 > Group 1, Group 2 < Group 3). Although the difference is not statistically significant, the interviews with the participants suggested that competition made the game more fun and satisfied because of participants' motivation to win their counterpart.

3.2 Flow State in Different Groups

The results echoed previous studies and suggested that situational simulation, role setting, collaboration and competition in serious games improved participants' engagement. The flow state of the three groups of participants was measured and compared accordingly. The results suggested that generally participants were more engaged with higher flow state when they played alone for their game tasks in competitive and individual modes. Compared with single-person learning, multi-person learning is better in several sub aspects of flow state such as self-awareness (F4), perceived importance of the game to the player (F10), perceived importance of the game to others (F11), suggested the benefits of peers, whether collaborative or competitive, to participants' learning experiences.

However, Group 2 (Collaborative) and Group 3 (Competitive) participants' scores of the flow in general were lower than Group 1 (Individual), although not statistically significant. Participants who played the game with peers reported lower scores in the sub-aspects such as perceived difficulty to remain concentrated (F2), perceived control over the progression (F5), whether the game meet my expectation (F6) and other's expectation (F7), and if the game is meaningful to me (F12). The findings suggested the participants tended to follow the game passively without thinking too much, but the social interaction with their partners or competitors distracted them from the game. Furthermore, Group 3 (Competitive) participants reported generally higher scores of flow state than Group 2 (Collaborative) participants. But participants who played the game with a partner were more aware of what they were doing in the game (F3), and perceived the game more meaningful (F12) to their learning than those who played the game with a competitor.

According to the interviews after the experiment, some participants reported they paid more attention to their partners over the game tasks in collaborative mode, it was possible that their social attention distracted their engagement in the learning content. While the situational simulation and role setting provide in collaborative and competitive modes had brought a certain degree of flow experiences, but the operation of online chat room communication could be complicated and interfered by the abilities of the partner. Therefore, the participants may feel less controllable over the learning environment, which could also decrease their scores of flow state.

4 Conclusion and Future works

Based on the historical importance of a special collection in a university library and the rich contextual resources provided in the literature of this collection, this study developed a simulation game about Tanaka Collection to investigate participants' experiences and performance in individual, collaborative and competitive learning contexts. The main mechanics of the game "The Citrus" was developed and implemented by Unity® with integration of protagonist-by-proxy character design and chatbots, to enable social interaction of the participants. The valid sample of 24 college students consisted of 11 males (45.8%), 13 females (54.2%) with similar prior knowledge and experiences participated in the experiment and were randomly assigned into three groups of individual (Group1), one-on-one collaborative (Group 2), and one-on-on competitive (Group 3) to complete the tasks of identifying 3 types of different citrus fruits.

The preliminary findings suggested that participants performed better and were more satisfied within multiple player interaction modes, whether it be with collaborative partners or competitive opponents. The results of participants' flow state also supported that the existence of peers affected participants' learning experiences positively. It was found that when participants collaborated with their partners in the game, their exposures to the related knowledge and information were increased and enhanced during the frequent communication and confirmation between them. The frequent exposures to the learning subjects therefore led to better learning performance. On the other hand, participants in the competitive relationship with their opponents were intrinsically motivated by their psychological pursuit to win before actually playing the game. They were more active in taking challenges by frequently thinking over, therefore they also could achieve better learning performance.

Based on the findings of the study, it is suggested that interweaving the elements of collaboration and competition in serious games was able to provide learners with sufficient exploration time and rich interaction to improve their learning performance. The current study investigated the history game implemented on tablet with simulation technologies. While the integration of collaborative and competitive learning in serious games require more empirical studies for the design guideline, different types of game and alternative instructional media will be explored and interwoven continuously among different storyline and game types in the future.

References

1. Ritterfeld, U., Cody, M., Vorderer, P.: Serious games: explication of an oxymoron: introduction. In: Ritterfeld, U., Cody, M., Vorderer, P. (eds.) Serious Games: Mechanics and Effects, pp. 3–9. Routledge, New York (2009)
2. Westera, W., Nadolski, R.J., Hummel, H.G., Wopereis, I.G.: Serious games for higher education: a framework for reducing design complexity. J. Comput. Assist. Learn. **24**(5), 420–432 (2008)
3. Prensky, M.: Digital game-based learning. Comput. Entertain. **1**(1), 21 (2003)
4. Werner, K.: Bringing them in developing: a gaming program for the library. Libr. Trends **61** (4), 790–801 (2013)
5. Michael, D.R., Chen, S.L: Serious Games: Games That Educate, Train, and Inform. Muska and Lipman/Premier-Trade (2005)
6. Felder, R.M., Brent, R.: Cooperative learning. In: Mabrouk, P.A. (ed.) Active Learning, pp. 34–53. North Carolina State University, Raleigh (2007)
7. Johnson, W.D., Johnson, R.T., Holubec, E.J.: Circle of Learning: Cooperation in the Classroom. Interaction Book Company, Edina (1986)
8. Kohn, A.: No Contest: The Case Against Competition. Houghton Mifflin Company, Boston (1986)
9. Sun, S.W.: Fantasia: cooperative computer games design. Instr. Technol. Media **37**, 2–9 (1998)
10. Tanaka Literature collection. http://cdm.lib.ntu.edu.tw/cdm/landingpage/collection/ta. Accessed 29 Jan 2019
11. Bonsignore, E., Hansen, D., Kraus, K., Visconti, A., Fraistat, A.: Roles people play: key roles designed to promote participation and learning in alternate reality games. In: Proceedings of the 2016 Annual Symposium on Computer-Human Interaction in Play, pp. 78–90. ACM, October 2016

Virtual Simulation Based Intercultural Learning

Guangwei Zhang$^{(\boxtimes)}$ (iD)

Shaanxi Normal University, Xi'an 710119, Shaanxi, China
zhangguangwei@snnu.edu.cn

Abstract. The communication across cultures is challenging, but it is more and more important with the development of economic globalization. Virtual simulation technologies could help create an immersive situated learning environment for improving the intercultural learning experience. Global Understanding (GU) is an international collaborative education community for improving the intercultural competence of the students. We study the approaches that virtual simulation technologies introduced into GU based on the analysis of virtual simulation in intercultural learning as well as the case of Shaanxi Normal University (SNNU) incorporating virtual simulation in teaching history and culture. The knowledge and communicating skills of different cultures are the two important factors in intercultural learning, and we believe they could be improved by virtual simulation based immersive experiencing and interactive virtual simulation respectively. The already-made virtual resources and the ones made collaboratively by the students, including 3D models, panoramic videos/images, and video games, together with the virtual reality content distribution methods could form an ecosystem for the virtual simulation based intercultural learning.

Keywords: Cultural learning · Global understanding ·
Virtual simulation · Situated learning

1 Introduction

People around the world have been pursuing better understanding of each other for hundreds of years. With the development of information communication technology (ICT), it is much easier than ever before for people from different countries getting connected with each other, with which people could work together, study together and even live together. Distance learning provides an important opportunity for the students learning many courses with students of different countries under the direction of a professor, which make the online education cross the boundary of countries. MOOCs have been the most successful distance learning pattern in recent years, which help students improve

Supported by the virtual simulation based teaching center for the history and culture along the Silk Road, Shaanxi Normal University.

© Springer Nature Switzerland AG 2019
P.-L. P. Rau (Ed.): HCII 2019, LNCS 11577, pp. 492–504, 2019.
https://doi.org/10.1007/978-3-030-22580-3_37

their learning mainly in their specialties. There exists another type of global collaborative learning projects, the main aim of which is to help the students understand different cultures to improve their intercultural competence, which is even more important than the professional knowledge in the globalization era. Global Understanding (GU) project[1], initialized by East Carolina University (ECU), involving more than 40 universities/colleges from more than 30 countries, is an international collaborative education community for the students studying different cultures. In every GU session, the students from a pair of partner universities discuss a certain culture topic together under the direction of the teachers from both sides, mainly through the video conferencing system. The intercultural learning in GU helps the students enhance a greater understanding of people from other cultures and form more positive attitudes according to the feedbacks of the GU students [7].

Learning different cultures is the essential goal of GU, and the virtual collaborative classroom of GU helps improve the cultural competence of the students. However, the traditional communication approaches in GU such as the video conferencing and text chatting limit the students' learning experience. Because the first-hand experience is very important to understand a foreign culture [8], and the learning happens in the context where the knowledge belongs to according to the theory of situated learning. As we know, it is the best to learn a culture by living in the environment for some time, however, it is not easy for most of the students studying abroad, and that is one of the reasons of establishing GU 15 years ago. Though GU provides a virtual classroom for students from different countries, where they can have the same class together at the same time, it is clear that the intercultural communication between two sides is not as good as studying abroad for the students. Virtual simulation can help create a virtual environment which could be used to show cultural objects and activities for foreign partners, in which the students can learn the culture immersively. Virtual simulation based cultural learning is more interesting and the students can get more knowledge while they experience in the virtual environment by themselves, and the guidance from their partners can help them understand the culture directly as they are really present in the environment. It would outperform the traditional communication methods which involve oral, video and image demonstrations because the knowledge they get is directly from what they experience. According to our practice in teaching history and culture in SNNU, the virtual simulation based teaching methods would promote the intercultural learning with the capability of generating situated learning environments and make the students understand foreign cultures better.

Culture usually has a close relationship with history as Nunn states: "historical events can have long-term impacts that continue to be felt today" [18], thus the virtual heritage resources (including sites, figures, and events) help the students understand past culture [13]. Most of the students of SNNU attending the GU course major in history, therefore we mainly discuss the virtual simulation based intercultural learning in the context of history and take the historical

---

[1] http://www.ecu.edu/cs-acad/intlaffairs/Global-Understanding.cfm.

resources as the main simulation target. The rest of the paper is organized as follows: Sect. 2 discusses the virtual simulation technology for improving intercultural learning and related work. The method we apply virtual simulation technologies in intercultural learning with GU as an example is discussed in Sect. 3.

2   Intercultural Learning and Virtual Simulation

The goal of intercultural learning is to improve the knowledge, skills of the students on the cultures different from their own [12]. In this section, we discuss the virtual simulation methods that improve the students' cultural knowledge and cultural communication skills with immersive experiencing and interactive simulation respectively.

2.1   Virtual Simulation for Intercultural Learning

Virtual simulation technologies such as virtual reality (VR), augmented reality (AR), mixed reality (MR), and video games provide new opportunities for learning different cultures in an experimental way. The XR (VR, AR, MR) devices, as well as portable devices such as smartphones and iPads are available in the classroom and home for many students. There are more and more virtual resources and the creation of them is getting easier. In a consequence, it is practical to introduce virtual simulation resources into the intercultural learning.

A virtual environment is created in computers that simulates the real world. It could be a social space, where educational interaction occurs and "the students are not only active, but also actors" [9]. They are widely used for the education in science, technology, and engineering [20], while they are less used and studied in cultural learning. The virtual simulation technologies could provide an immersive situated learning environment for better understanding cultures, which makes the virtual simulation more important for arts and humanities than natural sciences. Virtual reality (VR) is considered as a learning tool that helps increase meaningful social interactions and reduced social anxiety especially for the online courses [10]:

> "That makes it possible for students who live hundreds of miles apart to come together and share the same experience online. This is different from a discussion board or video chat in that students are actually seeing and hearing in a shared environment, erasing distance in the virtual space, rather than each being solely exposed to their own immediate surroundings as they sit at their computers. This simulated environment...contributes to a sense of presence."

VR makes it possible that the learning can happen "then" and "there" [4] as a result it increases the interest of the students and improves the performance at the same time. Cultural knowledge could be learned in an experiential learning pattern in an immersive virtual learning environment [19], and the learnability in a 3D virtual heritage is analyzed and proved in [25]. Virtual learning environments with virtual characters from other cultures, combined with authentic intercultural situations, hold potential for intercultural training [15], e.g. a situated cultural festival learning system is developed and used in teaching Chinese cultural festivals [5], and improving the learning motivations and outcomes compared with those of students who were taught using traditional methods. Virtual environments are even considered better than books and videos in history education in [14], where an ancient city Uruk around 3000 B.C. was reconstructed and populated with AI-controlled 3D avatars. The students could not only observe historical buildings, events, they could also interact with the simulated objects and persons. Besides immersive and interactive experiencing, a properly designed virtual world could "facilitate intercultural collaborative learning" [12]. VR games can help teach languages and culture as stated in [6], and VR could enhance remote collaboration [2,3].

Virtually reconstructed places provide opportunities for "authentic experiential learning activities that have the potential to re-mediate students' understanding of space and place through enacted interaction, and to make the learning more memorable" because of embodied experiences [21]. Immersive virtual reality could help enhance the spatial awareness and interest of students in the subject of history [22]. History could be simulated in historical virtual worlds (HVWs), and the historical re-enactment in the HVWs allows historians to criticize different interpretations of history and produce new knowledge on the past [16]. Historical events could be simulated in virtual environments, for example, the user could enact as different roles in a historical event as stated in [24], which give the students an overall experience of a historic event.

Virtual recreated materials are important sources for learning culture but they are new to most teachers and students, therefore they should do additional preparations, e.g. the user requirements for architectural heritage learning through virtual reality as stated in [1]. SNNU has set up a virtual simulation based teaching center for history and culture along the Silk Road for studying the virtual simulation technologies for teaching history and culture as well as training the students with the required skills for their further study and work. They provide the theoretical and practical basis for incorporating virtual simulation technologies in intercultural learning with GU as the testbed. According to the related research and our practices, the functions of the virtual simulation methods for intercultural learning could be classified into two categories: demonstration and interactive simulation.

2.2   Virtual Demonstration

There are various VR techniques as well as devices, but most of them are for personal experiencing. For culture communication, VR can be used to create a virtual object or environment, in which foreign students could explore and experience by themselves. There are lots of already-made VR materials, e.g. 3D recreated historical sites, 360-degree videos and images (e.g. YouTube virtual reality channel[2]), etc. We can use the virtual resources provided by museums, historical heritages such as digital Dunhuang Magao Grottoes[3], where virtual simulation technologies have been widely used. Some universities construct their own VR materials by their own faculties or together with some companies. Most of these already-made VR materials could be used freely, therefore, the teachers need to do good research to introduce suitable related VR materials into their courses based on the VR devices they have.

The students can feel and even touch what is demonstrated by VR, i.e. they are virtually brought into the cultural environment that they are going to learn. Though it is not the same with what they physically visit in the environment, what they can see and feel is even more real compared to the traditional methods, including oral explanations, demonstrations by image, videos, etc. Figure 1 shows a famous Chinese historical site, Dunhuang grottoes. When the students put on the VR headsets, they would feel like they are placed in the Dunhuang caves, where they can watch the murals on the wall and walk around, as shown in Fig. 2.

Fig. 1. Virtually Recreated Dunhuang Caves

2.3 Interactive Virtual Simulation

Interactive VR applications are much better than personal experiencing ones because experiencing a different culture usually needs the guidance from local people, which is similar to that a tour guide is usually needed when we travel to some new place and want to understand the culture better. The foreign students could meet the native students in the virtual simulated environments, for example, if our students want to show an ancient city of China to their partners, they

---

[2] https://www.youtube.com/channel/UCzuqhhs6NWbgTzMuM09WKDQ/.

[3] https://www.e-dunhuang.com/index.htm.

Fig. 2. Virtual experiencing in the virtually recreated Dunhuang caves

could construct the ancient city virtually and invite their partners to join them in the virtual city. Our students could introduce some famous buildings and historical events to their partners, such as how the Spring Festival is celebrated in China.

Interactive VR environments are mostly related to game platforms, where the interaction between users and the interaction between users and the environment is possible. In SNNU, we use virtual simulation technologies mainly in two parts: (1) immersive demonstration of historical sites (existing or non-existing); (2) game-based interactive virtual environments built by the students.

Minecraft[4] is a popular sandbox game, and it has been widely accepted as an education tool, in the virtual world of which players can build almost anything they want, and they can perform some collaborative activities together. Huge numbers of buildings as well as cities have been created with different kinds of blocks in Minecraft, e.g. the St. Peters Basilica in the Vatican[5] as shown in Fig. 3. Huge scale architectures could be virtually reconstructed in a crowdsourcing pattern [17], though it is an effective method, it is difficult, if not impossible, to reconstruct an ancient city completely with manually placed blocks. Some automatic or semi-automatic methods could be used for building a large city in Minecraft based on the GIS data and digital maps [11].

SNNU is located in Xi'an (called Chang'an in history), an ancient city of China, which 13 dynasties made as their capital city in history. It is difficult for a foreign students who know little about China and Xi'an to have a deep understanding about this city even after the introduction by their partners in Xi'an, according to our experience of GU, because it could only develop "with attention to experience" [8]. In SNNU, we are working on a project to recreate

---

[4] https://minecraft.net/.

[5] https://www.planetminecraft.com/project/lvl-60-special-beautiful-detailed-st-peters-basilica-world-download/.

Fig. 3. St. Peters Basilica in Minecraft

the Chang'an city in Tang dynasty. All the ancient buildings in the city are being built by our students in Minecraft collaboratively. The virtual Chang'an city would be a good environment for the foreign students to visit. It is historicaly accurate because it is recreated by the students of history major. Some of the buildings, e.g. the Big Goose Pagoda, Mingde Gate, the Temple of Heaven in Tang dynasty, virtually built by the SNNU students are shown in Figs. 4 and 5.

Fig. 4. Big Goose Pagoda in Minecraft (right) according to historical drawings (left)

Fig. 5. Ancient buildings in Chang'an city in Minecraft

3 Virtual Simulation in Global Understanding

3.1 Intercultural Learning in GU

GU provides the students around the world a platform for studying different cultures that they know nothing or very little with the native students of that culture face-to-face without going abroad. Existing cultural/traditional ceremonies and historical heritages are two important sources for cultural learning. In GU, cultural information is introduced to the foreign students in the form of words, pictures, audios, and videos. They worked indeed, however, nowadays the students know more about different cultures than ever before, because there are more and more methods for them to get to know the world. The expectation of intercultural learning of the students is getting higher than before. Therefore, GU should provide the students with intercultural learning of a new pattern that could enhance their interests and help them understand different cultures better, including cultural knowledge and communication skills.

Virtual simulation is a method that could potentially promote cultural learning in GU. We need to tailor these technologies to GU according to its topics. There are four main topics in GU: (1) college life, (2) tradition and family, (3) meaning of life, and (4) stereotype and prejudice. The first two topics are much easier to apply virtual simulation, and they are discussed as follows:

"College life" is the first topic for GU students. They would tell their partners some information about their universities, for example, where the university locates, how many hours they spend on learning every day, what they do in their spare time, etc. They would show some pictures or videos to their partners, most of which are related to their campuses. The students of both the partner universities can build their virtual campuses in Minecraft. When they talk about college life in the GU class, they can invite their partners to come into their virtual campuses and show them interesting things, such as important buildings, work together to do some games to simulate their real college life. They can also work together in Minecraft to build a building of their campuses based on their discussion. After working with several partner universities, they will build a complete campus and find how they could introduce them better to different partners.

The topic "tradition and family" is important for cultural learning in GU. Tradition and culture are closely related to history, and new technologies have been applied in many museums and cultural companies resulting in many virtually recreated historical sites. Most of them are free, and they provide even better experiences than we physically visiting them. In GU classes, the teachers and students collect this kind of resources and share with their partners, and give them some introduction of them as well as some manuals. Though most of them don't support multiple user viewing at the same time, it could be done asynchronously. After their virtual visiting, the students would discuss more deeply, because they have more knowledge about the partner country's culture. The technology is developing very fast, therefore in the near future the teachers and students might have the GU class in a virtual simulated world as the OASIS in the film "Ready Player One".

3.2   VR Materials Collaboratively Created by the Students

Most projects related to VR in education use already-made VR materials, which are built by companies or teachers. They enhance the students' interests, however, if the students can involve in the construction of the VR materials they can benefit more. With the development of IT and education, the students of different major, even the secondary students, are able to develop VR materials on their own. The 3D modeling tools such as Unity, Blender, Sketchup, as well as some game platforms such as Minecraft, SecondLife could be used in cultural learning. Here we classify the related technologies into two classes: VR content creation and distribution, which could make an ecosystem for virtual simulation based intercultural learning.

Creation of VR Materials. As to the creation of VR materials by the students, we are using Minecraft for the disappeared historical resources and 360° cameras for existing ones.

Minecraft is a sandbox game engine, which is widely used in education. Ancient cities or historical sites of large scale are usually needed for simulating history as well as virtual tours. GIS data and digital maps could be imported into Minecraft [11,23], in which the historical buildings could be reconstructed collaboratively by the teachers and students. 3D virtual worlds could be built using Second Life, OpenSim, etc., compared with which Minecraft has better adaptability, because the secondary students and college students could build anything they want in Minecraft; 360-degree videos and images are the most convenient means for the students recording existing cultural resources, e.g. museums, cultural activities/ceremonies, because the 360-degree cameras are popular and cheap, and they could be viewed from any perspective by the users.

VR Content Distribution. The distribution of VR materials could be through game platforms such as Steam, or VR device platforms such as Oculus store, however, the most popular and effective means is the web. WebVR helps present VR contents on the web, through which the 3D models, as well as the panoramic videos and images, could be immersively viewed with VR headsets on the web. Facebook's 360-React[6] and Mozilla's A-frame[7] are two of the most popular WebVR frameworks, and they are used in our laboratory by the students majoring in history and museology. Besides the recorded panoramic videos and images, some additional interactive information (e.g. background, navigation, history, etc.) could be integrated into the WebVR applications as the cases of Google Arts & Culture[8], which could serve as the tour guide for the users.

3.3   Requirements for Using Virtual Simulation in GU

Because the virtual simulation technologies are new to most teachers and students, the use of them in GU needs extra preparation besides what we do in traditional GU. First of all, we need to study the methods of how we can make effective use of virtual simulation in GU. The second thing is the resources and devices we need to implement the virtual simulation based learning in GU.

Resources and Methods. At first, we just collect some VR resources related to the GU topics and use them as a new kind of media in the class. We can also produce our own VR resources with some devices. For example, the virtual Dunhuang caves we use in teaching history as stated in Sect. 2.2 are produced by a company. For some traditional culture such as ceremonies and activities, we can use 360-degree cameras to record by ourselves.

The panoramic images and videos taken by the students could help to present the cultures, however, they are not good enough, interactive virtual environments could be constructed from the panoramic resources with the WebVR framework.

The SNNU students of history major go to Dunhuang to do academic investigation every year, and they take 360-degree videos and pictures as shown in Fig. 6. They present these cultural resources to their partners as a WebVR application, which could be viewed either with browsers on PC or smartphones or VR headsets.

---

[6] https://facebook.github.io/react-360/.

[7] https://aframe.io/.

[8] https://artsandculture.google.com/.

Fig. 6. A Dunhuang Mogao Caves in Dunhuang Museum Recorded by the students

Devices. In our practices of virtual simulation based intercultural learning, we use some VR devices such as VR headsets (e.g. Google Cardboard, HTC Vive, Oculus Rift, etc.), 360-degree VR cameras (e.g. Insta360 Pro2).

The VR resources and devices are important for implementing virtual simulation based intercultural learning, however, the virtual simulation based teaching/learning methodology is critical and needs further study.

4   Conclusion

We studied the approaches that virtual simulation technologies introduced into GU based on the analysis of virtual simulation in intercultural learning as well as the case of Shaanxi Normal University (SNNU) incorporating virtual simulation in teaching history and culture. Virtual simulation based immersive experiencing and interactive virtual simulation could improve the students' knowledge and communicating skills of different cultures. Already-made virtual resources and the ones made collaboratively by the students, including 3D models, panoramic videos/images, and video games, and the virtual reality content distribution methods together form an ecosystem for virtual simulation based intercultural learning. In the future, we are going to study the virtual simulation based methodology for intercultural learning, including the course design, learning assessment, etc.

References

1. Bakar, J.A.A., Jahnkassim, P.S., Mahmud, M.: User requirements for virtual reality in architectural heritage learning. Int. J. Interact. Digit. Media 1(1), 37–45 (2013)
2. Barakonyi, I., Fahmy, T., Schmalstieg, D.: Remote collaboration using augmented reality videoconferencing. In: Proceedings of Graphics Interface, GI 2004, pp. 89–96. Canadian Human-Computer Communications Society (2004)

3. Benko, H., Ishak, E.W., Feiner, S.: Collaborative mixed reality visualization of an archaeological excavation. In: Proceedings of the 3rd IEEE/ACM International Symposium on Mixed and Augmented Reality, ISMAR 2004, pp. 132–140. IEEE Computer Society (2004)
4. Black, E.R.: Learning then and there: an exploration of virtual reality in K-12 history education. Thesis (2017)
5. Chang, Y.H., Lin, Y.K., Fang, R.J., Lu, Y.T.: A situated cultural festival learning system based on motion sensing. Eurasia J. Math. Sci. Technol. Educ. **13**(3), 571–588 (2017)
6. Cheng, A., Yang, L., Andersen, E.: Teaching language and culture with a virtual reality game. In: Proceedings of the 2017 CHI Conference on Human Factors in Computing Systems, CHI 2017, pp. 541–549. ACM (2017)
7. Chia, R.C., Poe, E., Wuensch, K.L.: Attitude change after taking a virtual global understanding course. Int. J. Soc. Sci. **4**(2), 75–79 (2009)
8. Cushner, K.: The role of experience in the making of internationally-minded teachers. Teach. Educ. Q. **34**(1), 27–39 (2007)
9. Dillenbourg, P., Schneider, D., Synteta, P.: Virtual learning environments. In: 3rd Hellenic Conference Information & Communication Technologies in Education, Kastaniotis Editions, Greece, pp. 3–18 (2002)
10. Domingo, J.R., Bradley, E.G.: Education student perceptions of virtual reality as a learning tool. J. Educ. Technol. Syst. **46**(3), 329–342 (2018)
11. Formosa, S.: Neogeography and preparedness for real-to-virtual world knowledge transfer: conceptual steps to Minecraft Malta. Future Internet **6**(3), 542–555 (2014)
12. Hasler, B.S.: Intercultural collaborative learning in virtual worlds. In: Hinrichs, R., Wankel, C. (eds.) Cutting-edge Technologies in Higher Education, vol. 4, pp. 265–304. Emerald Group Publishing Limited (2011)
13. Ibrahim, N., Mohamad Ali, N., Mohd Yatim, N.F.: Cultural learning in virtual heritage: an overview. In: Zaman, H.B., et al. (eds.) IVIC 2011. LNCS, vol. 7067, pp. 273–283. Springer, Heidelberg (2011). https://doi.org/10.1007/978-3-642-25200-6_26
14. Ijaz, K., Bogdanovych, A., Trescak, T.: Virtual worlds vs books and videos in history education. Interact. Learn. Environ. **25**(7), 904–929 (2017)
15. Lane, H.C., Ogan, A.E.: Virtual environments for cultural learning. In: 14th International Conference on Artificial Intelligence in Education Workshops Proceedings, AIED 2009, p. 25 (2009)
16. Lercari, N.: Simulating history in virtual worlds. In: Sivan, Y. (ed.) Handbook on 3D3C Platforms. PI, pp. 337–352. Springer, Cham (2016). https://doi.org/10.1007/978-3-319-22041-3_13
17. Mol, A., Ariese-Vandemeulebroucke, C., Boom, K., Politopoulos, A.: The Interactive Past: Archaeology, Heritage, and Video Games. Sidestone Press, Leiden (2017)
18. Nunn, N.: Culture and the historical process. Econ. Hist. Dev. Reg. **27**(Suppl. 1), S108–S126 (2012)
19. Ogan, A., Lane, H.C.: Virtual learning environments for culture and intercultural competence. In: Virtual Learning Environments: Concepts, Methodologies, Tools and Applications, pp. 966–984. IGI Global (2012)
20. Potkonjak, V., et al.: Virtual laboratories for education in science, technology, and engineering: a review. Comput. Educ. **95**, 309–327 (2016)
21. Price, S., Jewitt, C., Sakr, M.: Embodied experiences of place: a study of history learning with mobile technologies. J. Comput. Assist. Learn. **32**(4), 345–359 (2016)

22. Rasheed, F., Onkar, P., Narula, M.: Immersive virtual reality to enhance the spatial awareness of students. In: Proceedings of the 7th International Conference on HCI, IndiaHCI 2015, pp. 154–160. ACM (2015)
23. Short, D.: Teaching scientific concepts using a virtual world—minecraft. Teach. Sci. J. Aust. Sci. Teach. Assoc. **58**(3), 55 (2012)
24. Slater, M.M., et al.: Virtually being lenin enhances presence and engagement in a scene from the russian revolution. Front. Robot. AI **5**, 91 (2018)
25. Zamora-Musa, R., Vélez, J., Paez-Logreira, H.: Evaluating learnability in a 3D heritage tour. Presence: Teleoper. Virtual Environ. **26**(4), 366–377 (2018)

Author Index

Printed in the United States
By Bookmasters